The Path of Philosophy

The Path of Philosophy

Truth, Wonder, and Distress

JOHN MARMYSZ
College of Marin

Australia • Brazil • Mexico • Singapore • United Kingdom • United States

***The Path of Philosophy:
Truth, Wonder, and Distress***
John Marmysz

Publisher: Clark Baxter

Senior Sponsoring Editor:
Joann Kozyrev

Assistant Editor: Nathan
Gamache

Marketing Manager: Mark T.
Haynes

Marketing Coordinator: Josh
Hendrick

Marketing Communications
Manager: Laura Localio

Content Project Manager:
Alison Eigel Zade

Senior Art Director:
Jennifer Wahi

Production Technology
Analyst: Jeff Joubert

Print Buyer: Mary Beth
Hennebury

Rights Acquisition Specialist -
Image: Amanda Groszko

Senior Rights Acquisition
Specialist-Text: Katie Huha

Production Service: Cadmus
Communications

Cover Designer: Kate Scheible

Cover Image: Jupiterimages
(ordered thru Getty)
sb10069763bg-001 (royalty
free) Greece, Athens, bust
inside Stoa of Attalos

Compositor: Cadmus
Communications

For product information and technology assistance,
contact us at **Cengage Customer & Sales Support,
1-800-354-9706 or support.cengage.com.**

For permission to use material from this text or
product, submit all requests online at
www.cengage.com/permissions.

Library of Congress Control Number: 2010936140

Student Edition

ISBN-13: 978-0-495-50932-5

ISBN-10: 0-495-50932-9

Cengage
20 Channel Street
Boston, MA 02210
USA

Cengage is a leading provider of customized learning
solutions with employees residing in nearly 40 different
countries and sales in more than 125 countries around the
world. Find your local representative at: **www.cengage.com**.

Cengage products are represented in Canada by Nelson
Education, Ltd.

To learn more about Cengage platforms and services, register
or access your online learning solution, or purchase materials
for your course, visit **www.cengage.com**.

Printed in the United States of America
2 3 4 5 6   24 23 22 21 20

Brief Contents

PREFACE   xii
ACKNOWLEDGMENTS   xv
INTRODUCTION   xix

Chapter 1   Myth, Science, Philosophy, and the Presocratics   1

Chapter 2   Socrates   22

Chapter 3   Plato   42

Chapter 4   Aristotle   64

Chapter 5   The Hellenistic Philosophers   89

Chapter 6   Medieval Philosophy   111

Chapter 7   René Descartes and the Transition from Medieval to Modern Thinking   143

Chapter 8   Hume   179

Chapter 9   Kant's Transcendental Idealism   211

Chapter 10   Hegel and the Manifestations of *Geist*   239

Chapter 11   Happiness, Suffering, and Pessimism in Kierkegaard, Schopenhauer, Nietzsche, and Mill   272

Chapter 12   Common Sense and Anglo-American Philosophy   311

Chapter 13   Existentialism and the Return to Being   355

CONCLUSION: PHILOSOPHY AND WONDROUS DISTRESS   392
GLOSSARY   401
BIBLIOGRAPHY   421
INDEX   427

Contents

PREFACE   xii

ACKNOWLEDGMENTS   xv

INTRODUCTION   xix

Analytic and Continental Styles of Philosophizing   xx

The Love of Wisdom   xxiii

Religion, Science, and Philosophy   xxiv

What Is Philosophy?   xxv

Philosophy as Wondrous Distress   xxvii

Chapter 1   Myth, Science, Philosophy, and the Presocratics   1

Mythic Thinking   2

Presocratic Thinking   6

The Milesian School: Thales and Anaximander   6

Heraclitus   10

Parmenides and the Eleatic School   12

The Atomist School: Democritus and Leucippus   15

From Mere Wonder to Wondrous Distress   18

Chapter 2   Socrates   22

The Difficulty of Perspective   22

Plato's Socrates   24

The Influence of Anaxagoras   24

Socrates' Inward Turn   26

The Socratic Method   27

The Trial of Socrates   29

Xenophon's Socrates   31

Aristophanes' Socrates   35

The Wondrous Distress of Socrates   38

Chapter 3   Plato   42

Plato's Divergence from Socrates   43

The Divided Line   46

The Myth of the Cave   51

Plato's Perfect Republic   55

Plato and Art   58

Wonder and Distress in Platonic Thinking   61

Chapter 4   Aristotle   64

Aristotle's Break with Plato   65

Aristotle and the Nature of Change   68

The Four Causes   70

Aristotle's Logic   74

The First Mover   76

Rationality, Emotion, and the Golden Mean   78

Aristotle's Philosophy of Art   80

Aristotle and Wondrous Distress   84

Chapter 5   The Hellenistic Philosophers   89

The Decline of Greek Power and Hellenistic Negativity   91

Cynicism   93

Stoicism   96

Epicureanism   101

Skepticism   103

Suicide and Hellenistic Philosophy   106

Wonder and Distress in Hellenistic Philosophy   107

Chapter 6   Medieval Philosophy   111

The Patriarch Abraham and the Covenant with God   112

Jesus   113

Muhammad   116

St. Augustine   118

The Question of Evil   121

Islamic Contributions to Early Medieval Thought   124

    Al-Kindi and Neoplatonism   124

    Al-Farabi   125

    Avicenna   126

    Averroes   127

Christian *a Priori* and *a Posteriori* Arguments for God's Existence   127

St. Anselm   128

    The Ontological Argument   129

    Criticisms of the Ontological Argument   131

St. Thomas Aquinas   132

    The Five Arguments for God's Existence   134

    Criticisms of Aquinas' Five Arguments   136

Wondrous Distress in Medieval Thought   139

Chapter 7 René Descartes and the Transition from Medieval to Modern Thinking   143

The Conflict between Science and Religion in the Early Modern Period   145

Modern Developments in Astronomy   146

    The Geocentric Model of the Universe   147

    The Heliocentric Model of the Universe   151

René Descartes   157

    The Cartesian Method   158

Meditations on First Philosophy   159

    Meditation I   160

    Meditation II   163

    Meditation III   164

    Meditation IV   168

    Meditation V   170

    Meditation VI   172

Descartes and Wondrous Distress   173

Chapter 8 Hume   179

The Mind/Body Problem   180

"Solutions" to the Mind/Body Problem   180

    Thomas Hobbes and Materialism   182

    George Berkeley and Idealism   183

    Arnold Geulincx, Nicholas Malebranche, and Occasionalism   184

    Gottfried Leibniz, Baruch Spinoza, and Monism   185

David Hume and the Empiricist Rejection of Cartesian
Metaphysics 189
John Locke *189*
The Good-Natured Hume 191
An Inquiry concerning Human Understanding 193
Impressions, Simple Ideas, and Complex Ideas *194*
Relations of Ideas and Matters of Fact *196*
The Ideas of God and the Self *199*
Hume's Skeptical Empiricism *200*
An Inquiry concerning the Principles of Morals 202
Utility *203*
Hume and Wondrous Distress 206

Chapter 9 Kant's Transcendental Idealism 211
Totalizers versus Critics 212
The Awakening of Kant 214
The Critique of Pure Reason 216
The Phenomenal and Noumenal Worlds *217*
The a Priori Intuitions of Time and Space *218*
The Categories of the Understanding *220*
Transcendental Idealism and the Impossibility of Metaphysics *224*
The Regulative Function of Transcendental Ideas *226*
The Critique of Practical Reason 227
The Good Will *228*
Hypothetical versus Categorical Imperative *228*
The Critique of Judgment 232
Beauty *233*
Sublimity *235*
Kant's Wondrous Distress 236

Chapter 10 Hegel and the Manifestations of *Geist* 239
The Difficulty of Hegel's Philosophy 241
Hegel's Vision of Unity 243
The Phenomenology of Spirit 247
Lordship and Bondage *248*
Stoicism, Skepticism, and the Unhappy Consciousness *250*
Dialectical Logic 252
The Abstract Side *254*
The Dialectical Side *254*

The Speculative Side   255

Absolute Knowing   256

The Doctrine of Being   257

God   259

Hegel's Influence   261

   Right, Center, and Left Hegelianism   261

   Ludwig Feuerbach   262

   Max Stirner   263

   Karl Marx   265

Wondrous Distress in Hegelian Philosophy   267

Chapter 11   Happiness, Suffering, and Pessimism in Kierkegaard, Schopenhauer, Nietzsche, and Mill   272

Søren Kierkegaard: The Knight of Faith   275

   The Sickness Unto Death   277

   Fear and Trembling   279

Schopenhauer's Synthesis of Plato, Kant, and Hinduism   282

   Piercing the Veil of the Thing-in-Itself   285

   The Will   287

   Anxiety, Suffering, and Distress   289

Friedrich Nietzsche and Positive Nihilism   294

   The Will to Power   295

   The Superman and the Death of God   297

Beyond Good and Evil: Nietzsche contra Utilitarianism   301

   The Greatest Happiness Principle   301

Wonder and Distress in Kierkegaard, Schopenhauer, Nietzsche, and Mill   304

Chapter 12   Common Sense and Anglo-American Philosophy   311

The Reaction against Hegel   312

William James   313

   Pragmatism   315

   The Tender- and the Tough-Minded   316

   The Pragmatic Method   317

   The Pragmatic Theory of Truth   320

   Religion   323

Bertrand Russell   327
   Russell's Rejection of Hegel   328
   Logical Atomism   329
   Epistemology   334
   Knowledge by Acquaintance and Knowledge by Description   338
   The Role of Philosophy   340
Ludwig Wittgenstein   341
   Tractatus Logico-Philosophicus   *342*
   Philosophical Investigations   *346*
Wondrous Distress in Anglo-American Philosophy   349

Chapter 13   Existentialism and the Return to Being   355
Nationalism, Imperialism, Technology, and War   356
Nihilism and the Decline of Civilization   357
   Friedrich Nietzsche   357
   Oswald Spengler   358
   Totalitarianism   360
   The Muselmann   361
Martin Heidegger   362
   The Question of Being   362
   Dasein   364
   Being-toward-Death   366
   Inauthenticity and Technological Thinking   367
   Authenticity   369
   Heidegger and Nazism   370
Jean-Paul Sartre   374
   Being-in-Itself and Being-for-Itself   374
   Freedom and Bad Faith   376
Simone de Beauvoir   378
   The Second Sex   *378*
   Otherness   381
   Women and Biology   382
Wondrous Distress in Existentialism   385

CONCLUSION: PHILOSOPHY AND WONDROUS DISTRESS   392
GLOSSARY   401
BIBLIOGRAPHY   421
INDEX   427

Preface

*T*he *Path of Philosophy: Truth, Wonder, and Distress* began as a guidebook written for my Introduction to Philosophy students at Corning Community College and the College of Marin. Over the many years that I have revised and polished this work, it has evolved into something more than a college textbook. In addition to offering an accessible and readable introduction to Western philosophy, this book also provides a critical perspective on the history of philosophy. This is a text that has been tested in the classroom but which will also be of interest to the educated reading public outside of the classroom.

The *Path of Philosophy* traces the history of Western thought from its beginnings in ancient Greece to contemporary developments in the Postmodern world. In this work, I have attempted to demonstrate how philosophy is unique and distinct from religion and science, while at the same time showing how all three disciplines are interrelated and woven together. The unique essence of philosophy, I argue, lies in its commitment to Truth, its enthusiasm for raising questions, and its willingness to defer final answers to those questions. By examining the arguments and contributions of influential figures from the Ancient, Medieval, Modern, and Postmodern periods, I show how philosophical thinking has historically served as a motivation for the pursuit of new developments in science, religion, and philosophy itself. Despite its successes, in the end, philosophical thinking always falls short of its real goal. It involves both the wonder of aspiring toward Truth and the distress of falling short of that Truth. In this way, philosophy can be characterized as wondrous distress.

Unlike many other introductory texts, *The Path of Philosophy* sustains a coherent and ongoing narrative throughout its length. I have written the book so that it tells a story in which particular philosophers appear as important participants. Rather than treating each thinker in isolation, I show how Western thinkers have built upon and critiqued one another's work. One reason for constructing the book in this manner is to counter the mistaken idea that philosophizing involves little more than brashly stating one's own opinion. I also hope to reverse a common impression that the study of philosophy is only focused on the analytical dissection of arguments and worldviews that have little, if any, relationship to one another. Rather, I have tried to show that philosophers are embedded in an ongoing tradition, and that there is a continuity of thinking in the West that explores and articulates an enduring, and insatiable, aspiration toward Truth and the comprehension of Being itself. In emphasizing this aspect of philosophical thinking, I have written a book that is unusual in its cohesiveness and that leaves readers with a vivid picture of philosophy as an extraordinary and spiritually important field of study.

The narrative structure of this book also serves the purpose of providing students with a framework within which they can contextualize and understand many of the primary works that are normally read in introductory philosophy courses. This book simplifies and explains those ideas and arguments, putting them into a context that helps readers to understand the interconnections between the thoughts of different philosophers over time. In addition, this book establishes the historical scaffolding necessary to appreciate and to make sense of thinkers outside of the scope of the work itself. It should be noted that this text, while spanning the whole history of philosophy in the West, is not intended as an encyclopedic catalogue of philosophers and their philosophies. I have carefully selected the thinkers who appear in this book to illustrate and clarify the theme of wondrous distress. In this way, the book attempts to walk a line between comprehensiveness and depth. Some books, in their attempt to be comprehensive, fail to linger with the important issues and arguments that make philosophy profound. Other books, in their attempt to be conceptually deep, fail to offer a panorama of the philosophical and historical landscape. This book walks a middle path between those two extremes.

An important feature that makes this book unique and accessible is the inclusion of original illustrations throughout each of the sections. These illustrations are the work of Juneko Robinson, and they provide vivid, moving, and often humorous depictions of the characters, events, and themes that are dealt with in this book. It may be a cliché to write "a picture is worth a thousand words," but in the case of Juneko Robinson's drawings, this is certainly the case. Her illustrations concretize some rather difficult and abstract concepts, thus providing the reader with a useful tool that assists in the comprehension of important ideas. Having worked closely with Juneko in the conceptualization of these drawings, I am delighted with the final product and amazed by her skill at bringing ideas to life. Her artistry and vision are integral parts of this work's composition.

Each chapter contains boxed features that amplify certain details appearing in the main body of the text and that point out connections to contemporary issues and topics. These features direct readers' attention to other books, films, events, and occurrences in popular culture that are relevant to the topics covered. In combination with numerous tables, diagrams, and illustrations, these boxed features impart a lively, entertaining, and visually interesting appearance to the text that will help students to understand the ongoing debates, questions, and controversies that are an integral part of philosophizing. Also included in each chapter are discussion questions that encourage students to draw their own connections and to relate the material to their own personal experiences and concerns.

I hope that *The Path of Philosophy: Truth, Wonder, and Distress* will serve as a useful, entertaining, and substantial introduction to the wondrous and distressing field of philosophical thinking. Those of us who have devoted our lives to philosophy know that in this discipline there is always more to explore, that there are always conflicting perspectives, and that there is never a final, authoritative verdict on how to interpret key issues. In giving expression to the wondrous distress of philosophical thinking, I hope that I have provided readers with something valuable that inspires them in their own search for Truth.

Acknowledgments

The Path of Philosophy: Truth, Wonder, and Distress is dedicated to the memory of my mother, Frances Marmysz. Without her, I would not be, and so neither would this book.

This book is the culmination of 10 years of thinking, discussing, teaching, studying, and writing. Over the course of these years, it has evolved and changed into something much more ambitious than it initially was intended to be. At the start, the chapters in this book were conceived as weekly lectures to be posted in my online Introduction to Philosophy classes, which I began teaching at Corning Community College in 2001. My first debt of gratitude, therefore, is to the students at CCC who indulged me as I started to articulate in writing the ideas found herein.

Corning Community College offered an atmosphere of collegiality without which this book's development would have been very difficult, if not impossible. My second debt of gratitude is thus to the faculty and staff at CCC who offered encouragement and support during the early phases of this book's conceptualization. In particular, I must thank Andrea Rubin, then chair of the Humanities and Communications Division, for her confidence in me and my work. Andrea's willingness to take the time to talk with me and offer her sincere and honest advice concerning issues both professional and personal helped to make my tenure at CCC both productive and fulfilling. Andrea, as I have told her often, is the best boss I have ever had. I also am grateful to Professor Vince Lisella, who was a good friend to me while I was at Corning, helping me to feel like I belonged even when I was unsure if I did. I will always cherish my memories of our philosophical conversations, and the passion, humor, and playfulness that Vince devotes to his thinking and teaching. Vince has helped me to pursue many ideas through to their end, including a number of those that appear in these pages. He is one of the best teachers I have ever met. Finally, I thank Professor Byron Shaw, who kindly took the time to read through and offer suggestions on an early draft of this text. Byron made me feel that this was a project worth undertaking.

The staff outside of the CCC Humanities Division were also extremely supportive and helpful as I began to get this project off the ground. A big boost of financial help came from CCC's Center for Professional Development, which granted me funding to commission some of the first original drawings by Juneko Robinson that accompany this text. I thank Les Rosenbloom and Joanne Moone, both of the Center for Professional Development, for their enthusiasm and belief in this project. No less important were all of the staff and faculty members at CCC who honored me with a SUNY Chancellor's Award for Scholarship and Creativity. This sign of their appreciation and respect will always be important to me, and it was a vital shot in the arm that helped me to retain my confidence and enthusiasm.

Andrea Rubin and Byron Shaw were also instrumental in helping me to secure a National Endowment for the Humanities (NEH) Fellowship for the summer of 2005, during which I was able to further research, think through, and polish the ideas in Chapter 11. I thank Andrea, Byron, and the NEH for the opportunity this fellowship gave me to participate in a six-week seminar titled "Terror and Culture: Revisiting Hannah Arendt's *The Origins of Totalitarianism*," held at Stanford University and led by Russell A. Berman and Julia C. Hell. I also thank the participants in that seminar, especially Scott Lukas, for helpful criticisms and input.

In 2005, I left CCC and accepted a position at the College of Marin, in Marin County, California, where I now teach philosophy. At COM, I have continued to be encouraged by supervisors, peers, and students. I therefore thank the numerous students from my Introduction to Philosophy courses at COM who have read and offered comments on the evolving versions of these chapters; in particular, Mike Williamson and Pietro Poggi. I also thank David Rollison, John Sutherland, David Snyder, and Janet Macintosh, all members of the COM English/Humanities Division, for their advice and concern with this project.

The editors at Cengage and Wadsworth deserve my gratitude for their help and guidance. In particular, I thank Marcus Boggs, Worth Hawes, Ian Lague, Patrick Stockstill, Joann Kozyrev, Nathan Gamache, and Alison Eigel Zade for their enthusiasm and professionalism as they steered me through the complicated and sometimes aggravating publishing process. Special thanks are due to Anne Talvacchio and Steven Burr at Cadmus Communications, who provided excellent suggestions in the course of copyediting the text.

I also thank the following reviewers who took the time to offer suggestions and comments:

Carlos Andres, California State University, Stanislaus; Babette Babich, Fordham University; Danielle Bertuccio, Suffolk County Community College; Joseph Campisi, Marist College; Lida Criner, Northwestern University; Stephen Daniel, Texas A&M University; Annette Neblett Evans, Lynchburg College; Charles Fethe, Kean University; Glenn Gentry, Columbia International University; Shahrokh Haghighi, California State University, Long Beach; John Holder, Pensacola Junior College; Deborah Holt, College of Southern Maryland; Mark Kosinski, Gateway Community College; Rory Kraft, York College of Pennsylvania; Flo Leibowitz, Oregon State University; Michael McClure, Prince

George's Community College; Elizabeth Meade, Cedar Crest College; John Millard, Boston College; Donald Morse, Webster University; Ronald Novy, University of Central Arkansas; David M. Parry, Pennsylvania State University, Altoona; Keith Putt, Samford University; Norman Rauls, Community College of Southern Nevada; Kent E. Robson, Utah State University; K. Rogers, University of Delaware; Chad W. Russell, University of Mississippi; Aimin Shen, Hanover College; Alex Snow, Cayuga County Community College; Joseph Ulatowski, University of Nevada; Craig Vasey, University of Mary Washington; Ann Voelkel, Blinn College; Shane Wahl, Purdue University; Nancy M. Williams, Wofford College; and Kenneth Williford, University of Texas at Arlington.

Randall Lake has done a wonderful job photographing, touching up, and digitally manipulating elements of Juneko's original drawings. I thank him for his hard work, his patience, and his reliability as we entered the final stages of production.

Many, many thanks are also due to my old friends Kent Daniels and Dario Goykovich who have read, critiqued, and argued with me about the contents of this book during our hikes in the hills of Marin County. I am pleased that the distress of life has only served to intensify our shared passion for philosophizing. I also thank my friends Jason McQuinn and Christopher Anderson for their helpful comments on Chapter 10, as well as for many stimulating conversations.

Finally, no words are adequate to express my thankfulness and love for my wife, Juneko Robinson, who has been a part of this project from its very beginning. Her creativity, philosophical insight, and encouragement have remained consistent throughout the years of this book's development. In addition to her extraordinary drawings, Juneko has contributed to this project in ways that are impossible to enumerate. Even at those points when we were separated by thousands of miles, Juneko inspired me to look to the future and to strive toward the realization of goals that are important to both of us. I am looking forward to the many adventures and experiences that we will share in the years ahead.

Introduction

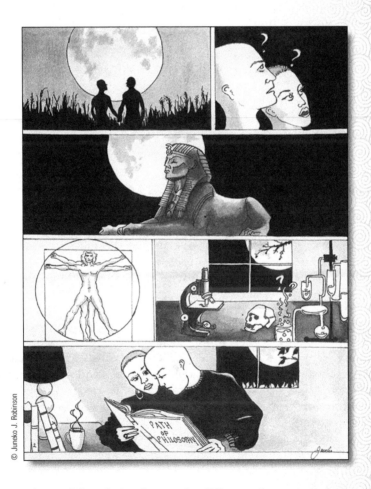

What is philosophy? What are the differences between analytic and continental styles of philosophizing? What is the relationship between religion, science, and philosophy? In what sense can philosophy be characterized as a kind of "wondrous distress"?

The study of philosophy is so varied and diverse in terms of its subject matter and in terms of the tools that are used to address that subject matter that it is virtually impossible to sum up in a neat and tidy fashion just what the field is all about. To complicate matters, the term "philosophy" can be, and is, appended to just about every other area of study. If you examine the catalogue of any major university, you are likely to come across courses with titles like "Philosophy of Science," "Philosophy of Religion," "Philosophy of Mathematics," "Philosophy of Art," "Philosophy of Technology," "Philosophy of Life," and on and on. It seems as if there is a philosophy of everything; perhaps even a philosophy of philosophy! Just what is it that all of these wide-ranging areas of study have in common?

An introduction to philosophy would do a disservice if it glossed over the controversies, the complexities, the disagreements, and the infighting that occur within the discipline. It is sometimes said that philosophy is the only academic domain in which practitioners are uncertain about what it is that they are studying. If you look at the field as a whole, this assertion is not so outlandish at all. Many philosophers do not agree among themselves what the proper scope of philosophical inquiry encompasses, or what tools are appropriate to it, and so we find an ongoing (and sometimes divisive and nasty) debate carried out within professional philosophy concerning its proper focus.

ANALYTIC AND CONTINENTAL STYLES OF PHILOSOPHIZING

For instance, in the contemporary world, one of the most pronounced and contentious divisions in philosophy has become that between the so-called "analytic" style of philosophizing and the so-called "continental" style of philosophizing. From the analytic camp we learn that the proper task of philosophy is to use the tools of logic and analysis to clarify and define problems, ultimately with an eye toward solving (or dissolving) those problems, thus providing us with clear and definitive answers to the questions that we have about the universe and our place in it. Philosophy, in this view, is closely allied with science, and its goal is thought to be the elimination of mystery and ignorance as well as the promotion of the progressive growth of human knowledge. In the words of Brian Leiter, one of the most vigorous proponents of the analytic style of philosophy in America today, "Analytic philosophers, crudely speaking, aim for argumentative clarity and precision; draw freely on the tools of logic; and often identify, professionally and intellectually, more closely with the sciences and mathematics, than with the humanities."[1] One of the central elements binding this category of philosophers together, and from which they take the name "analytic philosophy," is the emphasis on analysis. From this perspective, the job of philosophy is, by and large, to isolate and break apart particular issues and questions into manageable pieces so that they may be clarified and systematically scrutinized according to the procedures of logic and science. Just as scientists narrowly focus on clearly defined problems, according to the analytic perspective philosophers should likewise direct their attention toward issues that can be broken up into well-defined bits and pieces, which can then be addressed in isolation from other peripheral concerns. Philosophy, in this view, should treat the world as composed of pieces that can be taken apart and understood bit by bit. As in the natural sciences, analytic philosophers believe that progress is possible in philosophy if individual thinkers just commit to specializing in a particular area, focus their energies on individual problems, and then contribute their findings to the collective wisdom of the field.

From the continental camp, on the other hand, we learn that philosophy is not so much about logic and analysis as it is about ongoing contemplation and meditation on the grandest mysteries in the universe. In this view, philosophy should not be overly focused on providing unequivocal answers to questions. Rather, it should be content with lingering upon the enigmas and complexities of human experience, even if no answers are ever forthcoming. Here, philosophy is presented as more closely allied with the humanities, and as in art, literature, and cultural criticism, continental thinkers claim that focus should fall on exploring and appreciating the full depth of human experience. Bruce Wilshire, a passionate contemporary American critic of analytic thought and a proponent of the continental style of philosophy, writes:

> I understand philosophy in a traditional way. It is an activity the
> ultimate aim of which is to keep us open to the unencompassable, the
> domain of what we don't know we don't know. An obvious corollary
> is to strive to make our assumptions as clear and as grounded in
> experience as it is possible for us to make them. For our assumptions
> are just that: assumptions, which we formulate within a universe we
> cannot encompass in thought. Analytic philosophy tends to so sharply
> focus that it seals us from the vague but all-important background
> presence of the universe.[2]

The term "continental" stems from a tradition of philosophy that can be traced back to nineteenth-century thinkers from the European continent; in particular, certain post-Kantian thinkers like Kierkegaard, Schopenhauer, and Nietzsche. These thinkers were less concerned with the technicalities of logic and more literary in their approach to philosophizing. Though it is difficult to find a single element uniting all of the thinkers who today are classified as continental, they tend to have less faith in science, more interest in the history of ideas, and exhibit more of a tendency to engage in metaphysical speculation than analytic thinkers. Continental philosophers treat philosophy as an ongoing project in which the human thinker stands in awe of the universe and its overwhelming excess. Because the universe is so uncanny, it cannot be unambiguously or easily comprehended by breaking it into bits and pieces using logic or science. Thus, it is a common tendency of continental thinkers to critique logic and science as historically contingent devices that oversimplify, and thus cover over, the true nature of the world. For continental thinkers, deep contemplation seems more important than scientific progress or unequivocal answers.

Analytic thinkers often charge continental thinkers with being fuzzy-headed and mixed up. Because they do not emphasize problem-solving and the assertion of final conclusions, it is sometimes complained that continental philosophers are incomprehensible, equivocal, and purposefully opaque. Why can't they just say what they mean in a clear, straightforward fashion?! On the other hand, continental philosophers often charge analytic thinkers with being shallow and overly glib. Because the analytic tradition emphasizes solving problems and coming to clear conclusions, it is charged that analytic philosophers don't always take the time to linger with grander, "eternal issues" to appreciate the full depth, complexity, and mystery of human existence.

In this contemporary philosophical battle, we get the taste of an ongoing controversy that always has, and probably always will, be present in the field of philosophy. On the one hand, philosophers desire answers to questions. They pursue their inquiries because they want to make discoveries and come to know something about themselves and the world in which they live. On the other hand, some of the most important and enduring questions that humans ask themselves are of a sort that resist being answered. These questions have persisted precisely because human thought is too limited to fully comprehend the scope and depth of the issues that are involved. What is the meaning of life? Does God exist? What is Truth? What is Goodness? What is ultimately real? These sorts of questions may be unanswerable by anyone but a god, yet they are nonetheless among the most important and enduring questions, meriting contemplation regardless of whether or not we can produce answers to them.

T A B L E   I N T R O . 1   Continental versus Analytic Philosophy

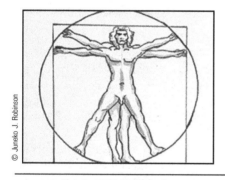 

Continental Philosophy	Analytic Philosophy
1. Tends to be aligned with the humanities	1. Tends to be aligned with the sciences
2. Tends to be more literary in style	2. Tends to emphasize the use of logic
3. Tends to be more friendly to the open-ended contemplation and exploration of human experience	3. Tends to focus on defining terms, resolving issues, and establishing answers to questions

THE LOVE OF WISDOM

Ironically, it is through the quarrels and disagreements of experts in the field that we can start to get an initial sense of what is essential, as well as what is non-essential, to the study of philosophy. Because those who engage in philosophical exploration don't necessarily agree on the subject matter or tools that are appropriate to their discipline, we might start to suspect that the essence of philosophy does not lie in a particular subject matter or in a particular set of tools at all. It may be that the essence of philosophy has less to do with subject matter and technique and more to do with something else. If this is the case, then trying to understand what philosophy is will require that we look past the superficial differences among particular philosophers and instead try to uncover the deeper similarities that both unite philosophers as philosophers and that separate philosophers from experts in other fields of study such as science and religion.

Among philosophers of all descriptions and dispositions there are a few characteristics that do seem to recur again and again, giving shape to a recognizable way of thinking that we call "philosophical." Part of the task of this book is to draw attention to those recurrent characteristics as they appear in the history of Western civilization. What we will find as our investigation progresses is that philosophy is, at the very least, a mode of thinking that is characterized by an enthusiasm for raising questions as well as a willingness to defer final answers to those questions in the quest for absolute Truth.

The term "philosophy" comes from two Greek words: *philos* and *sophia*. *Philos* means "love of." *Sophia* means "wisdom." The term "philosophy," then, literally means "the love of wisdom." It was the ancient Greek philosopher, mathematician, and religious figure Pythagoras who first coined this term. For Pythagoras, the study of the world was not simply a detached and academic exercise. Rather, it was an integral part of a much larger project that was focused on self-discovery and the aspiration toward personal perfection. As the genius who formulated the Pythagorean Theorem and the mathematical description of harmonies, and as the leader of a mystical religious cult, Pythagoras had, during his lifetime, developed a reputation as a very smart, profound, and spiritual figure. However, when asked by a fellow citizen whether he thought himself wise, Pythagoras is reported to have responded, "No, I only love wisdom."

Pythagoras' coinage of the term "philosophy," then, seems to have been intended as a way of articulating his *attitude* toward Truth and Wisdom. He didn't claim to be wise, in fact, but only to be a *philosopher* in the sense that he aspired toward, and loved, wisdom. If we follow him in this usage, then philosophy would turn out to be not so much a closed body of knowledge as an attitude of care and curiosity about what is true, good, and lasting. In fact, to be a philosopher, as we will see is the case with Socrates and the Skeptics, one need not know anything at all. One need only be willing to cultivate an attitude of openness to speculation and reflection concerning the world's mysteries. Philosophy is a quest and a process that inquires into and probes reality, asking questions about the world and our place in it. The philosopher is thus not an individual who knows Truth but rather an individual who strives toward, and is curious about, the undiscovered truths (or Truth) of the universe. It might even be said that as soon as one claims to have discovered final answers to the mysteries of the world, one ceases to be a philosopher. "No god is a philosopher or a seeker after wisdom," writes Plato,[3] because gods already know everything. Humans, however, do not know everything, and as long as they continue to aspire toward wisdom, Truth, and knowledge they remain philosophical creatures. If this is correct, then we can already see that the analytic and the continental perspectives on philosophy each have a part, but only a part, of the picture in proper focus. To be a philosopher is to be caught between the desire for answers and the realization that no answer is final. It is a way of thinking that is ambitious in its aspiration toward a perfect understanding of the world yet modest in its recognition of how far we must always fall short of this goal.

RELIGION, SCIENCE, AND PHILOSOPHY

Historically, philosophical thinking has had uneasy, though often fruitful, relationships with other forms of thinking. We can start to get a sense of these relationships if we take a brief moment to look at the distinction between philosophy, science, and religion. Over the course of this book we will trace the manner in which these modes of thinking are interconnected, and one of the major themes that will resound is the critical role played by philosophical thinking as a spur or motivation toward progress and development in other fields of human knowledge. It is clear that to expand and develop, it is necessary for the practitioners in an area of expertise to question, wonder, and speculate about things unknown and undiscovered. But this, in turn, requires an admission of ignorance concerning some of the very things that one seeks to explain. Both science and religion, therefore, require the sort of openness that is involved in philosophical thinking if they are to constantly move forward. Eliminate the philosophical elements of a field of study and it stagnates, or even worse, becomes corrupt.

Take, for instance, the field of religion. Like philosophers, religious thinkers probe and question reality, looking for the Truth behind the world's appearances. However, what makes religious thinkers distinctive is their claim that sacred texts or prophets and wise men hold the authority to reveal supernatural truths about existence. The religious thinker, in this way, differs from the philosopher who does not necessarily accept the authority of revelation but rather remains committed to ongoing questioning and the probing of Being itself in spite of, and sometimes in contradiction to, the proclamations and assertions of authority figures. The history of religious thinking is textured with conflicts between those believers who rely solely on faith and those who question their faith by reflecting philosophically on the nature and

TABLE INTRO.2   **Religion, Science, and Philosophy**

Religion	Science	Philosophy
1. Explains some things in terms of supernatural causes	1. Explains all things in terms of natural causes	1. Entertains the possibility of both natural and supernatural explanations
2. Uses faith, prayer, ritual, and narrative	2. Uses logic, observation, and hypothesis-testing	2. Uses logic, argument, narrative, dialogue, and questioning
3. Aspires toward mystical awakening	3. Aspires toward increasing knowledge of the natural world	3. Aspires toward wisdom
4. Offers answers	4. Offers answers	4. Raises new questions

justification of religious doctrines, traditions, and practices. During those periods of history when philosophical reflection becomes most muted and discouraged, we find that the institutions of religion tend to become much more dogmatic, insular, and closed off to innovation and progress. Religious authority, then, goes untempered, and voices of dissent are silenced. This is what occurred during the so-called "Dark Ages," and not until the spirit of philosophical thinking was later reinvigorated did new and exciting developments in religion begin to emerge.

Scientific thinking also benefits from, yet is distinct from, philosophical thinking. The scientist, like the philosopher, rationally inquires into the nature of Being. Yet unlike the philosopher, the scientist is predominantly concerned with the sorts of questions that can be answered by appeal to the tools of observation, measurement, description, and hypothesis-testing. The philosopher, however, cannot remain satisfied with such a limited range of inquiry and instead remains committed to asking more and more questions, many of which are impossible to answer in any empirically verifiable manner. Just as the history of religion is replete with instances when philosophical reflection has led to conflict, revolution, and reformation, so too does this occur in the history of science. Thus, we find Aristotelian science and astronomy being questioned and overturned by developments in Newtonian physics, and Newtonian physics, in turn, being called into question by developments in quantum physics, and so forth. These changes are not simply the result of science's own self-correcting nature, but, as Thomas S. Kuhn writes, of the formulation of different and "incommensurable ways of seeing the world"[4] on the part of scientists who actively, and philosophically, question the tools, methods, and paradigms that have been bequeathed to them by their tradition.

© Juneko J. Robinson

WHAT IS

PHILOSOPHY?

Because of the unrelenting nature of philosophical questioning, there is usually very little agreement among philosophers and very little hope of arriving at uncontroversial answers to the questions that they raise. The true spirit of philosophy lies in questioning assumptions, not in offering dogmatic answers. Philosophical thinking can, and does, work side by side with science and religion, pushing these fields further and further in their inquiries. Yet philosophers remain truly philosophical only insofar as they remain willing to question our most basic assumptions about reality. As we will see later, while philosophers have been instrumental in the development and progress of both science and religion, they have also sometimes been marked as the enemies of both of these fields. This is because at any given time a philosopher is willing to question, and thereby cast doubt on, the conventional beliefs and theories of the day. This may be perceived as threatening to the conservative forces within society's institutions. Yet without questions, there is no reason to look for answers. Without the recognition of what we don't know, there is no room made for discoveries. Without the distress of ignorance, there is no motivation to search for Truth.

Whereas the appeal of religious and of scientific thought is that they promise "Big Answers," the appeal of philosophical thought is that it poses "Big Questions." This propensity to raise "Big Questions" that don't necessarily have any clear-cut or uncontroversial answers is seen by many as troubling, and throughout the history of philosophy we find again and again that philosophers have been persecuted, ridiculed, and even killed for asking too many questions and challenging too many taken-for-granted assumptions. So it is that in asking questions about topics that others have never bothered to wonder about, philosophers not only expand the boundaries of human knowledge and learning, they also often expose themselves to public scorn. It can be comforting to live life thinking that what we know now is all that there is to know and to assume that our "common sense" is an adequate guide to the nature of reality. However, one of the important messages that philosophy has to teach us is that there are always more questions to be asked and that our "common sense" about the world is often wrong.

So what is philosophy? The perspective that will be taken in this book is that philosophy is a mode of thinking that is characterized by a commitment to Truth, an enthusiasm for raising new questions, and by a willingness to defer final answers to those questions. Philosophers love wisdom without necessarily believing themselves to be wise. They desire to know the truth about reality, yet in the process of their inquiries philosophers tend to discover that there are always more questions to be asked and more things to be investigated. In this way, philosophy is more like a quest and a process than it is a static and final body of knowledge about the world. In philosophy, anything may be questioned, and while this sort of openness allows for the continual development and pushing forward of human knowledge, it is also accompanied by a sort of distressing sense of doubt and incompleteness. Because there are always more questions to be asked, the answers that humans formulate to the mysteries of existence, whether they be in the language of science or religion, are never final. This is the double edge of philosophical thinking. It is filled with both wonder and distress: wonder at what we don't yet know, and distress that we will never know everything.

© Juneko J. Robinson

PHILOSOPHY
AS WONDROUS
DISTRESS

Reconstructing the history of philosophy is a formidable task, and there are innumerable ways that one might attempt it. The reader should understand that the narrative offered in this book is only one among many possible approaches to the subject matter, and yet I feel that what is articulated in this account comes closer than most to the expression of a neglected truth about the philosophical tradition. Throughout this book I will emphasize "wondrous distress" as the primary attitude that is indispensable for thinking philosophically. We will find this attitude present, to varying degrees, in all of the great philosophical figures this book will survey. Beginning with the ancient Greeks, we will follow the trajectory of Western philosophy through Medieval, Modern, and contemporary time periods, and we will repeatedly encounter ambitious thinkers who seek a target that they fail to strike. Truth, it seems, is an elusive objective. Philosophers have nevertheless found themselves aiming toward this mark no matter how often they fail to satisfy their ambitions. This is the engine that drives all of Western philosophy: the unsatisfied yet incessant pursuit of Truth. Many people find such a project puzzling, and they wonder why it is that anyone would be attracted to a kind of thinking that never seems to lead to final answers. If philosophy is characterized by wondrous distress, isn't it a fundamentally frustrating area of study? Why not abandon this endlessly inconclusive kind of thinking and instead focus on something more practical; something that will produce concrete results and that will grant us a degree of satisfaction, confidence, and assurance? These questions are familiar to any contemporary college student who is flirting with the idea of pursuing a philosophy major. They are good questions to ask, and they should be taken seriously. For many of us who have dedicated our lives to philosophy, these questions never go away. Yet there remain powerful reasons why the study of philosophy is good for us nonetheless.

When pursued authentically, philosophy instructs us in the virtues of intellectual modesty and curiosity while encouraging us to broaden our perspectives on the world indefinitely. There are no settled issues in philosophy, and thus it has no place for dogmatism, arrogance, snobbishness, or the proclamations of authorities. This may strike many readers as a peculiar assertion because some of the most dogmatic, arrogant, snobbish, and authoritarian figures in the history of Western thinking have at least *called* themselves philosophers! But in reality, such individuals have diverged from the true spirit of what it means to be a philosopher. It is not uncommon to see people adopting dogmatic and arrogant attitudes to avoid admitting the things that they really don't know, but when a "philosopher" does so, it is a true disgrace. Philosophical thinking, authentically pursued, ceaselessly reminds us of our separation from the final answers about the world while also provoking us to continue searching for Truth. In this way it promotes a sense of humility and openness to new learning. The wondrous distress that characterizes philosophical thinking can be frustrating, certainly, but perhaps this particular kind of frustration is not such a bad thing. It reminds us

that we are not perfect, that we have more to learn, and that our powers of understanding are limited. As we will see in the pages that follow, this is an important lesson that philosophy teaches us again and again.

NOTES

1. Brian Leiter, "Analytic and Continental Philosophy," *Philosophical Gourmet Report,* www.philosophicalgourmet.com/analytic.asp.

2. Bruce Wilshire, *Fashionable Nihilism: A Critique of Analytic Philosophy* (Albany: SUNY Press, 2002), p. 16.

3. Plato, *Symposium,* 204a.

4. Thomas S. Kuhn, *The Structure of Scientific Revolutions* (Chicago: University of Chicago Press, 1996), p. 4.

Chapter 1

Myth, Science, Philosophy, and the Presocratics

© Juneko J. Robinson

What characterizes mythic thinking? Who were the Presocratics? What characterizes Presocratic thinking? How do mythic thinking and Presocratic thinking complement and conflict with one another? How does Presocratic thinking pave the way both for philosophy and for science?

Traditionally, the first philosophers are considered to be a group of thinkers collectively known as the Presocratics. As their title suggests, the Presocratics were engaged in philosophical reflection at a time before Socrates made his mark on the world. Nevertheless, it is not quite correct to say that all of the individuals grouped together under this label actually *lived* before the time of Socrates. Some of them were, in fact, his historical contemporaries, and at least one of

1

these thinkers, Anaxagoras, was Socrates' teacher. Accordingly, the label "Preso-cratic" probably is intended more as a tribute to the importance and pivotal na-ture of Socrates in the history of philosophy than it is intended to denote a temporal sequence of thinkers. It is also, perhaps, meant to insinuate that the Presocratics anticipated, but did not quite perfect, a mode of thinking that only came into full bloom with the great Athenian philosopher. This last idea has be-come more and more controversial, and, as we will see later, some modern thinkers even assert that the accomplishments of Socrates are actually *regressive* when compared with those of his precursors. In any case, it is safe to say that those thinkers we now call the "Presocratics" did not refer to themselves by this label, nor would they necessarily have approved of its connotations.

Whatever we believe about their merits or shortcomings, however, it is pretty clear that with the Presocratics, sometime around 600 B.C., a change occurred that signaled a new and influential style in human thinking. The importance of this way of thinking lies in the fact that it was the first bold and concerted attempt to break away from a completely mythic and religious perspective on reality and in-stead to integrate rational and naturalistic elements into our picture of the world and its processes. In de-emphasizing mythic and religious accounts, the Presocratics initiated the growth of both philosophy and science. Yet in their revolutionary theories and ideas we can still, nevertheless, detect a concern for the sorts of issues that religion and myth always sought to address. These thinkers asked grand ques-tions about humans and their place in the universe, offering answers and specula-tions that were often articulated in the language of physics. The world they thus described was at once comprehensible, yet sublime; rational, yet filled with mys-tery; simple in its makeup, and yet awe inspiring in its scope. As a whole, the Presocratics represent a group of thinkers who attempted to understand themselves and their world in an unusually multifaceted and ambitious manner. In them, phil-osophical, scientific, and mythic thinking coexisted for a time, and yet it was an uneasy mix. With the later Presocratics, like Democritus, there progressively devel-oped a hostility toward myth and religion, which came to be seen as antithetical to rational, materialistic explanations of reality. In the end, as the scientific elements of Presocratic thinking came to overshadow all of the other elements, there appeared to be no room left for the mysterious and the nonphysical. It was then that ancient Greek science came into conflict with the myths of the ancient world.

MYTHIC THINKING

In order to understand how and why this conflict developed between myth and science, we need first to understand a little bit about the nature of myth and myth-making. A myth-maker tells stories about the world, and in so doing

© Juneko J. Robinson

provides an account concerning why things are the way that they are. In this way, myth serves as a kind of explanation for reality and so can be thought of as emerging from the same ground as science itself. Myth, like science, wants to understand the universe. One could only imagine what it would be like to live during a time and in a place where no explanatory framework existed for understanding the world. Under such circumstances things would just appear to happen for no reason. The phenomena of the world would flash across our field of experience in a never-ending stream of events, colors, sounds, smells, and feelings. Lightning would strike, but we would not know why it did so or what it was. People would be born, but we would have no idea where they came from or how it was that they were formed. The seasons would change, but there would be no indication of the mechanism or the purpose for this change. With the introduction of mythic or scientific explanations, however, all such phenomena may become woven into a comprehensible whole. What had merely been episodic and disconnected occurrences start to hang together, like the threads in a rug, and we begin to feel as if the world makes sense and has an order and pattern to it.

Yet the myths of the ancient world tended to have a somewhat different composition than the explanations of the physical sciences. In the physical sciences, the world is characterized in terms of the interaction of material constituents, like atoms. For the scientist, an appeal to supernatural entities is neither necessary nor desirable, and so all explanations are grounded in the elements and forces of nature. You might say that with science, nature is explained in terms of nature itself. The explanations of myth-makers are not necessarily restricted in this manner, however. The bulk of mythic stories formulated by the ancient Babylonians, the Jews, the Egyptians, and the Greeks before the time of the Presocratics were influenced by religious beliefs, and so they tended to focus on how the world came to be in terms of gods, goddesses, demons, angels, spirits, and other such supernatural entities. As the word suggests, *super*natural entities are things that exist above or apart from the natural world. They are not subject to the natural forces and laws that exist on Earth, but rather are the initiators of those forces and laws. Furthermore, it is usually the case that supernatural entities are not constrained or defined by a physical structure of their own. In their essence, they are something other than material substance, although they may occasionally inhabit or possess bodies in order to carry out their missions here on Earth. A supernatural entity, then, is neither essentially physical nor is it subject to physical forces, and so it may behave and act in ways that appear unpredictable and mysterious from our earthly perspective. Nevertheless, in conceiving of such entities the human mind gains assurance of a hidden order behind the confusing and grand diversity of phenomena that the world presents to our senses.

But if the supernatural characters of many ancient myths are so radically removed from the physical constraints and realities of our world, then it might appear that they could do just about anything. On the one hand, this would make it easy to use the gods to explain everything, because there is nothing that they cannot do. They would be absolutely powerful, occult, and inscrutable. On the other hand, if we cannot understand the workings of the supernatural world even a bit, then does an appeal to the gods really explain anything at all? If we cannot understand how or why the gods operate, then do such mythic stories really expand our knowledge of how the world around us operates? Without some sort of bridge between the gods and the realm of our own understanding, it may appear that all these myths give us is further mystery and so no real explanations at all.

It turns out that ancient myth-makers did offer a bridge between the human world and the supernatural world that purports to give us a way of understanding the hows and whys of godly action. This bridge is the attribution of human-like feelings, motivations, and desires to gods, goddesses, demons, and their ilk. Ancient myth-makers claimed that it is as a result of these inclinations that such supernatural entities are motivated to bring about the events that we see in the natural world around us. Because we can understand what it is like to be motivated by anger, love, or feelings of frustration, we might feel better equipped to understand the workings of the supernatural world itself in this manner, and if it is the hidden, supernatural world that determines how things unfold here in the natural world, then mythic stories might offer a way for us to better understand the world in which we live. For this reason, ancient myth-makers tended to rely not only on supernatural stories but also on "anthropomorphizations," which are characterizations attributing human-like qualities to non-human things. The first myths, in a nutshell, attempted to understand and explain the natural world by telling stories that often involved supernatural creatures motivated by feelings and desires that are a lot like the feelings and desires humans themselves experience.

By way of illustrating this aspect of mythic explanation, consider these opening passages from the Bible:

> And God said, "Let there be light"; and there was light. And God saw that the light was good; and God separated the light from the darkness. God called the light Day and the darkness he called Night. (Genesis 1:3)

> Thus the heavens and the earth were finished, and all the host of them. And on the seventh day God finished his work which he had done, and he rested on the seventh day from all his work which he had done. So God blessed the seventh day and hallowed it, because on it God rested from all his work which he had done in creation. (Genesis 2:1)

What we see here is an account of the world's creation by an all-powerful god, unconstrained by any sorts of physical laws, who magically brings the world into existence out of nothing. God experiences a sense of satisfaction and pleasure upon the completion of His task, just as human beings do when they successfully finish something. Like any human being who has exerted himself or herself physically, God desires rest after the completion of His project. Later on in the Bible, God experiences other sorts of feelings and emotions, like love and anger, and it is these sorts of motivations that are used to explain the occurrence of specific events in the world. When God is loving, there are certain natural consequences that result, and when He is angry there are other natural consequences.

As human beings we might feel as though we can understand the world around us a little bit better upon hearing this mythic tale. We know what it feels like to be happy, angry, or sad, and so we can empathize with a supernatural god who feels these same emotions. When we are angry, we might kick the wall and so put a hole in it. When God is angry, He might throw a fit and so, because of his supernatural powers, cause a thunderstorm. Just as our own anger explains why we kicked the wall and thus explains why there is a hole in the wall, so does God's anger explain why a thunderstorm occurred. Moreover, because the mythic story told in the Bible claims that the God with whom we empathize not only brought the world into existence but also sustains and intervenes in our lives, we may feel better able to cope and deal with all of the events, hardships, and challenges that we encounter throughout life. Such mythic storytelling assures us that there is a grand intelligence that has given order, significance, and meaning to the universe.

The author F. M. Cornford has likened mythic thinking to the mode of thinking that is present in human infants as they begin to emerge out of complete self-centeredness. At this point in mental development, a baby begins to realize that there are forces governing the outside world that are beyond its control. When the environment does not automatically respond to an infant's wishes, it may begin to suspect that nature possesses its own will. When a baby is hungry, food does not automatically materialize. When it wants peace and quiet, the world does not always cooperate. The infant, at this point in its development, learns that wishing for something does not make it so and that the state of the natural world is often at odds with human desire. It may seem to the infant as if some sort of conscious force "out there" is purposefully thwarting its desires and wants. These forces governing nature may then be likened to the only thing that is within the comprehension of the infantile mind; namely, the infantile mind itself. So it is that when a baby experiences its first frustrating and confusing encounters with the environment, it may formulate the belief that there is some sort of unseen intelligence standing behind the world's appearances. This unseen intelligence is thought of as possessing its own feelings, desires, and wants. This helps the infantile mind to make sense of what might otherwise seem completely incomprehensible.[1]

Cornford's characterization of mythic thinking is useful, but it also has pitfalls. One of its advantages is that it helps to clarify a major difference between the myths of ancient times, on the one hand, and the development of philosophical and scientific thought, on the other. Ancient myths were often supernatural and anthropomorphic. They explained the world by way of making reference to unearthly entities that have human-like qualities. This sort of explanation naturally reminds us of the sort of simple and naïve thought engaged in by young children. Yet mythic stories can also be quite sophisticated, complex, profound, and even sometimes non-supernatural. For these reasons it would be a mistake to allow ourselves to overextend Cornford's analogy. Mythic thinking is still engaged in by intelligent, rational, and educated adults today. It is not a sort of thinking that simply disappeared with the advent of science and philosophy, but one that continues to coexist with other ways of thinking about ourselves and the world. Mythic thinking is not necessarily an underdeveloped or immature form of thought, as some scientists and philosophers might like to claim, but rather a way of understanding and explaining the meaning of the world through narrative storytelling. It is not essentially inferior, but rather *different* from other non-mythic forms of explanation that rely more predominantly on argumentation, logic, and reason. In the ancient world, mythic stories very often were partnered with religious beliefs involving the gods, but myths can also be told that make no reference to the supernatural at all, as we will see in Chapter 3 when we encounter Plato's cave myth. The key point here is that myth-making is a form of storytelling, and in the ancient world before the emergence of the Presocratic philosophers, the stories that were most often told about the nature and origins of the universe involved little logic and many appeals to anthropomorphized supernatural entities.

PRESOCRATIC THINKING

Now, compare ancient, mythic accounts of creation, like that offered in the Bible to those provided by the Presocratic philosophers. While the Presocratic philosophers still incorporate mythic stories into their accounts, they tend increasingly to emphasize naturalistic explanations. In the thinking of these first philosophers, we begin to detect the earliest attempts to understand the natural world in a manner that relies less on stories about gods and more on logical analysis and naturalistic speculation.

The Milesian School: Thales and Anaximander

The majority of what we know about the Presocratic philosophers is secondhand. Most of their writing has been lost, and so our understanding of their way of thinking must be put together from fragments of texts and the accounts

© Juneko J. Robinson

of later philosophers like Aristotle. Traditionally, the first of the Presocratic philosophers was thought to be a man by the name of Thales. Thales lived in the Greek city-state of Miletus around 600 B.C., and he is credited with the assertion that everything in the world can be explained in terms of water. Now this is a strange claim, but it is one that we are still able to make some sense of. Even today it is said that the human body is composed largely of water, and we think that no life can exist without water. We believe that water is intimately connected with the cycle of existence on Earth, and so it is not that difficult to see why someone might claim that any explanation of life would necessarily have to include an account of how water is involved. Yet Thales seemed to be saying even more than this. According to him, not only do living things depend on water, but all material substances and natural phenomena are explainable in terms of water.

For instance, Thales apparently believed that the Earth itself floats in water. He seems to have reasoned that the Earth must be supported by something, and air is not substantial enough to offer this support: "... it [the Earth] can float like a log or something else of that sort (for none of these things can rest on air, but they can rest on water)...."[2] Earthquakes could then be explained, according to Thales, as the result of the agitation of the water in which the Earth rests. As the water becomes unsettled, this motion is then transmitted to the Earth and it shakes in the manner we experience during earthquakes. Notice that Thales' explanation here is not only naturalistic, but it involves an element of reasoning that is absent from completely mythic accounts of the world. Whereas a myth-maker might explain earthquakes by claiming that one of the gods became angry and shook the Earth in rage, Thales instead utilizes only the natural properties of water to explain the natural motions of the Earth. Furthermore, he reasons that because things are able to float in water, but not in other elements like air, water is the most likely candidate for the stuff that supports our planet. Not only is his explanation non-supernatural, then, but it is also logical in the sense that we can understand his reasons for believing it is true. In myths, on the other hand, there are no reasons offered in support of the mythic tales; there are only stories that you either empathize with or fail to empathize with. If you don't like the story told in a myth, the only recourse that you have is to tell another, different story. In myth-making, argumentation does not play the major role that it does in science and philosophy.

Water is capable of existing in a number of different states, and so, unlike other natural elements, it might be used to explain the differing forms of all the things that we see around us. Water can be a liquid, and so it might be thought to underlie all liquids. Water can also be frozen into a solid. Perhaps then all solid things are at some level frozen water. Water can be a gas. Maybe all gases, then, are composed of vaporized water. This line of reasoning is not quite valid, but it does suggest a way of thinking that is unique and remarkable for its time. When we look around us we see a huge diversity of shapes, textures, and forms. It takes a huge imaginative leap to speculate that all of this variety might be the result of one underlying substance. Thales' claim that everything is made of water is such a leap. In fact, the philosopher Friedrich Nietzsche claims that it is just this speculation about the underlying oneness of everything that really makes Thales a revolutionary thinker and worthy of the title "first philosopher."[3]

This first philosopher inspired an entire school of thought that has become known as the Milesian School, named after the city-state in which Thales lived. His first pupil was a man called Anaximander (ca. 610–547 B.C.). What is really interesting about Anaximander is the fact that he did not simply repeat the doctrines taught by Thales, but instead questioned these doctrines and critiqued them in a rational and logical fashion. Anaximander noticed that when we look at the world around us we see that some elements are in conflict with one another. If you pour a bucket of water on a small flame, the flame goes out. If you sprinkle a little bit of water into a raging fire, the water evaporates. These opposite elements—water and fire—are antagonistic to each other. If one of them predominates over the other, then the less plentiful element is destroyed. Now, Anaximander seems to have reasoned, we know that fire exists in our world. We see it everyday. Yet, if what Thales said is correct, how could this be? Thales claimed that water was the underlying substance of the entire world, but if this is so why hasn't it extinguished all of the fire in the world? If water and fire are opposites, how is it that they exist in the same world at the same time? One can't come from the other, Anaximander reasoned, so they must both come from some other thing that is not opposed to either element. He called this other thing "the Infinite." The Infinite is the underlying "stuff" of the universe. If all other things originate from it, then it must in some sense contain all of the other things. Yet it must contain them in such a manner that they are able to coexist with one another. It must be ambiguous in character, containing all of the other elements in an indeterminate state.

What Anaximander has done here is truly astounding, not because he is necessarily correct, but because he has attempted to think through all of the implications of his teacher's speculations, in the process finding what appears to be a logical inconsistency. On the basis of this inconsistency he rejects the premises of Thales' argument and goes on to offer a completely different set of speculations about the origins of our world. In mythic thinking this sort of thing does not normally happen. Myths are often full of contradictory claims, yet these sorts of logical inconsistencies are not seen as grounds for the rejection of the entire story. Mythic stories are intended to offer comfort and understanding to those who might otherwise be left without answers concerning the mysteries of reality. The sort of thinking that was introduced by the Milesian philosophers, on the other hand, seems less concerned with offering comfortable answers and more concerned with thinking through difficult questions.

B o x 1.1 Anaximenes

Anaximenes (sixth century B.C.) is considered to be a third member of the Milesian school. He claimed that everything is made of air. Some philosophers see this as a rather unoriginal contribution, as it only came after Thales himself had first proposed that everything is made of water. However, Anaximenes is also credited by some for performing the first empirical experiment designed to verify his speculation. In this experiment, Anaximenes is said to have slackened his mouth and blown air onto the back of his hand. The air hitting his hand felt soft and hot, like fire! When he pursed his lips and blew air onto the back of his hand in a compressed manner, it felt cold and hard, like earth! This, according to Anaximenes, substantiated his claim that all of the other elements were made of air in varying degrees of density.

This is not to say that the Presocratics did not offer any answers to the questions they raised. They certainly did. Anaximander, for instance, after critiquing his teacher's doctrines, went on to offer an account of how the world around us might have come to be. The Infinite, he said, may have been set into motion by a giant explosion. This explosion could have produced a sort of vortex, and as the Infinite began to spin faster and faster, the various elements it contained would have begun to separate from one another. The heavier elements, like earth, would have collected at the center of the universe. Water, being the next heaviest element, would have settled on top of earth. Air would settle over the water. Anaximander thought that fire was the lightest element and so it would settle over the air. This explains why when we look around us we see water settling on the earth and air occupying our atmosphere. Furthermore, it is because fire shines from beyond the vault of the atmosphere that we see what appear to be stars and bright spots in the sky. These heavenly bodies are actually holes in the blanket of air above us that allow the firelight beyond to radiate through. Sometimes these holes get blocked up, and that's when we have solar or lunar eclipses. Sometimes the fire actually rips through the air above, and that's when we get lightning strikes.

As with Thales, we see Anaximander attempting to think through difficult questions about the structure of reality, proposing speculations that are themselves open to question, criticism, and debate. Although they offer many theories that have the character of scientific speculation about them, it is not this that makes the Presocratics specifically philosophical. Rather, it is their openness to inquiry and their ongoing desire to question why things are the way that they are. It would have been easy for someone like Anaximander simply to follow along behind Thales, promoting his views and advocating the theory that "all is water." He could have probably carved out a nice little niche for himself promoting his teacher's theories and offering answers to those who cared to ask. Yet the philosopher in Anaximander was not satisfied with this. He was troubled by the nagging feeling that Thales' account of reality was substandard. He was probably unsettled by the realization that his mentor's teachings were fundamentally flawed, and this anxious realization spurred him to embark upon speculations of his own—speculations that would be questioned and criticized by others of a philosophical bent.

The Presocratic philosophers who came after Anaximander raised their own new sets of questions, theories, and speculations. Many of their names are well known to most of us today: Pythagoras, Empedocles, Anaxagoras, etc. It is in the thought of these men that we find the beginnings of important fields of study like mathematics, medicine, and psychology. We will have the opportunity to come back to some of these thinkers as we proceed along our path throughout this book. But presently I would like to introduce the ideas of Heraclitus and Parmenides in order to illustrate two contrasting Presocratic perspectives concerning the nature of motion and change as it takes place in our world. So far in our examination of the Milesian School of philosophy we have encountered an overwhelming concern with the reduction of the world's diverse and manifold appearances to just one underlying and stable physical element. In the case of Thales, this element is water. In the case of Anaximander, this element is The

Infinite. Both of these thinkers were predominantly interested in describing reality in naturalistic, logical, and monistic terms. In a way, both Heraclitus and Parmenides continue this tradition, and yet they also, in another way, represent a new innovation in Presocratic thinking. With them, questions concerning the nature of change and motion become a preoccupation. If the world is ultimately made of only one thing, are the changes that we observe around us real or just an illusion? In other words, what is ultimately more true, the apparent changes that we experience by way of our senses or the underlying and stable element that undergoes those changes? The conclusions of Heraclitus and Parmenides on this matter differ, and they offer a vivid illustration of two points of view that still divide people today. On the one hand, there are those who hold that our world is one in which change and flux are fundamentally real. On the other, there are those who believe that stability and uniformity are the most real features of our world. Heraclitus is the author of the first of these views; Parmenides is the originator of the second.

Heraclitus

Heraclitus lived in Ephesus around 500 B.C. Whereas Thales claimed water as the underlying element out of which the universe is composed, Heraclitus claimed that the basic "stuff" of reality is fire. We must be careful in our interpretation here, however, because it is somewhat unclear how literally Heraclitus intended this assertion to be taken. Heraclitus' writings are fragmentary, and even in his own time he had a reputation for being quite difficult to understand, hence his nicknames "the Obscure One," "the Dark One," and "the Riddler." It thus appears that Heraclitus did not always speak and write clearly or directly. How, then, should we interpret his claim that the universe is generated from fire?

In the fragments of his writing that remain, it is unmistakable that Heraclitus often engages in the use of metaphor. Taking this into account, it may be that he did not believe that the world was literally made of fire but only that it exhibits characteristics that are fire-like. What could this mean? Well, fire is an element that in many ways is quite insubstantial. It changes its shape constantly, and our

© Juneko J. Robinson

hands pass right through it if we try to grasp it. Fire is, nonetheless, very real and produces tangible effects on the objects with which it comes into contact. A small fire can spring up from almost nothing, expand to huge proportions, and consume an entire forest, in the end only to disappear into nothing once again. Fire is, thus, an element that is almost ghostly in its physical characteristics, yet powerful and destructive in its capacities. In saying that the world is fire, Heraclitus may have been calling to our attention the ongoing process of change and transformation that is part of reality. Like fire, our world is one that springs into existence, consumes itself in ceaseless movement, and finally is extinguished when it has exhausted the fuel on which it thrives.

Heraclitus explicitly tells us that reality is generated by way of the tension that exists between opposing qualities. Just as the heat of a fire requires an object cooler than itself to consume, so does the existence of the world depend on conflict between opposed forces. For this reason, Heraclitus writes, "War is the father of all, king of all."[4] Again, understood metaphorically, he seems here to be emphasizing war-like conflict and opposition as the generating force at work in the production of earthly, visible phenomena. Just as enemies collide with one another in a war, provoking movement and action, so in the world at large, movement, activity, and change are the result of conflict between opposites. Utilizing yet another metaphor, Heraclitus likens the structure of the universe to "a bow and a lyre."[5] In order for a bow or a lyre to function, there must be tension in their strings. If the tension in a bow's string slackens, the bow cannot propel an arrow through the air. If the tension in a lyre's strings fails, the instrument cannot produce music. Likewise, if all worldly tension were to disappear, the world as we know it would cease to exist. Without the tension between light and dark, we would not have days and nights. Without the tension between male and female, we would not have human beings. All of existence is made possible by the tension and conflict (the "war") that arises between these sorts of oppositions. Without distinctions of these sorts, everything would be the same thing and we would not be able to discern particular instances of entities that themselves change, move, and transform. The world, thus, metaphorically shares the qualities of fire, war, bows, and lyres insofar as all of these things move and function by harnessing the power of tension, conflict, and strife.

Perhaps the best known saying that sums up Heraclitus' understanding of the world is his assertion that "It is not possible to step twice into the same river."[6] A river consists of water that flows downstream, and although the banks of the river lend a kind of stability to the body of water, the contents of that body are never the same. So while we may be able to step into, say, the Russian River again and again over the course of years, the actual water that constitutes that river is always different. This is like our world; it "flows" onward, gaining whatever solidness it does possess from the consistency of its motions. Reality is just flux, change, and transition. Concrete things themselves are always passing into and out of existence.

Despite the fluid nature of reality, Heraclitus nonetheless sees a sort of unity in the diversity of nature's movements. This is why the fire metaphor is so apt for him. The movement of a flame, though ever changing and varied, still describes a distinct and singular entity; namely, the flame itself. In a similar fashion, the movements and flux of the universe, though diverse, complicated, and multifarious, also describe, in their totality, the distinct and singular entity that we call our universe. The universe itself is dependent on the tensions and conflicts that make up its content, and those same tensions and conflicts require the existence of the universe in order to be what they are. "From all things one and from one all things."[7] So it is that in a sense the universe is, as Thales and Anaximander before him had claimed, one thing. In another sense, however, the universe is also many things according to Heraclitus. We cannot accurately separate the one from the many and still hope to understand the nature of reality. True understanding comes from comprehending the ambiguous and intermixed character of opposites. Thus, Heraclitus tells us that the world is both "apparent and unapparent," "straight and crooked," "up and down," "pure and polluted," and that humans are both "living and dead." Real wisdom is attained once one masters the knowledge that our world exists somewhere in between these sorts of oppositions.

Diogenes Laertius tells us that by the end of his life Heraclitus claimed to have learned everything. It is no wonder then that he held most other people in utter contempt for their stupidity and went so far as to write of his fellow citizens that they "deserve to be hanged to the last man, every one of them: they should leave the city to the young."[8] Heraclitus eventually became so fed up with his fellow citizens that he abandoned his home in Ephesus to live a solitary life in the mountains. At the age of sixty he died after unsuccessfully trying to cure himself of dropsy by being buried in a heap of dung.

© Juneko J. Robinson

Parmenides and the Eleatic School

Whereas Heraclitus emphasized movement, flux, and change as the dominant characteristics of reality, Parmenides, who lived in the city-state of Elea around the same time that Heraclitus was alive, emphasized exactly the opposite sorts of attributes, arguing that stasis, stability, and eternal unchangeability are the true marks of reality. As with Heraclitus, much has been made of the difficulty involved in interpreting the writing of Parmenides, again largely because of the fragmentary nature of his work and its poetic style. Nevertheless, there does seem to be wide agreement that the emphasis on stability that we find in his philosophy is a result of the fact that Parmenides was the first of the Presocratics to rely so completely on pure logic that he willingly discounted the most seemingly commonsense observations that most people take for granted. Parmenides dismisses the testimony of our physical senses, which tell us that movement and change are real events in the world, and instead focuses his attention on the purely formal structure of thoughts and ideas. In so doing, Parmenides is the first philosopher to articulate what he saw as the eternal and unchanging rules of purely logical thinking and to claim, furthermore, that these rules govern not just our inner subjective world but also the outer objective world as a whole. In this, he anticipates the rationalism that we will see come to full expression in the ideas of Socrates and the writings of Plato.

The whole of Parmenides' philosophy is contained in a single poem that is divided into two sections. The first section, titled *The Way of Truth*, outlines what Parmenides holds to be the Truth about the world. The second section, titled *The Way of Opinion*, outlines what Parmenides claims to be the ideas accepted by most people as the truth, but which are in fact falsehoods. The poem as a whole thus delineates both what he believes is true and what is false about reality.

So what is false? In sum, Parmenides seems to hold that all of the doctrines of previous Presocratic philosophers are falsehoods. In the fragments that remain of the second part of the poem, Parmenides enumerates various cosmological doctrines that we have already become acquainted with in the course of the present chapter. We are told, for instance, to beware of views of the universe that propose the separation of elements into various "bands," perhaps in the manner of Anaximander's theory, which comprise differing levels of physical reality. We are also warned about those who view fire as the basic constituent of the universe. Any sort of cosmological speculation, it appears, is deceitful and uncertain, and thus Parmenides seems to be counseling us to cease such vain endeavors and instead to withdraw from discussion of the external physical world instead to meditate on the inner world of thought itself.

B o x 1.2 Pythagoras

Pythagoras (570–478 B.C.) was not only the first person to coin the term "philosophy" but he was also one of the great religious and scientific figures of the Presocratic era. The religious order led by Pythagoras held the belief that through the study of mathematics, people could cleanse their souls and be reincarnated into a higher form of existence. The Pythagoreans were vegetarians and engaged in a number of rituals reminding them of the sanctity of all life. They believed that all things, including music and even space itself, had an underlying mathematical structure. The Pythagorean Theorem and the Pythagorean theory of harmony are still studied today.

So what, then, is true? Parmenides delineates the truth as something that is "ungenerated and indestructible, whole, of one kind and unwavering, and complete."[9] It is, in other words, the exact opposite of Heraclitus' flux. Why is it that Parmenides claims this? The crux of the argument in *The Way of Truth* rests on what appears to be the assertion of a logical principle that is now sometimes referred to as "the Principle of Identity." According to this basic principle of logic, ideas must be considered as identical to themselves. The essence of the principle can symbolically be represented in the following way: A=A. When I use a word, say, "Apple," according to the Principle of Identity, I am being logical only if I continue to use that term consistently while speaking in the same context. Thus, according to this logic, if I assert "All apples are fruits," and then I also assert "All Macintoshes are apples," I must also hold it to be true that "All Macintoshes are fruits." If, on the other hand, I insist that "My Macintosh is a computer," I must, if I wish to be logical, clarify that I am using the term "Macintosh" in a different sense from the one I initially established. The context has changed and so the term "Macintosh" is revealed to be ambiguous. It can mean different things in different situations. According to the Principle of Identity, we must be clear about the precise meaning of a term and use the term in the same way when operating in the same context. If we don't follow this principle, then we cannot make any sense whatsoever and no one would be able to understand anything that anyone ever said. For instance, if the Principle of Identity is not adhered to, then I can legitimately says things like: All apples are fruits. All apples are not fruits. Therefore all apples are not apples! But this is obviously absurd.

In Parmenides' poem, he invokes something like the Principle of Identity in order to write about the nature of Being itself. When we talk about Being, we are talking about the totality of all that exists. Being is everything. Now, it is obvious that Being itself must exist, if this is correct, because it is, by definition, just the sum total of existence. Furthermore, Parmenides argues, if Being exists by definition, it is impossible for it ever not to have existed, for that would conflict with the Principle of Identity in the following way: if Being did not exist at one time, then at one time Being was not Being; but this is absurd. Being must have always been what it is according to the Principle of Identity. Thus, Being must be "ungenerated, indestructible, whole."

Advancing his argument further, Parmenides states that it is illogical to claim that Being ever changes. In order for change to occur within Being, it would have to become something other than what it is. But if it becomes something other than what it is, then it is no longer Being that we are talking about and therefore we have, once again, violated the Principle of Identity. What Parmenides takes this to imply is that there must be no divisions or distinctions within Being itself. It is "completed on all sides, like the bulk of a well-rounded ball, equal in every way from the middle."[10] Change, flux, and movement, then, are illusions. According to the rules of logic, and despite what observation reports to our senses, everything is one, whole, and unchanging.

Both Heraclitus and Parmenides agree, in a way, that everything is one. According to Heraclitus, however, the oneness of the universe is just the totality of tensions and the consequent motions generated by actually existing contradictions. The world, in his view, has no underlying substance but is simply an ongoing process of flux and motion. According to Parmenides, on the other hand, there is a oneness that underlies and is more real than any of the merely visible processes that our senses tell us exist. Like a good logician, Parmenides holds that contradictions are absurd and impossible. Because our senses tell us that the world appears to be rife with contradictions, it is necessary to find some way by which to resolve and eliminate those contradictions from our picture of the universe. We must turn inwards, to the mind itself, away from the senses, and use pure, logical thinking in order to understand the real truth that governs reality. When we do this, Parmenides holds, our intellects will cut through to the ultimate, indestructible, and ungenerated foundation of all reality that exists behind the world's merely apparent logical contradictions. As Bertrand Russell points out, in doing this Parmenides is among the first philosophers to logically conceptualize Being as a self-sustaining and stable substance that has reality beyond any of the particular things existing within its boundaries.[11]

While Heraclitus and Parmenides disagree on the ultimate nature of reality, we nevertheless detect in them a kind of spiritual kinship. Both of them exhibit a tendency toward mysticism insofar as they reverently view the universe in terms of unity, oneness, and interconnectedness. This is an interesting point, as both of these thinkers are otherwise quite rational in their discussion of the world, never making an appeal to supernatural entities and, especially in the case of Parmenides, utilizing the tools of logic in order to arrive at conclusions. The mixture of myth and logic in these thinkers may seem odd to us today, but this is only because we have been so greatly influenced by later developments in science and religion that have encouraged us to draw a separation between these ways of thinking.

One of the major contributors to this trend toward separation is a thinker to whom we will now turn. In what remains of this chapter we will examine the ideas of Democritus, a very influential figure who serves as an illustration of the culmination of the scientific emphasis in Presocratic thinking and its ultimate divergence away from both myth and philosophy.

The Atomist School: Democritus and Leucippus

Democritus was born in the city of Abdera around 460 B.C. He is remembered today as the greatest proponent of a theory called "atomism." Democritus agreed

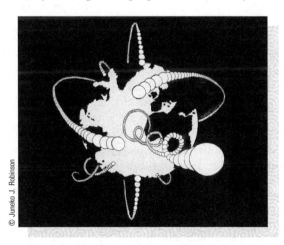

© Juneko J. Robinson

with those like Thales who claimed that there was ultimately only one constituent element that lay underneath everything else that we see around us. However, Democritus did not think that this element was water. When you crush a dry object like a rock you don't end up with liquid, after all, but with smaller particles of rock. The more that you smash these particles in turn, the smaller they get. Never are you able to pulverize a rock to the point that all of the material it is made up of disappears. So there must be some final level of material substance that always remains hidden within the objects of the world. This final level of substance Democritus called the "atom." The atom is a tiny, uncuttable particle of matter. When many atoms come together, they form objects, and all visible objects can be broken down into atoms.

According to Aristotle, the actual line of reasoning constructed by Democritus in order to come to his conclusion about the existence of atoms went something like this: if there was no limit to the divisibility of the objects in our world, then any object could, in theory, be divided everywhere at once. If this was the case, then all of the matter contained in a log, for instance, could potentially be broken down until nothing remained. But then where did the log come from? Because you can't get something out of nothing, the log must have come from some preexisting thing. If there was no preexisting thing out of which an object was formed, then the object would never have come into being in the first place. Furthermore, because the larger parts of an object come together by making physical contact with one another, the smallest parts out of which the larger parts are constituted must likewise be made up of parts that come together by making physical contact with one another. The smallest parts of physical objects, then, must not only preexist the objects that they constitute but they must also be made up of physical bits of material substance that are themselves uncuttable.[12] This is how Democritus, and his teacher Leucippus, came up with the idea of the atom. The word "atom" comes from the Greek terms *a*, meaning "not," and *tomos*, meaning "cut." Thus the atom is the smallest bit of matter that cannot be cut.

But how is it that atoms, these minuscule bits of material substance, come together in the first place? Democritus tells us that atoms are naturally in motion, traveling through a void of space. The motion of these atoms need not be explained, because motion just is their natural state. What needs explanation, rather, is that point at which atoms cease to move. This occurs when, by chance, they collide. When this happens, they sometimes stick together because of their varied shapes: "... for some of them are uneven, some hooked, some concave, some convex, and others have innumerable differences."[13] You can imagine a hooked atom colliding with another atom that has a hole in it. The hook of one might get caught in the hole of the other, and so the two atoms adhere to one another. This combination of particles might then collide with another set of connected atoms, and the whole mess would become entangled into a larger accumulation. The long-term aggregate of such chance collisions of atoms produce the physical things that we see in the world around us, claims Democritus.

Democritus' atomic theory seems almost modern and scientific in its nature. Even today, the Nobel Prize–winning physicist Leon Lederman fondly refers to Democritus as the grandfather of modern particle physics. According to this scientific way of thinking, the world is not designed by some higher, supernatural intelligence but is merely the result of chance. All things can be explained materialistically by analyzing the manner in which physical bodies happen to collide with one another. The manner in which such collisions occur is the sole determining factor of how things now appear.

This sort of explanation holds for human beings no less than for inanimate objects, according to Democritus. We also are made up of a variety of atoms, and the sensations that we experience are the result of atoms of differing shapes and sizes interacting with the atoms that make up our sense organs. In the case of taste, for instance, the atoms making up the food we eat have a particular way of interacting with the atoms of our tongues. Spicy foods are made up of sharp atoms and, as they poke and sting our tongue atoms, they create the sensation of burning. Sweet foods are made up of smooth atoms that roll across the tongue. Salty foods are made up of rough atoms that rub against the tongue. Likewise, our sense of sight is possible because of the impact of atoms on our eyeballs. Our sense of hearing is possible because of atoms that enter our ears and strike our hearing organs. From this Democritus concludes that all of the subjective qualities we humans experience and enjoy by way of our sensory perceptions are really just illusions that are created by atomic collision. Sights, sounds, tastes, and even feelings like love and hate are nothing more than the outgrowth of the movements of particles. As Democritus himself put it: "By convention sweet and by convention bitter, by convention hot, by convention cold, by convention colour: in reality atoms and void."[14] As we will see in Chapter 5, these ideas would later be taken as a starting point for the Hellenistic thinker Epicurus and his followers, who would then go on to develop them into an entire philosophy of life.

If Democritus is correct, then humans are themselves nothing more than lumps of matter. There is nothing especially spiritual or special about us. We are made up of atoms like everything else, and when we die our atoms will be released and dispersed into the void just like those that are liberated from any other physical object. This sort of claim was troubling to many of Democritus' contemporaries. How could Democritus claim such a thing? Isn't it obvious that humans are subject to different laws than are merely physical objects? What about the gods and the afterlife? Democritus answered simply:

> Some men who do not know mortal nature dissolves but are aware of
> the wretchedness of life spend their whole lives in troubles and fears,
> fashioning false stories about the time after death.[15]

And so it seems that for Democritus, all speculations about anything other than the atoms and the void are silly distractions that blind us to the real nature of our world.

Democritus appears to have enjoyed using his philosophy to debunk and overturn the conventional beliefs/illusions of his fellow citizens. An example of this can be found in his efforts to offer an explanation for the strange death of the tragic poet Aeschylus. This story illustrates the friction that was beginning to emerge between Presocratic science and the religious myths of the day. Aeschylus had been found dead on a beach with a massive wound to the head. It had been foretold by the Oracle at Delphi that this would happen. The Oracle had said that Aeschylus would be struck dead by a thunderbolt from the gods. What more certain proof could there be that the gods existed and did indeed intervene in human affairs than this? True to his skeptical nature, however, Democritus

TABLE 1.1 **The Presocratics**

Thales (625–547 B.C.)	"All is water."
Anaximander (610–547 B.C.)	"All is the Infinite."
Anaximenes (sixth century B.C.)	"All is air."
Pythagorus (570–500 B.C.)	"All is number."
Heraclitus (535–475 B.C.)	"All is fire."
Parmenides (535–? B.C.)	"All is one."
Democritus (460–370 B.C.)	"All is atoms."

questioned this explanation of Aeschylus' death. He went down to the beach where the poet had been found and observed that the sea birds in the area were in the habit of gathering clams to eat. In order to break open their shells, the birds would drop the clams from the sky onto the rocks below. Then they would swoop down and consume the flesh inside. This got Democritus thinking. He noted that Aeschylus was bald. Could it be that one of these birds mistook Aeschylus' head for a rock and so dropped an especially heavy clam on his head, striking him in such a manner that he suffered the fatal wound? Democritus, for one, thought that this explanation was a far better one than the supernatural explanation many other Greeks accepted as true.

With Democritus we see the triumph of non-supernatural thinking. His explanations for the objects and events in the world are entirely materialistic and deterministic. Many physicists today adhere to something like the Democritean view of the universe. It is about as far as you can get from a mythic or religious way of thinking. Yet we should also note that insofar as atomists, or any scientific thinkers, are committed unquestioningly to the basic premises of their science, they are also quite far from being philosophers. Physicists take it for granted that the world can be explained in a completely naturalistic and materialistic manner. Philosophers, on the other hand, don't take anything for granted. For the philosopher, everything is open to question. Indeed, insofar as Democritus questioned the validity and soundness of the mythic explanations of his day, he was exercising critical, philosophical thought. Insofar as he speculated on alternative explanations for the world's phenomena, again he should be considered a philosophical thinker. However, insofar as Democritus claimed to have discovered a final, naturalistic answer that unlocked the secret constitution of the universe, he was less like a philosopher and more like a natural scientist. With him, a scientific accent becomes pronounced over everything else, obscuring and making indistinct the mythic/religious and philosophical themes that his predecessors had exhibited before him.

FROM MERE WONDER TO WONDROUS DISTRESS

The theories of Democritus illustrate how in Presocratic thinking there was a progressive growth in the explanatory role played by naturalism and a progressive decline in the explanatory role played by myth and religion. The issues that concerned the Presocratics were of the sort that still concern physicists and other natural scientists today. They speculated and argued about the composition of the physical universe, proposing naturalistic answers to grand questions about the essence and origin of our world. In offering such answers, the Presocratics initiated a kind of non-mythic and rational way of thinking that shares affinities with both science and philosophy. Their naturalistic explanations were the first step toward modern science, but it was their willingness to question old beliefs and assumptions, while still aspiring toward the Truth itself, that made them philosophers.

The development of philosophical and scientific thinking, as exhibited in the ideas of the Presocratics, is often held up as a sign of progress, or even as a "miracle," in the history of human thought. This traditional judgment holds that the Presocratics were the first rebels against the superstitious nonsense of ancient myth-makers. Such assessments obviously have an agenda, and that agenda is to promote a non-supernatural, rational picture of our world; one that fits in comfortably with the later rise to dominance of science and technology in the West. Many people today, however, are quick to point out that modern scientific and technological developments are themselves not at all unequivocally positive. In the first place, we have become very aware of the negative effects that science has helped to foment in the form of technologized warfare, environmental degradation, global warming, etc. While mythic and religious thinking may be thought by some as key in the promotion of ignorance and blind obedience to authority figures, it is no less true that science has been key in the arrogant propagation of human power.

Of course, both mythic/religious thinking and scientific thinking have their positive sides. Along with technologized warfare, science has given us cures for diseases. Along with global warming, science has given us the ability to produce ample food for the hungry. Myth and religion have given us beautiful works of literature, art, and ceremony in addition to the Crusades and the Inquisition. As some of the most eloquent modern spokespersons for mythology have shown, myth also helps "us to cope with the problematic human predicament"[16] and to "render the modern world spiritually significant."[17] Both myth and science have their bright sides as well as their dark sides. Very few things in our world are unequivocally good or bad, as Heraclitus would remind us, and so the traditional view, which claims that science and philosophy are inherently superior to myth and religion, probably oversimplifies the truth. More likely, the transition to the Presocratic era contains a complicated mixture of good and bad elements.

The desire to declare one type of thinking the victor in the battle between myth and science reveals, I think, a very common propensity among human beings. We like to know that we have the right answers. We don't want to admit that we might be on the wrong side of an issue or that our beliefs might be mistaken. This sort of uncertainty makes us uncomfortable and causes us distress. As a result, many people recoil, almost instinctively, from considering issues from more than one perspective. Ambiguity and uncertainty make people anxious and so instead of confronting the full complexity of an issue, they jump to conclusions and stand firm on their own form of "common sense." This may succeed in helping us to feel confident and knowledgeable, but it very rarely succeeds in helping us to expand our thinking and to move closer to the real nature of the world. This is why we need philosophy. In addition to promoting the sort of wonder that both myth and science encourage in us, philosophy always reminds us to remain critical and unsatisfied with the conclusions at which we arrive. In the Presocratic thinkers, the questioning spirit of philosophy was largely directed toward the received myths of their time. This wondrous pursuit of the Truth led to the distressing undermining of the old ways of thinking, yet in the process it was also implicated in the establishment of a new set of doctrines that, over time, would become uncritically accepted by many people. Authentic philosophers would continue to fight against this sort of stagnation and insist that thinking remain unfettered by any sort of dogma, be it scientific or religious. This proved to be a dangerous mission. The promotion of wondrous distress challenges people to question their ideas and beliefs unceasingly. It offers little comfort other than a conviction that our lives will become fuller, richer, and more profound the further that we press ourselves to examine the mysteries of Being. As we will see in the chapter that follows, this was not comfort enough for those citizens of Athens whose beliefs were challenged by Socrates, one of the greatest philosophers who has ever lived.

QUESTIONS FOR DISCUSSION

1. In what ways are myth, science, and philosophy different from one another and in what ways do they overlap? Do you believe that one of these ways of thinking is superior to the others? Why?

2. Today we think of ourselves as benefiting greatly from modern scientific developments and the technology that has accompanied those developments. However, it may be the case that modern human beings still engage in forms of mythic thinking. What are some of the modern myths that people today endorse?

3. How do you think the insights and ideas of Presocratic thinkers have influenced the development of science? How have they influenced the development of philosophy?

4. Do you believe that the world is, at its foundation, one or many things? Is the true nature of reality flux, change, and chaos or is it ultimately stable, unchanging, and firm? What leads you to this belief?

5. Do you think the movement away from myth-making and supernatural explanation in Presocratic thinking a sign of progress and intellectual advance? Discuss why you do or do not think this to be the case.

6. In contemporary times, billions of dollars have been spent on the construction of supercolliders that are designed to reveal the underlying foundations of the physical world. In these facilities, scientists have broken matter down further and further, discovering the existence of smaller and smaller particles like quarks, leptons, and bosons. Do you think that there is an end to this search? Will scientists at some point finally identify the ultimate and fundamental physical particles that make up everything?

NOTES

1. F. M. Cornford, *Before and After Socrates* (Cambridge: Cambridge University Press, 1986).

2. Aristotle, *On the Heavens*, 294a28–34.

3. Friedrich Nietzsche, *Philosophy in the Tragic Age of the Greeks* (Washington, DC: Gateway Editions, 1994).

4. Jonathan Barnes (trans. and ed.), *Early Greek Philosophy* (London: Penguin Books, 1987), p. 102.

5. Ibid.

6. Ibid., p. 117.

7. Ibid., p. 114.

8. Ibid., p. 105.

9. Ibid., p. 134.

10. Ibid., p. 135.

11. Bertrand Russell, *A History of Western Philosophy* (New York: Simon and Schuster, 1972), p. 52.

12. Aristotle, *On Generation and Corruption*, 316a13–b16.

13. Barnes, *Early Greek Philosophy*, p. 247.

14. Ibid., pp. 252–253.

15. Ibid., p. 284.

16. Karen Armstrong, *A Short History of Myth* (Edinburgh, New York, Melbourne: Cannongate, 2005), p. 6.

17. Joseph Campbell, *The Hero with a Thousand Faces* (New York: Princeton University Press, [1949] 1973), p. 388.

Chapter 2

Socrates

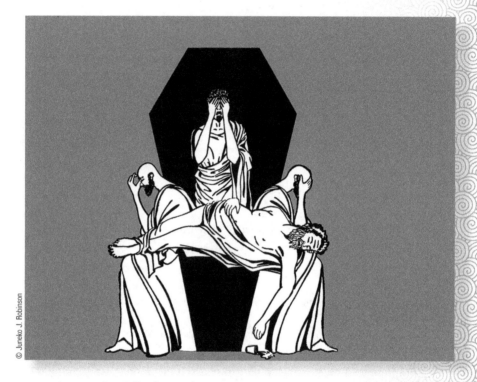

© Jureko J. Robinson

What are the difficulties we encounter when trying to understand the philosophy of Socrates? How was Socrates related to Presocratic philosophy? What is the Socratic Method? Why did Socrates write nothing? Why was Socrates put on trial by the Athenians? Why is Socrates considered by many to be the true father of philosophy?

THE DIFFICULTY OF PERSPECTIVE

As the thinking of the Presocratics drifted farther and farther away from religious concerns and closer and closer toward scientific ones, a philosopher emerged who rebuked and challenged this Greek trend. His name was Socrates. Socrates lived in the Greek city-state of Athens around 469–399 B.C., and he practiced philosophy verbally in the course of debating and arguing with others. Because Socrates himself never committed anything to writing, all that we know about him comes from the written works of others like Plato, Aristophanes, and Xenophon. Due to this fact, there is a great deal of controversy concerning how well we can reconstruct his life and actual way of thinking. As might be expected, because the character of Socrates appears in so many different dialogues and plays penned by so many different authors, the person who is thus represented takes on a different cast depending on who is telling the story. Aristophanes (ca. 446–386 B.C.) presents Socrates as a comic figure—a trouble-making buffoon who corrupts and misleads the people of Athens. Xenophon (ca. 430–354 B.C.) presents Socrates as a pragmatic, sensible, somewhat conventional, and down-to-earth citizen, while Plato (ca. 428–347 B.C.) paints a picture of him as rebellious and idealistic martyr for the Truth. Who are we to believe?

The traditional perspective on this issue holds that the early Platonic dialogues offer us the most accurate representation of Socrates and his life's mission. It is in these dialogues, the experts claim, that we find Socrates' student, Plato, most concerned with recording and accurately detailing the thoughts and ideas of his teacher for posterity. The later Platonic dialogues, it is claimed, represent the progressive development of Plato's own way of thinking, and though the character of Socrates still appears in these writings he is transformed into a mouthpiece for Plato's own thoughts and doctrines. This is why some of the ideas that appear in the later dialogues seem to conflict with, and in fact to contradict, what Socrates says in earlier dialogues. Like many bright students, the experts contend, Plato started off under the spell of his teacher but then went on to develop his own creative style and way of thinking.

This is all very plausible insofar as Plato's own intellectual development is concerned, but it doesn't tell us specifically why we should regard his early dialogues as more authoritative than what others wrote about Socrates. So why is it that contemporary interpretations of Socrates' philosophy rely so heavily on the Platonic texts? One reason is that these writings are extremely rich and intricate in philosophical detail. Here we get precise arguments and profound insights that are above and beyond those appearing in the other texts where Socrates speaks. Another reason, however, may be due to the skill and artistry of Plato's own writing and storytelling. One can't help but be entranced by Plato's dialogues, in which he utilizes metaphors, similes, and analogies that vividly and creatively bring to life the concepts and ideas that he is concerned with expressing. Because his dialogues are so artistically accomplished, as we read them we just feel as though some sort of Truth is being disclosed, and this may lead us to the conclusion that Plato's Socrates is in spirit, if not in detail, the real Socrates.

Others, like Xenophon and Aristophanes, nevertheless wrote accounts of Socrates and his life that probably have some truth in them as well. It is not sensible, as Bertrand Russell has done, simply to discount Xenophon as a "military man, not very liberally endowed with brains." Russell would bid us to set Xenophon's Socrates aside because "a stupid man's report of what a clever man says is never accurate."[1] Whatever Xenophon's IQ, it really has no bearing on the fact that Socrates did leave an impression on him, and from this impression we may be able to garner some sense of the Socratic message. Likewise with Aristophanes, who Socrates mentions in his speech to the court of Athens. Although the picture that Aristophanes leaves us is a comic one, this undoubtedly also reflects a facet of the complicated and profound personality that really was Socrates. All of those who encountered Socrates were affected by him, and they all came away with passionate opinions concerning his teachings. This fact alone attests to the power of his personality. Yet, like the impressions left by the same ink stamp on different sheets of paper, each encounter produced a slightly different mark depending on the nature of the engagement. Obviously there were many people in Athens who saw Socrates as a threat, just as there were many who saw him as a saint. Perhaps, if we pay due attention to a variety of the written depictions of this philosopher, we can begin to understand what it was in this man that had such a varied effect on so many different people.

PLATO'S SOCRATES

The Influence of Anaxagoras

In the Platonic dialogue *Phaedo*, Socrates tells us that he was at one time a student of the Presocratic philosopher Anaxagoras (500–428 B.C.), and was especially attracted to his notion that "nous," or "mind," was an important element in understanding the world. Anaxagoras, like most of the Presocratics, was concerned with speculations about the nature of the physical universe. However, unlike thinkers such as Democritus, Anaxagoras found it implausible that the complexity and order of the cosmos could be accounted for in terms of the chance collision of tiny, indivisible particles. Recall that according to Democritus, all of the qualities that exist in our world—like colors, tastes, and smells—are the

© Juneko J. Robinson

result of atoms, which themselves are colorless, tasteless, and odorless. But, wonders Anaxagoras, how can something that is odorless produce something with odor? How can something without color produce something with color? How, in short, could something come from something with which it shares no common qualities? Democritus himself ended up trying to resolve this difficulty by proclaiming that the qualities of color, taste, and smell are conventional "illusions"; they do not really exist objectively. Anaxagoras, however, was not content with such a "solution."

Instead, Anaxagoras taught that the material

substance making up the universe is limitlessly divisible. Like Anaximander before him, Anaxagoras speculated that our world arose out of an infinite cloud-like mass. Unlike Anaximander, however, he held that this mass was composed of distinct particles or "seeds," each of which contained, in differing concentrations, all of the qualities that exist in the universe. Everything in the physical world around us is made of these particles, and when a number of particles sharing a preponderance of one particular quality clump together, that quality overwhelms the others and becomes sensible to us. So it is that snow normally appears white because it contains more particles in which the color white dominates than it contains other sorts of particles. As Anaxagoras wrote, "each single thing is and was most patently those things of which it contains most."[2] Furthermore, this explains how it is that something like snow can change its color over time. As it loses those particles in which white predominates and leaves behind those in which, say, the color black predominates, the snow becomes black. The color black was there all along, claims Anaxagoras, it just was not noticeable to us.

Democritus taught that the world we live in is the result of chance. The apparent order and structure of the universe are really the outcome of probabilities; a lucky dice throw in which the atoms whizzing through the void collided just so for no good reason. Anaxagoras was especially unconvinced by such assertions. If you look around you at the order and harmony of nature, it does not appear as if what you see could be accounted for by mere accident. There are predictable regularities in our world. For instance, humans give birth to humans, always. It never has, nor ever will it, occur that a human gives birth to a pomegranate. But if worldly occurrences are just the product of luck, the probability of a human giving birth to a pomegranate would not be zero. It could, and would, happen at some point in the life of the universe. Yet it does not. On a more mundane level, it is obvious to even the most casual observer that there are cycles to the seasons, that night follows day, and that the sun always rises in the east and sets in the west. Are these sorts of apparent regularities nothing more than fluke occurrences?

Anaxagoras thought not. Instead, he taught that the world is organized and given shape by a rational, intelligent, and beneficent force called nous or mind. This is a very fine, nonphysical substance that is separate from, yet mixed in with, the "seeds" composing the rest of the universe. Mind surrounds and encapsulates the particles of the world, the way that the water in a stream surrounds the gravel in its bed, putting things into motion and giving them order and structure. This accounts for the fact that the world we see around us is not a chaotic jumble of confusion. Just as the downstream flow of water creates patterns in the arrangement of river stones, so does mind follow a logic of its own, creating patterns of structure and proportion in the cosmos. Mind also accounts for the fact that some things in our world are alive. Inanimate objects do not have minds of their own but have only been given form by the external influence of mind. Animate objects like humans, on the other hand, do have minds. Nous exists within their bodies and so they are self-moving, with the ability to create and impart order to the things around them.

With Anaxagoras we see a reaction against the pure materialism of Presocratic science, and it was this element of Anaxagoras' philosophy that first attracted Socrates. Socrates, however, ultimately became disillusioned with Anaxagoras because he thought that while recognizing the importance of mind for explaining the order of the universe, Anaxagoras still placed too much emphasis on material substance when actually forming his explanations. As Socrates says in Plato's dialogue *Phaedo*:

> What expectations I had formed and how grievously I was disappointed! As I proceeded, I found my philosopher altogether forsaking mind or any other principle of order, but having recourse to air, and ether, and water, and other eccentricities. I might compare him to a person who began by maintaining generally that mind is the cause of the actions of Socrates, but who, when he endeavored to explain the causes of my several actions in detail, went to show that I sit here because my body is made up of bone and muscle.... There is surely a strange confusion of causes and conditions in all this. It may be said, indeed, that without bones and muscles and the other parts of the body I cannot execute my purposes. But to say that I do as I do because of them, and that this is the way in which mind acts, and not from the choice of the best, is a very careless and idle mode of speaking.[3]

Socrates' Inward Turn

If the world had in fact been arranged according to a rational principle, then according to Socrates to truly understand the purpose of the world and our place in it would depend on our comprehension of that ruling principle and not simply on our comprehension of the superficial details of physical nature. If we want to understand the world, then we must attempt to pursue an investigation into the nature of mind. By coming to understand mind, we would become better able to understand how it shapes all of the world's details. Unlocking the secrets of the universe thus depends on unlocking the secrets of the mind. But how should one go about pursuing this task? It is one thing to observe the gross physical phenomena around us and to offer speculations concerning their nature, but it is quite another to grapple with something as intangible as the mind itself. How is one to begin such an investigation?

Anaxagoras had taught that mind is "infinite and self-controlling"[4] but that it remains distinct from the physical "seeds" with which it is mixed, like water remains separate from the gravel into which it is poured. Mind is "the finest of all things and the purest, and it possesses all knowledge about everything, and it has the greatest strength. And mind controls all those things, both great and small, which possess soul."[5] Humans, then, as thinking, self-directed, and ensouled creatures, are in possession of minds that are in control over their bodies, and though the human mind and body coexist with one another, they each remain distinct in their essences. Whereas the body can be observed and experimented on in the manner of scientific investigation, the mind is nonphysical and intangible, and an investigation into its operations must proceed by some means other than empirical ones. Because we cannot use our physical eyes in order to examine the mind, we must instead use the reflective power of the mind itself to do so. By "turning the eyes of the soul inwards," Socrates concluded, we might "gather the mind into herself"[6] and thus come to understand its true nature and design. In sum, Socrates argues that because each of us has a mind embedded within our own body, we are all capable of undertaking its investigation by marshaling the mind's power of reflection and directing it toward inner analysis, deliberation, and contemplation. In this manner, he claims, we can come to understand how the mind operates. Further, because our own minds are extrusions of a "divine, and immortal, and intellectual, and uniform, and indissoluble, and unchangeable"[7] reality that permeates the world, through inner reflection we might come to understand the governing principle of the entire universe.

So it is that Socrates comes to the conclusion that the proper task of philosophy is not, as the Presocratics had assumed, the investigation of the outer, physical world, but rather the investigation of the inner, mental world. The whole point and purpose of the philosophical life, then, is to concentrate on self-reflection and self-examination. "The unexamined life is not worth living for a human being," Socrates tells the jurors at his trial, and in so doing he sets a new course that widens the gap between philosophy and the natural sciences and which narrows the gap between philosophy and religious thinking. For this reason, F. M. Cornford claims[8] that it was Socrates who for the first time grants the human soul the significance that it deserves. With him, our nonphysical aspect becomes preeminently important, and its care, tending, and perfection become the focus of the good life.

The Socratic Method

But Socrates was not completely content to withdraw from the world around him like a religious mystic or like many of the later Hellenistic philosophers who would take some inspiration from his message. Quite the contrary. Instead, he devoted his life to engaging others in conversation with the hope that such interaction would not only benefit him in his own spiritual development, but that he might also help others to perfect themselves. It was in the course of such conversations that the Socratic Method, otherwise known as "dialectic," was developed and perfected. Dialectic refers to a process of conversation that takes place between two or more interested parties. In such a conversation, the participants agree to come together and discuss a particular topic with the goal of uncovering some sort of absolutely certain truth. By looking into themselves, the interlocutors can begin to reflect on the operations of their own minds, and by articulating their findings to one another, they may hone and clarify their thoughts as well as honing and clarifying the procedures and methods utilized in order to arrive at those thoughts. Disagreeing with one another and pointing out problems with each other's assertions, the participants in a dialectical exchange slowly begin to refine their own positions more and more precisely, with the ultimate goal of revealing the governing principles of thought and of the mind itself. With this process, Socrates encourages us to rediscover the normally obscure principles of order and rationality that exist naturally yet buried within our own consciousness. In conversation with each other Socrates hoped that we would all become wiser, more honest, and better than we had been beforehand. In this manner philosophical dialectic was intended to be personally transformative, cleansing and purifying one's soul of falsehood and illusion.

Suppose, for instance, that two people were concerned with the issue of happiness. At the outset of a dialectical exchange, the two participants would probably have a general, though somewhat vague, idea of what they mean by the term "happiness." One might venture the opinion that happiness means "doing what you want to do." The other might point out that sometimes people "do what they want to do" but nevertheless find themselves to be unhappy. Happiness, then, must be something other than simply "doing what you want to do." In fact, people who only "do what they want" oftentimes find themselves getting into trouble, and if they do not learn to do certain things that they initially do not want to do (like going to school, learning self-discipline, etc.), they end up living very unhappy lives indeed. Happiness, at least sometimes, seems to involve doing some things that you do not want or like to do.

The first participant in this exchange might counter, however, that if you never get to do what you want to do, then there is very little chance that you will experience happiness. Granted that happiness is not the same as "doing what you want to do," it at the very least involves doing those things that will ultimately contribute to a life in which you get to do many or most of the things that you want to do. Self-denial is worthwhile only if it allows us to work toward or obtain something else that we value; it is pain that is bearable only because we anticipate some sort of future reward for our sacrifices. One could never be happy if one were required to forgo all wants and desires without any hope of some sort of payoff.

A dialectical exchange like this could go on and on, and in fact most of the Socratic dialogues never reach any final resolution. Although Socrates himself seemed to be optimistic that this process might ultimately lead toward a full apprehension of the absolute Truth, he was also quite certain that he had not arrived at the point of knowing what that Truth was, which highlights an important point. We must understand that in order to engage in an authentic dialectical exchange, all of those involved must be concerned primarily with uncovering the Truth, and not primarily with winning particular arguments or with saving face. In this sense, Socratic dialectic presupposes a cooperative argumentative context. The interlocutors involved in such an exchange must cooperate with one another, conceding when a weakness in their own position has been revealed and recognizing when their conversational partner has a stronger argument than their own. What is important is not personal cleverness, but rather a reverence for those truths that become self-evident through the process of logical discussion. Socrates tells us that he himself would rather be proven wrong than to show someone else is wrong, and this precisely for the reason that by becoming aware of flaws in our own thinking we clear our minds to accept the real Truth, and thus, in the process, we become better and wiser than we were before.

However, one of the chief problems that Socrates often encountered was that many people he engaged in conversation were not willing to set aside their egos in order to pursue the Truth in a cooperative manner. Under such circumstances Socrates found it necessary to provoke, and even to embarrass and humiliate, his conversation partners. The point of such tactics was not necessarily mean-spirited. It was, rather, intended first and foremost as a way to dismantle the pretensions of those who claimed prematurely to know the final truths of the universe. Socrates believed that one must first admit to one's own ignorance before the real search for Truth could begin. He felt that we must stop blinding ourselves and others with lies and falsehoods so that we can clear the way for a genuine understanding of who we are and what our place is in the universe. According to Plato, in fact, Socrates claimed that he himself was completely ignorant and that he knew nothing. Consequently, it was quite aggravating to him that a whole variety of unreflective people in Athens, without even trying very hard, claimed to be in possession of the absolute truths of reality. These proclaimers of their own wisdom had all sorts of clever and glib answers to the very profound and troubling questions about which Socrates wondered. When Socrates prodded such individuals into a dialectical exchange, however, what he found was that their "wisdom" usually amounted to nothing. Under close scrutiny, the wise men of Athens proved their opinions to be full of inconsistencies, ambiguities, and flat-out falsehoods. Those who talked the loudest and with the most confidence were often those who spoke the most nonsense!

The Trial of Socrates

Among those whom Socrates found to be full of nonsense were the most powerful and influential people in Athens. According to Plato this was at least part of the reason why Socrates was finally dragged into court and charged with impiety and with corrupting the youth of the city. He had asked too many questions and made too many of the political and cultural leaders of Athens look like fools in public. However, for Socrates it was not so much their ignorance that was foolish, but their arrogant inability to acknowledge their own ignorance. Socrates came to the conclusion that he himself was the wisest man in Athens, but only because he knew that he knew nothing. The politicians, poets, artisans, and rhetoricians (Sophists), on the other hand, thought that they knew quite a bit when in fact they knew very little or nothing at all. At least, Socrates claimed, he was smart enough to recognize his own ignorance.

At his trial, as it is depicted in Plato's *Apology*, Socrates defends his continuing practice of dialectical questioning as essential to a meaningful life. In court, Socrates faces his accusers and utilizes the tools of logic in order to undermine the charges that are brought against him. Socrates' cross-examination of Meletus in the *Apology* is a perfect example of the dialectical method in practice. Socrates questions Meletus concerning the charges that have been brought against him and demonstrates that each and every one of these accusations is simply incoherent. It is interesting that Socrates, in the first portion of the dialogue, never asserts any positive position of his own. Rather he draws out of Meletus a series of statements and then proceeds to show that the things implied by these statements are nonsense. Today, philosophers call this form of argument "reasoning to an absurd conclusion." In this form of argument, one reasons from a set of premises in order to see what the premises imply. If the premises imply something that is false or incoherent, then there must be something wrong with the premises.

For instance, at one point in the cross-examination, Socrates asks Meletus about the charge of impiety that has been brought against him. Socrates says, "I suppose you mean, as I infer from your indictment, that I teach them [the youth] not to acknowledge the gods which the State acknowledges, but some other new divinities or spiritual agencies in their stead." Meletus answers, "Yes." A few minutes later Socrates asks Meletus again, "Do you mean that I am an atheist simply, and a teacher of atheism?" Meletus answers, "... you are a complete atheist."[9] But now Socrates has caught Meletus in an outright contradiction, for he can't both be an atheist and believe in new divinities and spiritual agencies. An atheist is, by definition, one who does not believe in gods. And so, as Socrates himself says, "... he certainly does appear to me to contradict himself in the indictment as much as if he said that Socrates is guilty of not believing in the gods, and yet of believing in them."[10]

But pointing out such logical errors and fallacies does little to convince the jury that Socrates is innocent. It probably doesn't help much that Socrates himself remains defiant throughout the trial, accusing the Athenian people of being lazy and in need of someone like himself to goad them into thoughtful reflection. Socrates tells the court that he will not demean himself by begging for mercy and that if they choose to sentence him to death, then so be it. However, he refuses to stop philosophizing and questioning people about the meaning of their lives. He seems to be unconcerned with the fact that he may be put to death, and he goes so far as to state, "Nothing will injure me, not Meletus nor yet Anytus—they cannot, for a bad man is not permitted to injure a better man than himself."[11]

This last statement reinforces something that is very important about Socrates' beliefs. Socrates thinks that his identity as a person is dependent on his mind and not his physical being. Though there may be those who can harm his body, he himself—his actual essence, or his mind and soul—is immune from the attacks of those "worse" than he. Those who are bad cannot harm those who are good because those who are good have confronted and understood something very precious about the nature of reality. They have looked deep within their own souls and honestly confronted the Truth. This is something that no one can take away from them. Those who are bad have not been honest with themselves and have ignored the truths that have been placed right before their noses. Meletus, for example, even when forcefully confronted with the Truth, cannot accept the fact that the charges he has brought against Socrates are incoherent and contradictory. In his denials, Meletus does not harm Socrates but only himself. He has chosen to allow his own vanity to get between himself and the Truth, and it is separation from the Truth that is the most wretched and miserable state of affairs imaginable to Socrates. Though Socrates may die as a result of the lies that have been told about him, the real losers in this affair are Meletus and the Athenian people. When given the opportunity to become better, they instead choose to become worse by moving farther away from, rather than closer to, the Truth.

It is no surprise when Socrates is condemned to death, and furthermore it is no surprise when Socrates expresses unconcern about this development. He remains quite committed to "the good life" and continues to philosophize with his friends up until the point at which he drinks the hemlock that will take his life. Toward the end of the dialogue *Phaedo*, Socrates becomes annoyed with his distraught friend Crito who still does not seem to get the point that Socrates is something other than the flesh and blood creature who will soon expire due to hemlock poisoning. The real Socrates, he keeps reminding us, is the mind that strove to discover the Truth by living a life of integrity, dignity, and commitment to Goodness. It is not necessary to be distraught, Socrates tells us, because the "real" Socrates never will die, although the body that housed him will.

Plato's depiction of Socrates shows us a man who skillfully and logically dismantled all of the charges that had been brought against him by the Athenian court, in this manner revealing that his accusers not only misunderstood him and his philosophy, but that they did not even have the honesty to admit when they were wrong. The force and power of Socrates' defense, as depicted by Plato, leaves readers with the impression that nothing Socrates could have truthfully said would have changed the minds of the jury members from their decision to convict. They seem to have already concluded before the trial that Socrates was guilty, but not necessarily of the charges formally brought against him. He was guilty, rather, of living his life in a manner that brought those in power to shame. What the jury really wanted, apparently, was for Socrates to stop talking and philosophizing with his fellow Athenians, or at least to stop making those in power look bad with his incessant questioning. Socrates, however, did not believe that he had done anything wrong. He believed that he had lived his life in the best way possible and that it was unjust to require him to conduct himself otherwise. So, on the one side we have a man who refused to change his way of life because he was convinced of the goodness and integrity of his actions. On the other, we have a jury that refused to pay heed to the force of logic and truth, but that was intent on silencing an annoying and dangerous "gadfly." What this trial came down to, it appears then, was a showdown.

XENOPHON'S SOCRATES

This impression of a showdown in the death of Socrates is reinforced by the writings of Xenophon. However, in his telling of the story, Xenophon

© Juneko J. Robinson

emphasizes an element of Socrates' motivation that others, like Plato, gloss over in their dramatic accounts of the same event. Plato makes it appear, most of the time, that Socrates did not care about how people viewed him and that he thought the opinions of the many should be disregarded when making choices in life. If we listen only to Plato, Socrates looks to be an especially stubborn and rebellious idealist with no concern for the fact that he will be leaving behind a wife, children, and many loyal friends when he is executed. As he tells his friend Crito, it doesn't matter what those around him think. All that matters is doing what is right, even if this leads to death. Contrary to this portrayal, however, Xenophon's depiction of Socrates presents us with a man who, in making his final stand, was quite conscious and concerned about the lasting mark his death would leave on those around him. Everyone must die at some point, and Socrates, Xenophon tells us, recognized his trial as a perfect opportunity to go to his death in the most appropriate and fitting way possible, thus leaving behind a positive image that would cement the Socratic teachings in the minds of all who followed. In stressing this point, Xenophon adds an extra dimension to our understanding of Socrates, helping to clarify the fact that in choosing to die, Socrates was not simply giving up on life, but was, rather, carrying out an important part of his life's mission. His stubbornness at the trial was not just a matter of selfish idealism. It was, rather, an attempt to extend his influence and teachings beyond his own lifetime and beyond Athens by dying a dramatic, attention-grabbing, and heroic death. In short, the death of Socrates, like the death of Jesus centuries later, was not incidental to his teachings, but was in fact an important capstone to the message that he worked to articulate throughout his life.

In Xenophon's version of Socrates' confrontation with the Athenian court, we get a picture of a man who is not only resigned to his own death but of a man who is downright eager to die, even before his trial begins. When asked if he should not be preparing a defense before going to court, Socrates is reported to have said, "Don't you think that my whole life has been a preparation for my defense?" Then, when reminded of the fact that the Athenians have often condemned even innocent men to death, Socrates replies:

B o x 2.1   Xenophon

Xenophon (ca. 430–354 B.C.) was a Greek general who, when young, was a student of Socrates. Although an Athenian by birth, later in his life he fought against Athens on the side of the Spartans. He is well known for a book titled *Anabasis*, which details his leadership of a Greek force of 10,000 mercenary soldiers on their journey back to Greece after a failed military campaign in Persia.

The story told by Xenophon in *Anabasis* details the dangers faced by the Greeks as they fought their way across Eastern Europe in order to make their way home. The book is still considered to be a classic in Greek literature and served as the inspiration for the 1965 novel *The Warriors*, by Sol Yurick, which in turn inspired a movie in 1979 and a video game in 2005. The plot of *The Warriors* concerns not a Greek army but a gang in New York City that must fight its way out of enemy territory in order to get back to its own neighborhood.

God in his kindness may even have my interests at heart and be arranging for me to be released from life not only at exactly the right age, but also in the easiest way possible. For if I am condemned now, then obviously I will be able to die in a way which those who have studied the matter judge to afford not only the least discomfort, but also the least trouble to friends, and which makes them miss those who have died. For when a person leaves behind in the minds of those around him no blot or ache, but passes away with a sound body and a mind capable of happiness, then it is inevitable that such a person will be missed, isn't it?[12]

Here, Socrates appears to be quite aware that the manner of his death is certainly going to have an enormous influence on how posterity assesses his life and his philosophy. Not only will it be quicker and easier to die from hemlock poisoning than to suffer the indignity of a slow and progressive physical decline, but to die at the height of one's intellectual and physical powers, fighting for what one believes in, assures a person the best chances of being remembered fondly and in a positive light. By choosing this mode of passing, Socrates believes that he will "benefit at the hands of both gods and men."[13] Although we get a hint of this notion in the Platonic dialogues *Apology* and *Crito*, the overall thrust of these dialogues is that Socrates believes it best to ignore the opinions of the masses. But perhaps Socrates was more concerned with his public image than Plato leads us to believe. Perhaps in the account of Xenophon we find a further reason why Socrates was so stubborn with the Athenian court. Perhaps he was looking forward to the sort of effect he would have on the world after his death.

This would not be unusual, for even today people with far less sense of personal mission than Socrates anticipate their own deaths and attempt to lay the groundwork for how they will be remembered in the future after they are gone. When people are diagnosed with terminal illness, for instance, it is common for them to make amends with enemies and to reach out to family members in order to settle old feuds. This sort of "fence-mending" might seem absurd if we remain too focused on the fact that the individual who is to die won't be around to reap the benefits of these renewed relationships. However, the purpose of this kind of reconciliation is not necessarily to make the dying person feel better but rather to leave a positive and dignified image in the minds of those who will be left behind. This may be especially important to individuals whose only mark on the world was made in the hearts and minds of their friends, loved ones, and close associates. For someone who has produced no great books, no great works of art, and no lasting artifacts, fond memories may be the only hope they have for continued influence after they are dead.

Recall that Socrates never did write anything. If he had, perhaps his manner of death might not have been so important to him. His words, then, might speak for themselves, and we wouldn't need to rely on the memories of others, like Plato, Xenophon, or Aristophanes, in order to give us a sense of who he was and what he taught. But in writing things down, Socrates probably also recognized that ideas have a tendency to become reified, taking on a meaning that may appear more certain and settled than really is the case. The dialectical method that Socrates practiced during his life, however, required constant and active questioning, not passive acceptance of a ready-made message. It required that the mind remain lively and engaged in the search for Truth. As it is very easy to allow a written text to take on authority of its own, given that the words on the page are right there in black and white, perhaps Socrates avoided committing his thoughts to writing precisely because he wanted to avoid making it appear that his message was completely worked out and unambiguous. This would be a violation of his own dictum that true wisdom consists in recognizing one's own ignorance, after all. By bestowing his memory to the minds of a variety of students who would then go on to write about him from an assortment of conflicting perspectives, perhaps Socrates anticipated that the meaning of his life and teachings would be endlessly debated and discussed after he was gone. This, in combination with his dramatic death, would maximize the chances that the spirit of his dialectical mode of philosophizing would be preserved forever, or at least for as long as there are minds active and curious enough to sort through the Socratic legacy. If this is correct, then the death of Socrates was not simply an injustice perpetrated against him by the Athenian people. It was also an opportunity for Socrates to bestow his last testament to the world, not just in order to be remembered as a great man, but in order to encourage all people to become wiser, better, and more profound through the practice of philosophy.

From the accounts of Plato and Xenophon we get a sense of Socrates as a figure concerned with cultivating critical thinking and active curiosity about the human mind and its mysteries. Although their depictions of Socrates emphasize different aspects of his personality, the message that speaks through these depictions is very similar: Socrates was a man of integrity, satisfied with nothing less than the absolute Truth, but always aware of how far he was from a final comprehension of the Truth. He was a man with a mission, and that mission was focused on making himself and others better and wiser, not through the accumulation of facts and figures but through encouraging the active and unceasing exercise of the mind's rational faculties. He was also a great teacher, not simply because of *what* he taught but because of *how* he lived and died. Unlike many professional teachers of his and our own time, Socrates tried to instruct not by setting himself up as an authority figure but by encouraging others to think freely along with him and to follow his lived example. As Xenophon writes, "[I]n my opinion he actually benefited his associates, partly by practical example and partly by conversation."[14] With Socrates, *how* one lives becomes just as important, if not more important, than *what* one believes.

ARISTOPHANES' SOCRATES

All of this might leave us with the impression that there really was nothing objectionable about Socrates and that the resistance he encountered from the Athenians was simply a matter of their own egotism, arrogance, and vanity. However, such an assessment would commit the error of trying to understand Socrates only from the perspective of those who loved him and agreed with his message. Imagine how, today, you would react if accosted in the street by an unkempt old man who wanted you to justify your manner of life. You would probably think him a crazy misfit and call the police! At the very least, you would view him as an annoyance and try to get away from him. Likewise in ancient Athens, Socrates was, understandably, thought of as a pain in the neck by many people for his unconventional methods. Furthermore, and more profoundly, there were also those who were critical of the overall character of his teachings precisely because in them they saw a dangerous movement away from the traditions that grounded Greek culture. Nietzsche is perhaps the most outspoken modern critic of Socrates, and his assessment of the Athenian philosopher highlights this destabilizing and revolutionary aspect of Socratic thinking:

© Juneko J. Robinson

Wherever Socratism turns its searching eyes it sees lack of insight and the power of illusion; and from this lack it infers the essential perversity and reprehensibility of what exists. Basing himself on this point, Socrates conceives it to be his duty to correct existence: all alone, with an expression of irreverence and superiority, as the precursor of an altogether different culture, art, and morality.[15]

This sentiment, that Socrates' mission acted to undermine social order, was exactly what he was charged with at his trial, and it is precisely this picture that is painted of him by another one of his contemporaries, the comic playwright Aristophanes. That there is some truth to this perspective is made very plausible if we consider the fact that with Socrates' dialectical method, everything is opened up to question and debate, and the only authority that one is subject to is the authority of logic and reason. Those who claim to know the Truth based solely on "instinct," "revelation," or "intuition" are open to suspicion in this view. If one cannot logically justify one's beliefs and ideas, then those beliefs and ideas are to be discredited as irrational and thus worthless. But then where does this leave those who ground their lives in the unquestioned routines of tradition and convention? What of those religious, political, and cultural leaders who claim authority not because they have reasoned through their ideas philosophically but because they have been endowed by the gods or by nature with special insight or understanding that transcends mere logic? In the eyes of Socrates and his followers, such individuals are to be interrogated, their lack of rationality exposed, and their authority dissolved. While to many this may seem like a legitimate triumph of reason over irrationality, to others it constitutes an attack on the very foundations of society.

B o x 2.2 Aristophanes

Aristophanes (ca. 446–386 B.C.) is considered to be among the greatest of Greek comic playwrights. He authored forty plays, eleven of which survive today intact. He was a representative of the "Old Comedy," which is a form of comic satire focusing on real people and events of the day.

Despite the fact that Plato holds Aristophanes' play *The Clouds* responsible for poisoning the minds of the Athenian public against Socrates, Aristophanes actually does appear as a friend of Socrates in one of the Platonic dialogues. In *Symposium*, Aristophanes is depicted as telling a very strange story about the origin of humankind. Originally, he says, humans had four hands, four legs, two faces, and two sets of genitals, one male and one female. Because these early humans were so strong, Zeus feared that they would challenge the gods. As a result, he cut them all in two, "as you might divide an egg with a hair," thus creating the two sexes. This is why men and women seek one another's company to this day!

The 1998 musical play and the 2001 movie version of *Hedwig and the Angry Inch* both include a song titled "The Origin of Love," which is based on Aristophanes' mythic story. In the movie version, an animated cartoon illustrates the events in the song.

In Aristophanes' play *The Clouds*, Socrates is portrayed as the leader of an institution called the "Thinkery." This institution is a school where students come and, for a fee, learn how to use the tools of logic. The story documents the efforts of Strepsiades, the father of Pheidippides, who desires to acquire the argumentative skills that will allow him to successfully get out of paying his debts. However, Strepsiades is not clever enough to master the techniques that Socrates teaches, and so he sends his son instead. As it turns out, Pheidippides learns all too well how to argue and he ends up finding a rational way to justify horsewhipping his own father and mother! It is at this point that Strepsiades is finally confronted with the error of his ways and renounces Socrates and his practices. As he exclaims at the end of the play, "By god, if you can prove that, then for all I care, you heel, you can take your stinking Logics and your Thinkery as well with Socrates inside it and damn well go to hell!"[16] He then burns down the Thinkery with Socrates inside of it, taking revenge on the man who tempted him into evading his "merely" conventional, legal obligations.

While *The Clouds* has an overall comic appeal, there is, nonetheless, a simmering sense of anger and hostility toward Socrates that is expressed in it. Aristophanes clearly wants to leave the impression that Socrates is a threat to the Athenian traditions of religion, law, and family. When we are first introduced to him, Socrates is depicted as denying the existence of gods and instead propounding the "Convection-principle" of the universe, whereby all things can be explained by the natural properties of gases. Thus, religious institutions are claimed to be based on falsehood. The laws, furthermore, may be manipulated by a process of logical trickery, and finally even the conventional hierarchy of the family unit might be turned upside down with the application of clever arguments. Naturalism and reason, thus, are comically depicted throughout the play as the enemies of tradition and polite society. This confrontation is finally dramatized when two fighting cocks take the stage, one representing the old ways of society and the other representing the new Socratic philosophy. The rooster symbolizing the old traditions is large and muscular, "powerful but not heavy, expressing in his movements that inward harmony and grace and dignity which the Old Education was meant to produce."[17] The rooster symbolizing Socrates, on the other hand, "is comparatively slight, with sloping shoulders, an emaciated pallor, an enormous tongue, and a disproportionately large phallus. His body is graceless but extremely quick moving; his every motion expresses defiant belligerence, and his plumage is brilliant to the point of flashiness."[18] This unflattering characterization is intended to cement the idea in the minds of the audience that Socrates and his followers, though clever and quick on their feet, are nonetheless lacking in reverence for the traditional values that made Athens the leader of the Greek world. Thus, at the end of the play, when Socrates is gagging and choking on the smoke from his own burning school, we are encouraged to laugh at the fate of such a ridiculous character who dared to challenge the common sense and wisdom of his own cultural heritage.

Obviously, the manner in which Aristophanes represents the content of Socrates' philosophy is in some conflict with the accounts of both Plato and Xenophon. Whereas Plato and Xenophon claim that Socrates is unconcerned with speculations about the physical world, Aristophanes claims that he has all sorts of unusual theories about the structure of the universe. Whereas Plato and Xenophon tell us that

Socrates is overwhelmingly concerned with the Truth, Aristophanes tells us that Socrates only cares about winning arguments. Despite these contradictions, there is one element that runs through all of the literature that centers on Socrates: he was certainly concerned with the practice of logic and the use of reason for the empowerment of the individual. It is this focus on thinking for one's self that is, perhaps, the key to understanding why so many people both love and hate Socrates.

Aristophanes' final comic portrayal of Socrates stands in stark contrast to Plato's tragic depiction of the same character as he dies from hemlock poisoning. We should keep in mind that Aristophanes was a well-established playwright when he produced *The Clouds* and had a firm stake in the traditions of Athens. From his perspective, the philosophy of Socrates was a threat to the institutions and the culture that supported him. Plato, on the other hand, was a very young man at the time of Socrates' trial and execution. From his perspective, the philosophy of Socrates was seen as an exciting and empowering method for doing away with the pretensions of the old guard and of clearing the ground for the contributions of a new generation. To the aging Aristophanes, Socrates was a threat. To the younger Plato, he was a hero. It would be superficial to say that only one of these perspectives is correct, for both sides express something of the hopes and the dangers that Socrates introduced into Western thinking. He was both a devil and a saint. In addition to encouraging individual freedom of thought and an active, critical engagement with the world, he also introduced a method that provoked the later development of cynicism, skepticism, and nihilism. Although Socrates himself was likely hopeful that his dialectical method of inquiry would eventually lead to the discovery of objective and absolute Truth, others were not so optimistic. Even today, he is loved by some and reviled by others for how he influenced philosophy.

THE WONDROUS DISTRESS OF SOCRATES

With Socrates we have encountered an individual who comes closer than anyone else, before or since, to a complete and pure distillation of the truly philosophical way of thinking. Wondrous distress manifests itself in his stubborn and uncompromising quest for Truth, which is coupled in him with an extremely unusual willingness to admit how little he really does know. If a real philosopher is, as I have been insisting, a person enthusiastic about raising questions but also willing to defer final answers to those questions in the pursuit of absolute Truth, then we have no better example of a philosopher than Socrates. Socrates repeatedly reminds us that to be philosophical is to be curious, to be open to dialogue with others and to remain agreeable to being shown when we are in error. This is what makes a person wise, he tells us, but it is not the sort of wisdom that is normally valued by the average, commonsense person in the street. The wisdom that Socrates teaches is a negative sort of wisdom. It is the wisdom that comes from recognizing, and admitting to, our own ignorance about the things in life that matter the most. "He, you human beings, is the wisest, who, like Socrates, knows that his wisdom is in truth worth nothing."[19] The value of wisdom, it seems, lies in its potential to remind us of our own separation from the Truth and thereby to spur us onward toward its reappropriation.

The element of wonder that we find in the ideas of Socrates is manifest in his optimistic supposition that the human mind is capable, through rational reflection, of moving closer and closer to an understanding of ourselves and the world we inhabit. It might be most accurate to call this element of Socrates' philosophy a hypothesis rather than a proven conclusion, because the only evidence that he has in its support is his own personal conviction that it is so. Socrates never presents us with objective evidence to verify the powers of reason and logic but rather appeals to us on the basis of our own inner experiences as thinking, willing, and rational creatures. He pleads with us to look inside of ourselves and to determine whether our inner world contains the same sorts of aspirational hopes and dreams that his inner world contains. At the times when Socrates sounds the most harsh and disgusted with his fellow Athenians, it is because he encounters either a lack of this inner drive in them or an unwillingness by them to listen to this inner drive. In either case, Socrates judges this as a disappointing shortcoming, making it impossible for him and his fellow citizens to walk along the same intellectual and spiritual path. According to Socrates, the only thing that makes life worth living is the desire and the drive to investigate, question, and wonder about reality. As he most famously states, "The unexamined life is not worth living."

The element of distress is no less present in the ideas of Socrates than is the element of wonder. Throughout the stories about Socrates we are haunted by three related, distressing issues. First of all there is our awareness that the life and mission of this great Athenian philosopher will culminate in his execution at the hands of the very people whom he hopes to help. Just as the story of Jesus, hundreds of years later, will be cemented by the tragic image of a man who has sacrificed his life for the good of humankind, so it is with Socrates. While we are captivated by the insights contained in the dialogues of Plato and Xenophon, or as we chuckle at the comedy by Aristophanes, in the back of our minds is the awareness that Socrates will die. This man who is so loved by those around him, who is so loving to those around him, and who is so ambitious in his aspiration toward the Truth; this man will be executed despite (or perhaps because of) his profound wisdom. His execution is a reminder to us that even the greatest figures in the history of the world are subject to death, and this is one of the most basic reasons why we must always fall short of complete and perfect understanding. We are finite creatures with a finite amount of time to explore ourselves and our world.

The second distressing element found in the life and teachings of Socrates is related to the issue of death. Because of the fact that we are all aware, at some level, that we will die, and because this awareness is customarily greeted with a sense of anxiety and dread, there is a common tendency on the part of many people to cover over this awareness, to try to forget about their finitude and consequently to assert themselves in the world as if they are all-knowing and god-like. This often becomes manifest in the unphilosophical and self-assured arrogance of individuals like Meletus, Anytus, and Lycon, who contrive to secure for themselves positions of power through the manipulation of the truth and of other human beings. Such exploiters are impervious to the lessons of reason and philosophy. They are driven not by the desire for Truth, but by the desire to assert their power and to make the world conform to their own ready-made conception of how things should be. The problem with this, as Socrates tells us, is that such individuals are caught in the grip of a very particular, and destructive, kind of ignorance. While Socrates teaches us that those who are conscious of the ways in which they are ignorant are on the path to wisdom, people like the power-hungry Meletus, Anytus, and Lycon are not even aware of their own ignorance. Being blind to the things that they don't know, such individuals have a tendency to sink further and further into the morass of complacency and unintelligence. "For herein is the evil of ignorance, that he who is neither good nor wise is nevertheless satisfied with himself: he has no desire for that of which he has no want."[20] Without a distressing awareness of the ways in which we are ignorant, we have no motivation to seek the real Truth. We remain satisfied with who and what we are and can conceive no reason to aspire toward anything more. One of the major messages that Socrates has to teach us is to avoid this sort of complacency and satisfaction by embracing the distress involved in recognizing our incomplete understanding of ourselves and the world.

The third distressing element in the teachings of Socrates involves the nature of the philosophical path itself. While Socrates, even when facing death, remains an optimistic figure, his image of philosophy has tinges of the tragic to it nonetheless. Given that, as humans, we have finite intellects and a finite allotment of time to explore the infinite mysteries of Being, we are, in a sense, doomed to failure in our quest for perfect and complete understanding of reality. We can never know everything, yet we should not give up on the pursuit of the Absolute. This incongruity between what philosophers aspire toward and what it is that they may potentially acquire sets up an impossibly distressing situation for the philosophical thinker. Philosophy, it seems, in its very core is a kind of systematic, methodical, and noble path to failure according to Socrates. The more ambitious our aspirations, the more intensely aware of our imperfection we become. Yet, ironically, it is through this very process that we also come to a deeper comprehension of who we really are. Through the failures of philosophy we come face to face with ourselves as the sorts of beings who must endlessly struggle and fall short of our highest goals. To do less than this is to be less than human. To do more is to be a god.

QUESTIONS FOR DISCUSSION

1. What are the problems involved in trying to reconstruct the philosophy of a person who never wrote anything? Do you think it is possible to sort through the various accounts we have of Socrates' life and thinking in order to discover his true philosophy?

2. It has been suggested by some thinkers that it may be that Socrates never actually existed as a flesh and blood human being. Just as many different people have written about fictional characters like Dracula and Sherlock Holmes, it could be that Socrates is simply a literary creation. Do you think this is possible? If it is, would it make any difference to the importance of the Socratic message?

3. The Socratic Method is still used today as a means of instruction in colleges and law schools. What are some of the advantages and the disadvantages of using this method of instruction? Do you think it an effective means of teaching?

4. What do you think Socrates' real purpose was for pursuing his conversations with fellow Athenians? Do you think he was really concerned with the Truth and with learning, or do you think he might have had other motivations?

5. Was the execution of Socrates just or unjust? Why do you think he was sentenced to death and why do you think he refused to flee? What would you do under the same circumstances? Explain.

6. What did Socrates mean when during his trial he said, "The unexamined life is not worth living"? Is it true that unreflective people might as well be dead? How important are self-reflection and self-examination to you in your own life?

7. Do you agree with Socrates that the real "you" is more than your physical body? Do you think that there is a life after death? What sorts of reasons do you have for believing as you do on this issue? Do you have any logical arguments to support your position?

NOTES

1. Bertrand Russell, *A History of Western Philosophy* (New York: Touchstone Books, 1972), pp. 82–83.

2. Jonathan Barnes (trans. and ed.), *Early Greek Philosophy* (London: Penguin Books, 1987), p. 230.

3. Plato, *Phaedo*, 98b6–d4.

4. Barnes, *Early Greek Philosophy*, p. 227.

5. Ibid., p. 228.

6. Plato, *Phaedo*, 66a.

7. Ibid., 80ba.

8. This is the theme of F. M. Cornford, *Before and After Socrates* (Cambridge: Cambridge University Press, 1986), pp. 27–28, 50.

9. Plato, *Apology*, 26b2–6.

10. Ibid., 26c1–8.

11. Ibid., 27a4–6.

12. Xenophon, "Socrates' Defense," in *Conversations of Socrates* (London: Penguin Books, 1990), pp. 41–42.

13. Ibid., p.143.

14. Xenophon, "Memoirs of Socrates," in *Conversations of Socrates*, p. 85.

15. Friedrich Nietzsche, *The Birth of Tragedy* in *Basic Writings of Nietzsche*, Translated and edited by Walter Kaufman (New York: The Modern Library, 1968), p. 87.

16. Aristophanes, *The Clouds*, Translated by William Arrowsmith (New York: Mentor Books, 1962), p. 126.

17. Ibid., p. 80.

18. Ibid.

19. Plato, *Apology*, 23b.

20. Plato, *Symposium*, 204a.

Chapter 3

Plato

© Juneko J. Robinson

Plato

How is Platonic philosophy distinct from Socratic philosophy? What is
Platonic Idealism? What is the significance of Plato's Divided Line
analogy? What is the significance of Plato's Cave myth? Who are the
Philosopher Kings? Why was Plato suspicious of artists? Why was Plato
hostile to democracy?

The powerfully dramatic life and personality of Socrates produced an effect on all
those who came after him, for better or for worse. The example he set would
become the standard of philosophical authenticity for a whole group of Greek
thinkers, although there would remain much dispute as to what his deepest and
most important message consisted of. Was Socrates most concerned with revealing
human ignorance? Was he most concerned with uncovering the absolute Truth? Or
was he most concerned with detailing how to live a good life? Even today there is
an ongoing debate among professional scholars concerning what Socrates really said

and meant. Such debate was just as contentious in the years following the death of this Athenian sage as it is now, and a wide variety of thinkers came to emphasize differing aspects of his legacy, producing conflicting, yet vital and exciting, schools of thought. Considering the open nature of Socrates' quest for Truth, perhaps nothing is more appropriate. Nonetheless, as has already been noted, of all of his followers, probably the most influential, and certainly the most eloquent, remains Plato. In his development, expansion, and formalization of Socratic insights, Plato produced a vision of reality that still has great appeal for many people today.

PLATO'S DIVERGENCE FROM SOCRATES

As was discussed in Chapter 2, Plato was the author of a variety of dialogues in which Socrates appears as a character. It is generally presumed that his earliest dialogues, like *Lysis*, *Euthyphro*, and *Apology*, more accurately represent the views of Socrates than do his later dialogues, like *The Republic*, *Theaetetus*, and *Timaeus*. In these later dialogues, Plato's own views are thought to become progressively more pronounced, and the character of Socrates is believed, finally, to be transformed into Plato's spokesman. Of course, because Plato's writing always takes

on a dramatic form, it is never entirely clear whether he is advocating the views of the characters in these dialogues. Instead, his philosophy must be ferreted out and reconstructed on the strength and conviction of the arguments that he puts into the mouths of others. Plato's own voice never shouts forth loud and clear in his writings but, as Irwin Edman writes, "one seems constantly to hear it whispered."[1] It becomes obvious, furthermore, as one compares the early with the later dialogues, that there is a difference in the overall message that is "whispered" through them. Whereas the early writings seem to reinforce the idea that human intelligence is unable to settle grand, metaphysical questions, the later writings seem

© Juneko J. Robinson

to suggest that such questions can be answered and that the wisest among us may potentially become aquainted with the governing principles of the entire universe.

Recognizing the difficulty involved in sifting out the uniquely original contributions that Plato made to philosophy does not preclude our attempts to understand a general mode or style of thinking that has come to be called "Platonic." The Platonic way of thinking is distinct from the Socratic way of thinking insofar as it focuses less on the critical recognition of human ignorance and more on a positive attempt to articulate an overall metaphysical vision of reality. Whereas Socrates appears to have spent most of his time clearing the ground of false beliefs and unsubstantiated dogma, Plato appears to have been most concerned with rebuilding an edifice of knowledge on the foundation that Socrates secured. With Platonic philosophy, we find a constructive effort to bring the human mind into congress with the Absolute and finally to settle an issue first raised by the Presocratic philosophers: what is it that is ultimately real? The Platonic answer to this question rejects the materialism of thinkers like Thales and Democritus and instead seeks to develop the insights of Socrates in a direction that will firmly ground all of reality in a transcendent, nonphysical world of pure ideas.

Plato founded the very first university in the Western world as an instrument to disseminate his ideas and to foster rational investigation into the mysteries of the universe. Whereas Socrates wandered the streets of Athens seeking out fellow citizens with whom to converse, Plato drew students to his school, which was built outside of the city in the suburbs of Athens. This *Academy* was so named because it was established in the Grove of Academus, a public garden honoring a Greek hero. Even today it is common to use the phrase "the Academy" in order to refer to our own system of higher education, and as is the case with contemporary universities, Plato's Academy drew students from great distances with its promise of insight and learning. This sort of arrangement, in fact, might give us an indication of another way that Platonism differs in spirit from the original philosophy of Socrates. The formality of Plato's institution suggests a manner of teaching that was hierarchical and top-down. Students came to his school to learn from his lectures and to follow his curriculum. Whereas Socrates seemed to have encouraged his friends to learn *with* him, Plato seems to have wanted strangers to learn *from* him. As Plato himself wrote in a letter to his friends, "... if these matters are to be expounded at all in books or lectures, they would best come from me."[2] So, just what are some of these "matters" that Plato "expounded" at his Academy?

Plato taught that we move out of a state of unmitigated ignorance when we come to appreciate that there is a reality more stable and lasting than the things that are immediately perceived by sight, touch, taste, hearing, and smell. Certainly, common sense tells us that when we examine our environment using the five senses, we find obvious evidence of a physical world that exists "out there." However, many people mistake the tangible qualities of this world for the most foundational of all realities. The Presocratics made this mistake, according to Plato, when they asserted that the most real and lasting things that exist must be made out of some sort of material substance like water, earth, air, or fire. The problem is that none of these elements remains unchangeable forever.

Rather, they all come into and go out of being, altering form and becoming different over time. When you strike a match, for instance, the flame comes into existence, and when you blow out the match, the flame goes out of existence. But, asks Plato, what is this "existence" that a thing like fire comes into and goes out of? Something can't just come out of nothing, so what is it that stays the same, unshakable and immutable, providing the ground out of which all other things like earth, air, fire, and water emerge and come into being? Whatever it is, Plato tells us this substratum, or characterless substance that underlies reality, must be of such a nature that it is capable of supporting everything that does, or that will potentially, exist. As Anaximander before him claimed, Plato tells us that if this ultimate foundation supports all things, even those that seem contradictory in nature, "then it ought to be devoid of any inherent characteristics of its own."[3] Plato likens this underlying substance, which is free of any unique features, to the base used by ointment makers in order to produce sweet smelling lotions. In order for the fragrances carried by ointments to fully assert themselves, the base into which they are mixed must be as neutral as possible; otherwise it will distort and possibly ruin the smell of the lotion. Likewise, the base substance that supports all that we see, taste, touch, and feel in the universe must be completely neutral in terms of its sensory properties so that it does not interfere with the attributes that it supports. This completely colorless, odorless, textureless, soundless, and "invisible" substance is more real than the properties that it supports precisely because it is unchanging and lacking in its own essential and distinct qualities. But now there arises a problem. How can we know and understand a reality that is so completely beyond our sensory comprehension? If we can't see, taste, touch, smell, or hear it, how can we know that it exists?

At this point, Plato draws on another of Socrates' most important teachings. If the nature of ultimate reality is such that it cannot be comprehended by the senses, then we should look to the rational faculties of the mind, rather than to the sensory organs of the body, as a way to understand the highest truths of the universe. What we need to do is withdraw our attention from the superficial and fleeting sights and sounds around us and instead inquire into the logical foundations that allow those sights and sounds to be. Anticipating a point later to be made by René Descartes, Plato writes in the dialogue *Theaetetus* that our senses are, in fact, a very poor judge of Truth overall because we know that they often, as in dreams, fool us into believing in the existence of things that are not truly there.[4] On this ground alone we should be skeptical of what the five senses show us and instead be more attentive to what our reason reveals to us. Reason, when properly used, never fools us. It is like a laser beam that unerringly cuts to the core of the Truth. The physical senses, on the other hand, are like lying friends who tell us what they think we want to hear, and as with lying friends it only takes the discovery of one instance of untruthfulness for us to become suspicious of everything else that they say. How do we know that what appears to our senses at this moment corresponds to the way things really are? We don't, because right now we could be dreaming, hallucinating, or experiencing an illusion. If we are to become consistently adept at sifting truth from lies, then we must learn to fully develop and utilize our capacity for logical thinking. The path to the Truth, then, is paved not with sensory observation but with the exercise of the mind and its capacity for rational reflection.

One of the things that reason tells us is that the "world of becoming"—the world of sight and sound, feel and smell—requires space in which to unfold. Space is not something that we can see, taste, touch, or feel in itself, but nevertheless it is something that logically must exist in order for the things in the sensory world to exist. Space is like the ointment maker's base substance. It remains hidden while allowing particular properties to become manifest in the world. All physical objects that come into being do so only insofar as they occupy a particular location. If space did not exist, then physical objects would not exist. Because our physical world depends on the pre-existence of this spatial, nonphysical reality, spatial reality is, therefore, more foundational than the physical objects it allows to be. Yet we could never know space simply through observation. If we never attempted to abstract away from the phenomena of sense, using the powers of the mind to figure out the logical conditions that make those phenomena possible, then we would never understand the reality that underlies the physical world around us. For this reason, Plato tells us that the study of abstract sciences dealing with spatial reality, like geometry, are at a higher level of sophistication than those dealing with merely gross, physical reality. In this he follows on the insights of the Presocratic philosopher Pythagoras who had claimed that the underlying unity of the world could be expressed in terms of geometrical and mathematical formulas. Mathematical order is more stable, lasting, and coherent than the physical world of change, generation, and destruction, and therefore more real. Because we can explain the physical world by reference to the nonphysical world of geometry and mathematics, the visible world around us must be dependent on a non-sensible realm of numbers and geometrical laws.

© Juneko J. Robinson

THE DIVIDED LINE

In *The Republic*, Plato likens the universe to a "line divided"[5] between a higher, intelligible realm and a lower, visible realm. In this manner, there are at least two levels of reality that contribute to the totality of existence. The level of "becoming" consists of all that is apparent to our physical senses. This "sensible world" really does exist, yet it is somewhat misleading, for it commonly distracts the mind from contemplating another higher, more stable realm of reality. Too often we content ourselves only with the things that we can see, taste, hear, touch, and feel, never developing beyond a desire for these sorts of entertainments. This is why the unchanging "intelligible world" normally remains hidden to us behind the phenomena of becoming. Yet as it remains hidden, it also provides the ground upon which the "lower," sensible realm is built. In a manner analogous to the Hindu notion of *Maya*, the world of sensory experience veils a deeper, more substantial, though immaterial, Truth of which most of us are not aware. Without this nonphysical world, the physical world would not exist. Yet because it is not dependent upon bodies for its own existence, the nonphysical realm could very well exist in the absence of the material realm. Because of this one-way dependency, the nonphysical world described by geometry and numbers is considered by Plato to be more real than the physical world that it provides a foundation for, and so knowledge of its details constitutes a higher order of wisdom.

Socrates was correct, according to Plato, when he asserted that the first step toward wisdom is the realization of ignorance. When we are born into this world, we take the things we see around us at face value and assume that what we perceive with our own eyes is real. For instance, it is natural for babies to think that their own reflection in a mirror is another baby, or that images flashed on a screen by a projector are three-dimensional objects. Though such judgments are mistaken, at a very young age all of us are deluded by these sorts of appearances because we don't make a distinction between the way that things seem to us and the way that things really are independent of our perceptions. We haven't yet developed the intellectual skills necessary to distinguish truth from illusion. Yet such naïveté is not wholly limited to children. Even into adulthood, many if not most people continue to rely on an unsophisticated confidence in their own "common sense." As long as our day-to-day routines serve well to keep us safe, comfortable, and happy, most of us assume that our unreflective way of being and acting in the world is correct, and any challenge to this everyday presumption is reacted against as abnormal and threatening. There are a variety of forces that conspire to encourage this sort of pedestrian thinking: cultural conditioning, peer pressure, and personal laziness are among them. The first step toward developing beyond this limited way of thinking is to question our commonsense beliefs and to admit that the way the world appears to us may not be the way that the world really is. Before we can aspire toward true wisdom, we must first turn our backs on old, comfortable illusions. It is then that real education can begin.

Education at Plato's Academy unfolded against this philosophical backdrop. As students became more and more adept at focusing the power of pure intellect on the abstract problems involved in mathematics and geometry, they would progressively become less attached to a dependence on the physical senses. You might say, in this way, that a Platonic education helped students to ascend the "divided line" of reality as if on a ladder, reaching higher and higher into the immaterial world that lies above the visible world of physical objects. Ultimately, claims Plato, as students advanced in their studies, they would move beyond even the contemplation of particular formulas and numbers and come to understand the very principles, or "Forms," that lie behind all systems of math and geometry. The Forms are the highest objects of contemplation. They stand in the same relation to math and geometry as math and geometry stand to the visible world. The Forms are more stable and unchanging, and thus more real, than everything else that lies below them on the divided line. Whereas even the student of mathematics must utilize written numbers and figures in order to make calculations, the student of the Forms moves beyond the need to utilize any sort of device that has a visible, physical component and learns to comprehend the object of study through the pure force of intellect alone. It is at this point in their education that students have risen to the highest level that formal learning can take them.

So what are these Forms that Plato tells us are the most real yet immaterial things that exist in all of the universe? Just as space itself stands behind the varying physical phenomena of the visible world, there must also be some sort of unifying substance that stands behind the varying formulas of math and geometry. What is it that provides the ground for all varieties of mathematical study, the way that space provides the ground for all physical phenomena? Plato's answer to this question is at once simple and profound. For all of those who pursue the abstract sciences, there are a handful of criteria that guide and direct their studies. First of all, they must be concerned with understanding the Truth. Without the guiding criterion of Truth itself, the student would be unconcerned with the accuracy or correctness of his or her discoveries. Such an individual could never focus attention on, and affirm, one set of ideas over another. Rather, a person unconcerned with Truth would simply be amused by the wide array of differing assertions and ideas in the world, seeing in them a "spectacle"[6] that is entertaining, the way that the sights and sounds of the visible world are entertaining to the uneducated masses. But this would lead the student nowhere except in circles, and not the sorts of circles that are appropriate to the study of geometry! In order to genuinely engage in the abstract study of math, the mathematician must be concerned with getting the correct answer, not just any old answer. There must be a Truth that stands behind the formulas, or else those formulas are mere illusions.

A reverence for the Truth is what makes one a real philosopher, but the Form of Truth coexists with other Forms that support and illuminate it and which are themselves distinguishable as necessary grounds for knowledge. Beauty is one of the other Forms that Plato singles out as foundational to human understanding. In Beauty, we find the motivation for pursuing the Truth. If Truth was itself ugly, then we might be tempted to ignore or overlook it in order to linger instead in the presence of something more pleasant and to our liking. But the real philosopher finds that Beauty always accompanies the Truth in such a way that it "gives birth to many gloriously beautiful ideas and theories, in unstinting love of wisdom."[7] Here we can see a kind of optimism in Plato that is missing from the writing of many later philosophers, but which was nonetheless a common element of the Greek worldview. For the Greeks generally (Democritus notwithstanding), and Plato in particular, the universe was conceived of as possessing an orderly and beautiful structure. Our world, in Greek terms, is a *cosmos*. It is not a haphazard or disorganized arrangement of physical bodies, but rather an elegantly structured and organic whole that is pleasing to contemplate.[8] The harmonies and patterns of geometry and mathematics reveal something of the beauty that exists in the world, but in order for particular beautiful patterns to be possible, there must be a Form of Beauty itself that stands behind and supports all of these individually aesthetically pleasing things. Once the philosopher fully comprehends the Form of Beauty, he or she also understands the Truth. Conversely, an understanding of the Truth always is accompanied by an appreciation of its Beauty. The two go hand in hand, yet they are still, in a conceptual sense, distinct from one another.

Besides the Forms of Truth and Beauty, Plato singles out the Form of Justice as also necessary to any sort of real knowledge, mathematical or otherwise. In order to understand the Beautiful nature of Truth and the Truthful nature of Beauty, one must be able to comprehend the manner in which these individual principles complement and articulate with one another. There is a relationship that holds between them, just as there are harmonic relationships that hold between all parts of the universe, and the Form of this relationship is the Form of Justice itself. When Justice reigns, all things play their proper role, fitting together like puzzle pieces that when snapped together allow the overall Beauty and Truth of an otherwise fragmented picture to shine forth. Truth, Beauty, and Justice, then, work together in order to prepare the ground for all forms of abstract scientific understanding that humans aspire to master. Furthermore, because the abstract sciences reveal a ground that is necessary in order to allow the physical world to be, our entire universe depends on the preexistence of the Forms of Truth, Beauty, and Justice. These are the governing principles of the universe, and without them we would not have the sort of universe that we do have.

There is one last component in Plato's metaphysical picture that must be put into place before we can fully understand the cohesiveness of his philosophical project. So far we have delineated at least three unchangeable and immutable Forms that underlie all of our knowledge about reality. Yet, so long as these Forms themselves remain un-unified, we cannot say that we have been completely successful in understanding them. Plato's purpose in introducing the Forms in the first place was to distill and clarify the underlying necessary conditions out of which the universe was built. But so long as the Forms remain ungrounded, it would be hasty to conclude that we have discovered the final governing principle of the universe. Something has remained unstated up to this point, and that is an articulation of the ultimate ground upon which the Forms themselves depend. What is this final point at which even the Forms converge into one?

The Good itself is this point. The Good is the Form of all Forms, providing the ultimate foundation upon which all else rests. The Good is to Truth, Beauty, and Justice what they in turn are to the abstract sciences, and for this reason "the Good must be honored even more than they."[9] It is the ultimate anchor point for everything that exists. Plato uses the image of the Sun to characterize the Good. Just as the Sun provides light so that our physical eyes may see the world around us, so the Good provides a sort of conceptual light so that our minds can make out the Forms underlying all reality. If this source of "light" did not exist, our minds would not be capable of making the sorts of distinctions that constitute the content of philosophical learning. It is because of the Good that we are able to make our way through the world and understand its structures and patterns. If we could understand the Good, we would understand that which throws light on everything, and thus "the Form of the Good is the greatest object of study."[10]

The problem with trying to study the Good itself, however, is that this Form is so general, so comprehensive, and yet so lacking in particular and distinctive characteristics, that it is impossible to articulate precisely what it is other than by saying "it is Good." Plato claims that our reason tells us the Good must exist; yet "it is not something that can be put into words."[11] The best that a teacher can do is to guide the pupil in the direction of the Good, leading the way toward its discovery, but at the end understanding of this Form comes "like light flashing forth when a fire is kindled; it is born in the soul and straight away nourishes itself."[12] Just as you cannot force another person to open up his or her eyes in order to see the firelight that is right in front of them, neither can the teacher of Good force the pupil to "see" this final object of study. Rather the teacher can only train the pupil in the various sciences and encourage the pupil's rational mind to think things through to their final ends. At the point at which one has come to understand the logical necessity of an anchor point that unites and grounds all other things in the world, knowledge of the Good will come in a flash, like a mystical conversion. Thus, where Platonic education begins in the systematic study of the mathematical sciences, in the end it culminates with a sort of religious awakening to the unspeakable, and yet the most ultimate, immaterial reality in the universe.

It is important for us to pause a moment and linger with this idea of the Good just a bit longer. Many past authors, I think, make it sound as if Plato's writings designate the Good as just one Form among all of the other Forms. However, if this were the case it would short-circuit the entire project that Plato undertakes in formulating his philosophy. The logical direction that Platonic thinking pursues is the unification of all things under a progressively narrower, yet more comprehensive, set of ideas. In the world of becoming, things are always changing, and so absolutely certain knowledge of its operations is impossible. For this reason, if we really are to claim knowledge of anything, we must look beyond the infinitely numerous phenomena of the visible world to the more stable laws and principles that govern that world. These laws and principles are fewer in number than the phenomena that they govern, and so we may potentially grasp them in their totality with the powers of the mind. Yet even these ideas are too numerous to hold in our minds all at once, and so the Forms are introduced in order to provide a manageable grounding for the principles and laws of the various abstract sciences. The Forms are an even smaller number of ideas that distill the essential properties of science to just a handful. We recognize the insights of the sciences because they reflect aspects of the Forms of Truth, Justice, and Beauty. These Forms are the criteria by which we judge the correctness of scientific insight. Yet the issue remains: by what criterion do we recognize the Forms of Truth, Justice, and Beauty as worthy standards in the first place? How do we recognize the Forms as Forms? What is needed is a final "Super Form," which is grasped intuitively and which anchors all other knowledge within its purview.

The Good is the Super Form of Truth, Beauty, and Justice. It defines the essential core that holds these ideas together, and thus it unites them underneath one simple, though infinitely grand, idea. Why are Truth, Beauty, and Justice good? Truth is good because it defines what really is the case. Beauty is good because it encourages us to linger in the presence of what really is the case. Justice is good because it delineates the relationship allowing us to find harmony in what really is the case. Where the Forms of Truth, Beauty, and Justice meet, Good itself becomes apparent and we come to understand that the universe and all of its otherwise confusing, distressing, and distracting details are part of one well-structured and comprehensible whole. Without the Good, we would not even have a universe in the sense of a unified reality. We would, instead, have only a diverse collection of phenomena, objects, ideas, and events. Thus, just as the concept of space sets the groundwork for the appearance of physical objects, the Form of the Good prepares the way for the appearance of all things, both physical and conceptual. In itself, it has no articulable characteristics, distinctions, or margins. Yet this is precisely what gives it the power that it does have: the power to collect together and unify all things, no matter how incongruous, contradictory, or inconsistent they may appear at first glance. It is to all reality what a neutral base is to fragrant lotions.

THE MYTH OF THE CAVE

Plato's account of reality as outlined above is quite abstract and complicated. In order to help us further understand what he is trying to get at in a more concrete and vivid manner, he introduces one of the most striking and effective allegories in the history of human thought: the myth of the cave. The myth of the cave is intended to illustrate the structure of reality as conceived by Plato and to help us comprehend the difficulties involved in the pursuit of the Good. It appears in Book VII of *The Republic*, following the discussion in Book VI of the divided line. As a myth, this story is, of course, not intended to be a literal account. Rather, it complements and augments the philosophical discussion that precedes it by telling the story of one individual's journey from ignorance to wisdom. In

© Juneko J. Robinson

telling this story, Plato reinforces the fact that myths are not necessarily opposed to scientific or philosophical thinking but rather may actually add an extra dimension to our understanding of a particular subject matter. In relating the myth of the cave, our emotions and our feelings are engaged, along with our intellect, and so the impression that is made on us is that much more profound and lasting. Instead of just reading about the structure of reality and the proper mode of education into its mysteries, we are taken along on a journey during which we come to empathize with the adventurer. We experience his struggles and his hardships, as well as his eventual triumph, ultimately coming away with a deeper appreciation of Plato's overall message. Because the struggles of the protagonist in the cave myth are intended to be analogous to our own experiences, this story speaks directly to us, helping us to see the significance that Platonic philosophy has for the way we live our lives.

According to Plato, the lives of most people are like those of prisoners in a cave. He asks us to imagine a bunch of people, strapped to posts in the depths of a "cave-like dwelling place."[13] They have been there all of their lives, staring at the walls, transfixed by shadows that flit and cavort over the surface of those walls. These shadows provide objects of entertainment and attention for the prisoners, and it would be no surprise if these individuals considered the shadows to be the most real and substantial things that exist. They have never experienced anything else and so they cannot imagine a world beyond the apparitions that they see. These prisoners are unaware that the shadows with which they are so entranced are, in fact, cast by people and objects positioned in front of a fire that burns in the cave behind where they are strapped. The sounds and echoes produced by the shadow-casters also seem to originate from the walls of the cave itself, and so the prisoners are treated to more than just a visual display. Their world of experience is one of both sight and sound. Furthermore, all they know of themselves is gathered from the shadows that they themselves cast, and so their sense of self-understanding is no more genuine than is their understanding of the rest of reality. Not only are they alienated from the real world, but they are self-alienated. They are literally and figuratively living in darkness, and Plato tells us "they are like us."[14]

Like the prisoners in the cave, most of us accept the world as it appears to our senses. "Seeing is believing," many people say. Yet, Plato points out, our senses only provide us with appearances. They do not reveal the underlying causes and principles that make the world of appearances possible. The real world is much more complicated than it looks, and until we are able to understand this, we will be like the prisoners in the cave whose perspective is very narrow and limited to the shadows cast before them. Until we ask questions about the causes of the things that we see, we will remain ignorant of the larger reality that makes possible the commonsense world that we take for granted.

Suppose one of the prisoners in the cave was freed to turn around and to look behind him. He would then see the causes of the shadows. The first reaction of the prisoner would probably be to turn away from the brightness of the firelight. His eyes, being accustomed to the dimness of the images on the cave wall, would hurt as they are directed all of a sudden toward a bright source of light. The pupils contract under such circumstances in order to protect the eyes from damage, and so the prisoner would most likely have a natural tendency to shut his eyes and turn away: "... his eyes would hurt, he would turn round and flee towards those things which he could see, and think that they were in fact clearer than those now shown to him."[15] The newly discovered reality behind him would be too much to take, and so he would reject it and instead want to go back to the shadows, embracing them as familiar and comfortable realities. The actual causes of the shadows would be strange and incomprehensible to this individual, and he would most probably be confused and disconcerted to learn that these things are more real than the shadows that they cast.

Likewise, when we are exposed to new truths we often find them painful to face. Our immediate reaction when confronted with uncomfortable truths is to deny them and to turn back to the comfortable old lies that we have lived our lives by for so long. Like the shadows on the cave wall, our old beliefs are familiar and easy to comprehend. The transition from one set of beliefs to another may be very difficult, as it destabilizes and calls into question everything that we at one time believed to be true. This is why the prisoner, like the rest of us, must be forced to behold these new and difficult truths. Without the help of a teacher who directs us and disciplines us in our education, we are too likely to remain content with the comfortable old lies. Most of us need someone who is willing to turn our eyes toward reality. Such a teacher cannot, of course, make us open our eyes, but this person can point us in the right direction and be persistent in pushing us at those times when we become most resistant to learning. This process of education is painful, and we are unlikely to continue ever forward unless someone who cares about our enlightenment is there to encourage us when it gets to be too much. Eventually, after much pain and effort the prisoner will become accustomed to the new sights and sounds within the cave, coming to accept the true relationship that exists between the shadows and their previously unseen causes.

The teacher will not be content to reveal only the fire that casts shadows on the cave wall, however. Once this new level of reality has been discovered, the prisoner will need to begin a long and arduous journey out of the cave itself and into the bright sunlight of the world beyond the cave. As Plato writes:

> And if one were to drag him thence by force up the rough and steep path, and did not let him go before he was dragged into the sunlight, would he not be in physical pain and angry as he was dragged along? When he came into the light, with the sunlight filling his eyes, he would not be able to see a single one of the things which are now said to be true.[16]

The sunlight that illuminates the outside world is thousands of times brighter than the fire that burns within the cave, and so it will be enormously more difficult and painful to become adjusted to its glare. The prisoner, in fact, will probably fight vigorously to avoid being dragged into the full light of reality. Once out of the cave, this individual will refuse to open his eyes. But the teacher must be persistent. Eventually the prisoner will find himself adjusting to his new surroundings, looking first at the shadows on the ground, which would be most familiar to him from his life in the cave, then at the trees and flowers that cast those shadows, and finally at the sun itself. It is at that point that the prisoner has emerged into a full understanding of reality. The cave that he once called home was a prison. It separated him from the world of Truth, keeping him ignorant of the greater reality that exists outside.

B o x 3.1   *The Matrix*: A Contemporary Version of the Cave Myth

---

The hit movie *The Matrix* (1999) represents a contemporary retelling of Plato's cave myth. In *The Matrix*, the main character, Neo, believes his life as an office worker and computer hacker to be all there is to his reality. This all changes when a teacher named Morpheus appears to him, offering the real Truth about the world.

Morpheus reveals to his student that the everyday world is just an illusion constructed in order to conceal a painful reality: humans are really slaves to intelligent machines that have taken over the world. These machines cultivate human beings as a form of energy, and in order to keep them placid, human brains have been plugged into an artificial dream world called the Matrix. The Matrix keeps human minds entertained and occupied at the very same time that their bodies are locked within cave-like enclosures.

The movie follows the process of Neo's movement out of his cave of illusion and his education into the Truth. As his understanding of the Matrix grows, Neo discovers that he gains greater and greater control of himself and his environment. Like the prisoner from Plato's cave, Neo progressively moves from a state of complete ignorance to a state of understanding and wisdom. He eventually becomes a teacher himself who descends back into the Matrix, sacrificing himself so that the entire human race may be released from bondage.

The journey out of the cave is the journey that all of us engage in when we embark upon a path of education. There are times when the exercise of our rational faculties will be painful. As we think beyond the superficial appearances of things, we often encounter truths that are difficult to accept or even to comprehend upon first contact. As we move farther away from the ignorant state that we once existed within, however, we begin to understand that the soothing darkness of conventional beliefs is quite pathetic. As we look back toward those who refuse to move out of the cave of ignorance, we feel sorry for them. Unless provoked, they will never develop. For the rest of their lives they will be like children who are naïve to the world outside of their own limited perspectives. For this reason, we may feel the duty to become teachers ourselves, showing others the path that we have uncovered, dragging them closer toward the blinding flames of Truth until they are no longer comfortable with their earlier ignorance.

Very few of us have ever taken the final step into wisdom that Plato likens to standing before the sun itself. The sun makes all life on earth possible. Everything is dependent upon it for existence. In Plato's cave myth, it is supposed to represent the Good itself. If we could stand before the Good and fully open our eyes to its glory, we would understand the meaning and significance of all that exists. But just as the power of the sun's rays make it nearly impossible to look directly at the sun, so too the power of the Good makes it nearly impossible to comprehend all at once. We get bits and pieces of it. We see its reflections and perhaps occasionally glance at it briefly, only to turn away a moment later. But those who have encountered the Good have come as close as possible to enlightenment. They know the way toward the highest reality in the world, and for this reason they are best equipped to show others where it lies. Yet, ironically, they are also the ones who are most likely to be misunderstood and resisted by the ignorant many. Because most people have never seen the Good, they may not recognize the wisdom of those who have seen it. There will be much mistrust and suspicion on the part of the ignorant many, and they may even try to destroy those who want to drag them out of their caves of ignorance. This is what happened to Socrates, according to Plato; Socrates tried to show the Athenian people the way toward Goodness, yet they reacted against him and ended up putting him to death for his efforts.

PLATO'S PERFECT REPUBLIC

The trial and execution of Socrates demonstrated to Plato the dangers faced by anyone who attempts to rescue the masses from their caves of ignorance. Teaching philosophy is no safe profession as it turns out! Most people would prefer to remain ignorant of the Truth and continue to find comfort in their familiar illusions. They will even persecute and kill those who try to shake them out of their waking dream. Because most people are so dangerously ignorant, Plato concluded that it is ridiculous to allow them to democratically decide on how to administer the state. When the masses are in charge, chaos and disorder result. Most people, being blind to the greater Good, instead act out of selfishness and a desire for personal gain. They are guided not by reason but by the desire to fulfill their lowest and basest appetites. A state governed by these sorts of people is among the worst that can be imagined, according to Plato. It is nothing more than mob rule, and under mob rule no one truly benefits. Instead, the best form of government would be one in which those who are guided by reason dictate policy to those who are not guided by reason. The few who understand the nature of the Good have the most authority to rule, and they should be in a position to enforce their vision of reality on those who would otherwise be ignorant of it. Instead of a democracy, then, Plato advocated an aristocracy, or "government by the best." Such a government should be led by "philosopher kings." As Plato wrote, "Cities will have no respite from evil ... unless philosophers rule as kings."[17] These philosopher kings would legislate policies that are enforced by a class of "guardians of the law." These guardians would consist of soldiers and police officers who understand the need for order and structure in society. They would willingly carry out the orders of the philosopher kings and make sure that their rational plan was enacted. Under such an arrangement, claimed Plato, Truth, Beauty, and Justice would be allowed to come into full flower, and the perfect state, or Republic, would be born.

There are many things to criticize about the political conclusions that Plato draws from his philosophical investigations,[18] but we should not lose sight of the fact that Plato intended his perfect Republic to be a place where all humans would have the opportunity to pursue, and aspire to, their chosen ideal. Even those who have a predisposition toward non-philosophical engagements would be given a place in his Republic and encouraged to live the sort of life that they desired to live. The lowest strata of society, for instance, would be allowed to go about their consumption of material goods in a relatively unfettered manner.

The masses love money and possessions, so in a well-ordered Republic they would be allowed to accumulate all of the wealth and goods that they desired. So long as these individuals carried out their social duties, there would be no harm done to the society as a whole by indulging their greed. The avarice of the many could be put to rational service by directing it toward the material sustenance of the state. The masses could be put to use producing food, weapons, shelter, clothing, etc., and for the most part they would be quite content with this role. Though they would never become spiritually enlightened, this is something that they don't care about anyway. Under Plato's plan, at least the masses are given the opportunity to pursue their own form of happiness and in the process to contribute to the overall functioning and well-being of the state.

The upper, spiritual strata of society is not concerned with money and goods, except to the extent that these things are needed for survival, and so if the masses are encouraged to follow through with their own desires, then the philosophers won't have to worry about the production of life's material necessities. Instead, they can direct the majority of their efforts toward the activity that they perform best, which is the contemplation and elucidation of Goodness. In the ideal Republic, thus, the philosopher kings would spend most of their time in contemplation of the Good and in enacting laws that reflect its spirit. Anything that distracted them from this duty would not be of overwhelming concern to them. Because the philosopher kings are more concerned with the Good itself than they are with ownership, Plato said that their lives should be relatively austere and spartan. They should live in a communal setting, owning very little. They would not even raise their own children but would rather entrust them to the care and upbringing of professional teachers whose sole purpose would be to train the children for their future duties in government. We can see here that the sort of life pursued by the philosopher kings would not be the sort of life that members of the lower classes would desire for themselves, even if given the choice. It is the kind of life appropriate only for those who have completely and unselfishly committed themselves to the pursuit of Goodness and to making sure that Truth, Beauty, and Justice remain the governing principles of society.

Plato's ideal Republic is thus structured hierarchically, like a human body. The few philosopher kings act like the head of the social body, rationally contemplating reality and legislating Goodness to the majority of citizens. This legislation occurs through the mediation of a police force that, on the one hand, understands and respects the moral authority of the philosopher kings, yet on the other hand, is not suited to the philosophical life itself. These "guardians of the law" are positioned somewhat like the chest in the human body. They mediate between the base, lower urges of the masses and the rational, higher aspirations that guide the philosophers. These guardians are motivated primarily by the drive that accompanies a spirited personality, and just as the other classes can find happiness in carrying out specific social roles, this class of people can also find contentment in enforcing the rule of law. Being action-oriented by nature, members of this police class need goals to pursue, and so they should look to those who are reasonable by nature in order to discover the best sorts of goals to follow. Thus, while the philosopher kings formulate the best kinds of laws according to their understanding of the Good, the police carry out the enforcement of those laws for the betterment of

the entire society. The masses, who, like the stomach, are guided by a desire to satisfy appetite, obey the laws and thereby secure the right to pursue their own sort of happiness in business, farming, craft, etc., in turn securing for all of society the material goods that it needs to survive. The philosopher kings are like the head in a well-ordered society, the police are like the chest, and the masses are like the stomach. Just as a healthy and well-functioning body needs all of its parts, so too does a healthy and well-functioning society need all of its social classes working together cooperatively for the good of the whole.

Plato also suggests that we think of the members of the various classes within society as having souls made from differing sorts of precious metals. The philosophers have gold souls, the police have silver souls, and the masses have souls made of bronze. Once again we see here how Plato encourages us to conceive of the relationship between the masses, the guardians, and the philosophers hierarchically. Gold is more precious than silver, which in turn is more precious than bronze. Strictly speaking, Plato tells us, it is not literally true that humans have souls made of metal; however, this is a useful sort of image by which to justify the various social rankings of the members of society. It is a "noble lie," which also helps to justify a kind of social mobility within society. Sometimes a person with a golden soul is born into one of the lower classes. When this does occur, that individual should be promoted within society in order to become one of the philosopher kings. Conversely, sometimes a person with a silver or a bronze soul is born into the circle of philosophers. When this occurs, that individual should be demoted to his or her appropriate place.

What many people object to in Plato's vision of a perfect republic is its top-down, elitist structure. To our modern ears, it sounds unfair, and dangerous, to put a small group of intellectual elites in charge of the rest of society without being subject to the wants and desires of the people. Wouldn't such leaders abuse their positions, after all? Doesn't the sort of dictatorial power that Plato wanted to put into the hands of philosophers inevitably lead to corruption and abuse? These are all legitimate concerns when considering the practical details of actually maintaining a government established on Platonic principles. However, in his writings about the perfect society, Plato seems more concerned with the philosophical task of contemplating and clarifying what sorts of people are ideally best suited to rule rather than with outlining a practical guide for how to manage them once they are in power. Plato believes that if people with the right sort of character are put in charge, then they will be self-regulating. A good head of state should be reasonable and concerned primarily with justice and the overall good of society, not primarily with making money or with exercising personal power and so, hypothetically, if you were to install such a ruler, he or she would be incorruptible by definition. How you actually go about identifying such people in the real world is another difficult question.[19] In modern democracies the assumption is that the best and most efficient way to find competent rulers is through popular elections. Plato was skeptical of this claim, and he condemned the idea of democracy, not because he detested human freedom but because he did not have much faith in the masses' ability to see beyond their own selfish wants and desires. If left to a vote, Plato thought that not only would the worst sorts of people be drawn to candidacy, namely, those most attracted to fame and power, but the voting population would most likely elect those leaders who promised them the most benefits, even if those promised benefits were detrimental to the overall health of the community. In a democracy, Plato wrote, people elect a candidate "if only he says that he wishes the crowd well,"[20] and this certainly is not the way to select legitimate philosopher kings.

Although Plato's aristocratic vision for government is not very popular among most modern people, his criticism of the democratic process, nonetheless, is not without some truth. In his day, and our own, democratic institutions and processes sometimes have led to injustice, including wars, the monopolization of resources, and the exploitation and abuse of minorities. Simply because the majority of people in a population approve of certain policies or laws, that does not guarantee that those policies or laws are good and just. Many times what the majority wants is wrong, and this is why democracies must be especially alert to the dangers of mass hysteria, moral panics, and mob rule. Not to recognize the weaknesses inherent in democracy is to blind ourselves to one source of much villainy in the world, although it is not necessarily to advocate some other form of equally flawed system of government. Considering that it was through a democratic vote that his teacher Socrates was condemned to death, however, it is not so mysterious why Plato was so alert and sensitive to the potentially negative aspects of democratic decision making.

PLATO AND ART

The distrust that Plato harbored for the rabble motivated him to go to great lengths detailing the means by which they should be managed and controlled. Whereas the philosopher kings are reasonable and rational, and so may always be trusted to do what is best, the masses are irrational, easily being moved by passion and desire. For this reason, rulers must be careful to put in place mechanisms that will regulate the population's exposure to provocative and emotionally inflammatory materials. Plato anticipated, thus, that strict censorship and control of the mass media would be essential in order to maintain harmony within the well-ordered republic. Before closing this chapter, I would like to briefly address the controversial measures introduced by Plato concerning the regulation of art and artists in the perfect society. This is an issue that we will return to in the following chapter on Aristotle, a pupil of Plato's who had very different thoughts on the same matter. The disagreement between these two philosophers concerning this topic is especially interesting because it is an issue that is still hotly debated today.

In Plato's time, the "mass media" consisted of tragedies, comedies, music, and artworks that were consumed by the Athenian public as entertainment in much the same way that movies, television, and music are used by us today. The creators of these media products were then, as they are now, revered by the public as talented and glamorous artists. Athenians especially loved flocking to the theaters in order to watch the newest tragedies and comedies, becoming enraptured by the stories and the messages that these dramas contained. The best of the dramatists were those who were most adept at provoking intense feelings in members of the audience, making them cry or laugh by means of the images, sounds, and portrayals that occurred on the stage. By manipulating these elements, artists transported viewers into another realm where, for the length of the performance, they forgot about the everyday real world and instead took part in the fictional universe that was created within the drama. Art, in this manner, was not only a means by which audiences were encouraged to forget about reality and to become embroiled in an unreal world, but it also spurred viewers to experience strong emotions about that fictive world. It was the combination of these last two elements that made art potentially threatening to the stability of society, according to Plato.

By encouraging audiences to become drawn into a fantasy world, art distracts from the world of reality. Take, for instance, Aristophanes' portrayal of Socrates in his comedy *The Clouds*. According to Plato, the inaccurate portrayal of Socrates in this play was one of the reasons why the Athenian public became so confused about the real message and philosophy of Socrates, consequently trying and executing him on charges that had no basis in fact. As Socrates states in his defense, the popularity of Aristophanes' comedy was key in promoting the widespread misconception that he, Socrates, was concerned with matters that he really was not concerned with at all:

> ... it is just as you have yourselves seen in the comedy of Aristophanes,
> who has introduced a man whom he calls Socrates, going about and
> saying that he walks in air, and talking a great deal of nonsense concern-
> ing matters of which I do not pretend to know either much or little.[21]

This play, insofar as it was loosely based on the life of Socrates, was a reflection of reality, yet it was a very dim reflection, containing more distortion than clarity. True, Socrates was a philosopher who used the tools of logic to pursue his topics of interest. However, this exhausts the truthful content of *The Clouds*. Aristophanes otherwise presents Socrates as a man who takes money for his teaching, who is concerned with speculations about the physical world, and who uses logic to trick and mislead people. All of these details are false, according to Plato, and contrived by Aristophanes because he was more concerned with entertaining his audience than with educating them about the Truth. Using artistic license, he fabricated scenes in order to produce chuckles rather than understanding, and in

---

B o x 3.2 Censorship in Contemporary American Culture

Plato advocated state censorship of the mass media because he believed that most people were not capable of distinguishing between reality and fantasy. Today, the issue of media censorship remains a controversial topic that gains attention every time someone imitates harmful actions portrayed on television or in the movies.

In the movie *The Program* (1993), members of a football team are depicted testing their courage by lying in the middle of a freeway while cars speed by. Soon after the release of this film, members of a high-school football team were killed after replicating the stunt on a public roadway.

In 1999, two students at Columbine High School in Denver, Colorado, went on a shooting spree, killing fifteen of their fellow students and themselves. In the aftermath of the shooting, the violent lyrics of rock bands, like Marilyn Manson and Rammstein, were blamed by some for inspiring the killings.

In 1999, an appeals court in San Francisco ruled that computer-generated child pornography did not violate federal law because no real children appear in such material. However, those opposing this ruling argued, as Plato did, that such material could inspire would-be child molesters to harm real children.

---

doing so, Aristophanes was guilty of distracting viewers from the real world of Socrates' life, leading them to be more influenced by a false portrayal than by the actual man. It might all be fine and good if people recognized that this depiction was false; however, the viewing public is not always that sophisticated. Too often they mistake the artistic portrayal for fact itself. They become confused about the distinction between fantasy and reality and, as in the case of Socrates, when this happens, some very real, negative consequences may result.

Artists are powerful because in their distortion of reality they are capable of moving audiences to great emotional depths. In the exercise of their creative abilities, artists are able to generate feelings of amusement, joy, sadness, despair, and pride, but they do so only by creating representations that, while perhaps inspired by real things, nevertheless are not the things themselves. Whether playwright, painter, or sculptor, the artist works with appearances and images, and these appearances and images are very far removed from the unchanging Forms that are the highest and most real objects of knowledge. In fact, Plato tells us that the product of the artistic imitator is "at three removes from nature,"[22] and thus not much more than a delusion or a hallucination. If the Forms are the primary source of Truth, the theories of math and science are secondary, and the objects of the physical world are third in order of veracity, then the artist who creates imitations of physical objects for the sake of entertainment is working at a very low level of reality. The artist is like a person who casts shadows on a cave wall in order to delude, misguide, and, most dangerously, emotionally titillate those who are transfixed by the display.

Because art generates intense emotions in an audience, the artist does indeed possess a unique talent, but that talent is too powerful to go unsupervised according to Plato. Often we see artists irresponsibly working people up and encouraging them to do things that are disruptive to the smooth functioning of society, and in these situations Plato tells us that the government should step in and set guidelines for what the artist may and may not create. In recent years, our own government has stepped in to regulate the content of movies and television shows, for instance, demanding that appropriate guidelines be put in place in order to delimit what may and may not be shown, the fear being that impressionable children (and some ignorant adults) might be moved to imitate the sorts of antisocial behaviors that they see in popular programming. Plato would be very sympathetic with such measures, for he was among the first to fully recognize, and take seriously, the powerful influence that the mass media can have on the minds of a population. Because artists are so talented at influencing the feelings of the masses, he thought that they should be held accountable for what they do, and if they are allowed to remain in the community at all, they should be required to produce only works that uplift and improve the souls of citizens.

WONDER AND DISTRESS IN PLATONIC THINKING

Plato is a remarkable figure in the history of human thought. His is one of the most sophisticated and comprehensive attempts to think reality to its foundations and then systematically build up an understanding of the world that follows rationally and logically from what he has discovered. The Platonic manner of thinking sees all of the world's details as having a proper function and place within the grand structure of Being itself, and so humans, as a part of the universe and its fabric, have a purpose. That purpose is to struggle to learn about the order of reality. Though we are born into ignorance, Plato tells us that we ennoble ourselves as we strive toward greater and greater levels of knowledge and wisdom. We are all capable of this task; however, many of us are lacking in the motivation that is needed in order to pursue fully the most abstract forms of knowledge. Thus, Plato seems to be telling us, we must rely on one another for help. We must gather together in communities, united behind leaders who have our best interests at heart, in order to realize a system of social organization that will efficiently and effectively allow for the revelation of absolute Truth. This Platonic vision places philosophy at the center of all concerns, and it sees politics, religion, science, and art as avenues through which the love of Truth and wisdom may potentially gain expression. Ultimately, according to Plato, all things are a reflection of an overarching and unifying principle of Goodness. Sometimes we get distracted from this fact, but if we are persistent and serious enough, he tells us, we will finally be successful at discerning the real Truth from mere imitations of the truth. When this happens we will become as good as we possibly can become.

It is worth emphasizing that for Plato, there is no inherent incompatibility between the truths of politics, religion, science, art, and philosophy. All of these fields of study make a contribution to the spiritual quest that is the proper concern of human beings. Although at times there may be points of friction between philosophers and those who focus their attentions in other areas, these points of friction are not inevitable. In the search for Truth we need all the help that we can get, and at various points in our progress toward wisdom we may find different vocabularies and tools useful for different purposes. As long as the wondrous *desire* for Truth underlies and motivates the creation of art, the governing of the state, the study of physical reality, or the worshiping of the gods, we can remain optimistic that we are headed in the right direction. Any artist, scientist, politician, or worshiper who wants to know the Truth is also a philosopher, and as philosophers their guiding aspiration will not end until the words they use to articulate the nature of reality finally fail and they find themselves directly in the presence of the Good itself.

Thus, the affirmative wonder that spurs one to investigate the universe and its mysteries is a necessary, but not a sufficient, condition for the pursuit of philosophy, according to Plato. Also present must be the painful awareness of our distressing separation from the Truth. Wisdom may be the final goal of the Platonic thinker, but philosophers are only "lovers of wisdom" who are caught in an in-between world of incompleteness and longing. Because they love wisdom so dearly, their separation from this ideal is especially unbearable. The imagery of Plato's cave myth vividly illustrates for us the pain, the struggle, and the torment that is implicated in the expansion of our perspectives on the world, emphasizing that the path and process of education is not a tranquil or easy one. Upon advancing up the "steep and rocky path" out of the cave, we experience a kind of intellectual vertigo as we leave behind the familiar and everyday world in pursuit of higher forms of reality. This is necessarily arduous, distressing, and dangerous, but if the drive to persist remains strong, and if we surround ourselves with like-minded philosophers, then, Plato tells us, it will all have been worthwhile.

QUESTIONS FOR DISCUSSION

1. There is a great deal of controversy concerning how to distinguish between the true philosophy of Plato and the true philosophy of Socrates. Do you think this a fruitful debate? Is it a debate with philosophical, or merely historical, significance?

2. It has been claimed that Plato is the father of totalitarianism. Why do you think someone would make this claim? Do you agree or disagree with it?

3. Why do you think that Plato settled on the Good as the highest reality in the world? Do you think this view is consistent with the discoveries of modern science?

4. Plato's criticisms of art were based in the mimetic view of art, which claims that all art is a form of imitation. Is this a correct theory of art? How do you think Plato might react if he were exposed to examples of contemporary conceptual art?

5. In the realm of interpersonal association we make a distinction between sexual and "platonic" relationships. How do you think Plato's philosophical worldview is reflected in this usage?

6. Plato was quite critical of democracy, but in the Athens of his time, democracy was a very different institution from what it is in the contemporary United States. Do you think that modern American democracy is immune to any of the criticisms of Plato?

7. Using Plato's myth of the cave as a guide, discuss a period in your own life when you moved from a state of ignorance to a state of wisdom. What were your own "shadows"? Who was casting them? Who was the teacher who guided you out of the cave? What was your "steep and rocky path"? What was the ultimate Truth that you discovered? Once you escaped, did you feel inspired to return to the "cave" in order to rescue others?

NOTES

1. Irwin Edman (ed.), "Introduction," *The Works of Plato* (New York: The Modern Library, 1956), p. xi.
2. Plato, *Letter VII*, 341d2–3.
3. Plato, *Timaeus*, 51a2–5.
4. Plato, *Theaetetus*, 158c9–d6.
5. Plato, *The Republic*, Book VI, 509d5.
6. Ibid., Book V, 475c6–e7.
7. Plato, *Symposium*, 210d5–6.
8. In Plato's *Timaeus*, the main speaker (Timaeus) tells the story of how the universe was created to be beautifully ordered by an intelligent and all-powerful "Demiurge" who used the geometry of triangles to structure everything from the four basic elements to the human body. Furthermore, the universe as a whole is depicted as a living organism, and everything in it is claimed to play a part in its healthy functioning. See *Timaeus*, especially 27b5–42e4.
9. Plato, *The Republic*, Book VI, 509a4.
10. Ibid., 505a2–3.
11. Plato, *Letter VII*, 341c7.
12. Ibid., 34c9–d1.
13. Plato, *The Republic*, 514a2–3.
14. Ibid., 515a4.
15. Ibid., 514e1–4.
16. Ibid., 515e4–516a4.
17. Ibid., 473d.
18. For a lengthy criticism of Plato's *The Republic*, see Karl Popper, *The Open Society and Its Enemies* (London: Routledge & Kegan Paul, 1945). Also see Bertrand Russell, *A History of Western Philosophy* (New York: Simon and Schuster, 1972), pp. 108–119 (Plato's Utopia).
19. Plato did have some involvement in trying to get his political ideas put into practice. When he was forty, he traveled to Sicily in order to try to educate the tyrant Dionysus in the ways of the philosopher kings. His efforts failed. Dionysus was more concerned with personal power and influence than he was with ruling according to the law of goodness. Eventually, after much intrigue and danger, Plato returned to Greece without having any positive effect on the character of Dionysus. See *Letter VII*.
20. Plato, *The Republic*, Book VIII, 558c1.
21. Plato, *Apology*, 18d–e.
22. Plato, *The Republic*, Book X, 597e2.

Chapter 4

Aristotle

How does Aristotle's empiricism differ from Plato's rationalism? What are the four causes? What is a syllogism? What is the First Mover? What is the Golden Mean? What is catharsis? How do Aristotle's ideas on art differ from those of Plato?

Plato was the first Greek philosopher to establish a formal institution of higher learning. His Academy was the prototype of today's university, and it was there that many of the greatest minds of the ancient world gathered in order to investigate the nature of reality and to learn about the insights of Platonism. Yet, as we have seen with many of the thinkers already examined in past chapters, true philosophers are never uncritical of their teachers, and so it should be no surprise that some of the students at Plato's Academy came to question their master's wisdom and break free of his influence, moving in their own unique intellectual directions. Perhaps the most important, and certainly the most well known, of these rebels against Platonism was a man named Aristotle. Aristotle studied at Plato's Academy for twenty years, beginning at the age of 18, and was such an intellectual force within the school that he became known as the nous. (This, I suppose, is similar to the teasing manner in which today's bright students are sometimes referred to as "brains.") He was also, allegedly, referred to as "the scholar," as well as "the reader," all nicknames that reinforce our sense of his commitment to study and his philosophical seriousness.

ARISTOTLE'S BREAK WITH PLATO

Aristotle's break with Plato's Academy began when, upon Plato's death, the philosopher Speusippus was bequeathed control of the school in 347 B.C. Speusippus was Plato's nephew, and his focus within philosophy was, presumably, heavily influenced by the nature of his uncle's thought. Diogenes Laertius, in his book *Lives of Eminent Philosophers*, lists thirty works written by Speusippus, yet none of them remains, and so the precise content of his teachings is impossible to know for certain. We do know, however, that Aristotle disagreed with certain aspects of Speusippus' philosophy, specifically his view that goodness and beauty are *effects*, rather than *causes*, of natural phenomena.[1] Whether because of this sort of philosophical disagreement, or

© Juneko J. Robinson

because of his resentment at being passed over as the head of the Academy, or simply because he felt it a natural time to move on, Aristotle left the school at Athens and for the next twelve years traveled from city to city, teaching and conducting research. It was during this time that he made the acquaintance of Philip of Macedon and became the tutor for Philip's son Alexander, the man who would eventually come to be known as Alexander the Great. Twelve years after departing from the Academy, Aristotle finally returned to Athens and established his own school called the Lyceum. For thirteen years he remained there until 323 B.C. when he was, like Socrates before him, charged with impiety. Instead of staying to fight the charges, as had Socrates, Aristotle fled, saying that he would not allow the Athenians to sin twice against philosophy. Finally, at the age of 63, Aristotle died in exile.

The contemporary philosopher Martin Heidegger once said that all we need to know about Aristotle's life was that he was born, that he thought, and that he died. While Heidegger's intention in saying this was to encourage us to focus on the content of Aristotle's writing rather than on the superficial details of his biography, the particulars recounted above are nonetheless useful in helping to illuminate something of an overall pattern in Aristotle's life that is indicative of his way of thinking. Throughout his life, Aristotle moved from place to place, exploring the world and encountering different sorts of people and things outside of Athens. Unlike Socrates, who was reluctant to leave his city even when it meant that he would be killed, Aristotle was eager to make firsthand observations of the world "out there," experiencing for himself the grand diversity of phenomena that were to be found outside Athens. He spent at least three years in Asia Minor, where he made detailed observations of marine life, the descriptions of which were incorporated into his book on animals. During his travels he collected the constitutions of 158 different cities for study and comparison. This sort of enthusiasm for observation and direct experience sets Aristotle apart from his teacher Plato who, as you will recall, downplayed the role of these things in philosophy. Whereas Plato suggested that we withdraw our attention away from the senses, Aristotle seems to have lived the sort of life that reveled in the use of his senses, and his system of thought reflects this fascination.

Plato reportedly once said, "Aristotle spurns me, as colts kick out at the mother who bore them."[2] While it is undeniable that Aristotle learned much from his teacher, it is also clear that he wanted to move in a more observationally grounded direction with his philosophy. Consequently, he tried to leave behind some of the "otherworldly" aspects of Platonism. Whereas Platonic philosophy tends toward a quasi-religious view of reality, Aristotelian philosophy develops toward a more scientific, down-to-earth outlook. While Plato stresses rational contemplation and its role in personal, spiritual transformation, Aristotle stresses the role of reason and sensory observation for understanding the mechanics of the world and its processes. This is not to say that Aristotle is completely unconcerned with things of a divine or spiritual nature, and there is still a great deal of scholarly debate concerning just how far Aristotle does in fact depart from the doctrines of Platonism. However, it is handy to keep these general differences in mind. It is not making too much of a generalization to say that with Aristotle, concerns of a scientific nature come to the fore, just as they did with the

Presocratic philosophers of earlier years. Nonetheless, we also need to be sensitive to the fact that Aristotle's science is of a different sort than the crass materialism of a Thales or a Democritus. Having had the benefit of Plato's insights, Aristotle attempts to create a science that pays heed to the formal, nonmaterial aspects of reality as well as to the concrete, physical constituents of the world. In doing so, Aristotle created a system of thinking that has had a powerful influence on the development of all succeeding Western thought, both religious and scientific, up to the present day.

Plato had claimed that our world is like "a line divided" between a lower level of reality and a higher level of reality. The world that we can see around us is a world of illusion, being a mere reflection of a more stable realm consisting of indestructible and eternal Forms. The Forms can be understood only through the exercise of our rational capabilities. They cannot be observed with the eye or measured with a stick. Rather, they can be intuited only after we have honed our intellects through the study of abstract sciences such as mathematics and logic. Note that for Plato, the development of our minds, and an understanding of nature's true reality, depends on our ability to transcend our preoccupation with the sensual world around us. Though investigation into the visible world is the first step toward wisdom, if we become obsessed with that visible world we will remain blind to the more stable and unchanging realm that lies above and behind it. We will be like the prisoners in a cave of illusion who mistake the shadows on the walls for reality itself. This view, that we can come to know the nature of reality simply through reflecting on the operations of our minds, has come to be called "rationalism." Rationalists, like Plato, tend to advocate skepticism toward information that is gathered through the senses. Instead, they suggest that we reflect on the ideas that we reason with and that we try to analyze and understand the logic and structure of this nonphysical, conceptual world. For the rationalist, it is the form of the mental world that is really important because it is that world that corresponds to a "higher" and more stable reality. In this vein, following Socrates, Plato turned his back on the study of physics and became overwhelmingly concerned with the nonphysical world of Forms.

Aristotle thought that this was overdoing things. He recognized that Socrates and Plato had discovered something very important that had been overlooked by the Presocratics, but he also thought that the Presocratic philosophers had touched on something important as well. The Presocratics, in trying to analyze everything in terms of material substance, had discovered one particular aspect of reality. But Socrates and Plato in their focus on the Forms had discovered and developed an understanding of a different aspect of that same reality. Whereas the Presocratics had focused on material explanations, the Socratics had focused on formal explanations. As Aristotle writes in his book *Physics*, "Since 'nature' has two senses, the form and the matter, we must investigate its objects as we would the essence of snubness. That is, such things are neither independent of matter nor can be defined in terms of matter only."[3] Socrates' "snub nose," for example, cannot be described only in terms of the matter that makes it up, although it would not exist as a part of our actual universe in the absence of its material constituents. In order for a snub nose to exist, there must be some sort of matter (flesh, blood, cartilage) that is shaped or "formed" into the arrangement that we identify as "snubness" and "noseness." If there was no form to the matter, all you would have would be a glob of unformed "stuff," or what Aristotle calls "prime matter." If there was no matter to take on the form of snubness, all you would have would be an idea or concept of snubness and not an actual, existing "snubby" thing. According to Aristotle, therefore, neither the Presocratic philosophers nor the Socratic philosophers have given a complete description of the underlying nature of our world, because each group neglected to investigate a necessary aspect of the universe as it actually exists. Part of Aristotle's genius lay in his observation that something had to be added to the theories of past thinkers in order to create a comprehensive description of all reality.

ARISTOTLE AND THE NATURE OF CHANGE

According to Aristotle, our entire universe is composed of particular things possessing both form *and* matter. As we look around us, we see a grand diversity of objects and entities, each possessing its own unique nexus of both formal and material substance. For instance, on the other side of my room I see both a wooden chair and a wooden desk. Both are made out of the same sort of material substance—wood—but that material substance, in each case, is shaped into a different sort of form. It would be a mistake to conclude that the chair and the desk are really the same type of thing simply because they are both wooden. By focusing only on the material aspect of these objects we miss an important distinguishing characteristic of each. One of them is formed in such a manner that it is meant for sitting on, while the other is formed in such a manner that it is meant for writing upon. The same sort of material substance is able to support differing kinds of forms. You can take a block of wood and form it into a chair or into a table or, in fact, into any number of things. For this reason, Aristotle tells us that material substance is a kind of "potentiality" that exists in the world. It may take on any number of different forms, and until it does so it has not reached its full "actuality." As he writes in *Metaphysics*, "... matter exists in a potential state, just because it may come to its form; and when it exists *actually*, then it is in its form."[4] So it is that in order for an actual, sensible object to come into existence, a form must express itself through some sort of material substratum. Understanding the nature of the real world, then, starts with an understanding of the ways that material substance takes on and actualizes forms.

Aristotle's focus on the relationship between material and formal substances brings together insights from both the Presocratic and the Socratic philosophers, and it also helps to explain something that had never before been addressed satisfactorily. How is it that things in our world change? It is obvious to even the casual observer that the universe is full of things that shift from one state to another. Trees sprout, grow, and decay. Humans are born, age, and die. Caterpillars metamorphose into butterflies. Mountains rise and erode. Past philosophers were so concerned with understanding the nature of the invariable, foundational substructure of reality that their systems of thinking often ended up insinuating that the phenomenon of change was simply an illusion. In truth, they seemed to suggest, nothing really changes. Underlying the appearance of transition, something always remains the same, either a primary material essence or a primary form, and it is this sameness that defines the real substance of the universe. In fact, the idea that things in our world could change was seen by some philosophers as a violation of the very laws of reason and logic. For instance, the Presocratic thinker Parmenides wrote:

> ... being, it is ungenerated and indestructible,
> whole, of one kind and unwavering, and complete.
> Nor was it, nor will it be, since now it is, all together,
> one, continuous. For what generation will you seek for it?
> How, whence did it grow? That it came from what is not I shall not allow
> you to say or think—for it is not sayable or thinkable
> that it is not. And what need would have impelled it,
> later or earlier to grow—if it began from nothing?
> Thus it must either altogether be or not be.
> Nor from what is will the strength of trust permit it
> to come to be anything apart from itself. For that reason
> Justice has not relaxed her fetters and let it come into being or perish,
> but she holds it. Decision in these matters lies in this:
> it is or it is not. But it has been decided, as is necessary,
> to leave the one road unthought and unnamed (for it is not a true
> road), and to take the other as being genuine.
> How might what is perish? How might it come into being?
> For if it came into being it is not, nor is it if it is ever going to be.
> Thus generation is quenched and perishing unheard of.
> Nor is it divided since it all alike is—
> neither more here (which would prevent it from cohering)
> nor less; but it is all full of what is.
> Hence it is all continuous; for what is approaches what is.
> And unmoving in the limits of great chains it is beginningless
> and ceaseless, since generation and destruction
> have wandered far away, and true trust has thrust them off.
> The same and remaining in the same state, it lies by itself,
> and thus remains fixed there. For powerful necessity
> holds it enchained in a limit which hems it around,
> because it is right that what is should not be incomplete.[5]

Parmenides is telling us here that it is illogical to think that anything in the world could either come into or go out of being. This is because in order for something to come into being, it would first have to be nothing, and for something to go out of being, it would have to become nothing. But both of these are impossible, claims Parmenides, because you can't get something from nothing, and if you have something it can't just disappear into nothing. From this it follows that change is impossible, because the very process of change presupposes that an object becomes something that it is not. This is the same sort of logic that led Plato to posit the existence of eternal Forms that remain stable and fixed behind the "illusion" of changing sensory experiences. Despite what our senses tell us, the real universe, the one that lies behind the appearance of flux, is eternal and unwavering. This is what reason tells us must be so according to thinkers like Plato and Parmenides.[6]

Yet when we actually look at the world around us, change does seem to occur. We can see it with our eyes and detect it with our other bodily senses. As opposed to rationalists like Plato and Parmenides, Aristotle takes such observation seriously and thus may be categorized alongside those thinkers who are termed "empiricists." Empiricists claim that true knowledge comes through observation, not through mere logical reflection on the contents of the mind. To know what is true, we must first look out into the world and through the use of our sensory organs collect experiences that may then be sorted through and organized into systems of knowledge. According to empiricists like Aristotle, this is the only way that we can learn anything. To ignore the data of experience is to close oneself off from a rich and promising source of real information about the nature of reality. "[I]f one perceived nothing," Aristotle tells us, "one would learn and understand nothing."[7] The appearances of things around us are not distracting illusions, according to this way of thinking, but are, rather, an accurate and dependable indication of the way things really are. Used carefully and properly, our sensory organs provide us with a sound understanding of the world and its structure.

THE FOUR CAUSES

So, given that our senses tell us that things in the world are subject to change, how do these changes take place? Aristotle suggests that change is possible because matter is capable of taking on differing forms, and it is through such "trans-form-ations" that things become other than they once were. Matter, as pure potentiality, may become anything. Form, on the other hand, is a pure actuality. When matter takes on a particular form, we identify the composite substance that is thus created by the type of form that becomes manifest. So, for instance, we distinguish between a wooden chair and a wooden table by reference to the forms exhibited through the wood, and not by reference to the wood itself. The form defines what kind of thing an object is, while the matter simply allows the "whatness" of the form to express itself. Thinking of the modern notion of a quark helps to make sense of what Aristotle is getting at here. According to modern physicists, a quark is the smallest particle of matter that exists in our universe. Everything is made up of quarks. They are like Aristotle's notion of "prime matter" insofar as they have the potential to be anything. Yet because they are potentially anything, the quark is unique to nothing. If I say that something is made up of quarks, I haven't told you what is special about the thing I am referring to. I could be referring to a

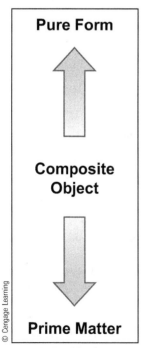

Pure Form

Composite Object

Prime Matter

© Cengage Learning

FIGURE 4.1 The Form/ Matter Distinction

table, a human, a cat, haggis, a pomegranate, or anything else in the universe. In order to talk about the peculiarities of things, I must say something about the unique, actual structure and form of the object in question, and this requires going beyond its merely material components. By talking about how quarks are arranged, I am able to say something about the peculiar traits of the object under scrutiny. Indeed, the quarks that make up one object could be broken up and refashioned in order to create a completely different object, and changes in our world take place when such transformations occur. Democritus hypothesized something like this when he talked about the existence of the atom. However, he, like Plato and Parmenides, ultimately concluded that appearances are deceiving and that change is an illusion because the atom always remains unaltered throughout its various recombinations. Only the atom is real, according to Democritus. Aristotle, on the other hand, takes change as something that is indisputable and real in its own right. According to him, understanding the shifting, formal *arrangement* of material substance is just as important as understanding the nature of material substance itself. Although matter is a component of everything in our world, according to Aristotle, it is inseparable from the forms that it supports, and the vast and varied changes that we see taking place around us occur as differing forms express themselves through shifting arrangements in the material substrate.

Our world is not, according to Aristotle, stretched between higher and lower levels of reality. Instead, there is only one level of reality, and that is the level in which we live. Everything in our world is a "composite substance" made up of both matter and form. When we look at the things in our world, the reason that we are able to recognize them for what they are is that we can recognize the forms of things as they become manifest through matter. "To each form there corresponds a special matter."[8] Matter and form work together in order to bring reality into existence. Except in thought, they cannot be separated. So how does matter take on differing forms? How is it that matter becomes "informed"? Aristotle suggests that this is a question completely neglected by his predecessors. Whereas some past thinkers had focused on material explanations of the universe and others had focused on formal explanations of the universe, no one had yet speculated on the force or energy that brought the universe into existence in the first place. In addressing this issue, Aristotle introduces another sort of explanation in addition to the material and formal sorts. This he calls the "efficient" explanation. Form is imparted to matter through the exercise of some sort of force. In the case of chair building, it is the builder who imparts this force, and so it is the chair builder who is the "efficient cause" of the chair. Such an individual has the formal idea of a chair in his or her mind and then proceeds to bring that idea to life by way of building a chair out of some sort of material. Thus, change occurs when some sort of force imparts form to matter or, conversely, takes form away from matter.

But Aristotle recognizes that there is even more to the world than this. The chair builder, after all, does not just go around haphazardly imparting chair forms into any material whatsoever. Rather, this individual has a notion of the purpose for which the chair will be used and so tries to build a chair that will serve this purpose in the best manner possible. Chairs are intended for sitting, and so the chair builder must be concerned with how the finished product will best suit this purpose. Aristotle claimed that this directs our attention to a further sort of explanation that can be offered for the things in our world. Whereas a "material" explanation focuses on the stuff that a thing is made of, and a "formal" explanation focuses on the nature, essence, or arrangement of the thing, and an "efficient" explanation focuses on the force that imparted form to matter, a "final" explanation tells us the purpose or goal that a thing is intended to serve. According to Aristotle, things in our world are organized in such a fashion that they serve their own distinctive and unique purposes. When we observe the cycles of the seasons, the structure of our anatomy, or the interrelationships of the ecosystem, we see that all objects in the universe promote some goal and perform some function. The universe, in Aristotle's way of thinking, is like a big organism, the parts of which all have a reason for existing. To understand a thing, then, we must not only understand what it is made out of, what kind of thing it is, and who made it, but we must also understand its purpose. To know the purpose played by an object is to know its final cause, and this, perhaps, is the highest and most important kind of knowledge that one can have concerning an object.

Whereas Plato had claimed that there is one unifying and overarching principle of Goodness of which all things in the world are mere reflections, Aristotle, with his discussion of the final cause, suggests that "goodness" is more a matter of how well an individual object fulfills its own unique purpose than it is some sort of universal principle applying to all things across the board. The "good," in other words, is relative to how well or poorly an object meets its own, individual goals. So, for instance, a good knife is one that cuts well. A good roof is one that protects a house from rain. A good politician is one who carries out the duties of his office. It would be silly to say that a knife is not a good knife because it can't carry out the tasks of political office. That would be holding the knife to the wrong standard. Instead, each worldly, composite substance has embedded within its essence a purpose that is appropriate to its proper functioning as a particular object. To understand the final cause of a thing, we must understand what purpose that thing is supposed to serve, and to understand a thing's purpose, we must understand what kind of thing it is; we must understand its form. Form and function are intimately connected with one another in this manner, and in the very structure of an object we can glimpse the purpose that it is best suited to serve. For instance, when you walk into a gym, you might at first be mystified by the different sorts of weight machines that you discover on the floor. They are all very complicated looking and confusing, consisting of systems of levers, cables, weights, and pulleys. However, once you start to investigate the forms of these machines by sitting in them and seeing how they conform to the contours of your body, you may start to understand the kinds of purposes they are intended to serve. As you start to use a curl machine, you realize that it is designed to exercise your bicep muscles. As you use a chest press machine, you understand that its final cause is to exercise your chest muscles. Each of these machines, furthermore, is good insofar as it effectively performs its intended purpose. The "good," therefore, does not exist above and apart from entities, but is, rather, embedded in their formal structure. This is yet another example of how

Aristotle brings philosophy right down to earth in opposition to his teacher, Plato. Everything in the universe is, indeed, striving toward a good, as Plato taught. However, according to Aristotle, the good that is being striven toward rests within the very composition of each and every existent entity, and not in a separate, otherworldly realm of pure, formal being.

According to Aristotle, a complete understanding of the world and its processes starts with an appreciation of the parts that make up that world. By observing the particular things that we can see, taste, touch, and feel, we collect facts that beg for explanation, and complete explanations of the things in the world may be articulated in terms of four distinct, yet interrelated, causes: the material cause, the formal cause, the efficient cause, and the final cause. We can claim to fully understand something when we are able to enumerate all of the causes that contribute to its existence. In other words, Aristotle is claiming that it is not enough to simply know "that" something is the case. He also demands that we know "why" things are the case, and knowing "why" something is the case involves offering explanations that spell out the causes that contribute to a thing's being. While the pursuit of scientific knowledge starts in observation, the systematic explanation of observed facts is no less important than the observations themselves. Observation produces a kind of immediate, intuitive knowledge, but it is only through the further construction of causal accounts that genuine, scientific understanding is produced. For Aristotle, gaining wisdom is a matter of collecting, cataloging, and systematizing more and more descriptions of the causal mechanisms at work in the world around us. Philosophy, as we have already discovered, is the "love of wisdom," and for Aristotle, "Wisdom is knowledge about certain principles and causes."[9]

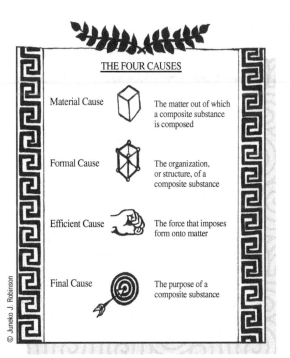

THE FOUR CAUSES

Material Cause — The matter out of which a composite substance is composed

Formal Cause — The organization, or structure, of a composite substance

Efficient Cause — The force that imposes form onto matter

Final Cause — The purpose of a composite substance

© Juneko J. Robinson

Aristotle's philosophical science is both empirical and systematic. Yet it differs from modern science in at least a couple of ways. First of all, Aristotle's notion of cause is much broader than that of most modern scientists. When a modern scientist refers to a cause, normally he or she has in mind only something like Aristotle's efficient cause. Today, causation is normally spoken of in terms of the transfer of energy, and you will rarely find contemporary scientists talking of anything like a final or formal cause. Sometimes the material cause is appealed to, but even that is normally overshadowed by the notion that cause and effect relationships can be reduced to the transfer of energy from body to body.[10] Second, modern science is focused on predicting events, and we moderns consider it the sign of a science's correctness when it consistently allows us to accurately predict future states of affairs. Aristotle's science, on the other hand, is less focused on prediction and more on explanation. He wants to give us a way to make sense of the world after the fact, even if the explanations so produced serve no predictive or practical purpose whatsoever. "All men by nature desire to know,"[11] Aristotle writes, and for him knowing "why" something is the case is more important than foretelling or controlling the future course of nature.

Many of the "truths" that Aristotle claims to have known, nevertheless, turn out to be false. He claimed that men have only eight ribs, that the heart is the seat of intelligence, and that the brain is simply a cooling unit for the body. He asserted as fact that women have fewer teeth than men and that the Earth does not move. These observations were all backed up by Aristotle with explanations for why they must be so, and this suggests one of the problems with his systematic empiricism. Whereas Plato may not have placed enough trust in the senses, Aristotle may have placed too much trust in the unsophisticated, commonsense observations of his day. According to him, final judgments on truth or falsehood must be rooted in actual, observable sensory data, yet how can we be certain that what we see always corresponds to the way things really are? It is one of the taken-for-granted presumptions of Aristotle's philosophy that, for the most part, we can rely on the testimony of our senses because our minds and the world outside of our minds share a common structure. What we see, taste, touch, and feel, according to Aristotle, corresponds to an objective and concrete reality that really does exist independent of our perceptions. We can know the structure of the universe because our mind is an appropriate tool for accurately deciphering its secrets. Certainly we must be cautious, for errors do sometimes occur due to sloppiness in method and laziness in character, but with careful observation and the use of logic, Aristotle believed that the human intellect is capable of comprehending the absolute and final truths of Being itself. In this he echoes the optimism of his Greek ancestors and their confidence in the rationality and the order of the universe; a confidence that would begin to radically deteriorate in the post-Aristotelian era.

ARISTOTLE'S LOGIC

Aristotle never seriously entertained any skeptical doubts about the powers of our observational capacities, and building on the optimism of his predecessors, he was the first thinker to develop a precise and elaborate system of logic in order to delineate the orderly pattern he thought to be shared in common by the human mind and nature itself. This logic starts from the supposition that in thinking, as in nature, qualities exist within substances. In the structure of human thought, we always attribute predicates to subjects, such as in the sentence "Man is rational." Here the concept of "rationality" is predicate to the subject "man." This grammatical structure found in our thinking, Aristotle assumes, corresponds to a naturally occurring structure that also exists objectively in the world, independent of our thinking. What appears as a predicate in our language corresponds to a quality in nature, and what appears as a subject in our language corresponds to a substance in nature. A substance is more stable and foundational than the qualities it supports, and without substances in which to manifest themselves qualities would not exist. For instance, rationality could not just float around on it own. A substance, such as a man, must possess or display it as a quality. Thus, there is congruence between the way that humans think and the world that we think about. The very grammar of our language corresponds to the structure of nature, and this is what makes it possible for us to know our world. If this were not the case, if there was not a common structure shared by human thinking and the world, then we could never know anything about objective reality.[12]

A "primary substance" is that subject/substance that underlies other things: "… they are entities which underlie everything else, and … everything else is either predicated of them or present in them."[13] A primary substance is the widest, most comprehensive of categories, and any of the qualities predicated of a primary substance are termed by Aristotle "secondary substances." You can think of the relationship between primary and secondary substances as something like the relationship between the nested circles in a Venn diagram. The widest circle is the primary substance, while the circles within are the qualities or secondary substances. In the statement "Man is rational," "Man" is primary and "rational" is secondary.

Notice that it is illogical to predicate "Man" of "rational." To say "rational is man" makes no sense. This is because there is a natural relationship that exists between the categories involved such that the substance "Man" is more primary, and substantial, than is "rationality." Furthermore, because this is the case in our language, Aristotle also assumes that it must be the case for the world of nature that our language is used to talk about. The world, thus, like our language, is composed of a series of nested substances. Secondary substances "convey a knowledge of primary substance"[14] such that they allow us to understand something of the essence or form of the primary substance that they exist within. So, for instance, "rationality" tells us something of the nature of "Man." By exploring and unpacking the relationships between the subjects and predicates in our language, and thus the relationships between primary and secondary substances in nature, we are able to gain greater and wider knowledge of reality.

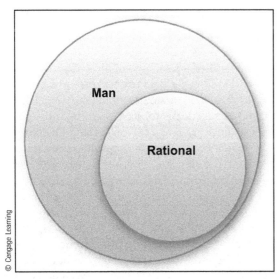

© Cengage Learning

FIGURE 4.2 The Relationship between Primary and Secondary Substances

Aristotle introduced the "syllogism" as the technical device by which we may explore the formal relationships that exist between subjects/primary substances and predicates/secondary substances. The syllogism is an argument that consists of two premises and one conclusion. The premises in a syllogism are statements that, taken together, necessarily imply the conclusion of the argument. For instance, consider the following syllogism:

All men are rational.
All Greeks are men.

_____

All Greeks are rational.

The first two statements, "All men are rational" and "All Greeks are men" are the premises. From them, we may conclude "All Greeks are rational." Notice that each of the statements in the syllogism is made up of a subject/predicate construction. Note also that the two premises share a common term ("men") that links them together. This common term, called a "middle term," does not appear in the conclusion, but it is the link that allows us to bring together the subject of the second premise (Greeks) with the predicate of the first premise (rational). All valid, deductive reasoning, Aristotle discovered, must include such a linking term, and without this term an argument must necessarily fail. With this discovery, Aristotle took the first step toward formalizing the process of reasoning, showing that there is a consistent order and structure to the way that we think when we think well. In addition to demonstrating the valid forms of thought, Aristotle also outlined the common, invalid ways of thinking to which humans often fall prey. In so doing, he not only offered guidance for how to reason properly, but he also sharpened our sensitivity to the errors in thinking that often lead us astray.[15]

THE FIRST MOVER

Aristotle claimed that all scientific/philosophical reasoning could be expressed in the form of the syllogism, and that by doing so we could systematize our learning and ultimately reason our way back to the broadest, most comprehensive primary substance that underlies all other secondary substances in the universe; namely, "God." Aristotle's God is the final grammatical subject and therefore the most foundational of all primary substances as well. If all qualities must exist within something more stable than they are themselves, then there must be some ultimate, unchanging substance that contains and sustains all of the changing and transitory worldly qualities that we observe in our environment. This ultimate substance grounds all Being and acts as the source from which everything else issues. Aristotle, of course, was a pagan thinker and so his God is not the Judeo-Christian God. It is in no way a personal deity that cares about humans and their condition. Rather, it is simply the most extensive subject within which all other predicates are nested. It is the widest circle of the Venn diagram. It is the "first cause" of everything that exists. It is the preeminent explanation. This

"First Mover" must necessarily exist, he tells us, because all of the changes, distinctions, motions, and purposes that we see, taste, touch, and feel in the world around us had to originate from some prior source. Like all of the changeable and transient qualities in the universe, such things must take place within something more stable and substantial than they are themselves. God provides the ground out of which all changing things arise. It is "something which moves without being moved, being eternal, substance, and actuality."[16]

For Aristotle, the existence of God is a scientifically necessary condition for explaining the existence of change and impermanence in the world that we see around us. There must be a first cause of the universe, and in order to qualify as a first cause a thing must be eternal and unchanging. But in order to be eternal and unchanging, God must be complete actuality, or put in another way, a substance that is perfectly formal in character. Recall that any substance made of matter has an aspect of potentiality about it, and if something has an aspect of potentiality, then it is subject to change. Only pure form is fully actual and so immune to alteration. Thus, the first cause of the universe, God, must be a nonmaterial, formal substance. Furthermore, this formal substance, insofar as it has the inexhaustible power to sustain the changing movements of the universe over an infinite period of time, must itself possess an endowment that, while capable of compelling other things to move and change, is itself immovable and unchangeable. It must exhibit a fully actual yet powerful force that is self-contained, unending, and unfluctuating. Aristotle tells us that the only sort of power that has this quality about it is that of pure thought, and so God must be a purely formal, thinking substance! Of course, God doesn't think about humans or existence or anything outside of itself, for then God would be dependent on those things. Rather, God thinks only about its own thinking, and so is completely self-dependent. It is the rest of the material universe, Aristotle tells us, that aspires toward the self-dependency of God, and this is the ultimate reason why we see change and transition all around us. Things in our world are constantly striving to actualize their own full potential in emulation of God's perfection. As they strive and struggle to be like God, material objects become transformed, yet insofar as nothing that participates in the material world is yet fully actualized, all things in this world remain in perpetual transition. The only things in the visible realm that are even close to God's self-completeness, according to Aristotle, are the heavenly bodies that rotate around the Earth in perfectly circular orbits. The paths of these circular orbits have neither a beginning nor an end, and so they are the nearest reflections of the self-contained activity that is God's thinking. Otherwise, the Earth is made up of things and creatures whose final purpose is perpetually out of reach, and only God is flawless and whole. As Aristotle writes:

> If, then, God is always in that good state in which we sometimes are, this compels our wonder; and if in a better this compels it more. And God *is* in a better state. And life also belongs to God; for the actuality of thought is life, and God is that actuality; and God's self-dependent actuality is life most good and eternal. We say therefore that God is a living being, eternal, most good, so that life and duration continuous and eternal belong to God; for this *is* God.[17]

So it is that Aristotle, according to many scholars, seems to fall back into the old Platonic way of thinking against which he originally chafed. Whereas he had originally rejected the notion of unchanging and transcendent Forms that stand behind the material world of change, Aristotle ultimately returns to this idea, claiming that a purely formal, unseen, and unchanging substance is the true anchor point of the universe. Furthermore, we can detect in Aristotle's notion of the First Mover an echo of Socrates' claim, picked up from Anaxagoras, that the universe is organized and given form by the power of nous, or mind. As it turns out, for Aristotle, God is the most powerful, nonmaterial, thinking substance that exists, and it causes everything in the universe to become organized by way of inspiring aspiration toward its perfection. Thus, despite his insistence on recognizing the importance of material causes in science, Aristotle, it could be argued, still remains within the Socratic tradition of philosophy in that he elevates a nonmaterial cause of the universe to the highest and most important of all positions.

RATIONALITY, EMOTION, AND THE GOLDEN MEAN

According to Aristotle, all things in the universe are striving toward self-perfection, attempting to be God-like in their own ways. There is, however, one creature who does, in actual fact, possess a small degree of the First Mover's perfection as part of its very essence. This creature is the human being. Humans, like all things in the world, have been caused to come into existence and thus may be analyzed in terms of the four causes. It is pretty obvious that part of what makes us human is that we are made up of flesh, bone, fat, blood, etc. This is our material cause. But what is our formal cause? Following Socrates and Plato, Aristotle suggests that the soul is the formal cause of human Being. The human soul is what gives us life and intelligence, and it is what makes us different from plants and animals. All living creatures have souls, according to Aristotle, but the souls of humans are more complicated than those of other creatures. We share with all other living creatures the need to take in nutrition, and we share with animals the ability to feel pain and pleasure, but we also have something unique that is not shared with other living creatures. Only we have the capacity for reason. Rationality is our highest and most unique capacity that sets us apart from all other living creatures.[18] This capacity for reason is what makes humans, among all other animals, most God-like. This being the case, Aristotle tells us that our final cause consists in pursuing a reasonable life in which we strive to exercise our rational faculties to the fullest extent possible. In so doing we achieve happiness and fulfillment.

But what about emotions? If human beings should always strive to be rational, how do our emotions fit into the happy life? Plato had argued that the passions are dangerous, clouding our rationality and leading us astray, thus making us worse than we might potentially be. Because artists are experts at stirring up the emotions, Plato even went so far as to advocate expelling them from his well-ordered society. Aristotle, however, rejected Plato's stance on this issue. He did not think that emotions are necessarily dangerous, but that they could

TABLE 4.1   The Four Causes of Humans

Material Cause	Flesh, blood, bone, etc.
Formal Cause	Soul
Efficient Cause	Parents, grandparents, etc.
Final Cause	Rationality

be harnessed in order to motivate us toward virtuous behavior. This is possible only if we would use our reason in order to moderate our feelings. Instead of allowing ourselves to swing from one extreme type of emotion to another, Aristotle tells us that in our everyday life we should strive to achieve a "golden mean" in our behavior. This is, he thought, the most reasonable and virtuous way to be. For instance, when faced with an enemy it is certainly natural to feel fear and angry conviction. Aristotle would not dispute this. But such feelings, he claims, originate from the lower, irrational portion of our soul. The reasonable human being does not automatically act on such feelings the way an animal does, but rather enlists the aid of the higher, distinctively human part of the soul in order to temper these sorts of base impulses. Rationality tells us that it is cowardly to run away from a fight when we allow ourselves to feel too much fear, just as it is rash to fly headlong into battle because we feel too much conviction. "Of those who go to excess[,] he who exceeds in fearlessness ... would be a sort of madman or insensible person if he feared nothing ... while the man who exceeds in confidence about what is really terrible is rash."[19] It is far more virtuous to be courageous, which results from a moderate compromise between fear and conviction. "As we have said, then, courage is a mean with respect to things that inspire confidence or fear ... and it

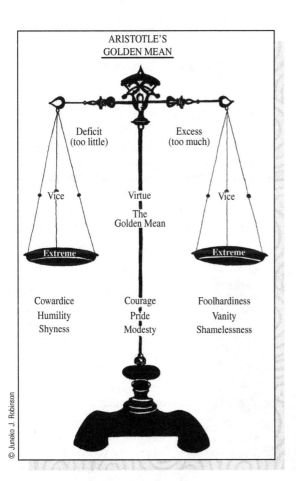

ARISTOTLE'S
GOLDEN MEAN

Deficit (too little)   Excess (too much)

Vice   Virtue   Vice
The
Golden Mean

Extreme   Extreme

Cowardice   Courage   Foolhardiness
Humility   Pride   Vanity
Shyness   Modesty   Shamelessness

© Juneko J. Robinson

chooses or endures things because it is noble to do so, or because it is base not to do so."[20] The golden mean between extremes, Aristotle tells us, is usually the best guideline for leading a morally virtuous life.

There is, however, a non-moral, purely intellectual realm of virtue as well, according to Aristotle, which is not subject to the constraints of the golden mean. In the life of pure intellect the guideline of temperance does not play the same sort of role that it plays in our moral decision making. As the highest, reasonable portion of our soul is the most God-like, it must be free to pursue its own ends without moderation or constraint. In the full enjoyment of intellectual contemplation, humans mirror the activity of God, and in so doing come as close to happiness as is possible for composite, earth-bound creatures. It is true that as long as they live humans are tied to their material endowments and so must heed the irrational demands of the lower desires. However, at their best and happiest moments, they are able to act as if they are self-contained, thinking substances, not subject to the contingencies of material existence. Intellectual virtue, as opposed to moral virtue, consists in following reason where it leads us, giving it free rein to explore the most extreme boundaries of thought. While in everyday life we must make compromises and temper our feelings, in the world of pure thought we may allow our minds to exercise their full powers without moderation.

ARISTOTLE'S PHILOSOPHY OF ART

Aristotle recognized that emotions do play a role in everyday human life, and though we should not ever allow ourselves to get overwhelmed or to be carried to extreme kinds of behavior by them, there are times when it is healthy to allow ourselves to express and share the full potency of our feelings with others. Just as the complete force of pure intellect may be allowed expression in schools of philosophy, an appropriate venue for the full and passionate expression of emotion, according to Aristotle, was at the theater. It was at the theater that people could gather to watch tragedies and comedies in order to experience the mental release that results from crying and laughing. Aristotle agreed with

© Juneko J. Robinson

Plato that artists were experts at provoking emotions in people, but unlike his teacher, he thought that there were reasons to admire and encourage them in this talent. According to Aristotle, having our feelings stirred up by artistic performances allows us the opportunity to vent them in a safe environment. It is healthy, he thought, to laugh and to cry, but such displays should occur under

---

B o x 4.1 Aristotle's Lost Book on Comedy

In the introduction to *Poetics*, Aristotle tells us that he will write about the structure of both tragedy and comedy. However, as the book progresses, most of the discussion centers on tragedy leaving the topic of comedy almost completely ignored. Scholars today believe that the reason for this omission is that the sections dealing with comedy have been lost, perhaps when the library at Alexandria was destroyed sometime around A.D. 390.

The mystery of what happened to the lost book on comedy is the subject of *The Name of the Rose*, a novel written by Umberto Eco in 1980, which was also made into a popular motion picture starring Sean Connery and Christian Slater in 1986.

In *The Name of the Rose*, a Medieval monastery provides the setting for a murder mystery that begins as a number of monks turn up dead, apparently from poisoning. A monk/detective and his assistant arrive in order to solve the murders, and in the course of their investigation they discover that this monastery houses the lost writings on comedy from Aristotle's *Poetics*. As it turns out, the librarian at this monastery has poisoned the pages of the manuscript so that anyone who touches it with unprotected fingers will die.

Why did the librarian poison the book? Because he claims that comedy is dangerous. It encourages people to feel superior and powerful by encouraging them to laugh at others. If the impulse toward laughter is not guarded, claims the librarian in the story, people might be tempted to laugh at God Himself!

---

controlled circumstances. Artistic performances provided this circumstance, and so he thought the public staging of tragedies and comedies to be a good idea.

In his book *Poetics*, Aristotle offers an analysis of the popular entertainment of his day in terms of the four causes. As it comes down to us, *Poetics* primarily focuses on the subject of tragedy and deals only in an incomplete manner with comedy, probably because a whole portion of the text has been lost or destroyed.[21] Nevertheless, this book offers one of the most clear, clever, and convincing applications of Aristotle's method of analysis to a subject that many people assume immune to causal, scientific explanation. As such, it is a great testament to the power and creativity of Aristotle's way of thinking. Before closing this chapter, a brief examination of Aristotle's treatment of comedy and tragedy in *Poetics* offers a final illustration of his method and his genius, highlighting his divergence from Plato in matters of aesthetic appreciation. What follows is also intended to show that even when we are concerned with something as seemingly subjective and personal as aesthetic appreciation, scientific and philosophical modes of analysis may enrich and augment our experience rather than simply explain it away.

Aristotle agrees with Plato that the arts are a type of imitation. However, unlike Plato, Aristotle does not think of imitation as necessarily bad. "Imitation is natural to man from childhood, one of his advantages over the lower animals being this, that he is the most imitative creature in the world, and learns at first by imitation."[22] Imitation allows us to focus our attention on unfamiliar things, taking pleasure as we invest work in the simulation and replication of reality. For Aristotle, rather than presenting a distraction from Truth, imitation is an activity that encourages us to understand the meaning of the world around us. Though the product of imitation is not, in fact, the real thing, it is a means by which we can get to know the real thing.

Tragic and comic plays, as forms of artistic poetry, are types of imitation. But rather than imitating physical objects (as in painting or sculpture), plays imitate the *actions* of human beings. In a comic play, the actions imitated are those of people inferior to us, and because we find these actions "ridiculous" but "not productive of pain or harm to others,"[23] we are amused by them. In a tragic play, on the other hand, the actions imitated are serious and performed by noble characters that we care about and respect. When a misfortune befalls the noble characters in a tragedy, the emotions of pity and fear are aroused in the audience: pity, because we care about the noble protagonist, and fear, because we become upset in anticipation of what will happen. In a successful comedy, the feeling of superior amusement triggers a laughing response, whereas in a tragedy, the feelings of pity and fear trigger a crying response. We can judge the quality of a comedy or a tragedy on the basis of their ability to make us laugh or cry, and so any good play should aim at the final cause that is appropriate to its type. "Catharsis" is the name given by Aristotle to that moment when the pent-up feelings generated by a play break free and are expressed outwardly by members of the audience. Venting feelings in this manner acts as a safety valve so that powerful emotions are not allowed to build up to dangerously high levels in everyday life. Instead of exploding in anger, it is much preferable, and more rational, to sit in the theater and cry or laugh off all of your frustrations.

The final cause of a play, then, is catharsis. This is the end that an artistic performance is aimed at producing. So how is this end produced? What are the material, formal, and efficient causes of a play? The material causes are easy enough to identify. The most basic of the material causes is the set of words out of which the play is constructed. These are the building blocks of a story, whether we are considering it as a script that is written down on paper or as a performance that is spoken out loud. Aristotle devotes large sections of *Poetics* to the analysis of the parts of language, starting with letters and going on to write about the words and sentences that are constructed out of those letters. Yet, without authors to write down the words and actors to speak them, no performance would ever be possible. Thus we naturally come to the conclusion that the efficient cause of the play must be the people who put their energy into the work, structuring the words in such a manner that they produce the final effect that is intended. A play then, whether comic or tragic, is made up of a series of words that have been organized by artists in such a way as to produce catharsis in an audience. But how specifically must these words be organized? What is the formal cause of a play?

You will recall that Aristotle referred to the soul as the form of the human being, and likewise, in *Poetics*, he tells us that "the life and soul, so to speak, of Tragedy is the Plot."[24] The plot consists of the overall structure and organization of the actions and events in a play. It defines the actual story line, insofar as it is the plot that connects all of the incidents together into a cohesive whole. When someone asks "What was the play about?" the natural response is for us to explain the plot. A well-structured plot should carry the audience along in such a manner that, for the length of the play, they become absorbed in the story and forget about the world outside of the play. The audience should not become confused by the action, and they should not be distracted by implausible motivations or improbable occurrences. These sorts of things pull the viewer out of the fantasy world created by the performance and thus short-circuit the effect it is supposed to have. If during a performance we find ourselves thinking, "I don't understand what is going on!" or "That could never happen!" then it is unlikely that our emotions will be engaged enough to experience catharsis at the appropriate times. We will be too busy thinking about the problems in the plot, rather than empathizing with the characters and their plight.

Thus, a good plot should be well structured, and this means that not only should it follow the rules of probability but that it should be "complete" and of the proper "magnitude." To be complete, according to Aristotle, is to have "beginning, middle, and end."[25] The beginning introduces the characters and situations of the story. This is the part that prepares us for the unfolding actions in the middle of the play. In the best cases, the middle portion of a play involves complications of the initial situation. These complications entangle both the characters and the audience in a web of difficulties that need to be sorted out or suffered through. Without this kind of complication, the plot would be uninteresting, going from point A to point B with none of the roller coaster thrills that we expect when we go to see a performance. An engrossing plot is normally one that is complicated by twists, turns, and unanticipated "reversals" that surprise us and provoke our concern for the characters along the way. These twists and turns, furthermore, should be given a resolution and conclusion in the end of the play. There is nothing more frustrating than developing an attachment to characters in a story that leads nowhere. For this reason, a well-structured plot should wrap up all of the loose ends that were unraveled during the middle portion of the performance in a satisfying, and cathartic, denouement.

To be complete, then, a play needs to have a beginning, a middle, and an end. But what does it mean for the play to be of the proper magnitude? Aristotle tells us that the proper magnitude for a play is such that it not be too short, for then there is no time for the complications and reversals to occur that make the story interesting, nor too long, for then we become confused and bored and thus lose interest. The proper magnitude for any particular play is impossible to pin down precisely, but in general terms it should be of "a length to be taken in by the memory."[26] What Aristotle means by this is that we, the audience, should be able to hold the entire plot in our heads all at once. This allows us to appreciate the structure, form, and organization of the piece and to contemplate its beauty. Because we cannot easily discern the structure of things that are very, very small, nor the structure of things that are very, very big, the magnitude of any beautiful piece of art is going to have to be of a moderate dimension.[27] Of course, the tastes and intellectual capacities of audiences vary, and so the plots that some audiences find immoderate may prove to be just right for others, and in fact differing subject matter needs to be treated in differing ways. The structure of a plot that adequately details the life of Socrates may not be adequate to the story of the rise and fall of the Egyptian Empire. Yet in either case, the beauty of the final product demands that the artist, who is the efficient cause of the piece, impart the appropriate form to words, which are the material cause, in a manner that produces the desired final effect on the intended audience.

T A B L E 4.2   The Four Causes of a Drama

Material Cause	Letters, words, and sentences
Formal Cause	Plot
Efficient Cause	Author, director, and actors
Final Cause	Catharsis

What is really remarkable about *Poetics* is not necessarily that Aristotle is correct in his assessment of comedy and tragedy, but rather that he was imaginative and creative enough to realize that his philosophical/scientific insights into the four causes could be applied to something like the arts. Aristotle's love of art and his love of philosophy and science in no way contradict but rather reinforce each other, acting as congruent avenues to the Truth itself. Today, it is all too common for some scientists to relegate issues of aesthetic appreciation to the realm of mere subjectivity, or worse yet, to attempt a reduction of aesthetic experience to processes and components that discount its genuine power. To claim that the experience of laughing or crying, for instance, can fully be understood simply as the result of a stimulus that floods the brain with a particular chemical is not only superficial, but insulting to the depth and profundity of human experience. Aristotle does not make this sort of error, and his analysis in *Poetics* is an example of how scientific, philosophical, and artistic thinking can coexist without crowding one another out of the picture.

Yet, it is also true that Aristotle's treatment of art is not final and complete. As the popular success in recent times of such films as *Memento* and *Pulp Fiction* demonstrate, the particular details of Aristotle's philosophy of drama is riven with faults. The structure of these films defies the traditional beginning, middle, and end order that Aristotle thought indispensable for audience enjoyment. They produce their own unique sorts of artistic effects by breaking with conventional story-telling techniques and experimenting with forms of organization that would probably have been baffling to Aristotle's tastes. Nonetheless, because the last word on the success or failure of a piece of art rests in the effects that it produces in the audience, Aristotle would, like any good scientist, be receptive to the empirical evidence at hand in these cases. Given that these films did meet with widespread audience approval, if he was around today, Aristotle would no doubt be driven to speculate on the reasons why this was the case, opening up new questions and areas of investigation. As a philosopher, the prospect that his theories might be wrong would not be threatening to him but rather a challenge to further thinking.

ARISTOTLE AND WONDROUS DISTRESS

The poet Samuel Taylor Coleridge claims that humankind can be divided into two general groups: those who think Plato is right and those who think Aristotle is right. While it is the case that Aristotle and Plato do pursue ways of thinking that in many senses diverge radically from one another, it is also the case that

Aristotle was greatly influenced by his teacher, and we can detect the traces of this influence both in the subject matter that he studied and in the method that he used. Like Plato, Aristotle was ultimately concerned with trying to unify all knowledge under a simple and comprehensive set of ideas. Unlike Plato, he did not want to turn away from the visible world in order to do this. This last point is the key characteristic that marks Aristotle as an empiricist and that sets his thinking apart from the rationalism of his teacher. Aristotelian philosophy, consequently, has a markedly scientific flavor as opposed to the more pronounced religious overtones of Platonic philosophy. Granted that Aristotle tends toward a scientific view of the world, what is it that makes his thinking distinctively philosophical?

Aristotle wrote that "philosophy begins in wonder."[28] In order to pursue wisdom, one must ask questions and be curious enough to undertake the investigation of reality; in short, one must wonder about the things that one does not know. In this contention, Aristotle articulates one of the guiding themes that has been our concern from the beginning of this book. All philosophers possess the desire to know.[29] Wonder is an indispensable part of the philosophical way of life. Without it there is no motivation to aspire toward wisdom, and as we have already established, it is the love of wisdom that is the essence of philosophy. Aristotle, in telling us that philosophy begins in wonder, then, pinpoints something very important. Yet notice that what he has pinpointed is just a *beginning*. What else is required by philosophy?

The works that Aristotle has left to us are amazing in their logic, in their empirical detail, and in their drive to offer explanations for the visible phenomena of the world. Aristotle is considered to be one of the giants of Western philosophy, and it would be indiscreet to exclude him from this illustrious club. I don't intend to do this, but I would like to point out something that is obvious to all who read the writings of this legendary Greek thinker. In Aristotle's texts, while there is certainly an emphasis placed on the importance of human wonder, there is little or no emphasis placed on what I have been characterizing as distress. Aristotle seems not to be the sort of man who tormented himself over the things that he did not know, but rather was concerned with investigation into the things that he could know. In his written works we find the thoughts of an author who is confident and assured of the powers of the human mind and who has little doubt that the conclusions he has derived are the correct ones. The questions that he asks are sometimes ambitious, yet he always successfully formulates sensible, down-to-earth answers that appeal to our commonsense views on how things operate. This sort of confidence is bracing to many readers, especially those who appreciate the concreteness of the empirical sciences, but it also leaves many of us with the feeling that perhaps Aristotle was overconfident. We know today that many of the established "facts" that he deduced from observation are not facts at all. So where did he go wrong?

There are many possible responses to this question. First of all it is clear that any system that holds empirical verification as the final judge on the correctness or incorrectness of a view is only as strong as the correctness of its observations. In Aristotle's time observations were conducted in a manner that today would be considered unsophisticated. Technology was lacking, and there were no established methods for careful experimentation. Aristotle's observations were thus quite casual compared to what the sciences would demand today, and so we might expect that many of his assertions would, consequently, be suspect. Secondly, and related to the previous point, Aristotle relied heavily on argumentation in order to establish his conclusions about the nature of the physical world. He established logic as a science and was certain that by reasoning carefully he could uncover the truths of Being itself. While proper reasoning is important, it is also true that (1) an argument is only as sound as the content that goes into the argument and (2) differing and contradictory conclusions can be reached by logical means. As regards the first point, we have already touched on the problems with the content that Aristotle embedded in some of his arguments. Bad observations coupled with good arguments led Aristotle to false conclusions in many cases. With regard to the second point, Aristotle seems often times to presume that simply because he has produced a good argument for a conclusion, that conclusion must be true. For instance, Aristotle argued that the planets must orbit the Earth in perfectly circular patterns. When you look up in the sky it appears that the planets consistently trace out arcs in the sky. Because circular motion is the only form of motion that is unbroken, consistent, and perfect, it must be the case that the planets orbit the Earth in circular patterns. There is nothing wrong with this argument other than the fact that the conclusion is wrong. Aristarchus of Samos, appealing to the same evidence, argued that it was, in fact, the Earth that circled the Sun along with the other planets! Mere argument establishes nothing in these cases. What is needed is further inquiry and investigation into what appears to be the case.

If Aristotle had more of a sense of his own fallibility, then perhaps he would have been more cautious about coming to final assertions about the world. Like the Presocratic philosophers before him, Aristotle stops being a philosopher and starts being a natural scientist at those points when he allows his wondrous desire for answers to overtake his finite capacities to understand the world. This is not to discount his accomplishments but simply to point out that the complacency that sometimes characterizes Aristotelian thinking, and the embarrassing conclusions that result, could have been circumvented with the infusion of a fresh dose of philosophical distress. Philosophy begins in wonder, no doubt, but it is nourished and preserved by the distressing thought that our answers fall short of the complete Truth. Aristotle was a philosopher when he raised new questions, subverted old dogmas, and speculated on unsolved mysteries. Sometimes, however, he stepped out of his philosopher's shoes and took on another, more authoritative role as "the master of all who know." I like to imagine that if transported into contemporary times, it would be the philosopher in Aristotle who would break free and, in both wonder and distress, come to embrace the ongoing, endless, and incomplete nature of human understanding.

It is ironic that both Plato and Aristotle, each of whom built their own elaborate and systematic accounts of the structure of reality, should have been inspired by an Athenian gadfly whose most powerful claim to fame was that he knew nothing at all. One wonders what Socrates would have thought of his students.

QUESTIONS FOR DISCUSSION

1. Samuel Taylor Coleridge claimed that all people can be classified as either Platonists or as Aristotelians. Which one are you? Discuss the aspects of each of these philosophical systems that you admire and those with which you disagree.

2. Aristotle is considered the third of the three major Socratic philosophers. What in his thinking is inherited from Socrates? In what ways do you see his philosophy as diverging away from Socrates? In what ways does Aristotle appear to be influenced by Plato? In what ways does his philosophy diverge from Plato's philosophy?

3. It is claimed by some scientists and historians today that Aristotle's philosophy single-handedly held back the progress of science until the dawning of the seventeenth century. Why do you think some people would say this? Do you think it is a fair charge?

4. It has been claimed by some people that Aristotle's discovery of the syllogism is the single most important discovery in the history of Western thought. Why do you think someone would make this claim? Why, on the other hand, do you think Bertrand Russell disputed the truth of this claim?

5. Is it true that the most virtuous course of action is always the most moderate? Discuss Aristotle's Golden Mean and its usefulness as a guide for ethical behavior.

6. Using Aristotle's theory of drama as outlined in *Poetics*, analyze the structure and the effect on audiences of a contemporary film or television show. According to Aristotle's criteria, is the film or show a good drama? What would Plato think of it?

7. According to Aristotle, unlike Socrates or Plato, there is no such thing as an afterlife for human beings. Drawing on what you have learned about the four causes, why do you think Aristotle would hold this view?

NOTES

1. Aristotle, *Metaphysics*, XII.7.30.
2. Diogenes Laertius, *Lives of Eminent Philosophers*, R. D. Hicks (trans.) (London: Harvard University Press, 1959), p. 445.
3. Aristotle, *Physics*, 194a.12–15.
4. Aristotle, *Metaphysics*, IX.1050a15317.
5. Jonathan Barnes (trans. and ed.), *Early Greek Philosophy* (London: Penguin Books, 1987), pp. 134–135.
6. Even the Presocratic thinker Heraclitus, who is famous for the assertion "All is flux," claimed that fire was the underlying substance of the universe. "We remember Heraclitus for saying "all is in flux" (Fr. 65A3), but he was much more excited about his discovery that underneath the flux of the phenomenal world exists *aiezoon pyr*, "everlasting fire" (probably a symbol of consciousness, for which the Greeks as

yet had no single term), which ordinary human beings do not perceive but to which they owe such knowledge as they possess." Michael N. Nagler. "Reading the Upanishads," in *The Upanishads*, Eknath Easwaran (trans.) (Tomales, CA: Nilgiri Press, 1987), p. 298.

7. Aristotle, *De Anima, III*, 8.432a.9–10.

8. Aristotle, *Physics*, 194b9–10.

9. Aristotle, *Metaphysics*, I.982a.

10. This is at least true of the Newtonian model of modern physics. "An essential feature in the Newtonian paradigm is that the world, or a part of it, can be ascribed a state.... When things happen in the world, the states of physical systems change. The Newtonian paradigm holds that these changes can be understood in terms of forces that act on the system, in accordance with certain dynamical laws that are themselves independent of states." Paul Davies, *The Cosmic Blueprint* (New York: Simon and Schuster, 1989), p. 11.

11. Aristotle, *Metaphysics*, A.1.980a.1.

12. Bertrand Russell considers this all to be a mistake involving the "transference to the world-structure of the structure of sentences composed of a subject and a predicate." *A History of Western Philosophy* (New York: Simon and Schuster, 1972), p. 202.

13. Aristotle, *Categories*, 5.2b.16–18.

14. Ibid., 5.2b.31.

15. Aristotle's discovery of the syllogism is generally considered to be one of the most important events in the history of Western thought, although Bertrand Russell, curmudgeon that he is, considers it to be "unimportant." See Russell, *History of Western Philosophy*, p. 202.

16. Aristotle, *Metaphysics,* XII.6.1072a.25.

17. Ibid., XII.7.1072b.22–30.

18. Aristotle, *De Anima*, Book II.

19. Aristotle, *Nicomachean Ethics*, III.7.1115b.25–29.

20. Ibid., III.7.1116a.10–13.

21. The book and the film *The Name of the Rose* deal with the possible fate of Aristotle's lost writings on comedy. In this story, it is the Medieval Catholic Church that is to blame for the suppression and destruction of this portion of Aristotle's work. Comedy, because it teaches people to laugh, is dangerous to religion, according to the characters in the story. It primes observers to take things lightly and may even encourage them to laugh at God! A Platonic theme is clearly evident here. See Umberto Eco, *The Name of the Rose* (New York: Harvest Books, 1994); *The Name of the Rose* (DVD), Warner Home Video, 2004.

22. Aristotle, *Poetics*, III.1449a.34–35.

23. Ibid., III.1449a.35.

24. Ibid., 1450a.39.

25. Ibid., 1450b.26.

26. Ibid., 14511a.5.

27. Ibid., 1450b.35–40.

28. Aristotle, *Metaphysics,* I.2.

29. It is not so clear, as Aristotle also holds, that "all men by nature desire to know." I am reminded of a popular anti-philosophical T-shirt that I used to see quite often. Across the chest of this T-shirt were the following words: Don't know. Don't care.

Chapter 5

The Hellenistic Philosophers

© Juneko J. Robinson

Why is Hellenistic philosophy claimed by some to represent a decline in Greek thinking? Who was Diogenes and how did he live out the philosophy of Cynicism? How did Stoicism attempt to systematize the insights of the Cynics? What is *apathia*? In what ways did the Epicureans disagree with the Stoics? What is *ataraxia*? Who were the Skeptics?

As we have seen in the past two chapters, both Plato and Aristotle drew a great deal of inspiration from their intellectual mentor Socrates. Neither Plato nor Aristotle, however, was content simply to repeat or blindly propagate these ideas. On the contrary, both thinkers were eager to construct religious or scientific systems that developed their teacher's insights in ways with which Socrates would likely not have been satisfied. Recall that for Socrates, the greatest intelligence consists in the knowledge that "the wisdom of men is worth little or nothing."[1] Those who claim to know the final Truth about reality are usually the ones who are least aware of their own ignorance. Yet both Plato and Aristotle came to some very firm conclusions about humans, the structure of the universe, and the nature of goodness. In this, perhaps, they began to depart from the influence of their philosophical precursor. Stanley Rosen writes, "Aristotle does not merely love or pursue wisdom; like Hegel, he regards himself as possessing it."[2] The same might be said of Plato as well,[3] and if philosophy consists in the *aspiration* toward the Truth, then as soon as an individual claims to have achieved this goal, it might be said that person no longer remains a real philosopher. For instance, in *The Symposium*, Socrates, quoting Diotoma, states:

> No god is a philosopher or seeker after wisdom, for he is wise already; nor does any one else who is wise seek after wisdom. Neither do the ignorant seek after wisdom. For herein is the evil of ignorance, that he who is neither good nor wise is nevertheless satisfied: he feels no want, and has therefore no desire.[4]

Viewed in this manner, Plato and Aristotle come to look either like wise gods or ignorant fools. In any event, from the perspective of a purely Socratic standpoint, they may appear not to be authentic philosophers at all, because in asserting the truth of their final conclusions they abandon the desire to continue questioning those conclusions. In sum, they no longer are *lovers* of wisdom who harbor the motivation necessary in order to continue the search for Truth.

But perhaps this is too harsh. Maybe it would be more accurate, and fair, to say that Plato and Aristotle were not *simply* philosophers in the Socratic sense, but that they were also system builders in their own right. It might be said that just as the Presocratic philosophers combined philosophical questioning and speculation with scientific thinking, so did Plato and Aristotle utilize philosophical reflection as a means to develop religious and scientific systems of their own. In doing so, these two intellectual giants of ancient Greece may have turned against the example set by Socrates. Yet as we have already seen with Thales and Anaximander, there is something ironically philosophical about this nonetheless. Those who take part in philosophical investigation are not shy about moving in new directions and exploring new ways of thinking. Simply mimicking and repeating the ideas of one's teacher is not true philosophy; developing new thoughts and challenges to old orthodoxies is. If we grant this, then Platonism and Aristotelianism might be viewed as two notable systems that work to extend the scope of philosophical inquiry in order to try to understand some of the mysteries about which Socrates himself wondered. In consolidating their positions, Plato and Aristotle were, perhaps, philosophers, but they were also more than philosophers. Plato was a philosophical religious thinker, and Aristotle was a philosophical scientist.

There were, however, individuals at the time who saw in Plato's and Aristotle's attempts at system building a vain exercise that distracted students away from the underlying spirit and purpose of the original Socratic teachings. These individuals viewed the schools of Plato and Aristotle, the Academy and the Lyceum, as monuments to arrogance; places where brainwashing rather than philosophizing took place. According to these critics, what people needed was a call back to simplicity and a rejection of the sorts of conventional modes of living and learning that squelched the individual human intellect. What had been forgotten, they claimed, was the nonconformity, rebellion, and skepticism that Socrates displayed. As a result, a countermovement in philosophy developed that would gain steam and come to dominate the tumultuous and troubled world that emerged after the death of Aristotle.

THE DECLINE OF GREEK POWER AND
HELLENISTIC NEGATIVITY

Socrates, Plato, and Aristotle lived during a time when the Greek city-states were starting to slip into a period of political and military chaos. Athens lost the twenty-seven-year-long Peloponnesian War in 404 B.C., after which Sparta and her allies tore down the walls of Athens. Sparta went on to try to replace Athens as the leader of the Greek world, but her allies rebelled and the Spartan army was later destroyed by the army of the city-state of Thebes. In a condition of disarray and exhaustion, the warring city-states proved too weak to fend off the imperialistic advances of the northern kingdom of Macedon. In 338 B.C. Philip and his army defeated the armies of Athens and Thebes, expanding Macedonian rule southward.

Philip of Macedon was assassinated in 336 B.C., and his son, who became famous as Alexander the Great, took control of the empire. Alexander was successful at conquering even more of the ancient world, extending his rule all the

way from Spain to India. However, after his death, Alexander's generals began to fight among themselves and they divided up the empire into a number of warring kingdoms. None of these kingdoms ever gained the upper hand over the others, and so for many years the Mediterranean was in a state of war and instability until the Roman Empire began its expansion around 300 B.C. Under the power of Rome, the Mediterranean was eventually unified politically and militarily as it never had been before. Yet, in contrast to the war and chaos of earlier times, the cost of this later unity was a great deal of oppression by Roman rule. In any case, the world felt like it was out of the average Greek's control or reckoning, and the philosophies that gained a foothold during this period give expression to this mood of popular distress. If Socrates had been a pessimist, he might very well have resembled many of the key figures who emerged during this "Hellenistic era" of philosophy.

The term "Hellenistic" means "Greek-like." Traditionally it has been claimed that the Hellenistic philosophies represent a decline in the vigor and originality of Greek thinking. As Greek culture was disseminated throughout the ancient world, by means of the inevitable exchange that occurs during times of war and empire consolidation, it was, in turn, affected by the ideas and cultures of faraway people. Many critics claim that this sort of interchange diluted Greek thought and that the ideas thus produced represent a "degenerate" development. Not only did philosophy become tainted by Eastern pessimism, they claim, but it also gained no new substantial insights over those formulated by the past Presocratic and Socratic thinkers.

Hellenistic philosophers may have borrowed ideas from previous thinkers, and they may also show signs of pessimism, but this does not erase the fact that they did indeed offer interesting, practical, and positive insights into the implications of philosophy for everyday life. Instead of representing a decline in philosophical vigor, the Hellenistic philosophers might be interpreted as returning to the zealous and vital spirit of Socrates himself. With them, the central question of philosophy becomes, once again, "How should we, as incomplete and ignorant beings, live in this world?" Furthermore, with the influence of Eastern religious insights and ideas, Hellenistic thinking takes on a concern for spiritual issues, offering practical diagnoses and treatments for the emotional pains endured by human beings. Cynicism, Stoicism, Epicureanism, and Skepticism are all philosophies that, to one degree or another, propose ways of life that will allow us, as individuals who must necessarily fall short of perfection, find peace and contentment in life. To some people, their solutions appear rather pessimistic and extreme, but in them we can detect the influence of popular religious views culled from Judaism, Hinduism, and Buddhism, as well as catching a glimpse of some of the incipient ideas that would play a central role in shaping later Christian doctrines.

Collectively, Hellenistic philosophies tend to advocate the switching off of emotional attachment to things in the outer world as a means toward the alleviation of pain and suffering. According to these philosophies, life as it is unreflectively lived is painful because we desire many things that we cannot possibly have. If we just stop wanting what it is impossible for us to get, then we could be content with the world as it is. Virtue, wisdom, and the good life result from reigning in our desires and learning how to submit to objective reality rather than trying vainly to change it. As Socrates taught, happiness might be obtained if only we could train ourselves to be concerned with the "tendence of the soul" above all other things in life. Power, money, prestige, and all of the conventional social rewards offered to us are merely distractions that pull us away from the contemplation of our own inborn nature. If we could ignore the artificially contrived temptations of the outer world, we would have more time to inspect the inner world of our souls, and in so doing we would discover something firmly within our control. Each of us was born with a mind, and this mind is capable of breaking through the socially constructed delusions that have led us to confuse our real needs with our merely superficial desires.

Cynicism

The doctrines of Cynicism offer a vivid illustration of this trend in Hellenistic philosophy. The term "cynic" comes from the Greek word *kynikos*, which means "dog-like,"[5] and it appears initially to have been used as a term of insult aimed at the Greek philosopher Antisthenes (ca. 444–366 B.C.) who once taught at a school called the "Cynosarges" around the time that Plato and Aristotle were still alive. Antisthenes was a follower of Socrates,[6] and when his mentor was executed by the Athenians, he abandoned his previous aristocratic lifestyle and turned his back on mainstream Athenian culture. He dressed in rags, lived in the streets, and advocated the abolition of government, religion, and private property. Indeed, he seems to have been the first anarchist! It appears to have been this unconventional lifestyle, and his insistence that a formal education was unnecessary in order to acquire wisdom, that brought him into conflict with both Plato and Aristotle, and which led Aristotle to refer to "Antisthenes and other such uneducated people" in his book *Metaphysics*.[7] Antisthenes, however, must have found Aristotle's aspersion amusing, for his own contention was that the truly wise man has no need for the traditions and institutions of conventional society. Real education results not from the collection of facts or the acceptance of tradition but from living a self-sufficient and virtuous life. Echoing the message of Socrates, Antisthenes advocated continuing and ongoing self-reflection and a simple life as the way to free one's self from the distractions and perversions of a decadent culture.

The writings of Antisthenes are gone, but his message has been transmitted, and perhaps even amplified, by the lived example set by his most famous student, Diogenes (ca. 413–327 B.C.). Diogenes came to Athens from the city of Sinope,

© Juneko J. Robinson

from which he was exiled for defacing the official coins of the state.[8] This crime, apparently, was intended as an act of rebellion against the government and its claim to have authority to regulate the economic lives of its citizens. In perhaps one of his most famous utterances, Diogenes purportedly said that he held no allegiance to any single country but

---

B o x   5.1   Diogenes

Diogenes remains a figure whose memory still inspires and influences many people today.

The Diogenes Award is bestowed annually by the Public Relations Society of America in the San Diego area on PR professionals who "demonstrate candor when dealing with the public and the news media, regardless of any potential negative outcome" (see www.prsasandiego.org/content.asp?itemid=81).

Diogenes Syndrome is the name for a rare medical condition in which elderly people neglect their personal hygiene and the tidiness of their surroundings.

In Sacramento, California, an organization called Diogenes Youth Services offers counseling and support for runaway and homeless youth. The Web site for this organization credits Diogenes as being the "first youth advocate, who gave up his possessions and, lantern in hand, went in search of truth, honesty, and self enlightenment" (see www.diogenesyouthservices.org/).

The Japanese anime film *Reign: The Conqueror* depicts the life of Alexander the Great. One episode is devoted to the depiction of Diogenes' influence on Alexander. In this episode, Diogenes is depicted as a Yoda-like sage who provokes others and helps them to see the truth.

---

that he was a "cosmopolitan," or citizen of the entire world! Furthermore, when told by the court judges in Sinope that he was condemned to be expelled from their city, he is reported to have responded, "And I condemn you to stay here!" For Diogenes, confinement to one particular set of conventional customs or beliefs was the worst of all possible punishments. His life would be spent spreading this idea.

When Diogenes arrived in Athens, he overturned a discarded urn and lived beneath it. This was now his house. His choice of shelter was a message to the Athenians: a person can live a perfectly happy and healthy life without a luxurious home. Later, when he saw a young slave boy using his cupped hands to scoop up water and drink it, Diogenes threw away his own drinking cup, realizing that it was an extravagance he could do without. These were the sorts of actions performed by a man who was concerned with simplifying his life by owning as little as possible. Too often humans come to think that happiness rests on the acquisition of things and that we can demonstrate our worth by displaying vast amounts of ornamentation to those around us. Diogenes boldly and dramatically showed us that this is not the case. His life was a happy one, but he owned hardly anything. In his efforts to convince the Athenians that wealth and luxury were distractions that encouraged neglect of the simple joys in life, Diogenes performed other stunts calculated to grab their attention. For instance, he masturbated in public, laughing at those who were shocked, claiming that if the starving could alleviate their hunger simply by rubbing their stomachs, they should certainly not hesitate from doing it! How strange it is, Diogenes seems to be saying, that the simplest and most natural activities are the ones that human beings go to the greatest pains to complicate and hide behind a curtain of social convention. Sex, defecation, and urination, for example, are all things that human beings naturally engage in, yet we have developed a sense of embarrassment about them. You don't see dogs rebelling against nature in this way. Better, then, to live like a dog and reap the simple joys of life than to allow artifice and convention to repress us. Because of social conventions, we have become used to denying our basic, animal urges and thus have arrived at the false conclusion that our happiness and contentment rest on the acquisition of material comforts and adherence to artificial rules of propriety and politeness. This sort of corruption had become so bad, Diogenes claimed, that when he walked through the streets of Athens in the middle of the day with a lantern, he was unable to find even one honest man.

Diogenes taught that the virtuous and happy life was not to be found in the acquisition of fame, fortune, or power. To be truly happy, one must live according to nature, disregarding all convention. Convention pulls us away from an awareness of who we really are, and the feelings of despair and depression that often overcome people are a result of striving to attain those things that don't really matter and are not really fulfilling. Society encourages us to reach for many things that are not natural. Jobs, political office, wealth, fine clothes; none of these things is important or worthwhile. However, we are often fooled into thinking that they are important due to the influence of the many ignorant people around us. Plato called Diogenes "Socrates gone mad!," because even more than Socrates before him Diogenes advocates a disregard for popular opinion. Instead, we should listen to our own inner, natural needs and try to live a modest, simple existence in accordance with those needs. The simple, natural life is the best and healthiest form of life, according to Diogenes. We all need to eat, sleep, drink, defecate, and satisfy our sexual desires. None of these things is shameful, he claimed, and it is a sign of the perverting influences of conventional society that we have come to think that they are so.

Diogenes' way of life, not surprisingly, proved to be quite shocking to the middle classes of his time. Yet, he seems also to have been admired and loved by quite a large following of people as well. Alexander the Great is supposed to have been one of his most well-known admirers. Alexander sought out Diogenes, hoping to meet the wise Cynic. He found him reclining in a field, basking in the sun. Upon approaching Diogenes, Alexander introduced himself and offered the philosopher anything that he wanted. Diogenes reportedly opened one eye, looked at the great leader of the Macedonian Empire and said, "Anything I want? OK. Please move out of my sunlight!" The moral of the story is that even Alexander, the greatest conqueror of the ancient world, had nothing that Diogenes wanted. The only thing that this powerful, rich, and prestigious man could do for Diogenes was to get out of his way. This sort of self-sufficiency and contentment has a power of its own, and this is no doubt why Alexander himself is quoted as saying, "Truly, if I were not Alexander I would wish to be Diogenes."

The teachings of Diogenes were not only directed against the unthinking habits and customs of the men and women in the streets. He also attacked what he saw as the pretensions and conceit of the intellectuals at the Academy and the Lyceum. All of their abstract theorizing and conjecture was seen by Diogenes as just as much a distraction from inner human nature as material wealth was to the average citizen. Recalling the example of Socrates, Diogenes took it upon himself to unmask the underlying ignorance of these pretenders to wisdom, and he utilized his characteristic wit and knack for showmanship to make fun of and expose their intellectual arrogance. One story has it that when members of the Academy had made a big deal over finally formulating an adequate definition of "Man" as "a featherless biped," Diogenes plucked a chicken and threw it into their classroom! With this simple counterexample Diogenes dispatched their definition. Did this chicken suddenly become a man once its feathers were plucked? Of course not. In their preoccupation with abstraction, Diogenes seems to be saying, these "wise men" could not even anticipate how a simple, everyday chicken could bring their ideas to nothing.

Today cynics are usually thought of as people who are contemptful and distrustful of others. They presume that everyone is motivated by the lowest and most selfish of desires. In this we can detect an echo of the original sense of the philosophy; however, ancient Greek Cynicism is a bit more complex than this. Its philosophical foundation rests upon the belief that human beings have become alienated from their true nature because of the influences of conventional society. "Getting back to nature" entails disregarding what the culture tells us is important and listening to our own inner drives. Happiness and contentment are only possible if we understand who we are and how we fit into the natural world. All conventions are hollow, artificial, and distracting according to the Cynics. As a result, we should not allow them to influence us. Instead, we need to utilize our rationality in order to understand who and what it is that we really are. By reflecting on our inner nature, we will come to understand that we have been endowed with some very simple needs that can be efficiently satisfied as long as we stay focused and don't allow ourselves to be led astray by the temptations of the outer world. This message should remind us of the words spoken by Socrates as he defended himself in front of the

Athenian court: "The unexamined life is not worth living." Antisthenes, Diogenes, and their followers were recalling these words as they challenged people to think about what it is that is really important in life and not to waste time and energy pursuing empty goals.

Stoicism

Although many people may have appreciated the insights and the rebelliousness of the Cynics, the lifestyle they advocated was no doubt too extreme ever to become part of a popular movement. In its rejection of the mainstream, Cynicism had to stay a philosophy for outsiders.

However, some of the ideas expounded by Antisthenes and Diogenes did appeal to many people during the tumultuous times of the early Hellenistic period, and these ideas were powerful enough to inspire developments that would eventually culminate in a philosophical system that became known as "Stoicism." Stoicism found its roots in the Cynic claim that peace of mind was to be found in a return to nature and a withdrawal of emotional attachment from things in the world. However, unlike the Cynics, Stoic philosophers would come to the conclusion that, as Aristotle had claimed, human beings are social creatures by nature and so should not abandon the world of convention but dutifully, and unemotionally, play their assigned role within it. Stoicism has a long and complicated history that would take it through at least three major periods of development over the course of 400 years. It would evolve from a belief system held by just a few people, to the de facto philosophy/religion of the pre-Christian Roman Empire. Its doctrines would be advocated both by slaves and emperors alike. In what follows, I shall offer only a rough outline of some of the most consistently held doctrines that characterize this philosophy. The main idea that will be emphasized is the manner in which Stoicism expresses the renunciation of worldly attachment and a willing acceptance of nature's plan. This theme, as we will see in the following chapter, prepares the way for some of the later developments in Christian thinking.

Stoicism is first supposed to have been formulated by a man named Zeno (ca. 335–264 B.C.), who, after finding himself shipwrecked in Athens, was browsing in a book shop reading about Socrates. Asking the shop keeper if he could find someone like the legendary Athenian sage still alive today, the proprietor told him to follow a man who was just then passing by the shop. This man was a Cynic named Crates. Zeno followed Crates, listened to him, and absorbed his teachings. However, Zeno seems to have desired more than just to live an outsider's lifestyle. He wanted to develop a system of thought that would help to explain the nature of reality itself. Consequently, he began the project of systematizing the scattered insights that he learned and teaching about his discoveries from a painted porch called a *stoa poikile*. Thus Stoicism was born.

Stoicism begins with the assertion that all existing things are rooted in the material world. Drawing on Aristotle and rejecting Plato, Zeno claimed that there is no such thing as a nonmaterial reality. Even things like the soul, numbers, and God are physical entities.[9] However, the substantial foundation that grounds our world is not simply passive matter, according to the Stoics, but rather a mixture of passive matter and an active element called *pneuma*. Pneuma is a combination of air and fire, and it is this substance that interpenetrates and thus shapes the structure of all the inert stuff in the universe. Our world, then, while it is wholly composed of matter, is not simply a dead, passive thing. It is infused with an active force that is rational and intelligent. The Stoics referred to this force, this all-pervading pneuma, as "the soul of the world," "the mind of the world," "nature," "God," or "artistic fire."[10] The active and passive forces that constitute the universe work together, like form and matter in Aristotle's system, to produce the order and structure that we see around us. We can also detect the influence of Anaxagoras and Socrates here, and the notion that nous, or mind, is the ordering and rational principle of all reality. In the case of the Stoics, however, this mind substance that pervades all reality is a completely physical thing.[11]

The universe is alive, according to Stoic philosophy, and pneuma is the soul of the universe. It permeates all that exists, bringing everything together in a continuum of connectedness. Quite literally, everyone and everything are touched by pneuma. It fills up the spaces between all objects with the result that there is no such thing as a void within our world. You and I, the table and the trees outside, are all physically connected with one another. This fact is demonstrated by the occurrence of movement at a distance. If you yell into the air in the direction of a piece of paper suspended from the ceiling by a string, you will see the piece of paper vibrate. The reason why this happens, according to the Stoics, is that the sound emitted by your voice sets up waves of motion in the surrounding pneuma, and as it propagates outward, those waves make contact with the paper and thus cause it to move. The same explanation holds for our ability to hear and see things at a distance.[12] Because there is a medium all around us that allows for the transmission of movement, we are able to affect, and be affected by, the things in our environment.

Understanding our connectedness to one another, and to everything else in our world, is the first step toward understanding our place, purpose, and responsibility within reality. Because all things are physically connected, everything affects everything else when it moves. Thus, when a tree drops its fruit somewhere on the earth, it has an effect on me and all other creatures. When I become angry and yell at my neighbor, there are real, physical effects that result from my actions. When a bug flies from a leaf in the woods, there are aftereffects. Any action sets in motion a series of disturbances in the pneuma that have an infinite number of consequences.[13] Furthermore, all of these actions have themselves been caused by motions that occurred prior to them. All events are like links in a long chain of cause and effect that can never be broken. Our world and the lives that we live in it are thus predetermined according to the past states of the universe.[14] There is little that we can do about this according to Stoicism except resign ourselves to the way things are and accept them as part of God's plan.

This element of fatalism has led many commentators to see Stoicism as a despairing and passive philosophy. Because everything in the universe—including your own status in society, the particular circumstances of your life, your economic standing, etc.—has been predetermined according to past events, it is useless and vain to try to alter the order of reality. Add to this the doctrine of the "eternal return," and things just seem to become even bleaker. According to the Stoics, the present state of the world is destined to repeat an infinite number of times into the future, and it has been repeated an infinite number of times in the past. Every little detail of existence will recur again and again into infinity. This follows, they claim, from the fact that everything in the universe is composed of material substance. Because there is a finite amount of matter in the universe, there are only a limited number of combinations and states that it can take over the infinite amount of time that it exists.[15] Over an infinite length of time, it just stands to reason that all things will repeat again and again and again. All of our triumphs and failures, all of the beauty and the ugliness, all of the things we hoped for and dreaded, will recur ad infinitum, as if on an eternally looping filmstrip. The universe itself goes through an infinite number of cosmic cycles of creation and destruction by fire as well, and thus there is no end to the wheel of existence.[16]

We, and the world that we live in, are fated eternally to repeat everything. As stated in the Old Testament book of Ecclesiastes, "That which is, already has been; that which is to be, already has been."[17]

Bertrand Russell writes, "To a modern mind, it is difficult to feel enthusiastic about a virtuous life if nothing is going to be achieved by it.... A destruction of the present world by fire, and then a repetition of the whole process. Could anything be more devastatingly futile?"[18] Certainly, this may be our first reaction to the Stoic worldview, but on further reflection we might also find something comforting in it as well. As a whole, claim the Stoics, the ongoing cycles of cause and effect that take place within the universe are good, insofar as they contribute to the overall structure and order of reality. If we were able to step outside of our world and observe all these interactions from a detached perspective, we would see that there is a harmony that emerges out of the tension created by the motions within the pneuma. From the panorama of eternity, everything is just as it should be. It is only from the fragmented and partial perspective of creatures within the universe that things sometimes appear bad, unfair, or cruel. Nature is, in fact, a self-regulating, perfectly organized, and rational system, and if we truly come to understand this fact, claim the Stoics, we would never wish anything to be any different from how it already is. There is comfort to be taken in this knowledge, for it reminds us that even when it appears things are out of control and headed for disaster, ultimately it will all turn out for the best. As the Stoic Roman emperor Marcus Aurelius (A.D. 121–180) wrote:

> From providence all things flow. And side by side with it is necessity, and that which works to the advantage of the whole universe, of which you are a part. But that is good for every part of nature which the nature of the whole brings to pass, and which serves to maintain this nature. Now the universe is preserved, both by the changes of the elements and by the changes of the things compounded. Let these principles be enough for you; let them always be fixed opinions.[19]

Becoming educated about the rational and harmonious order of nature is thus an important part of the Stoic philosophy. The truly wise and educated person, realizing that the world is governed by a principle of goodness, actively aligns his or her wants, hopes, and desires with the realities of the universe as they have become manifest. This is what the rational life entails. By becoming more and more rational in our thinking, we come to understand the logic and the necessity of reality itself, seeing it for what it actually is: the best of all possible worlds. The best and most virtuous life is found, then, not in fighting against the way things are but in embracing them. We should not try to change the world according to our wishes, but rather come to wish for the world to be the way it actually is in reality. "For good or for ill, life and nature are governed by laws that we can't change. The quicker we accept this, the more tranquil we can be."[20] Once this way of thinking has been achieved, we become truly wise and emerge into a state of tranquility that the Stoics called *apathia*, which means apathy, acquiescence, or resignation. In apathia, the Stoic sage becomes completely at ease with the way things are. All extreme emotional states, like fear, anxiety, and manic joy, melt away and are replaced with a sense of peaceful contentedness. A.A. Long points out that although the popular view of the Stoic is of a person who feels no emotions whatsoever, this is not the way that the original Stoics characterized their ideal. The Stoic sage "is not entirely impassive, contrary to the popular conception," but rather "his disposition is characterized by 'good emotional states.' Well-wishing, wishing another man good things for his sake; joy; rejoicing in virtuous actions, a tranquil life, a good conscience … ; and 'wariness,' reasonable disinclination."[21] These sorts of feelings result from giving oneself over to nature and its necessities. If we could become emotional allies with the world, we would find contentment and tranquility in everything that it requires of us and others.[22]

The Stoics conceptualized their philosophy metaphorically as an egg. The shell of the egg plays a similar role to logic in their system. It holds everything together and allows things to take on a recognizable order and shape. The white of the egg is like the realities of the physical world, which logic allows us to understand. Embedded inside of the white of the egg is the yolk, which is like human life. Because we exist as part of a physical world, knowing our purpose and place requires that we understand that world to the best of our abilities. Therefore, a good human being must study and understand the three basic Stoic disciplines: logic, physics, and ethics. These areas of study fit together naturally, the way the parts of an egg fit together, but ultimately it is ethics that is the point and purpose of all studies. To know how to live well; that is the most important thing according to the Stoic sage.

It is a long way between the fully developed system of Stoicism that was espoused by the Romans and the relatively simple and straightforward ideas that were expounded by the early Greek Cynics. Whereas Antisthenes and Diogenes rejected the importance of formal education, the Stoics demanded it. Whereas the Cynics refused to capitulate to the conventions of society, the Stoics found peace of mind in acquiescing to their social duties. Whereas the Cynics abstained from speculation on metaphysical issues, the Stoics created complicated metaphysical systems. However, despite all of these differences, there is at least one core characteristic that remains constant across these philosophies, and this is the concern for sincerity and a return to nature. Both Cynics and Stoics preached that the source of our unhappiness and anxiety about life is rooted in a misconception about what is really important. Too often we allow ourselves to be led astray by the distractions of the social world, and instead of seeking happiness within our own minds we seek it through our attachments to things and people in the world around us. But real contentment, these philosophers remind us, must come from within. We can't control the outer world. It is too complicated and independent of our will. The only hope lies in controlling our inner world, and we can do this if we just focus our attention on the appropriate goals. "Do things external which happen to you distract you? Give yourself time to learn something new and good, and cease to be whirled around."[23] By sincerely committing ourselves to the perfection of the mind, we may become the sorts of individuals that nature intended us to be and thus come to live life simply, authentically, and without friction. Both Cynics and Stoics hold this to be the most important goal in life, and in its pursuit they advocate a turning away from the outer world. In the case of the Cynics, this turning is quite literal, taking the shape of nonconformity and poverty. In the case of the Stoics, the turning is more subtle, consisting of an emotional detachment from the things, commitments, and roles that one is duty-bound to perform in life. In either case, however, mental anguish is to be conquered by a return to the inner self.

It is unclear whether Socrates would have approved of the Stoic philosophy. On the one hand, he would have appreciated its focus on the individual soul and its concern with wisdom. On the other, he may have reacted against its ideal of apathia. For Socrates, wisdom is an ongoing and endless quest whose guiding ideal is Truth. It is a process rather than a destination, and those who believe themselves already to have unlocked the secrets of the universe miss the point of the philosophical life. The wise person understands that there is always much that he or she does not know but does not take this as an excuse to stop searching for the absolute Truth. In apathy, it seems, a state of mind is achieved that undercuts the sort of feeling that is necessary for continued searching and questioning. Without the unsettled and anxious feeling of incompleteness that accompanies the sense of our own ignorance, we lack the motivation to aspire toward a deeper and more extensive understanding of reality. While the Stoic sage may have been someone who achieved a sense of inner tranquility, one wonders whether this tranquility might have been more the result of weariness with the world than of an eagerness to continue exploring it. This would make all the difference as to whether we should consider Stoicism more a philosophy or more a religion. Did it offer final, comforting answers to the suffering we endure in the world, like a religion, or did it encourage more questions, as philosophy does?

Epicureanism

This last issue is one that must also be raised when exploring Stoicism's most popular competitor, Epicureanism. Epicureanism was a philosophy founded around the same time as Stoicism by none other than a man named Epicurus (341–270 B.C.). Though most of their particular doctrines are quite different from those of the Stoics, the Epicurean promise of a serene and untroubled mental

state is the same. However, instead of apathia, the Epicureans called this state of mind *ataraxia*. Ataraxia is a feeling of joy and pleasure that results when one has satisfied all worldly desire and thus extinguished it. In Buddhism, a similar state is likened to the final goal of enlightenment, and one sometimes gets a sense of the Epicureans, likewise, as quasi-religious seekers whose use of philosophy is directed toward a sort of mystical loss of self and thus toward the end of human suffering.[24] Like enlightenment and apathia, ataraxia is offered by the Epicureans as the final, heaven-like aim of following their system of belief. It is not simply the love of wisdom but rather wisdom itself.

Epicurus would bristle at the characterization of his philosophy as a religion, however, because part of his motivation for formulating this system was to counter what he saw as the destructive effects of religious thinking during his times. Contrary to what they claim, religious people actually promote fear and suffering according to Epicurus. The threat of supernatural punishment after death is the greatest source of human unhappiness, he taught, and so his philosophical system is premised on the assumption that if there are gods, it is much better for us to act as if they take no interest in human affairs whatsoever. This idea may have first taken root during his time as a youth when he was forced by his mother to lend her assistance as she traveled from place to place making money as a soothsayer and spell-caster. It was then that the young Epicurus encountered people whose fear and anxiety concerning their fate after death made them willing to spend large sums of money in order to try to appease the gods with rituals and magical incantations. Perhaps being close to the operations of his mother's business exposed him to the sorts of experiences and behind-the-scenes details that so easily lead to disenchantment. Whatever the reason, he went on to formulate a philosophy firmly rooted in the here and now world of material existence and which denied any power to supernatural entities.

Epicurus was a follower of the Presocratic atomist Democritus, and like Democritus Epicurus believed that nature is made up only of atoms in motion. Atoms, because they have weight, fall downward. Once in a while, however, they may swerve unexpectedly, thus causing the sorts of collisions that ultimately lead to the creation of objects. As atoms collide and stick together, things come into existence. As atoms fall away from one another, the objects that they constituted decay and disappear. Humans, as part of nature, are also made up of conglomerations of atoms, and when humans die, like all material things, their atoms are dispersed into the void. There is no such thing as an afterlife and so there is nothing to fear in death. When you die, you simply cease to exist as a unified combination of atoms. "Death is nothing to us; for that which has been dissolved lacks sensation; and that which lacks sensation is no concern to us."[25] It is best then to enjoy life to its fullest while you are here in the world and to reap as much pleasure and happiness as possible while you are able to do so.

Epicurus taught that the goal of life is happiness. But what is happiness? Epicurean philosophy takes a very straightforward approach to this question. Happiness is the same as pleasure, and pleasure is just the absence of pain. Pain and pleasure, furthermore, can be accounted for in terms of atomic collision. The human soul is made of very fine and subtle particles. We perceive things when other particles from our environment make impact with our sense organs and transmit their motions to our souls. When these motions are violent and disturbing, we feel pain. On the other hand, when our soul atoms regain their natural arrangements, we experience pleasure. True pleasure, then, is a static state of the soul in which the atoms that compose us remain undisturbed and at peace. If the point of life is to be happy by maximizing pleasure and minimizing pain, then we should seek to withdraw as far as possible from the sorts of experiences that stir up our souls and thus cause upset. We should avoid all of those entanglements and commitments in life that involve us in activities causing pain. If we could live life in such a manner that we never encountered painful situations, then we would be truly happy.

Though we cannot completely withdraw from the world, Epicurus advocated that we should at least withdraw as much as possible. Like the Cynics, he claimed that there are certain needs and desires that are natural and some that are unnatural. Unnatural needs and desires agitate our souls to the point where, instead of experiencing a sense of pleasurable tranquility, we instead experience tension and anxiety. If we could avoid the unnatural desires, then we could keep ourselves from becoming involved in activities that are destined to bring us more pain than pleasure. Natural desires, on the other hand, cause pain if they are not satisfied, and so we should devote our energies toward fulfilling these desires in a moderate fashion. The key here is moderation. The desire for food is a natural desire that brings pleasure if fulfilled. However, overindulgence in food brings more pain than pleasure and is thus unnatural. When you eat too much you get a sore stomach and become fat and unhealthy. This only multiplies pain and so brings unhappiness. Likewise with sex; although sex is a natural desire, if you overdo it and become obsessed with sex you get entangled in relationships that bring quite a lot of heartache. It is best, thought Epicurus, to avoid such problems by moderating indulgences and learning to enjoy and appreciate the simple, natural pleasures that can be fulfilled easily. Those desires that tend to lead to more and more desires are unnatural and vain and so should be avoided. Think of how some people pursue fame and fortune, never resting satisfied with what they have. According to Epicurus, such individuals will never be happy.

The Epicurean emphasis on happiness and moderation should remind us of Aristotle. Yet unlike Aristotle, Epicurus taught that humans should seek their happiness away from the public and political world. Involvement in the public world only serves to stir us up and to mix us up in relationships that inevitably lead to more pain than pleasure in the long run. For this reason, Epicurus set up a commune where his friends and followers could live lives of "repose," taking it easy and relaxing in peace and quiet. The state of mind that resulted from a life of untroubled repose and friendship was ataraxia. The state of ataraxia is a mental condition of serenity and peacefulness achieved when all unnecessary desires are extinguished, all necessary desires are satisfied, and all anxiety and worry melt away, leaving the Epicurean happy and content with the world as it is.[26]

Skepticism

Ataraxia was a state of mind advocated by many Hellenistic philosophers, though different groups had different takes on how it was to be achieved. According to the Skeptics, for instance, it was the desire to know the Truth that led to anxiety and upset, and so to give up that desire was to become truly happy. The founder of Greek Skepticism was Pyrrho of Elis (ca. 360–270 B.C.). Inspired by the

teachings of Socrates, Pyrrho went so far as to claim that we can never know anything for certain. Because striving to understand that which is beyond our comprehension can only lead to frustration, Pyrrho advocated the complete withdrawal of judgment on factual matters. We should, he claimed, cease to worry about truth or falsehood and instead simply renounce such evaluations, remaining content with uncertainty. Pyrrho took this so seriously according to some accounts that when his own teacher was in danger of drowning in a bog, Pyrrho refused to pull him out because "There was no way to know for certain whether such action would result in help or harm."[27] In this, it seems as though the Skeptic's pursuit of ataraxia comes quite close to the Stoic's pursuit of apathia. Mental detachment is what leads to happiness in both cases, but in both cases it is a strange kind of happiness that results, consisting of the elimination of any sort of positive conception of pleasure, feeling, or knowledge. Happiness becomes a complete withdrawal of mental effort and culminates in an attitude of aloofness.

We find another way in which Skepticism harmonizes with Stoicism in its stance toward the conventions of society. According to Pyrrho, because the Truth cannot be known, there is no reason to question the conventional wisdom of one's own culture. One set of laws, rules, or morals is as good as any other because none of them can be justified, and so people should not rebel against the standards of the community to which they belong. Rather, Pyrrho taught, one should follow convention and not cause any social upset. Whereas the Cynics pointed to the mere conventionality of social rules as a reason for their abolition, Pyrrho followed the Stoic example more closely. As in Stoicism, the Pyrrhonic Skeptic submits to playing his conventional role within society, not making any waves and supporting a conservative attitude toward social norms. Because no justification for the ultimate truth or falsehood of anything can be discovered, we should just accept everything the way it is. One could not imagine a belief system more perfectly suited to maintaining the oppressive demands of Roman imperial rule.

Skeptical philosophy was further propagated by Pyrrho's student Timon (320–230 B.C.), who developed an argument to show clearly why it is that any knowledge of the Truth is impossible. Timon's reasoning focuses on a very Socratic issue; namely, the potentially ongoing nature of our investigation into the world. Any argument that claims to establish the Truth, Timon observed, must be based upon a set of premises. Yet any set of premises may be questioned, and so we may legitimately demand a justification that establishes the premises themselves as true. But such justification must itself take the form of an argument, which in turn must be based upon a set of premises. Because we can demand an argument in support of any premise set, there is no way that we can establish a final justification, once and for all, for any statement of Truth. All we can hope for is endless argumentation. I wonder if anyone asked Timon whether this criticism also applied to his own skeptical argument!

The legacy of Skepticism was carried on, after the death of Timon, by members of Plato's Academy, who came to emphasize those aspects of Platonism that teach us to distrust our senses and to be suspicious of the appearances of things in the world. Under this "New Academy" there was a drift toward the view that the best we can do in trying to understand reality is to calculate probabilities. The more consistently that we have experiences of a certain type, the more likely we are to accept those experiences as revealing some stable condition of the world. If I strike my hand with a hammer fifty times and if after each strike of the hammer I feel a sensation of pain, then I can come to the tentative, probabilistic conclusion that striking my hand with a hammer causes me pain. This is not a certain fact, according to the Academic Skeptics, but it is more likely than not to be true; further, this is the best that we can do in our attempts to establish knowledge. In the end, members of the Academy taught that nothing was absolutely true, only more or less probable. Gone was the ambitious and quasi-religious hope for a mystical awakening to the Good. In its place was an empirical and quasi-scientific method for establishing probabilities.

It is doubtful whether it is even proper to call the Skeptics "philosophers" in the sense that we are using the term in this book. If a philosopher is a lover of wisdom, and so a person concerned with discovery of the Truth, then it would appear that in Skepticism we have the antithesis of philosophy. The Skeptics have given up on the Truth in order to alleviate the suffering and anxiety that are involved in its endless pursuit. For them, peace of mind is the most important

---

B o x 5.2 Contemporary Epicureans and Skeptics

A number of popular products, Web sites, magazines, and associations exist today that continue to promote ideas inspired by Skepticism and Epicureanism.

Though perhaps straying from Epicurus' advice concerning moderation in food and drink, the Web site epicurean.com has links to hundreds of gourmet recipes.

Epicure Magazine, published in Boston, Massachusetts, is a popular food periodical found in many supermarkets.

Epicurean brand kitchen utensils and cutting surfaces borrow the ancient Greek philosopher's name as a marketing gimmick to sell cooking implements.

Epicurious.com bills itself as a Web site "for people who love to eat."

Skeptic magazine and Skeptic.com are publications of the Skeptics Society that, in their own words, are devoted to "promoting science and critical thinking."

The Skeptic magazine (skeptic.org.uk) states that it is committed to "Pursuing Truth through Reason and Evidence."

The Committee for Skeptical Inquiry (csicop.org) publishes *Skeptical Inquirer*. Both the committee and the magazine focus on debunking claims of supernatural and paranormal occurrences.

thing toward which to strive. Distress and wonder are simply annoyances that upset mental quietude.

SUICIDE AND HELLENISTIC PHILOSOPHY

The desire to flee from the world and to retreat from the pains and frustrations of reality ultimately became so pronounced in Hellenistic thought that even suicide became a legitimate option for many of these figures. The "philosophical suicide" of this period of time was not necessarily the sort of suicide that we are familiar with today. Normally we think of suicide as something that is provoked by despair and sadness, but for many of the Hellenistic philosophers suicide was instead conceived as an avenue to increased happiness and joy. One argument in favor of suicide originated in Epicurean presuppositions with the following line of reasoning: if there is no afterlife, then in death there is nothing, including anxiety or pain, and if the point of life is to eliminate anxiety and pain, then death would be the ultimate good. Because pleasure is just the absence of pain, and because in death there is the complete absence of pain, then in death there is, by definition, the absolute form of pleasure! You can see how this argument relies on the negative conception of pleasure that was offered by Epicurus and his followers. If we think of pleasure as a positive quality in life, then this entire argument falls apart. However, for the Epicureans, pleasure is not a positive quality in the world but rather a state that is reached when we withdraw from pain and anxiety. The Epicurean philosopher Hegesias (third century B.C.), who was known as "The Death Persuader," taught this very thing, and as a result many of his students killed themselves. His public lectures, consequently, were suppressed by the authorities and he was forbidden to continue teaching. Nevertheless, Hegesias himself is reported to have lived to a very old age.

Another argument for suicide originated in the ideas of the Stoics and seems also to have been advocated by some Skeptics. Recall that both of these schools of thought promoted the cultivation of a state of mind: apathia in the case of the Stoics and ataraxia in the case of the Skeptics. Because the struggle to achieve these mental states was so difficult, anyone who was successful in their apprehension would naturally want to avoid backsliding into the previous condition of anxiety and worry. To avoid such a decline, then, it was held by some Stoics and Skeptics that one should kill oneself once apathia or ataraxia were grasped. Because there is nowhere to go but down once you have reached the highest state of mental perfection, why run the chance of losing the very thing you have worked so long and hard to achieve? By killing yourself you become assured that your life ends in perfection and not on a sour note.

Throughout the Hellenistic and Roman periods there are many stories of individuals who killed themselves in pursuit of bliss. Lest we think of this as a completely bizarre notion, we should not forget that among the devoutly religious even today, one must die as a prerequisite for entry into Heaven. We should also remember that many of these Hellenistic thinkers saw themselves as following in the footsteps of Socrates, who himself chose what he believed to be a noble death over a life of tedium and oppression. The term "euthanasia," in fact, comes from this Greek notion of a "good death" that is freely chosen and carried out in order to minimize pain and suffering. Today many people advocate euthanasia in cases of extreme and incurable physical suffering, but there remains a hesitancy on the part of most people to likewise advocate it in cases of mental suffering. Why is this so? Perhaps it is because most people today believe that there is normally a cure for mental unhappiness and that those who experience psychological torment can be helped through drugs or therapy. Those Hellenistic philosophers who advocated suicide, however, would dispute this contention. According to them, life, by its very nature, produces suffering. There is no cure other than the end of life. Sophocles seems to have anticipated this lament when he wrote, "Never to have lived is best, ancient writers say; never to have drawn the breath of life, never to have looked into the eye of day. The second best's a gay goodnight and quickly turn away."[28]

WONDER AND DISTRESS IN HELLENISTIC PHILOSOPHY

To sum up the discussion in this chapter, we should note that all of the philosophies of the Hellenistic period share at least a couple of characteristics with one another. First of all, they exhibit a great degree of weariness with the world. As has already been noted, the period of history during which these philosophies were formulated was a time in which there was a decline in Greek power and autonomy and an increase in exposure to foreign ideas and philosophies. Perhaps this shift had some role in making Western thinkers experience feelings of helplessness and a loss of control over their own destinies. All of the major Hellenistic thinkers seem to express a sense of passivity and pessimism about their own ability to control the changes taking place in the world. It might thus seem better to just withdraw from that world and find happiness and peace within one's own mind.

This leads to the second thing that should be noted. In all of these philosophies there is an emphasis on perfecting the self. When people feel unable to control the world around them they may seek to control the one thing that is always within their power. They may instead seek to change their attitude toward the world. For instance, if you come to the conclusion that you will never become a famous movie star, you might become depressed and sad that the world is so unfair. On the other hand, you might just decide to give up on the desire for stardom and look for something that you can obtain. The Hellenistic philosophers taught that the one thing that we can all obtain is control over our own souls. If we focus our energies inward, disregarding all of the titillating distractions that the world has to offer, then we can become better and happier with ourselves.

Are the teachings we have surveyed in this chapter truly philosophical in the sense of cultivating a stance of wondrous distress? On the one hand, there seems to be something constructive and wondrous in the Hellenistic emphasis on self-perfection and the drive for peace of mind. The effort to gain control of one's own perspective and to change one's own attitude about the world is a useful and important skill to master, especially in times of cultural transition, change, and social chaos. The individual who is not able to find peace in the objective world cultivates a truly valuable skill in gaining control of the inner, subjective world of consciousness. Even in times of comparative social stability this sort of skill is important, as it encourages us to take responsibility for ourselves and how we live our lives. In this sense, the Hellenistic emphasis on the quest for peace of mind, whether it be in the form of cynical contentment, apathia, or ataraxia, represents a positive drive toward a better state of being. In setting up ideals to pursue, the Cynics, Stoics, Epicureans, and Skeptics retain the spark of wonder, which is an indispensable ingredient in the forward movement of consciousness. This philosophical element of wonder is preserved in these figures insofar as the active commitment to, and aspiration toward, a higher state of development remains active in their way of thinking.

On the other hand, the final state of being striven toward by the Hellenistic thinkers is one in which all development, activity, and aspiration come to a close. Contrary to the open-ended nature of purely philosophical thinking, among the Hellenistic thinkers the goal of life is not to struggle and strive endlessly for the Truth but to struggle and strive until such time as one's own mind is able to detach itself from the pains and frustrations of the world. While the notion of distress is clearly a predominant element of Hellenistic thought, this distress is seen as the world's main problem. It is something to be conquered, overcome, and left behind. In this way, these systems of thought remind us of religious teachings with their focus on curing human suffering and establishing a heaven on earth. In philosophical thinking, however, the element of distress acts as an ongoing motivation that spurs the individual to the perpetual expansion of his or her horizons. A sense of incompleteness and longing pushes the philosopher to continue a search that is endless in its scope. In this regard, it diverges from the religious emphasis on final answers and peace of mind. So, whereas in Hellenistic thinking we certainly encounter the theme of distress and dissatisfaction, it is always with an eye toward the alleviation and elimination of this distress and dissatisfaction. The most extreme manifestation of this world-weary drive for quietude is in the advocacy of suicide by many Hellenistic figures. Even death, it seems, is a more desirable option for some than a life without final answers.

To the extent that wonder and distress remain present in the Hellenistic thinkers, we may consider their work to be philosophical in nature. They do, nevertheless, have a tendency to emphasize a way to move beyond the distress of this world, and to that extent, we also find an element of religion in their thinking. In the doctrines of the New Academy, additionally, we find a kind of scientific solution to the issue of mental anguish. Being a philosopher is a matter of degree, perhaps, and it may be most charitable simply to point out that most of these Hellenistic thinkers are philosophers of a sort, but none of them is a philosopher to the same degree as the person from whom they took inspiration.

In reacting against the authority of Plato and Aristotle, and in trying to recapture the spirit of Socrates, the Cynics, Stoics, Epicureans, and Skeptics contributed much that is of value to the world of human culture and also prepared the way for the emergence of a religion/philosophy that was just beginning to develop during the ascent of the Roman Empire. This system of thought is Christianity. Christianity did not develop in a vacuum, and it did not spring into existence out of no-where. Rather, it slowly gained root and blossomed through the efforts of a whole lineage of prophets, martyrs, saints, and philosophers who interpreted and developed the message of a man named Jesus. Many of these Christian thinkers were influenced by the insights and reasoning of the Hellenistic philosophers.

QUESTIONS FOR DISCUSSION

1. What are some of the historical, cultural, and sociological influences that might have been involved in the rise of the various Hellenistic philosophies?

2. Cynicism, Stoicism, Epicureanism, and Skepticism are all terms that still have current usage today. How do the modern uses of these terms differ from the ancient philosophies themselves? Are there aspects of our own culture that are similar to the culture out of which these ideas emerged?

3. Diogenes was supposedly called "Socrates gone mad" by Plato. Why? What aspects of Diogenes' message mirror the message of Socrates? In what ways was he different from Socrates?

4. The Stoic philosophy has many characteristics of a state religion. What are some of those characteristics? Are there any aspects of Stoicism that seem anti-religious to you?

5. The Stoic state of mind called "apathia" and the Epicurean state of mind called "ataraxia" share some common characteristics, but they also seem distinct. Discuss the commonalities and the differences between them.

6. How is ancient Greek Skepticism both similar and distinct from modern scientific skepticism?

7. What sorts of similarities do you detect between the various Hellenistic philosophies and Eastern philosophies/religions like Hinduism, Buddhism, and Taoism?

8. Cynicism, Stoicism, Epicureanism, and Skepticism are sometimes referred to as "decadent" philosophies that promote pessimism and negativity. Why is this? Do you think this is a correct assessment of these philosophies?

NOTES

1. Plato, *Apology*, 23b.
2. Stanley Rosen, *Hermeneutics as Politics* (New Haven, CT: Yale University Press, 2003), p. 59.
3. Rosen would dispute this.
4. Plato, *Symposium*, 204a.
5. W. L. Reese, *Dictionary of Philosophy and Religion* (Atlantic Highlands, NJ: Humanities Press, 1980), p. 116.

6. It is interesting to note that Socrates himself swore "by the dog" at times in order to emphasize his point. See Plato, *The Republic*, Book III.399.e.3.

7. Aristotle, *Metaphysics*, 1043.b.24.

8. The stories about Diogenes that follow are taken from the accounts of a different Diogenes, namely, Diogenes Laertius, in his book *Lives of Eminent Philosophers*, R. D. Hicks (trans.) (Cambridge, MA: Harvard University Press, 1942).

9. Bertrand Russell, *A History of Western Philosophy* (New York: Simon and Schuster, 1972), p. 253.

10. A. A. Long, *Hellenistic Philosophy* (Berkeley and Los Angeles: University of California Press, 1986), p. 148.

11. Long, for these reasons, claims that it is a mistake to call the Stoics simple materialists. He writes, "The Stoics are better described as vitalists." *Hellenistic Philosophy*, p. 154.

12. S. Samsbursky, *Physics of the Stoics* (Princeton, NJ: Princeton University Press, 1987), p. 23.

13. This reminds one of recent speculations in modern chaos theory, particularly the Butterfly Effect. "Unless we know the initial state of a system to infinite precision, our predictability soon evaporates. This extreme sensitivity on the initial data implies that the circulatory patterns of the atmosphere might be ultimately decided by the most minute disturbance. It is a phenomenon sometimes called the butterfly effect, because the future pattern of weather might be decided by the mere flap of a butterfly's wings." Paul Davies, *The Cosmic Blueprint* (New York: Simon and Schuster, 1989), p 52.

14. Something similar to the Hindu and Buddhist notion of karma seems to be operating here.

15. This argument would later be resurrected by the German philosopher Friedrich Nietzsche as a cornerstone of his own philosophy. See, for example, §341 of Nietzsche's *The Gay Science*, Walter Kaufmann (trans.) (New York: Random House/Vintage Books, 1974).

16. In this we can detect the influence of Semitic and Hindu cosmological doctrines.

17. Eccles. 3:15.

18. Russell, *History of Western Philosophy*, p. 255.

19. Marcus Aurelius, *Meditations* (Roslyn, NY: Walter J. Black, 1945), p. 20.

20. Epictetus, *A Manual for Living* (San Francisco: HarperCollins, 1994), pp. 27–28.

21. Long, p. 207. In this we can see that Russell was incorrect to write that in Stoicism "Not only bad passions are condemned, but all passions." Russell, p. 255.

22. The Taoist idea of *wu wei* is very similar to this. Perhaps there is an influence?

23. Marcus Aurelius, p. 21.

24. The basis of Buddhism lies in the assertion of "Four Noble Truths": (1) Life is suffering; (2) Suffering is caused by desire; (3) If desire is extinguished, suffering will end; (4) Desire can be extinguished by following the Eight-Fold Path. See Huston Smith, *The World's Religions* (San Francisco: HarperCollins, 1991), pp. 99–119.

25. Quoted in Long, *Hellenistic Philosophy*, p. 49.

26. There is, in fact, a modern anti-anxiety medication still in use by doctors today called hydroxyzine that is sold under the brand name "Atarax."

27. Wallace Matson, *A New History of Philosophy*, Vol. 1 (New York: Harcourt Brace Jovanovich, 1987), p. 171.

28. Sophocles, *Oedipus at Colonus*, Third Choral Ode.

Chapter 6
Medieval Philosophy

© Juneko J. Robinson

What is a covenant and how is it important to Judaism, Christianity, and Islam? What sorts of philosophical elements do we find in the teachings of Abraham and Jesus? What is the difference between the *a priori* and *a posteriori* arguments for God's existence? What is the Ontological Argument? What are Aquinas' Five Arguments for God's existence? How did Islamic thinkers contribute to the development of philosophy in Medieval times? How do religion and philosophy overlap in the Medieval world?

By the year 133 B.C., the Roman Empire had conquered the entire Mediterranean world, but by around A.D. 300 this empire was already beginning to crumble. The Romans came to call the Mediterranean Sea *mare nostrum,* or "our sea," and they swept it clear of pirates, policing its shores, thus allowing safe travel and trade throughout the region. In addition, they built roads and brought political stability to an area that previously had seen much war and chaos. Despite all of this, the Romans were not universally applauded by the people whose lands they occupied. In particular, we know that there existed a great deal of animosity and distrust between the Romans and the Jews, a people that inhabited a strip of land called Palestine, located on the eastern coast of the Mediterranean Sea. The Jews considered Palestine to be their promised land, given to them by their God, "Yahweh," consequent to the repeated exile, suffering, and struggle that they had endured over the course of their history. Through all of this upheaval, and despite many lapses, the Jews had striven to fulfill the obligations of their covenant, or contract, with God, and in so doing they affirmed their status as a chosen people.

THE PATRIARCH ABRAHAM AND THE COVENANT WITH GOD

As a chosen people, the Jews believed that they possessed a special relationship with God. This relationship was not one that granted them moral superiority over non-Jews, but was, rather, one that placed special and stringent responsibilities on their community. The Jews were obligated to recognize only one God, to offer tributes and sacrifices to that God, and to observe various dietary restrictions and ritual duties that periodically reaffirmed their allegiance to Yahweh. In this sense, the Jews saw themselves as the conscience of humankind; a living reminder to the world that all humans owe gratitude to their maker. According to the Jewish holy text, the Torah, God willfully created all human beings as a mixture of earth and spirit: "[T]he Lord God formed man of dust from the ground, and breathed into his nostrils the breath of life; and man became a living being."[1] However, it was Abraham who was the first human being to commit himself in a serious and single-minded fashion to living according to God's law and plan for the universe. This was demonstrated by Abraham's willingness to sacrifice his son when asked to by God[2] and to obey a command to circumcise himself and his male children. These acts demonstrate quite a rare and unshakable trust in God's plan, to say the least! While other human beings selfishly pursued wealth, fame, and personal

© Juneko J. Robinson

power, forgetting that they owe everything to God, only Abraham kept Yahweh in the forefront of his mind at all times. For this reason, Abraham is considered to be the first of the Jews, and his descendants were thus destined to receive Palestine as "an everlasting possession."[3]

But Abraham was not simply a submissive instrument of God's will. A covenant, by its very nature, requires that there be two sides to an agreement, and both of these sides have a duty to uphold their own part of the bargain. After he had demonstrated his own commitment to Yahweh, Abraham also demanded of God that He fulfill a set of obligations and remain open to disagreement and debate with those who love Him. We can see this illustrated in the story of Sodom and Gomorrah, where Abraham enters into an active negotiation with God, actually changing one of God's plans through the use of reason and argumentation. In this instance, Yahweh was displeased with the inhabitants of the cities of Sodom and Gomorrah because of their sinfulness and so He told Abraham that He was going to completely obliterate them. Abraham was horrified by this pronouncement and bargained with God, getting Him to agree, finally, that if he were able to find ten good men in Sodom, the cities would be spared. As it eventually turned out, there were not even this many good men in the city, and so Yahweh "rained on Sodom and Gomorrah brimstone and fire,"[4] killing everyone. What is interesting about this story, however, is not the fact that God carried through with His intentions, but that He listened to Abraham at all and, indeed, was willing to alter His plans for Sodom and Gomorrah according to the reasoning that Abraham articulated. Thus, the first Jew, the model for all others to come, was not just a passive and unthinking follower of Yahweh. Rather, Abraham was a committed, yet critical, individual who attached himself to a God who is, in essence, reasonable and willing to enter into negotiation with His followers.[5] This illustrates something that is important to keep in mind. The Jewish faith, and its Christian and Islamic descendants, from the very beginning expressed high regard for the active use of intellect, reason, and the critical faculties, even at the same time that an equal emphasis was placed on the importance of faith in God's wisdom. Members of this Abrahamic tradition are expected to have faith in God but never to use this as an excuse to stop thinking and questioning or to stop utilizing the rational capacity that God has breathed into us. This fact will be key in helping us to understand the later development of philosophy in the Medieval world.

JESUS

Under Roman rule, the Jews in Palestine were subject to oppression that was made especially distasteful by virtue of the fact that it occurred in the very land that God had given to them in recognition of Abraham's loyalty. Although the Romans did attempt to make some special accommodations for Jewish monotheistic belief, ultimately it became clear that the worldly demands of Roman imperial rule were expected to outrank the Jews' allegiance to Yahweh. This culminated in attempts by corrupt Roman governors to steal from Jewish religious funds, the destruction of the Second Temple in Jerusalem, and eventually the slaughter and murder of Jews who rebelled against such injustices. The Romans proved themselves to be no friends of the Jews or of anyone else who challenged their power and authority. In the face of such ruthlessness, the Jews, like many other oppressed people under the Romans, despaired of their own ability to throw off the yoke of their oppressors. Among many Jews,

© Juneko J. Robinson

consequently, there developed the hopeful idea that a messiah, or savior, like Moses or David, would again arrive to rescue them from their terrible state of subjection. Thus, the scene was set for the arrival of Jesus, a Jewish teacher who promised his people release from the suffering of this world and entrance into the Kingdom of God.

As we have seen, many people within the Hellenistic culture of the Roman Empire were ready to receive a message like that preached by Jesus. As with many of the philosophies that were popular at the time, Jesus taught that conventional social constraints were a barrier to true happiness. He taught, in fact, that one need only love God and one's neighbor in order to be saved and transported to a realm of heavenly bliss.[6] Though this world is full of pain and suffering, through love and purification of the soul the individual could overcome and leave behind this substandard earthly world, ultimately to emerge into another world of eternal peace and happiness (somewhat like the state of ataraxia).

Furthermore, it appears that Jesus wanted to reinvigorate in his followers the spirit of critical, rational thinking that had been practiced by Abraham but that had largely been forgotten by the convention-bound Jews and Romans of his day. This is apparent from the fact that Jesus delivered his message in the form of parables. Parables are stories that illustrate and communicate important moral or religious lessons in a nonliteral fashion, thus requiring those listening to them to exercise their own skills of interpretation. Though part of the reason why Jesus taught in parables was certainly to avoid persecution,[7] I think another, perhaps more important, reason was to cultivate in his followers the sorts of critical thinking skills that are involved in the exegesis and understanding of difficult texts. Jesus thus encouraged his followers to have faith in God at the same time that he encouraged them to think for themselves and to actively utilize the rational capacities that God gave them. This was the path to spiritual liberation.

The parable of the "sower of seeds" helps to illustrate this point. In the Gospels, Jesus tells a gathering of his followers a story about a sower who spreads seeds on the ground. Some seeds fall along the path unprotected and so are quickly eaten by birds. Some of these seeds fall on rocky ground where they immediately sprout and begin to grow but quickly die for lack of soil. Other seeds fall among thorns and cannot grow because they are crowded and choked out of existence. Finally, some seeds fall on fertile soil where they take root and develop in a healthy manner. Jesus tells his followers that the seeds in this parable represent his message. The first instance, where the seeds fall along the path, represents those unprotected from Satan, or the pretenders to wisdom, who are ready to pounce and "take away the word which is sown in them."[8] The second instance, where the seeds fall on rocky ground, represents those who are ready to uncritically accept the word of Jesus and who "immediately receive it with joy; and they have no root in themselves, but endure for a while; then, when tribulation or persecution arises on account of the word, immediately they fall away."[9] The third instance, where the seeds fall among thorns, represents those who are distracted by the temptations of the world around them and so ignore the message. Finally, the last instance, where the seeds fall on fertile ground, represents those who listen to the message, allow it to penetrate into their minds slowly, the way that a seedling takes root, and to blossom naturally. In this last case, Jesus seems to be telling his followers to think about the lessons that he is delivering, to turn them over in their heads and to contemplate them intelligently. Those who uncritically accept a teaching, those who don't understand things on their own terms, will not absorb the full depth and meaning of what is communicated. The message won't "take root" in their minds. To be an unthinking follower, then, is not the point. The point is to exercise one's own rationality and to see the Truth for oneself, not simply to follow the dictates and dogmas of those in power.

This message was met by established Romans and conservative Jews as a challenge to their worldly authority. It appears these mainstream forces feared that Jesus was a revolutionary figure who was preparing to usurp their power and overthrow their institutions. As a result, Jesus was captured, tortured, and executed in the standard Roman manner: crucifixion. Shortly after his burial, rumors began to circulate that Jesus had been resurrected, ascended to Heaven, and would shortly return to lead the righteous to salvation. It seemed to many that the messiah had finally arrived. As time passed, however, it became apparent that Jesus was not coming back immediately, and so the faithful resolved to prepare themselves for his eventual Second Coming. This preparation consisted of accepting Jesus as the son of God and as the savior of mankind. Those who did accept these ideas became known as "Christians," because they followed the *Christos*, which means "messiah" in Greek.

After Jesus' death, a number of individuals wrote down their memories of his message and life, but it was Paul of Tarsus who was the most influential interpreter and popularizer of Jesus' teachings. Whereas Jesus himself never broke completely with Judaism, Paul did, and it is he who really established Christianity as a new faith.[10] Paul taught that after his death, Jesus' spirit found a place on earth in the collective mass of the faithful. These followers, in fact, together constituted the mystical body of Christ. By joining with one another in union, the faithful became Jesus' body on earth. As Paul writes in the New Testament book Corinthians, "Do you not know that your bodies are members of Christ?"[11] Each individual believer's body was thought to contribute to the whole, and together this mass was the avenue through which the teachings of Jesus could be continued and propagate throughout the world. Such was the founding of the Catholic Church. In addition to the Jewish scripture that became the Old Testament, the new Christian faith accepted the books of the New Testament as a continuation and completion of God's covenant with human beings.[12] With this, Christians claimed that the special relationship between the Jews and Yahweh had been extended to all people, so that everyone now had an obligation to uphold the law of God.

Initially, Christians were horribly persecuted, but eventually Christianity usurped Stoicism and Epicureanism as the most popular faith of the Romans. Around A.D. 325 the Emperor Constantine made the practice of Christianity legal, and in 380 the Emperor Theodosius declared it to be the official religion of the Empire. In a way, the fears of those who had executed Jesus seemed to be coming true as his spiritual kingdom emerged to dominate and overthrow the old order. In a manner similar to Socrates in ancient Greece, the image of a man willing to oppose the conventions of the day, to think for himself, and to die for the Truth was a stinging reminder of humankind's spiritual alienation, and this notion proved to be a powerful force for centuries thereafter. The Catholic Church would become one of the most potent influences on human culture that the world has ever seen, and it was within this institution that the philosophies of various thinkers like St. Augustine, St. Anselm, and St. Thomas Aquinas were articulated. These Medieval philosophers were primarily concerned with carrying on the tradition, begun with Abraham, which attempted to understand God's design and plan for the world. Utilizing logic, argumentation, and reason, these thinkers attempted to clarify and make sense of the ideas in the Bible in order to understand the nature of God and our proper relationship to Him.

MUHAMMAD

After Augustine, but before the time of Anselm and Aquinas, in the year A.D. 570, a child was born in the city of Mecca, Saudi Arabia, who would grow up to have an immense and lasting influence on the worlds of religion, philosophy, and politics. This child was named Muhammad. Muhammad's father died before his son's birth, and Muhammad's mother died only six years after his birth. His grandfather died when Muhammad was eight. Thereafter, under his uncle's care, Muhammad settled into life as a sheep trader. He was eventually married, at the age of twenty-five, to Kadija, a woman of forty who owned her own trading business. Out of these difficult and humble circumstances, Muhammad would mature to become the founder of Islam, a religion that today is second only to Christianity in its number of followers.

As an adult, Muhammad retreated each year to a cave at Mt. Hira in order to meditate and pray. In the year A.D. 610, on the seventeenth night of his retreat, Muhammad claimed he was visited by the Angel Gabriel who held him in an embrace and commanded him to "Recite!" After Muhammad protested that he was not a prophet, the angel demanded that he proclaim the Truth nonetheless. It was then, on what is now called "the Night of Power," that Muhammad began to recite and proclaim the words that would eventually constitute the text of the Islamic holy book, the Koran, a title which in Arabic means "the recitation." The words that flowed out of Muhammad's mouth on that night were not his own, he insisted, but the words of the one true God, "Allah":

1. Proclaim! (or read) in the name of thy Lord and Cherisher, Who created—

2. Created man, out of a (mere) clot of congealed blood;

3. Proclaim! And thy Lord is Most Bountiful—

4. He Who taught (the use of) the Pen—

5. Taught man that which he knew not.

6. Nay, but man doth transgress all bounds,

7. In that he looketh upon himself as self-sufficient.

8. Verily, to thy Lord is the return (of all).

...

19. ... Bow down in adoration, and bring thyself the closer (to God)![13]

These words, recorded in Chapter 96 of the Koran, were not greeted by Muhammad with immediate or enthusiastic acceptance. His initial reaction was to fear that he had lost his mind! After receiving reassurance from his wife Kadija, however, Muhammad accepted that he had indeed been chosen as God's messenger, and so for the next twenty-three years God's words came pouring out of him. These words, written down and compiled by those who were his followers, eventually became the text of the Koran.

The Koran is claimed by the faithful to be a continuation, as well as the culmination, of the story told throughout the course of the Old and New Testaments. In the Koran, Jews and Christians are referred to as "People of the Book"[14] because they are believers in the books of the Bible. Both Jews and Christians worship the one true God, which is the God of Abraham and which is also the same God who spoke through Muhammad. However, whereas the Jews and Christians trace their lineage to the bloodline that passes from Abraham through Isaac, Muslims (followers of Islam) trace their own lineage in the bloodline that passes from Abraham through Ishmael, who is the son that Abraham produced with his servant, Hagar. Jews, Christians, and Muslims, therefore, are like siblings who share a common father and who worship the same deity. As is often the case with siblings, all three of these Abrahamic religions historically have had problems getting along with one another. From the perspective of Muslims, the problem with the Jews is that they are too exclusive in their understanding of their relationship with God. The Jews refer to themselves as a "chosen people," meaning that their own bond with God is special and unique. Muslims bristle at this idea and, like Christians, claim that anyone may enter into a covenant with the one true God. Unlike Christians, however, Muslims do not accept the idea of a trinity in which God, Jesus, and the Holy Spirit are aspects. "They do blaspheme who say: God is one of three in a trinity; for there is no God except One God."[15] Muslims insist on the unbroken unity and oneness of God to such a degree that it is considered blasphemous to conceive of anyone, be it Jesus or Muhammad, as the embodiment of God. Both Jesus and Muhammad are messengers of God, but they are not to be confused with God Himself.

According to Muslims, the revelations contained in the Old and the New Testaments, though they are in substance true, nonetheless have been distorted and garbled over time. The strength of the Koran, on the other hand, is that it not only contains God's latest revelations as they have been channeled through Muhammad, but it is also one and complete. Unlike the Old and New Testaments, which have been written by many hands over a long period of time, the Koran is the literal word of God, revealed over a short period of time through one person. For this reason, according to Muslims, it is the most complete and accurate account of God's Truth. Thus, while Muslims consider Jews and Christians to be their brothers, these People of the Book are a bit misguided and primitive in their understanding of God. The full Truth lies only in the Koran.

While the Koran contains the final and complete revelation of God, and while it claims to be the literal word of God, it is also the case that the literal word of God is not intended always to be taken literally. Surah 2:7 of the Koran states: "He it is Who has sent down to thee the Book: in it are verses basic or fundamental (of established meaning); they are the foundation of the Book: others are allegorical." In other words, while some fundamental truths are explicitly articulated in the Koran, some of what is written also is allegorical, meaning that some of its truths are expressed through the nonliteral use of metaphor and other sorts of figurative or symbolic language. Thus, it is not enough simply to take everything in the Book at face value. Rather, as with the parables of Jesus, one must exercise reason and critical thinking skills in order to understand and interpret the metaphorical and symbolic meanings of certain portions of God's message. This is where philosophy comes in.

The major contributions of Islamic philosophers during the Medieval era centered on three tasks. First, they rescued, translated, and then transmitted back to the West ancient Greek philosophical texts that would have otherwise been destroyed by antipagan Christian fanatics. Second, they attempted to apply the insights of Greek philosophy and logic to the interpretation of the Koran itself. Third, they were concerned with formulating reasonable arguments that would demonstrate to nonbelievers the Truth of Islam. These three accomplishments are incredibly important, and without Muslim philosophers like Al-Kindi, Al-Farabi, Avicenna, and Averroes, the world would have lost much of the ancient wisdom of the Greeks. Whether Jewish, Christian, or Muslim, it appears that faith and belief are not enough. Believers have always needed to think through and understand their religious faith and commitments. They are not content simply to believe; they also want to understand why they believe. Philosophy provides the motivation and tools with which to undertake this sort of exploration.

ST. AUGUSTINE

St. Augustine (354–430) was one of the first and most influential of the Medieval Christian thinkers. Today there are those who question Augustine's right to be called a philosopher, mostly because he was a religious man first and foremost.

© Juneko J. Robinson

Wallace Matson, for instance, claims that Augustine accepts the Christian God on faith and thus is not really a philosopher at all. "[T]o be philosophical [a worldview] must be defended by an appeal to reason, as distinguished from authority or tradition. Augustine's thought does not in general meet this requirement."[16] This same criticism, if true, would apply to all religious thinkers, who to one degree or another root their thinking in faith. The presumption that authors like Matson operate under holds that religion and philosophy are necessarily opposed to one another. Faith and reason are opposites, in this view, and anyone who holds a belief on faith must therefore, in a sense, be unreasonable or, in other words, unphilosophical. But while thinkers like Augustine may not seek to establish all of their beliefs by an appeal to reason, they do, in fact, use reason, argumentation, and logic as a way to clarify and analyze those beliefs that they already hold on the basis of faith, and so logic and reason are, contrary to what Matson and others claim, very important indeed in the articulation of their worldviews after all. One may be both philosophical and religious at different times, and this is, I think, the case with individuals like Augustine. Religion and philosophy are not necessarily contradictory but rather may complement and augment one another, overlapping and diverging at various points in the thinking process. A person may be both a religious thinker and a philosopher, and this is, I believe, the case with Augustine.

But even more, what is truly philosophical about figures like Augustine is not just their use of logic. After all, scientists also defend their worldviews through the use of reason as well, and not all of them are philosophers. What truly establishes Augustine and other Medieval thinkers as philosophers is their ongoing and unfulfilled aspiration and desire for Truth itself. Recall that philosophy, as described in this book's introduction, is more like an attitude than it is a set of techniques or tools. It is a "love of wisdom," and Augustine, no less than any of the Ancient Greeks we have surveyed so far, is an individual who exhibits this sort of philosophical drive and desire. As is demonstrated by the examples of Abraham, Jesus, and Muhammad, even religious people may be philosophical about their beliefs as long as they are willing to examine, question, and wonder about the truth of those things that they accept on faith. Authors like Matson draw too sharp a distinction between faith and reason, failing to recognize that the two usually (if not always) work in concert with one another. We cannot engage in philosophy unless we have faith that there is some sort of, as yet unrealized, Truth to philosophize about. To be truly philosophical is to desire Truth but also to feel oneself to be separated from a full understanding of that Truth. Philosophy takes place in that in-between zone where a desire for the absolute clashes with the limitations of the human intellect. As we will see, this is one of the major lessons that the Medieval thinkers have to teach us, and it is their concern with this issue that really highlights the philosophical nature of their writing. According to the Medievals, if you love wisdom, then you must have faith because God's truths are too big to be comprehended all at once. To paraphrase St. Anselm, to know anything we must first believe in something.

Augustine came to understand this last fact the hard way. He began his life as a non-Christian, pulled this way and that by his bodily desires and inclinations. As he writes in Book II of his autobiography, *Confessions*:

> I was among the foggy exhaltations which proceed from the muddy cravings of the flesh and the bubblings of first manhood. These so clouded over my heart and darkened it that I was unable to distinguish between the clear calm of love and the swirling mists of lust. I was storm-tossed by a confusing mixture of the two and, in my weak unstable age, swept over the precipices of desire and thrust into the whirlpools of vice.[17]

As a youth, Augustine experienced this rush of confusing and unsettling lower desires and realized that if left to their own devices, they threatened to pull him away from any sort of higher calling. In all human beings, the bodily cravings for sex, food, and pleasure are the sorts of things that are necessary to a certain extent, but they may destroy us spiritually if we allow them to be the sole driving forces of our lives. We all know people who pursue this sort of hedonistic lifestyle, and very rarely (if ever) do such people seem to be truly happy, and even more rarely do they seem to have acquired any degree of wisdom. Such people are more like animals than humans, and it is only when they learn to set aside the desire for immediate, bodily gratification that they might begin to develop their higher capacities. Even the Cynics and the Epicureans recognized this fact of human life. Augustine, though acquainted with the philosophical thoughts of the Greeks, found their ideas too difficult initially and so drifted away from the wisdom of the ancients toward the teachings of Mani, a religious leader who preached that the world is a battlefield upon which the forces of good and evil fight for control. For Augustine this was, perhaps, the first step toward understanding and coming to terms with his own difficult situation. If the world was characterized by a process of struggle between opposing forces, then maybe this would explain why he felt such a great degree of inner turmoil and torment. Perhaps all was not lost, and there was hope that the force of good within him might ultimately triumph over the force of evil.

Despite the hope that he found in Manichaeanism, Augustine eventually became frustrated with its actual doctrines and he lost confidence in his teachers, who he discovered "could not possibly give me a reasoned answer to what I wanted to know."[18] It seems, in particular, that many of the claims that the Manicheans made about the nature of astronomy were self-evidently false, and Augustine could not continue to adhere to a belief system that perpetuated such nonsense. Consequent to this disillusionment, Augustine turned back to Greek philosophy and the Bible for answers to his questions, and it was here, after a long and difficult inner struggle, that he began to find those answers.

The Question of Evil

The main question that Augustine harbored had to do with the existence of evil in the world. If it is true that God is all knowing, all powerful, and all good, then why do bad things happen? Why, for instance, do people suffer and die in a world that was created by a perfect God as described in the Bible? In Genesis, it is written that God made the world and that His creation is good. So where did evil come from? The Manicheans claimed that evil is an active, tangible force and that it causes earthly suffering by struggling with God for control of humankind and the world itself. The Devil opposes the Creator and exists as a force of darkness in a universe that would otherwise consist only of light. But why would a perfect God allow such a situation? If God truly is all-powerful, good, and perfect, then why does He permit evil to exist at all? This just didn't make rational sense to Augustine, and he believed that there had to be some sort of logical solution to this apparent paradox.

B o x 6.1 The Question of Evil Today

Augustine's treatment of the question of evil still has relevance today. The questions he raised are asked again and again every time awful catastrophes occur in our world.

The murder of six million Jews by the Nazis during World War II forced people to ask how it is that God could allow such a holocaust to occur. The PBS drama *God on Trial* depicts the prisoners in a Nazi concentration camp who stage a legal trial in which they charge God with "murder, collaboration with the enemy, and breach of contract with His chosen people" (www.jewishjournal.com/television/article/pbs_presents_god_on_trial_in_auschwitz_20081106/).

In the PBS program *Faith and Doubt at Ground Zero*, religious people of all faiths ponder the question "Where was God on 9/11?" Those who witnessed this terror attack felt themselves profoundly shaken and their previous understanding of God altered. Though very few religious believers lost faith altogether, they still struggled with how and why a good and all-powerful God would allow such a thing to occur (www.pbs.org/wgbh/pages/frontline/shows/faith/).

After the devastating 2010 earthquake in Haiti, Pat Robertson made public comments that attributed this disaster to his belief that the Haitian people must have "made a pact with the Devil." These comments sparked outrage, partly because the Haitians are Christian. Robertson's comments are perhaps a result of his own inability to understand why God would allow such a disaster to befall a Christian nation (www.cbsnews.com/8301-503544_162-6096806-503544.html).

After much contemplation, the answer finally came to him. The question of evil arises out of the obvious fact that all things in the world are subject to corruption and decay. Death, sickness, suffering—all of these ills are examples of a kind of distress that is caused by the deprivation of goodness. When people become sick, it is because they have lost their health. When people die, it is because they have lost their lives. When people suffer, it is because they have lost their happiness. The states of health, life, and happiness are good things that pass away, being replaced by things we consider evil. But we consider such things to be evil precisely because they represent a lack of that which they replace. So it is, Augustine reasons, that evil is simply a lack or absence of goodness. Evil, then, is not a positive quality in the world at all, but rather the nothingness that remains when all positive qualities are taken away. Because God created the world as good, everything that actually exists is good. Evil, which is just the absence of goodness, consequently does not exist as an actual, tangible thing. In short, evil does not exist! As we humans observe the decay and dissolution of objects in our world into nothingness, we only perceive this as evil because it draws our attention to the gap that may always develop between ourselves and God, the ultimate source of the world's goodness. This acts as a reminder that only God is absolutely good and that we benefit by aspiring to be closer to Him.

To clarify: if something is corruptible, then it must have some sort of good and positive quality that is subject to corruption. Because everything in the world is corruptible, it logically follows that everything in the world is good to the degree that it may be sapped of its goodness. Evil, then, does not exist as a thing in itself. If a thing became absolutely evil, it would "cease to exist altogether." Thus, evil "is not a substance,"[19] but a process of deprivation that leads to nothingness. This is the line of reasoning that led Augustine to understand how it is that the all-powerful, good, and knowing God that Jesus proclaimed could have created the world in the manner that it presently exists. God did not introduce evil into the world, and in fact the world as God created it is perfectly good. So it is that Augustine concludes, "It is the mark of an unsound mind to be displeased with any single thing in your creation, and so it was with me when I was displeased with many of the things which you made."[20] As we can see, Augustine's faith in God does not become weaker as a result of his philosophical thinking but rather becomes much stronger. It blossoms by becoming firmly rooted in the fertile soil of his mind through the cultivation of logic, reasoning, and rational contemplation. In this, Augustine continues a tradition of philosophical thinking that not only reflects the concerns of the ancient Greeks but those of Abraham and Jesus as well.

Thomas Altizer writes, "Although seldom recognized, Augustine is of overwhelming importance in Western philosophical thinking, for he was the first thinker to draw forth and to understand the subject of consciousness, or to understand the subject of consciousness as a true center and ground."[21] This is clearly indicated by Augustine's treatment of the problem of evil. As he articulates, evil turns out to be a quality attributable not to the objective world of God's creation but to the subjective, time-bound world of the finite human mind. Our displeasure at certain aspects of reality is the result of an inability to understand how it is that all things harmonize and interconnect according to God's infinitely wise plan, and we are unable to understand God's overall plan for the universe precisely because we are not God but instead only finite consciousnesses within the universe that we seek to comprehend. Because we are inside of this world that has overflowed out of God's infinite goodness, we can't completely understand how it is that all of the pieces of this world fit together. It is like we are trying to understand the floor plan of a multistory skyscraper that is still under construction while we are locked in a room on the first floor. God is like the architect of that same building who already knows all of the steps that are necessary in order to make things come together properly. God, standing above and beyond the world of creation, sees the whole as a whole. Existing beyond time and space, God understands everything at once. Whereas the history of the world unfolds for us like an ongoing construction project, for God the history of the world is like a blueprint in which all relevant details are present simultaneously and understood to contribute to the comprehensive excellence of his intended project. Our consciousness is too puny to comprehend all of creation at once the way God does, and so we can only approach it piece by piece and moment by moment. Thus, when something appears evil to us, it does so only as the result of our own intellectual failing.

Augustine writes that those who can't understand the goodness of God's creation "do not yet understand how these things are made by you and in you, and they are trying to taste eternity while their mind is still fluttering about in the past and future moments of things."[22] The problem we have as finite creatures is that we cannot comprehend the whole of God's plan for the world once and for all. We think in terms of past, present, and future, while these distinctions do not exist for God. Augustine is, in this regard, making a point that would be rediscovered hundreds of years later when Immanuel Kant, Albert Einstein, and Edmund Husserl would speculate on the relativity of the concept of time. Time, according to Augustine, is a quality of the human mind, not of the world outside the human mind. For the world as it exists in itself, there is no passage from past to future. Being itself is one and whole and unchanging, and in fact, for Augustine, Being itself is equivalent to God Himself.[23] As we aspire to understand God, then, we aspire to understand Being, yet because we view the world through the lens of time, we must always fall short of total and complete comprehension. Yet, with the use of pure reason, we can begin to grasp something of the general form of God and the world that He has brought into existence.

The world that we live in was not created in order to alleviate some sort of want or imperfection in God's nature, according to Augustine.[24] Because God is perfect, He has no wants or desires. Thus, God did not create the world because he had a desire to change or to manipulate the structure of reality, but simply because His goodness was so great that it "overflowed." "From the fullness of your goodness every created thing has its being...."[25] This overflowing goodness manifests itself as our world, and our world, therefore, is whole, perfect and complete as well. All of Being is dependent for its existence on God, and the more we come to learn about God, the more we understand Being itself. There is a distinctively Platonic influence in Augustine's thought here. Just as Plato claimed that the only evil is ignorance of the Good, Augustine claims that the only evil is ignorance of, or separation from, God. Goodness shines down and illuminates everything, according to Plato. Yet the farther away from Goodness that we find ourselves, the dimmer its light appears to us. Likewise, Augustine seems to be saying that God overflows into everything, yet the farther that we find ourselves from the source of this overflowing goodness, the less aware we are of its excellence. If we have faith in God, however, then we will be able to detect a relative degree of goodness in all things insofar as they fit into the pattern of creation as it emanates from the creator. In retaining our faith in God we may thereby attain knowledge of Being itself.

Augustine is considered to be primarily a theologian, yet the issues he is concerned with are eminently philosophical in nature. The manner in which he articulated his thoughts was, of course, greatly influenced by the culture of his day, but in substance the questions that he dealt with are the same sorts of questions that have always been of interest to philosophers: What is real? What is good? What is the structure of Being itself? How can I know Truth? In addressing these questions, Augustine exercised a philosophical mode of thinking in order to articulate a coherent and comprehensible Christian worldview. Starting from the revealed premises that he found in the Bible, he questioned, reasoned, and argued about the meaning and significance of those premises for life here on Earth. Even more importantly for our purposes, Augustine was a lover of Wisdom insofar as he aspired to understand the ultimate Truth of the universe. The fact that he called this Truth "God" is only of superficial note. Whatever term is used, a lover of Truth is also a lover of Wisdom and thus a philosopher. As exemplified in his ongoing struggle to understand God rationally, Augustine typifies that inexhaustible drive to grasp the nature of Being itself; something that constantly eludes full comprehension by human beings.

ISLAMIC CONTRIBUTIONS TO EARLY MEDIEVAL THOUGHT

Al-Kindi and Neoplatonism

The Library at Alexandria was established on the north coast of Egypt during the third century as a repository for important texts, including ancient Greek philosophical works. At its peak it was purported to contain 500,000 volumes. During the third century, a civil war erupted in Alexandria, and the main buildings of the complex were destroyed. In 380, at the decree of the Roman emperor Theodosius, Christianity was declared the official religion of the Roman Empire, and as a result the rest of the library was destroyed because it promoted pagan learning. It is only thanks to the efforts of Medieval Muslim scholars, who preserved and translated works of ancient Greek philosophy into Arabic, that many of these texts were rescued from complete oblivion. After the fall of the Roman Empire sometime around A.D. 476, and during the ensuing Islamic Golden Age, Islamic culture spread westward and Muslims established schools and research institutions, such as the library in Cordoba, Spain, which surpassed the Library at Alexandria in the number of books it owned. At these institutions, philosophical inquiry and investigation continued to be pursued while in the Christian world such exploration was discouraged.

Among the major figures of the Islamic Golden Age was Al-Kindi (ca. 800–873), an early Islamic philosopher who lived and worked in Baghdad during the eighth century A.D. He was a patron of the Caliphates of the Abbasid Dynasty, the second of the great Islamic dynasties to spread and consolidate the power of Islam. During the reign of the Abbasid dynasty, philosophy, science, and literature flourished, because these sorts of endeavors were encouraged by the rulers as a symbol of the culture's sophistication. Al-Kindi's output in this regard was purported to be voluminous (although most of this work has been lost). In the realm of philosophy, it appears that his most all-consuming concerns were with the issues of how to reconcile faith with reason and with the application of logic and rational principles to the interpretation of the Koran. Following the teachings of Aristotle, Al-Kindi claimed that philosophical understanding results from our ability to delineate the four causes (material, formal, efficient, and final) of particular things in the universe. The universe, being made up of both material and immaterial substances, furthermore, must be investigated both through the power of sensory observation as well as the power of "rational cognition."[26] Physics, Al-Kindi claimed, is the branch of learning that focuses on data derived from the senses while metaphysics is the branch of learning focused on data derived from pure thinking and meditation on "first principles."

One of Al-Kindi's most influential accomplishments, ironically, also involves a major mistake. He translated parts of *The Enneads*, a book by a second-century Neoplatonic writer named Plotinus (205–270), and wrongly attributed the original work to Aristotle.[27] Plotinus' Neoplatonic philosophy elaborates a mystical version of Plato's "divided line" analogy in which all things in the universe emanate from a divine, uniform, and unitary force called "the One." Like Plato's Good, the One is the source of all things in the world, and true knowledge ultimately comes when a person is able to comprehend this first principle through pure thinking and thus liberate himself or herself from the finitude of material existence. Al-Kindi, by mistaking the author of *The Enneads* for Aristotle, set a path for future Islamic philosophy in which elements of Platonism and elements of Aristotelianism became intertwined. All things come from the One, according to Al-Kindi, which is identical with the one God, Allah, who the Bible and the Koran state created the world out of nothing. Articulating many of the same Aristotelian arguments that we will shortly encounter in the work of St. Thomas Aquinas, Al-Kindi establishes the necessity of such a first cause of the universe on purely rational grounds. Because this first cause is prior and superior to everything else, it can "have no analogy with anything created."[28] This reinforces the dictum from the Koran that no images of God should ever be created, because such things would merely falsify and make finite that which is infinite and beyond representation. In this and other ways we find in the work of Al-Kindi an intermingling of the insights of Aristotle, Plato, and the Koran. These insights are interpreted in such a way that they are claimed to overlap and illuminate, but not contradict, one another. Reason and faith are complementary.

Al-Farabi

Al-Farabi lived during the tenth century A.D. He was born in Damascus and traveled between Baghdad, Egypt, and Syria. He is well known for his commentaries on Aristotle and his attempts to reconcile Platonism with Aristotelian philosophy.

Drawing influence from Al-Kindi, Al-Farabi proclaims the emanation of the world from the one God. God must exist, he argues, because there must be a first cause of motion in the universe and secondly because the contingent things of the world must find their root in something necessary. The world, he claims furthermore, "overflowed" out of God's perfection by a "necessity of nature."[29] This assertion runs contrary to the standard Islamic view that God created the world willingly and as a matter of choice, but it is a clear reflection of the Neoplatonic element that seems to pervade much of early Medieval Islamic philosophical speculation. Mankind, according to Al-Farabi, is the necessary culmination of a series of emanations out of God, and thus the cosmic "process of development is consumated"[30] in the human species. Humans, consistent with the Biblical and Koranic worldview, thus are designated by him as the pinnacle of God's creation.

Avicenna

Avicenna (980–1037), whose name is the Latinized version of the Arabic *Ibn Sina*, is unusual in the history of Islamic philosophy in that he wrote an autobiography. This act is frowned upon by some Muslims for placing too much emphasis on Avicenna the man and distracting attention from God or Muhammad. Nonetheless, Avicenna's autobiography might be thought of as following in the tradition of Augustine who also set his own life's story down in writing, not as an act of self-aggrandizement but as a way to show how God's wisdom and power manifested themselves through him. Avicenna tells us in his autobiography that by the age of ten he had completed his study of the Koran, and by the age of eighteen he had read Aristotle's book *Metaphysics* forty times. Despite this, he was unable to fully understand Aristotle's philosophy until he read the commentary of Al-Farabi. The development of Avicenna's philosophical views was thus highly influenced by the Neoplatonic perspective of his predecessor.

Like Al-Kindi and Al-Farabi, Avicenna establishes the existence of the one God from which all else emanates. God must exist, he argues, because anything that exists, as Aristotle had held, must arise as the result of a previous cause. Because causes can neither go back infinitely nor loop back on one another in an eternally recurring circle, there must be a first cause of the universe. This first cause is, of course, God. Once Avicenna establishes the existence of a Prime Mover, he proceeds to describe the production of the entire universe as the consequence of a necessary overflowing of God's essence. As was the case with Al-Farabi, this leads Avicenna to promote a deterministic view of the unfolding of reality. There are, he claims, "ten intelligences" or "emanations" that emerge from God to the visible, tangible world. These emanations terminate in the human mind and its reasoning capacity. This capacity, Avicenna concludes, gives humans the ability to mirror, dimly, the formal ideas that are found originating in God. This is how prophesy and revelation are possible. Rare, unusually reasonable individuals are able to perceive God's thoughts and then communicate them to other human beings. This is why Muhammad was able to transmit God's words that were later captured in the Koran. He had a highly developed and sensitive reasoning capacity.

Like Plato and Augustine, Avicenna insists that there is, in truth, no evil in the world. Because God is good, and because the world has emanated from God, the world is good. What appears evil to us is really just a matter of our ignorance, and there is always a perspective to be adopted from which what appears to be evil actually serves some sort of purpose in the grand design of the universe. All is as it must be.

Averroes

By the eighth century, Islam had extended its political and religious influence all the way into Spain, and the city of Cordoba became an exciting and vital center of Islamic learning. In the year 1126, Averroes (1126–1198), whose name is a Latinized version of the Arabic name *Ibn Rushd*, was born in Cordoba, and within this atmosphere he absorbed and contributed to the development and clarification of Aristotelian influences in Islamic thinking.

Averroes argued against those who claimed that philosophy was the enemy of religion. In response to a book titled *The Destruction of the Philosophers*, he wrote a book titled *Destruction of the Destruction*. According to Averroes, the ignorance of those who reject philosophy lies in their unwillingness to take seriously the explicitly stated assertion of the Koran that much of what appears in this holiest of books is allegorical in nature. As noted above, Surah 2:7 is clear: some verses in the Koran are meant to be interpreted figuratively and metaphorically. The techniques of philosophy are thus important in order to clarify and understand the nonliteral truths that are given voice in the Koran.

The bulk of Averroes' writings are commentaries on Aristotle, and one of his major concerns was to demonstrate that the ideas of Plato had mistakenly become mixed up with the ideas of Aristotle. He criticized both Al-Farabi and Avicenna on this account, emphasizing that the entire doctrine of emanation is a Neoplatonic, and not an Aristotelian, teaching. In clarifying this point, and in producing elaborate analyses and commentaries, Averroes' writings became indispensable not only to other Islamic philosophers but also to Christian philosophers who relied on Latin translations of his work in their own interpretations of Aristotle.

Islam spread west through the thirteenth century, and during this time many texts and ideas that had been lost during the suspicious and unphilosophical years of the Christian "Dark Ages" were reintroduced to the West. As Europe emerged out of its Dark Ages and into the Middle Ages, the works of Islamic philosophers like Al-Kindi, Al-Farabi, Avicenna, and Averroes would exert a powerful influence on Christian thinkers like St. Anselm and St. Thomas Aquinas, who were not hostile to the mixture of religious ideas with philosophical thinking. During this time, Christians established serious schools of learning and philosophy again began to prosper. This ushered in the era of Christian Scholastic Philosophy, a movement that enthusiastically pursued the application of logic and reason to the analysis of religious texts.

CHRISTIAN *A PRIORI* AND *A POSTERIORI*
ARGUMENTS FOR GOD'S EXISTENCE

None of the later Medieval thinkers, Christian or Muslim, ever seriously doubted that God exists any more than most of us doubt the existence of the objective world. God's reality was considered a piece of revealed truth that was obvious to anyone with the mental capacity to understand the meaning of the holy texts. However, according to Medieval philosophers, many people are too lazy or unthinking to plumb the deepest depths and meaning of this truth, and so Scholastic Christian philosophers, inspired by previous Islamic thinking, took it upon themselves to demonstrate, using the most absolutely clear, logical arguments possible, that God must exist.

St. Thomas Aquinas suggested that there are basically two general strategies that may be used in order to demonstrate the existence of God. The first strategy starts with the definition of God and goes on to show that God's existence follows from this definition. This is a purely rational, *a priori* method of argumentation that relies solely on an intellectual understanding of the concept "God." The second strategy begins with God's effects in the world and then argues backward to the first cause of those effects. This is a more empirically based, *a posteriori* form of argumentation, relying as it does on our ability to actually make observations of the world around us and then to reason back to the first cause of the phenomena that we discern.[31] St. Anselm of Canterbury chose to follow the first strategy, while St. Thomas Aquinas himself chose to follow the second.

ST. ANSELM

St. Anselm (1033–1109) was a Benedictine monk who died in 1109, but his importance to the world of philosophy and religion stretches all the way into

contemporary times. One of his great insights concerned the overlapping and complementary nature of faith and reason. Unlike Matson and other modern authors, Anselm was keenly aware of the indispensable role played by faith in the quest for knowledge. We can't even attempt an understanding of reality unless we choose a starting point from which to initiate our process of investigation. We need to begin somewhere, and so belief in a set of foundational ideas is absolutely necessary in order to get the operations of rational thought moving. For Anselm this foundation was provided by the doctrines and proclamations of the

© Juneko J. Robinson

Christian Bible. But Anselm did not simply content himself with unquestioning belief in these doctrines and proclamations. Instead, he used them as a springboard for ongoing philosophical contemplation. According to Anselm, there is little danger that rational analysis will undermine real religious faith. Such a fear suggests, in fact, that one's faith is not strong enough in the first place. The authentically faithful see critical study and philosophical questioning as an opportunity that may potentially strengthen their beliefs by producing a deeper understanding of the significance of revealed Truth. Thus, the desire to question, argue, and think philosophically about articles of faith is the hallmark of a fully devoted and serious Christian. While faith remains primary, Anselm nonetheless claims that rational understanding grows out of this unreasoned foundation. In his book *Proslogium*, Anselm writes, "For I do not seek to understand that I may believe; but I believe so that I may understand. For I believe this also, that 'unless I believe, I shall not understand.'"[32] If we attempted to understand the world without first believing in anything, we would have to begin from nothing. But then out of nothing, nothing would be produced. Faith, then, is an instrument of the understanding and it allows us to gain knowledge of things beyond the articles of faith themselves. Faith and reason are thus interconnected.

Anselm's complicated arguments and philosophical speculations serve a purpose similar to prayers for the religious non-philosopher. His arguments, like prayers, focus the mind and sharpen his awareness of God, drawing him ever closer to the Holy. Through philosophical meditation, Anselm celebrates God, finds comfort and solace, while also shutting out annoying distractions from the mundane world:

> Come now, insignificant man, fly for a moment from your affairs,
> escape for a little while from the tumult of your thoughts. Put aside
> now your weighty cares and leave your wearisome toils. Abandon
> yourself for a little to God and rest for a little in Him. Enter into the inner
> chamber of your soul, shut out everything save God and what can be of
> help in your quest for Him and having locked the door seek Him out.[33]

Continuing in the tradition of Abraham, Jesus, Augustine, Al-Kindi, Al-Farabi, and Avicenna, Anselm considers rational thinking to be a means of cementing one's relationship with God. A person need not pray in order to have faith, but prayer is one sign of faith as well as tool for focusing and strengthening one's religious convictions. Likewise, reason, logic, and argumentation are tools that might serve the purpose of helping one to better understand God and to linger in His presence. Nowhere is this prayer-like use of logic more apparent than in Anselm's famous Ontological Argument for God's existence.

The Ontological Argument

Ontology is the study of Being itself, and it was the eighteenth-century philosopher Immanuel Kant who first referred to Anselm's most well-known argument for God's reality as the "Ontological Argument." In this piece of reasoning, Anselm attempts to prove the Being or existence of God by means of "one single argument that for its proof required no other save itself."[34]

Anselm begins this task by marshaling the definition of God upon which Augustine had already elaborated: God is absolute goodness and perfection. Anselm's way of articulating this definition is "Now we believe that You are something than which nothing greater can be thought."[35] We can think of nothing greater or more perfect than God. Even a fool, or an atheist, says Anselm, understands this as the correct definition. When we use the word "God," even if we go on to deny the objective existence of God, we use the term to refer to a perfect being, the absolutely incorruptible creator of the universe. The word itself, if it is meaningful at all, denotes the greatest, most perfect being imaginable. The foolish atheist, Anselm tells us, understands this, and by claiming that God does not exist this individual is trying to convince us that there really is no such thing as a perfectly good creator of the universe.

But this does not make logical sense, according to Anselm. The fool accepts the definition of God as absolute perfection and in so doing admits that God exists in his intellect, because even to argue about this issue in the first place, the idea of God must be present in the mind. When the fool claims that God does not exist, then he cannot be claiming that God does not exist in the mind, but rather that God exists nowhere except in the mind. The fool is saying that God is only an idea in our heads. Yet in making this claim, St. Anselm tells us, the fool demonstrates that he does not really understand the idea of God at all. The next part of his argument will focus on demonstrating that if one truly does have the idea of God in one's head, it is logically impossible also to deny the objective existence of God outside of one's head.

If we accept that God is an idea in our heads, then it is possible to imagine God existing outside of our heads as well. Anything you can think in your mind can also be imagined to exist outside of your mind, claims Anselm. Of course this alone does not mean that such things do really exist objectively. It only means that it is conceivable for any idea that you can formulate in your head to correspond to something outside of your imagination. Even though I may doubt that unicorns or fifty-foot-tall aardvarks actually exist outside of my imagination, I can still conceive of them doing so. When I picture something in my mind, I can immediately raise the question as to whether or not such a thing actually exists in the outside world. Scientists do this as a matter of course when they formulate a hypothesis and then go on to test it in order to see whether it is true or not. Likewise, if the idea of God is conceivable to our minds, the question of God's objective, nonmental existence also comes to our mind. So, even if God is only an idea in our heads, then we can at least conceive of God also existing outside of our heads as well.

But, Anselm continues, if it is conceivable that God exists outside of our heads, then it is possible to conceive of something greater than the idea of God as it exists only inside of our heads. To exist in objective reality is greater than to exist only as a thought in our minds. For instance, it is greater to really have a million dollars than it is only to think you have a million dollars, isn't it? Likewise, for God to exist outside of our minds would be greater than to have him exist only in our minds. But if this is so, then we can conceive of something greater than the idea of God in our minds, and therefore the idea of God in our minds is not the greatest thing conceivable. But the definition of God that

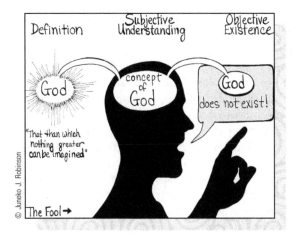

even the fool accepts as true is "a being than which nothing greater can be thought." Anselm's line of reasoning thus leads us to the conclusion that if we have the idea of God as the highest, best, and most perfect being imaginable, then it is contradictory to claim such a being only exists as a thought in our heads. A perfect being would not really be perfect if it only existed as an idea. When a fool claims "God does not exist," it is obvious, then, that the fool doesn't understand the concept behind the word "God." If the very meaning of "God" is the most perfect being imaginable, then by definition such a being must exist.

Anselm concludes his argument/prayer by thanking God for allowing him to understand through reason what he already believed by means of faith. "I give thanks, good Lord, I give thanks to You, because what I believed before through Your free gift I now so understand through Your illumination, that if I did not want to believe that You existed, I should nevertheless be unable not to understand it."[36] The strength of his faith is thus buttressed by the power of his intellect, and through philosophical contemplation Anselm feels himself to have been brought closer to God, Truth, and Being itself.

Criticisms of the Ontological Argument

St. Anselm's Ontological Argument for God's existence has many detractors, but it also still has many supporters. The argument proceeds by getting us to accept a very common definition of God and then demonstrates that this definition implies the existence of a perfect being. Just as it would be contradictory to accept the definition of "bachelor" and then go on to claim that there are married bachelors, it is contradictory, claims Anselm, to accept the definition of "God" and then go on to say He doesn't exist. It is precisely this *a priori* nature of the argument, however, that makes it so controversial. Anselm tries to move from a purely conceptual notion of God to the assertion of His objective, extra-mental existence. But is this legitimate? May we plausibly make arguments that seek to establish the extra-mental existence of things based solely on conceptual definitions? If I have the idea of a perfect cookie or a perfect car, does that mean that these things, too, must necessarily exist by virtue of their defined perfection?

Anselm addressed this sort of issue when a monk by the name of Gaunilon confronted him with a similar example. Suppose, Gaunilon suggested, that someone tells me about the greatest, most perfect island that "is superior everywhere in abundance of riches to all those other lands that men inhabit."[37]

By the same reasoning that Anselm proved the existence of God, would not the objective existence of this island be a logical necessity?

Anselm's response to Gaunilon's challenge rests on the uniqueness of God and His perfection. God is the only thing that truly can be conceived of as perfect. There is nothing in the definition of "island" that necessarily involves the idea of perfection, let alone in the definitions of "cookie" or "car." The true definition of God, on the other hand, does necessarily involve this idea. In fact, the definition of "God" is the only thing that involves the idea of perfection necessarily. Anselm does grant that if someone was truly able to conceive of a perfect island, then it would necessarily have to exist. However, no one can truly conceive of such a thing because the concept of an island does not contain perfection as part of its essence in fact. Just as you cannot truly conceive of a square circle, neither can you truly conceive of a perfect island. On the other hand, to truly conceive of God is to understand Him as perfect. Before discounting Anselm's response too quickly, notice that he does have a point. If someone told you that he or she was thinking of the greatest, most perfect being imaginable, and that there was nothing greater than this thing that was being thought about, you would probably guess that this person had God in mind. When talking in such superlative terms, it is natural for our thoughts to be drawn to ideas of holiness. This might suggest that it is really only correct to apply the notion of perfection to God Himself. Nothing else in the world is perfect, perhaps, except God, if He exists. And if God is by definition perfect, He must exist. Or so Anselm claims.

But if this is so, then it seems as though Anselm's argument runs the risk of circularity by presupposing the very thing that he is attempting to prove. If I start with the assumption that necessarily perfect things must exist, then the conclusion "God (the only necessarily perfect thing) exists" is simply a restatement of my previous assumption. It doesn't prove anything, except that the definition of God involves the idea of perfection, which in turn involves the idea of existence. All that has been accomplished is unpacking the meaning of the term "God." This was the very criticism made of the Ontological Argument by Kant, who wrote, "The concept of a highest being is a very useful idea in many respects; but just because it is merely an idea, it is entirely incapable all by itself of extending our cognition in regard to what exists."[38] It is clear, in other words, that the idea of God exists, but there is no plausible way to show that the existence of the idea of God proves the objective existence of God Himself.

ST. THOMAS AQUINAS

Before Kant, there were many other philosophers skeptical of Anselm's "proof," and like Kant, many of these other philosophers believed in God nonetheless. St. Thomas Aquinas (1225–1274), one of the great minds of the Medieval world, was one such individual. According to Aquinas, the definition of God offered by St. Anselm is the right one, yet it is also a definition that is too sophisticated for the human mind to truly grasp. Though it is correct that the essence of God is

© Junako J. Robinson

perfection, we don't really understand what this means. Our minds are too puny to accurately understand God's nature, and even though we commonly use the word "God," the full profundity and depth of its real significance always evades us. Therefore, Aquinas writes, "… because we do not know the essence of God, the proposition [God exists] is not self evident to us, but needs to be demonstrated by things that are more known to us, though less known in their nature—namely, by His effects."[39]

We cannot understand those things with which we have no experience, according to Aquinas, and so in order to begin a study of something unfamiliar, we must relate it to something that is more familiar to us. A male doctor, for instance, cannot experience childbirth, and so to gain some appreciation of the experience he must make observations, ask questions, and perhaps draw analogies between his own experiences and those of women giving birth. Though he will never really "know" in an absolutely certain sense what childbirth is like, he can approximate an understanding of the experience that brings him emotionally closer to his patients. Likewise, the transcendent God of the Christian faith is so far beyond common human experience that the only way for our minds to start to gain an understanding of God is by relating God to things with which we do have experience. In this way, according to Aquinas, St. Anselm got things backward by trying to move from the definition of God to a demonstration of His existence. Echoing the insights of Augustine, Aquinas claims that because we are finite human beings, we cannot understand the infinite perfection of God directly through the process of pure thought. We only get bits and pieces of the Truth in this manner. Therefore, we must look to the world around us and ask how it is that the things we can actually see, taste, touch, and feel relate to the existence of God. In this way, we may then start to understand God indirectly as He is manifested through the world with which we are familiar. By starting from our everyday experience and reasoning back from there, we may start to get a sense of the necessary role played by God as the first cause of the universe and, like the doctor with his patient, be drawn closer to the object of our investigation.

The Five Arguments for God's Existence

St. Thomas Aquinas was a follower of the Greek philosopher Aristotle, and like Aristotle, he believed that scientific knowledge of reality begins with empirical observation and the understanding of cause and effect. When we look around us, Aquinas points out, we observe a whole variety of worldly phenomena. We see bodies in motion, we see things changing from one state to another, we see things coming into and going out of existence, we see things that exhibit differing degrees of perfection, and we see earthly order and structure. From these five sorts of observations Aquinas claimed it is possible to construct five differing causal arguments that demonstrate the existence of a being to which we all give the name "God."

First of all, our observations of the world reveal immediately to us that things are in motion. We see trees swaying and clouds floating through the air. But what is it that caused this motion? Well, the wind of course. It is the blowing of the wind that causes trees to move and clouds to float. But what is it that causes the wind to blow? Well, we might answer, fluctuations in the Earth's atmosphere cause the wind. But what causes these fluctuations? Solar energy, we might reply. But what causes the Sun to emit this energy? Nuclear reactions within the Sun's core, of course. But what causes these reactions? Questions about the preceding cause of any observable movement might go on and on in this manner forever. But, says Aquinas, if there was no first cause of movement in the universe, then none of the movements that we do observe would exist, because "whatever is in motion must be put in motion by another."[40] Therefore, there must be something that is the first moving cause of the universe, and whatever it is, this is what "everyone understands to be God."[41]

Aquinas' second argument starts from the nature of efficient cause. Recall that according to Aristotle, an efficient cause is the force that allows matter to take on differing forms. When we observe the world around us, we see matter taking on differing forms on an ongoing basis. For instance, male and female humans and animals join sexually, each contributing a certain quantity of material in order to produce offspring. These adult creatures are the efficient cause of their children. But what was the efficient cause of the parents? Well, their parents of course. But what was the efficient cause of their parents? Another set of parents. Just as we can continue to question the origins of motion, we can continue to question the origins of efficient cause. But if there was no first efficient cause, then there would be none of the efficient causes that we observe around us. Therefore, writes Aquinas, "it is necessary to admit a first efficient cause, to which everyone gives the name God."[42]

T A B L E 6.1   St. Thomas Aquinas' Five Arguments for God's Existence

1. The Argument from Motion
2. The Argument from Efficient Cause
3. The Argument from Possibility and Necessity
4. The Argument from Degrees of Perfection
5. The Argument from Design

Aquinas' third argument for God's existence starts from the observation that things in our world arise and decay. Nothing that we see around us is permanent. Humans are born, but then they die. Mountains arise, but then they are worn down. Buildings are constructed, but then they are destroyed. If it is true that all worldly things pass into nonexistence, this means that no worldly thing is necessary. They are merely possible, or contingent. But if this is true, then at one time none of the things that constitute this world existed. Because we know that nothing can be created out of nothing, the world that we now live in must have come into existence out of something that was noncontingent, necessary, and eternal. This noncontingent, necessary being is just what is meant by the term "God."

Fourth, when we look around us we see things that exhibit differing degrees of qualities like goodness, truth, and nobility. Some people are more ethical than others, some warriors more courageous than others, and some statements are more true than others. But how is it that we recognize these various degrees of gradation? The only way that we could know that something was better, truer, or more noble than something else is if we had a standard against which we measure all of these things. So it is that there must be something that is the highest Good, the highest Truth, and highest in Nobility. This ideal standard, says Aquinas, is what we call God.

The fifth and final argument that Aquinas gives for God's existence proceeds from the observation that there is structure and order in the world. When we look at the world around us we see that things are not in a state of chaos. Things proceed in an orderly and predictable pattern. Even those objects that do not possess an intelligence of their own, like plants, water, and other natural elements, obey certain rules of nature. Plants always turn toward the Sun, take in nourishment, and carry out photosynthesis. Water always runs downhill, freezes at a certain temperature, and vaporizes at a certain temperature. It is obvious when we observe the world that it has a pattern and that it follows a plan. But if this is so, there must have been some intelligence that designed the world according to this plan. "Therefore some intelligent being exists by whom all natural things are directed to their end; and this being we call God."[43]

All of St. Thomas Aquinas' famous five arguments for God's existence are what philosophers call *a posteriori* arguments, which means that they rely on evidence that comes from actual experience. Each argument starts from a commonsense observation and then moves on to seek an explanation for this observation. In contrast, the Ontological Argument of St. Anselm is an *a priori* argument, or an argument that relies on evidence that is not derived from experience but instead from a ready-made definition. It is interesting to note that in the arguments of Aquinas, he never claims to understand the true essence of God. Rather, starting from his sense experiences he tries to reason back to the causally necessary conditions that underlie what he sees around him. Though he cannot give us a detailed picture of God, Aquinas tells us that there must be some sort of first cause of the universe, and that whatever this first cause is, we are used to calling it God. The term "God," then, is a kind of pointer that not only indicates the logical necessity for some kind of prime mover of the universe but also a word that exposes our ultimate ignorance of the full essence of that prime mover. The best that we can accomplish with logic and observation, Aquinas seems to be claiming, is to grasp a few, scattered facets that help to highlight and start to bring God into focus for us. Reason and rationality can only take us so far in our understanding of the universe, according to Aquinas, and if we want to go farther, we may just have to take a leap of faith.

Criticisms of Aquinas' Five Arguments

To many modern minds, at least some of Aquinas' five arguments still retain a degree of plausibility. This derives from the causal nature of his reasoning. Influenced as we are by scientific thinking, most of us are likely to give credence to arguments that rely on empirical evidence and an appeal to the notion of cause and effect. Furthermore, the fact that Aquinas does not insist, at least in these arguments, on any particular detailed characterization of God's nature helps to disconnect his arguments from any particular, traditional religious conceptualization of God. God, as far as these arguments go, is simply the first cause of the universe. If you think that the universe must have a first cause, then you must believe in Aquinas' notion of God, by whatever name you decide to call it. Notice, in this regard, that many current, scientific explanations for the genesis of the universe are compatible with Aquinas' reasoning.

For instance, according to the Big Bang theory, our universe originated from an infinitesimally small point of matter called a "singularity." This singularity comprised all the material that now exists in the universe, except that before the time of the Big Bang, it was densely packed into an immeasurably small location. For some reason (scientists today still do not have an explanation for this

---

B o x 6.2 Francis S. Collins and the Genome Project

The Human Genome project was completed in April 2003, resulting in a complete genetic map of human beings. This blueprint reveals that we have approximately 20,500 genes that act as the basic set of instructions governing the growth, development, and functioning of the human organism.

The original director of the Genome Project, Dr. Francis S. Collins, was at one time an atheist. However, after reading about religion and being exposed to the intricate complexity of the human genome, he became a Christian. The genome, he decided, was the language of God.

Dr. Collins developed a "theory of theistic evolution" that he calls "Biologos." While distinct from the theory of Intelligent Design, Biologos suggests that there is nothing inconsistent in the belief that at the moment of the Big Bang God imparted a plan to the universe that we are now in the process of carrying out. Evidence of this plan is found in such places as the human genome:

> ... science, with all of it appropriate demands to rigor, really only applies to investigating the natural world. If one decides that the natural world is the only interesting place to study, well, then science will do. But ... there are a lot of really important questions that science can't help you with, like, What's the purpose of my life? Is there a God? What happens after I die?

(http://articles.sfgate.com/2006-08-07/news/17305535_1_dr-francis-s-collins-human-genome-project-atheist)

event), there was a cosmic explosion[44] that propelled matter in all directions, thus creating the universe that we now inhabit. Although many contemporary scientists assert that the Big Bang theory has done away with the need to talk about God as the creator of the universe, it seems as though the theory itself is asserting something very similar to Aquinas' first argument for God's existence. Recall that in his first argument, Aquinas makes the claim that in order for things to be in motion, they must have been put into motion by a previous, initial event. Aquinas attaches the name "God" to this event, but in substance, the label "Big Bang" plays the same role. Whether you call it God or the Big Bang, in essence it amounts to the same thing: the first cause of motion in the universe. For this reason, the physicist Stephen Hawking writes that the Big Bang theory "does not preclude a creator."[45] The Big Bang, like the concept of God, is just one way of articulating something about an event that initiated, and explains, creation. In fact, as Hawking points out, the Catholic Church declared in 1951 that the Big Bang theory was not counter to Biblical teachings.[46] So it seems that scientific and religious explanations are not always incompatible with one another, and in some cases they may even amount to the same thing.

Another example of a modern, scientific theory that is often cited as overturning the need for arguments such as those proposed by St. Thomas Aquinas is the theory of evolution. Bertrand Russell, for instance, has claimed, in his essay "Why I Am Not a Christian"[47] that the argument from design, which corresponds to Aquinas' fifth argument, is a load of nonsense. The main reason he gives for this conclusion is that Charles Darwin, the author of the theory of evolution and natural selection, has given us a much more plausible explanation for the regularities that are apparent in our world. Recall that in Aquinas' fifth argument, he observes that the pattern and order of nature are too predictable to be the result of chance or happenstance. Instead, there must have been an intelligence, God, to put things in order. Darwin, on the other hand, proposed that the regularities of our world can be explained by means of an unintelligent, slow, and purely probabilistic process, which he named "natural selection." Why is it that we are so well suited to our lives here on earth? According to Darwin, it is because we have adapted to the conditions of the universe, not because God antecedently created everything to interact as a harmonious system. Those creatures that cannot adapt die out, and so from the perspective of the survivors, it only appears as if the world was designed to meet our needs. Yet, as with the Big Bang theory, the theory of evolution is not necessarily in conflict with Aquinas' line of reasoning. In both cases there is an attempt to explain how it is that the world has achieved the state in which it now exists. Aquinas calls "God" whatever it is that allowed this to happen, but remember that he never claims to understand the means or mechanisms by which God operates. The word "God" is just a place-holder that belies our ignorance of the true nature and process of creation. The theory of evolution, likewise, offers an explanation for the state of the world. In this way it serves the same purpose that God serves in Aquinas' fifth argument, although instead of theological language, it is cloaked in probabilistic/scientific language. I imagine Aquinas himself, if introduced to this theory, might well respond, "Ahhh. So you have a different name for God!"

Despite the above charitable reading of Aquinas' arguments, there remains embedded in his reasoning an assumption that would soon be thrown into question by the emerging sciences of the Modern Era. According to Aquinas, it is inconceivable that the chain of causality could reach back infinitely far. There must be some sort of first cause that got the ball rolling. Following Aristotle, Aquinas continues to hold that the world we see around us is composed of purposeful and goal-directed processes, and because of this it is completely unthinkable that there is no overarching principle like Goodness or God that holds the universe together. It is unimaginable to him that the universe, and all of the processes that it encompasses, stretches back into infinity. Yet, as Bertrand Russell writes:

> If everything must have a cause, then God must have a cause. If there can be anything without a cause, it may just as well be the world as God, so that there cannot be any validity in that argument. It is exactly of the same nature as the Hindu's view, that the world rested upon an elephant and the elephant rested upon a tortoise; and when they said, "How about the tortoise?" the Indian said, "Suppose we change the subject." The argument is really no better than that. There is really no reason why the world could not have come into being without a cause; nor, on the other hand, is there any reason to suppose that the world had a beginning at all. The idea that things must have a beginning is really due to the poverty of our imagination.[48]

And so it is with the sum of Aquinas' arguments for the existence of God. Because they all rest on the assumption that an infinite regress of causes is absurd, and because that assumption is not necessarily true, the arguments themselves rest on shaky ground.

Yet, on the other hand, perhaps this was Aquinas' point all along. Coming back to the notion that the term "God" is really no more than a pointer, or a place-holder for our ignorance, St. Thomas Aquinas may very well have been sympathetic to Russell's critique of his arguments. As Aquinas himself writes, "By faith alone do we hold, and by no demonstration can it be proved, that the world did not always exist.... Hence that the world began to exist is an object of faith, but not of demonstration or science."[49] For Aquinas, the idea that things must have a beginning really is due to the poverty of our imagination. This is, in fact, the purpose that the idea of God serves for our finite intellects in the first place. We cannot fully imagine the infinite, the absolute, and the unbounded, and so we try to encompass it with ideas, words, and concepts that in truth do not match up perfectly to the way things really are separate from human thinking.[50] Yes, we do lack the imagination, the intellect, and the understanding to conceive of a universe without a cause, and so we have created the languages of science and religion to organize our thinking. In these ways, Aquinas would probably not object to criticisms like those of Russell, yet this would have no effect on his religious will to believe nonetheless. For Aquinas, philosophy and science cannot prove everything, and for those truths that elude the grasp of reason, faith offers a foundation that is steady and comforting.

WONDROUS DISTRESS IN MEDIEVAL THOUGHT

In the autumn of 1273, Aquinas was busy at work when something uncanny happened to him. He experienced a mystical awakening, which led him to abandon writing with the claim that all of his words were like "mere chaff in the wind." Over the course of his lifetime he had authored thousands of pages of text, and now a single experience of the Holy proved to him that, as stated in the Old Testament book Ecclesiastes, "The more words, the more vanity, and what is man the better?"[51] As was the case with his Jewish, Christian, and Islamic predecessors, the point of writing, studying, and philosophizing was to struggle and strive in order to gain an understanding of God, Being, and Truth. If a single experience brought one to this understanding, then so much the better. In that moment of mystical illumination, the usefulness of philosophy melted away for Thomas Aquinas, and as the ultimate significance of the universe was laid bare to him, the need to argue and reason became superfluous. Plato wrote, "None of the gods philosophize," and neither, it seems, do those saints who stand with God.

Medieval thought represents an interesting and instructive point in time when philosophy and religion meet at a crossroads. Beginning with the patriarch Abraham, the Jewish, Christian, and Islamic traditions have established commitment and faith in one God as the foundation for all of their other beliefs, and yet they have never completely done away with philosophical questioning and openness in their quest to understand the nature of God and the nature of human obligation. In these traditions, God is wholly other and separate from the universe in which we live. He is truly super-natural. God exists outside of our world, and so philosophy, logic, and science must, in the end, ultimately fail as tools for uncovering God's real nature. When it comes right down to it, faith and intuition succeed where philosophy and science give out. Because what is really important is a grasp of the Truth and an understanding of God, medieval thinkers willingly set aside philosophy in order to finally obtain what it is that they are after. Yet, philosophy is not altogether useless to these individuals. The questioning, reasoning, and argumentation that is a part of philosophy offers medieval thinkers a way of struggling with their faith, adding texture to their beliefs and giving substance to their thinking. In this, it pulls the faithful closer and closer to God. Once they have exhausted the usefulness of philosophy, however, these medieval thinkers willingly cut their ties with the field and give themselves over to communion with the Holy.

The aspiration toward God is very much akin to the philosopher's aspiration toward the Truth. In fact, medieval thinkers would no doubt equate these two states of being, as they claim that a communion with God necessarily also represents a communion with Truth. In this we can see how the twin aspects of wonder and distress are a part of the medieval way of thinking. Insofar as a religious worshiper aspires toward God and the Truth, this individual embodies the wondrous desire for fulfillment of a superlative ideal. Yet, so long as human consciousness falls away from God and experiences the pain of separation from the Holy, distress is nevertheless part of this life as well. Wonder and distress are thus an integral part of medieval thinking, and to this extent we can see that these religious men are also philosophers.

The point at which people like Augustine, Anselm, Aquinas, Al-Kindi, Al-Farabi, Avicenna, and Averroes depart from philosophy and follow a divergent path is when they claim an immediate and intuitive awareness of God that resists all attempts at articulation. Because the use of words, arguments, and reasoning requires a sort of conceptual space to allow for the unfolding of ideas, and because in communion with God all conceptual space evaporates proportionally as distance between the individual and the infinite consciousness shrinks to nothing, philosophy vanishes in a flash with the occurrence of the mystical experience. Really, this is the point of all religion after all. It is not aimed at intellectual knowing, but rather at an experience of unity with something greater than the finite self. Philosophy sometimes serves as a tool that aids the individual consciousness to move in the direction of this experience, but in the end, it always gets in the way of taking the final step. Whereas the religious mystic ultimately needs to stop asking questions, the philosopher must always ask questions and admit to his or her fallenness and separation from Truth. This situation may prevent the philosopher from alleviating distress once and for all, but it also keeps wonder alive forever.

QUESTIONS FOR DISCUSSION

1. How are the arguments of Stoicism similar to some of the arguments that are offered in medieval times for God's existence? How is the Stoic understanding of God different from the Abrahamic religions' understanding of God?

2. Why do you think Jewish, Christian, and Islamic thinkers might be suspicious of ancient Greek thought? What aspects of ancient Greek philosophy do you think these same thinkers found useful?

3. What is the "problem of evil" and how did St. Augustine address this problem? How are his insights relevant today when we are confronted with catastrophes like 9/11, destructive earthquakes, and wars?

4. In your own words, try to clearly articulate St. Anselm's line of reasoning in his Ontological Argument. Can you concisely sum up the entire argument syllogistically, with two premises leading to one conclusion? Do you think this argument has merit? Do you think this argument is fallacious?

5. In your own words, clearly articulate St. Thomas Aquinas' five arguments for God's existence. Explain what all of these arguments have in common and how their strategy differs from the strategy of argumentation pursued by Anselm in his Ontological Argument.

6. What are some of the objections that modern-day scientists might raise against Anselm's Ontological Argument and Aquinas' five arguments for God's existence? Do you agree with these objections? Why or why not?

7. Do you think there is an inherent conflict between religious faith and philosophical argumentation, or do you think the two modes of thought are compatible with one another? Discuss the ways that faith and reason both overlap and diverge in the teachings of the medieval philosophers.

8. The modern philosopher Friedrich Nietzsche claims that scientific thinking is actually an outgrowth of religious philosophizing. Why do you think he would make this claim? In what ways were the medieval philosophers concerned with ideas and speculations that might be considered scientific in nature?

NOTES

1. Gen. 2:4.

2. God, of course, rescinds this request and replaces a ram in the place of Abraham's son. Gen. 22:9.

3. Gen. 17:8.

4. Gen. 19:24.

5. The contemporary Jewish philosopher Martin Buber calls this relationship, which he claims is the core of Jewish faith, an "I and Thou" relationship. See Martin Buber, *I and Thou* (New York: Book-of-the-Month Club, 1999).

6. Mark 12:28.

7. Ibid., 4:10.

8. Ibid., 4:15.

9. Ibid., 4:16–17.

10. It is for this reason that Nietzsche suggests that it is more accurate to speak of "St. Paulism" than it is to speak of "Christianity." It also calls into question the accuracy of the conventional Christian interpretation of Jesus' message.

11. 1 Cor. 6:15.

12. It is worthwhile to note that the actual order and organization of the books in the Jewish Tanakh and the Catholic Old Testament differ. In the Catholic Bible, the books of the prophets have been grouped toward the end of the text, presumably to emphasize the coming of the Messiah in the New Testament. In the Tanakh, these same books are not grouped at the end but are instead mixed in with the other books.

13. *The Holy Qur'an: English Translation of the Meanings of the Qur'an with Notes*, Abdullah Yusuf Ali (trans.) (Indianapolis, IN: H&C International, 1992), p 506. Muslims believe that the Koran, as recited in Arabic, is the literal word of God. Thus, any translation into a language other than Arabic is an alteration of God's word. A note in the English edition of the Koran that I have cited reads: "Important Note: This is only the translation of the meanings of the Qur'an, and it by no means replaces the need for the original Arabic which is the only revealed message of God verbatim."

14. Surah, 3:64; 4:47.

15. Surah, 5:72.

16. Wallace Matson, *A New History of Philosophy,* Vol. 1 (New York: Harcourt Brace Jovanovich, 1987), p. 196.

17. St. Augustine, *The Confessions of St. Augustine* (New York: Mentor Books, 1963), pp. 40–41.

18. Ibid., p. 98.

19. Ibid., p. 151.

20. Ibid., p. 152.

21. Thomas J. J. Altizer, *Godhead and the Nothing* (Albany: State University of New York Press, 2003), pp. 53–54.

22. Ibid., p. 265.

23. Scott Macdonald, "The Divine Nature," in *The Cambridge Companion to Augustine* (Cambridge: Cambridge University Press, 2001), pp. 70–71.

24. Later thinkers, like Hegel, would dispute this claim.

25. Augustine, *Confessions of St. Augustine*, p. 317.

26. Majid Fakhry, *A History of Islamic Philosophy* (New York: Columbia University Press, 1970), p. 88.

27. According to Majid Fakhry, Al-Kindi himself did not translate any works, but rather commissioned translations and revised or paraphrased them. Ibid., p. 83.

28. Ibid., p. 95.

29. Ibid., p. 137.

30. Ibid., p. 138.

31. St. Thomas Aquinas, *Summa Theologica*, Fathers of the English Dominican Province (trans.) (Westminster, MD: Christian Classics, 1981), Vol. 1, p. 12 (Q. 2 Art. 2).

32. St. Anselm, *Proslogium*. M. J. Charlesworth (trans.) (Notre Dame, IN: University of Notre Dame Press, 1979), p. 115.

33. Ibid., p. 111.

34. Ibid., p. 103.

35. Ibid., p. 117.

36. Ibid., p. 121.

37. Ibid., p. 163.

38. Immanuel Kant, *Critique of Pure Reason*, Paul Guyer and Allen W. Wood (trans. and ed.) (Cambridge: Cambridge University Press, 1998), p. 568.

39. Aquinas, *Summa Theologica*, pp. 11–12 (Q. 2 Art. 1).

40. Ibid., p. 13 (Q. 2 Art. 3)

41. Ibid.

42. Ibid.

43. Ibid., p. 14.

44. Recall the philosophy of Anaximander, Chapter 2.

45. Stephen Hawking, *A Brief History of Time* (New York: Bantam Books, 1990), p. 9.

46. Ibid., p. 47.

47. Bertrand Russell, *Why I Am Not a Christian* (New York: Touchstone Books, 1957), pp. 9–11.

48. Ibid., pp. 6–7.

49. Aquinas, *Summa Theologica*, p. 243 (Q. 46 Art 2).

50. In this way, Aquinas does appear to disagree with a basic Aristotelian assumption.

51. Eccl. 6:11.

Chapter 7

René Descartes and the Transition from Medieval to Modern Thinking

© Juneko J. Robinson

What is the geocentric model of the universe? What developments led to the formulation of the heliocentric model of the universe? Why was the Medieval Catholic Church resistant to the heliocentric model? What is the Cartesian Method? What is Cartesian Doubt? What is the *Cogito*?

What is the relationship between mind and body in the Cartesian system? How does Descartes offer a way to resolve the conflicts between science and religion?

Transitions are seldom easy, and often they can be rather traumatic. In the history of human thought there have been many transitions, some more difficult than others. In previous chapters we scrutinized a number of these periods of change, emphasizing the tensions and commonalities that have emerged between religious, scientific, and philosophical modes of thinking. From our contemporary perspective, it may be tempting to look at the ground covered so far as mere history; a quaint reminder of the long and difficult path that has led up to, and culminated in, the modern worldview. Many people imagine that we present-day humans have collectively arrived at a high point in our learning and that our civilization represents a kind of summit from which we see Truth more clearly than any of those who came before us. In this regard, thinkers such as Thales, Democritus, Socrates, Plato, Aristotle, Diogenes, Epicurus, Augustine, Anselm, and Aquinas might be regarded by some people as interesting historical figures who have little of substance to teach us today, other than to show how far we have come in our drive for Truth. "If they knew what we know now," some people might be tempted to claim, "those guys would be astounded!" This sort of attitude presumes that human thinking is progressive and that it inexorably tends to move forward toward a more finely tuned and advanced state of accomplishment.[1] However, I advise against this way of viewing our subject matter, and it will be especially important for us to keep this advice in mind as we begin this chapter on the transition from Medieval to Modern thinking. Because many of the developments that we will encounter in this and future chapters have been especially influential in shaping our contemporary worldview, it may be natural for us to presume that the thinkers we are discussing are finally getting things right. But, I wish to emphasize, this opinion may largely be a matter of perspective.

As I mentioned in Chapter 1, it is probably a distortion to claim that scientific thinking is, in its essence, somehow more advanced or progressive than religious thought. There are profound thinkers in all areas of specialty, regardless of the content of those specialties. The ideas of Plato and of St. Augustine, St. Anselm, and St. Thomas Aquinas are some of the most sophisticated in all of human history, yet they are shot through and through with religious themes and assumptions. It would be a mistake to suppose that because these individuals operated from a position of religiosity that they were substandard intellectually. Likewise, simply because thinkers like Democritus, Aristotle, Diogenes, and Epicurus rejected what they saw as superstition in those around them, this does not automatically qualify them as superior intellects. What does set these individuals apart from less interesting minds, I claim, is not so much the content of their thinking as their readiness to entertain *new ways* of conceiving the world and their willingness to open up new questions about the nature of Being. It is this philosophical element that augments and fortifies both the religious and scientific ideas of the individuals that we have examined so far, raising them above run-of-the-mill thinkers and transforming them into exemplary figures in the history of human thought. As such, they serve as important role models for all times, and they are reminders that regardless of how clever we believe we have become, the world still retains endless mysteries to challenge and frustrate our understanding.

The dynamics and conflicts that we have seen exhibited in the ideas of the ancient Greeks and the Medieval philosophers are not simply things of the past but rather are indicative of processes that are always at work in human thought and culture. The struggle to uncover and understand Truth continues today, and it will no doubt continue indefinitely into the future, unless of course everyone eventually becomes either a god or a super-scientist. Until then, the love of wisdom will motivate deep thinkers to pose new questions, propose new solutions, and offer new speculations about the mysteries that continue to distress us and make us wonder.

THE CONFLICT BETWEEN SCIENCE AND RELIGION
IN THE EARLY MODERN PERIOD

In Modern times, we see this process at work no less than in the Ancient and Medieval worlds. However, whereas religious themes came to dominate in Medieval times, in the Modern world, as in the times of the Presocratics, the discoveries of the new and emerging sciences would begin to chafe against the old, traditional, and accepted ways of thinking. In the growing conflict between science and religion, Modern thinkers began to find themselves caught between the revealed "truths" of the Church and the "truths" revealed through reason and observation. These two sources of truth, it turned out, were often in conflict with one another and so a decision had to be made. To whom do we listen, the Church or the scientists? The transition from Medieval to Modern times is characterized by an ongoing conflict between the authority of these two forces and the attempted reconciliation of their respective insights. This is a conflict that is still playing itself out today with greater or lesser degrees of fruitfulness and hostility.

As the Modern era progresses, we find that philosophical thinking gains a renewed sense of vigor, innovation, and brashness. The inconsistencies between religious and scientific worldviews seem to act as a spur, revealing the weaknesses in both fields and encouraging thinkers to philosophically consider original ways of conceptualizing reality and our place in it. It is during this time that we begin to witness the emergence of two separate, yet related, currents in philosophical inquiry itself, both of which were mentioned briefly in the introduction to this book. On the one hand, some philosophers begin to focus their attention on issues and problems of a tangible and empirical nature. These individuals tend to ally themselves with the insights of science and so emphasize the sorts of questions that are down to earth and that admit of clear and distinct answers. This current of thought would develop into the so-called analytic tradition in contemporary philosophy. The other current of philosophical thought continues to be fascinated with issues and problems of a more abstract and metaphysical nature, which do not necessarily lend themselves to clear answers or empirically verifiable results. The questions pondered by these thinkers retain an aura of religious wonder and awe concerning the unplumbed mysteries of existence. This orientation would develop into the so-called continental tradition in contemporary philosophy.

Today, the analytic and continental traditions are often just as hostile toward one another as were science and religion in the sixteenth and seventeenth centuries.[2] However, the threads that run through these two ways of philosophizing were much more tightly woven together at the commencement of the Modern era than they are today. Many of the groundbreaking thinkers of this time were less concerned with asserting the primacy of one set of dogmas over another and more concerned with trying to harmonize what they believed to be legitimate insights of the Church with the new discoveries of the sciences. This reconciliation of science and religion was most famously attempted by the French philosopher René Descartes in the seventeenth century, and so it is to him that tradition has bestowed the distinction of being the first truly Modern philosopher. We will turn to a discussion of his *Meditations* during the latter half of this chapter. But first, in order to understand the challenge he faced, we need to set the scene and look at some of the controversies that were raging at the time Descartes was writing and thinking.

MODERN DEVELOPMENTS IN ASTRONOMY

We will initiate our investigation into the transition from Medieval to Modern times by examining the field of astronomy, taking special note of how the old earth-centered view of the universe began to be called into question around 1543. This is an appropriate place to begin, because this change signals a radically new way of thinking about the structure of the universe and how humans fit into it, vividly illustrating the unsettling, and sometimes traumatic, effects that can be produced when prevailing suppositions begin to lose their plausibility. At the same time, we will see that these events also illustrate the sense of excitement and creativity that often go along with the undermining of old beliefs and the creation of new ones. During such periods of crisis, philosophy becomes an especially potent force in the world precisely because, as Thomas Kuhn writes, philosophical thinking is "an effective way to weaken the grip of tradition upon the mind and to suggest the basis for a new one."[3] When the old dogmas and beliefs begin to break down, creative, philosophical thinking is called for in order to make sense of things. In the new astronomy of the Modern era, we see just this sort of breakdown, reorientation, and the establishment of a new tradition.

The Geocentric Model of the Universe

The Medievals inherited their view of the universe from the ancient Greeks. It was Aristotle who was considered by philosophers like St. Thomas Aquinas to be the only true authority on issues concerning the natural world,[4] and it was to his authority that Medieval astronomers commonly appealed. Aristotle had taught that nature consists of two separate realms: the heavenly and the earthly. On the Earth we see change, generation, and decay, all of which may be explained and comprehended by way of the Four Causes. Yet, when we look to the skies—the heavens—we see no such change. Rather, in the heavens we observe only perfect cycles of circular movement. The planets and other heavenly bodies, Aristotle explained, rotate around the Earth in circular orbits precisely because such movement is simple and eternal. The circle is uniform, without beginning or end, and so is the closest thing to purity that exists. This is why the heavenly bodies can remain in endless movement. Furthermore, it is clear both to observation and pure reason, claimed Aristotle, that "the earth does not move and does not lie elsewhere than at the center [of the universe and of the orbits of the heavenly bodies]."[5] Reason tells us that the Earth lies at the center of the universe because it is a heavy mass, and the appropriate place for a heavy mass is the center. In addition, observation shows us that the Earth does not move either from its spot or around its own axis. If it did move around its own axis, a falling body would not simply drop straight downward but would, as the Earth rotated underneath it, travel parallel to the surface of the Earth. Observation of the regularity with which the stars rotate around us also proves that the Earth does not move from its central spot, for if it did, "there would have to be passings and turnings of the fixed stars. Yet no such thing is observed. The same stars always rise and set in the same parts of the earth."[6]

The cosmology described by Aristotle, and accepted by the Medieval thinkers, is both "geocentric," or "earth-centered," and "geostatic," meaning that the Earth does not move. The Earth sits at the center, immobile, while the heavenly bodies rotate around it (see Figure 7.1). Though we no longer believe this to be an accurate model of the universe, it is easy to understand why the Greeks and the Medievals accepted it as true. When you look up in the sky at the paths of the sun, moon, planets, and stars, it does, at least to the casual observer, appear as though they are in circular motion around us. The Earth itself, on the other hand, seems to remain stable and fixed. From our own perspective on its surface, no earthly motion is immediately apparent. Aristotle's geocentric and geostatic theory of the universe, then, seems to square with

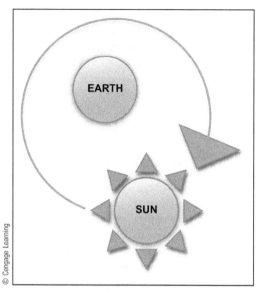

FIGURE 7.1 The Geocentric Model

common sense and basic observation. In fact, it even held up in the face of a competing theory, proposed by Aristarchus of Samos in the third century B.C., which stated that the Earth was just another planet in motion around the sun. This proposal was considered to be preposterous at the time, as it flew in the face of common sense and clear observational evidence. Aristotle's model of the universe, on the other hand, worked pretty well in order to explain what was clearly the case according to the naked-eye observations of the time.

But there were complications, and the Greeks knew this. The word "planet," in fact, comes from a Greek word meaning "wanderer," and this name was bestowed on some of the heavenly bodies because of their observed tendency to wander in their paths across the backdrop of the stars. If you watch the movements of the planets very closely over a period of time, you will see that they don't really travel in perfectly circular paths across the sky at all. Rather, there are points in their orbits where they stand still and even move backward. Astronomers have given this phenomenon the name "retrograde motion" (see Figure 7.2). Today, of course, we attribute retrograde motion to the fact that the Earth is not at the center of the universe but is hurtling through space along with all of the other heavenly bodies. There are points in the Earth's orbit where it overtakes and leaves behind other planets in their orbits, and so, from our observational perspective, it only appears as though those other planets are moving backward in the sky.

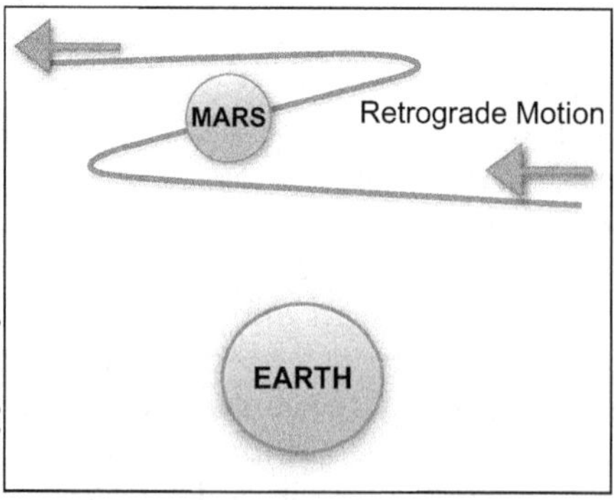

The ancient Greek philosopher and astronomer Eudoxus (408–355 B.C.) was able to develop a way of explaining this motion which managed to retain the geocentric and geostatic character of Aristotle's system. He proposed that the planets were embedded in a series of perfect concentric spheres, one nested in the other. Retrograde motion could then be accounted for by the fact

FIGURE 7.2 Retrograde Motion of Mars as Viewed from Earth

that sometimes a sphere within a sphere rotates backward, thus carrying its planet in the opposite direction of the larger sphere containing it. This contrivance allowed the Greeks to retain the idea that the heavenly bodies moved in perfect circles around the Earth. When this system was later elaborated upon and fine-tuned by Islamic philosophers, Eudoxus' spheres were imagined to be made of crystal and to produce a kind of "music of the spheres" as they rubbed and rotated one within the other (see Figure 7.3).[7]

This cosmological model remained intact until around A.D. 140 when the astronomer/astrologer Ptolemy modified and systematized it so that it was even more consistent with observational evidence. In the Ptolemaic system, the Earth is not directly at the center of the orbits of the planets but is slightly off-center. Regardless, it still is the body around which the planets revolve. The motions of the planets themselves are described by a complicated series of forty cycles-within-cycles (much like the spheres-within-spheres of Eudoxus) called "epicycles" (see Figure 7.4). This number of epicycles proved necessary to describe the apparent motions of the planets as long as these orbits were still assumed to be perfectly circular. The thought still had not occurred to Ptolemy, despite the

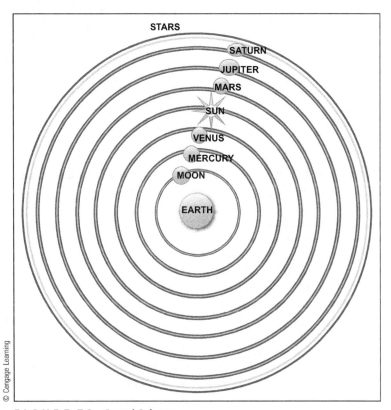

FIGURE 7.3 Crystal Spheres

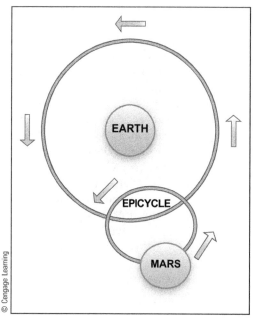

© Cengage Learning

F I G U R E 7.4   The Epicycle

increasing complication of his system, that the shape of planetary orbits might be something other than circular. But then, the traditional authority of Aristotle, and common sense, encouraged this way of thinking. It would later take a very bold and brave break with tradition, and with common sense, to initiate a different way of conceptualizing the relationship between Earth and heavens. For the time being, however, the Ptolemaic model worked very well at making accurate predictions concerning the positions of the planets, and it would remain the accepted model of the universe for a long time to come.

We should pause here, momentarily, to say something about the manner in which the development of the geocentric and geostatic theory of the universe advanced. Some writers on the history of science are too quick to point an accusing finger at Aristotle, claiming that it was because of him and his authority that the progress of astronomy and physics was held back for thousands of years. But it is a misunderstanding of the Aristotelian worldview to level this charge against him. No doubt, Aristotle himself would have encouraged those who came after him to continue to formulate new theories that better explained the nature of our world. He was, as discussed in Chapter 4, a philosopher very much attuned to the importance of observation and scientific discovery, and so it is not really fair to claim that he himself retarded scientific development in Medieval times. In fact, it might be argued that it is only because of Aristotle that science was encouraged to develop at all. In constructing a theory of nature that was based on logic and observation, the influence of the Aristotelian worldview provided a positive and powerful stimulus to the later development of the empirical sciences.

Furthermore, the manner in which the Medieval view of the universe did develop is not so misguided by tradition and religious dogma as some would lead us to believe. What we see during this period is a progressive honing and perfection of the most generally accepted scientific theory of the time. Even today, this is the way that science develops. Scientists don't just throw away old theories in which they find problems. Rather, they try to modify and alter the most accepted theories in order to accommodate new facts and observations. As theories become more and more complicated and sophisticated, they are able to account for more and more phenomena. However, if another theory comes along that is able to account for the same phenomena in a simpler and more elegant fashion, it is often presumed that the simpler theory is the better one, and so there is a change in how things are conceptualized. This is precisely what occurred during Medieval times with the geocentric and geostatic model of the universe. As problems in it were detected, changes were made in order to better account for observational evidence. As we will see, however, as observational techniques developed and as new facts emerged, there would come a time when a simpler explanation for the apparent motions of heavenly bodies would become appealing to many, though not all, scientific minds. Ironically enough, it would be the ideas of the ancient Greek philosopher Aristarchus of Samos, whose sun-centered theory of the universe had earlier been dismissed as scientifically untenable, that would come to displace the commonsense theory of Aristotle.

The Ptolemaic system was accepted by just about everyone during the Medieval period. It not only made accurate predictions about the positions of the planets, but it was consistent with common sense, Aristotle's authority, and Church doctrine. Aristotle had asserted: "… it is clear that the earth does not move and does not lie elsewhere than at the centre,"[8] and in the Bible (Psalms 93:1) it is written "Yea, the world is established; it shall never be moved." To the Christian minds of Medieval times, the Earth, as the center of the universe, seemed the appropriate place for God's human creation. After all, aren't we the focus of the Lord's love and attention? Furthermore, the Ptolemaic model left open a space where God, Heaven, and Hell could exist as actual, physical realities. Because the universe was finite, its boundary being the final orbiting backdrop of stars, God had a place to exist, watching all of creation from the outside, the way that we might gaze at a snow globe. It was easy to imagine Heaven in some location above our universe and Hell existing in some location beneath it. Everything seemed neat and tidy and so the Church, over time, became increasingly wedded to this cosmology and took it as given that this was the correct picture of the universe. The science of the Medieval period and the doctrines of the Catholic Church were able to coexist harmoniously for a while.

© Juneko J. Robinson

The Heliocentric Model of the Universe

As already mentioned, in the third century B.C., Aristarchus of Samos had speculated that the Earth might move along with the other planets, but such an idea seemed incomprehensible. Why wasn't there a constant wind blowing across the surface of the

Earth if this was true? Why didn't all of the objects on the Earth fly off of its surface? These sorts of simple questions led most people to reject the theory that the Earth moved. Up until the sixteenth century A.D., no one really questioned that the Earth stood still while the heavenly bodies orbited around it. It was, ironically, a harbinger of modern times when, in 1543, Nicoli Copernicus (1473–1543) resurrected Aristarchus' ancient idea that perhaps the Earth was not immobile and stable, thus calling into question the commonly accepted geocentric and geostatic theory of the universe. Copernicus was a Polish priest who was searching for a way of simplifying the existing model of the universe while retaining the ability to produce accurate predictions of heavenly movements. His procedure was purely mathematical rather than observational, and what he found was that if one were to shift the Earth into a circular orbit around the sun, then the number of epicycles needed to explain the planets' movements was reduced from forty, the number in the Ptolemaic system, down to twenty (see Figure 7.5). As it turned out, the model was simpler, yet it produced predictions no more accurate than the Ptolemaic model. Furthermore, by shifting the Earth from the center of the universe, Copernicus was breaking with what at the time was the commonsense view of reality. In fact, Copernicus was quick to point out that his speculations were not intended as a true model of the real motions of the planets but rather as a way of simplifying the calculation and prediction of planetary positions as viewed from our perspective on Earth. Because it wasn't even very

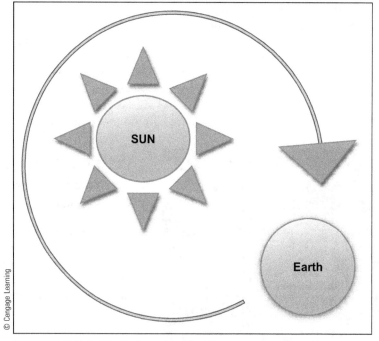

FIGURE 7.5 The Heliocentric Model

successful at doing this, his book, *On the Revolutions of the Heavenly Orbs*, was largely ignored, or laughed at, by both scientists and religious leaders when it was published close to his death in 1543.

But Copernicus was living in a time of transition. The Catholic Church had already experienced a split once in 1054,[9] and in 1517 it experienced another when Martin Luther (1483–1546) initiated the Protestant Reformation. Luther had become disgusted with what he saw as corruption and dishonesty on the part of Church leaders who increasingly seemed to be consolidating power and influence by retaining for themselves the authority to interpret and mold religious practices. Luther challenged this authority by suggesting that the laity did not need authorities to interpret the Bible for them. If only the Bible was translated into the language of the people, they could read it for themselves, and so Luther produced a translation of the Bible from Latin into German. The Lutheran Church grew up around this movement, holding that each individual member of the Church could relate to God on one's own without the interference of the Pope. Although Luther himself thought that Copernicus was a fool, these individuals nonetheless share a sort of philosophical courage that is characterized by their willingness to think beyond officially sanctioned doctrines and to entertain new ideas and interpretations of reality. Just as Copernicus, in the field of science, was willing to take his thought in new directions, so was Luther, in the field of religion, willing to do the same thing. The transition to Modern times would be facilitated by the efforts of these sorts of freethinkers, and as their ideas gained more and more attention, a collective shift in perspective would follow.

Philosophical theories and worldviews are important, but if they are not supported by empirical evidence and observations that offer some objective corroboration, then they have little hope of becoming accepted by minds of a more scientific bent. In the case of Copernicus' heliocentric, or sun–centered, model of the universe, there was nothing that could be offered as conclusive evidence in support of its truth until a man by the name of Galileo Galilei (1564–1642) began to closely scrutinize the heavens with a new invention called the telescope. The telescope was not invented by Galileo himself, but he was apparently the first person to put it to use in the service of astronomy. With it he was able to observe things that no one had seen before, and these discoveries would lend increasing support to the theory of Copernicus and to the undermining of the old Aristotelian/Ptolemaic system of astronomy. First of all, contrary to what Aristotle had claimed, it became clear to Galileo that the heavenly bodies were by no means perfect and unchanging. When viewed through a telescope, the moon appeared to have a surface covered with seas, valleys, and mountain ranges. It was not a smooth and perfect orb at all but instead a body whose terrain resembled that of the Earth! Furthermore, Galileo was able to discern that the moon received reflected light from the Earth, just as the Earth received reflected light from the moon. The Earth and the moon were beginning to look very similar to one another indeed, and if this was so, why shouldn't the laws that apply on Earth also apply to what happens on the moon? Additionally, when looking at the sun, Galileo found that it had spots moving across its surface. The existence of these spots suggested that the sun also underwent changes, that it moved, and that it was, therefore, imperfect like the Earth.

When Galileo turned his telescope to the other planets, he discovered more startling things. First of all, some of the planets had satellites circling around them. Jupiter, for instance, had four moons orbiting it. If this was the case, and if Jupiter itself was in orbit, then it was clear that a planet in motion could retain satellites. Therefore, it was possible that the Earth, with its moon, could also be in motion. In addition to this, when he observed the planet Venus, Galileo saw that it went through phases during which its surface was illuminated by sunlight. However, the patterns of illumination were such that they did not coincide with what should happen according to the Ptolemaic theory. Instead, they were more like what should happen if Copernicus' theory was correct.

Observation after observation seemed to contradict the expectations that one would have given Ptolemy's system and instead to corroborate the predictions that would follow from Copernicus' theory. This mounting evidence led Galileo to become ever more confident in his Copernicanism, yet it had the opposite effect on many of those with whom he worked at the University of Padua. Many of his colleagues, afraid of what they might see, refused Galileo's invitation to look through his telescope. They preferred, like the prisoners in Plato's cave myth, to ignore the truth and to remain comfortable and content in their old ways of thinking. Galileo was worried that the influence of these traditionalists might inhibit the progress of scientific advancement, and so he traveled to Rome in order to defend, and advocate for, the legitimacy of his research. He was disappointed when the Catholic Church instead "declared Copernicanism false and erroneous in 1616."[10] Despite this, in 1623, Galileo published a book in which he presented a dialectical exchange between an Aristotelian and a Copernican. This might not have been so threatening except for the fact that in his book Galileo depicts the Copernican as having much more convincing arguments than the Aristotelian. In response, Pope Urban VIII, who earlier in life had written a poem praising Galileo, now brought him to trial, and after being shown the instruments with which he would be tortured, Galileo was compelled to denounce his own work and writing. He was then sentenced to house arrest for the remainder of his life. Legend has it that although Galileo did publicly renounce his heretical beliefs, when bowing before the judges at his trial he muttered under his breath, "Nevertheless, the Earth still moves!" Whether this is true or not, it is the case that while imprisoned at home he completed yet another book detailing his views on physics, which was smuggled out of the country and secretly published in Holland.

Though perhaps not as bold and defiant as Socrates, Galileo was a hero to science and philosophy nonetheless. In the face of religious dogma and bigotry, he refused to abandon his desire for Truth or to mouth the words of a tradition in which he no longer believed. His willingness to look at the world and to describe it the way that he honestly saw it still serves as a source of inspiration to those today who view Galileo, along with Copernicus, as one of the founding fathers of the modern scientific worldview. The observations that Galileo made, in combination with the theoretical work of Copernicus, produced a new way of looking at the relationship of the Earth to the rest of the planets. However, one further contribution would be needed before this way of looking at the universe could be made to precisely fit all of the most carefully collected data concerning planetary motion. This contribution would come from a man named Johannes Kepler (1571–1630).

Kepler was a follower of the Presocratic philosophy of Pythagoras, and his driving desire was to articulate a model of the universe that described planetary motion in terms of the five mathematically perfect solids. Pythagoras had observed that there are only five three-dimensional solid shapes whose surfaces are all of uniform configuration. The tetrahedron has four uniformly triangular faces. The cube has six uniformly square faces. The octahedron has eight uniformly triangular faces. The dodecahedron has twelve uniformly pentagonal faces. Finally, the icosahedron has twenty uniformly triangular faces. Kepler thought it more than a coincidence that there were only five perfect solids and that there were also only six known planets. Perhaps the regularities of these solid shapes described the orbits of the planets around the Earth, he thought, and so Kepler embarked upon a passionate attempt to show how planetary motion could be described according to this geometrical plan. He speculated that instead of crystal spheres, the planets were separated by these perfect shapes and were carried through the heavens and around the Earth according to a mathematically harmonious plan designed by God Himself. If Kepler could unlock the secrets of this plan, as revealed in the beauty of mathematics, then the Pythagorean hope of explaining everything in the universe in terms of numbers would be one step closer to completion.

As we know today, there are more than just six planets, and so from the outset Kepler's initial theory was based on a false assumption. It is no wonder, then, that he became more and more frustrated as he found that his attempts to map the orbits of the planets onto the shapes of the perfect solids met with repeated failure. Yet, Kepler was not eager to throw out his hypothesis. Instead, he considered the possibility that the observations of the actual movements of the planets might be inaccurate. Perhaps the reason why his Pythagorean-inspired project was not working was due to poor observational evidence, and so Kepler accepted an invitation to work with Tycho Brahe (1546–1601), the keeper of the most accurate astronomical observations of that time. Brahe made naked-eye observations of heavenly movement and kept extremely detailed records. However, he himself had trouble making sense of these data. As a result, he invited Kepler to help him in his work to formulate a cosmological model that would accurately account for the observed data.[11]

Brahe died before Kepler was successful,[12] but ultimately Kepler did formulate a new picture of the universe that accurately predicted all of the planets' movements without the complicated use of epicycles. His bold theory consisted, first, of following the example of Aristarchus and Copernicus by moving the Earth from the center of the universe and placing it in orbit around the sun. However, the shapes of planetary orbits, Kepler claimed, were not circular, as everyone had always assumed they must be, but elliptical. An ellipse is like an elongated circle, resembling the outline of an oval. Instead of having one central point of focus, it has two. In Kepler's new system of planetary motion, the sun lay at one of the foci of the ellipses that made up the planetary orbits, much in the same way that Ptolemy had claimed that the Earth sat just off-center of the middle of the universe (see Figure 7.6). Furthermore, Kepler produced a mathematical description of the movements of the planets that showed them traveling at different speeds depending upon their distance from the sun. His model worked simply and perfectly to predict the positions of the planets in the skies at any given time.

However, not only did Kepler's theory conflict with Aristotle, the Bible, and Church doctrine, but it was psychologically painful for those who had assumed that humans were the center of the universe and that God had set the heavens in perfectly circular motion around us. Not only is the Earth not the center of the universe, but the planets don't move in circles and, as if to cement the imperfection of God's creation, the planets don't even move at a uniform speed! But it gets even worse. One of the implications of Kepler's theory that was especially troubling to the Medieval mind was that the universe did not end at the boundary of the stars. In order to make his theory accurately reflect the observational data, Kepler was forced to assert that the stars constituting the constellations are infinitely far away. This means that the universe is infinitely large. Where then was the place for God, Heaven, and Hell? If the universe is infinite and the Earth is just one of many planets rotating around the sun, then how special are human beings? The Church found these questions very disturbing and so suppressed the new heliocentric, or sun-centered, view of the solar system. It persecuted those who

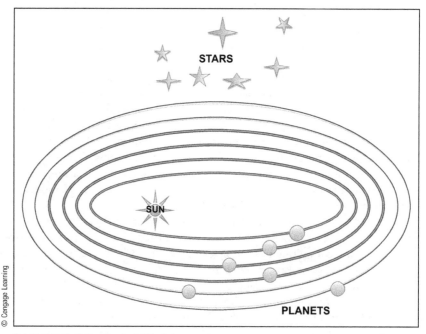

© Cengage Learning

FIGURE 7.6 Kepler's Model

advocated this theory, torturing and killing people who refused to submit. Kepler himself was excommunicated and even his mother was arrested, threatened with torture, and imprisoned by the Inquisition.

There were, however, some religious people who, even as Galileo and Kepler were developing their theories, were also developing interpretations of their faith that opened the way for reconciliation between these new developments in science and traditional religious beliefs. Giordano Bruno (1548–1600) was one such religious man. According to Bruno, the universe is interpenetrated with God's infinite substance throughout. Because God Himself is infinite and the universe is an expression of God, it only makes sense that the universe would be infinite as well. Consequently, it has no center. The only reason why it appears to us as though it must have a center is because of our finite human perspective.[13] However, through the development of our capacity for love, we may be able to break through this arrogant and egocentric way of viewing the universe and thus forge a bond between ourselves and the infinite goodness of God Himself.

Bruno's departure from Church-sanctioned geocentrism was responded to when the Catholic Church burned him at the stake for his claims. This was a reminder to everyone that heresy would not be tolerated and that official Catholic doctrine was to be accepted as true solely on authority of the Church's say-so. Asking too many questions and doubting the correctness of religious proclamations was not tolerable, and those who did so risked their lives during these times. However, the fact that the Church was so threatened by the philosophical and scientific speculation of people like Galileo, Kepler, and Bruno suggests that its leaders were well aware that change was in the air. As the old ideas about the structure of reality were called into question, the Church must have feared that its power and influence were starting to slip away. After all, the Church claimed to be an instrument of God, and thus to be infallible in its proclamations of Truth. If it was to become apparent that many of the "truths" held by the Church were not true at all, where did this leave its authority? How would the Catholic Church retain followers if the emerging sciences proved that religious revelation was flawed? For those Catholics who sincerely believed that their faith was the authentic road to salvation, this was an especially upsetting issue. How many souls would burn in Hell if the Church was unsuccessful at showing them the path to righteousness?

RENÉ DESCARTES

The incongruity between Catholic doctrines and the insights of science in the seventeenth century presented a very troubling circumstance for those who, like René Descartes (1596–1650), were both good Catholics and devoted scientists. Descartes fully understood the power of the emerging sciences of the Modern era, and he was concerned that if the Church did not learn to accept and accommodate these newly discovered insights it would be in danger of collapse. The more that science revealed about the real structure of the world, the more obvious it became that the Church was wrong about quite a bit. Was there any

© Juneko J. Robinson

possible way that science might be capable of existing in concert with religious faith? Could new discoveries in math, astronomy, and physics coexist with Catholic doctrines so that the intellectual and spiritual reputation of the Church could remain strong?

Descartes seems to have thought so. But in order for this to happen, good Catholics like himself would have to look deep within their own minds and reflect philosophically upon their beliefs in order to separate those things they knew to be true from those things about which they were uncertain. If this could be done, then the possibility lay open to eliminate nonsensical convention from those things that were absolutely true, certain, and knowable according to our God-given faculty of reason. If an absolutely certain bedrock could be discovered upon which to build all beliefs about the world, then we would never run into the problems that the Church had already encountered in being led astray by false theories and assertions concerning the structure of the universe. Both religion and science might rest on the same foundation, and if carefully examined, we might find that they both express important truths about the world. Descartes would, in the end, claim that science and religion held authority in two separate realms of Being, and that as long as each field stuck to its own domain of authority there would be no necessary conflict between them. Science gives us truths about the physical world, while religion gives us truths about the spiritual world. Both the physical and the spiritual worlds are real, according to Descartes, but one must use the appropriate tools for unlocking their particular secrets. Thus, both science and religion are important for different reasons and are able to coexist with one another. Furthermore, the spiritual and the physical worlds are both parts of an even larger reality that emanates from God, and so they in turn are rooted in a common foundation, which is itself knowable to human reason.

The Cartesian Method

In a book titled *Discourse on Method,* Descartes formulated a procedure for conducting an inquiry into the foundations of things. His method, now called the Cartesian Method, consists of four steps: First, accept nothing as true that is not

T A B L E 7.1   The Cartesian Method

1. Doubt	Anything that is not absolutely clear and distinct is to be rejected.
2. Analyze	Once an indubitable truth is found, break it down into its component pieces.
3. Synthesize	Take the pieces and put them back together.
4. Repeat	Steps 1–3 should be repeated to assure that no mistake has been made.

clearly and distinctly recognized as such. Second, divide the problem at hand into as many parts as possible. Analyze it into its component elements. Third, reflect upon the problem by proceeding from the simplest elements and then move on to what is more complex. Fourth, repeat this procedure again and again in order to make sure that no errors were made.[14] Each of these steps plays an important role in structuring and organizing our reasoning processes, according to Descartes, making it more likely that we will be successful in thinking issues through correctly, thus helping us to arrive at conclusions without error. The problem with our everyday commonsense way of approaching problems is that too often we proceed from assumptions that are false and then move on to reason in a confused manner that only makes issues more unclear. The Cartesian Method helps to guard against this sort of loose thinking.

The first step in Descartes' Method delineates what is now called Cartesian Doubt. Cartesian Doubt is a very specific form of doubting strategy that is not to be confused with the sheer destructiveness of ancient Greek skepticism. Instead of a plan directed toward undermining all belief, Descartes' form of doubt is intended as the first step toward the apprehension of those beliefs that are absolutely true. As Descartes writes, "In this I did not wish to imitate the skeptics, who doubted only for the sake of doubting and intended to remain always irresolute; on the contrary, my whole purpose was to achieve greater certainty and to reject the loose earth and sand in favor of rock and clay."[15] His excavational metaphor is apt. The purpose of doubting, for Descartes, is to clear away the rubble and shifting "sand" of conventional nonsense that has accumulated in our minds and which only acts to obscure the real Truth. Once this nonsense is cleared away, a firm and solid foundation will be revealed upon which we may then confidently build the rest of our knowledge.[16]

MEDITATIONS ON FIRST PHILOSOPHY

Nowhere is the dramatic strength of this first step in the Cartesian Method more apparent than in the first two chapters of Descartes' most famous book, *Meditations on First Philosophy*. In this work, as proclaimed in its letter of dedication, Descartes sets out to utilize his method in order to show through the use of pure reason that "the human soul does not die with the body, and that God exists."[17] Descartes goes to great lengths in order to circumvent any fears that the Catholic Church may have had that his strategy of doubt might potentially undermine belief in God. From the very beginning, Descartes assures "the most wise and distinguished men, the dean and doctors of the faculty of sacred theology of Paris ... who have always been the greatest pillar of the Catholic Church,"[18] that he will show the human soul and God to be two of the most indubitable truths available to human reason. They constitute a firm foundation upon which all real knowledge ultimately rests. However, he warns, readers must understand his overall plan first, and then carefully follow his reasoning, step by step. His proof is lengthy and difficult, and so it is imperative that the reader be "particularly attentive" to his arguments. Otherwise, there is the potential for misunderstanding. As it turned out, despite his pleas, Descartes' intentions were misunderstood, and his book was banned by the Catholic Church in 1663 for introducing too many dangerous doubts.

Meditation I

Meditations on First Philosophy is divided into six chapters, or meditations.[19] In the first meditation, Descartes establishes the point and scope of his doubting strategy. He begins by clarifying his reasons for demolishing his existing opinions:

> Several years have now passed since I first realized how numerous were the false opinions that in my youth I had taken to be true, and thus how doubtful were all those that I had subsequently built upon them. And thus I realized that once in my life I had to raze everything to the ground and begin again from the original foundations, if I wanted to establish anything firm and lasting in the sciences.[20]

In order to avoid erecting a tower of belief upon a foundation of false opinion, Descartes must be certain that his most basic principles are incontrovertible. To assure this, he decides that it is best to start from scratch; but to do so is no easy task. He has become so habituated into taking so many "truths" for granted and self-evident that, for thoroughness' sake, a systematic and exhaustive strategy of doubt is required to assure the complete dismantling of his beliefs and opinions. He proceeds in this manner by doubting from the inside out: first, his sense perceptions; second, the existence

© Juneko J. Robinson

of his own body and the physical world; third, the physical sciences; and fourth, mathematics. If upon examination he finds even a modicum of uncertainty in a given idea, he vows to dispose of the entire belief.

The first set of beliefs on which he turns his doubt loose are those based upon information received through the senses. Even though sense perceptions may appear to be the most real and direct kind of evidence for the existence of a world "out there," Descartes recognizes that the images in dreams likewise often seem direct and real. Yet the realistic images and experiences that occur in dreams are, in fact, merely illusions. This is all that is necessary to sabotage his confidence in the accuracy of sense perceptions. Just because something *seems* real, that does not mean that it *is* real. This is a notion that we have already encountered through Plato. Our senses are very often fooled by optical illusions, hallucinations, and other sorts of sensory mistakes. If we have been led astray even once by our senses, how can we be sure that we are not always being led astray? How can I be certain that the things my eyes tell me exist in the world are not merely phantasms and delusions? How, indeed, can I be certain that I am not living in a dream world? Often we have dreams that seem very real, and it is not until we wake up that we come to understand that we were, in fact, dreaming. Is there any way we can be certain that is not happening at this very instant? No, there is not. Anything that can happen in real life can also happen in a dream, and so there appears to be no absolutely certain way to determine whether I am, at this moment, dreaming or awake. I might pinch myself in order to see if I suddenly wake up, but then there remains the possibility that I dreamed pinching myself and waking up. The Taoist sage Chuang Tzu made this same observation thousands of years before Descartes, reporting that he awoke from dreaming that he was a butterfly and wondered whether he was not now a butterfly dreaming that he was Chuang Tzu!

This dream hypothesis is a very powerful aid in Descartes' attempt to doubt as much as he possibly can. It is important to recognize that Descartes is not asserting that he is in fact dreaming, but that it is possible that he is dreaming. The point is to highlight the lack of a criterion or an anchor point between waking and dreaming that would allow us to distinguish between the two with 100 percent certainty. We just don't know whether we are really awake or really dreaming right now, and so we must suspend our judgment about what we see, taste, touch, and feel around us. From here, a suspicion about the independent existence of the supposed objects of sense is a natural step. How can we know that the objects in the physical world (including our bodies) exist if we only know these things through potentially faulty sense perceptions? And if the existence of physical objects is uncertain, then how can we retain faith in the results of the physical sciences? All science rests upon observation and hypothesis testing, but if we can't trust our senses, how can we trust our observations? Thus, the dream hypothesis undermines our confidence in both sensory observation and the results of scientific inquiry.

Descartes finds it more difficult to challenge his belief in mathematical truths. "For whether I am awake or asleep, two plus three makes five, and a square does not have more than four sides."[21] Are the truths of math and geometry impervious to doubt, then? Descartes decides that there is a way even to doubt these things.

Our belief in the truths of math and geometry are ultimately dependent upon the assumption that we are not constantly being deceived by some sort of "evil genius" who delights in tricking us. How do we know, in other words, that God is not evil and that He doesn't get a kick out of intervening in our understanding of numbers in such a manner that every time we attempt to calculate $2 + 3$ we make a mistake? Maybe God "… has directed his entire effort at deceiving me."[22] Think about the sort of scenario depicted in the popular movie *The Matrix* and you will have a contemporary parallel to Descartes' evil genius hypothesis. In that movie, it is not God but evil machines that deceive human beings by manipulating their brains. If we proceed on the assumption that a tireless and powerful deceiver God or machine is at work in the world, we would have to be on guard against falsehoods everywhere, and we would even become skeptical enough to doubt mathematical "truths."

It should be noted that Descartes is not claiming that he really believes there is an evil God deceiving him at all times; that would be contrary to his strategy of systematic doubt. Rather, the evil genius hypothesis is introduced, like the dream hypothesis, as a way to shore up his doubt about the things that seem most self-evident to him. It is part of pushing the first step in his own method to its farthest limits. On this hypothesis, just about anything can be doubted; and that is the point. Descartes wants to doubt everything that he possibly can so that he will avoid falling into error about anything. Some philosophers have claimed that with this last hypothesis Descartes forever doomed his hope of discovering any certain truth. If we act as if there is a malicious God constantly tricking us, how could we ever be sure of anything? It is at this point that Descartes has reached the point of absolute skepticism. He has suspended judgment concerning the truth or falsehood of all things and so cleared the way to search for something that he hopes can be known for certain. Despite the power of the evil genius hypothesis, Descartes still hopes to discover something that he is unable to doubt.

B o x 7.1 Depersonalization and Derealization Disorders

Descartes, through philosophical reflection, came to wonder whether the outside world might be a mere dream or an illusion of his own mind. There is a documented psychological disorder called "derealization" in which sufferers likewise come to feel as if the outside world is not real. Those afflicted with this malady sometimes also report feeling that the people around them are mechanical, just as Descartes wonders when, in *Meditation II*, he looks out of his window at the people passing by on the sidewalk.

Another related condition that Descartes avoids is called "depersonalization." In this disorder, people come to feel as if they themselves do not exist. Descartes reasons that it would be impossible for him not to exist so long as he is thinking. However, those who suffer from depersonalization actually do come to feel as if they themselves are unreal.

These disorders are documented and described in the *Diagnostic and Statistical Manual of Mental Disorders*, published by the American Psychiatric Association.

These are the basics of Cartesian Doubt. Cartesian Doubt works rather ironically. It approaches the quest for absolutely certain knowledge by doubting everything. It strives to be systematic and as all-encompassing as possible. Its point is to eliminate all false opinions held simply by force of habit and to clear the ground in order to discover a foundation upon which we may base our beliefs without anxiety. Doubting, for Descartes, is intended as a way to secure the very basis for certain knowledge. It serves the double function of being both the eliminator of all false belief and the mechanism by which to discover Truth. But how is one to get anywhere or learn anything from the position of absolute skepticism with which we are left at the end of Meditation I? Addressing this dilemma is the task of Meditation II.

Meditation II

In Meditation II, Descartes stumbles upon his hoped-for foundation of certainty. The act of doubting is, in fact, an act of thought. In order for a person to engage in the activity of doubt, it is absolutely obvious that person must be thinking, and in order for a person to think, it is absolutely obvious that person must exist. It follows, then, that every time Descartes doubts, he knows that he exists. The content of what he is thinking about does not matter in this regard. Even if deception is taking place, it is immediately self-evident that there is someone who is being deceived. "'I am, I exist' is necessarily true every time I utter it or conceive it in my mind."[23] In this axiom Descartes finds his secure foundation, and from here he will go on to build up a system of beliefs, secure in the knowledge that they rest on solid ground. In *Discourse on Method*, Descartes articulates this absolutely certain foundation in a formulation that is known as the *Cogito*, because it comes from the Latin phrase "*Cogito ergo sum*," which means "I think, therefore I am."[24] This is perhaps one of the most famous, and ingenious, insights in the history of philosophy. Later thinkers, such as Edmund Husserl and Jean-Paul Sartre, would, for this reason, take it as the departure point for their own systems of philosophy. Every time that I think, I am assured that I exist, because if I didn't exist I wouldn't be here to think! What could be more certain? I must exist as a thinking thing!

There is a joke concerning Descartes that goes something like this: Descartes was having a drink in a bar one night when a drunk walked in and recognized him. "Hey! You're René Descartes, the famous French philosopher!" the drunk exclaimed. "You wrote that book *Meditations on First Philosophy*!" Descartes tried to ignore the drunk but was accosted further. "You must have plenty of money, smart guy! Writing a famous book like that must have made you rich. Why don't you buy me a drink!?" Descartes, hoping to dissuade the drunk, turned to him and replied, "I think not!" Promptly, Descartes disappeared from the bar and ceased to exist!

This joke, whether you find it funny or not, raises some important issues about the *Cogito* and Descartes' line of reasoning in the second meditation. If the only thing that assures me of my own existence is the act of thinking, what happens if I stop thinking? Do I no longer exist? Some philosophers have complained that this is precisely what is implied by Descartes' argument and that there is something terribly wrong here. When I go into a dreamless sleep, or if

I go unconscious, obviously I don't cease to exist altogether. You can see this when I wake up or come out of unconsciousness. Therefore, there must be something wrong with the *Cogito*. It is flawed and so it cannot act as an absolutely certain and true foundation for the rest of our knowledge.

This objection, I believe, misses Descartes' point. Descartes, at this stage of his argument, is not making the claim that our existence is dependent upon our act of thought, but rather that the act of thinking gives us evidence of our own existence as thinking things. Without thoughts to think about, I would not have any point of focus toward which to direct my mental attention, and so if there is an "I" that exists independent of thoughts, it would have no means of demonstrating its own borders. The German phenomenologist Husserl would later call this quality of thinking "intentionality," which means that mental processes must be directed toward something in order to manifest themselves. You can't think without thinking about something, in other words. However, this does not imply that when your mind is not thinking about something that your mind ceases to exist. What would the sky look like if there were no light to illuminate it? What would a textured surface feel like if there were no hand to touch it? I don't know, but the lack of light or of a hand's touch does not mean that the sky or textured surfaces do not exist. Likewise, if you are not thinking about something, this does not automatically imply that there is no "you" that still exists. In fact, it appears that Descartes conceived of the mind as a sort of substance, which supports thoughts and feelings the way that a piece of paper supports words and doodlings. When you erase the words and drawings off of a piece of paper, the paper remains, and analogously, the mind may remain even if there are no thoughts in it. Nonetheless, as long as I do think, this gives testimony to the fact that there is an "I" that is doing the thinking. This, I believe, is all that Descartes wants to show at this point in his *Meditations*, all jokes aside. Every time that he thinks, he has absolutely certain evidence that he exists.

Meditation III

But how is one to proceed from this insight toward the reestablishment of science and religion? That step is taken in Meditation III. Note that the only thing Descartes is certain of is his own existence. If left here, Cartesian Doubt would culminate in solipsism, which is the belief that the only thing that exists is one's own mind. Everything else that appears to exist, according to the solipsist, is merely a dream or projection of the mind. Descartes does not want to end up in this position and so, in the third meditation, he decides that he must look for evidence of something that exists outside of his mind in order to escape the solipsist's conclusions. But how to go about this while remaining on an absolutely certain foundation?

Descartes has already doubted away his confidence in the senses, and so any proof that he offers for the existence of something outside of his own subjectivity will have to steer clear of claims based upon empirical observation. He will have to proceed completely *a priori* (prior to experience). Because the only thing that he is absolutely certain of is the existence of himself as a thinking thing, he decides to examine the ideas that are contained within his own thinking substance

TABLE 7.2   The Origins of Ideas

Innate Ideas	Originate from within the mind.
Adventitious Ideas	Originate from outside of the mind.
Imaginary Ideas	Imagined into existence by the mind.

to see whether they give any indication of the existence of a reality outside of themselves. He looks inward instead of outward, and what he finds are three natural classes of ideas. Some ideas, those that he calls "innate,"[25] seem to come from within himself (like the idea of his own mind); some ideas, those he calls "adventitious,"[26] seem to come from outside of himself (like ideas of God and the physical world); and some ideas, those that are "produced by me,"[27] seem to be the result of his own imagination (like ideas of unicorns and other illusory creatures). Descartes commits to examining the ideas that appear to come from outside of himself in order to see whether they contain any evidence that will give him absolute proof that they do in fact depend on something other than his own mind for their existence. It should be stressed that in noticing that some ideas appear to come from outside of himself, Descartes is not yet committing to the position that they really do come from some exterior reality. All that Descartes has committed to at this point is the self-evident claim that some ideas, like ideas of God or physical reality, seem to be inspired by an influence independent of his own will. Of course, just because it seems like some sort of outside influence has produced these ideas in him, that does not mean that this is really the case. It could be a delusion or a dream that makes him think this way. But Descartes decides to examine this class of adventitious ideas more closely nonetheless in order to see what sorts of clues they might hold about the nature of a reality beyond his own thoughts.

Descartes tells us that ideas of all types really do exist, and we know that they exist by the fact that they are immediately present in the mind; the mind itself being the most certain truth of all. All ideas at least exist in the mind that perceives them. This quality of existence Descartes calls "objective reality"[28]: "… the objective mode of being belongs to ideas by their very nature."[29] In other words, all ideas have objective reality insofar as they exist as ideas, regardless of their content. The idea of a unicorn has as much objective reality as the idea of anger, simply by virtue of the fact that both thoughts exist as ideas in the mind. However, there are some ideas that purport to represent a reality that also exists outside of the mind. These ideas have a certain amount of content, or "formal reality," and this content must come from somewhere: "… the formal mode of being belongs to the causes of ideas."[30] Because it is impossible for something to come from nothing, any idea that possesses so much formal reality, or content, that it could not have been produced by the mind itself must have been caused by something outside of the mind. Are there any ideas like this? When Descartes examines the contents of his ideas, he finds that most of them could have been conjured up by the force of his own imagination. Ideas of finite objects such as pencils, bits of clay, unicorns, and other human beings are so

T A B L E 7.3   Types of Reality

Objective Reality	The mere existence of an idea.
Formal Reality	The content of an idea.
Eminent Reality	The source of the content of an idea.

unspectacular that it is not that difficult for him to accept that they could have been caused by his own equally finite being. They could be the product of his own imagination.

However, Descartes does find one idea whose content he thinks is beyond his own capacity as a finite creature to bring into existence. This is the idea of God. Along with St. Anselm, Descartes recognizes the idea of God as an idea whose content is infinite and perfect. But how could a finite creature like Descartes be the cause of such an idea? He couldn't, claims Descartes, because the cause of an idea must have at least as much formal reality as the idea itself has. A finite creature could not possibly create an idea with infinite formal content, and so the idea must have originated from somewhere other than Descartes' own finite mind. But the only possible origin of such an idea is a being with as much formal reality as the idea itself, and because the idea itself has infinite formal content, so too must the being that created it. But the only possible candidate for such a being is God Himself. Therefore, Descartes concludes that God must exist outside of his own mind.

Descartes' argument for God's existence in the third meditation owes much to both St. Anselm's Ontological Argument and the causal arguments of St. Thomas Aquinas. Like Anselm's argument, Descartes starts with an *a priori* recognition of the idea of God as contained in the mind. He argues from the inside out in order to establish the existence of an infinitely perfect being. Like Aquinas' arguments, Descartes relies on a causal principle in order to show that the *a priori* idea of God must have originated from a first cause that exists independently of Descartes himself. Descartes' argument is, thus, subject to many of the same sorts of criticisms that have been leveled against the arguments of both Anselm and Aquinas. Perhaps one of the strongest objections raised against Descartes disputes the assertion that the idea of God must have been caused by something as formally real as God Himself. Why couldn't the idea of God be a matter of imagination, pieced together from other ideas in the same fashion that the thought of a unicorn came into existence? Descartes' response is quite similar to the response of Anselm to the same criticism; "But we used the idea of God which is in us to demonstrate God's existence, and such immense power is contained in this idea that we understand that, if in fact God does exist, it would be contradictory for something other than God to exist without having been created by him."[31] In other words, the formal content of the idea of God is so infinitely great that if you are really thinking of God, it is logically contradictory to claim that God exists only as an idea and not also as the cause of that idea. But is this conclusion as absolutely certain as the *Cogito*?

Descartes' argument for God's existence rests on a causal principle that seems more than a bit shaky today: "what is more perfect ... cannot come into being from what is less perfect."[32] Because the idea of God is filled with the formal reality of infinite perfection, it could not, according to Descartes' reasoning, come from anything less than an infinitely perfect being. The idea expressed here is superficially plausible, and on an intuitive level it is a presumption that many people probably take for granted. In fact, Descartes claims that it is an assumption that is "manifestly true."[33] A thing cannot come from something that is lesser in reality than itself. Thus, a piece of lumber cannot come from a tree that is smaller than the plank itself; a child cannot be born to a parent who weighs less than the child itself; a crop of corn cannot come from a field that contains less vegetable matter than the yield of the harvest; etc. As these examples suggest, it is commonly presumed that a lesser substance cannot produce a substance greater than itself. However, recent developments in the branch of physics known as chaos theory undermine this presumption on a fundamental level. As Paul Davies writes, "... we have found that the existence of complex and intricate structures of behaviour does not necessarily require complicated fundamental principles. We have seen how very simple equations that can be handled on pocket calculators can generate solutions with an extraordinarily rich variety of complexity."[34] In fact, as it turns out, very complicated phenomena can be produced by simple, uncomplicated causes. The simple act of a butterfly flapping its wings can ultimately produce the complicated and powerful result of a hurricane in another part of the world. This may lead us to question the "manifest truth" of Descartes' presumption that a thing with "more reality" cannot be produced by something with "less reality," and if this presumption is not necessarily true, then it would seem that Descartes' claim for God's necessary existence is a rather weak link in his chain of argument.[35]

Nonetheless, at the end of Meditation III Descartes believes that he has found the correct route back to the world and away from solipsism. Because he has an idea of a perfectly good and infinite God, and because that idea could come from nowhere else than God Himself, a perfectly good and infinite God must exist. Furthermore, a perfectly good and infinite God cannot possibly be a deceiver. Therefore, the evil genius hypothesis is disproved. Therefore, the world as it was created by God and as it appears to Descartes must be pretty much the way that it really is. Therefore, the dream hypothesis is disproved, Cartesian Doubt is overcome, and the commonsense world that we see around us can be reestablished. Descartes may thus reassert his confidence in the senses and his trust in all that he sees, tastes, touches, and feels. All of this hinges on the claim that God exists, for it is only through the assurance of God's goodness that we are able to trust that our sensory impressions correspond accurately with the world "out there." Lest this seem too contrived to be plausible, consider the fact that what Descartes has done here is not so different, and perhaps is even more sophisticated, than what modern-day empirical scientists take for granted. The scientist today claims that we can trust our sensory observations of the world because nature assures us that our sense organs are well suited to survival in our environment. But how do we know that this is really the case? Is the appeal to nature any more satisfying than the appeal to God? Whatever one appeals to, as long as there is a distinction drawn between the way the world really is and the way that the world appears to us, we must find some sort of link between reality and perception. God and nature provide just this sort of link. Yet, in either case, it is still clear that perceptions and reality do not always coincide. How can we consistently tell the difference between those perceptions that are true and those that lead us astray? Addressing this distinction is the task of the fourth meditation.

Meditation IV

In the fourth meditation Descartes embarks upon an investigation into the question "Why do I so often fall into error?" In the previous meditations he discovered what he believes to be an absolutely firm foundation for his understanding of himself and God, yet when he tries to move beyond this foundation, Descartes realizes that he is still prone to making many mistakes and taking many things for true that are in fact false. Why does this happen? Descartes wants now to take the next step and move from an absolutely certain knowledge of himself and God toward an understanding of the world around him. In this meditation he seeks "a way by which I might progress from this contemplation of the true God, in whom, namely, are hidden all the treasures of the sciences and wisdom, to the knowledge of other things."[36] If he is successful, Descartes will now be able to establish a set of criteria by which he is able to distinguish between perceptions reflecting the real nature of reality and those perceptions that are mistaken illusions.

In establishing both his own and God's existence, Descartes has discovered two "clear and distinct ideas" that exist in his own mind. These ideas are clear insofar as they strike him with the powerful force of undeniable truth, and they are distinct insofar as they are unambiguous and unmixed with any other ideas. The clearness and distinctness of these ideas are, Descartes believes, the marks of true knowledge. Yet there is little in his experience of the world that strikes him with the same sort of clearness and distinctness as his ideas of himself and God. His own skeptical method of doubt has, in fact, made him aware of the numerous ambiguities and uncertainties that accompany his perceptions of the physical world. In order to reestablish the authority of the sciences, however, he must find a way of moving past this uncertainty and gain an understanding of the world as it clearly and distinctly presents itself to him. The manner in which Descartes attempts to accomplish this task is to apply the third step in his method. Recall that Descartes' method, first, begins with doubt, then, second, moves toward analysis of those simple ideas that cannot be doubted, and, third, attempts to reflect from simple toward more complex ideas. In this third step, absolutely certain ideas are brought together so that more complex knowledge might result from their combination. Because the parts that make up the more complicated systems of knowledge are indubitable, Descartes reasons that the complex itself must also be absolutely certain. A house that is skillfully built of quality materials will be a quality house, and likewise Descartes believes that a system of knowledge that is carefully constructed of indubitable bits will itself be indubitable.

Descartes has found that it is clear and distinct to his mind that God exists, and through the analysis of this idea of God he has also discovered that it is impossible that God is a deceiver. From this, Descartes reasons that all of the faculties that have been granted him by God are not intended to lead him into falsehood. Descartes' ability to make judgments about the world, then, has the capacity to lead him toward the truth, and this must be the purpose for which God intended his judgment to be used. God did not endow him with the ability to make judgments to draw him into a web of deception. Rather, this judging faculty of the mind was given to him to use in a particular manner for finding Truth. In other words, there is a correct and an incorrect way to use our ability to consider and evaluate the things that appear to us in the world. If we use this ability in the correct way, as God intended, then we will not fall into error. However, if we persist in using bad judgment, we will constantly fall into error, not through God's design but because of our own laziness and lack of discipline.

Descartes writes that human beings are "constituted as a kind of middle ground between God and nothingness, or between the supreme being and non-being."[37] What he seems to be claiming here is that while human beings aspire toward absolute wisdom and knowledge, they are nevertheless tied to their own finitude in such a way that they can never actually become omniscient gods. Humans are bound to the earth and all of the imperfections that accompany that situation, yet they constantly strive to overcome their imperfections. They have an unlimited will toward infinite knowledge, yet their actual, finite ability to understand things always holds them back. This, thinks Descartes, is the source of all human error. Our unlimited will pushes us constantly to judge things as true or false, and it does so, often times, before we actually understand all of the intricacies of the things that we are making judgments about. It seems to me that Descartes has a very good point here. Most of us at one time or another have been guilty of forming judgments and making assertions about things that we don't truly understand. We sometimes jump to conclusions about people and things before we have all of the facts, and when we do so, we risk forming faulty opinions about those people and things. Descartes suggests that the way to avoid this sort of error is to restrain our will in accord with the powers of our understanding. In other words, if we refrain from making judgments until all of the facts are in, we will minimize the probability that we will form false conclusions about the things in the world. God has endowed us with the freedom to judge, and if we use this freedom correctly and carefully, we can avoid most cases of error. The world and all of the things in it can be known as long as we use our mental powers in the manner that God intended.

So ends the fourth meditation, in which Descartes has reestablished his confidence that the way the world appears to the careful and analytic mind is pretty much the way that the world is in reality. God could not possibly have allowed it to be any other way, claims Descartes. If we restrain our will to judge and limit ourselves to reasoning that proceeds from ideas that are clear and distinct to our understanding, we will not fall into error. In the fifth meditation, Descartes carries through with this insight and inquires into the nature of the material world, mathematics, and, yet again, into the nature of God Himself. He wants to apply what he has learned about the functioning of the human mind in order to

eliminate all skepticism and doubt about the independent existence of the physical world.

Meditation V

His first step in this direction is to carefully enumerate all of the impressions that he clearly and distinctly has of the things he sees around him. What he comes up with is a list of basic qualities that all physical objects seem to possess: extension in length, breadth, and depth; size; figure; duration of motion; etc. These qualities in isolation from one another may not seem that interesting or informative, but when considered in combination with one another they produce a description of the world that is grounded in the most fundamental understanding that we can have of physical reality. The world around us consists of extended bodies of particular sizes and shapes that are in motion. Descartes proceeds from reflection on the physical world to reflection on mathematics and geometry. What he discovers as he scrutinizes the ideas of number and figure is that he clearly and distinctly understands that even though he has never observed numbers or the perfect figures of geometry in the world, they nevertheless must exist in some manner separate from his thinking about them. It is impossible for him to conceive of these things as not existing. No matter how stridently he wills himself to believe something to the contrary, he cannot make himself believe that a triangle, for instance, does not exist as a figure with three sides. This idea strikes him so forcefully that the only way that he could doubt it would be to assume that God was actively trying to deceive him. However, as he has already discovered in the third meditation, this is impossible. So, it must follow that the apparent truths of arithmetic and geometry are in fact truths.

What Descartes has done now is to reestablish not only his confidence in his ideas of the concrete physical world but also his confidence in his ideas about the abstract world of pure mathematics. His intention for doing both of these things is to demonstrate that in combination with one another, these ideas will yield a precise and absolutely certain understanding of the way that the world around us works. By sorting through our ideas of the physical world with mathematical precision, we may construct an absolutely certain science of the physical world. A careful understanding of the world will restrict itself to these sorts of insights. However, any attempt to extend understanding beyond such insights is liable to fall into error. Indeed, Descartes observes that the farther away he finds his mind wandering from the basic clear and distinct ideas, and the more complicated the systems that he builds out of those ideas become, the more uncertain and hesitant he finds himself feeling about the results. Think about the way that you proceed when you are figuring an especially long mathematical equation and you will get a sense of the problem that Descartes is facing. When you start your calculations, you begin from a very simple foundation. You add particular numbers and carry out particular operations that are in themselves quite simple and uncomplicated. But as you proceed through the mathematical proof, the operations that you carry out become more and more numerous. Once you reach the solution to your problem, you may forget the details of all of the operations that you performed. When you look at the full solution to your mathematical problem, it may appear bewildering and confusing as a whole. Yet because it was you yourself who carried out each step in the proof, you have a certain level of confidence in the result. In fact, you could go through the problem again and again to check your work, and the more times that you do so, the more confident you become that you have been correct in your calculations. In a like manner, Descartes realizes that because of his finite capacity for understanding, he is liable, as he proceeds along in his meditations, to lose confidence in the whole system that he is constructing. However, as in a mathematical proof, he can regain greater and greater levels of confidence in what he has produced if he repeats his reflections again and again; this is the fourth step in his method. Ultimately, it is not necessary that he be able to apprehend the truth of everything at once. It is sufficient that he carries through with all of the requisite steps in an orderly and careful manner and that he recall this to mind when he worries about the soundness of his conclusions. As a human being he recognizes himself as possessing a finite intellect, and so though he aspires towards full and complete comprehension of the world he also knows that this full comprehension will never present itself to his mind all at once. He can only get bits and pieces at a time. But through a careful application of method, he can put those bits and pieces together and understand the connections between them.

It is only God, Descartes claims, who can know everything at once and as a whole. This is why confidence in the existence of God is the final foundation of all our knowledge. If we don't believe in God, writes Descartes, then we are "incapable of achieving perfect knowledge about anything else."[38] It is only because God created a comprehensible world comprising consistent and knowable regularities that we are in a position to scientifically investigate and explain those regularities. Science depends upon the belief that the world is somehow rationally ordered and constructed. Without this assumption, all science would collapse, and the only thing that assures us that this assumption is correct is the understanding that God exists and that God is not a deceiver. As mentioned earlier, the notion of God is replaced today by many scientists with the idea of nature as a self-regulating system. In either case, however, the same point remains: without the presumption that the universe is orderly and that our minds are well suited to understanding its structure, science would be impossible.

At the end of the fifth meditation, Descartes has come to the realization that science and religion are not necessarily contradictory to one another. Rather, they may be complementary entities that work together in order to bring us closer to an understanding of who we are and what our place is in the universe. Science is the method by which finite creatures like ourselves unlock the order that God has imparted to reality. Though we must accept that something like a master planner has structured the universe, we cannot comprehend God's design all at once because it is too complicated.[39] The best that we can do is to understand that there is a master planner and then proceed to try to understand His blueprint bit by bit.

Meditation VI

In the sixth and final meditation, Descartes sums up and draws ultimate conclusions from his reflections. He observes that the only thing that assures him of the real and independent existence of the objects of sense are his own clear and distinct ideas of them, and the only thing that assures him that these ideas do represent what they purport to represent is the existence of God. As long as he is careful to restrain his willingness to make judgments in such a manner that he doesn't go beyond what the evidence permits and what his understanding can comprehend, then he may discover the sorts of truths that are accessible to the finite human mind. But one question remains. Given that it is clearly and distinctly apparent to the understanding that he exists as a thinking being, Descartes wonders how it is that the nonphysical substance composing the mind is related to the purely physical substance that composes the body. In other words, how is it that the mind and body interact? Descartes thinks it obvious that his identity is distinct from his physical being. If he were to lose a part of his body, he wouldn't be less of himself. His identity would remain intact regardless of how much of his body was taken away. It must follow, therefore, that the world that God brought into existence consists of two distinct yet interrelated substances. Physical substance is the sort of substance that extends into space and is divisible into parts. Nonphysical substance does not extend into space and cannot be divided into parts. The mind is nonphysical, whereas the body is physical (see Figure 7.7). Descartes writes, "nature also teaches not merely that I am present to my body in the way a sailor is present in a ship, but that I am most tightly joined and, so to speak, commingled with it, so much so that I and the body constitute one single thing."[40] Yet how is it that two completely different substances are commingled so that they compose a unity? Descartes doesn't answer this question in *Meditations on First Philosophy*, but he thought it obvious that such an interaction did occur.

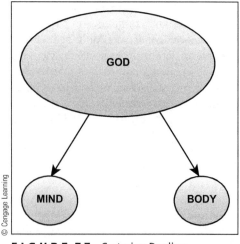

FIGURE 7.7 Cartesian Dualism

Descartes would speculate elsewhere that the interaction of mind and body occurred through the mediation of the pineal gland in the brain. The pineal gland is a tiny organ in the midbrain whose function, even today, has not been clearly determined.[41] Descartes thought that the human spirit is contained in this tiny organ, and that through a system of veins and capillaries, the spirit interacts with the body and directs its motions. The problem with this solution to the question of how the mind and body interact is that it really does not answer the deeper issue. If the spirit (or mind) is completely nonphysical and does not extend into space, then it seems impossible, no matter what the hypothesis, to explain how it can impinge upon and affect a substance that is entirely physical. The movement of physical substance is explained by impact, yet nonphysical substance cannot come into direct contact with anything and so it cannot impact anything, let alone physical substance. If we accept the idea that mind and body are composed of two completely distinct substances, then in principle it seems as though the interaction between the two must remain mysterious. This is what is today known as the "mind/body problem."

Descartes resolved the conflict between religion and science by suggesting that whereas science has authority in explaining the physical structure of the universe, the Church retains ultimate and final authority as the institution that holds the truths about God and the soul, mind, or spirit of human beings. The Church is to be obeyed in matters of mind and soul, while science is to be obeyed in matters of physical explanation. Yet the cost of this new division of labor was to introduce the mind/body problem into philosophy. Many later Cartesian philosophers would devote their careers to trying to resolve this problem with a variety of bizarre and sometimes quite clever proposals. However, none of the solutions could ever work as long as the substances of mind and body were conceptualized as absolutely distinct. Today, some contemporary philosophers continue to wrestle with the Cartesian assumption of a duality between the mind and body, yet most of their solutions remain as bizarre as some of the solutions of Descartes' followers. As we see continually throughout the history of human thought, the resolution of one problem has led us face to face with yet further mysteries.

DESCARTES AND WONDROUS DISTRESS

Descartes is one of the most important figures in the history of Modern philosophy, not only because he offered a serious and sustained defense of science but because he reminded the world that keeping an open mind and being willing to raise uncomfortable questions is necessary to the growth and nurturance of human thinking. The transition between Medieval and Modern times was characterized by a great deal of friction between the old beliefs that were championed by the Church and the new discoveries of science. From the perspective of those committed wholeheartedly to either side of this battle, the times must have seemed dire. From the religious viewpoint, the world seemed to be falling away from God. From the scientific viewpoint, it appeared as if old-fashioned bigotry and superstition had the upper hand over reason and rationality. What Descartes tried to show was that both religion and science stand to benefit from the philosophical impulse to question the foundations upon which ideas rest.

Asking questions and being open to new speculations about the nature of the universe do not need to make us fearful. If approached with a sense of wonder, such philosophical activity can help us to advance the cause of human thinking as a whole. When we are able to set aside the appetite for power, prestige, and authority, and when we no longer concern ourselves overwhelmingly with the desire to control and dominate the imaginations of those around us, then we can get on with the much more important task of seeking Truth itself.

This wondrous impulse toward knowledge is balanced in Descartes' thinking with an equally well-developed sense of distressing uncertainty. Although he explicitly sets himself against the destructive project pursued by the ancient Greek skeptics, Descartes realizes that the positive and constructive part of his own philosophy cannot move forward until such time as he addresses the nagging, skeptical doubts that present a challenge to his plan. It is a testament to Descartes' serious commitment that he is willing to so thoroughly question many of the beliefs which he ultimately reestablishes as truths by the end of *Meditations on First Philosophy*. Some readers of the *Meditations* have balked at this strategy, especially when it comes to the "dream" and the "evil genius" hypotheses, complaining that Descartes has gone too far with such speculations and that, in the concluding sections, he just ends up where he started anyway. Why then even bother to question the existence of the physical world and the truths of math when in the end the intuitions of common sense are vindicated? But the more we consider Descartes' intentions, the more apparent his philosophical genius becomes. Descartes is so devoted to absolute Truth that for him, any degree of uncertainty is intolerable. This same intolerance to uncertainty leads many less philosophically minded people to simply close their eyes and to turn away from the evidence and the difficult arguments which present challenges to their intuitively held beliefs. For such nonphilosophical minds, mental comfort and the unperturbed serenity of unquestioned belief is always preferable to an exhausting, unsettling, and potentially hazardous journey into the depths of skepticism. Instead of recoiling from the dangers of such an undertaking, however, Descartes embraces this quest and utilizes his own distressing uncertainty as a tool for the potential discovery of a solid foundation which will anchor his convictions. He does take chances and he does run the risk of reaching a point of no return with his method of doubt, but this is precisely what makes his writing and his thinking so exciting to so many of us. Like Socrates before him, Descartes reveals how little it is that we do know for certain, but in the process he also shows us how important it is to dig deep in order to try to justify our ideas nonetheless.

In contrast, the least philosophically satisfying parts of the *Meditations* are those in which Descartes becomes too anxious for Truth, and where he seems to forget the importance of his doubting strategy. At these times it seems as if the distressing nucleus of skepticism fades away from his thinking and Descartes becomes overeager to find his bedrock foundation. In these sections, the real criticism of Descartes may be not that he is too dubious but that he is not dubious enough. Such, I feel, is the case in his arguments for God's existence in the third meditation. It is here, in his anxious desire to reestablish a connection between the subjective realm of thinking and the objective realm of the world outside of the mind that Descartes appeals to a variety of "manifest truths" that have themselves not been subjected to the cold, hard inspection of Cartesian Doubt. This, I think, reveals what may be an underlying problem in the way that Descartes sometimes uses his method.

The Cartesian strategy presupposes that the way toward finally uncovering the Truth about reality is in the direction of doubting everything that we can possibly doubt. When we find something that cannot be doubted, Descartes claims, then we have discovered a truth. But as we have seen in this chapter's discussion, different people may have different levels at which they are able to tolerate doubt. Just because one person finds it impossible to doubt some particular assertion does not mean that some other person will not be able to doubt that very same assertion. In short, the inability to doubt something does not make that thing true. Descartes was unable to doubt the "manifest truth" of a principle stating that something greater cannot be produced from a cause lesser than itself, yet today we can easily doubt this principle. What this shows us is that it is overly hasty to claim that our subjective inability to doubt things establishes anything as objectively necessary about the world. At best, doubt works to undermine our unquestioned confidence in opinions we have held unreflectively. It does not, however, necessarily lead to the discovery of final truths. Descartes sometimes oversteps the legitimate bounds of his own method by mistakenly using doubt in order to establish truths rather than simply to eliminate falsehood. In so doing, he ends up abandoning the true spirit of philosophy by allowing his enthusiasm for final answers to overwhelm his sense of uncertainty. This is why, as Bertrand Russell has pointed out, the destructive part of Descartes' project is often more convincing than the constructive part.

All of this calls to mind Descartes' discussion in *Meditation IV*. It is in this section that Descartes advises us, with a great deal of philosophical wisdom, always to be careful not to allow our infinite will for knowledge to overpower the finiteness of our intellectual capacity to understand the world. When we are too eager to reach final answers, we tend to jump to conclusions. When we ignore the nagging doubts and uncertainties that always accompany human claims to knowledge, we fall into dogmatism and ignorance. Descartes was well aware of these dangers, and yet he himself often falls prey to them. When he does so, Descartes also falls short of the ideal of philosophy. However, at his best and most philosophical moments, Descartes exemplifies both the wondrous desire for Truth and the distressing awareness of his own separation from the Truth. The formulation of the Cartesian Method, in fact, is probably best understood as a means by which Descartes and his followers could remind themselves of the importance of keeping both wonder and distress alive in their thinking. Like a ritual practice, the Cartesian Method offers a form of discipline that is designed to keep us on the path of philosophy.

QUESTIONS FOR DISCUSSION

1. What are the reasons that the geocentric theory of the universe was accepted for so long? What are the arguments against this theory? Imagine that you were living in Ancient or Medieval times. Can you imagine any evidence that would lead you to reject this theory?

2. Do you think that Galileo is a coward for giving in to the demands of the Catholic Church? What do you imagine that Socrates would have done under these circumstances?

3. Why was the Catholic Church so resistant to the insights of thinkers such as Copernicus, Galileo, and Kepler? Do you think that it was necessary for the Church to resist their insights, or could the Church have prospered in spite of these new scientific discoveries?

4. Descartes claimed that the Church and science should have authority in differing realms. Do you agree with Descartes or do you think that the Church and science must necessarily be in conflict with one another?

5. What is the Cartesian Method? Discuss the ways that this method is still used today.

6. In what ways does Descartes draw upon Medieval arguments in order to establish the existence of God? Do you think his arguments are sound? Why do you think he felt it necessary to prove God's existence?

7. The mind/body problem is a puzzle that is still debated today. Do you think there is any possible solution to this problem? By what mechanism do you think the mind and the body interact?

NOTES

1. This is an attitude encouraged by both religion and science, two fields that claim to give voice to ahistorical truths. In this regard, Robert Paul Wolff notes that mathematics and the sciences "consign even their classics to the farthest corners of the library." See Robert Paul Wolff, "Introductory Remarks to the Reader," in *Ten Great Works of Philosophy* (New York: Mentor Books, 1969), p. ix. Thomas Kuhn likewise observes, "The depreciation of historical fact is deeply, and probably functionally, ingrained in the ideology of the scientific profession.... The result is a persistent tendency to make the history of science look linear or cumulative." See Thomas Kuhn, *The Structure of Scientific Revolutions* (Chicago: University of Chicago Press, 1962), pp. 138–139.

2. For a book-length treatment of this hostility, see Bruce Wilshire, *Fashionable Nihilism: A Critique of Analytic Philosophy* (Albany: SUNY Press, 2002).

3. Kuhn, *The Structure of Scientific Revolutions*, p. 88.

4. In fact, Aquinas referred to Aristotle as "the Philosopher."

5. Aristotle, *On the Heavens,* II.14. 296b.27.

6. Ibid., II.14.296b.5. It would be much later in history that the phenomenon of parallax would be measured and thus disprove Aristotle's contention in this passage.

7. I. Bernard Cohen contends that the phrase "sphere of influence," used today in a nonastronomical sense, may derive its origins from this theory. See I. Bernard Cohen, *The Birth of a New Physics* (New York: W. W. Norton & Company, 1985), p. 27.

8. Aristotle, *On the Heavens*, ii.14.296b26.

9. This is when the Roman Catholic and the Eastern Orthodox Churches officially divided.

10. Stephen Hawking, *A Brief History of Time* (New York: Bantam Books, 1990), p. 180.

11. Tycho Brahe had his own pet theory about the structure of the solar system, which was known as the "Tychonic System." In it, the moon orbits the Earth while all of the other planets orbit the sun, which in turn orbits the Earth. Thus, the Earth remains the center of the system.

12. There is recent speculation that Tycho Brahe may have been murdered by Kepler so that he, Kepler, could get a hold of all of Tycho's secret observational data. Tycho died a sudden and painful death that may have been due to mercury poisoning, and because Kepler stood to benefit from Tycho's elimination, some suspicion has fallen on Kepler. See Joshua Gilder and Anne-Lee Gilder, *Heavenly Intrigue: Johannes Kepler, Tycho Brahe, and the Murder Behind One of History's Greatest Scientific Discoveries* (New York: Anchor Books, 2005).

13. Eliot Albert claims that this makes Bruno a far more radical thinker than Copernicus. Albert claims that we should stop talking about the "Copernican Revolution" and instead talk about Bruno as the instigator of the modern viewpoint. See Eliot Albert, "The Shattering of the Crystal Spheres: 'rolling from the centre toward X' in *Nihilism Now!* (New York: St. Martin's Press, 2000), pp. 1–17.

14. René Descartes, *Discourse on Method* (Indianapolis, IN: Library of the Liberal Arts, 1983), p. 12.

15. Ibid., p. 18.

16. Michael Williams points out that this tactic points to a sort of metaphysical commitment in Descartes' philosophy that may not be immediately apparent. The idea of a "foundation" for knowledge is assumed, but never argued for, in Descartes' works. "Only Descartes' artful method of exposition ... prevents this from being immediately apparent" (p. 47). "Descartes and the Metaphysics of Doubt," in *Descartes*, John Cottingham, ed. (Oxford: Oxford University Press, 1998), pp. 28–49.

17. René Descartes, *Meditations on First Philosophy* (Indianapolis, IN: Hackett Publishing Company, 1993), p. 1.

18. Ibid.

19. Presumably, on the seventh day Descartes rested!

20. Descartes, *Meditations*, p. 13.

21. Ibid., p. 15.

22. Ibid., p. 16.

23. Ibid., p. 18.

24. Descartes, *Discourse on Method*, p. 21.

25. Descartes, *Meditations*, p. 26.

26. Ibid.

27. Ibid.

28. Ibid., pp. 27–28.

29. Ibid., p. 28.

30. Ibid.

31. René Descartes, "Third Set of Objections with the Author's Replies," in *Modern Philosophy: An Anthology of Primary Sources*, Roger Ariew and Eric Watkins (eds.) (Indianapolis, IN: Hackett Publishing Company,1998), p. 69.

32. Descartes, *Meditations,* p. 28.

33. Ibid.

34. Davies, *The Cosmic Blueprint,* p. 52.

35. This is why Russell claims "The constructive part of Descartes' theory of knowledge is less interesting than the earlier destructive part. It uses all sorts of scholastic maxims, such as that an effect can never be more perfect than its cause, which have somehow escaped the initial critical scrutiny. No reason is given for accepting these maxims, although they are certainly less self-evident than one's own existence, which is *proved* with a flourish of trumpets." Bertrand Russell, *A History of Western Philosophy* (New York: Simon and Schuster, 1972), p. 567.

36. Descartes, *Meditations,* p. 36.

37. Ibid.

38. Ibid., p. 47.

39. Recall the arguments of the Stoics and of St. Augustine in this regard (Chapters 5 and 6).

40. Descartes, *Meditations,* p. 53.

41. The pineal gland gets its name from the fact that it is shaped like a tiny pine cone. According to *Black's Medical Dictionary,* "there is increasing evidence that, in some animals at least, it is affected by light and plays a part in hibernation and in controlling sexual activity and the colour of the skin." *Black's Medical Dictionary,* 35th Edition, edited by C. W. H. Harvard (Totowa, NJ: Barnes and Noble Books, 1987), p. 542.

Chapter 8

Hume

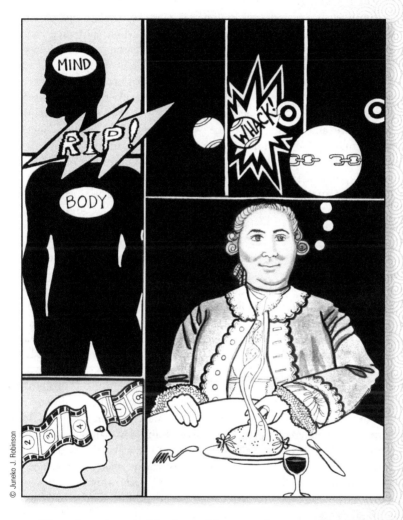

© Juneko J. Robinson

How does the mind/body problem reveal a potential incoherence within Cartesian metaphysics? In what ways does David Hume turn away from the assumptions of Cartesian philosophy? From where does knowledge of the world originate according to Hume? How does the mind organize simple ideas into complex ideas? Why does Hume think ideas like causation, God, and the self are nonsense? What is the basis of morality according to Hume?

THE MIND/BODY PROBLEM

Descartes' dualistic metaphysics left Western philosophy with a picture of a world in which mind and body exist as completely different sorts of substances. Body, the material substance that forms the physical portion of the world, is completely inert and nonthinking; it possesses the quality of extension into space but has no consciousness of its own. Mind substance, on the other hand, is conscious. It thinks, feels, judges, understands, and allows for the existence of ideas and concepts, yet it is completely nonphysical and so does not extend into space. These two substances, Descartes claims, mix and intermingle with one another in such a manner that in human beings they "compose a certain unity,"[1] thus accounting for the everyday relationship between our physical and mental existence. One is reminded here of Socrates' teacher Anaxagoras and his claim that the universe is made up of "seeds" of matter that are interpenetrated by the intelligence of nous or mind.[2] Mind guides the body, intelligently making decisions concerning its movements. It is a sort of "ghost in the machine" that directs and controls the body, and after the death of our physical being, because mind is itself completely nonphysical in composition, it may even conceivably continue to exist apart from the body.

Mind and body, in this way of thinking, are completely different sorts of things, and yet they are presumed to causally affect one another. However, because of their radically opposed qualities, it is quite puzzling how it is that one of these things really can causally influence the other thing. Common experience shows us that when our minds desire for our arms to move, generally our arms do move, and so it appears that, in fact, the mind can produce effects in the body. Conversely, when our bodies fall victim to injury, our minds experience pains that seem to be triggered by the violent physical events. So it appears as if the body can, in fact, produce effects in the mind. Furthermore, there are certain emotional states that are associated with both physical and mental qualities at the same time. When I am nervous, for instance, I not only feel mentally agitated, but my body sweats and my hands shake. But if mind is nonphysical, and thus has no parts, how can it make the body do anything? Likewise, if the body has only parts, how can it make a substance like mind, which has no parts, feel anything? Mind and body must somehow succeed in interacting with one another if they are to produce the sort of mind/body unity that we experience on a regular basis, but how is all of this possible if the mind and body are two completely different sorts of substances? By what mechanism does their interaction occur?

"SOLUTIONS" TO THE MIND/BODY PROBLEM

This last question has troubled many philosophers and has led to the proposal of many different answers, but as long as one adheres to a Cartesian–dualistic

---

B o x 8.1 The Mind/Body Connection

Descartes was convinced that the mind and the body do, indeed, interact with one another. The problem was to explain just how it is that a completely nonphysical substance (mind) could interact with a completely physical substance (body). What is the mechanism?

Today, many schools and hospitals offer classes that focus on the connection of mind and body, even though scientists themselves still puzzle over this problem. Usually, classes in the mind/body connection focus on insights and techniques that are drawn from Eastern forms of religion, spirituality, and philosophy. Ancient systems such as Hinduism and Buddhism suggest that meditation and yoga are ways that we can come to understand the link between our physical selves and our spiritual (mental) selves.

The therapeutic effect of these practices seems to be especially effective in treating anxiety and depression. Through bodily discipline and the conscious control of breathing, meditation helps to produce calming effects on a person's state of mind. Investigation into why and how this works may lead to new discoveries about the connection between mental and physical states.

Western psychologists and psychiatrists believe that there is often a chemical/physical cause for our mental states. The prescription of antidepressant and mood-altering medications indicates that there is some sort of consistent and predictable connection between bodily and mental states. It is interesting, however, that while it is clear that mood-altering medications do in fact produce results, it is still unclear how and why they do so.

---

separation between mind and body, any answer must proceed in one of two ways: either by attempting to find a bridge between mind and body, or by showing that what seems like an interaction between the two is really not an interaction at all but an illusion that can be accounted for in some other way. Descartes, of course, followed the first of these strategies and tried to argue that it was God who created a mysterious connection between mind and body. He claimed that within the brain's pineal gland there is an articulation of mind with body that we humans can't really explain or fully understand, but that God in his goodness and wisdom has seen fit to make actual. But this is just another way of saying "God works in mysterious ways," which is fine, but it doesn't really answer the original question "*how* do mind and body interact?" Any attempt to show a bridge between mind substance and body substance, it appears, will always be subject to this sort of problem. If we continue to accept that mind and body are completely different from one another, then in order to explain their interaction there must be a bridge between them. However, any bridge between mind and body must itself be partly mind and partly body, and so we run into the original problem all over again: how do mind and body interact to form this bridge? This trajectory inevitably leads to an infinite regress, and the only solution that will produce a final answer will be to assert that some mysterious force, like God, makes it so.

Because there is in principle no way to understand the nature of a bridge between two completely incompatible substances, there are only a few possible solutions that remain to the mind/body problem. First, you might deny that mind really exists and claim that what appears as mind is really just a form of the body. Second, you might deny that material substance really exists and claim that what appears as body is really just a form of the mind. Third, you might claim that while both mind and body substances do exist, the apparent interaction of one with the other is really just an illusion. Finally, while claiming that mind and body substances really do exist, you might argue that at a more fundamental level they are actually manifestations of a single all-inclusive substance.

Thomas Hobbes and Materialism

Materialism is a doctrine that argues for the first of the above-mentioned solutions. The philosophy of Thomas Hobbes (1588–1679) will exemplify this viewpoint for us. A contemporary of Descartes, Hobbes denied that mind and matter interact by asserting that the material world is the only world that actually exists. Because there is no such thing as mind, there is no need to explain its interaction with matter. The universe, Hobbes held, is composed of bodies in motion and nothing else. All motion, furthermore, is determined by the ironclad rule of causal law. This holds no less for human beings than it does for nonhuman things. In truth, Hobbes claimed, the apparently free actions of human beings are not free at all; instead, they are governed by the same natural laws that control the rest of physical reality. Most of us tend to think that at least our own thoughts are free and undetermined, but according to Hobbes even this is not the case. Our inner, mental world does not consist of a distinct nonmaterial substance independent of the laws of cause and effect, but rather is a direct causal result of the physical motions that affect our bodies both from within and from without. Sensory perception results from observing physical objects in motion external to our own bodies, while emotions and feelings result from motions internal to our bodies. All mental thoughts, ideas, and conceptions, Hobbes claims, are in reality just mere "phantasms" that may be explained away as the result of various sorts of physical activity that originate from within or outside of the brain. Appeals to mental substance are unnecessary in this view. All that really exists is physical substance.

Hobbes' teaching is just one example of materialism. What we describe as "mind," claim the materialists, is just an artifact of the physical functioning of the brain, a mere epiphenomenon that emerges unintended out of the brain's complex physical structure, and the language of mental phenomena serves no real purpose. It simply fools us into thinking that we have some sort of freestanding soul or mind, when in fact we are only very complicated machines that act according to the rules of physics. This view recalls the ancient claims of Democritus and his follower Epicurus, and it is a perspective that has many adherents in the scientific world today. Philosophical materialism has led directly

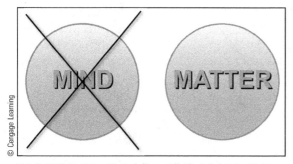

FIGURE 8.1   Materialism: All That Exists Is Matter

to contemporary work in the field of artificial intelligence, which presumes that out of the material components of computers, something like a human mind or thinking machine can be produced.[3] With this viewpoint, mind and matter are not incompatible properties of the world precisely because mind does not exist as a freestanding substance. At best, the term "mind" is just a way of speaking about matter and its motions. At worst, it is a useless and distracting term that deludes us and encourages us to believe in something that just does not exist. In any case, according to materialism, the mind/body problem is premised on the false assumption that mind is a substance that actually exists. Once we eliminate this false belief, claim the materialists, we no longer have a problem because we no longer need to explain the interaction between mind and matter (see Figure 8.1).

George Berkeley and Idealism

If the materialists are right, then Descartes was wrong, and the human soul cannot exist after the death of the body. This is one of the disturbing implications of materialism. Materialism also seems to imply that free will is an illusion, because most materialists claim that matter is governed by the ironclad laws of physics and not by choice. Machines, after all, don't freely decide to do what they do; they act out of causal necessity. What does this mean for our ideas about morality and justice? How can we hold anyone ethically responsible for actions that are the result of natural, physical causes? These sorts of problems make materialism quite implausible to many people, and so it should be no surprise that some philosophers have found themselves more attracted to the claims of Idealism.

Idealists, like George Berkeley (1685–1753), suggest that it is the language of physical substance, rather than mental substance, which is dispensable from our vocabulary. Following on the insights of Descartes, Berkeley observed that the only things that we ever have absolutely direct contact with are the ideas in our minds. Even when I claim to see a physical object like a table, it is really the idea of a physical object that I am experiencing directly. All perceptions, in fact, are made possible only through the mediation of ideas, and it is only by a further inference that I can come to the conclusion that my ideas somehow correspond to a physical world "out there." But if this is so, what need is there to appeal to a physical world outside of ideas at all? Why not just eliminate the unnecessary assumption of a separate world of physical existence and instead assume that the mental phenomena appearing to us are all there is to reality?[4] Perhaps all of reality is just made up of ideas.

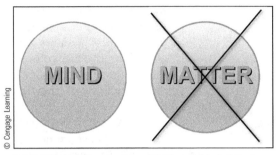

FIGURE 8.2 Idealism: All That Exists Is Mind

Berkeley asserts that "to be is to be perceived." This principle consistently dovetails with an empirical perspective on knowledge insofar as empiricism holds that the only way that we know anything is first by perceiving it with the senses. Berkeley agrees with this perspective wholeheartedly, and he develops the empiricist's position to a rather startling conclusion. If all knowledge originates in sense perceptions, then we have no solid reason to believe in anything outside of sense impressions. Our reality is just a world of ideas perceived by our minds. "To be is to be perceived." Does this mean, then, that when I stop perceiving my reality, as happens when I go to sleep or when I die, that the world disappears? Berkeley says that this is not the case. Instead, there must be an objective all-encompassing mind, the mind of God, that goes on perceiving the world even when my own finite mind ceases to do so. It is the ongoing perception by God that assures the objective existence of reality independent of any particular human mind. In effect, the entire universe is made up of the thoughts in God's mind. Thus, there really is no such thing as matter; only ideas. Idealism thus dissolves the mind/body problem by denying the existence of body altogether, eliminating the need to show how a nonphysical thing like an idea can interact with a physical substance (see Figure 8.2).

Arnold Geulincx, Nicholas Malebranche, and Occasionalism

The third of the above-mentioned solutions to the mind/body problem was proposed by the Cartesian philosophers Arnold Geulincx (1624–1669) and Nicholas Malebranche (1638–1715). These two thinkers suggested that what appears to us as the causal interaction between our minds and our bodies is just an appearance. In fact, the two substances of mind and matter, though both real, are forever separate, one never having any affect on the other. What appears as an interrelation between the two is really just a parallelism set up by God. When I will my arm to move and it proceeds to move, it is not really my mind that is producing movement in my arm, claim Geulincx and Malebranche. It is actually God who has produced in my mind a desire to move, and has also simultaneously yet separately caused my body to move. God is like a puppeteer who manipulates

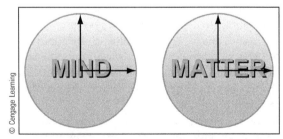

FIGURE 8.3 Occasionalism: Mind and Matter Are Synchronized but Have No Causal Interaction with One Another

both the thoughts and the bodies of human beings in such a manner that mind and body seem to work together, when in fact they never really have any direct contact with one another. To use another analogy, the physical and the mental worlds are like two synchronized clocks that appear to run together only because a clockmaker (God) has made it so.[5] This solution to the mind/body problem is known as "Occasionalism." It is so named because thoughts in the mind are treated not as causes of bodily movement but merely as occasions for movements that in fact result from a third cause; namely, God (see Figure 8.3).

Gottfried Leibniz, Baruch Spinoza, and Monism

Materialism, Idealism, and Occasionalism are all rather awkward and, quite frankly, implausible solutions to the mind/body problem. There is an artificiality about these doctrines that strikes us as desperate. How is it that mental ideas and physical bodies are related to one another? Materialism, Idealism, and Occasionalism all end up by concluding that there is no relationship between ideas and bodies either because mind doesn't really exist, or because matter doesn't really exist, or because the two substances, even if they do exist, are forever separated from one another. But each of these "solutions" appears to deny something that most of us take to be true: both mind and body are real, and they do interact with each other. Is there any way of saving both mental and physical substance in the process of addressing the mind/body problem?

In the work of Gottfried Leibniz (1646–1716) and Baruch Spinoza (1632–1677), we find two separate, yet similar, attempts to do just this. The strategies pursued by these two thinkers are similar, and they remind us of the work first undertaken by the Presocratic thinkers Anaximander and Anaxagoras, who suggested that the underlying substance of the universe must be of some sort of ambiguous constitution such that it may support all of the apparently contradictory qualities that we really do observe in the world. In the case of Leibniz and Spinoza, an attempt is made to explain the coexistence of mind and matter by digging deep into the ontological structure of reality and showing that at its foundations, the world is rooted in some single substance that transcends and yet also encompasses the properties of both mind and matter.

Let us first examine the philosophy of Leibniz. Leibniz is rightly considered a genius, not just for his ideas in metaphysics, but also for the fact that he invented calculus independent of Newton's own simultaneous work. There was a nasty battle between these two thinkers over who made the discovery first and thus over who would take credit for it. As Bertrand Russell writes, it appears to be Leibniz who, in the end, "died neglected" in this matter. In any case, Leibniz's contributions to the history of philosophy are today well recognized, and his main fame lies in a very strange metaphysical vision of the universe. This vision drew from the insights of the Occasionalists, who have already been discussed briefly, and from the ideas of Spinoza, who will be discussed later.

Leibniz begins by observing that the basic substance out of which the universe is composed cannot be material in nature. All matter has the quality of extension into space, as Descartes had already observed. But if this is the case, and if the universe is composed of material substance, then it is infinitely divisible. Anything that has extension has length, and if something has length, it can be divided into parts. Because all matter by its very nature has extension, it always has length and can therefore always be divided into smaller and smaller parts. If the universe is ultimately composed of matter, then it makes no sense to speak of a fundamental material foundation. Any supposed material foundation could always be divided into an even more fundamental foundation, and so on, thus the idea of a basic material substance that grounds all reality must be nonsense.

So what is the alternative? Leibniz is led to the conclusion that if there is a final foundational substance that grounds our world, it must be extensionless, and he seems convinced that some such substance must, in fact, exist. The name he gives to this extensionless substrate out of which everything else around us arises is the *monad*. As in the doctrine of Occasionalism, monads are self-enclosed substances that never have any causal interaction with one another. They do tend to group together and to form "colonies," however, and it is out of these colonies that our world is formed. The inner character of each monad is something like a mind that mirrors the entirety of the universe in itself, and yet it also is something like a point in space that occupies a place. Thus, even though each monad contains a reflection of the universe within it, no two monads are the same because their reflection of the universe comes from a unique spatial perspective. Each monad is, consequently, distinctive and unique from all other monads. In this way, Leibniz seems to be suggesting that the universe is made up of an infinite number of discrete substances, but in another way he also seems to be asserting that all of these discrete substances are of the same kind. Like the "seeds" of Anaxagoras, the monads come together, and in their diversity they harmonize to produce the universe of which we ourselves are a part (see Figure 8.4).

How does this harmony between the monads emerge? In the famous words of Leibniz, it is a harmony that has been "preestablished" by God. Among the monads, there is a hierarchy. Some of them reflect a very clear picture of the rest of the universe, and some of them reflect a very confused picture of the rest of the universe. Think about a group of people watching a football game. Imagine that some of these people

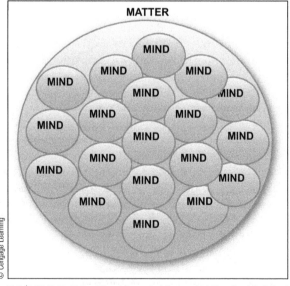

FIGURE 8.4 The Monad: Matter Is Mixed with Mind

view the game from up close with no impediments to their perspective. Others, however, are sitting far away, in the back of the stadium, and so must crane their necks and peer around columns to see the action on the field. Those spectators who are close to the action would have a better understanding of what is going on during the game than would those who are far away and whose view is obstructed. Likewise, some monads have a better understanding of the structure of their own colonies than do others. The monad with the clearest understanding of the structure of the totality of reality is God, and it is the God monad that has, in fact, established harmony between all the other monads. There are many other possible alternative realities that could have been established, just as there are many possible alternative ways of seating people at a football game. However, because God has a perfectly clear and unlimited understanding of what would be entailed by these possibilities, He is also able to anticipate which reality will be the best and most harmonious one. Thus, God has made the choice of bringing into existence this particular world, the one which we now inhabit, precisely because it is the best of all possible worlds. Though the world may not be perfect, like a well-built football stadium, it is intelligently designed to fulfill its purpose in the best manner possible.

The monad is a substance that is neither mind nor matter but something that encompasses the qualities of both mind and matter. It is, as W. L. Reese puts it, something like a "center of force" by which reality is held together as a whole. By positing this entity, Leibniz is able to establish the fundamental origins of the world and to show how it is that mind and matter are rooted in one and the same underlying substance. The mind/body problem is thus solved. Mind and matter are really just appearances that arise out of the harmonious coexistence of large numbers of monads. There is still a bit of cheating going on here, however; like Descartes before him, Leibniz leaves it up to God to explain exactly how it is that all of this works. In the end, we are left with the view that God makes it so.

As mentioned previously, Leibniz was influenced not only by the Occasionalists, from whom he adopted the metaphor of synchronized clocks in order to describe the preestablished harmony of our world, but also by the philosopher Baruch Spinoza. Spinoza was, like Leibniz, concerned with offering a resolution to the apparent incompatibility between mind and matter, and he also ultimately concluded that it is God who makes such interaction possible. Spinoza's philosophy is different from Leibniz's, however, in that Spinoza claims that God is the only substance that actually exists. Whereas Leibniz grounded our world in the existence of a multitude of distinct and unique monads, Spinoza grounds the world in God Himself.

According to Spinoza, by definition there can only be one substance. The very meaning of the term "substance," he asserts, refers to something which does not depend upon anything else for its continued existence. A color, for instance, must inhere within something other than itself in order to exist. You don't find a color floating around in the air, after all. It must actually be in an object that is tangible and substantial. Thus, you may have a red apple, but not just "red." The apple in this case is a substance, and the color red is a quality of that substance.

Yet, apples also rely on other things, like trees and water and soil for their existence, and so they cannot truly be considered as fully self-subsistent. As we saw in our discussion of Plato, Aristotle, and St. Thomas Aquinas, this is the case for anything that exists in our world. No particular things that we can see, taste, touch, or feel are completely self-dependent. All things arise and decay, and so they require something beyond themselves to exist. But if this is so, then there really is no such thing as a substance that exists in our world. There are only transitory qualities. If this is so, then there must be some universal substance beyond our sensory experience that supports all other things and that allows them to actually become manifest.

The one substance that does exist, and upon which all other things are dependent, is God. In Spinoza's philosophy, God is the only thing that does not depend upon anything else, and so by definition God is the one true substance. All other things that we see in our world are "modes" of God. God, being infinite, contains an infinite number of modes, not all of which we perceive. The two modes that we can detect, however, are the modes of mind and body. Mind and matter exist together in God, but from our perspective they come to appear as separate qualities, the way that the sweetness and the redness of an apple are experienced separately by us but are known nevertheless to exist together in the apple itself. God, not the monad, is the foundation of all that exists, according to Spinoza (see Figure 8.5). The mind/body problem is resolved when we understand that neither mind nor body is really substance at all. They are both simply modes of God. Because they are not substances, there is no inherent difficulty with their interaction. The answer, once again, to how mind and body are related to one another is that God makes it so.

The views of Leibniz and Spinoza, despite some key differences, are nonetheless examples of a monistic solution to the mind/body problem. Both thinkers have attempted to show how, at a fundamental level, both mind and body are grounded in some substance that is not simply mental or material, but which has aspects of both mind and matter within its nature. Like many of the Presocratic philosophers, these two thinkers claim that there exists an eternal, fundamental, and ambiguous sort of "stuff" from which all other things arise. For Leibniz it is the monad. For Spinoza it is God. In either case, neither mind nor matter is ultimate. Something lies behind both mind and matter, and this unseen "something" is what guarantees that the order and structure of our everyday world are maintained.

© Cengage Learning

FIGURE 8.5 Monism: Mind and Matter Are Part of a Single, Greater Whole

DAVID HUME AND THE EMPIRICIST REJECTION OF CARTESIAN METAPHYSICS

It is ironic, but eminently philosophical, that in his attempt to discover an absolutely certain foundation for his knowledge of himself and the world around him Descartes introduced a metaphysical system and a way of thinking that was successful in promoting much continued speculation and a whole host of questions concerning some very abstract topics. Descartes' philosophical system leaves a lot of unsolved problems and puzzles for us to consider. This is not the situation that Descartes had claimed he wanted to bring about. He had hoped that his *Meditations* would provide an absolutely certain foundation for all science and religion, yet what it seems to have done is to open up the door to unending conjecture and more than a little bit of mystery.

Recall that Descartes began his search for absolute certainty not by looking out into the world around him but by closing his senses off from the world and reflecting on the contents of his own mind. By looking inward instead of outward, Descartes hoped that he could eliminate error and ground his knowledge on a firm foundation of clear and distinct ideas. These ideas, he thought, existed in his mind *a priori*, or before experience. Descartes, in this respect, falls into a category of thinkers who are referred to as "rationalists." Rationalists, like Descartes and Plato before him, believe that the human mind is completely self-transparent, and that it contains certain innate ideas that can be meditated upon and sorted through by means of the sheer force of structured thought. All knowledge, rationalists claim, can be grounded with certainty in the necessary relations of innate ideas that appear in all minds regardless of experience.

John Locke

But not everyone thinks that the rationalists are right. Empiricists claim that instead of looking inward for knowledge, the proper place to look is outward. All of our ideas, or the most important ones, the empiricists say, come from the information we gain through our sense organs, and though our senses may not exactly mirror the true nature of reality, they are the best tools at our disposal. The most extreme empiricists, in fact, hold to the claim that there are no such things as innate ideas at all. Upon birth your mind is, as John Locke (1632–1704) claimed, a *tabula rasa*, or "blank slate."[6] It is experience that writes upon the blank slate of your mind, giving you ideas that you then proceed to rearrange and use as the basis of reason. According to this empiricist view, Descartes' assertion that he was at birth endowed with the ideas of selfhood and God is nonsense. Such ideas, the empiricists claim, come to the mind only after it has been exposed to sensory input.

According to Locke, all ideas come to the mind the way that writing comes to a piece of paper. Something must impinge upon the mind and place ideas into it, the way that a hand inscribes letters onto a page. Our sense organs receive impulses from the environment, and these impulses are received as perceptions of the mind, producing what Locke refers to as "simple ideas." Simple ideas cannot be broken down or analyzed because they are composed of the qualities our senses immediately convey to our minds. "Red," "rough," "soft," etc.; these are qualities that cannot be described any further. They represent raw experience. If you encounter someone who has never seen the color red, for instance, there is really no way that you can describe the color to this person. All you can do is give them exposure to the color so that they too have the same simple idea of red that you have. Or you might try to explain the color red as being like other colors that this person is immediately acquainted with. You might say that it is sort of like orange and brown mixed together. In so doing, however, you are presuming that the person is already acquainted with the simple ideas of orange and brown.

Now, Locke claims, some simple ideas correspond with the world as it really is, and some simple ideas correspond only to the way that our minds interpret sensory input. For instance, the shape and texture of an apple really do exist in the apple itself. On the other hand, the color and the taste of the apple exist only for us when we look at it or bite into it. There is no such thing as "red" independent of the observer, and there is no such thing as "sweet" independent of the taster. Those qualities that actually exist in the apple Locke calls "primary qualities." Primary qualities are stable and independent of interpretation. They actually exist objectively in the world. "Secondary qualities," on the other hand, exist only in the mind of the observer. A colorblind person and a person with normal sight both see the shape of the apple, but they do not see the same color of the apple. This suggests that the shape of the apple exists independent of the observer while the color is more like an interpretation of the individual observer's mind.

There must be some sort of underlying substances that ground both primary and secondary qualities, allowing them to occur together consistently, claims Locke. As we have seen again and again, it is hard to imagine a quality existing without some sort of stable substance within which it can exist. For this reason, Locke argues that there must be primary substances in which all other qualities exist. Why is it that I consistently discover red, round, sweet, and crunchy objects in the produce section of the supermarket? Because there are substances, called "apples," that exist in this world. But this is where Locke runs into problems. By its very nature, a substance is not subject to direct inspection by the senses. Only the qualities that inhere in the substance are discernible to our senses. Never do you see, taste, touch, or feel substance. You feel a particular texture. You see a particular shape. You taste a particular flavor. You never see, taste, touch, or feel substance itself. Try to imagine, for instance, what an apple would be like absent any particular color, shape, texture, flavor, smell, etc. It would be nothing at all! Plato encountered this problem and was thus led to the conclusion that ultimate reality must go beyond the world of sensory experience. The ultimate substances, Plato claims, are knowable only by abstracting them away from sensory input. It is the rational power of the mind that gives us the truest ideas about reality. Locke, however, refuses this conclusion and stubbornly hangs on to his empirical presuppositions. But in doing this, his philosophy runs into an insurmountable contradiction. A philosophy based on empirical assumptions cannot arbitrarily introduce nonempirical ideas like substance. What appears to have happened with Locke is that his empiricism only went part of the way; he still found it difficult to abandon some of the rationalist assumptions that Descartes had tried so vigorously to establish. In particular, this idea of substance seemed so "clear and distinct" to his reason that it was an impossible idea to shake.

But if empiricism is correct, then the rationalist Cartesian project was doomed from the start. If this is so, then it is no wonder that Descartes' metaphysical system results in a characterization of the world that is full of bizarre and unanswerable paradoxes like the mind/body problem. Maybe what is needed is a new form of skepticism that takes a critical look at the very ideas Descartes thought beyond doubt. Maybe those ideas like substance, selfhood, and God on which Descartes based his entire philosophy are not so certain after all. Maybe, instead of assuming that such supposedly "clear and distinct" ideas are inborn and necessary, we should initiate an inquiry into the sensory origin of such ideas. This was the challenge taken up by the Scottish philosopher David Hume (1711–1776).

David Hume was fed up with the sorts of abstract philosophical systems that had been constructed by Cartesians and other such metaphysicians. He sought to demolish these systems by demonstrating that they rested upon nothing other than "sophistry and illusion."[7] The major point he wanted to argue is that as long as beliefs and philosophies are ungrounded in observation and sensory experience, they must remain little more than superstitious fantasies that have no relation to reality. He believes that the appropriate way to rectify this situation is to undertake a full inquiry into the functioning and nature of the human mind. Hume's inquiry will take us into some unexpected territory. At the outset it may seem as though Hume's intention is, like Descartes', to rediscover a truly certain foundation, once and for all, for our knowledge of the world. But this is not what Hume ends up doing. Instead, Hume proceeds to argue that there is nothing in our experience of the world that is absolutely certain for all times. Because all of our ideas are gathered from observation of the world, and because the world changes through time, our observations of the world will likewise change through time. This being the case, we can never be certain from one moment to the next that our knowledge of the world will remain valid into the future. Alhough we may think it probable that the world will continue to appear to us as it has in the past, we can never be certain of this and thus we should always be sensitive and open to what further observation and experience have to teach us. With Hume, knowledge of ourselves and the world around us becomes probabilistic and open to constant revision rather than being mathematically certain and final.

THE GOOD-NATURED HUME

Hume was born in 1711, in Edinburgh, Scotland. In an autobiographical essay titled "My Own Life," he writes that his "ruling passion" was the study of literature and the desire for the attainment of his own "literary fame."[8] Hume was repeatedly frustrated in the second of these passions, as his earliest writings failed to gain a wide and popular audience. He tells us, however, that such disappointments and frustrations "never soured my temper,"[9] and he not only continued to

© Juneko J. Robinson

write and to publish, but he revisited his older books and rewrote and polished them for republication in the hopes that they would be better received. This detail gives us an interesting insight into Hume's overall approach to the world. For many academics and authors, lack of popular acceptance for their work is viewed as a symptom of the public's shallowness or, put another way, as proof of their own extreme depth of thinking. Often, the philosophical writer views himself or herself as a sort of sage who need not strive for clarity but who puts all of the responsibility for understanding on the shoulders of the audience. David Hume did not do this, and this is no doubt one of the reasons he has come to be so beloved by so many readers. When his first book, *A Treatise of Human Nature*, was a complete failure with the reading public, falling, as he himself writes, "dead-born from the press,"[10] Hume reworked it and subsequently republished it as two separate volumes; *An Inquiry concerning Human Understanding*, and *An Inquiry concerning the Principles of Morals*. The latter work, Hume claims, "is of all my writings, historical, philosophical, or literary, incomparably the best."[11] Hume, then, was the sort of man who didn't become bitter over his own failures or over the criticisms leveled at him by others. Instead, he took these as opportunities to refine his ideas and his presentation of those ideas. He seems to have believed that through this process his writing would become better, clearer, and closer to the truth. Through it all, he strove to remain in good humor and to keep his outlook positive. In the end, even as he lay dying from a "disorder of the bowels," Hume writes:

> I have suffered very little pain from my disorder, and what is more strange, have, notwithstanding the great decline of my person, never suffered a moment's abatement of my spirits, insomuch that were I to name the period of my life which I should most choose to pass over again, I might be tempted to point to this later period. I possess the same order as ever in study, and the same gaiety in company. I consider, besides, that a man of sixty-five, by dying, cuts off only a few years of infirmities; and though I see many symptoms of my literary reputation's breaking out at last with additional luster, I know that I could have but a few years to enjoy it. It is difficult to be more detached from life than I am at present.[12]

The good-natured Hume sounds, here, very much like Socrates, who also went to his death willingly, calmly, and without distress.

In what follows, I will treat *An Inquiry concerning Human Understanding* and *An Inquiry concerning the Principles of Morals* as containing the most well-articulated foundations of Hume's philosophy. This is not uncontroversial. Many authors claim that Hume "dumbed down" these books and that his true masterpiece remains the unaltered *Treatise of Human Nature*.[13] Whether this is true or not, I agree with Hume that what is found in the *Inquiries* represents some of his best and clearest writing. The *Treatise*, written while Hume was still very young, may be passionate but it is not polished.[14]

AN INQUIRY CONCERNING HUMAN UNDERSTANDING

Hume begins *An Inquiry concerning Human Understanding* by pointing out the "mixed nature" of human life. "Man is a reasonable being,"[15] he tells us. Humans, as Descartes already quite correctly observed, are thinking, rational creatures. We take pleasure from using logic and science to unlock the mysteries of the world. We enjoy solving puzzles and utilizing our reason to come to firm conclusions about things. However, "man is a sociable no less than a reasonable being."[16] We could never live happy lives without enjoying the company of others. All humans need to have friends with whom they talk and spend time. Finally, "man is also an active being."[17] Humans need to occupy themselves with work and projects in order to acquire a sense of meaning and accomplishment in life. Though humans are reasonable, sociable, and active, no one is all of these things all of the time, and Hume tells us that at points in our lives we need relaxation and rest from each of these aspects of our nature. None of us could ever be happy if all we did was think or socialize or work, and for this reason, "It seems, then, that nature has pointed out a mixed kind of life as most suitable to the human race, and secretly admonished them to allow none of these biases to draw too much, so as to incapacitate them for other occupations and entertainments."[18]

But neither must we neglect any of these aspects of our nature. The desire for relaxation may often encourage people to draw back from mental efforts that lead into difficult and obscure metaphysical territory. Thus, you will find those who refuse to engage their own intellects and who instead leave it to charlatans and cranks to offer answers to really difficult issues that could, with the proper effort, be answered instead with the application of rationality and logic. According to Hume, this is what produces popular superstition. People often turn to superstition when they feel incapable of thinking things through for themselves. They reject the power of reason to solve problems because reason requires work that is "painful and fatiguing,"[19] and so it is much easier to bestow on religion or some other sort of irrational power the authority to provide answers to the metaphysical mysteries of existence. This propensity should not be tolerated, according to Hume. The philosopher, especially, must submit to the "fatigue" that is involved in using rationality to unlock the secrets of the universe and try to think things through to their foundations. Like Descartes, Hume wants us, at least once in our lives, to attempt an inquiry into the very basis of human understanding so that we may, once and for all, appreciate how it is that we know what we know, and also appreciate those sorts of things that are beyond our comprehension. Unlike Descartes, Hume does not want to leave the Church or God with final and ultimate authority over affairs of the spirit. According to him, it is only when philosophers address the principles that govern human understanding and morality that we will be immunized against the nonsense perpetuated by superstition and "religious fears and prejudice."[20]

Impressions, Simple Ideas, and Complex Ideas

So from where is it that all of our understanding of the world originates? Hume tells us that our knowledge begins with ideas, and that all the ideas we have in our minds derive their origins from previous sense impressions. These sense impressions come either from the outer senses, like taste, sight, smell, touch, etc., or from the internal senses, like inner feelings and emotions. Wherever they come from, these impressions lead to the immediate creation of ideas in our minds. The only difference between impressions and the ideas that they give rise to is the fact that impressions are more "strong and vivid"[21] than ideas, although ideas are more long-lasting. For instance, if you put your hand in a fire, you will have an impression of burning heat as long as your hand is in contact with the flame. After you remove your hand from the flame, the impression will vanish but the idea of burning heat will remain in your mind. This sort of idea, claims Hume, is a "simple idea." By this he means that it corresponds almost exactly to a single impression that is received through an organ of sense. All legitimate knowledge, Hume claims, is traceable back to simple ideas that have their origin in simple impressions. Any idea that is not rooted in a simple impression is nonsense.

Simple ideas can be collected together in the mind over time and retained in the memory. The mind, however, is not completely passive in how it treats these ideas. Rather, it has a habit of organizing and connecting them together in strings of associations. When it combines and connects simple ideas together, the mind produces "complex ideas." Hume claims that there are basically three principles by which the mind connects simple ideas into complex ideas. These principles are: "Resemblance, Contiguity in time or place, and Cause and Effect."[22] For instance, suppose that you have an idea of your mother and an idea of a picture of your mother in your mind. It would be quite natural in this case for you to associate these ideas with each other according to the principle of resemblance. The picture itself is really nothing more than a piece of paper with patterns on its surface. Your mind, however, senses that there is some sort of resemblance between those patterns and the physical appearance of your mother. Thus, when the memory of the picture is called to consciousness, so is the idea of your mother. In fact, this is the reason why people carry pictures of loved ones with them. Pictures help call to mind the memory of a particular person or persons. This is possible by virtue of the principle of resemblance, which draws our minds from one idea to another to the degree that those ideas share some sort of likeness to one another.

Sometimes, furthermore, we associate ideas that have no necessary resemblance to one another but that simply follow one another in a temporal or spatial stream of consciousness. As an example, Hume asks us to consider the ideas of apartments in an apartment building.[23] It is natural, he claims, for our minds to be drawn from the idea of one apartment to the next by the principle of contiguity in time or place. Because apartments in apartment buildings are built right next to one another, the thought of one apartment leads our minds to consider its contiguity with other apartments in the building. I'm not sure that Hume's example is really the best one to illustrate his intention here because apartments in apartment buildings also usually resemble one another pretty closely. Perhaps a better example would be the ideas of differing foods that are shelved near one another in a supermarket. Our minds might be drawn, for instance, from the idea of vinegar to the idea of canned haggis not because they resemble one another in any significant way but because they are shelved next to each other (contiguously) in the market. Or perhaps we work in that supermarket as stock clerks and our minds are drawn from the idea of vinegar to canned haggis because we consistently shelve these products one after the other. In any case, the more times that we sense one thing occurring before, after, or next to another thing, our mind has the tendency, due to the principle of contiguity, to connect those things together. In the case of things like vinegar and canned haggis, we don't make the mistake of thinking that there is any sort of necessary connection between the things so associated. We realize that it is just a matter of happenstance or convention that they occur together, and so we would not be utterly shocked to find, upon walking into the supermarket one day, that the vinegar no longer appears next to the canned haggis. We would simply look for it somewhere else, assuming that the store manager had decided that this item should be shelved next to some other thing in the store; perhaps next to the Scotch whiskey.

Sometimes, however, people do make the mistake of thinking that two or more ideas that are merely associated with one another are instead necessarily connected with one another. This is what often happens with prejudice and superstition. Sometimes people have a few experiences of a certain type, and then they draw hasty generalizations from those experiences. For instance, suppose that a person has three bad experiences with a Scotsman. We would not be surprised to hear that that person developed a prejudice against the Scots, even though we know that it is probably not rational to do so on the basis of such limited experience. Or suppose that a person three times had a black cat cross his or her path and three times afterward suffered some sort of bad luck. Again, we would understand why such experiences might lead to a superstitious fear of black cats, but we would nonetheless know, rationally, that such fear was unfounded. Although our minds have a habit of wanting to draw hard and fast connections between contiguous events, Hume tells us that we must be on guard against doing so when it is unwarranted. Events that are merely associated with one another on the basis of resemblance or contiguity in time or place are not connected *necessarily* with one another. Rationally we know this; in practice we sometimes forget this fact.

There is, however, a third principle by which the mind associates ideas, which does involve the notion of a necessary connection. This is the principle of cause and effect. Imagine the idea of a wound, writes Hume, and your mind is naturally drawn to consider the idea of a cause for the wound. The wound is thought to be an effect of a previous event, such as a gunshot or a blow to the head. Normally, the cause is believed to precede the effect and the effect to

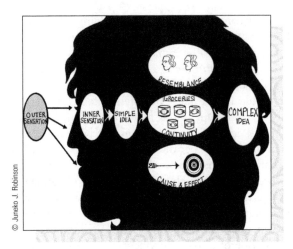

follow the cause. Any time that we connect two ideas together in a necessary manner, such that one idea is thought to represent an essential force that brought another idea into existence, the principle of cause and effect is utilized. Our minds tend to search for causes and to look for effects all of the time, claims Hume, even if we don't actually observe one or the other as it takes place. We do this because we don't believe that things just happen out of the blue. As Aristotle observed, we believe that all things occurring in the universe do so because some previous and objective cause has produced observable effects. Reasoning that proceeds by connecting ideas according to the principle of cause and effect is one of the most common ways that we claim to build up our knowledge about the world around us. Notice that it is different from mere contiguity in time and place insofar as the connection of cause and effect is claimed to be unbreakable. The same causes always result in the same effects.

Relations of Ideas and Matters of Fact

With these three principles—resemblance, contiguity, and causality—Hume thinks that he can explain the functioning of the human mind. All of our knowledge is built from the association of simple ideas into complex systems of ideas by means of these principles. With our senses, we take in sense impressions. Those sense impressions are copied by the mind as simple ideas, and those simple ideas are associated into strings of complex ideas that in turn define our claims to knowledge. But there is an important further distinction to be made between two separate categories of knowledge that have been produced by this process of human thinking. Hume tells us that while much of our reasoning takes place by way of the "relations of ideas" that already exist in our memories, some of our reasoning also tries to draw inferences beyond the ideas that we hold in our memories to reach conclusions about "matters of fact" about the world outside of our minds. "The relations of ideas" and "matters of fact" form two separate categories of human learning.

All of the ideas in our memory have an origin in experience. When we confine our reasoning to these ideas by simply inspecting the relations that hold between them in terms of resemblance and contiguity in time and space, we produce the sort of knowledge known as the "relations of ideas." This sort of knowledge derives from analyzing and inspecting the ideas we have already stored up in our memories, delineating how these ideas fit together in our minds independent of how they relate to anything outside of our minds. Hume seems to think that this is where we get such analytic systems of knowledge as are found in geometry, math, and logic. This sort of knowledge is absolutely certain, claims Hume, but its certainty comes at the price of telling us absolutely nothing about the state of the world outside of our minds. The truths of mathematics, geometry, and logic are truths that hold only in the abstract world of thought. Nowhere in the actual world of concrete reality will you find perfect circles or triangles, but it will always be certain, says Hume, that "... truths demonstrated by Euclid [will] forever retain their certainty and evidence."[24]

It may seem a little bit puzzling that an empiricist like Hume would claim that we can have knowledge of abstract entities which exist nowhere "in nature." Don't all ideas come from previous sense impressions, after all? What I think Hume is getting at here is that while you can be certain of the ways that ideas in your mind relate to one another, those relations tell us nothing about the *current* state of affairs in the actual concrete world after the time at which those ideas were stored, analyzed, and reflected upon by the operations of thought. Like the pictures in a photo album, the ideas in our heads may derive their initial existence from some sort of outside reality, but as time goes on, we can remain certain only of the internal relationships holding between the pictures themselves. As the real people depicted in the pictures change and die, the pictures retain an independent reality that has nothing to do with the current state of affairs in the world. Likewise, the ideas in our memories share no necessary resemblance to the state of the world outside of our memories after they have been stored. As the world around us changes from moment to moment, there is nothing to guarantee that the ideas we formed an instant ago are not now out of sync with objective reality, like the pictures from an old family photo album.

Yet, in addition to reasoning about the relations of ideas that already exist in our heads, humans have a desire to try to draw inferences from their ideas to the actual state of affairs in the world. This is what scientists do when they attempt to make predictions about the future based upon their past observations of reality. They collect observational data, analyze it, and then attempt to say something beyond what the ideas themselves contain. For instance, a chemist might repeatedly mix two chemical compounds and observe the reaction that occurs again and again, storing the ideas in his mind and sorting through them with the tools of logic. He then might predict, on the basis of what he has seen in the past, that every time he mixes these chemical compounds together in the future they will react in a like manner. Hume says that this sort of reasoning involves the principle of cause and effect. The chemist is claiming that the mixture of these chemicals is a cause and that the reaction that follows is an effect. This sort of reasoning falls into the category of what Hume calls "matters of fact," and when we reason about matters of fact, Hume claims, we always utilize the principle of cause and effect. But what does this mean? Hume embarks at this point on an investigation that will attempt to decode the very meaning of the idea of cause and effect.

What is cause and effect? Normally we think that the connection existing between a cause and its effect is a necessary connection. In other words, we think that every time we see an event that is a cause, it is followed inevitably

T A B L E 8.1   Relations of Ideas and Matters of Fact

Relations of Ideas	Matters of Fact
1. Absolutely certain	1. Never certain
2. Tell us nothing about the world	2. Tell us something about the world

by an event that is its effect. But does this ever really happen? Causes and effects can only be discovered through observation, claims Hume, but where in the world do we ever see a necessary connection between two events? Surely, we often see events that resemble one another, and we often see events that are contiguous in time and place, but do we ever see two or more events that are always and necessarily connected together in a relation of cause and effect? Hume asks us to consider the example of a couple of billiard balls in this regard. When one ball strikes another and the second ball proceeds to move, we assume that what we have observed is the first ball causing the second ball to move. But if this is what we have seen, then we must have seen a necessary connection between ball one and ball two. However, we never really in actual fact observe such a thing. All we see, no matter how many times we observe ball one strike ball two, are two distinct events: (1) one ball strikes a second ball; (2) the second ball moves. "They seem *conjoined*, but never *connected*."[25] It is quite imaginable that at some time in the future the first ball might strike the second ball but the second ball would not move. But if this is possible, then how can we say that there is a necessary connection of cause and effect occurring between these two events?

Hume concludes that we cannot. Any time that we talk about cause and effect as a necessary connection we are, in fact, going beyond the actual impressions we have experienced and thus simply talking nonsense. Yet the principle of cause and effect lies at the very heart of our reasoning about the matters of fact in the world. What Hume concludes, then, is that none of our knowledge about the world outside of our minds is certain. When we reason according to this principle what is really occurring is that our minds are expressing an expectation that something will follow from what we take to be a cause. Because we have seen things happen in conjunction with one another time and time again, we have developed the *habit* of concluding that they always happen together. But our future observations of the world might be different from those in the past, and so any conclusions that we draw on the basis of past experience are not necessary but merely probabilistic. We are willing to bet, in other words, that the future will be pretty much like the past, and because we are willing to make this bet we tend to think in terms of cause and effect. But there is no real certainty that this will always be the case. As Hume writes:

> Our idea, therefore, of necessity and causation arises entirely from the uniformity observable in the operations of nature, where similar objects are constantly conjoined together, and the mind is determined by custom to infer the one from the appearance of the other. These two

circumstances form the whole of that necessity, which we ascribe to matter. Beyond the constant *conjunction* of similar objects, and the consequent *inference* from one to the other, we have no notion of any necessity or connexion.[26]

Hume's analysis of cause and effect ends with a skeptical refutation of its legitimacy as a basis for our certainty about the nature of objective reality. We never actually see cause and effect, and so the idea is itself a kind of empty concept. At most, it is a habit of our minds. Because it is always possible that the future state of affairs in the world will change, our habit of thinking in terms of cause and effect really says nothing about the world itself. It only tells us about the things that we ourselves anticipate on the basis of what we have already observed about the world around us. Although we tend to think that the world around us is governed by this principle, Hume demonstrated that according to strictly empirical criteria, the notion of a necessary connection between events as they occur in the world is nonsense. Because we never have, and never can, see a necessary connection, we have no good empirical reason to believe it exists. Our minds may be in the habit of thinking in these terms, but that does not mean that cause and effect actually exists outside of our minds. The idea of cause and effect is, according to strictly empirical standards, a kind of superstition.

The Ideas of God and the Self

Hume contends that any legitimate idea must be traceable to a previous sense impression, and thus any idea that is not so traceable is empty nonsense. The idea of a necessary connection between the events in the world, then, is vacuous; or perhaps to put the matter more accurately, the idea of cause and effect is mistaken and confused. But so are a whole host of other ideas that philosophers, scientists, and everyday people have taken for granted throughout history. Take, for instance, the idea of God. Hume asks us to consider the sense impression from which we derived this idea. Recall that God is supposed to be the Supreme Being, infinite in goodness, truth, wisdom, and love. Is it possible that we have ever had a sense impression of a being possessing any of these infinite qualities? No, of course not, and so we have no reason to believe that such a being exists in the world. We may have a desire to believe that God exists, and believing in God may make our lives easier and happier, but we have no empirical proof that our idea corresponds to a matter of fact in the world of objective reality. At most, the idea of God derives from an internal hope or fear or longing. Its root is in a subjective feeling, not an objective matter of fact.

The concept of the self is another idea that Hume examines with devastating effects.[27] Descartes had claimed that he discovered his "self" by looking inward and unearthing the clear and distinct idea of a thinking substance. Yet Hume asks us to consider what exact impressions this idea derives from. According to Descartes' own words, his "self" is that thing that "… doubts, affirms, denies, knows a few objects, and is ignorant of many,—[who loves, hates], wills, refuses,—who imagines likewise, and perceives…."[28] But where in all of this is the sense impression of "self"? There is none, claims Hume. "For my own part, when I enter most intimately into what I call *myself*, I always stumble on some particular perception or other.... I never can catch *myself* at any time without a perception, and never can observe any thing but the perception."[29] All that Descartes discovered was a series of thoughts that occur in a temporal sequence. There is no impression of a thinking substance that underlies these thoughts, and so an objectively existing self that exists independent of those thoughts is nonsense. We have no really good empirical evidence that such a thing exists. All that the self is, according to Hume, is a "bundle or collection of different perceptions, which succeed each other with an inconceivable rapidity, and are in perpetual flux and movement."[30]

Hume's Skeptical Empiricism

As we can see, Hume takes his basic empirical assumptions and carries them to the most logical extremes. In strictly adhering to the claim that we cannot know about anything that does not first present itself to our senses, Hume demolishes many of the ideas and beliefs that Descartes had attempted to put on a firm foundation. Descartes had tried to show that all of science and religion could be grounded in the absolutely certain ideas of self and God. Hume, on the other hand, demonstrates that even these apparently foundational ideas are empty. Although we are accustomed to believing in them, we have no observational proof that they correspond to any sort of objective and independent reality. So what are the consequences of this for human knowledge? According to Hume, none of our speculations about matters of fact will ever yield any certitude. Science—insofar as it concerns itself with cause and effect—and religion—insofar as it concerns itself with God and the soul—can never produce absolutely certain knowledge about the world. This does not mean that we should abandon them altogether, but rather that we should recognize their limits and understand that we are fallible creatures who must forever remain unsure about objective matters of fact. Human beings are locked into a world of impressions and ideas that they have access to only through the perceptions of the mind. "The mind has never anything present to it but the perceptions, and cannot possibly reach any experience of their connection with objects."[31] Any claims about the world as it exists outside of the mind, and the ideas the mind contains, are subject to uncertainty. Knowing this, we can continue to live our lives exercising a kind of "mitigated skepticism" about the way the world appears to us. For instance, we can live and speak as if the laws of cause and effect are real, all the while understanding that this is not necessarily the case. Our impressions of the world may change in the future, and we should be sensitive to this possibility. But until we actually encounter such changes, our normal, everyday way of thinking about the world seems to be adequate for life. We are, after all, creatures of habit, of a "mixed nature," says Hume, and until our habits prove counterproductive, there is no good reason for us to change them.

Notice that Hume has completely rejected the Cartesian claim that our systems of knowledge must be grounded in absolute certainty. According to Hume, because all ideas come from experience, if you were to seriously undertake the project of Cartesian Doubt, you would end up discovering that there are no foundational, clear, and distinct ideas that exist in the mind *a priori*. Descartes' absolute skepticism, if consistently carried to its logical extreme, would in the end leave us with nothing to believe in whatsoever. So instead of doubting everything that can be doubted, Hume suggests that we should instead consider what seems more or less probable to us according to our experiences. While it is useful to ponder the sorts of philosophical suspicions that Descartes entertained, Hume tells us that we can't live our entire lives speculating about the world beyond our experience and worrying about whether it corresponds to our perceptions. It is good enough to trust in probabilities and live our lives according to the best odds. With this conclusion, Hume echoes the insights of the ancient Greek Skeptics, but he also turns against an entire tradition of philosophy that began at least with Socrates. Recall that while Socrates never claimed to have reached Truth itself, he still aspired toward absolute certainty. His dissatisfaction with those around him stemmed from the fact that they did not likewise strive for absolute Truth. Instead, they contented themselves with living unreflectively, accepting the world at face value, the way that prisoners in a cave accept the shadows on the wall as reality. Hume in effect tells us that all we can ever have are the shadows on the cave wall, and so while we might once in a while wonder about what casts the shadows, we should really not spend too much time in such speculations. Out of habit we can still believe in God, the self, and cause and effect, but if we want to talk and write about things that we really know well, we should stick only with those ideas that are rooted in our experiences. At the very end of *An Inquiry concerning Human Understanding*, Hume writes the following:

> When we run over our libraries, persuaded of these principles, what havoc must we make? If we take in our hand any volume—of divinity or school metaphysics, for instance—let us ask, Does it contain any abstract reasoning concerning quantity or number? No. Does it contain any experimental reasoning concerning matter of fact and existence? No. Commit it then to the flames, for it can contain nothing but sophistry and illusion.[32]

So it was that Hume himself took up the study of history, a discipline that, at least in certain ways, is more concerned with simply describing events as they appear to us rather than with metaphysical speculation upon the nature and causes of those events, and appropriately it was with the publication of his book, *A History of England*, that Hume finally found the success and fame he had so long desired.

Hume's philosophy is both empirical and skeptical, two qualities that are at the root of the scientific method. A scientist needs to be skeptical to see beyond the superstition and nonsense of common, everyday thinking. Galileo, for instance, was skeptical of the Aristotelian view of the universe, and by clearing his mind and actually looking at the skies through his telescope he was able to see the heavens as they really are, rather than as the Church wished for them to appear. Skepticism works like a ground-clearing device in this way, allowing the scientist to open up a space for accurate and careful empirical observations that tell us something more accurate about the true structure of the world. Yet Hume discovers that skepticism and empiricism can take us only so far in unearthing the world's mysteries. Because all observations must be filtered through the human mind, they are always subject to the distorting lens of human perspective. If we want to talk carefully about what it is that we really know, it is clear, claims Hume, that we must restrict ourselves to those simple ideas that clearly make themselves present to our consciousness, and not about the shadowy forces that lie behind those ideas. Our perceptions may or may not correspond to an objective reality beyond our own consciousness; we can't be sure. The best we can do is to recognize the diversity of possible experiences and be open to those experiences as they manifest themselves to us.

AN INQUIRY CONCERNING THE PRINCIPLES OF MORALS

There is no area of human experience that invites more diversity of opinion, and disagreement, than that of ethics and morality. In his book *An Inquiry concerning the Principles of Morals*, Hume attempts to apply his skeptical and empirical method to an analysis of just this topic. *An Inquiry concerning the Principles of Morals* complements *An Inquiry concerning Human Understanding* by highlighting the important role played by ethics and morality in promoting the overall smooth functioning of society as a whole. Whereas in the first *Inquiry* Hume presented an outline of the principles governing the "reasonable" side of human nature, in this second *Inquiry* Hume delves into different territory and attempts to uncover the principles that govern the "sociable" side of human nature. His discussion of this topic is much briefer than the discussion pursued in the first *Inquiry*, and in what follows I shall likewise try to be quite concise, outlining only the general contours of Hume's ethical theory.

Hume embarks on his investigation of morality by first making the empirical observation that in different societies and cultures we find widely diverse and seemingly conflicting moral rules and regulations. In New Guinea, for instance, it is a moral demand that the practice of cannibalism be engaged in. In Europe, on the other hand, cannibalism is considered to be immoral. Is one of these cultures correct about the real ethics of cannibalism? This is a difficult question to answer with certainty, and Hume suggests that we entertain an element of skepticism concerning the actual content of these sorts of rules and regulations in order to dig deeper into the possible function that they serve in a more general sense. The idea that Hume wants to drive home is that the apparent contradictions we find between the explicit moral rules advocated by differing cultures actually mask a deeper, underlying similarity. The common function served by all moral rules, claims Hume, is to bind human beings together into prosperous and smoothly functioning societies. Different cultures find themselves facing different sorts of concrete situations over the course of history, yet if they are to survive and prosper, all cultures must promote the general welfare and happiness of their populations. Morality is the means by which this goal is accomplished. Because different cultures find themselves struggling to survive under different sorts of circumstances, differing—and sometimes conflicting—systems of moral rules have come into existence. Cannibalism in New Guinea has served to promote social cohesion while, conversely, in Europe it is the injunction against cannibalism that has served to promote social cohesion. In either case, moral rules serve to hold a society together.

Utility

Recall that Hume, in the beginning of his first *Inquiry*, wrote that humans have a "mixed nature." Part of that nature is governed by rationality and intellect. However, another part of that nature is to be "sociable" and "active." Morality, Hume claims, can be found in all cultures precisely because it fosters interaction between people, allowing us to come together and to get along so that we may pursue the sorts of activities that make us happy and bring us pleasure. Morality is, in this way, "useful" above all else. For this reason, Hume claims that it is the principle of "utility" that governs and directs all ethical and moral systems. This is proven, he claims, by virtue of the fact that when a rule of moral conduct begins to bring more pain than pleasure to society, or when it begins to interfere with the peace, harmony, and order of society, people are apt to consider the rule unnecessary, and in fact, immoral, and this precisely because the rule no longer serves the purpose of bringing pleasure and harmony to society as a whole. Because we have a natural passion to be around others, when that passion is interfered with, we believe that something has gone wrong. What we call "good," then, comes from just those rules and modes of behavior that allow us to indulge our social passions and to express a "sentiment common to all mankind."[33]

Theories of ethics have generally followed one of two paths, Hume tells us. There are those who claim that moral rules are derived through the exercise of "reason," and then there are those who claim that moral rules rest on unreasoned "sentiment." Those who claim that moral rules are based on reason hold that "we attain knowledge of them by a chain of argument and induction," while those who claim that moral rules are based on sentiment hold that we know right from wrong by way of "an immediate feeling and finer internal sense."[34] The distinction that Hume is highlighting here is the distinction between intellect and passion. Is the realm of morality based on logic and reason, or is it based on feeling and emotion? Hume comes down squarely on the side of feeling and emotion in this debate. While reason is an important tool by which human beings may calculate, compute, and plan a course of action, no amount of calculation, computation, or planning can tell us what sorts of goals or actions we *should* pursue, according to Hume. There are many reasonable criminals in the world who are very clever at cheating, stealing, and murdering, yet we do not consider them to be moral individuals. What they lack is an internal feeling of regard for others. Such a feeling cannot be deduced through logic and argument, according to Hume. Rather, it is something that you feel or fail to feel. If you do feel this sense of benevolence toward others, it is considered a moral virtue. If you fail to feel it, we consider it a moral vice. Morality, then, at its foundation, has to do with having a sense of compassion for ourselves and others. An unreasonable person may be a moral person as long as he or she has the appropriate

---

B o x 8.2   Public Memorials to Hume

David Hume, a notorious atheist, is buried on Carlton Hill in his home city of Edinburgh, Scotland. Ironically, the inscription on his tomb reads:

> Behold I come quickly,
>
> Thanks be to GOD which
>
> giveth us the victory, through
>
> our LORD JESUS CHRIST
>
> DAVID HUME
>
> BORN APRIL 26th 1711 DIED AUGUST 25th 1776
>
> ERECTED IN MEMORY OF HIM
>
> IN 1778

On the Royal Mile, which runs through the old section of Edinburgh, in front of
the High Court Building stands a larger than life statue of Hume that was completed
in 1995 by the artist Sandy Stoddart. The statue depicts Hume in flowing Greek-
inspired robes. According to the official Web site for Edinburgh (http://www.edin-
burgh-royalmile.com/interest/statue-hume.html) the statue was intended to be an
"extremely grave and serious representation."

One wonders whether Hume is rolling over in his grave!

---

sorts of benevolent feelings, while a reasonable person may, on the other hand,
be immoral if he or she lacks those same sorts of feelings. Hume concludes, "It
appears evident that the ultimate ends of human actions can never, in any case,
be accounted for by reason, but recommend themselves entirely to the sentiments and affections of mankind without any dependence on the intellectual
faculties."[35]

This last statement may seem quite extreme, but Hume's point does make
some sense. Suppose that you like haggis and your friend does not. All of the
arguments in the world are not going to change your friend's mind about the
desirability of haggis. You can describe the qualities that you adore in this dish
and argue about its virtues until you are blue in the face, but such disquisitions
will do no good. Why? Because appreciation of the flavor of food is based purely
on an internal experience of taste. It has nothing to do with intellectual arguments or lines of reasoning. You either like certain foods or you do not. Now
of course, tastes may change and it may happen that at some time in the future
your friend will also come to savor the flavor of haggis. However, this will not
be the result of argumentation. It will, rather, be the result of a change in his
internal experience of the food's flavor.

Hume claims that a similar situation holds for morality. Just as our like or
dislike of a food is traceable to an internally generated impression of the food's
flavor, so are ideas about morality traceable to an internally generated impression of sympathy for humankind. All of the arguments in the world cannot
convince a human being to feel a sense of comradeship with other human

beings. A person either has such feelings or fails to have such feelings. If he does have these feelings, then the basis for moral behavior is present in his psychology. If he fails to have such feelings, then the basis for moral behavior is absent. Hume claims, nonetheless, that it is natural for human beings to have such feelings, and that it is "impossible for such a creature as man to be totally indifferent to the well or ill-being of his fellow creatures."[36] All cultures, therefore, being collective entities built of individual members who naturally feel concern for others, come to formulate codes of conduct that serve to promote the general welfare of the whole. Discretion, industry, frugality, honesty, fidelity, cheerfulness, courage, and tranquility are just some of the qualities that people find agreeable and useful to themselves, and so they naturally wish to cultivate these as individual virtues. Furthermore, because humans harbor a natural desire for those around them to prosper and flourish, qualities like justice and benevolence are also considered virtues because they promote "the good of mankind"[37] and contribute to the "good of society."[38] Thus, there is no conflict between the individual and the collective good, according to Hume. Humans are naturally bound together socially and so rely on one another to foster a prosperous and favorable living circumstance for all. Morality and ethics are useful for this very reason.

The desire for fame, Hume writes, illustrates how it is that good behavior and moral conduct are consistent with both self-love and love of the community. An individual who desires fame is concerned with a certain type of personal pleasure that, by its very definition, is dependent upon others for its fulfillment. In the process of trying to become famous, a person must be aware of how he or she is affecting others, what sorts of behaviors invite attention and approval, and how these behaviors are useful or harmful to the public. Popular opinion encourages the person seeking fame to reflect on himself or herself while considering how to alter his or her behavior for the desired effect. "This constant habit of surveying ourselves ... keeps alive all the sentiments of right and wrong, and begets in noble natures a certain reverence for themselves as well as others, which is the surest guardian of every virtue."[39] A person motivated by the desire for fame, then, cannot be condemned for being selfish. Rather, such a person exemplifies the sort of social sensitivity that is absolutely indispensable for truly moral behavior. It is probably no accident that Hume was driven to utilize this particular example in the conclusion of his *Inquiry concerning the Principles of Morals*, considering the fact that he admitted that one of the driving passions in his own life was the desire for fame!

Morality, then, is not a matter of putting aside one's interests, as some people claim, but of fulfilling one's interests and of playing a useful role in the society of which one is a part. The individual and community support one another, and moral rules are the expression of that mutual support. Hume claims that this fact can be discovered through empirical observation, and that conclusions to the contrary are the result of being misled and "perverted" by artificial theories and philosophies that are themselves not grounded in observation. Just as notions of God, the self, and causality are nonsense, so are those theories of morality which claim to be based either in reason or any other foundation than the feeling of benevolence toward humankind.

HUME AND WONDROUS DISTRESS

Hume has been referred to as a Scottish wrecking ball because of the devastating criticisms he directed against the systems of science, religion, and morality.[40] Whereas Descartes believed that his own skeptical method had uncovered a number of indubitable truths about the nature of the world, Hume, likewise utilizing a method of skepticism, showed that the foundations Descartes had "discovered" are not as secure as they first seemed. While Descartes attempted to tame skepticism in order to make use of it in the service of knowledge, Hume, on the other hand, is a true inheritor of the totality of the Skeptical project, and he follows through fearlessly with its destructive aims. Hume shows us how little there is that we can be certain about in our world, and like the original Skeptics, he counsels us to give up on the abstract notion of Truth itself and instead to focus our attention on the concrete calculation of probabilities. Insofar as Hume advocates extinguishing the wondrous desire for absolute Truth, we find something quite unphilosophical in his writings. The fact that he finally abandoned philosophy in order to take up the study of history is a very strong indication of his impatience with the endlessness of philosophical speculation and questioning. Hume wanted to uncover and eliminate nonsense from the human worldview, and once he had done this, he wanted to get on to other matters. The fitting irony is that he had to use philosophy in order to destroy philosophy.

The impression with which one is left upon reading Hume's work is that he was a down-to-earth, commonsense individual who believed he had a bona fide and simple cure for the abstract and out-of-control world of philosophical speculation. In this, there is much to admire. In the Modern world after Hume, it becomes impossible to make assertions concerning the structure and order of reality without also providing an account of how we go about knowing such things to be true. In this way, Hume holds philosophers accountable for their ideas and demands that they justify their assertions by appeal to real-life experience. What sorts of impressions ground and give content to our ideas? With this simple and straightforward question, Hume summons philosophers to offer an empirical account of their thinking. He also offers a litmus test for the detection of nonsense. If you cannot trace an idea back to a previous sense impression, Hume tells us, then the idea is empty and should be dispensed with. This bold and quite extreme call for the empirical justification of all claims to knowledge is still regarded by many as a healthy and productive counterreaction to the abstractness of metaphysical systems like those produced by Descartes. In this, Hume has taught us a lesson from which we still benefit today.

Ultimately, Hume does prove himself to be an authentic philosopher in his ability to raise new questions, undermine old dogmas, and think things through in a new and profound manner. In his own way, he is concerned with Truth, of course; for Hume, the real Truth has become obscured by too much empty-headed nonsense, and he sees himself as the skeptic who can finally get to the bottom of things. In this way, he is not so much different from Descartes. However, whereas Descartes found Truth in that which cannot be sensed, Hume found it only in the senses. His wondrous distress led him to look past tradition, convention, and the established wisdom of the day. He desired Truth, yet he was distressed by the undemonstrable nature of much philosophical speculation. Hume retains a philosophical orientation even as he seeks to undermine much of the work that has been done in the field. This is a familiar part of the philosophical world, stretching all the way back to its beginnings in the disputes between Thales and Anaximander. Philosophers have always sought to do something new, to question old beliefs, and to argue against their predecessors. Hume fits the bill of the philosophical rebel in all of these ways.

And yet, Hume also seems to want us to accept, once and for all, the legitimacy of his empirical orientation on knowledge. In all of Hume's writings there is a clear sense that he was never willing to seriously question his own empiricism but rather took it as a starting point for everything else that he did. Empirical verification is always the court of last appeal for Hume; it stands as the ultimate criterion against which all else is compared. I suppose the simple and straightforward question that we have learned from Hume could be directed toward this very issue: how do you know that all knowledge begins in sensory impressions? Whatever answer he potentially could give, it would have to be grounded in something other than experience, and this alone should lead us to wonder about the true finality of Hume's position. In any case, while his willingness to raise questions and reveal the shortcomings of other ways of thinking produced important philosophical insight, Hume's unwillingness to question the basis of his own empirical presupposition demonstrates the limits of his patience with philosophy.

Hume's insights have had a tremendous influence, especially in the various fields of science where the need to verify and substantiate theories through direct observation is emphasized. The ultimate lesson that Hume has to teach us is that Truth is always one step ahead of us, always slipping from our grasp as the world unfolds and changes around us. For this reason, it is especially imperative that we remain open to new observations as we endlessly refine and transform our understanding of reality. In this there is a great deal of wisdom. But one also wonders whether Hume himself was not driven by some unexamined presuppositions that could benefit from further philosophical reflection. In particular, Hume never questions that all real knowledge is rooted in sensory experience. But how do we know this to be true? Can such an assertion be established empirically? We shall keep this question in mind as we move on to the next chapter.

QUESTIONS FOR DISCUSSION

1. What is the mind/body problem, and why is it a problem? Do you think that modern science has resolved this problem, or is it still an issue?

2. Are you a materialist, an idealist, a monist, or an occasionalist? Why? What sorts of reasons and arguments can you marshal in support of your position?

3. Are you a rationalist or an empiricist? Why? What sorts of reasons and arguments do you have in support of your position?

4. In modern psychology a point of consistent controversy is the question that is sometimes formulated simply as "nature or nurture?" This controversy focuses on the question of whether human psychology is more a result of experience (nurture) or more the result of inborn programming (nature). What is your view on this issue, and how does it relate to the philosophical debate between empiricism and rationalism?

5. Do you agree with Hume that the idea of cause and effect has no empirical justification? If so, what consequence do you think this has for the empirical sciences? If not, explain the empirical evidence that you think supports the idea of cause and effect.

6. Is Hume correct that there is no empirical evidence for the self? Explain why or why not.

7. Hume's moral philosophy suggests that all systems of ethics are based on feeling, emotion, and sentiment rather than on reason and logic. If this is true, what sorts of implications do you think it might have on relations between different cultures? Is it possible for cultures that have differing systems of ethics to coexist?

NOTES

1. René Descartes, *Meditations on First Philosophy* (Indianapolis, IN: Hackett Publishing Company, 1993), p. 166.

2. See Chapter 2, *Socrates*.

3. Modern materialists fall into a number of differing camps. "Materialist reductionists" claim that all phenomena can be reduced to, and thus explained by, material circumstances. Hobbes seems to represent this viewpoint. "Epiphenomenalists" claim that mental phenomena are not reducible to material conditions but that they emerge out of the functioning of material structures. Without matter, what we call "mind" would not exist in this view. This is a perspective that goes back to Ancient Greece; we read about it in Plato's dialogue *Phaedo* (85e–86d), and we also read there how Socrates undermines this claim. Contemporary adherents to this view include the philosopher John Searle. "Dialectical Materialism," a view discussed in Chapter 10, holds that all human culture emerges out of material and economic circumstances. This is a view held by Marx and Engels.

4. The modern philosophical movement known as "phenomenology" (founded by Edmund Husserl) follows this approach, not by denying the existence of an independent physical world but by "bracketing out" the question of its existence and focusing attention on the consciousness of phenomena. See, for example, Chapter Three, "The Thesis of the Natural Standpoint" (particularly §32), in Edmund Husserl, *Ideas: General Introduction to Pure Phenomenology*.

5. Wallace Matson, *A New History of Philosophy*, Vol. 1 (New York: Harcourt Brace Jovanovich, Publishers, 1987), p. 282.

6. Locke actually writes the following: "Let us then suppose the Mind to be, as we say, white paper void of all characters, without any Ideas; how comes it to be furnished?" John Locke, *An Essay concerning Human Understanding*, Peter H. Nidditch (ed.) (Oxford: Clarendon Press, 1975), p. 104.

7. David Hume, *An Inquiry concerning Human Understanding* (Chicago: Open Court, 1927), p. 176.

8. David Hume, "My Own Life," in *An Inquiry concerning Human Understanding*, pp. v and xvi.

9. Ibid., p. xvi.

10. Ibid., p. vii.

11. Ibid., p. x.

12. Ibid., p., xv.

13. This is the position of Bertrand Russell. See *A History of Western Philosophy*, p. 660.

14. Hume writes in an "advertisement" that precedes the text of *An Inquiry concerning Human Understanding* that he had been in error and "gone to press too early" when he published the *Treatise* (p. xxvii). He writes, furthermore, "Henceforth, the Author desires, that the following Pieces [*An Inquiry concerning Human Understanding*] may alone be regarded as containing his philosophical sentiments and principles" (p. xxvii).

15. Hume, *An Inquiry concerning Human Understanding,* p. 4.

16. Ibid., p. 5.

17. Ibid.

18. Ibid.

19. Ibid., pp. 7–8.

20. Ibid., p. 8.

21. Ibid., p. 19.

22. Ibid., p. 22.

23. Ibid.

24. Ibid., p. 23.

25. Ibid., p. 76.

26. Ibid., pp. 84–85.

27. Hume writes about the self in the *Treatise* but leaves this account out of *An Inquiry concerning Human Understanding*.

28. Descartes, *Meditations*, pp. 133–134.

29. David Hume, *A Treatise of Human Nature* (Mineola, NY: Dover, 2003), p. 180.

30. Ibid., p. 180.

31. Hume, *An Inquiry concerning Human Understanding*, pp. 162–163.

32. Ibid., p. 176.

33. David Hume, *An Inquiry concerning the Principles of Morals* (New York: Library of Liberal Arts, 1957), p. 93.

34. Ibid., p. 4.

35. Ibid., p. 111.

36. Ibid., p. 56.

37. Ibid., p. 80.

38. Ibid., p. 97.

39. Ibid., p. 96.

40. T. Z. Lavine, *From Socrates to Sartre: The Philosophical Quest* (New York: Bantam Books, 1989), p. 145.

Chapter 9

Kant's Transcendental Idealism

© Juneko J. Robinson

How did Hume influence Kant? What is the distinction between the noumenal and phenomenal worlds? What are the *a priori* intuitions? What are the categories of the understanding? What is a hypothetical imperative? What is the Categorical Imperative? What is the difference between beauty and sublimity?

TOTALIZERS versus CRITICS

What are the limits of knowledge? Throughout the history of human thinking this question has been raised again and again, and those who have been concerned with confronting it fall, roughly speaking, into two separate camps. First, there are those who claim that there are no inherent limits to human knowledge. The Presocratics, Plato, Aristotle, St. Anselm, the Epicureans, the Stoics, and Descartes might be classified, more or less, as representatives from this first camp. Their optimistic and ambitious attitude toward human learning includes a vision of totality, and they believe that through its powers the human mind is capable of unlimited and complete knowledge of the cosmos and its first principles. The human mind, according to this group of thinkers, is like a mirror that, when properly polished, reflects back an accurate and dependable image of the world in which we live. These are the metaphysicians, the systematizers, and the "big thinkers" whose philosophical speculations steer a course toward certainty. They are the ones who believe that philosophical thinking is capable of uncovering the vast entirety that is the universe and of making it wholly present in our thinking once and for all, thereby overcoming the need for any further philosophizing.

In the second camp are those who claim that human knowledge is inherently limited, and that no matter how far we push our inquiries we will always fall short of a total and final comprehension of reality. At their most philosophical moments, all of the individuals we have so far surveyed express this sentiment to one degree or another; however, it is in the thoughts of Socrates, Diogenes, the Skeptics, St. Augustine, St. Aquinas, and Hume that we have seen this attitude highlighted most vividly. These are the individuals whose major purpose is to humble us in the face of the infinitely unknowable, whether that be the universe, God, or ourselves. Human knowledge, they emphasize, never quite encapsulates the whole Truth, and so we should always remain modest about our intellectual claims. These sorts of thinkers have, from time to time, been accused of pessimism (and even nihilism) insofar as at least part of their philosophical projects are focused on demonstrating the shortcomings, and in fact the vanity, that is involved in the drive for absolute knowledge. There is always a facet of Being that eludes our intellectual grasp, according to these thinkers, and we are most wise when we are fully aware of, and willing to own up to, our ignorance of the Absolute.

This tension between what I will call the "totalizers" and the "critics" has, I believe, always been a part of philosophy. On the one hand, the totalizers represent that aspect of philosophy that strives for knowledge of absolute Truth and desires nothing more than its fulfillment. However, in their desire for the Absolute there is, perhaps, always a danger that these sorts of individuals will jump too quickly for the "golden ring" and thus come away with something less than the grand prize for which they had hoped. I think this is what many of us find awe-inspiring, yet also frustrating, in the totalizing visions of Plato, Aristotle, Descartes, etc. They aspire to so much, yet in the end their final systematic philosophies always deliver less than we hope for.

This is precisely why the critics, like Socrates and Hume, can be so delightful. They represent that aspect of philosophy that is always attuned to our separation from absolute Truth. They remind us that we are not gods, but humans with finite intellects who must digest the world one bite at a time. It is satisfying, for many of us, to see arrogant totalizers brought down to earth and be reminded of their failures by these critics. However, just as there is the danger of overambitiousness in the efforts of the totalizing philosophers, there may also be the danger of *underambitiousness* in the critics. There is a kind of smug safeness that very often goes along with the critical viewpoint. Many of these thinkers exhibit an uncreative tendency toward attacking the weaknesses in others while themselves lacking the sort of boldness required to build new systems of their own. It may be that these critical philosophers give up too easily and that they lack the courage and audaciousness that can be so inspiring in the totalizing visions of other thinkers.

Like the ends of a stretched rubber band, these two tendencies—the drive toward totality and the critical recognition of our failure to truly grasp totality—exist side by side and define the constant tension that underlies all real philosophy. Particular philosophers have been drawn to focus their attention on one or the other end of this "rubber band" at different times, yet a rubber band that is stretched too tightly snaps, and one that is left too slack stores no energy and falls limp. So it is with philosophy. If the drive for the Absolute is not tempered by the recognition of our intellectual limits, the field of philosophy "snaps" and relinquishes its questioning posture, giving in to the answers provided by science or religion. Conversely, if the margins of our intellectual boundaries are not constantly pushed by a passionate desire for the Absolute, philosophy "falls limp" and collapses into mere criticism and skepticism. At its most vital and active, philosophical thinking exists between these two poles. It is a tension that is never at rest with itself. Insofar as all of the thinkers we have surveyed in this book exhibit some degree of philosophical wisdom, even as they may be pulled to one extreme or another, this sort of tension is always present in their thinking.

David Hume, whose ideas we examined in the previous chapter, is an example of an individual who undertook one of the most ambitious and extreme attempts in history to force philosophy into falling limp. He thus typifies the radical end of the critical spectrum of the field. There are certain things that we can never know, Hume tells us, and so we should not speculate too vigorously on whatever it is that lies beyond the grasp of our knowledge. Cause and effect, the soul, and God in particular are things of which humans have always desired knowledge; however, because there is no possible empirical evidence that these things really exist, Hume tells us that we should just stop thinking about them. If we restrict our thoughts to those things that are within our grasp, Hume concludes, then we can live content and unperturbed by vain speculations. By talking only about those things that are empirically verifiable and in making ourselves useful to those around us, we can achieve happiness and reap the rewards that society has to offer us in the here and now. Of course, in counseling us not to worry too much about grand metaphysical issues, Hume himself gave these issues a great deal of thought and thus, ironically, created his own form of metaphysical system. It was this system that would exert a massive influence on one of the most pivotal figures in modern philosophy, Immanuel Kant (1724–1804).

THE AWAKENING OF KANT

Hume's conclusions were disturbing to many people, and Kant was one of those people. Kant had been a dogmatic rationalist before encountering Hume's ideas, but he tells us that reading Hume "interrupted his dogmatic slumber."[1] Hume had conclusively shown, thought Kant, that the ideas of cause and effect, the soul, and God can never be found ready-made in the objective world. Because we never see, feel, taste, smell, or touch them, we have no empirical proof that they exist. Of particular concern to Kant was the idea of cause and effect. If cause and effect is an illusion, as Hume's philosophy implies, then we can never be certain whether or not the events we perceive in the world will consistently be followed by other events that we have come to expect. How do I know when I drop a ball off of a tower that it will fall downward and strike the ground? How do I know when I put my hand in a fire that it will be burned? How do I know that water freezes at zero degrees Celsius? If Hume is correct, then I don't know these things with certainty. I only think them probable because I have observed them to occur again and again in my past experience. But who says that the future may not be different from the past? If this is possible, furthermore, then what does this do to science, which is a field of inquiry that takes for granted the idea of cause and effect? Is science even possible after Hume?

© Juneko J. Robinson

It is this last question that propelled Kant as he began to write his most famous and influential work, *The Critique of Pure Reason*. This book was to be one of three critiques that would attempt to unearth the foundations of our thinking and to expose the necessary conditions that underlie our systems of knowledge, ethics, and aesthetic judgments. In the first critique, *The Critique of Pure Reason*, Kant addresses the topic of "what we can know" and attempts to delineate the outline of a science of human knowledge. In the second critique, *The Critique of Practical Reason*, Kant addresses the topic of "what we ought to do," attempting to demonstrate the basis of all human morality. In the third critique, *The Critique of Judgment*, Kant addresses aesthetics and attempts to show what it is that makes our judgments of beauty and sublimity possible. Taken together, the three critiques represent an ambitious attempt to comprehensively examine the structures of human thinking and to show that while our knowledge does have limits, those limits are precisely what make human forms of science, morality, and aesthetics possible. Kant's work, in this way, truly embodies the tension that is a unique part of philosophical thinking. On the one hand, he will argue that the human mind is incapable of knowing everything that there is to know about objective reality. On the other hand, he will argue that our subjective reality is shaped not just by the inborn structures of the mind but also by the human desire to transcend the pregiven boundaries of our thinking. Ultimately, the picture that Kant paints is one in which humans constantly strive, yet fail, to achieve an understanding of the Absolute. Despite our failures, we nevertheless do achieve progress in our thinking through our constant aspiration toward the unattainable. Thus, while Kant's philosophy is critical of those who claim to have perfected a final understanding of absolute reality, he at the same time grants that the drive toward totality has an important purpose in human thinking and should for this reason not be discouraged.

Kant lived a life that was by all accounts very structured, regular, and conventional. Otfried Höffe writes, "Nothing extravagant taints his life-style: no unusual clothing or hair style, no moving gesture such as the 'Sturm und Drang' period loved."[2] Kant was, it appears, not a very dramatic or exciting figure in terms of his day-to-day activities. Though he was a well-loved teacher, he never experienced any grand adventures, and in fact during his lifetime he never even left the city of Königsberg where he was born. It is claimed that his neighbors would set their watches according to his daily routines, so regular were his habits. This sort of stable and predictable way of life may have been a reflection of his underlying desire for orderliness and structure, which would in turn contribute to his later attempts to systematize all human thinking in his three *Critiques*.

Over the course of his early writing career, before his "critical period," Kant was fascinated with science and astronomy, publishing works that speculated on the origins of the universe and earthquakes. Philosophically, he was at first a dogmatist who believed that our understanding of the world proceeded by the analysis of ready-made concepts and their connections to one another. During this early "precritical" period, the philosophical works that he produced were sometimes tedious and uninspiring. One prime example of this is his essay *Observations on the Feeling of the Beautiful and Sublime*,[3] a work that simply regurgitates uncritically a variety of old stereotypes about men, women, and the world:

> Women have a strong inborn feeling for all that is beautiful, elegant, and decorated. Even in childhood they like to be dressed up, and take pleasure when they are adorned. They are cleanly and very delicate in respect to all that provokes disgust. They love pleasantry and can be entertained by trivialities if only these are merry and laughing. Very early they have a modest manner about themselves, know how to give

themselves a fine demeanor and be self-possessed—and this at an age when our well-bred male youth is still unruly, clumsy, and confused.[4]

These sorts of generalizations today strike us as silly and unwarranted, and if Kant had never broken free from this sort of dogmatic and conventional way of regarding the world he would not have become such a pivotal figure in the development of Western thinking. To his credit, and in contrast to his otherwise conventional, comfortable, and predictable lifestyle, Kant was not unwilling to take chances and break new ground intellectually. It was only upon emerging from his early precritical period that Kant was to become one of history's most important philosophers.

As mentioned above, Kant credits Hume for rousing him out of his "dogmatic slumber." Upon reading Hume's works, Kant realized that there was no possible way that universal laws and rules, such as the law of cause and effect, could be deduced from observation. Does this mean then, as Hume had concluded, that ideas like cause and effect are nonsense? According to Kant, the answer is "no." Certainly Hume was correct that our idea of cause and effect is not derived from experience, but this does not show that the idea is gibberish, only that it must be derived from something other than experience. Kant points out that the idea of cause and effect is entirely indispensable for the scientific knowledge that we do claim to have about our world. Without cause and effect we would live in a weird world that is unpredictable and strange; a world in which it would be unsurprising to find that balls dropped from towers fall upward, or that hands placed into fires become cold, or that water freezes at 1,000 degrees Celsius. This is not the world that we live in, however. The human world of experience is the world that makes sense to us, and it is one that takes for granted the relationship of cause and effect. Hume's mistake, Kant would claim, was that he looked for the origin of causality in the wrong place. Cause and effect does not exist somewhere "out there," independent of human experience. It is, rather, one of the preconditions for human experience. It is not found in any of the impressions we have of the world but is imposed by our minds upon the ideas that arise from those impressions. According to Kant, Hume's criticism of the idea of cause and effect is misguided because Hume forgot that like the principles of resemblance and contiguity in space and time, cause and effect is an important organizing principle of the mind itself. Without the imposition of some form of organization upon sensory input, the world would appear like a chaotic mass of unconnected and disassociated ideas. Because this is not the way that the world does in fact appear to us, our minds must indeed impose some kind of order on ideas. Cause and effect is just one of those principles of order.

THE CRITIQUE OF PURE REASON

At the very beginning of *The Critique of Pure Reason*, Kant makes the keen observation, "… though all our knowledge begins with experience, it does not follow that it all arises out of experience."[5] With this, he disputes the basic assumption that empiricists like Hume take for granted. We cannot account for the way the world appears to us if we presume, as Hume does, that our physical senses are the only guide that we have to reality. Instead, it must be the case that in addition to sensory experience, the mind itself contributes certain modes of organization that it imposes on the data of perception. Knowledge, then, is not simply the collection of sensory impressions, but rather the collection *and* the organization of sensory impressions. In other words, to really *know* something our minds must both take in information and process that information to make sense of it. Knowledge is constituted in this way and is the product of an active mind that sifts through data and systematizes it according to a schema of conceptual categories.

The Phenomenal and Noumenal Worlds

Kant suggests that we shift our attention away from speculation about the constitution of the objective world and instead focus our attention on the world as we subjectively experience it, asking the question, "What makes that world of subjective experience possible?"[6] Think about how different creatures experience their surroundings. Bats, for instance, make sense of their surroundings predominantly by using something called "echolocation." They send out sound waves that bounce off of objects and return to their auditory sensors with information that helps them to determine where things like trees, rocks, and other creatures are. Their world is built up out of information that is mostly auditory. This is a much different world from that of an earthworm, which has no auditory sensors. The earthworm's world is a world of touch. It feels the earth's soil on its body and navigates accordingly. Likewise, there are many other creatures that build worlds around them by relying upon one or more or the other senses. The manner in which they experience things differs according to how they encounter and impose structure upon the sensations that are created in them by way of interaction with the outside environment.

While there is presumably a world "out there" that exists independently of experience, no creature can know that world independently of experience. All creatures, humans included, must process their impressions of the world through a perspective, and while that perspective gives a hint of the world beyond experience, it also distorts and hides certain aspects of reality. Kant calls the world as it is perceived the "phenomenal world." The phenomenal world is the world of experience that emerges from the interaction between the mind and the reality that exists independently of the mind. That which exists independently of the mind Kant calls the "noumenal world."[7] It is the world of uninterpreted reality that would be there regardless of whether or not we encountered it. The phenomenal world is the only world that we have direct experience with, while the noumenal world is the "thing-in-itself" beyond our direct powers of perception. We only encounter the noumenal world by way of filtering it through the lens of the mind. But as we filter our perceptions in this fashion, the phenomenal world emerges, and thus any time that the mind encounters reality, the reality that it encounters is the world of subjectively interpreted phenomena and not the objective world as it exists in-itself. Think about the way that we perceive tastes or colors, and you will get a good idea of what Kant is driving at here. Tastes and colors are phenomena that exist wholly within the mind of the perceiver. They do not exist in the objective world itself as they are perceived,

PHENOMENA

NOUMENA

SUBJECTIVE
REALITY

OBJECTIVE
REALITY

© Juneko J. Robinson

but rather are produced through the interaction of human sensory mechanisms with something from the objective world. The interaction between a sensory organ, say the eye, and something in the environment, say a wavelength of light, produces in the human mind the perception of a color, say red. As Kant writes, "The taste of wine does not belong to the objective determinations of the wine ... but to the special constitution of sense in the subject that tastes it. Colours are not properties of the bodies to the intuition of which they are attached, but only modifications of the sense of sight, which is affected in a certain manner by light."[8] And so it is for all of our encounters with reality according to Kant. Our minds are constantly interpreting and processing information, and because we can never step outside of our own minds, all that we know of the world is the interpretation that constitutes our phenomenal reality.

Who has a better idea of what the world is really like: the bat or the earthworm? In a way, this is a silly question. The bat and the earthworm live in subjectively different worlds. The earthworm knows its world, and the bat knows its own world. They have differing phenomenal experiences by which they conceptualize reality. Certainly, their worlds may overlap at points, such as when the earthworm feels itself being eaten by a bat that has hunted it down by means of echolocation. But to say that the phenomenal world of the bat more accurately represents objective reality than does the phenomenal world of the earthworm misses the point that neither of their phenomenal worlds corresponds precisely with the noumenal world, or the world as it is in and of itself. Both creatures must filter through and organize the sensations they receive through their sensory organs to know any world at all. But the world that they come to know is not necessarily anything like that which exists apart from their perceptions of it. Any knowledge that a mind has of the world "has only to do with appearances, and must leave the thing in itself as indeed real *per se*, but not known by us."[9] Thus, whatever the noumenal world consists of, there is no creature, no matter what its perspective, that can possibly know its true and objective nature. Because knowledge consists in the interpretation and organization of sensory data by the mind, all knowledge is locked into one perspective or another. There is no such thing as a mind that knows uninterpreted reality.

The *a Priori* Intuitions of Time and Space

So what is it that makes the *human* perspective distinctive? Like any conscious creature, humans must interpret the sensations drawn from their environments, and we do so, claims Kant, by means of organizing sensory input according to a unique schema that already exists inside our minds. While our mode of perception is "not necessarily shared in by every being,"[10] the first stage of every *human* being's perception involves what Kant calls the "*a priori* intuitions of space and time." All humans, according to Kant, understand the world as unfolding within the domain of space and time, and yet because space and time are not sensations that we can perceive with our senses, our awareness of them must be derived from something other than empirical, sensory data. Space and time, in fact, must originate *a priori*, or before experience, because they are the preconditions for all of our experiences. Therefore, space and time do not exist outside of us in the objective, noumenal world but rather are intuitions of the mind itself that are imposed upon the data of experience as the first mode of phenomenal organization. The human, phenomenal world always occurs within the constraints of space and time, claims Kant, precisely because the human mind itself necessarily imposes this structure on all of its experiences.

Space is the precondition for the mental representation of outer experience, while time is the precondition for the mental representation of inner experience. What Kant means by this is that to think about objects existing in the world outside of us, we must first presuppose open space in which those objects may appear.[11] Though we never actually see space, our minds must conceive it to distinguish distinct objects existing independently of one another and separate from us. If there was no space, there would be no place for our representations of objects to unfold. Everything would be one thing; or more accurately, everything would be nothing, because there would be no things! Likewise, time is something that we never empirically observe; however, to be aware of our inner world of representation we must think thoughts in temporal order, one after the other. If our minds did not impose this sort of sequential ordering on our representations, then everything would appear to us to occur all at once. Furthermore, it is only because of the ability to organize representations according to a "time sequence" that we are able to become aware of our own inner state of consciousness. The power to think things in sequence attunes us to the world of inner thought, which is a world that we never empirically observe but only experience intuitively during the temporal process that is thinking.

Kant's analysis of the intuitions of space and time explains how it is that the pure sciences of geometry and mathematics are possible. A pure science is a science that is completely *a priori* and not based on empirical observation. According to Hume's metaphysical system, pure sciences are not possible, because all ideas must be traced back to sensory impressions to be meaningful. Kant, however, claims that our knowledge of geometry is completely based on our inborn intuition of spatial relationships as they appear ready-made in the mind. Likewise with mathematics. Pure mathematics is possible as a science because we are endowed with an inborn intuition of time, which makes possible the temporal ordering of particulars, one after the other, enabling us to count, as in arithmetic. We need not observe anything at all to learn these sciences; we are already hardwired for them. Furthermore, and contrary to Hume, Kant asserts that these pure sciences are informative. Through their productive synthesis, the *a priori* intuitions give us new information and not just the completely empty formalism that Hume had claimed was the earmark of any analytic system. When we add 1,023,000 to 2,800,000,000 and then divide the sum by 6.5, we learn something new, according to Kant. We gain new information from this *a priori* synthesis that was not apparent beforehand. According to Hume, such a procedure only teases out information that was already there, and so nothing new is learned; it is merely a "relation of ideas." For Kant, however, there is such a thing as *a priori* synthetic knowledge; or in other words, knowledge that is completely free from experience but also meaningful and informative.

With his account of the *a priori* intuitions of time and space, and with his claim that these intuitions are sufficient to ground the pure sciences of geometry and mathematics, Kant believes that he has undermined the empirical presumptions of Hume. It is simply not the case, Kant concludes, that all meaningful knowledge comes from observation and experience. Rather, the mind possesses within itself a set of structures that work in concert with one another, producing knowledge and information that is absolutely certain, and that acts as the ground for the nonobservational sciences. Now that he has discovered the foundation for these nonobservational sciences, Kant considers what it is that grounds the observational sciences.

The Categories of the Understanding

While geometry and math deal with abstract entities that are completely generated from within the mind, the observational sciences, like physics and astronomy, purport to deal with objectively real entities that exist outside of our minds. But if these objects exist outside of our minds, how can we be certain about the manner in which they will always behave? Hume had tried to convince us that because the future can always be different from the past, there is no possible way of predicting with certainty how the world of natural objects will operate into the future. Kant, however, is not satisfied with this. He points out that we do, in fact, have a science of nature that seems to work well, as is apparent in fields like physics and astronomy. So instead of skeptically dismissing these accomplishments, Kant instead seeks to inquire into the conditions that make these sciences possible. "Since these sciences actually exist, it is quite proper to ask how they are possible; for that they must be possible is proved by the fact that they exist."[12] So how is it possible that we have a science of nature?

Natural science is the study of the relationships between natural objects, and as such it presupposes not only a field of time and space within which these objects may appear but also a logic by which the connections between them may be known. Unlike the pure sciences, the natural sciences utilize empirical input that the mind collects from its sensory mechanisms. While the mathematician need only think about numbers, the astronomer must actually look to the skies and the physicist must actually make measurements of the physical world. Thus, the natural sciences utilize *a posteriori* observation in addition to *a priori* forms of mental organization. This is what is distinctive about the science of nature, then. It brings the mind together with sensation in order to build up a picture of the world around us. Without sensory input, our mind would have nothing to work with. Without innate organizational structures, sensory input would have no logic or order. As Kant writes, "Without sensibility no object would be given to us, without understanding no object would be thought. Thoughts without content are empty, intuitions without concepts are blind."[13] In order to have a science of nature you must have both an object of sensation and a way of thinking about that object of sensation in connection with other objects of sensation. It is clear that particular objects of sensation are given to us by way of the mind's space- and time-bound perceptions, but what is the pattern of logic by which we connect these perceptions together into a coherent and orderly whole?

Kant finds an answer to this last question in the philosophy of Aristotle. Recall that Aristotle was the first person to offer a systematic account of logic, which he claimed was the basis of all human thinking. Kant picks up on this and applies Aristotle's logic to an analysis of the very structure of human understanding. The mind, Kant tells us, not only intuits objects within the context of space and time, it also has in place a system of twelve categories by which it understands the connections between these objects. These twelve "categories of the understanding" represent an exhaustive list of the ways that perceptions may be synthesized within the human mind, and they are enumerated by Kant as in Table 9.1.

TABLE 9.1   Kant's Categories of the Understanding[14]

I. Of Quantity	II. Of Quality
Unity	Reality
Plurality	Negation
Totality	Limitation
III. Of Relation	IV. Of Modality
Of Inherence in Substance	Possibility–Impossibility
Of Causality and Dependence	Existence–Nonexistence
Of Community	Necessity–Contingency

What is interesting to notice in this list of the categories is how Kant has completely subjectivized a number of relationships that had previously been assumed to exist outside of the human mind in the objective world of nature. Take, for instance, the first group: "Of Quantity." Here we have the categories of unity, plurality, and totality listed as organizing structures of our thinking. What Kant is telling us is that when we look at the world and process the information that we receive from that world, it is the mind, and not the world in-itself, that is organizing what we perceive according to quantity. Quantity, in other words, does not exist "out there" independent of us, but is rather a way for us to make sense of our environment. There is no such thing as "unity" or "plurality" or "totality" out there in the objective, noumenal world. Rather, we sift through and interpret whatever it is that is "out there" and make sense of it in these terms. Physicists today tell us something quite similar to this when they point out that what appear to us as solid objects in our environment are really not solid at all but mostly made up of empty space. A table, for instance, is made up of subatomic particles that have more space between them than they have firm matter. Why is it, then, that a table appears solid to us? Because our minds have a tendency to group particular particles together and to see them as unified objects. Experiments have shown, in fact, that when objects are multiplied beyond a certain number, test subjects begin to have problems distinguishing between individual members of the group and so begin to see them as a unified whole. Consider what happens when you gaze out at a vast number of trees. Instead of seeing individual trees you are likely instead to see a forest. This is just the difference between interpreting what you see as a plurality or a unity, and it is all going on inside your mind. The trees themselves stay the same. It is only your way of thinking about them that changes.

Just as the categories that define "quantity" are contributions from the mind, so are the categories that define "relation." Subsumed under this third grouping are particular classes of relationships like "substance" and "causality." These two latter categories are especially interesting given that they are the very things that Descartes claimed to discover by meditating on the structure of his own thinking and that Hume claimed were absent from his sensory impressions of the world itself.[15] According to Kant's analysis, neither substance nor causality exist independent of human thinking; rather, they are actually part of the mind's own organizational structure, just like all of the other categories of the understanding. A "substance" is an underlying and unchanging foundation that supports the sorts of properties that cannot exist in and of themselves. For instance, Descartes concluded that mind substance must exist because thoughts, which cannot exist without someone to think them, obviously exist. Yet one cannot empirically observe mental substance, and for this reason Hume concluded that Descartes was wrong about its existence. Kant, on the other hand, makes the claim that mental substance does exist, but only as an organizing strategy that allows us to impart coherence to impressions that would otherwise seem quite fleeting and unpredictable. For instance, if we didn't have the idea of a mental substance, all we would be aware of would be transitory thoughts that pop into and out of consciousness. By activating the category of substance, however, we bring all of our thoughts together, in a sense, and ground them by rooting them in a common underlying concept that persists through time even as the thoughts themselves change.

Cause and effect is another idea that Descartes claimed was clearly and distinctly real, while its existence was disputed by Hume. Recall that cause and effect involves the necessary connection between two or more ideas. We say that the appearance of one thing is a cause if it always brings about the appearance of another thing, the effect. Hume rejected the idea of causation because it is impossible to empirically observe a necessary connection between two or more things. According to Hume, all we can observe is a relationship of constant conjunction by which ideas repeatedly accompany one another, but we can never be sure that they will always accompany one another because we cannot see into the future. Kant, however, asserts that while Hume is correct that evidence of causation is not to be found in our observations of the world, it is nonetheless one of the ways that we make sense of our observations of the world. It is one way that the mind imparts structure to ideas. Of Hume, Kant writes, "... it never occurred to him that the understanding might itself, perhaps, through these concepts, be the author of the experience."[16] Thus, Kant puts a new slant

---

B o x 9.1 Autism and Kantian Philosophy

Autism is a mental disorder in which people are unable to interact normally with others. Symptoms become apparent within the first three years of life. Typically, autistics seem withdrawn and internally preoccupied. They engage in behaviors like rocking, hitting themselves, and various other forms of self-stimulation.

In the past it was thought that autistics were completely unable to function in the normal world. However, in recent years there have been a number of people, previously labeled as autistic, who have come out of their shells, not only describing their experience but also becoming professionally successful.

Temple Grandin was diagnosed with autism, yet she has earned a PhD in animal science and has become one of the most successful designers of livestock facilities in the United States. In her book *Emergence*, Dr. Grandin describes the experience of being autistic in terms that recall Kant's description of the human mind. She reports that in autism, one is not capable of properly filtering the stimuli that come through the senses. As a result, the autistic person becomes overwhelmed by input from the outside world and so withdraws.

Grandin's account matches that of Donna Williams, who in her book *Nobody Nowhere* also discusses the subjective experience of being autistic. Like Grandin, Williams describes being unable to filter out the chaos of the objective world's stimuli. Williams has now published ten books while also painting and working on a screenplay.

Autism might be thought of as a breakdown of the categories of the understanding. Those who are not able to mentally organize experience are perhaps apt to withdraw from the overwhelming chaos of the noumenal world.

---

on Hume's own assertion that the mind has certain "habits" when it comes to the association of ideas. But while Hume dismissed the idea of cause and effect as a "bad habit," Kant upholds it as a necessary mechanism for the organization of our thoughts.

In combination with one another, the *a priori* intuitions of space and time and the twelve categories of the understanding give order and coherence to our phenomenal experiences. These experiences, it needs to be reiterated, are not an exact mirror of the noumenal world that lies behind them but are rather interpretations that together constitute our shared human version of reality. While the human, phenomenal world may be different from that of a bat or an earthworm, it is nonetheless our reality. Time, space, substance, causality; all of these things really do exist for us, although they do not exist independent of us. As our minds encounter sensory stimuli, they organize and synthesize these stimuli, constructing a pattern of phenomenal appearances that constitutes the world we are conscious of and within which we make our lives.

The picture that Kant gives us of the human mind characterizes it as something like a very sophisticated computer program. It has in place a whole set of formal structures that await the input of content so that it can begin to categorize data and organize them into useful information. Consider the way that a web browser functions. If you were to look directly at the source codes constituting the raw data that web browser programs read, they might look like a bewildering array of nonsense. However, when you run this seeming nonsense through the

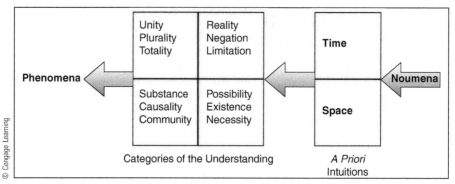

FIGURE 9.1   The Constitution of Phenomenal Reality

web browser program, the program makes sense of the data, interpreting them in terms of a well-organized screen of information. Comprehensible pictures, text, and sounds emerge through the organizational powers of the web browser. Likewise, the human mind, according to Kant, possesses certain innate structures that allow us to give significance to the data reaching us through the senses. Our phenomenal world emerges in our minds like images, words, and sounds emerge onto a computer screen. By organizing data according to the *a priori* intuitions and the categories of understanding, a comprehensible world-picture emerges, and though it may bear only as much resemblance to the objective world as the image on a web browser bears to its source code, it is this emergent world that we call our own (see Figure 9.1).

Transcendental Idealism and the Impossibility of Metaphysics

Kant's philosophy is called "Transcendental Idealism" because it attempts to transcend the ideas in our minds in order to get at the conditions that make those ideas possible. Transcendental Idealism can be thought of as an attempt to synthesize the insights of both rationalism and empiricism. On the one hand, Kant agrees with the rationalists that there are certain innate structures of the mind that provide grounding for our knowledge of the world. On the other hand, he agrees with the empiricists that without sensory input, these innate structures cannot do their job. Without experience, our minds would be like empty file cabinets or computer programs without data input. So it is that Kant walks a middle ground between the extremes of Descartes and Hume.

Though his philosophy seems very sensible and moderate in a number of ways, there is at least one troubling consequence to be drawn from Kant's characterization of human knowledge. If Kant is right, then what we call "knowledge" is not knowledge of the world as it objectively exists. We can never know with certainty what the world is like independent of our experience because all we can experience and know with certainty are the phenomena that arise out of an interaction between our minds and the noumenal world. We always experience the noumenal world only through the subjective lens of our minds, which color and distort reality as it objectively exists independent of us. Whatever objective reality is like, we cannot know its essence. If this is true, then all of our knowledge is only subjectively valid. If Kant is correct, then truly objective knowledge is impossible. We must forever be separated from the world as it is in–itself by our uniquely human perspective. Locked into the human perspective, we can never know what lies beyond that perspective. We are like prisoners in a cave.

Kant's Transcendental Idealism was intended as a means of rescuing our knowledge from the sort of skeptical attacks that Hume had undertaken. We do have absolutely certain knowledge, claims Kant, but this absolutely certain knowledge is not of the noumenal world. Rather, it is knowledge of the phenomenal world of human experience. All knowledge is subjectively constituted, according to Kant, and for this reason, while a science of phenomena is possible, a science of metaphysics is not. Metaphysics is the science of being–in–itself, but because we never have experience of being–in–itself, any attempt to argue about its nature is doomed to failure. Because our human perspective cuts us off from the world as it is in–itself, the only science that is possible for us is a science of appearances.[17] Now, this has not stopped past philosophers from arguing endlessly about things like the nature of the soul, the beginning of the universe, and the existence of God, but according to Kant such arguments must always fail precisely because there is no observational evidence that can ever be produced in order to settle these issues. The problem with philosophical debates of this sort, Kant tells us, is that they rely on "pure reason." When pure reason is exerted without sensory input, the human mind is capable of producing all sorts of competing and inconsistent arguments that have the appearance of being logical but which always leave us with some sort of unresolved problem. For instance, you can offer formally valid arguments concluding that the universe has a beginning, but you can also offer formally valid arguments that the universe is eternal, says Kant. These arguments on their own will never settle the issue at hand because they attempt to derive conclusions about things that are not within the realm of potential experience. When you have good arguments on either side of an issue, the only way to figure out which argument is correct is to test the arguments against observation. However, because metaphysical arguments concern the noumenal world, and we cannot possibly ever experience the noumenal world, these arguments must remain unresolved.

Metaphysical arguments are examples of what Kant calls "transcendental illusions" produced by the exercise of pure reason. At the same time that the various categories of the understanding serve to sort through and coherently unify our sensations, the faculty of pure reason "secures the unity of the rules of understanding under principles."[18] Pure reason, in other words, works toward the completion of the task that the understanding only begins, which is the absolute unification of all thinking under a supreme and unconditioned principle. It is this tendency toward the absolute unification of thinking that is the source of the "transcendental illusion" as it is found in arguments about the soul, the origins of the universe, and God's existence. Pure reason desires a final end to the series of conditions that the mind sets in place over the course of attempting to synthesize an understanding of the world, and for this reason it has a tendency to reach beyond its grasp, trying to come to conclusions about issues that it cannot possibly establish through the function of the understanding alone. In the course of this aspiration, pure reason produces "transcendental ideas," or principles that go beyond all possible experience, but which also serve to focus and consolidate the manifold variety of all the other ideas we have in the course of our thinking lives. As we saw with St. Aquinas' arguments for God's existence in Chapter 6, for example, the transcendental idea of God serves as a final anchor point in which all else is rooted. Everything culminates in God, and so the idea serves the function of giving pure reason a sense of completion and satisfaction. All of the loose ends get tied together, and thinking can come to an end. Pure reason, Kant claims, always strives toward this sort of culmination.

The Regulative Function of Transcendental Ideas

Though the exercise of pure reason results in transcendental illusion, according to Kant this is not such a bad thing. In fact, it is only natural and in some ways it is downright useful. While "all those conclusions of ours which profess to lead us beyond the field of possible experience are deceptive and without foundation," it is also the case that "human reason has a natural tendency to transgress these limits."[19] This natural tendency of reason to go beyond all possible experience and to strive toward the unification of all knowledge serves to give thinking an ultimate purpose, directing it toward a goal that, while quite unattainable, is nevertheless useful in its "regulative" function. If our thinking was always pulled this way and that way without any focal point, progress would never be possible in any area of our intellectual lives. The transcendental ideas, while illusory, serve the purpose of beckoning us in a particular direction and of motivating us to develop and hone our way of thinking so that it becomes progressively more unified, concentrated, and organized (see Figure 9.2). As Kant writes:

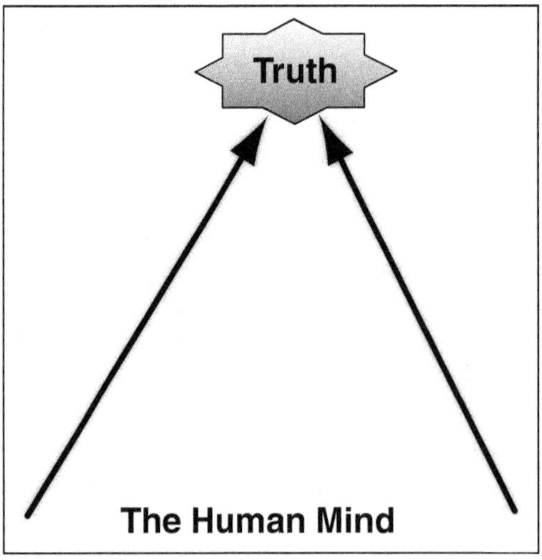

FIGURE 9.2 The Mind's Aspiration Toward the Unification of Knowledge

© Cengage Learning

[Transcendental ideas] ... have an excellent, and indeed indispensably necessary, regulative employment, namely that of directing understanding towards a certain goal upon which the routes marked out by all its rules converge, as upon a point of intersection. The point is indeed a mere idea, a *focus imaginarius*, from which, since it lies quite outside the bounds of possible experience, the concepts of the understanding do not in reality proceed; nonetheless it serves to give these concepts the greatest unity combined with the greatest extension. Hence arises the illusion that the lines have their source in a real object lying outside the field of empirically possible knowledge—just as objects reflected in a mirror are seen as behind it. Nevertheless this illusion ... is indispensably necessary if we are to direct the understanding beyond every given experience ... and thereby to secure its greatest possible extension, just as, in the case of mirror-vision, the illusion involved is indispensably necessary if, besides the objects which lie before our eyes, we are also to see those which lie at a distance behind our back.[20]

THE CRITIQUE OF PRACTICAL REASON

Human reason, Kant claims, is always trying to overreach its own boundaries. As it pushes toward greater and greater degrees of theoretical unification, reason will never rest until it has formulated a single principle under which all knowledge can be subsumed. While this task can never be completed, the human mind naturally desires its completion and thus endlessly aspires toward a theoretical principle that is beyond its grasp. But in addition to this *theoretical* application, reason also has a *practical* application. Just as in the theoretical realm reason seeks the unification of all knowledge under a single principle, in the practical realm it seeks the subsumption of all actions under a universal action-directing principle. This is the task of practical reason, which involves the use of the faculty of reason for the formulation of universal laws delineating how we ought to act in the world. Whereas pure reason seeks an absolute unity of knowledge, practical reason seeks an absolute principle of morality.

In the preface to *The Critique of Practical Reason*, Kant notes that there was a certain "critic" who once complained that Kant's moral writings "contain no new principle of morality."[21] Kant's amused response to this criticism is to joke, "Who would want to introduce a new principle of morality and, as it were, be its inventor, as if the world had hitherto been ignorant of what duty is or had been thoroughly wrong about it?"[22] The point that Kant is driving at with this humorous remark is one with which thinkers like Socrates and Plato would also agree. It would be ridiculous and misguided to consciously contrive a new principle of "morality" because that which is truly moral is so independent of what people say or think. You cannot just make up new moral principles. The purpose of reasoning about morality and ethics is not to come up with novel, clever, and unprecedented rules but to clarify and elucidate the guidelines of proper action that our intuition tells us are true already. In our world, people sometimes act morally and sometimes they act immorally. We make these sorts of determinations every day. How is it that we do so? The task of practical reason is to answer this question. Just as Kant, in *The Critique of Pure Reason*, purported to uncover the *a priori* conditions that make science possible, so too in *The Critique of Practical Reason* does he attempt to demonstrate the underlying *a priori* conditions that make morality possible.

The Good Will

Kant is no skeptic. He never questions whether morality really exists but starts with the commonsense observation that in our world, our human, phenomenal realm, there are certain sorts of actions that we deem moral and some that we deem otherwise. What is it that allows us to make such distinctions? Kant claims it to be obvious that to act morally, it is required that an actor strive toward the performance of actions that are good. Any formulation of an overarching principle of morality must reflect this idea or else it will fail, by definition, to be a truly moral principle. Morality then, by definition, has to do with acting in accordance with the good. So what does it mean to act in accordance with the good? What, in fact, is the good? In his book *Grounding for the Metaphysics of Morals*, Kant writes, "There is no possibility of thinking of anything at all in the world, or even out of it, which can be regarded as good without qualification, except a *good will*."[23] A good will is the only unqualified good thing that we can think of because it is the only thing that always aims at the production of good actions. The will produces the desire to act, and a good will, consequently, produces the desire to act in a good fashion. If a person has a good will, we can be assured that he or she need not be cajoled or strong-armed into doing the right thing. Such a person is self-motivated toward goodness, already having the natural predisposition to strive toward action that is in accordance with morality. Even if this desire to do good produces bad consequences, we can't really hold it against the person. Moral action is a matter of motivation, and even if the world does not cooperate with the good intentions of the good will, the good will itself can't be blamed for this state of affairs.

This still doesn't tell us precisely what the good is, but it does give a sense of the direction of Kant's argument. According to Kant, morality and goodness have very little to do with outcomes and consequences and much more to do with motivations and the pursuit of one's duty. A person who produces bad outcomes, yet who was motivated out of a desire to do good, is not considered by us to be immoral. Conversely, a person who produces good outcomes, but who was motivated by evil desires, is not considered by us to be a moral person. Morality and goodness have to do with the willful desire by an individual to do the right thing regardless of consequences. The good person is one who acts out of a sense of duty to goodness and not out of a selfish desire for rewards or out of a desire to avoid punishment. "A good will is good not because of what it effects or accomplishes, nor because of its fitness to attain some proposed end; it is good only through its willing, i.e. it is good in itself."[24]

Hypothetical versus Categorical Imperative

If a perfectly good person is someone who is motivated by the pure and unselfish commitment to perform good actions for their own sake, then this helps us to understand how moral actions differ from other sorts of nonmoral actions. When we act according to the principle of utility, for instance, we are motivated by the desire to be rewarded for our efforts. When motivated by utility, you wish to profit from your deed, like when you go to work to earn a paycheck, or when you do things to obtain fame and fortune. Contrary to what Hume had argued, this sort of behavior is not really moral in character, according to Kant, precisely because it is concerned primarily with the anticipation of rewarding outcomes. Moral behavior, on the other hand, is not concerned with outcomes but only with what is right universally, whatever the outcomes might be. Morality, strictly speaking, rejects utility in favor of absolute devotion to the good, and so all truly moral actions, claims Kant, have the character of principles that are universally binding regardless of circumstance. Morality tells us that we are obligated to act for the good no matter what situation we find ourselves in and no matter what sorts of negative consequences might be incurred. For this reason, Kant claims that authentically moral principles are examples of "categorical imperatives." An "imperative" is an action-directing statement that tells you what to do. A "categorical imperative" is an action-directing statement that is categorically (or universally) binding. This is in contrast to principles of mere utility, which Kant calls "hypothetical imperatives." A "hypothetical imperative" is an action-directing statement that tells you what to do under specific, hypothetical conditions. For instance, the statement "If you want to make money, you should get a job" is a hypothetical imperative. It tells you what you should do under the hypothesis that you want to make money. No one, of course, would confuse this sort of statement with a moral principle. It is simply a directive that tells you the means by which you can achieve the end that you want to achieve. As Kant writes, "If the action would be good merely as a means to something else, so is the imperative hypothetical." On the other hand, "if the action is represented as good in itself ... then the imperative is categorical."[25] The directive "Don't kill" doesn't give a set of conditions under which killing is wrong. It unconditionally and categorically forbids killing regardless of circumstances, and so, unlike a merely hypothetical imperative, it is truly moral in character.

T A B L E 9.2   Hypothetical versus Categorical Imperatives

Hypothetical Imperative	Categorical Imperative
1. An action-directing statement	1. An action-directing statement
2. Conditional in nature	2. Unconditional in nature
3. Nonmoral	3. Moral

The human will is capable of making free choices, and it is the good will that freely chooses to do good. If there was a person who had a perfectly good will, then that person would always freely choose to act in accordance with goodness and so would always act in a perfectly moral fashion. Because such a person's actions would always be in accordance with the universal good, his or her actions would offer us concrete examples of categorical imperatives. Of course, no such person really exists, but we are able to imagine such a person, and in doing so we recognize that such perfect moral decision-making depends upon the ability to freely and unerringly choose to act in accordance with what

---

B o x 9.2   Various Formulations of the Categorical Imperative

---

Nietzsche accused Kantian morality of affirming Christian values in a language that the average, everyday Christian could never understand. In fact, the various formulations of the Categorical Imperative do sound very much like the "Golden Rule": "Do unto others as you would have them do unto you."

The ways that Kant formulates the Categorical Imperative varies, and different authors have identified differing numbers of formulations in Kant's writings. All of these formulations, Kant insists, are nonetheless variations of only one underlying and supreme formulation.

In his book *Grounding for the Metaphysics of Morals*, there are at least three ways that Kant articulates the Categorical Imperative. They are as follows:

1.   "Act only according to that maxim whereby you can at the same time will that it should become a universal law."
2.   "Act in such a way that you treat humanity, whether in your own person or in the person of another, always at the same time as an end and never simply as a means."
3.   "Act in such a way that your actions are in willful accord with a kingdom of ends." (In this formulation a "kingdom of ends" means a perfect world. This formulation is not as explicitly articulated as the first two.)

---

categorically ought to be done. The real world offers all sorts of temptations and incentives to act in a variety of ways, but when we do act morally, it is always in a manner that (1) is freely chosen, (2) is motivated by a good will, and (3) is unconcerned about resulting costs or benefits.

Let's entertain a couple of examples in order to illustrate Kant's message. First, imagine a man who suffers from a convulsive condition that is triggered by stressful situations. Suppose that he is eager for money and that his friend suggests to him that they engage in a bank robbery together. The man agrees, stipulating that he will only act as a lookout while his friend commits the actual robbery. Suppose that in the course of the job, the man suffers a convulsive episode and unintentionally knocks his friend to the ground as his friend is pointing a gun at the teller. The robbery is foiled, and those in the bank mistake the man's actions for a heroic intervention. The man, hoping for some sort of reward, plays along with all this and claims that he did indeed intend to thwart the robbery. His friend is thrown in jail, the man is hailed as a hero, and he receives the key to the city and a new car as a reward for his actions.

Most of us would probably agree that this individual did not act according to the dictates of morality, although there were a number of good consequences that resulted from his actions. For one thing, his initial motivation for getting involved in this scenario was not a devotion to do good but a greedy desire for money. Second, his actions in the bank were involuntary, being triggered by the stress of the situation, so he didn't even freely choose to stop the robbery. Finally, he took advantage of the circumstance, calculating how to achieve maximum benefit for himself, even though this meant that his friend would take the fall for the whole crime. All of this adds up to a picture of a person exhibiting a greedy and opportunistic streak in his personality; hardly the type of person who we would consider to be a font of morality!

Now consider a person who is motivated by a desire to do good. Let's say that she is a medical researcher who is searching for a cure for cancer. Suppose that her only motivation for conducting her research is to alleviate human suffering and that she freely chooses to engage in this research even though it pays poorly and she must sacrifice time with her family and friends. Imagine, furthermore, that this researcher at one point believes that she has discovered a drug that is successful at destroying cancer cells and that she decides to conduct human experiments to verify her findings. In the course of the experiments it turns out that the drug kills both cancer cells and the patients! All of the test subjects die. The drug is a failure, and our researcher is completely devastated by the extra suffering she has introduced into the world. Her reputation is ruined, her funding is cut, and no one trusts her anymore. Despite her despair, however, she goes back into the lab to try again, because she believes that she has a duty to continue the fight against disease.

In contrast to the convulsive bank robber discussed above, this medical researcher is motivated by a desire to do good. For this reason alone, most of us would naturally hold her in higher moral regard than the bank robber, whose actions produced positive consequences only unintentionally. Second, the cancer researcher has freely chosen her calling. She could have chosen any number of other easier jobs in life that would have allowed her to earn more money and to spend more time with her family, but instead she freely chose to commit herself to research that would help others. Finally, even when her research failed to produce the ends she had hoped for, she continues along the path that she feels duty-bound to pursue. Most people would probably hold that the potential for failure and negative consequences are the unavoidable risks we face when we undertake important projects. The motivation to do good, however, overshadows any sorts of bad outcomes in the case of someone like our cancer researcher, and we feel that despite the unfortunate outcome of her experiments, she was nonetheless acting in an ethical manner by at least trying to make life better for those around her.

These admittedly hyperbolic examples are intended to illustrate Kant's point that morality as we intuitively conceive of it involves unselfish and universal commitment to a principle of goodness. The main thing in moral actions, Kant tells us, is motivation. The truly moral person is the person who desires nothing other than to do good, and although the real world may thwart our grandest plans, this does not reflect on the moral character of pure intentions themselves. To conduct yourself according to your categorical duties, no matter what the consequences, is the pinnacle of Kantian morality. We always fall short of this pinnacle, but we should always continue to strive toward it, attempting to perfect and purify our motivations as long as we live. Kant concludes from all of this that we can sum up the supreme law of morality in the following manner: "So act that the maxim of your will could always hold at the same time as the principle giving universal law."[26] This is the supreme formulation of the Categorical Imperative and thus is the guiding principle of all morality. This imperative directs us to always strive toward a way of life that we authentically could will for all other human beings. Imagine if everyone acted in the way you are about to act, Kant suggests, and you will be able to determine how pure your will is. If you are motivated by greed, selfishness, the desire for fame, or some other sort of nonmoral concern, this will be revealed when you consider what sort of world would result if everyone acted in a like fashion. Only actions motivated by a good will can authentically be willed as universal principles, claims Kant, because it is only such actions that do not contradict practical reason's desire for absolute consistency. For instance, you may be able to will yourself to steal money out of greed, but if you attempt to will stealing as a universal law it would justify the conclusion that others should steal from you, which would itself undermine the very purpose of your greedy intentions in the first place. This brings home the point that your original motivation was selfish, meaning that you desired some sort of personal benefit or reward that you would deny to others, and thus that it was based on a hypothetical rather than a categorical manner of thinking. Truly moral principles apply to everyone, and by testing our actions against the supreme form of the Categorical Imperative, we can determine how well or poorly we are living up to the demands of moral consistency.

Kant's ethical theory ends up echoing the traditional admonitions that we find in the moral systems of most societies and religious systems of thought. "Do unto others as you would have them do unto you." "Don't do to others what you would not want them to do to you." These sorts of imperatives are nothing new, but what Kant has attempted to do, using the guideline of reason, is to clarify the principles he claims all people already naturally recognize. We all intuitively know right from wrong, yet we often fail to act properly because we become distracted by selfishness.[27] What Kant has done is to provide us with an account that helps us to see clearly the difference between morality and mere utility, as well as to construct a method by which we may test ourselves when we are uncertain about our true motivations. In substance this is nothing new, but as Kant himself would remind us, true morality is universal and so should not be subject to novelty and innovation in any case.

THE CRITIQUE OF JUDGMENT

In what remains of this chapter, I very briefly sketch the outlines of Kant's insights into aesthetics as he presents them in the last of his critiques, *The Critique of Judgment*. In this book, Kant constructs an aesthetic theory that continues a pattern he has already established in the first two of his critiques. In *The Critique of Pure Reason*, knowledge is shown to be dependent on a set of *a priori* principles rooted within the structure of the human mind. In *The Critique of Practical Reason*, morality is shown to be dependent on an *a priori* categorical imperative preexisting in the human mind. In *The Critique of Judgment*, Kant goes on to claim that our experiences of beauty and sublimity are likewise based on certain mind-dependent conditions. The overall pattern of Kantian philosophy thus becomes very clear. Our entire world is one that is based in, and that depends on, the human perspective. Kant's "Copernican Revolution" thus repositions the human mind, making it the center of its own universe; a universe that has no necessary resemblance to the domain outside of human consciousness. All knowledge, morality, and aesthetics are universally valid, but only within the realm of subjective experience. What lies beyond this phenomenal realm, only God knows.

Beauty

The purpose of *The Critique of Judgment* is to address the issue of how aesthetic judgments are possible. Kant observes that when we speak of beautiful things, there is a strange quality to our assertions. On the one hand, we all recognize that matters of taste vary from person to person. What one person finds beautiful, another finds ugly. On the other hand, when we ourselves claim that something is beautiful, there is also an objective aspect to our determination. It appears to us that the thing that we are referring to as beautiful really is beautiful; or in other words, that the quality of beauty actually does exist within the thing we are regarding. For instance, if I say, "That is a beautiful painting," I am trying to say something about the painting itself, although at the same time I recognize that other people might not share my viewpoint. But how can this be so? How is it I can claim that something possesses the quality of beauty while at the same time recognizing that other people may not be affected by such an object in the same way that I am? How can a painting be both beautiful and not beautiful at the same time?

Kant solves this puzzle by making a distinction between immediate sensations and the generalized concepts that are involved in making judgments. Sensations of sight, sound, or taste are immediately experienced as pleasant or unpleasant. This part of the aesthetic experience is wholly subjective. When I look at a painting, there is an immediate component of sensory input that my eyes receive: the colors and shapes of the paint splotches on the canvas. Upon the reception of these stimuli, I personally experience a simultaneous feeling that is then associated with the visual stimulus. In the case of the shapes on the canvas, I feel a sense of pleasure, perhaps. Now my rational mind attempts to generalize this experience by utilizing a concept. The problem is that the experience itself is entirely singular, and so when I do apply a general concept to the experience I am only making a universal judgment about my experience. I am claiming that all experiences of this type are cases of pleasing things, and yet there is in fact only one case of an experience of this sort; namely, the experience that I myself have when I am looking at the canvas and feeling pleasure. This second part of the aesthetic experience, the part in which I apply a general concept to my singular experience and thus make a universal claim about the experience, describes the objective part of aesthetic judgment. Thus, the aesthetic

© Juneko J. Robinson

experience has both an individual (subjective) and a universal (objective) component. This is why differing people can disagree about whether or not a particular thing really is beautiful. The thing itself affects different people in differing ways so that what brings one person pleasure brings another person displeasure. When I say that a painting is beautiful and another person disagrees with me, our disagreement is not really about the painting itself but about how the painting affects us. We are not disagreeing about what beauty itself really is but only about whether or not this particular painting is an instance of a beautiful thing.

If, however, there was a stimulus that was accompanied by the feeling of pleasure in all people, all people would agree that the thing producing the stimulus was beautiful. This is how Kant at one point formulates his definition of the beautiful: "Beautiful is what, without a concept, is liked universally."[28] In other words, if everyone found that a particular thing affected them pleasurably, everyone would like that thing, calling it beautiful. Is there anything that has this effect on people in fact? Is there anything the perception of which fills all human minds with pleasure and thus which all human minds find beautiful?

Just as Kant claimed that there are an array of *a priori* formal structures in our minds ensuring the universal validity of science and morality, so too does Kant claim that the human mind is structured in such a manner that it naturally finds beauty under a set of consistent and universal conditions. These conditions are such that they always necessarily produce a feeling of pleasure in us and thus always provoke in us the judgment of beauty. Kant tells us that when we perceive some sort of orderly form in an object, our understanding strives to comprehend the purpose that the form of the object is intended to serve. But in objects of aesthetic appreciation, like paintings, there is no objective purpose. A painting is not like a cog in a machine that has a well-delineated function we can deduce by examining its relationship to all of the other parts in the machine. No, a painting's only goal (if it is a true piece of art) is to be subjectively contemplated by an audience. When the human understanding encounters a thing such as a painting, the imagination is activated and it attempts to conjure up some sort of meaning and significance for the artwork being regarded. Because there is no objective meaning or significance to be found, the imagination endlessly deliberates, playing with a variety of possibilities, which it then supplies to the understanding. Because the only function of the form embedded in an artwork is to provoke "unstudied and purposive play by the imagination,"[29] it is precisely in the endless play of imagination that the mind comes to find the purpose that it was after all along. The purpose of the painting, as it turns out, is precisely to be contemplated endlessly by the human mind. Any time that the understanding, the imagination, and an object come into reciprocal harmony, resonating with one another in the back-and-forth contemplation of such "purposeless purposiveness," pleasure is produced in us, and we then make the judgment that the thing we are contemplating is beautiful. Notice, however, that the quality of beauty is not really in the object itself but in the relationship that exists between the mind and the object. It is this relationship that "sustain[s] the free play"[30] of the imagination and that is the true source of beauty according to Kant.

Sublimity

© Juneko J. Robinson

The experience of the sublime is a related but distinct aesthetic experience. In the experience of the sublime, the mind initially finds no harmony whatsoever between itself and an object in the world. Instead, it finds only disorder and chaos. Normally this situation would cause a human being to feel a sense of distress and to run away from the object encountered. However, when we have a sublime experience, the mind is successful at imposing its own subjective form of order on the object. Our understanding produces the concept of "infinity," and it then utilizes this as a sort of lens through which it can view the otherwise disorganized phenomenon. In so doing, the human mind, in a subjective sense, dominates the chaos by bringing it under the purview of a concept. The result is a feeling of pleasure produced by a recognition of the mind's own seeming power to bring order to disorder. As Kant puts it, "… sublimity is contained not in any thing of nature, but only in our mind, insofar as we can become conscious of our superiority to nature within us, and thereby also to nature outside us."[31] When we encounter things such as vast waterfalls, thunderstorms, expanses of starry skies, the open ocean, or any other sort of overwhelming natural phenomena, we rescue ourselves from sheer terror only by mentally conquering the unlimited power or expanse of the thing we perceive by subsuming it under the concept of "infinity" and consequently judging it as sublime. There is something exhilarating about this capacity, and the feeling of sublimity thus has a different character to it than the feeling of beauty. Beauty is relaxing, easy, and amusing. Sublimity is invigorating, difficult, and bracing. A flower is beautiful. Niagara Falls is sublime. A stroll in the park is beautiful. Skydiving is sublime. The love you have for a puppy is beautiful. The fear you have of God is sublime.

With his aesthetic theory, Kant has once again shown us how certain ideas that have traditionally been thought of as denoting objective states of affairs in the world might actually be more properly characterized as matters of subjective human interpretation. If Kant is correct, nothing in the world as it exists in-itself is truly beautiful or sublime. Rather, beauty and sublimity are ways that we experience and aesthetically appreciate our minds' own relationship with the world. In aesthetics, no less than in the rest of his philosophical project, then, Kant has exercised, as he himself puts it, a kind of "Copernican Revolution" that places human beings at the center of their own universe. Our minds actively generate our phenomenal reality, and even our experiences of things beautiful and sublime are in large part reflections of how much we appreciate our own powers of interpretation.

KANT'S WONDROUS DISTRESS

"Two things fill the mind with ever new and increasing wonder and awe, the oftener and the more steadily we reflect on them: the starry heavens above me and the moral law within me."[32] In this, one of the most famous quotes from Kant, is summed up his sublime respect and reverence for both the inner and the outer worlds of human experience. Kant began his writing career distressed by a crisis in human knowledge, and his systematic critique of human thinking represents a sustained attempt to demonstrate the universal and necessary *a priori* principles that our minds rely on to organize, synthesize, and interpret the sensations we receive from the objective world.

Kant, however, did not end up offering us final answers to all of the mysteries of existence. At the heart of the human soul, and in the depths of the outer universe, there remain mysteries that we can never fully understand. While our innate drive for unlimited knowledge pushes us forward, our separation from the objective world by way of the distinctively human perspective will continue to foil our plans for a final apprehension of the absolute. Kant in this way was both a systematizer and a critic. In offering a systematic account of how human thinking works, he also offered a criticism of those philosophers who claimed to have transcended the boundaries of all possible experiences. Kant tells us that he has "found it necessary to deny knowledge, in order to make room for faith."[33] He denies absolute knowledge of the objective, noumenal realm, while granting us knowledge within the purely human, phenomenal realm. Beyond the phenomenal realm one may have faith in what one wishes, but such claims can never be substantiated by reason.

In these ways, Kant clearly exhibits the elements of wondrous distress that characterize truly philosophical thinking. In genuine wonder and awe, Kant strains to pursue ideas to their limits, only to find in the end that these limits constantly recede into the distance, the way that parallel lines disappear into a vanishing point and never converge. The distressing awareness that absolute knowledge constantly eludes our grasp, however, is presented by Kant as an opportunity for endless investigation of the world rather than as an excuse to give up on learning. The innate tendency of the human mind to strive toward complete and final knowledge of reality, though doomed to failure, can be harnessed in the service of ongoing and productive advancement in the human sciences. This is typified by the regulative power of transcendental ideas, which while technically presenting us with an illusory hope for completeness give us the practical motivation to act in the world. As we strive to encompass more and more knowledge under a more and more comprehensive and unified set of conceptual principles, our own human interpretation of reality progresses to become more panoramic, well textured, and sophisticated. Though the phenomenal world of human experience will always remain alienated from the noumenal world as it is in-itself, it is precisely this alienation that promotes our collective movement forward toward the ideal of Truth itself.

Kant's philosophical system promoted both inspiration and despair in those who came after him. As we will see in the following chapters, wonder and distress would be renewed in a whole new generation of philosophers as a result of Kant's work.

QUESTIONS FOR DISCUSSION

1. Discuss the differences between rationalist and empiricist approaches to philosophy. Explore the ways that Kant integrates both of these approaches into his own philosophy. Which perspective do you most agree with? Why?

2. Kant claims that all possible experience must be of the phenomenal world. This is the world that is filtered through the intuitions of time and space and organized by the categories of the understanding. What do you think Kant would say about those individuals who claim to have had mystical experiences in which they came to know God or in which they reached nirvana?

3. Kant believes that all humans share the *a priori* intuitions and the categories of understanding. Is this true? Do you think it possible that the ways we organize our experiences might be more flexible than Kant claims? How much of a role do you think socialization plays in the formation of our mental lenses?

4. Kant believes that the insights of science are true; however, they are only subjectively true. Is Kant correct about this, and if so, what are the implications of this claim?

5. Discuss a time in your life when you had to wrestle with a difficult ethical decision. What was the situation you had to deal with, and how did you confront it? Describe how you reasoned your way to a decision. How closely did your line of thinking match the details of Kant's ethical system?

6. Kant's ethical system is mostly focused on the intentions behind actions rather than on the consequences that follow from actions. Do you think this is the right way to think about morality? Aren't there occasions when good intentions lead to immoral actions?

7. Discuss the differences between a beautiful and a sublime experience. Describe in these terms some experiences that you have had. Do you agree with Kant that beauty and sublimity are judgments of the human mind rather than objective qualities found in the world itself?

NOTES

1. Robert Paul Wolff (ed.), *Ten Great Works of Philosophy* (New York: Mentor Books, 1969), p. 302.

2. Otfried Höffe, *Immanuel Kant*, Marshall Farrier (trans.) (Albany: SUNY Press, 1994), p. 7.

3. Bertrand Russell is dismissive of this work: "Like everybody else at that time, he wrote a treatise on the sublime and the beautiful. Night is sublime, day is beautiful; the sea is sublime, the land is beautiful; man is sublime, woman is beautiful; and so on." Bertrand Russell, *A History of Western Philosophy* (New York: Simon and Schuster, 1972), p. 706.

4. Immanuel Kant, *Observations on the Feeling of the Beautiful and the Sublime*, John T. Goldthwait (trans.) (Los Angeles: University of California Press, 2003), p. 77.

5. Immanuel Kant, *The Critique of Pure Reason*, Norman Kemp Smith (trans.) (New York: St. Martin's Press, 1965), p. 41.

6. Kant, in fact, phrases this in terms of four separate questions: How is pure mathematics possible? How is pure science possible? How is metaphysics, as a natural disposition, possible? How is metaphysics, as a science, possible? *The Critique of Pure Reason*, pp. 56-57.

7. Ibid., pp. 257–275.

8. Ibid., p. 73.

9. Ibid., p. 24.

10. Ibid., p. 82.

11. Recall Plato's similar discussion from *Timaeus*.

12. Kant, *Critique of Pure Reason*, p. 56.

13. Ibid., p. 93.

14. Ibid., p. 113.

15. Ibid., pp. 335–336.

16. Ibid., p. 127.

17. In *The Critique of Pure Reason*, Kant sums it up like this: "For we are brought to the conclusion that we can never transcend the limits of possible experience, though that is precisely what this science is concerned, above all else, to achieve. This situation yields, however, just the very experiment by which, indirectly, we are enabled to prove the truth of this first estimate of our *a priori* knowledge of reason, namely, that such knowledge has only to do with appearances, and must leave the thing in itself as indeed real *per se*, but not known by us" (p. 24). This same insight would motivate Edmund Husserl to formulate the science of phenomenology in the twentieth century.

18. Kant, *Critique of Pure Reason*, p. 303.

19. Ibid., p. 532.

20. Ibid., p. 534.

21. Immanuel Kant, *The Critique of Practical Reason*, Lewis White Beck (trans.) (Upper Saddle River, NJ: Library of Liberal Arts, 1993), p. 8.

22. Ibid.

23. Immanuel Kant, *Grounding for the Metaphysics of Morals*, James W. Ellington (trans.) (Indianapolis, IN: Hackett Publishing, 1981), p. 7.

24. Ibid.

25. Ibid., p. 25.

26. Kant, *Critique of Practical Reason*, p. 30.

27. This is what led Nietzsche to remark cynically, "Kant wanted to prove, in a way that would dumbfound the common man, that the common man was right: that was the secret joke of his soul. He wrote against the scholars in support of popular prejudice, but for scholars and not for the people." See Friedrich Nietzsche, *The Gay Science*, Walter Kaufmann (trans.) (New York: Vintage Books, 1974), pp. 205-206.

28. Immanuel Kant, *The Critique of Judgment*, Werner S. Pluhar (trans.) (Indianapolis, IN: Hackett Publishing, 1987), p. 64.

29. Ibid., p. 93.

30. Ibid., p. 95.

31. Ibid., p. 123.

32. Kant, *The Critique of Practical Reason,* p. 169.

33. Kant, *The Critique of Pure Reason,* p. 29.

Chapter 10

Hegel and the Manifestations of *Geist*

© Juneko J. Robinson

What did Hegel find dissatisfying in Kantian philosophy? What is the difference between "picture thinking" and "conceptual thinking"? What is *Geist*? What is Hegelian logic? What is Hegel's Doctrine of Being? What is absolute knowing? How do Hegel's followers develop and apply his insights?

Just as Kant had been troubled by the skeptical assertions of Hume, so were many post-Kantian thinkers troubled by Kant's own philosophical conclusions. The German author Jacob Hermann Obereit went so far as to claim that Kantian philosophy is "nihilistic" insofar as it reduces the world of objective existence to nothing. If Kant is correct, claims Obereit, then we each live in a world of complete subjectivity and we have no reason to believe in any sort of objective reality outside of our experience at all. What we are left with are the mere appearances of things. Heinrich von Kleist, in a similar vein, laments:

> I recently became acquainted with Kantian philosophy—and now I must quote you a thought from it, though I do not imagine that it will shake you as deeply or as painfully as it did me. We cannot decide whether that which we call truth is real truth or whether it only seems so.... My sole, my highest goal has foundered and I no longer have an aim.[1]

Kleist's lament expresses a sentiment that became more and more common once the insights of Kant started to be seriously considered. If the human mind never knows things directly but only by way of a process involving mental interpretation, then we cannot discern how closely our knowledge parallels objective existence. Because the very operation of our thinking works like a lens that distorts and filters the world as it is in-itself, we are left only with a subjective picture of reality. It doesn't matter how clever or dedicated we are to discovering the secrets of the universe; ultimately we must fail in our attempts to know these secrets. Furthermore, if this is the case, then the grand desire that has propelled philosophy from the very start is doomed to failure. Philosophers have never been satisfied with the comforts of convention but have always sought after absolute Truth, Justice, Goodness, and Reality. As lovers of wisdom, philosophers desire to know how the world really is, not merely how it appears to us. If Kant is correct, however, it is impossible to know the world's true, objective nature. What is a philosopher to do? Why strive for wisdom when true wisdom will always allude us? Kant's advice is that we should explore the phenomenal world of subjective human experience and be satisfied with its ever-growing yet finite boundaries. We can capture a subjective sort of truth in this regard. But according to many philosophers, this is not good enough. Giving up the desire for absolute, objective Truth is unthinkable for them. After all, Socrates died for Truth and his followers have for centuries struggled against conventional ignorance and small-mindedness to aspire toward that which is objectively real and good. How could one abandon this tradition and still call oneself an authentic philosopher?

Accepting the claims of the Kantian system functioned, in these ways, to alienate many thinkers from their highest aims and aspirations, producing an atmosphere of hopelessness and despair that is palpable in much post-Kantian philosophy. If Kant is right, then humans are forever separated from that which is objectively real and thus most desirable and of highest value. If this is so, then there is no option but endlessly to desire, yet never to obtain, the most valuable thing imaginable: absolute Truth itself. In reaction to this viewpoint there develops, among those operating in the shadow of Kant, an overwhelming concern with how to surmount our alienation from Truth and our feelings of despair in regard to this situation. The solutions offered by the post-Kantians are many and varied, but in this and the following chapter, I will be concerned with tracing a particular thread within the post-Kantian tradition that begins in the writings of Georg Wilhelm Friedrich Hegel (1770–1831).

THE DIFFICULTY OF HEGEL'S PHILOSOPHY

Hegel is an exasperating figure in the history of Western thinking. His tremendous influence on the development of later philosophy is unquestionable, and yet trying to understand the content of his own original philosophy is a frustrating, and sometimes an impossible, undertaking. Bertrand Russell writes, "Hegel's philosophy is very difficult—he is, I should say, the hardest to understand of all the great philosophers."[2] This opinion is held by just about all commentators who have, to any degree, attempted to decipher his texts. Part of the difficulty surely has to do with the simple fact that Hegel was a terrible writer. Henry Hatfield, for one, characterizes Hegel's writing as part of a "widespread intellectual disease"[3] in which German authors came to believe that profound thoughts cannot be expressed in clear language. Robert Solomon, furthermore, characterizes Hegel's

writing as "intentionally obscure"[4] and in particular points to Hegel's most famous book, *The Phenomenology of Spirit*, as being "filled with infelicities that would not have survived a second draft: mixed metaphors that are almost embarrassing and such unfortunate devices as 'on the one hand ..., on the other hand ..., and thirdly ....' References are obscured, pronouns ambiguous, subordinate clauses left dangling, and worse, there are leaps in logic that on no account can be defended...."[5] In fact, it would largely be in reaction against the opaque style of Hegel's prose that later analytic philosophers would reemphasize the need for clarity in the articulation of philosophical concepts.

Nevertheless, in Hegel's defense we should recognize that it sometimes is the case that difficult ideas do require difficult language in order to gain expression. Hegel certainly goes to the extreme in this regard, but his writing is not all smoke and mirrors. Granting that it is not on account of his technical brilliance as a writer that he came to be regarded as one of the most important figures in nineteenth-century philosophy, what was it that led to Hegel's tremendous influence? The answer, simply stated, is that there is a profound core of philosophical insight in his thinking, and it was this core that eventually came to attract a large group of followers who would utilize these elements of Hegelian philosophy for a wide and diverse variety of purposes. Once we dig through the obscurity and longwindedness of Hegel's prose, I believe that what we find are two central and important core ideas that are responsible for his immense impact.

First, we find a rejection of the Kantian claim that humankind is necessarily and forever alienated from ultimate and absolute reality. The phenomenal and noumenal worlds, it turns out, are not forever separated according to Hegel, but rather are aspects of a grander, comprehensible whole. Hegel contends that humans, and the world we are part of, are involved in an ongoing and unfolding historical process that is meaningful and purposeful. Ultimately this process will culminate in the conceptual realization that all things in the universe are unified and connected, like the parts of an incredibly complex organism. Comprehending the totality of this process is within human grasp, and once this comprehension occurs the apparent rift between our subjective experience of reality and the actual objective truth of that reality will be overcome.

Second, Hegel articulates the logic by which our understanding of this grand, comprehensive totality can take place. Hegel's logic is not the traditional logic of Aristotle but rather a novel kind of reasoning that is structured in terms of an ongoing synthesis of contradictory concepts. This logic, called "dialectic," owes much to the method of Socrates, except that for Hegel, it describes not only the interaction between individual human minds but also the structure and nature of the entire universe itself. According to Hegel, we become attuned to the nature of this logic first by examining the concrete details of history's events and then by abstracting from those events the rhythms and the regularities operant in the manner of their unfolding. Though each particular occurrence in history is singular and unique, when understood from a panoramic perspective we come to see that taken as a whole, the sum total of these singular and unique incidents give substance and shape to the recognizable contours of a rational pattern. This pattern is encapsulated in Hegel's dialectical logic.

In attempting to simplify the complicated and very often obscure details of Hegelian philosophy, I shall focus my discussion on these two topics: Hegel's vision of unity, and the system of dialectical logic he believes will unlock the secrets of that vision. Once we have explored these key points in Hegel's system, we will then examine some of those thinkers who have been influenced by one, the other, or both of these aspects of Hegelian thought. As is the case with many great thinkers in the history of philosophy, the influence of Hegel's ideas becomes manifest most dramatically in those who have reacted against his conclusions. Ironically, there is a sense in which this fact serves to confirm much of what Hegel has to teach us.

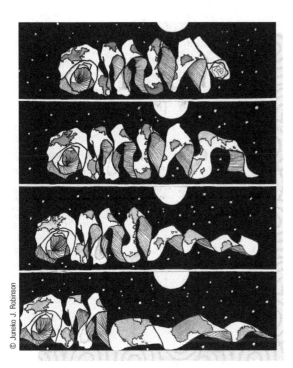

© Juneko J. Robinson

HEGEL'S VISION OF UNITY

Hegel was an active figure in Prussian intellectual circles during the late eighteenth and early nineteenth centuries, and the development of his philosophy was greatly influenced by the atmosphere of these times. During this period, Enlightenment thinking was coming into conflict with an opposing movement of thought known as Romanticism. The tension between these two cultural currents largely involved a disagreement about the roles that reason and passion should play in human life. Enlightenment thinkers, like Kant, emphasized the role played by rationality. They focused on the power of human intellect to transform and guide the human condition toward a brighter future in which freedom and autonomy would be advanced. Thus, the ideals of freedom, progress, rationality, and humanism were the sorts of goals that proponents of the Enlightenment sought to realize. The Romantics, on the other hand, feared that this emphasis on humanism and rationality was undermining the organic interconnection between human beings and nature. Whereas the Enlightenment perspective represented humans as autonomous, calculating, and free, the Romantic perspective was one in which human beings were more like conduits through which nature gained expression. Thus, according to the Romantics, humans are not so much free as they are driven by primal forces that are best known through feelings, passions, and emotional responses. Insofar as the Enlightenment thinkers privileged reason over passion, the Romantic thinkers objected to this privileging as a denial of the deeper and more profound essence of human nature.

Caught between the Enlightenment and the Romantic movements, Hegel was torn between a view of humans as free and reasonable and a view of humans as driven by deep and obscure natural forces. Accordingly, Hegelian philosophy attempts to synthesize these ideas by characterizing the world as a place where the natural forces that drive all things are governed by an underlying rationality. As Hegel writes in *Reason in History*, "[T]his *Idea* or *Reason* is the True, the Eternal, the Absolute Power ... it and nothing but it, its glory and majesty, manifests itself in this world...."[6] Again, in *Philosophy of Right*, Hegel most famously states,

"What is rational is actual and what is actual is rational."[7] Our universe, then, is not an irrational and haphazard place. It is, rather, a place where observable occurrences are the result and expression of more profound, rational causes at work in the heart of existence. Hegel, in fact, recalls Anaxagoras in this regard and explicitly appeals to Anaxagoras' concept of nous or "mind" in order to buttress his own point.[8] You will remember from Chapter 2 that Anaxagoras was Socrates' teacher, and that he held the universe to be interpenetrated by a non-material, rational substance that gives order and structure to all that exists. Likewise, Hegel believes the universe to be a manifestation of a similar sort of rationality. In claiming this, he is able to satisfy both the Enlightenment assertion that human reason is an important part of our lives and the Romantic demand that we pay tribute to the deeper and more hidden powers of nature.

Hegel thinks it a mistake to conceive of the world's underlying rationality as a particular being or "thing," however, and in this sense he is in disagreement with Anaxagoras. Anaxagoras encouraged us to visualize rationality as something like a stable and well-defined entity that exists within the universe, the way that the water flowing through a river bed is a fixed substance contained within the confines of the river's banks. Hegel teaches us, instead, that rationality really is not an object of this sort. It cannot be accurately visualized and pictured in our minds the way that we can visualize the eddies and currents in a body of water. Instead, it is a *process* that can only correctly be grasped through the ongoing exercise of conceptual thinking. "Conceptual thinking" is an advance over Anaxagoras' primitive form of "picture thinking." Picture thinking attempts to understand the world through visualization, through actually "seeing" particular objects in our minds. If we mentally visualize rationality as if it were a flowing river, we are engaging in picture thinking. This manner of reflection has always been used by people because it is a beneficial aid in helping us to make difficult and abstract ideas more concrete and tangible and thus more comprehensible. However, the drawback of this form of thinking is that it induces us to oversimplify and to reify concepts. When you reify a concept, you treat it as if it were more concrete and stable than it really is. Thus, in utilizing picture thinking, we tend to reify the concept of rationality and mistakenly think of it as something "familiar, fixed, and inert" when in fact it is more correctly conceived of as a fluid and "self-moving"[9] activity.

Because the language we use has a form that expresses thoughts in terms of subjects and predicates, we are always in danger of lapsing into picture thinking and thus of reifying concepts. For instance, because we are able to use the word "rationality" as the subject in a statement—as in the statement "Rationality is the essence of the universe"—we may be deluded into thinking that there exists a distinct entity to which this word applies, just as the label on a can of peaches refers to the product inside of the package. If we make this mistake, the subject "rationality" inadvertently becomes a fixed entity to which the predicate "essence of the universe" applies as a quality. We can detect here Hegel's first step away from the assumptions of Aristotelian logic. Whereas Aristotle claimed that the subject/predicate structure of language accurately mirrors the true nature of the world, picturing it as a series of nested substances, Hegel disagrees. Instead, Hegel tells us that this structure is an oversimplification of reality that distracts the mind from the deeper truth of the matter. Hegel cautions us not to think of subjects and predicates as completely distinct and separate entities that are simply added together with one another like interchangeable links in a decorative chain. In actuality, the subjects and the predicates we use in order to form statements are concepts that constitute a kind of natural unity in which each seamlessly and organically passes away into the other. When you break apart a statement and only scrutinize the subject and the predicate in isolation from each other, they make no logical sense and meaning is lost. "Rationality is ..." expresses nothing until it is coupled with a predicate such as "... the essence of the universe." This demonstrates the interconnectedness of these ideas and shows how the full meaning, or truth, of the statement requires that subjects and predicates commingle with one another.

This insight, Hegel concludes, is indicative of the fact that meaning and truth emerge out of an interaction and blending of distinct, and apparently opposed, worldly particulars. These worldly particulars may take many forms. They may be material circumstances, historical events, words, or concepts, but ultimately it is in a gestalt arising out of the interaction between particular individuals existing in our world that ultimate Truth resides. "The Truth is the whole. But the whole is nothing other than the essence consummating itself through its development," Hegel writes.[10] To know the truth is to understand how and why everything fits together, and for this reason we cannot understand reality only by way of analysis. We must also be aware of the synthetic relationships between the parts of the system which constitute our universe. The world itself is a unity, but it is a unity characterized by a ceaseless process of ongoing synthesis.

Rationality, properly understood, is the overall structure and rhythm of this ongoing action of synthesis as it occurs in the universe. The universe is rational, but we must be careful to understand that for Hegel, rationality is not a static state but a *movement* of reality. "It is the process of its own becoming."[11] The term that Hegel uses to refer to this rational structure, this movement, is *Geist*. The term *Geist* is translated into English alternately as "mind" and as "spirit." It thus suggests a kind of nonphysical substance that is intelligent, sensitive, and aware. On the one hand, in characterizing the substance of the universe as mind, Hegel is emphasizing the rational and logical aspects of the world. On the other hand, in characterizing the substance of the universe as spirit, Hegel is likewise emphasizing the obscure, occult, and feeling aspects of that same world. The ambiguous term *Geist* is thus perfect for bridging the gap between the Enlightenment and the Romantic perspectives on reality because it encompasses both reason and feeling within its purview. The world is not a dead "thing," Hegel wants us to understand, but rather a living, moving, and evolving organism. Furthermore, it is an organism that operates according to a logic knowable to the human mind. The world is *Geist*, or more accurately, it is the unfolding of *Geist*.

Because humans live in the world, we are a part of *Geist* and so we necessarily participate in its life. It is this insight that is key in Hegel's refutation of Kant's nihilistic division between the noumenal and phenomenal realities. According to Hegel, Kant was no less guilty of picture thinking than were any number of other individuals in the past. The noumenal or objective world was claimed by Kant to be a vast, unknowable "thing-in-itself," and this according to Hegel was one of Kant's main delusions. By designating the objective world to be a thing, Kant committed the fallacy of reification. He stabilized, objectified, and fixed a definition of reality which placed it at odds with the character of the subjective domain of the human mind. The mind is an active, thinking, and reasoning thing that possesses its own set of interpretive structures. The objective world, on the other hand, is something that exceeds the interpretive structures of the mind according to Kant. Because the mind is defined by a finite set of intuitions and categories of the understanding, and because the "thing-in-itself" cannot be encompassed (pictured) by these finite structures, human knowledge must always lack correspondence with noumenal reality. Subject and object, in Kant's philosophy, then, must always remain alienated from one another.

But, Hegel responds, the Truth of the world is not that it is a "thing-in-itself," separate and distinct from human thinking. Rather the Truth of the world is that it is a process of synthesis, and part of the process of synthesis involves human existence. Human beings, as part of the unfolding movement of *Geist*, play a part in that unfolding. Thus, the objective and the subjective worlds interpenetrate and participate in each others' domains. They cannot arbitrarily be torn apart but must be considered as an organic unity if the real Truth and meaning of the world are to be salvaged. Because the penetration of the subjective realm into the objective realm means that the objective realm participates in the life of the phenomenal world, and because the penetration of the objective realm into the subjective realm means that the subjective realm participates in the life of the noumenal world, we have discovered the bridge between these two worlds that Kant had denied. The objective and subjective aspects of reality are just different sides of the same landscape, according to Hegel. By bringing the reflective powers of the human mind to bear on the objective side of this landscape, we may incorporate an understanding of the structures we find there into our subjective thinking, raise them to consciousness, and in so doing synthesize subject and object into a higher conceptual unity. In the final completion of this project, we potentially elevate our understanding of the whole to the point where the very processes that govern our own relationship to the whole are themselves embodied in our way of thinking. If this highest level of conceptual thought could be actualized, our understanding of the world as a subject/object synthesis would then be promoted to the most refined and perfect level that is possible. Hegel calls this most advanced level of conceptual thinking "absolute knowing," and it appears as if he believes himself to have been successful at bringing it to a climax.

Absolute knowing is a state of wisdom insofar as it entails bringing Truth to presence in the mind of a thinker, and Hegel believes himself capable of guiding us to this point of ultimate understanding. In leading us to a state of wisdom, furthermore, Hegel seeks to bring philosophy to an end. As he writes in the preface to his *Phenomenology of Spirit*, "To help bring philosophy closer to the form of Science, to the goal where it can lay aside the title of '*love* of knowing' and be *actual* knowing—that is what I have set myself to do."[12] Hegel's purpose, then, is quite an ambitious one. He wants, once and for all, to bring the Truth of the universe to full consciousness and thus to make us wise. As we have seen, this is an extremely difficult thing to do from a Hegelian perspective because Truth is a thoroughly unstable sort of target. It is an ongoing movement that ceaselessly incorporates all that it encounters, synthesizing opposites and converting them into ever more complicated and ambiguous manifestations. How exactly are we to get our minds around this ceaseless process, raise it to a conceptual level, and thus finally gain possession of Truth?

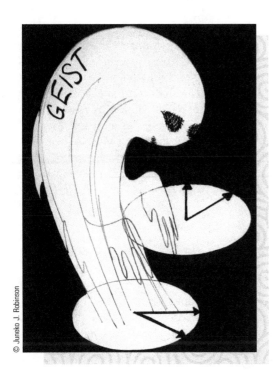

© Juneko J. Robinson

Hegel has an answer to this last question. If we are able to master the details of dialectical logic, then we will have acquired the tools needed to lay bare the purely formal structure of the self-moving movement of *Geist* and in so doing make comprehensible its superficially bewildering appearance. What this will result in is our capacity to see how the constant flow of the movements of *Geist* actually adhere to a consistent and rational pattern that is reflected within each and every finite detail of the universe. We will be able to "see" the infinite in the finite and the finite in the infinite if we just train ourselves to look at the world through a logical and rational perspective. Of course, the logical and rational perspective that Hegel has in mind, as alluded to above, is not wholly in accordance with traditional kinds of logic. Rather, Hegel wants to start afresh with a more natural kind of logic that he himself has discovered in the course of undertaking his own phenomenological investigation into reality. A phenomenological investigation consists of simply describing the details of experience as it presents itself to us. Kant had claimed that the phenomenal world, the world of experience, is the only world we have direct access to, and Hegel starts with this insight, scrutinizing the world of phenomenal appearances in order to unearth the coherent, logical form that runs through the entirety of observable circumstances. In so doing, he hopes to find a structural thread that holds together all of reality. The universal logical structure that Hegel claims to have discovered is embodied in his dialectical logic. Before discussing the specific details of Hegelian logic, let us first briefly look at how Hegel came to its discovery.

THE PHENOMENOLOGY OF SPIRIT

Hegel wrote his most famous book, *The Phenomenology of Spirit*, as a prelude to his later writings on logic. In the *Phenomenology*, Hegel undergoes an extensive, often exhausting, and sometimes incomprehensible investigation into the details of the history of consciousness. The ultimate purpose of this investigation is to distill a logical system that finally will be presented in his other works, *The Science of Logic* and *The Encyclopedia of the Philosophical Sciences*. I shall not attempt to go into a great amount of detail here concerning all of the particular transitions in the *Phenomenology*—they span the entire history of human thinking, running from prephilosophical beliefs on the immediacy of sense experience to the development of sophisticated forms of art, morality, and religion. In the end, what Hegel discovers amid all of the convolutions of this concrete intellectual history is an underlying logical, triadic structure that propels human history forward. We will examine the formalities of this structure more closely in the pages that follow. Presently, however, let us scrutinize one well-known, vivid, yet brief example from the *Phenomenology* that helps to demonstrate both the strategy that Hegel follows and the logical pattern that he claims to have discovered at work in the world of real human experience.

Lordship and Bondage

In Part B of *The Phenomenology of Spirit,* Hegel discusses a relationship that he calls "lordship and bondage" to illustrate how it is, through conflict and struggle, that the world evolves and moves forward by means of the synthesis of opposing forces. What Hegel attempts to do here is something like a reconstruction in his own mind of events that have already been carried out over the course of past philosophical history. The theme of lordship and bondage that he emphasizes appears to be his own subjective reconstruction of a process of thought that began with Socrates and ended in Christian philosophy.

Hegel begins by positing a lone, self-conscious individual, existing "in and for itself."[13] This individual becomes aware of itself as a consciousness by virtue of the fact that it reflects upon itself. It is thus "in-itself" insofar as it exists as a consciousness, and it is "for-itself" insofar as it is aware of its own existence as a conscious being. The fact that this self-conscious awareness develops only by way of reflection leads the individual to realize that acknowledgment and recognition are necessary for the development of self-identity. If an individual was completely unselfconscious, unreflective, and unaware of his or her existence as a thinking thing, there would be no self to speak of. An act of mental recognition is required for us to emerge into the world as unique thinking individuals. The first step in this emergence, Hegel seems to suggest, is the recognition of the mind by itself. This reminds us of Socrates and his claim that the "unexamined life is not worth living."

But soon this self-enclosed consciousness is compelled to project outside of itself, desiring recognition from something beyond its own boundaries. It wants to be acknowledged by something other than itself, and so it looks to the world for affirmation. It immediately becomes obvious that to gain this sort of affirmation, the individual must turn to other consciousnesses that exist in the world. Nonconscious beings will not do, as they do not have the capacity to register thought and so remain inert and unmoved. Thus the individual seeks out other conscious beings with whom to interact, and as these beings come into contact with one another, "They recognize themselves as mutually recognizing one another."[14] Once again, Socrates and his desire to engage his fellow citizens in conversation comes to mind.

This recognition, according to Hegel, is not a friendly event as it turns out. The two selves, as they encounter one another, enter a "life and death struggle"[15] and vie for dominance in their newly formed relationship. Why? The answer

---

B o x 10.1   The Master/Slave Dialectic

Hegel's discussion of the master/slave dialectic, or the lordship and bondage relationship, has influenced an enormous number of philosophers, psychologists, sociologists, and political and theological thinkers. Among these are the following:

- The existentialist thinker Jean-Paul Sartre (see Chapter 13) drew on Hegel's ideas
  in order to characterize the dialectical give-and-take that occurs in all concrete
  human relationships.
- The sociologist W. E. B. Du Bois applied the master/slave dialectic to his descrip-
  tion and analysis of the African American experience.
- Simone de Beauvoir (see Chapter 13) characterizes the battle between the sexes
  in terms of Hegel's master/slave dialectic.
- The Jewish theologian Martin Buber described the I–Thou relationship between
  God and Man in Hegelian dialectical terms.
- In psychoanalysis, the master/slave dialectic is claimed by many practitioners to
  describe the relationship between doctor and patient.
- According to Karl Marx (see later in this chapter) the master/slave dialectic gov-
  erns the relationships between social classes.
- Hegel's ideas on the master/slave dialectic have influenced the contemporary
  neoconservative political thinker Francis Fukuyama, who writes that the worldwide struggle between political ideologies is soon to come to an end.

---

seems to be that in their mutual recognition, each consciousness must objectify the
other, each treating the other as the focus of its attention. These minds come to
know one another from the outside, not from the inside the way that they know
themselves. As a result, others become "things" to be mastered and dominated in
the demand for self-recognition. Think of how it is that you yourself encounter
other human beings, and I believe that this will make some sense. When you meet
people, you cannot jump inside of their minds. Instead you must assess who they
are in terms of how they dress, how they speak, how they act, etc. You come to
understand them through external appearances primarily, and only after you have
interpreted those appearances are you able to make an inference to their internal
states of mind. You learn, through trial and error, how it is that various people
react in various circumstances. If the purpose of your relationship with others is
to gain recognition, you will no doubt learn how to manipulate their reactions
and responses for the desired effect. You learn how to treat them as instruments
for the fulfillment of your own egoistic desires. According to Hegel, when this sort
of relationship develops, and one person submits to another in order to fulfill the
first individual's desires, lordship and bondage, or the master/slave relationship, is
the result.

The lord, or master, desires recognition from the bondsman, or slave, but
the problem is that in demanding this recognition, the lord "holds the other in
subjection,"[16] and in so doing dehumanizes the bondsman. The bondsman, who
was initially approached precisely because he was a conscious being, comes to be
dominated so totally that he is transformed into nothing more than property for
the lord. "What now really confronts him is not an independent consciousness,

but a dependent one."[17] The bondsman becomes enslaved to the purposes of the lord and master, and in this way the lord's search for recognition in the mind of the other ultimately comes to an ironic defeat. The slave ceases to be viewed as a subject capable of furnishing recognition of the lord's own consciousness. He becomes, instead, a mere thing to the lord; a nonhuman tool, an object.

Furthermore, Hegel tells us, the lord suffers an even greater, and even more ironic, setback in his domination of the bondsman. The bondsman is forced to work and labor for the lord, and in so doing it is the bondsman who develops the capacity to permanently alter and creatively shape the objective world. The lord, on the other hand, becomes alienated from his own creative powers to mold reality because it is only through his workers, whom he dominates like slaves, that he can create effects. Thus, in the end, the master, who initially sought recognition in the eyes of the other, must now retreat back into himself and suffer continued alienation. The slave, ironically, is the one who triumphs over his subjection by the master, coming to a new realization of his own creative powers.

Lordship and bondage is a condition that Hegel draws upon to demonstrate how it is that opposing forces collide in the world, and in their collision interact to produce something greater than the sum of their initial parts. In the end, one force, the lord, retreats back to his initial position of self-enclosed existence. The other force, the bondsman, is transformed by this relationship and flowers forth into something greater than he was before his encounter with the lord. Through struggle, suffering, and toil the bondsman learns to develop his creative capacities and to become much more than the self-enclosed consciousness that he initially was. In Hegel's terminology, each of these forces "negates" the other, and in this negation they contribute to a new state of being that is a dialectical synthesis of the two sides of the interaction. The transformed slave has become a master over the world and may now go on to produce even more transformations in that world. On the one hand, he is both master and slave. On the other, he is neither master nor slave anymore but something new and more lively. As happened in the case of Socrates, the life and death struggle with an opposing power motivates the slave to mature and expand his creative potential.

Stoicism, Skepticism, and the Unhappy Consciousness

In the history of Ancient Greece, we know that the Socratic philosophers left a legacy that was built upon by the Hellenistic philosophers. If we take Hegel's discussion of the lord and bondsman relationship to be in some way an expression of the current of thinking engaged in by Socrates, then it is no surprise that he follows this section of the *Phenomenology* with a discussion of Stoicism and Skepticism. With Stoicism, Hegel tells us, we find a literal synthesis of the lord and bondsman in the very fact that this philosophy was adhered to by both rulers and their subjects. Both emperors and slaves in the Roman Empire accepted Stoicism. Why? Because it offered a solution to the Roman oppression of all humankind. Recall that Stoicism advocates a withdrawal of emotional attachment to things in the outside world, promising an inner life of peace and spiritual quietude. Under the domination of the mighty Roman Empire, all people were slaves as they became aware of their impotence in the face of the law and military might. "Stoicism could only appear on the scene in a time of universal fear and bondage,"[18] writes Hegel, and the only way that one could find freedom under these conditions was to identify with the inner world of the mind. In Stoicism we see both rulers and subjects thinking of themselves as something other than purely physical beings subject to the forces of external coercion. Instead, they become free thinking and independent consciousnesses. They flee toward an inner world of thinking to find a kind of mastery that cannot be found in the outer world of physical existence. Stoicism thus unites the lord and the bondsman with a common belief system and shows them all how to become masters of their own souls.

This inward flight, Hegel tells us, advances to the development of Skepticism. The Skeptical philosophy treats the outer world as a veritable nothingness in that the skeptic claims to possess no certain knowledge of anything external at all. "What Skepticism causes to vanish is not only objective reality as such, but its own relationship to it."[19] In other words, the Skeptic is alienated from anything other than what is immediately present to the mind. Nothing that is separated from the mind is predictable or knowable with certainty. Whereas the Stoic begins the inward movement by asserting the mind's freedom from the contingencies of the objective world, the Skeptic brings this freedom a step further, negating the existence of objective reality and affirming only the existence of subjective reality. The Skeptic is like the master who has encountered and objectified as "other" something outside of himself. Yet the Skeptic is also like the slave in that his negation of the objective world has formed within him an awareness of his own inner duality as both a subject that thinks and reflects and an object that is thought about and reflected upon. Just as the slave was both subject to himself and object to the master, so too does the Skeptic become an internal synthesis of subject and object. For this reason, Hegel concludes that in the Skeptic "the lord and the bondsman [are] now lodged in one."[20]

Christian philosophy followed Hellenistic philosophy in the progression of history. Similarly, Hegel comes to see "the unhappy consciousness" as the final outgrowth of Stoicism and Skepticism. The unhappy consciousness is indicative of a mind that is divided against itself. It is an "inwardly disrupted consciousness"[21] that is aware of its own self-alienation. Inheriting from Skepticism the view of mind as both a reflecting subject and the object of its own reflection, the unhappy consciousness commences an outward movement, in contrast to the inward movement of Stoicism and Skepticism, externalizing and projecting its own essential qualities onto the world "out there." In so doing, it creates the idea of a perfect, objectively existing consciousness (God) that is separate and apart from its own merely subjective existence. What we see here is the final irony of the mind's attempt to gain recognition. With the unhappy consciousness, the mind finally creates its own lord out of itself. Sadly, it must remain forever alienated from its creation, because the unhappiness of this form of consciousness lies precisely in the fact that it is not aware of what it has done. It truly believes that God exists as an independent and separate entity and does not understand its own role in the creation of God out of the movements of its own inner reflection.

The trajectory of thought that begins with the lord and bondsman and ends with the unhappy consciousness is Hegel's own very unusual and abstract way of reconceptualizing the history of philosophy from Socrates to Christianity. What Hegel thinks he has revealed in the course of this examination are the vicissitudes of a conceptual unfolding that progresses by means of opposition and conflict. For anything to happen in the course of human thought, there must be a break or division between two or more ideas. It is as if the history of consciousness rushes in to fill the gap created by this division, manifesting itself as a flowing movement that works to mend fractures. Repair is accomplished by taking elements from either side of divisions and blending them together in a synthesis that reconciles conflicts. History moves forever forward in this fashion. If there were no conflicts, there would be no such movement. Everything would be one and whole, fixed and stable. The phenomenological fact of history, then, proves that opposition and conflict are a part of reality.

Perhaps the most vivid and beautiful image that Hegel utilizes in order to convey the dynamic relationship he sees existing between all opposed forces in the universe appears at the very opening of the *Phenomenology*. It is here that Hegel likens the unfolding of the world to the growth of a plant. Just as the struggle between the lord and bondsman produces Stoicism, Skepticism, and the unhappy consciousness in turn, so too does the growth of a plant manifest itself in successive stages, each of which negates the previous stages:

> The bud disappears in the bursting-forth of the blossom, and one might
> say that the former is refuted by the latter; similarly, when the fruit
> appears, the blossom is shown up in its turn as a false manifestation of
> the plant, and the fruit now emerges as the truth of it instead. These
> forms are not just distinguished from one another, they also supplant
> one another as mutually incompatible. Yet at the same time their fluid
> nature makes them moments of an organic unity in which they not only
> do not conflict, but in which each is as necessary as the other; and this
> mutual necessity alone constitutes the life of the whole.[22]

Like a plant, the world unfolds according to an organic and fluid pattern. Dialectical logic, Hegel tells us, is the truth of that pattern.

DIALECTICAL LOGIC

Frederick G. Weiss writes, "If the totality of the universe were viewed as a vast puzzle of interlocking pieces, Hegel's *Logic* would be its pure form, the essential structure and method governing the articulation of the pieces qua organic parts and in such a way that they constitute that universe not as a puzzle, but as a whole."[23] Hegel's logic is not the symbolic kind of system that contemporary philosophers and mathematicians are used to studying and working with today. It is not a method that has been designed to distinguish valid from invalid lines of reasoning and thus to encourage the pursuit of good arguments. Instead, Hegel's

logic is, first, a description of the order and structure of relationships that govern everything in the universe, and second, it is a method that allows us to comprehend those relationships.

As we have already seen, Hegel believed the world to be governed by an ongoing process of synthesis. Hegel's logic attempts to articulate the manner by which this synthetic movement commences and perpetuates itself. It is important to remember that what Hegel wants to describe here is not really a temporal or a historical process but a *logical* process. Whereas the *Phenomenology* described a temporal process that has taken place over time, the logical system described in Hegel's works on logic always is whole and complete in–itself. It is not time-bound, even though our understanding of it may require that we break it into pieces and that we think one piece after another. In–itself, however, the portions of a logical process all exist together, simultaneously and independent of our thinking about them. For instance, take the equation "1 + 1 = 2." When we think through this equation, our minds consider each of its components in sequence. First we think "1." Then we think "+." Then we think "1." Then we think "=." Finally we think "2." Nevertheless, we know that all of these components form a synthetic unity that is not dependent on our own need to consider each digit and operator in isolation from the others. The sequence represents a timeless, purely formal relationship that nevertheless is actually reflected in how the world concretely operates. Likewise, the logical system that Hegel describes is one in which all components exist together simultaneously, and even though we must begin understanding this system by analyzing and separating it into parts, at a more sophisticated and advanced level of understanding, we should strive to comprehend how these parts dissolve back into a natural, organic unity.

Thus Hegel tells us, "In point of form Logical doctrine has three sides,... [however] these three sides do not make three parts of logic, but are stages or 'moments' in every logical entity."[24] Hegel uses the term "moments" to stress the idea that the parts of his logical system meld and disappear seamlessly into one another in the way that one instant of time melds and disappears into the next. Each of the three parts that he will delineate are thus to be understood as integral to each other. Each one presupposes and implies the other parts, so that in a very real way their distinctiveness dissolves when properly understood.

The Abstract Side

First in the order of our thinking is the "abstract side" of logic. This aspect of logic describes the starting point at which, from our own perspective, we have to commence. All reasoning must begin from a standpoint, and without such a point of departure the reasoning process cannot even get under way. The standpoint from which logical reasoning commences is one in which a seemingly fixed, stable, and distinctive particular is grasped by the mind as an entity possessing well-defined boundaries. It may seem strange that Hegel refers to this as the "abstract side" of logic, but his reason for doing so is that this starting point is many steps removed from the underlying fluidity of the real world. Nothing is really fixed, stable, and distinctive, and so when we start thinking about the world as being made up of these sorts of entities we are actually thinking in a very abstract manner that is quite withdrawn from the concrete and actual nature of *Geist* itself. In any case, to begin reasoning we must start at some point, and so we treat some idea in our minds as if it were a stable foothold; something like a springboard that in its rigidity will allow us to be propelled toward other ideas. For instance, in the equation "1 + 1 = 2," I begin by thinking of the idea "1" as a distinct, separate, and stable entity from "+" and "1" and "=" and "2." This allows the second "moment" of logic to unfold.

The Dialectical Side

The second side of logic is the "dialectical side." Here, the stable and fixed character of the entities we encountered initially becomes superseded and broken down. Things "pass into their opposites,"[25] and we encounter a conflict between one thing and another. The boundaries that we initially took to be fixed and stable are suddenly breached by the appearance of another apparently fixed and stable entity that forces the first entity into a relationship, as we saw in the relationship between the lord and bondsman. Hegel refers to this as the stage of "negative reason"[26] because it is during this moment that the unique distinctiveness of our starting point is destroyed and forced to commingle with something other than itself. Negative reason, however, is not purely destructive because in breaking the field of thought in two it creates conceptual room in which movement may now take place. This is when the process of reasoning can actually get under way. For example, when we first encounter the numeral "1," there is no motivation to think things through or to speculate on other things beyond "1." However, with the appearance of the operator "+," things change. When we see "1 +," already there is an anticipation built up in us. We wonder "1 + what?" "1" can no longer stand alone and undisturbed. We demand that it yield its fixity and tell us something more about its relationship with other things in the world. This continues when we see "1 + 1." Now we are confronted with further questions. What does it mean to bring this numeral into a relationship with itself? These can't be the same "1s" if they are being added to one another. What could it possibly mean to add a thing to itself? Now we see "1 + 1 =" and we want to know where this is all leading. In a sense, the instant that "+" appeared we knew that there was more to come, and when the second "1" appeared we knew that "=" was on its way. This demonstrates that each of these parts already contains something more than we initially imagine when we consider them only from the "abstract side" of thinking. Now, as we go through the concrete operations of seeing how these particular entities interact with one another, we start to understand that there is a very complicated and interdependent web of meaning that runs through these symbols. They are dialectically related to one another in such a manner that their own "one-sidedness" is negated and they are shown to be anything but self-contained and independent entities.

The Speculative Side

If logic is not carried to its third moment, Hegel tells us that dialectic results in skepticism. What he seems to mean by this is that absent a concern for the final synthesis of knowledge, our reasoning process, once begun, has no necessary stopping point. Logic that reaches only the dialectical phase becomes embroiled in an ongoing and open-ended battle of mutual negation between the particular entities that first came into a relationship with one another. This calls to mind Socrates and his endless debates with his fellow Athenians. There was very rarely a satisfying and final culmination to these conversations, and so each of the interlocutors departed from the interaction with a distressed and uncertain mind. But what was the good of all this except to foster skepticism and despair?

Hegel thus tells us that the third and final movement of logic is found in the "Speculative stage, or stage of Positive Reason."[27] Here, the conflict and opposition between initial terms is resolved in a synthesis that "sublates" their differences. When a difference is sublated, it means that the apparent contradictions between things are finally revealed as obscuring or disguising a deeper bond of commonality. In the stage of Positive Reason, the conflict between two terms is overcome as the essences of the seemingly contradictory elements are proven not to be contradictory at all. Rather, they conjoin with one another and rise to a more elevated level of synthetic unity, just as the slave incorporated aspects of the master into his own being and thus was transformed into a creative worker. In Positive Reason, a new concept emerges that encompasses both previous ideas and accommodates them in such a manner that their differences contribute to something greater than the sum of their parts. This is the synthesis that we examined earlier and that Hegel claims as the governing

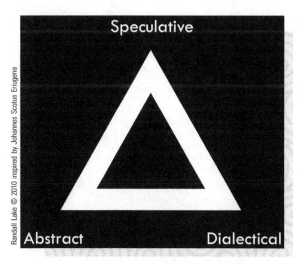

Speculative

Abstract   Dialectical

principle of all reality. Notice how this ongoing process of synthesis is only made possible by way of the logically anterior separation and conflict that already exists between particulars. So it is that "2" represents the synthesis and sublation of "1 + 1" only because of the separation and conflict that exists between the particular symbols of the equation in the first place. "2" encompasses "1 + 1" and brings into existence an idea that is more than just the sum of its parts. Notice that "2" also encompasses "1.5 + .5," "1.75 + .25," etc. It is an idea that accommodates "1 + 1" but whose meaning is not exhausted by "1 + 1." It is an idea that has been raised to a higher and more meaningful level.

Absolute Knowing

All of the three sides of logical reasoning—the Abstract, the Dialectical, and the Speculative—require and imply one another as long as the movement of reason takes place. However, as our own thinking becomes progressively more sophisticated and as we gain greater facility with synthesizing ideas, we may reach a final culmination in the synthesis of ideas that results in something that Hegel calls "absolute knowing." When we reach the stage of absolute knowing, all of the seemingly contradictory and conflicting details of the world are sublated and our minds become capable of piercing through to the underlying unity that ties reality together as an organic whole. At this stage of thinking, all things are integrated into, and accommodated by, a universally enveloping concept, an "absolute Idea," that leaves out nothing that has ever transpired in the universe. On the surface of it, this sounds impossible, for how could anyone hold all of the world's details in his or her head all at once? Hegel's response, I think, would be that you don't literally hold all of the world's details in your head but only the formal essence of the relationships those details share with one another. In absolute knowing, what you know is not an infinite number of facts, but the essence, or form, of *Geist*. Knowing the meaning of the number "2" does not imply that you know all of the infinite variety of ways that people have deduced that number, and likewise in absolute knowing it is not implied that you can recall all of the events in history. What it does imply is that you have comprehended the underlying pattern of meaning in existence. Just as a piece of fruit in some sense embodies all of the processes of growth that were necessary in order for it to come into existence, so too does the absolute Idea embody all of the processes that contribute to reality as a whole. A wise man need not know all of history's details in order to engage in absolute knowing. All that is necessary is to grasp the fruit of history; its absolute Idea.

Hegel's logic is aimed at the production of wisdom in the individual. Through the dialectical understanding of reality, a philosopher moves closer and closer toward Truth until a concept emerges that finally and completely embodies all possible relationships that exist in the world. At that point, the love of wisdom ceases and wisdom itself comes into full presence, like a fruit emerging out of a plant's blossom. Philosophy ends at this moment and the newly emerged "wise man" becomes a "perfect and satisfied man who is essentially and completely *conscious* of his perfection and satisfaction."[28] If I may engage in a bit of picture thinking myself, I visualize the Hegelian wise man as analogous to a person standing at the center of a multifaceted diamond, and who, in gazing outward, sees himself and the world reflected in a staggering number of aspects. Each of these aspects finds its focus in this person's mind, and so he is able to tie them together and to think all of them at once and as a unity. For this person, the world manifests itself as a kaleidoscope of phenomena, but this kaleidoscope is not bewildering or distressing. Rather it is fascinating, meaningful, rational, and harmonious. Furthermore, contained within this vision is the very mind that collects these aspects together and conceives of them as a singularity. The Hegelian wise man is as one with his world, not separated from it as Kant had suggested must be the case.

The Doctrine of Being

I would like to address one final point that is relevant to Hegel's work in logic. This concerns what he refers to as the "Doctrine of Being." The Doctrine of Being is Hegel's attempt to ontologically ground his system of logic so that it avoids the criticism of being merely historical and thus subjective. Hegel claimed to have discovered the details of dialectical logic through the careful examination of historical events that appears in *The Phenomenology of Spirit*. In doing this, he wanted to allow the world to speak for itself, rather than trying to artificially impose some sort of structure on its Truth. However, once the form of *Geist* became manifest to him through history, Hegel needed to demonstrate that what he detected really was Truth, and that as such it was necessarily rooted in a rock-solid foundation. If he could show that the process embodied in dialectical logic emerges from a starting point that is certain and does not presuppose anything false, then it would be worthy of recognition as the primary foundation for all thinking. Hegel's attempt to reveal the ultimate, necessary, and unquestionable ontological ground out of which the movement of rationality grows is carried through in the Doctrine of Being.

To be legitimate a science must be based on as few assumptions as possible, and any assumptions that it does take for granted must be true. It seems throughout the history of philosophy, however, that there are always people who come up with ways to doubt and question just about any assumption that is taken for granted. Is it possible, then, to found a system of thought that is completely free of presupposition? This is the task that Hegel takes up as he attempts to show that dialectical logic is worthy of being regarded as primary to all other forms of human thinking. To do so, he tells us, we must find a beginning that is "absolute," which means that it must be "an immediacy, or rather merely immediacy itself."[29] What he means here is that the starting point for an absolutely infallible science should be one that is immediately and intuitively recognized by any rational individual as correct. It should not depend on anything outside of itself but instead be rooted in a singular idea that is completely indubitable. This sounds very much like the task that Descartes set for himself in *Meditations on First Philosophy*,[30] and likewise, Hegel seeks a foundation that is unshakable upon which to erect the rest of his philosophy. Unlike Descartes, however, Hegel wants to steer clear of subjectivism, and so he will not be satisfied to establish the thinking "I" as his beginning. If you start with the subject, then inevitably you must explain how the subject relates to the objective world, and thus you have introduced a dualistic division between subject and object into your thinking from the start. It is just this sort of division that culminated in the alienation of subject from object in the Kantian system, and this is precisely what Hegel wants to avoid. How best to proceed then?

Hegel's solution is to establish Being itself as his starting point. In the concept of Being we find a singular and powerful idea that, Hegel tells us, is both all-encompassing and empty at the same time. Being is everything. There is nothing we can conceive that falls outside of the boundaries of Being, because Being designates everything that exists. This aspect of the concept demonstrates its power to ground anything, because all things, no matter what other differences they may exhibit, have in common the fact that they exist and thus have Being. Yet, in encompassing all particular things that exist, Being is also the emptiest of concepts. If we try to pin down any particular characteristics of Being itself, we are left speechless. Being itself is nothing without reference to particular beings, and so while Being is everything, it is also at the same time Nothing. Being and Nothing form an organic unity with one another such that each acts as both subject and predicate to the other: Being is Nothing, and Nothing is Being. This means that with Being we have found a ground that is itself grounded in Nothing and so is completely presuppositionless. It quite literally takes Nothing for granted! Because the content of the concept of Being is Nothing, that means it has no real content other than a sort of formal self-reference. Its content is its form and its form is its content.

Being and Nothing, in addition to being identical, are also opposed to one another in such a fashion that they create an "onward movement"[31] that is synthesized in the concept of Becoming. Concretely, the world we inhabit is neither pure Being nor pure Nothingness, but something in between. Things come into and go out of existence. Change, as Aristotle has claimed, is a very real characteristic of the world, and the manner in which change is constituted, according to Hegel, is by way of the natural self-generated movement of Being as it comes into conflict with itself, in the guise of Nothing, and then goes on to resynthesize itself into a unity. "The Truth of Being and of Nothing is accordingly the unity of the two: and this unity is Becoming."[32] Becoming is the process by which all we experience comes to actuality and then passes away. A thing that "Becomes" is more than Nothing yet less than Being. It is caught in between these two extremities, and its own nature is defined by this in-betweenness.

Being and Nothing are the abstract poles between which the concrete world makes its appearance. They are conceptual realities, co-generated in the presence of actual, particular things already existing in a state of Becoming. Let me stress that, as I understand it, Hegel does not intend to suggest that Being and Nothing somehow *historically* precede the existence of the universe and that the universe thereby emerges, within time, out of their conflict. Being and Nothing are not separate or independent of the universe, nor do they precede its creation. These concepts exist atemporally, outside of time, in logical space, and are dependent upon the state of the world as it is presently manifested. Hegel is not interested in issues dealing with the historical origins of the physical universe but rather restricts his comments to issues dealing with the *logical* composition of the universe as it now exists. To take

an analogous example, a triangle does not slowly come into existence with the appearance, over time, of three angles. More correctly speaking, a triangle just *is* a figure with three angles. It presupposes these angles as part of its very definition. Until three angles exist, you don't have a triangle, and if three angles do exist, you already have a triangle. The angles and the triangle are codependent upon one another and thus always exist concurrently. Likewise, Being, Nothing, and Becoming depend on one another to be what they are, and so the existence of one also implies the existence of the others. Just as the idea of a triangle logically presupposes three angles, so too does our presently existing world logically presuppose Being, Nothing, and Becoming. They describe the form of our concrete universe just as the existence of three angles describes the form of a triangle.

In time, then, Being, Nothing, and Becoming neither precede nor follow one another, and yet in a *logical* sense, the universe of Becoming can be said to be generated by the dialectical opposition between Being and Nothing. They constitute the engine that drives our unfolding reality. Furthermore, because Becoming is the synthesis of Being and Nothing, and because Nothing *is* Being, Being is the logical primary ground upon which all other things stand. In order to fathom the logical unfolding of reality, then, all we really need to grasp is Being. Being itself is Truth. But in conceptualizing the unity of Being, we must also strive to comprehend the diversity within that unity. This is the tricky part. Genuine wisdom does not come merely from mouthing the word "Being." It also requires the authentic ability to understand the diverse ways in which Being becomes incarnate. Being, in other words, is not a separate "thing" that exists independently from all of its particular manifestations. It is, instead, the overall form and constitution of the sum total of those manifestations. Being is the form of the universe as it concretely exists. For this reason we may not disregard anything at all as we strive to conceptualize this universal Truth. "The Truth is the Whole," Hegel has told us. It manifests itself in a dazzling variety of phenomena, and all of these manifestations contribute to its substance. In the concept of Being we encounter the mind's manner of encapsulating and thinking the Whole of Truth all at once.

God

When the mind thinks Being, it also thinks God, according to Hegel. Thus, the dialectical logic, which is rooted in the Doctrine of Being, leads us to a theological epiphany. God does exist, according to Hegel, but there is a great deal of controversy over just what sort of God it is in which Hegel believes. On the one hand, there are those commentators who point to Hegel's own commitment to the Lutheran Church as evidence that the God he believes in is the God of Christianity. There is a problem with this, however, because the Christian God is the God of Abraham, and as we have seen in past chapters, Abraham's God is the creator of the universe, existing apart and separate from the world. But this is something that Hegel denies of God. Hegel's God is identical with the form of the world, not separate from it. Furthermore, Hegel's position implies that God is actually *dependent* on, and emergent from, the interrelationships that exist between the total sum of concrete particulars that make up the universe. This is certainly not a typical Christian belief, and it is what leads Robert Solomon to conclude that Hegel is actually an atheist.[33] According to Solomon, the god of Hegel is really no God at all, because it is in no way a supernatural entity but a fully natural and world-bound presence. Solomon points out that, long before Nietzsche made the same proclamation, Hegel announced the "death of God"[34] as a self-standing being that exists independent of and apart from human thinking. If we take Hegel at his word, as articulated in *The Phenomenology of Spirit* at least, then it would appear as if his philosophy rejects the existence of any sort of traditional, Christian way of believing in God.

Frederick Beiser, on the other hand, suggests that Hegel should not be considered an atheist but a "vitalistic materialist" who sees "God as the whole of nature."[35] In vitalistic materialism, the supernatural realm is denied existence, yet the material world is claimed to have the self-organizing properties that we find in all natural organisms. According to this view, taken as a whole the universe is just an organism that we call God. If this is Hegel's position, then it runs very close to what is known as pantheism, which is the belief that "everything is God." However, as Peter Singer points out, Hegel certainly did not claim that every individual and particular thing in the universe literally is God. Singer thus concludes that Hegel is actually a panentheist.[36] This differs from pantheism insofar as the panentheist holds that the world of material reality is only a part of God. God, in other words, is not wholly identical with the universe but rather includes the universe as a portion of its constitution. The universe is something like God's body, in this way of thinking, but while God may be dependent upon its body for existence it also is more than just a body. God is more than the sum total of its parts, just as you or I are more than just the sum total of our bodily parts.

I agree with Singer that this last position, panentheism, pretty well characterizes Hegel's view on the nature of God. However, in the final evaluation it also seems rather silly and simple-minded to be overly concerned with putting a final and distinct label to Hegel's views on this subject. Unlike many other things in Hegel's philosophy, the content of his theology is pretty clear. God is Being. Being is Truth. Truth is the Whole. Therefore, God is the Whole. The Whole, furthermore, is defined as more than simply a collection of distinct and unconnected parts. It is the sum total of the interrelationships that exist between the parts as well. Therefore, God is the sum total of all the parts, and of all the interrelationships that exist between the parts, of the universe. This may not be a conventional way of thinking about God, but it is also not that difficult to comprehend. Perhaps it is the only thing in Hegel's philosophical system that is not difficult to comprehend.

HEGEL'S INFLUENCE

Right, Center, and Left Hegelianism

Hegel's philosophy attracted a great deal of attention and a massive following, first in Europe and then in the United States, spawning a movement in nineteenth-century thinking that was eventually to become complicated by serious theological and political disagreements. These disagreements led to the development of a number of divisions among Hegelians. Initially, after Hegel's death, the main point of contention proved to be the implications of Hegelianism for the realm of religion. It was this topic that precipitated the fragmentation of the philosophy into three separate schools of thought, labeled by David Friedrich Strauss (1808–1874) as "Right," "Center," and "Left" Hegelianism.[37]

As we have seen, Hegel's thoughts on the topic of God are unconventional but not all that obscure. What is unclear is how to reconcile these thoughts with traditional Christianity. The Right Hegelians undertook the project of showing how Hegel's God was compatible with the God of Christianity, and they also became concerned with defending Hegel's conservative political views. In general terms, this group was focused on maintaining the status quo. Hegel himself had claimed that the Prussian state, which was his own home, represented the collective social and political culmination of the self-conscious manifestation of *Geist*. In effect, history and philosophy had come to an end in Prussia because this is where Hegel brought his ideas to fruition. Truth had become actualized and absolute knowing became a reality in Prussia. This being the case, Hegel and the Right Hegelians advocated the preservation and perpetuation of the conditions under which this event had occurred. For them, among the things that this entailed was the conservation of the Prussian system of government.

However, times were changing and the Center Hegelians emerged as a force that utilized Hegelian philosophy as a means toward gradual, evolutionary political change. These individuals were liberal reformists who saw in Hegel's philosophy a way to promote productive negotiation within the Prussian system. This, they hoped, would result in the ongoing alteration of political conditions to suit the needs of contemporary circumstances. In their view, although it was the case that *Geist* had become self-conscious through Hegel and in Prussia, there was still an incongruity between this fact and the concrete political structures that the state had in place. More work had to be done to make "appearances conform to the 'essential' reality of actualized reason."[38]

Neither the Right nor the Center Hegelians ended up having a lasting impact on philosophy in the long run. Their concerns were too focused on their own times and their own political circumstances. Once the Prussian state withered away, their concerns would be of little more than historical interest. However, in the thoughts of the third group of Hegel's followers, the Left Hegelians, we find ideas that would go on to affect the future not only of philosophy but also of the world as a whole. The Left Hegelians were neither conservatives nor reformers; they were theological and political radicals who believed that the true message of Hegelianism was revolutionary. For one thing, they believed that Hegel's views on God implied that Christianity, and indeed any religious system based on faith in the supernatural, was a lie. Religion, according to the Left Hegelians, is simply a delusion that keeps people from focusing on real, concrete human affairs. This is perhaps the most pronounced theme that we find in Left Hegelianism. There is a rejection of the transcendent and the abstract and a reaffirmation of the worldly and the concrete. Second, in Left Hegelianism there also develops a political message that calls for the revolutionary overthrow of political institutions that oppress individual freedom and equality. To take hold of their own lives, human beings need to live under circumstances that are conducive to free choice. The Left Hegelians rejected the idea that their present political conditions represented those circumstances. Rather, economic and social inequality were perpetuated by the powers that be, and thus, far from embodying the authentic manifestation of *Geist*, they felt that Truth had been retarded and covered over by the traditional institutions of the state. It was time to get rid of those institutions and to usher in a new era of history.

Ludwig Feuerbach

Among the first, and most influential, of the Left Hegelians was Ludwig Feuerbach (1804–1872). Taking inspiration from Hegel's theological conclusions, Feuerbach claimed that the Christian God was nothing more than an abstraction that distracted our attention from the concrete realities of this world. Because we are dissatisfied with this world and our sufferings in it, we imagine that there is a heaven in which all suffering will end. But this heaven is just an illusion, claims Feuerbach, and the sooner that we realize this, the sooner that we can get on with the task of making the world that we now live in better. Instead of giving money and time to the Church, we should be taking care of our fellow human beings. The more energy that we devote to solving worldly problems, the less

© Junako J. Robinson

energy we will devote to otherworldly illusions, and in the process we will be on the road to bettering mankind as a whole. Feuerbach tells us that if we abolish the ideal of the Christian God, we will be more likely to devote our attention toward the real problems of everyday existence. If we just stop desiring abstract, otherworldly things that we can't have, then we can start working toward getting those things that will make life better for us in the concrete world of the here and now. Feuerbach suggests that we should abandon religion and abstract illusions instead to embark upon a program of social revolution and the improvement of mankind.

For Feuerbach, all religion is an exercise in projection. Echoing Hegel's discussion of the "unhappy consciousness," Feuerbach claims that the religious consciousness takes purely human qualities and objectifies them as something existing outside of concrete, particular humans. God is the ultimate objectification of these qualities, and when humans worship God they are thus unconsciously worshiping themselves. "[R]eligion is man's earliest and also indirect form of self-knowledge.... Man first of all sees his nature as if out of himself, before he finds it in himself. His own nature is in the first instance contemplated by him as that of another being."[39] Thus, when God is conceived of as a being of pure understanding, or as the source of morality, or as a suffering being (as with Jesus), these conceptions are in reality just a reification of human qualities, like intelligence, moral sentiment, and feeling. They are an exercise in the sort of "picture thinking" that Hegel had warned against.

Furthermore, claims Feuerbach, this propensity to project human qualities onto a being called God is motivated, in actual fact, by real-world suffering and poverty. "The more empty life is, the fuller, the more concrete is God. The impoverishing of the real world and the enriching of God is one act."[40] Feuerbach's solution to this situation is to make humans fully conscious of the process of religious abstraction, to unmask it for what it is, and thereby to undermine its authority so that human energies can be refocused on the problems of the concrete, everyday problems of living life. Religion interferes with the alleviation of real suffering because "duties towards God necessarily come into collision with common human duties,"[41] and so only by eliminating the worship of God can we get back to what is really important; namely, the worship of mankind. "The beginning, middle, and end of religion is Man."[42]

In Feuerbach's writing, we find a concern with the development of theological themes that Hegel had first formulated. While Hegel did not advocate the rejection of God, he did open the door to thinking of God as something that emerges out of, and thus is dependent upon, human thinking. Feuerbach radicalizes Hegel's views on this topic and draws what to many was a shocking conclusion: Man creates God. This was enough to lose Feuerbach his teaching position and to ostracize him from the mainstream intellectual community of his time. Nevertheless, his book *The Essence of Christianity* became a worldwide sensation, coming to influence a whole new generation of "Young Hegelians" who would continue to boldly develop his critique of religious abstraction.

Max Stirner

Max Stirner (1806–1856) takes Feuerbach's radical ideas and makes them even more radical. Stirner noticed that Feuerbach tended to use the term "Man" with as much reverence as religious thinkers used the term "God." With Feuerbach, Stirner writes, "... Man, has ascended to the highest being, religiously."[43]

The only known image of Max Stirner, drawn by Freidrich Engels, 1892.

Stirner tells us, however, that "Man" is no less an abstraction than is "God." As such, this idea distracts us from the needs of concrete individuals. "God has become man, but now man is the gruesome spook which he seeks to get back of, to exorcise, to fathom, to bring to reality and to speech."[44] If we are ever to overcome our alienation from reality, claims Stirner, then we must stop aspiring toward this ideal and abstract notion of Mankind. We must stop desiring to be something that we are not. Instead, we should live in the moment and do what we desire in the here-and-now. We must strive after nothing that is abstract, concerning ourselves only with the concrete world around us. Stirner closes his most famous book, *The Ego and Its Own*, with these words:

> I am the owner of my might, and I am so when I know myself as *unique*. In the *unique one* the owner himself returns into his creative nothing, of which he is born. Every higher essence above me, be it God, be it man, weakens the feeling of my uniqueness, and pales only before the sun of this consciousness. If I concern myself for myself, the unique one, then my concern rests on its transitory, mortal creator, who consumes himself, and I may say:

> All things are nothing to me.[45]

According to Stirner, all that really exists are unique, individual human beings. But society and culture try to shape and distort these "unique ones." Through schooling especially, societies attempt to force individuals into molds, creating "educated" and "cultured" citizens who will be useful to the society as a whole.[46] They try to make the concrete individual conform to an abstract ideal. But this is no better than religious indoctrination, claims Stirner. The ideal can never be made real, because all ideals are abstractions. As a consequence, we will always suffer alienation as long as we allow ourselves to be tempted by abstract notions of "mankind." All that exists are individual human beings struggling for power and happiness in a world that offers nothing else beyond this life. Once we realize this, Stirner claims, we can then truly be happy without worrying about some world of "higher" achievement and success.

Both Feuerbach and Stirner tell us that overcoming the alienation and despair of life requires that we turn our backs on ideas that distract us from the concrete world. Like Hegel before them, they see traditional religion as a substandard way of thinking that keeps the mind from conceptualizing the real nature of the world. Unlike Hegel, however, these thinkers do not believe that the societies they presently inhabit embody a state of final and enlightened perfection. They are, unlike Hegel, social revolutionaries who believe that humans still have a long way to go and that the road to satisfaction starts by learning to switch off the desire for things that are beyond our worldly grasp. If you just stop striving toward God and Heaven, then you may potentially become satisfied in the here and now with what you've got. The trick is to dissolve the incongruity between what you aspire toward and what you can actually obtain by recalibrating your desires. If you constantly strive toward the abstract, then your hopes are doomed, because the abstract can never be made real. Better, then, to focus attention on the concrete and to mold and shape the world so that it suits our wants, desires, and needs.

The Left Hegelian thinkers believe that our relationship to the world can be improved through a program of philosophical, psychological, political, social, and economic action. All of these thinkers see something wrong with our present relationship to the world, and they envision their task as providing both a diagnosis and a treatment for this sick state of affairs. The culmination of this current within Hegelianism is found in one of the most politically aggressive and revolutionary philosophies of our times: Marxism.

Karl Marx

Marxism is a philosophy that has had a tremendous impact, for better and worse, on the social and political landscape of our world. Its influence may currently be on the wane, but its effects will be with us forever. It is from Marxism that the ideals of communism were developed. It may seem a long way from the politically conservative nature of Hegel's thought to the revolutionary philosophy of communism; however, there are at least two threads that connect these ways of thinking. The first thread is found in the dialectical view of history. The second thread is found in utopianism, which is the belief in the perfectibility of our world.

© Juneko J. Robinson

Karl Marx (1818–1883), while rejecting much of Hegel's abstract philosophizing, nevertheless retained many of his ideas concerning the productive force of the dialectical relationship between opposites. Marx reinterpreted Hegel's "dialectical idealism" in materialistic terms, claiming that it was not the progressive unfolding of ideas and their distillation into an absolute concept that propelled history forward but rather the concrete process of class conflict between laborers and the capitalist owners of the means of production. The movement of history, according to Marx, is primarily the result of material and economic forces that come into collision with one another. Through this collision of concrete forces, synthesis is produced and the world moves forward. In his own time, Marx predicted the coming synthesis of owners (the bourgeoisie) and workers (the proletariat) in a new, universal kind of human being who would embody both ownership and the creative energy of the worker. This new human being would institute a new form of communist government that would supplant capitalism. Under communism, there is collective ownership of productive institutions and a redistribution of wealth throughout society so that all inequalities between human beings are eliminated. With the elimination of inequality, Marx claimed that the source of material conflict in the world would disappear and thus so would the movement of history. A perfect society free of conflict would thereby be ushered in.

The perfect communist society will be resisted by the owning classes, according to Marx, and for this reason before things get better they will have to get worse. As workers become more and more self-conscious and aware of their own class interests, conflict between capitalists and workers will intensify until there is a revolution of the workers in which they seize the factories and centers of production for their own. Marx writes, "The proletariat will use its political supremacy to wrest, by degrees, all capital from the bourgeoisie, to centralize all instruments of production in the hands of the State, i.e., of the proletariat organized as a ruling class."[47] The forward march of history thus leads to a revolution of the proletariat who will themselves take control of production and institute a revolutionary state.

The revolutionary state, however, is merely a temporary measure, according to Marx. It too is destined to fade away once human beings become socialized into the new communist way of life. Once this occurs, human nature itself will be transformed. Greed will be bred out of people, and cooperation instead of competition will be the rule. Class conflict will evaporate, and everyone will live together freely and harmoniously. "In place of the old bourgeois society, with its class antagonisms, we shall have an association, in which the free development of each is the condition for the free development of all."[48] At this point, the state itself, with its laws and formal governing mechanisms, will become superfluous. Once everyone has all of their material needs met, and when everyone has been bred to cooperate with others, then the state will no longer serve any purpose and so will simply fade away. An anarchist utopia, instead of Hegel's absolute Idea, will finally signal the crowning achievement of history.

Marx claimed that he had "turned Hegel upside down" by asserting the power of economic and material forces over the power of ideas. Despite this fundamental difference, Marx owed a huge debt to Hegel's dialectical logic and its vision of perfect knowing. Although Marx himself was less of a philosopher than a social activist and political revolutionary, he could not have accomplished all that he did without the Hegelian system of thought. Whether this is a good thing or a bad thing is left to the reader to decide.

WONDROUS DISTRESS IN HEGELIAN PHILOSOPHY

Both wonder and distress lie at the core of Hegelian thought, but in the end Hegel's system is also an attempt to vanquish these philosophical qualities. Hegel's thinking was initiated by his own distressed reaction to Kant's division between the noumenal and phenomenal realms. Consequently, the guiding mission of Hegelian philosophy is to seek a way to mend this division and to finally bring the human subject back into commerce with the Absolute. This goal, Hegel tells us, is equivalent to the pursuit of Truth itself. Truth is the Whole; it is the sum total of all that exists, and Hegel will be satisfied with nothing less than the realization of Truth. Here we find evidence of the sort of vigorous curiosity and wondrous excitement that are the necessary conditions of all authentic philosophizing. Hegel desires the Truth; yet he is also distressed by his separation from it. This is fertile ground for the commencement of ambitious and dynamic philosophical striving.

The method of dialectic is the key with which Hegel believes we can finally unlock the secrets of Truth, alleviate our alienation from reality, and arrive at the point of absolute knowing. As we have seen above, Hegel explicitly states that he is ultimately concerned not with the "love of wisdom" but with wisdom itself. He wants to move past being a mere philosopher to become a wise man who is able to hold the "absolute Idea," Truth, in his mind once and for all. The enthusiasm and the passion that he expresses as he pursues this goal are awe inspiring, and yet in his final claim to success we feel as if we have reached a dead end. At this point, not only is distress alleviated, but wonder evaporates as well. There is no use for wonder when you actually possess the most profound Truth of the world, and Hegel's concluding position seems to be that he himself has accomplished the task that all other philosophers have failed to complete. Hegel has dialectically thought his way past time itself and has come to a position of eternal and absolute knowing. All that is left for the rest of us to do is to learn about Hegel!

There is, however, a hint in Hegel's own writing that maybe he was not so confident of his final grasp of Truth after all. In the culminating chapter of *The Phenomenology of Spirit*, the chapter that concerns "absolute knowing," we encounter a short, easy to overlook passage suggesting, perhaps, that the process of understanding does not end but rather moves in cycles. Hegel writes, "The movement is the circle that returns into itself, the circle that presupposes its beginning and reaches it only at the end."[49] Is Hegel saying here that a grasp of Truth is something that comes and goes, like the movement around a circle? Is absolute knowing a point, among other points, that comes and goes? Does the mind reach its destination and then move away from that goal, only, once again, to embark upon the journey home? This could be, and if it is so, then Hegel has rescued philosophical wonder and distress from becoming dissolved in the confidence and satisfaction of wisdom.

The initiating question of Hegelian philosophy focuses on how we may solve the problem of human alienation from absolute Truth. In this alienation,

Hegel saw the source of much intellectual and spiritual suffering, and so his life's project focused on developing a strategy by which to alleviate this distress. It is no coincidence, then, that many of Hegel's more down-to-earth and practical followers, like Feuerbach, Stirner, and Marx, were drawn to the development of systems of their own that are predominantly concerned with psychological, social, and political solutions to related but more concrete forms of human suffering. Lying latent within the arguments of Hegel and these followers is an assumption that is so much a part of our "common sense" that we may not even think to question it. This is the view that more than anything else, the purpose of philosophy (and perhaps even of life itself) is to promote human happiness and satisfaction. It is through philosophy that the secrets of the universe might be revealed and then utilized to transform our human world into a more comfortable, happy, and satisfying place. I shall return to this point in the following chapter, but suffice it to say here that such an assumption, while certainly reasonable, is not altogether indisputable. In fact, if philosophy is, in its purest sense, a way of thinking that endeavors toward continual questioning, the deferral of final answers, and the opening up of new perspectives on Truth, we might even come to the conclusion that happiness and contentment are antithetical to pure philosophy. If happiness and contentment describe a state of mind in which desire has been extinguished and frustration has been eliminated, then what would be the motivation for happy and content humans to continue philosophizing? As we heard Socrates say in Chapter 2, the real shame of human ignorance is that the ignorant are satisfied and happy with their current state of being and so they have no desire to seek wisdom. Perhaps, then, those philosophies that seek an end to human unhappiness also seek an end to philosophy itself.

This is not to suggest that thinkers such as Hegel, Feuerbach, Stirner, and Marx have nothing philosophical to say. To return to a metaphor I used in the preceding chapter, I would, indeed, characterize them as existing at an extreme end of the "rubber band" that is philosophy. If philosophy strains between the desire for answers, on the one hand, and the recognition of how little we really know, on the other, then these thinkers are individuals who have stretched philosophy as far as it will go in one particular direction.[50] Their philosophizing has produced answers, and these answers are now intended as guides to our mastery and manipulation of the world around us. All of these figures seem to believe that, because they have revealed the true nature of the world, philosophizing may end and the task of scientific, political, and social action may now begin. They have stretched the rubber band as far as it can go and have now been propelled beyond the need for philosophizing. Marx was quite explicit in this when he wrote "The philosophers have only interpreted the world, in various ways; the point is to change it."[51] This is an attitude that we will see disputed in the chapter that follows by another group of philosophers who were both inspired by, and critical of, the ideas of Kant and Hegel.

QUESTIONS FOR DISCUSSION

1. Do you think that Hegel was successful in his attempt to think the "absolute Idea"? Why or why not?

2. The two-party system in our own country operates by way of conflict and compromise. Discuss this system of political dialogue in terms of Hegel's dialectical logic.

3. Hegel's master/slave dialectic has been used by philosophers, sociologists, and political scientists as a model for discussing such things as race relations, the relationship between men and women, and the relationship between nations. Using the master/slave dialectic, discuss some of the ways that people and nations can become dominant over those who previously dominated them.

4. In traditional Christianity, God exists as the creator of the universe and thus stands outside of and apart from the universe. In Hegel's system of philosophy, God is the form of the universe itself. Nevertheless, Hegel claimed that he was a Christian. Do you think Hegel's views on God can be made consistent with a Christian worldview?

5. Feuerbach claimed that religion distracts people from making the actual, concrete world a better place. However, isn't it true that the only reason some people help the poor and act kindly to others is because of their fear of punishment by God? Discuss the ways that religion both benefits and damages the world.

6. Stirner is sometimes called the father of philosophical anarchism because he teaches that individuals can get along just fine without the state. Do you think this is true? Do you think a society of Stirnerite "unique ones" is possible?

7. With the fall of the Soviet Union and China's increasing openness to capitalism, it has been claimed that Marxism and communism have been shown to be unworkable. Do you think this is true? What do you make of recent claims that the U.S. government is drifting closer and closer to a form of Marxist socialism?

NOTES

1. Quoted in Johan Goudsblam, *Nihilism and Culture* (Lanham, MD: Rowman and Littlefield, 1980), pp. 36–37.

2. Bertrand Russell, *A History of Western Philosophy* (New York: Simon and Schuster, 1972), p. 730.

3. Henry Hatfield, "The Myth of Nazism," in *Myth and Mythmaking*, Henry A. Murray (ed.) (Boston: Beacon Press, 1968), p. 205.

4. Robert Solomon, *In the Spirit of Hegel* (Oxford: Oxford University Press, 1985), p. ix.

5. Ibid., p. xi.

6. Georg Wilhelm Friedrich Hegel, *Reason in History, A General Introduction to the Philosophy of History*, Robert S. Harman (trans.) (New York: The Liberal Arts Press, 1954), p. 11.

7. Georg Wilhelm Friedrich Hegel, *Philosophy of Right* in *Hegel: The Essential Writings*, Frederick G. Weiss (ed.) (New York: Harper Torchbooks, 1974)

8. Ibid., pp. 13–14. See also G. W. F. Hegel, *The Phenomenology of Spirit*, A. V. Miller (trans.) (Oxford: Oxford University Press, 1977), paragraph 55.

9. Hegel, *Phenomenology*, paragraph 32.

10. Ibid., paragraph 20.

11. Ibid., paragraph 18.

12. Ibid., paragraph 178.

13. Ibid., paragraph 178.

14. Ibid., paragraph 184.

15. Ibid., paragraph 187.

16. Ibid., paragraph 190.

17. Ibid., paragraph 192.

18. Ibid., paragraph 199.

19. Ibid., paragraph 204.

20. Ibid., paragraph 206.

21. Ibid., paragraph 207.

22. Ibid., paragraph 2.

23. Frederick G. Weiss (ed.), *Hegel: The Essential Writings* (New York: Harper Torchbooks, 1974), p. 87.

24. Weiss, *Logic* in *Hegel: The Essential Writings*, p 92.

25. Ibid., p. 95, paragraph 81.

26. Ibid., p. 92, paragraph 79.

27. Ibid., p. 99, paragraph 82.

28. Alexandre Kojeve, *Introduction to the Reading of Hegel: Lectures on* The Phenomenology of Spirit, James H. Nichols, Jr. (trans.) (Ithaca, NY: Cornell University Press, 1980), p. 85.

29. Weiss, *Logic*, p. 105

30. See Chapter 7.

31. Weiss, *Logic*, p. 118, paragraph 87.

32. Ibid., p. 119.

33. Solomon, *In the Spirit of Hegel*, p. 34.

34. Hegel, *Phenomenology*, paragraph 785.

35. Frederick C. Beiser, "Introduction: Hegel and the Problem of Metaphysics," in *The Cambridge Companion to Hegel* (Cambridge: Cambridge University Press, 1993), pp. 8–9.

36. Peter Singer, *Hegel: A Very Short Introduction* (Oxford: Oxford University Press, 2001), p. 106.

37. Allen W. Wood, "Hegel and Marxism," in *The Cambridge Companion to Hegel*, p. 414.

38. John Toews, "Transformations of Hegelianism, 1805–1846," in *The Cambridge Companion to Hegel*, p. 389.

39. Ludwig Feuerbach, *The Essence of Christianity*, George Eliot (trans.) (New York: Barnes and Noble Books, 2004), p. 15.

40. Ibid., p. 76.

41. Ibid., p. 262.

42. Ibid., p. 186.

43. Max Stirner, *The Ego and Its Own*, Steven Byington (trans.) (London: Rebel Press, 1993), p. 58.

44. Ibid., p. 41.

45. Ibid., p. 366.

46. In addition to his major work, *The Ego and Its Own*, Stirner also wrote a short paper published in 1842 criticizing the educational system titled *The False Principle of Our Education, or Humanism and Realism*, Robert H. Beebe (trans.), James J. Martin (ed.) (Colorado Springs, CO: Ralph Myles, 1967).

47. Karl Marx, *Selected Writings* (Oxford: Oxford University Press, 1977), p. 237.

48. Ibid., p. 238.

49. Hegel, *Phenomenology*, paragraph 802.

50. Along these lines, in his book *The Poverty of Philosophy*, Marx attacks the French socialist thinker Pierre-Joseph Proudhon for being "too philosophical."

51. Marx, *Selected Writings,* "Theses on Feuerbach," p. 158.

Chapter 11

Happiness, Suffering, and Pessimism in Kierkegaard, Schopenhauer, Nietzsche, and Mill

© Juneko J. Robinson

Why does Kierkegaard claim that all humans are in despair? Who is the knight of faith? What is the "will"? Why did Schopenhauer consider himself to be a pessimist? In what ways did Nietzsche accept Schopenhauer's philosophy? In what ways did Nietzsche reject Schopenhauer's ideas? What is the *Übermensch*? What is the Greatest Happiness Principle? How does Mill's Utilitarian moral philosophy conflict with the insights of Nietzsche?

As was illustrated in the previous chapter, many philosophers after Kant became preoccupied with the problem of how to reconcile our merely subjective understanding of reality with the objective nature of the universe as it exists independent of human experience. Kant had presented a rather convincing picture of the human mind, depicting it as an active instrument that sifts through our sensory perceptions, organizing, synthesizing, and interpreting ideas according to a set of *a priori* intuitions and categories of the understanding. If this depiction is accurate—and it does seem likely that something of the sort is the case— then the human mind understands the world not as it really exists in-itself but only as it appears to us as filtered through the human perspective. For many philosophers this is a troubling situation because it implies that any of our possible knowledge of the world is merely subjectively valid. If Kant is right, then all we can ever know are the subjective appearances of things but never the real objective nature of things-in-themselves.

Hegelian philosophy sought a way to mend this rift between the subjective and objective domains of reality, with an eye toward demonstrating the interconnectedness of the two realms. Hegel claimed that dialectical logic gives us the tool needed to demonstrate how the world of objective spirit, or *Geist*, is a rational and unfolding process that includes the human mind within its boundaries. This being the case, the subjective realm of human thinking is not, in truth, split off from the world of objectivity but is rather an integral part of the universe. Because there is no necessary division between subject and object, we humans have the potential to transcend our limited time- and space-bound perspective on reality to truly comprehend the whole of the universe. To do this we must discipline ourselves, leave behind "picture thinking," and raise our understanding to the level of the pure concept. If successful, we may hold within our minds the "absolute Idea," which makes present the pure form of the universe itself. This experience of "absolute knowing" is also God's perspective, and in gaining this viewpoint, Hegel believed that we could cease being philosophers who merely aspire toward wisdom and finally become actual possessors of wisdom.

Hegelian philosophy, as we have seen, was very influential and attracted a huge number of devoted followers who saw in Hegel's system a path toward the alleviation of human ignorance and alienation, not only in the intellectual realm but also in the down-to-earth world of concrete, everyday living. With its quasi-religious overtones and its optimistic outlook on the human capacity for absolute knowledge, it is no wonder that Hegelianism would prove to be popular. Optimism and hope always attract more people than do pessimism and despair, and it is certainly the case that Hegel's philosophy is a philosophy of hope.

And yet, Hegelianism was also regarded by some as a philosophy of arrogance. According to many thinkers, the Kantian dilemma was not adequately solved by Hegel but simply set aside. In proclaiming the triumph of the "absolute Idea," all Hegel did, according to these critics, was establish himself as the ultimate philosopher king for the entire world, offering a premature and fraudulent path to happiness through reason and logic. Consequently, in contrast to the Hegelian trend in post-Kantian thought, there developed another more fatalistic, less popular, but ultimately important and influential current of philosophizing that I shall, in what follows, characterize as "nihilistic." This tradition is best represented by its three most famous proponents, Søren Kierkegaard, Arthur Schopenhauer, and Friedrich Nietzsche.

Kierkegaard, Schopenhauer, and Nietzsche were not at all pleased with what they regarded as the abstract utopianism of Hegelian philosophy. All three of these thinkers go to great lengths to emphasize how the alienation and despair of life are unavoidable and how the attainment of "absolute knowing" or of a perfect society are mere pipe dreams conjured up by arrogant pretenders to wisdom. However, although they do not believe that perfection in this life is possible, they also do not believe that we are able simply to give up the desire for absolutes. They teach that humans, as long as we live, are trapped in a world of striving, aspiration, and hardship. The human condition is inevitability torn between the desire for absolutes and the frustrating realization that absolutes are beyond our capacity to actualize. All we can expect from this life, therefore, is an endless cycle of struggle. Any attempt to flee from this state of affairs is a delusion that blinds one to the real, lived nature of human existence. For Kierkegaard, who was a proponent of Christianity, the absurdity of such earthly trials may inspire one to take a leap of faith and thus commit oneself to love of God. For Schopenhauer and Nietzsche, on the other hand, the absurdity of life leads away from faith in the Christian God. The best that we can do, according to Schopenhauer, is to understand our situation and, according to Nietzsche, take hold of and embrace the struggles of life. This last point highlights a major difference between the Schopenhauerian and Nietzschean perspectives. Whereas Schopenhauer took a dim, passive, and pessimistic view of the human condition, Nietzsche attempted to rescue some sense of vitality and optimism from the depths of nihilistic despair. Kierkegaard, with his unique form of Christian nihilism, walks a strange middle path between hope and despair. Like Schopenhauer, he suggests that we must, in one sense, acquiesce to the absurdity of existence. Like Nietzsche, however, he sees such acquiescence as opening the door to a new perspective on life, one in which we may go so far as to actively embrace and savor the difficulty, forlornness, and despair required by our existence.

Despite differences in their particular attitudes concerning life's absurdity, all of these thinkers claim there is something in the natural constitution of human beings that prevents us from attaining a final, satisfying reconciliation with the world around and within us. Humans must forever strive, struggle, and fail in their attempt to grasp the ultimate. While Schopenhauer sees this as a bad thing, Kierkegaard and Nietzsche see it as a good thing; whether good or bad, the characterizations of the world offered by these philosophers steer clear of proclaiming final solutions to human alienation and instead emphasize the necessity of ongoing interpretation and the unending exploration of ourselves and of Being itself. If authentic philosophy dwells in the realm of never-ending aspiration and never-ending thinking, then it is here within this nihilistic tradition that we may, perhaps, find philosophy to once again truly thrive.

In this chapter, I shall outline the major doctrines of Kierkegaard, Schopenhauer, and Nietzsche, placing emphasis on their preoccupation with the issues of intellectual striving and suffering. With these thinkers we will encounter a set of doctrines that some people have found detestable due to what is perceived as the denigration of the masses and callousness to the problem of widespread human unhappiness. Other people, however, are enthralled and delighted with these very same ideas because of what they see as a heroic glorification of the individual. To highlight the controversy surrounding these thinkers, I shall, at the end of this chapter, briefly introduce readers to the moral philosophy of John Stuart Mill, a contemporary of Nietzsche, whose own philosophical ideas provide a stark contrast to the doctrines of the nihilistic thinkers. Mill's philosophy presents arguments in many ways counter to Kierkegaard's, Schopenhauer's, and Nietzsche's, and which are rooted in the belief that human happiness and the alleviation of suffering are indeed of paramount importance. Mill's moral philosophy thus serves as an interesting foil to the rest of the contentions with which we will be predominantly concerned throughout this chapter.

SØREN KIERKEGAARD: THE KNIGHT OF FAITH

Although Søren Kierkegaard (1813–1855) predicted that he would not live past the age of thirty-three, in fact he died of a lung ailment at the age of forty-two. In Danish, his name means "graveyard," which seems apt considering the dark and grim nature of his thought, his preoccupation with death, and the tragic nature of his life. When he was young, Kierkegaard fell in love with a girl named Regine Olsen, but he cancelled his engagement to her because he felt himself called to a solitary and difficult life of suffering and struggle in the aspiration to seek God. At the end of his lonely existence, after collapsing on a Copenhagen street and then lying ill in a hospital for six weeks, Kierkegaard's final words were reportedly, "The bomb explodes, and the conflagration will follow."[1] He seemed confident that his lonely struggles in life had resulted in powerful ideas that would soon engulf the world. Fittingly, the inscription on his tombstone reads simply "The Individual."

© Juneko J. Robinson

Kierkegaard's father was a wholesale importer who, upon his own death, left a very large fortune to his son as an inheritance. This wealth allowed Kierkegaard the leisure to pursue the life of a socialite, chasing pleasure as a "man about town." Beneath all of this, however, Kierkegaard was a deeply troubled and depressed individual who was incessantly worried that his life lacked meaning. He longed for something more stable and eternal than the diversions offered by wealth and the company of fashionable society. The pleasures of this world, he seemed to feel, were too fleeting to offer real satisfaction and comfort. Even the rich must die, after all, and then what? If all humans must die, then what sense can life possibly make? Are we thrown into the world simply to exist for a short period only to be extinguished forever? The entirety of Kierkegaard's philosophical career is spent trying to understand how we, as human beings, may salvage purpose from our seemingly absurd situation in life as mortal, finite, and time-bound creatures.

If the desire for meaning at any cost was Kierkegaard's only goal, he may well have simply adopted the "system" of Hegel and contented himself with the idea that all things in the universe are an expression of *Geist*. In fact, Kierkegaard did study Hegelian philosophy, which he first encountered through the lectures of Friedrich Wilhelm Schelling (1775–1854), a romantic thinker who was critical of Hegel's system. Along with his teacher, Kierkegaard concluded that Hegelianism was a fraud. Though it does purport to bring meaning to life, Hegel's philosophy nevertheless objectifies thinking by making it something that exists prior to concrete, living human subjects, and this was something that Kierkegaard could not accept. On the contrary, Kierkegaard insists that thinking is not some sort of disembodied unfolding of ideas but rather a process that is grounded in individual human minds. Humans exist first and then ideas are thought, not the other way around. In this way, Kierkegaard emphasizes the primacy of the individual over the more abstract view that Hegel presents of universal *Geist*. Whereas Hegel often makes it sound as if humans emanate from the unfolding of a cosmic mind, Kierkegaard tells us that ideas emanate from individual, thinking human beings.

In contrast to Hegel's abstract way of characterizing the universe, Kierkegaard adopts a more concrete way of understanding the world, approaching reality from an unabashedly subjective perspective. It is the concrete, living individual who is the foundation of his philosophy, and from the perspective of the individual knowledge always remains incomplete and unfinished. Any attempt to adopt a detached, universal perspective on the world is thus doomed because such a perspective would require a person to step outside of the finite confines of the human mind itself. As Kant had already argued, this is impossible. We must always remain locked into our own unique perspective, seeing the world from the standpoint of finitude. For these reasons, Kierkegaard dismisses the "system" of Hegel as sheer arrogance. It represents the failed attempt of a finite individual to become perfect and infinite. Hegel seems to have mistaken himself for God, Kierkegaard would say, and we are well advised to avoid this sort of mistake at all costs. It is this emphasis on subjectivity, human finiteness, and the inevitability of ongoing, worldly struggle that distinguishes Kierkegaard's approach to philosophy and which has led many to classify him as the first truly "existentialist" thinker. Melville Chaning-Pearce summarizes the characteristics of Kierkegaard's existentialism in the following manner:

> In the meaning of Kierkegaard "existential thinking" is thus a mode of thought which accepts the tension of life and is therefore concrete not abstract, subjective and personal not objective and impersonal, passionate (in the sense of suffering) and not dispassionate, which seeks not rational proof for thought but the assurance of faith for life and claims to explore a dimension of reality closed to the analytical reason....[2]

The search for Truth, Kierkegaard always insists, begins from the perspective of the individual and never, as long as we live, are we able to abandon our individual perspective to "see" Truth objectively and fully. At best, human life consists of an endless struggle, making it ever clearer that the intellect must always fall short of absolute understanding and that consequently a "leap of faith" is necessary if we are to find any sort of spiritual peace. The leap of faith is an important act, according to Kierkegaard, for it is the only thing that offers hope for the reconciliation of our finite selves with the infinite nature of true reality. Such a leap, however, is by far the most difficult project that a human being can undertake. At times, Kierkegaard himself confesses he does not even really understand how it is done. Nonetheless, he insists that it is only in such a leap that serenity may be gained.

The Sickness Unto Death

The human condition is one of despair, Kierkegaard tells us, and as long as we live we must remain in this state. For this reason, "despair is the sickness unto death."[3] We need to understand, however, that Kierkegaard's use of the term "despair" is rather idiosyncratic, referring not to a psychological state of mind but to an ontological state of being. When he speaks of human despair, Kierke-gaard is referring to our state of existence; a state in which we find ourselves hopelessly separated from, and yet also hopelessly longing for, the infinite. While Hegel had sought to show that there is no such necessary separation, Kierkegaard insists that as embodied flesh-and-blood creatures, we human beings must always be separated from the eternal by virtue of the restrictions imposed upon us by our embeddedness in the physical world.

The reason why this sort of despair is a necessary part of human existence, claims Kierkegaard, is that in their essence all humans are a "synthesis of the in-finite and the finite."[4] All humans are bodily creatures who also possess souls. The body is finite. The soul is infinite. This mixture of finite body and infinite soul is an uneasy one. Psychologically, this condition leads us to experience a mental state of chronic anxiety.[5] Because we are unable to bring the finite and infinite within us into harmony, we feel ill at ease and not-at-home in our everyday lives. However, this psychological anxiousness is merely a superficial symptom of our deeper spiritual separation from the true infinity of God. Despair, unlike anxiety, is a state of being rather than a state of thinking. While mental disquietude alerts us to a misalignment in our being, the state of that be-ing itself is one of despair.

Separation from God is sin, and so despair is also sin. However, according to Kierkegaard, this does not mean that despair is unequivocally bad. "Is despair an excellence or a defect? Purely dialectically, it is both."[6] The reason why he claims this is that, in despair, we find ourselves in a position to pursue a better state of being. Movement toward God is possible only if we are first separated from Him, and so in despair we find the possibility for "upbuilding and awakening." If we were never in despair, we would never become aware of our own finitude, and thus we would never become aware of our own depen-dence upon God. Thus it is that despair is the source of our "superiority over the animal,"[7] and for this reason "it is the worst misfortune never to have had this sickness: it is a true godsend to get it."[8]

Kierkegaard is very clear, however, that he is not simply advocating that hu-man beings wallow in their despair, congratulating themselves for how aware they are of their own separation from God. Rather, Kierkegaard wants us to move toward God and to struggle and strive to mend the rift between our own souls and the infinite creator who grounds and sustains us. Despair is good, in other words, insofar as it motivates us to action. You will recognize here something of the "wondrous distress" that I have been emphasizing throughout this book as the essential element of philosophy, and it is clear that as long as humans are alive as embodied individuals, Kierkegaard believes that productive philosophizing may take place. As we strive to fill the gap between our own finiteness and the infinity of God, we humans may remain involved in the drama of life and of thinking. However, according to Kierkegaard, this drama will come to an end; not while we are still embodied, as Hegel had sug-gested was possible, but when we are dead and have left the finitude of the body behind. It is only because of the ill fit between body and soul that we experience mental anxiety and that we exist in a state of despair. Once this incongruity is dissolved, however, something else is possible. The soul may rest peacefully with God. The problem is, of course, that there is no way to philosophize or to put into words what it is like to be in perfect harmony with God. Philosophy ends precisely where despair ends. Thus, philosophy has nothing to tell us about the state of being that occurs beyond despair.

Fear and Trembling

"If there were no eternal consciousness in man ... what would life be but despair?"[9] Because our consciousness is godlike in its freedom from finitude, there is hope for the reconciliation of the self with the infinite. According to Kierkegaard, this is the goal of Christianity. The Christian is a person who, in the experience of anxiety, has come to an awareness of despair and is now on the path toward God. But Christians are still embodied human beings, and so the struggle and despair of life are ongoing conditions even for them. This fact highlights one of Kierkegaard's major complaints about conventional Christians.[10] Like Hegel, many such individuals mistake themselves for something far greater than what they really are. The arrogance of the Church and of its ignorant followers speaks to their "outwardness," meaning their concern with worldly appearances, rather than to the sort of "inwardness" that is the mark of a true Christian. The inward human being is one who eschews the opinions and the expectations of the public to instead focus attention on the development and the "upbuilding" of a personal relationship to the Holy. Socrates is pointed to by Kierkegaard as a perfect example of a pre-Christian thinker who cultivated this sort of inwardness, and indeed Kierkegaard venerates Socrates almost as much as he does Jesus. He sees both men as authentic examples of simple, honest, and caring individuals who have accepted their own suffering in this world as a chance to move toward something greater. Most churchgoing Christians, ironically, are less devout than the pre-Christian Socrates! The real Christian, like Socrates, should be concerned with his or her own soul rather than with appearances. However, what we see in conventional "Christendom" is an overwhelming concern with outward ritual, manners, and pretense. Socrates, like Jesus, was willing to die for Truth. Today, Kierkegaard tells us, most "Christians" do not even respect the Truth upon which Christian faith was founded.

As discussed in Chapter 6, Christianity, along with Judaism and Islam, is one of the Abrahamic religions. It was the patriarch Abraham who first made a covenant with the one true God, willingly circumcising himself and obeying God's command to kill his own son Isaac as proof of his faith and commitment to God. Because of his extreme faith, Christians came to regard Abraham as someone to emulate. However, Kierkegaard points out, most contemporary Christians would be horrified if today someone like Abraham heard a call from God and acted on it. In fact, Kierkegaard tells us that if a modern-day priest heard that one of his own flock acted as Abraham had, that priest would explode with indignant rage, perhaps exclaiming, "Loathsome man, dregs of society, what devil has possessed you that you wanted to murder your own son?"[11] This is how radically Christianity has become alienated from its true foundations. Today, the actions of Abraham himself are condemned as evil and immoral according to Kierkegaard[12] Christians today cannot even understand what it is that Abraham accomplished, and although they pay lip service to him as a patriarch of the religion, they have no true appreciation of his real greatness.

Kierkegaard tells us repeatedly that he himself is also unable fully to empathize with the inner experience of Abraham. However, Kierkegaard is able to articulate the paradoxical nature of Abraham's situation and to appreciate the tremendous accomplishment of this man. The astounding thing about Abraham, and the reason why he is an authentic representative of faith according to Kierkegaard, is that Abraham was able to accept that he must transgress the moral command against murder to obey a holy command to sacrifice his son to God. Being thrown into this situation, most of us would collapse into inaction and despondency. But Abraham did not. He found himself placed in a seemingly impossible situation; a situation of contradictory demands. As Kierkegaard writes, "in this contradiction lies the very anguish that can indeed make one sleepless; and yet without that anguish Abraham is not the one he is."[13] Abraham is a great man because he was able to endure the anguish generated by the absurd demand made upon him and yet still retain his faith in God. Abraham loved his son Isaac with all of his heart. At the same time he had absolute faith in God. The paradox in Abraham's situation was that he was willing to sacrifice his beloved son to his beloved God, all the while believing that God would never allow Isaac to die. This is absurd, of course, because Abraham is the one who willingly raised his hand against Isaac, ready to plunge a knife into his own son's chest. Nonetheless, while Abraham fully intends to kill his son, he also fully believes that his son will be spared by God's grace. "He believed on the strength of the absurd, for there could be no question of human calculation, and it was indeed absurd that God who demanded this of him should in the next instant withdraw the demand."[14] So, the greatness of Abraham lies in the fact that, at one and the same time, he intended to kill his own son and he believed that God would not allow his son to die. This is an amazing accomplishment, according to Kierkegaard, because it attests to a state of mind in which reason and logic are suspended in favor of infinite faith. This, of course, is the state of mind toward which a true Christian must also aspire.

Abraham took a "leap of faith" and thus is, perhaps, the most well-developed example of what Kierkegaard calls a "knight of faith." The knight of faith is an individual who is "continually making the movement of infinity"[15] while still embodied as a finite individual. Anguish and despair never disappear from the life of such an individual, and yet the knight of faith moves on, facing the absurdity of existence with vigor and fortitude. Like a brave Medieval knight riding into battle, the knight of faith incessantly, tirelessly, and impossibly struggles to reconcile the finite with the infinite. His life is one of hardship, despair, and anxiety, but it is a noble life nonetheless because through this sort of turbulence spiritual purity is approximated in greater and greater degrees. Life for the knight of faith is suffering, and yet this suffering is worthwhile insofar as it brings the individual ever closer to God.

The knight of faith has attained the highest level of spiritual development possible for an embodied human being. As we saw in the case of Abraham, however, there are always conflicting demands in the world that tempt and distract the faithful from their commitment to God. One of these demands stems from the realm of morality and ethics. According to Kierkegaard, the human being who only leads life according to ethical rules is not as spiritually developed as a human being who is also, like Abraham, sensitive to the demands of a God beyond the realm of ethics. There are times when the commands of God trump the commands of ethics, and at such points in life, there occurs a "teleological suspension of the ethical."[16] The term "teleological" refers to the end or the goal that a thing pursues, and so when Kierkegaard asserts that there are times when ethical commands are "teleologically suspended," he is claiming that the goals embodied in morality and ethics are not absolute and that they may potentially be superseded by some greater demand; namely, the command of God. From the perspective of a person who holds duty to the moral law as absolute (perhaps like Kant?), individuals like Abraham appear to be immoral; strictly speaking, they are. However, what the merely ethical person does not realize is that morality does not represent the highest expression of Truth. The ethical human being has not ascended to the level of the knight of faith and so cannot understand that an inarticulate commitment to God is a higher imperative than commitment to the articulable rules of this world. Thus, the life of faith is a higher calling than the life of morality.

Some people never even ascend to living a life guided by ethics, however. The ethical life, Kierkegaard holds, is a more developed level of existence than the sort of life lived by those who participate in a merely "aesthetic" mode of existence. In the aesthetic mode, a human being makes no movement toward the infinite but simply delights in the immediate pleasures of the finite world. "The first immediacy is the aesthetic,"[17] claims Kierkegaard, because in regarding the world aesthetically a person simply takes in and appreciates the world as it immediately presents itself to him. Such a person delights in immediate pleasures and seeks the avoidance of pain and is not concerned with good or evil, and certainly not God. To such an individual, the finite world of sights and sounds, smells and sensations is all that there is. The irony of living this sort of life is that the aesthetic individual is, superficially, quite content. He gives no thought to the absolute and so does not experience the mental torment involved in trying to reconcile the finite with the infinite. Yet as Kierkegaard points out, because this sort of person is so far from consciously recognizing his or her separation from God, this person is, in fact, in despair to a greater degree than anyone else. Recall that despair is separation from God. The aesthetic individual, in not even being aware of his or her separation, is in worse shape than even the ethical individual, who at least has a sense of something greater than the self. The person who leads an aesthetic life may be superficially happy, but in a deeper, spiritual sense, he is in the depths of despair.

The three stages of life—the aesthetic, the ethical, and the religious—seem to mirror Kierkegaard's own biography. Born into wealth, Kierkegaard, like the Buddha, came to recognize that there must be something more to life than mere pleasure. To live without a challenge, without hardship to overcome, is perhaps the worst curse that a human being can face. Human beings discover their deeper capacities through struggle, trial, and suffering. Without these we stagnate and remain content with the way things are in the moment. This is the conclusion reached by Kierkegaard himself, and so he moved beyond a merely aesthetic appreciation of the world to develop a grander and more ambitious aspiration toward infinity. Ethics offered the first step, but even here we find something constructed within the human world. Ethical rules and commands are formulated by humans as presumed reflections of some grander and more universal Truth. To move beyond the reflections and toward Truth itself is the task of faith. The knight of faith gazes beyond the institutions, the conventions, and the rules of this world, trying to become one with the infinite reality of God's holiness. This is impossible, but in striving to realize this impossibility, the authentic Christian comes to stand in the presence of something awe-inspiring and uncanny. In "fear and trembling" he or she approaches God and submits to the absurdity of existence.

"[T]he real reason why men are offended by Christianity is that it is too high, because its goal is not man's goal, because it wants to make man into something so extraordinary that he cannot grasp the thought."[18] This quotation sums up not only what Kierkegaard sees as mainstream society's objection to true Christianity, it also sums up the complaint of many people against Kierkegaard himself. Kierkegaard forsakes happiness and contentment in this world in the name of endless struggle, despair, and anxiety. He admonishes us to strive for the unattainable to affirm our freedom and to ennoble ourselves in the aspiration toward God. What happens after death we cannot truly say, but as long as we live we may become more and more profound by looking "inward" and seeking the Holy as it manifests itself in our souls. While such endless struggle may testify to Kierkegaard's own sincerity, does it not ask too much of us? Perhaps in rebelling against the arrogant finality of Hegel and of "Christendom" Kierkegaard went too far in the opposite direction. This is Walter Kaufmann's contention when he writes of Kierkegaard, "He was a man in revolt, and even if one quite agrees that a revolt was called for, one may regret that he went much too far."[19] But Kierkegaard was not the only philosopher to rebel violently against the mainstream thinking of his day, and as we will see in what follows, he may not even be the most extreme of the nihilistic rebels. At least in Kierkegaard, the possibility of heaven remains. In the thinking of Schopenhauer and Nietzsche, even this hope evaporates.

SCHOPENHAUER'S SYNTHESIS OF PLATO, KANT, AND HINDUISM

Although Arthur Schopenhauer (1788–1860) did not make his reputation as an academic, he did, for a short period of time, lecture at the University of Berlin, the same university at which Hegel taught. Schopenhauer's lectures were not at all popular due to his stubborn insistence on scheduling them at the same time that Hegel held his own classes. Hegel was the most popular philosopher in the German-speaking world at the time and Schopenhauer was a nobody, so it is no surprise that Schopenhauer's lectures were never well attended. Schopenhauer's decision to engage in this sort of one-sided competition is indicative of an obstinate

© Juneko J. Robinson

streak in his personality that would get him into trouble more than once over the course of his lifetime. Troubles with his mother, paternity disputes, accusations of assault, and repeated legal difficulties were just some of the messes that Schopenhauer had to deal with during his lifetime. Perhaps, in addition to his various philosophical influences, it was his unsettled and tumultuous personal relationships, coupled with his bitter and pigheaded disposition, that inclined him to formulate a philosophy he himself would proudly label as a form of pessimism.

Schopenhauer was a man greatly influenced by Kant's philosophical system, and though he was quite critical of much that his predecessor wrote, Schopenhauer nonetheless believed firmly that the basic insights of Kantianism were correct. As he writes in the appendix to Volume I of his masterpiece *The World as Will and Representation*, "Kant's works … will themselves eternally extol their master, and will always live on earth, though perhaps not in the letter, yet in the spirit."[20] The most important insight that Kant introduced into philosophy, according to Schopenhauer, "is the distinction of the phenomenon from the thing-in-itself, based on the proof that between things and us there always stands the intellect, and that on this account they cannot be known according to what they may be in themselves."[21] That there is a gap between our subjective understanding and the objective reality of the world around us guarantees that we are always at least one step separated from the true nature of things, and Schopenhauer explicitly connects this Kantian insight with the much earlier thoughts of Plato. Recalling Plato's myth of the cave, Schopenhauer reminds us about the image of a prisoner, chained in the depths of a dark cavern, watching shadows and reflections as they dance across the interior walls. The prisoner thinks that these shadows and reflections are all there is to reality. However, in truth there is much more to the world than the prisoner's perspective reveals. The sun and the firelight burning behind the prisoner are what give the shadows shape and form, and even after the shadows and reflections themselves cease to exist, these sources of illumination remain. But the prisoner is not privy to this knowledge. Like us, he is bound to a limited perspective through which he filters and interprets reality, and it is this limited perspective that blinds him to the real truth of his situation. According to Kant's philosophy, we are all like the prisoners in Plato's story, trapped in our own cave-like human perspective.

That Kant's philosophy seems to echo the earlier thoughts of Plato is compelling, but it is not a surprise. After all, both philosophers take part in a common, Western tradition, and Kant himself was certainly well acquainted with Plato's writings before he undertook his own philosophical investigations. However, Schopenhauer points out, there is an even more ancient, non-Western tradition that seems to communicate the same thoughts as those of Plato and Kant. The religion/philosophy of Hinduism, especially as articulated in the *Upanishads*, also characterizes our everyday perceptions as a "veil" that separates us from the absolute and true nature of things. The *Shvetashvatara Upanishad* speaks of *Maya*, which is the totality of appearances that present themselves to our consciousness, but which are themselves not the most stable or foundational truth that exists. According to the *Upanishads*, all of reality is a process during which *Brahman*, the source and origin of everything that is, manifests itself in various forms. In our everyday manner of living, we take the manifestations of *Brahman* as distinct, separate, and discrete phenomena. In actual fact, however, this is an illusion, because all of these phenomena are, at a more fundamental level, interconnected and find their origin in one underlying, indestructible, and eternal source. *Maya* is thus the lens through which humans understand and perceive *Brahman*, yet is also by the same token the veil that separates us from the absolute. The first chapter of the *Shvetashvatara Upanishad* puts it this way:

> What is the cause of the cosmos? Is it Brahman?
> From where do we come? By what live?
> Where shall we find peace at last?
> What power governs the duality
> Of pleasure and pain by which we are driven?...
>
> The world is the wheel of God, turning round
> And round with all the living creatures upon its rim.
> The world is the river of God,
> Flowing from him and flowing back to him.
> On this ever-revolving wheel of being
> The individual self goes round and round
> Through life after life, believing itself
> To be a separate creature, until
> It sees its identity with the Lord of Love
> And attains immortality in the indivisible whole....
>
> Conscious spirit and unconscious matter
> Both have existed since the dawn of time,
> With maya appearing to connect them,
> Misrepresenting joy as outside of us.
>
> When all these three are seen as one, the Self
> Reveals his universal form and serves
> As an instrument of the divine will.[22]

This passage articulates a number of themes that were important to Schopenhauer, and it illustrates why, along with Plato and Kant, he cites Hinduism as one of the most potent influences on his own thinking. First of all, like Plato and Kant, the *Upanishads* suggest that the way the world appears to us is not identical with the way the world really exists independent of our perceptions. Plato talks of an "intelligible realm" that lies behind the world of sensible phenomena, while Kant writes of a "thing–in–itself" that exists independently of the phenomenal realm. Likewise, the *Upanishads* speak of *Brahman*, which is the ultimate reality hidden behind appearances. Furthermore, our understanding of the nature of the singular, underlying substance of the universe, according to Plato, Kant, and the *Upanishads*, is actually *distorted* by the very operation of our minds as we attempt to understand it. For Plato, it is our senses; for Kant, it is the *a priori* intuitions and the categories of the understanding; whereas in the *Upanishads* it is the veil of *Maya* that interferes with our ability to grasp the objective Truth of the world as it exists independent of our minds. So not only are we separated from the real nature of things by the way we think, but our thinking, by its very operations, interprets and filters reality, producing a kind of counterfeit depiction of what exists "out there." Finally, while Kant insists that we are forever cut off from the thing–in–itself, both Plato and the Hindus suggest that there is a path beyond rational thinking that will allow us to experience the overwhelming and sublime nature of the world beyond appearances. For Plato, it is the leap into the "Good" itself, while according to the *Upanishads* the practice of yoga promises to bring one into mystical union with *Brahman*. The intellectual process of philosophizing can take us only to the point of understanding how ignorant we are of the real nature of the world around us, but Plato and the Hindus also tell us that there are experiences that may potentially take us beyond the intellect. Religion and mysticism pick up where philosophy leaves off. In point of fact, Kant also came very close to agreeing with this last assertion when he claimed that he had "denied knowledge to make room for faith." So the ideas of Hinduism, Platonism, and Kantianism all seem to share some very close affinities with one another.

Bertrand Russell notes that two busts decorated Schopenhauer's study: one of Kant and one of the Buddha.[23] East and West seem to have found a point of contact in Schopenhauer's thinking, and his original synthesis of ideas from these two traditions produced a philosophy that he himself described as a kind of "pessimism." Why pessimism? To understand this, we need to understand how Schopenhauer applied the basic insights of Plato, Kant, and the Hindus to draw a rather gloomy assessment of the world and our place in it. The picture that he will paint for us is very different from the picture painted by the Hegelian philosophers. Whereas despair and alienation are hardships that thinkers like Hegel, Marx, Feuerbach, and Stirner believe may be overcome, according to Schopenhauer as long as we live we will never escape from suffering. Indeed, for Schopenhauer, as for Kierkegaard, "... all life is suffering."[24]

Piercing the Veil of the Thing-in-Itself

Schopenhauer draws a correlation between the Hindu notion of *Maya* and Kant's notion of the *a priori* intuitions and the categories of the understanding. According to the Hindus, if we could pull back the veil that hangs between our minds and the world, then we would be able to see reality in all of its rawness. Schopenhauer asks us to consider the following: is there any way of drawing aside the *a priori* intuitions and categories of the understanding as the Hindus suggest be done with the veil of Maya? Kant claimed that this could not be done because these are the very structures by which we organize and interpret our experience of the world. You can't step outside of your own mind to see the world independent of your mind. However, Schopenhauer suggests that we may at least be able to pull aside a number of the "veils" screening our vision to get a clearer picture of reality, if not a completely unobscured one. Recall that Kant had claimed that among the *a priori* intuitions acting as the primary lenses through which we view the world are time and space. In addition to time and space, the categories of the understanding contribute organizational structures like cause and effect to our picture of the world. According to Schopenhauer, when we look to the world outside of us our minds automatically constitute experience by means of precisely three principles—time, space, and causation— thus producing what he calls "representations." "What is the world of perception besides being my representation?"[25] The "outer," perceptible world appears to stretch out before us in space, containing bodies that over the course of time interact with one another causally. But we must be careful to realize, as Kant has already pointed out, that all of this is a product of the mind's powers of interpretation and not an indication of the real nature of the world as it exists initself. It is the mind that interprets the world "out there" in terms of time, space, and cause and effect. But suppose we could reduce the number of lenses that stand between us and the thing-in-itself? Could we then get a clearer representation of reality? And if so, how could we possibly go about this task?

The lenses through which we experience the "outer" world are three. But, claims Schopenhauer, there are far fewer lenses through which we experience the "inner" world of our own consciousness. Kant had claimed that the intuition of time was the source of inner representation, and Schopenhauer interprets this to mean that there is only one "veil" standing between the mind and ultimate reality as it is manifested within us. Because we ourselves are a part of Being, it should be possible for us to reflect inward and come very close to an immediate encounter with the core of the thing-in-itself:

> … *we ourselves are the thing-in-itself.* Consequently, a way *from within* stands open to us to that real inner nature of things to which we cannot penetrate *from without.* It is, so to speak, a subterranean passage, a secret alliance, which, as if by treachery, places us all at once in the fortress that could not be taken by attack from without.[26]

At times, Schopenhauer writes as if inner reflection brings one into direct contact with the thing-in-itself, but at other times he is more hesitant and restrained in his assertion to this effect. Kant had already pointed to the impossibility of knowing the thing-in-itself directly, and Schopenhauer largely concurs with this Kantian insight.[27] Schopenhauer's main point, however, is that because the inner world of consciousness relies only on the intuition of time for its representations, it is here that we come the closest to seeing ultimate reality for what it is. It is here within ourselves that "the thing-in-itself is manifested under the lightest of all veils, and still remains phenomenon only in so far as my intellect, the only thing capable of knowledge, still always remains distinguished from me as the one who wills, and does not cast off the knowledge-form of *time*, even with inner perception."[28] As we reflect on our inner state of conscious existence, we are engaged in a process of thinking, and thus we are still separating ourselves as thinking subjects from the object of our thought. Therefore, we are not in *direct* contact with the thing we want to know. Nonetheless, inner consciousness involves only the time sequence of thinking one thought after another, and thus it is able to dispense with the interpretive crutches of spatial and causal representation. We thereby bring ourselves two steps closer to the thing we really want to make contact with the deeper we descend "inward" and the farther we leave the "outer" world behind.[29]

The Will

So what is it that we find buried deep within ourselves once we are able to pull aside the multiple obstructions between our minds and ultimate reality? Schopenhauer tells us that what we find seething and boiling beneath the surface of our thinking, and what we can discern in a relatively clear manner through the single veil of inner time consciousness, is the will. The will is a substance that is beyond time, space, and causation. It defies the principles of reason but energizes and gives life to all forms of thought, feeling, and physical existence. It is a blind force of dynamism that expresses itself in an infinite number of ways, yet is itself unitary, unbroken, and singular. The will is what the Hindus call *Brahman* and what Kant calls the thing-in-itself. It is the primal and eternal source of all that exists. As Schopenhauer writes, "Just as a magic lantern shows many different pictures, but it is only one and the same flame that makes them all visible, so in all the many different phenomena which together fill the world or supplant one another as successive events, it is only the one will that appears, and everything is its visibility, its objectivity; it remains unmoved in the midst of this change."[30]

In Hinduism, it is the image of the ocean that is used to characterize the comprehensive unity, and yet the apparent diversity, of all things that have existence in the universe. The ocean is a deep, expansive body whose waters touch and interpenetrate everything that exists within it. On its surface waves form, and although each individual wave has a shape and contour of its own, these waves are not, in their essence, separate from the ocean itself. The appearance of diversity on the ocean's surface is a mask for the underlying oneness of the ocean as a whole. Waves come into existence, they travel across the surface for a short period of time, and then they dissolve back into the ocean's depths once again. This surface-level drama, though it is in one sense real, is in another sense a distraction that pulls our attention away from the more enduring and fundamental reality that lies below the surface. According to the Hindus, this is what reality itself is like, and Schopenhauer agrees. Beneath the superficial appearances of things, there is a unity that binds all apparent phenomena in the world together into one unbroken and enduring well of Being, just as the water of the ocean binds the waves together. According to Schopenhauer, the will is to all existence what the deep waters are to the ocean's waves.

TABLE 11.1   Our Separation from Reality

	Objective reality is:	What separates us from objective reality is:
Hinduism	Brahman	The Veil of Maya
Plato	The Good	The Senses
Kant	The Thing-in-Itself	The *a priori* Intuitions and the Categories of Understanding
Schopenhauer	The Will	Time, Space, and Causality

But why the will? For what reason does Schopenhauer insist that the substance tying everything together is will? The answer to this question is to be found in Schopenhauer's reflection on his inner state of consciousness and the intimate relationship it shares with his own body. Schopenhauer observes that as individual human beings, we occupy bodies. Obviously, the way that we experience our own bodies is different from the way we experience other sorts of bodies outside of us. Outer bodies are known only through the senses. We see, taste, touch, hear, and smell them, collecting information about them from a distance. Our own body, however, is known intuitively, from the inside as well as being observable to us from the outside. This leads Schopenhauer to conclude that the human body is a phenomenon that has two "sides" and that it presents itself to us in two different ways. On the "outside," there is a physical manifestation. When I look at the movement of my own toes, I experience them in the same manner that I would any other exterior object that is in motion. Their wiggling movements appear as an objective phenomenon that unfolds in front of my visual field. From the "inside," however, I experience this same movement in an entirely different manner. From the perspective of my inner subjectivity, I immediately and intuitively have the sense of being in charge of my toes. I can "will" them to move, and even when such actions are not consciously executed, I still have the sense that it is the inner "me" that does the moving. This experience of an inner "stirring"[31] that on the outside manifests itself empirically as bodily movement is what Schopenhauer calls the will. The body is just the will "objectified" and observed from the outside, while the mind is just the will as it is subjectively experienced from the inside.[32]

Contrary to Descartes, who had posited a causal connection between the separate substances of mind and body, Schopenhauer asserts that there is no distinction to be made between an act of will and movements of the body. In fact, willing and moving are one and the same thing. Willing does not cause the body to move; willing *is* the movement of the body. "Every true act of his will is also at once and inevitably a movement of his body."[33] Willing, then, is just movement. From our inner perspective, we experience the will as an inner movement or stirring that never ceases. Try to sit and think about nothing and you will quickly find that your inner state of consciousness refuses to cooperate. It constantly wants to do something, to think something, or to feel something. This is an indication of the unsettled nature of the will itself, which is never at rest but always pushing outward. In its most primal and unadulterated manifestation, the will is a blind striving, an "urge" or an "impulse" of force. It doesn't care how it manifests itself, it simply needs to expand outward. It is a pulsating force that is the inner you, always the same yet always in motion and always seeking to express itself in some manner or fashion. Like electricity, the will naturally conducts. As it wells up and discharges itself, the will produces representations, which like waves on the surface of the ocean are merely eruptions of an unending turbulence that carries on deep below. In the case of human beings, the eruptions of the will may manifest themselves as thoughts, feelings, or the body itself. Thus, the will is neither mind nor matter but something out of which both mind and matter become manifest as representations.

Schopenhauer explains the existence of the world as the manifestation of the primal will in various "grades." In this, he harkens back to Plato who claimed that all of existence is arranged in a hierarchy extending from the most real "Forms" down to the least real appearances. For Schopenhauer, the "grades" of existence start with the lowest manifestations of gravitation and impenetrability and then move up the scale to the highest manifestation, which is human life. At the lowest level, it is the conflict between the forces of attraction and repulsion that give evidence of the will's activity. "This constant pressure and resistance can be regarded as the objectivity of the will at the very lowest grade."[34] Out of the struggle of these forces, the will "objectifies" itself, creating manifestations that become more and more complicated and sophisticated by degrees. Thus, inorganic nature emerges at the next level after gravity, followed by plants, then animals, and finally humans.[35] "They form a pyramid, of which the highest point is man."[36] It is with humans that we find the development of the reasoning faculty, and it is this faculty that is both a testament to our elevated nature as well as a curse that transforms our specific form of life from one of unthinking instinct to one of "deliberation," "irresolution," and "uncertainty."

Anxiety, Suffering, and Distress

Will is movement, and in humans this movement finds its highest manifestation in the reasoning faculty. Reason, according to Schopenhauer, is what separates humans from animals, although human life, it needs to be emphasized, is continuous with animal life. There is no sharp break between humans and nonhumans, only an increasingly greater level of "objectification" of the primal will. This increasing complexity manifests itself in the capacity for abstract thinking. Animals are motivated, Schopenhauer claims, purely by direct perceptual representations. An animal responds instinctually to the things that it sees, feels, hears, tastes, and smells. It fears or desires only those things in its immediate environment and has no capacity to worry about the future or regret things that have occurred in the past. While human beings are also often motivated by the things they immediately perceive, reason additionally gives us the capacity to think abstractly and so to project beyond the immediate moment and to ponder both the past and the future. In this way, humans are able to plan, learn, develop, and adapt. We experience things, retaining memories of the consequences of actions, and thus become able to predict and anticipate the course of the world's unfolding process. Because of this, humans, unlike animals, can choose to forsake momentary, fleeting pleasures in anticipation of something desired but not yet manifest. We often subject ourselves to transient pains to acquire some sort of reward that is yet to be. In fact, according to Schopenhauer,

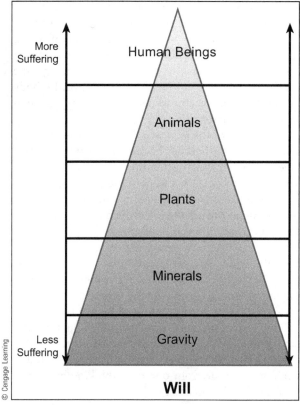

More
Suffering

Human Beings

Animals

Plants

Minerals

Less
Suffering

Gravity

Will

FIGURE 11.1 Grades of the Will

most of human life is lived abstractly and our greatest joys, as well as our greatest pains, actually derive from thinking rather than from sensation. On the one hand, we are able to hope for a better future and savor cherished memories from the past. On the other hand, we endlessly subject ourselves to anxiety, worry, and fear over the nonconcrete past and future, creating mental anguish and pain. These mental pains are of a sort that in comparison "all the sufferings of the animal kingdom are very small."[37] Animals suffer in the moment and then move on. Humans, in contrast, endlessly turn things over in their minds and fill themselves with ongoing hypothetical worries. So it is that the capacity for reason is both a blessing and a curse. While it gives us the tool with which we may accomplish great things, it also introduces the condition of deep suffering into human life (see Figure 11.1).

When reading Schopenhauer's writing, it is the issue of human suffering that strikes one as the main focus of his concern. This preoccupation places him alongside other post-Kantian thinkers, but unlike Hegel, Feuerbach, Stirner, and Marx, Schopenhauer leaves us with a sense that ultimately there is not much that we can do to bring about the final alleviation of human pain and unhappiness. According to Schopenhauer, all human beings are driven by a will that constantly desires to do more and more. It is the will that drives us to engage in the activities of life, pushing us forward toward the completion of our goals. However, when we actually finish a project that we have begun, the will becomes bored and desires to engage in renewed activity. The will never rests content with the fruits of its labors, and so our entire lives are spent either feeling bored with our completed tasks or feeling anxious about the work to be done. There is no escape from life's pain, according to Schopenhauer. Between life and death lie boredom and anxiety. Beyond death lies nothing. All life, then, is ceaseless striving, punctuated by boredom, as the primal will constantly finds ways to express itself through us until the point at which we die. As long as we live we suffer, and to stop suffering is necessarily to stop living. "Thus that there is no ultimate aim of striving means that there is no measure or end of suffering."[38]

The process of living life is inextricably connected to suffering. Schopenhauer calls the dynamism of the will that pushes us to continue striving, struggling, and suffering "will-to-live." It is this will-to-live that is the culprit in our unhappiness, and so Schopenhauer counsels us to turn against it if we want to find peace. This might initially lead us to think that Schopenhauer, like some of the Hellenistic philosophers, advocated suicide. If life is suffering, then it would seem that willing our own physical death would offer a possible escape from suffering. However, Schopenhauer does not agree with this line of thinking. In suicide, he claims, we do not find the denial of the will-to-life but rather "the will's strong affirmation"[39] and thus the very antithesis of an escape from suffering. Schopenhauer characterizes the suicide as a person who is frustrated with the world and who vainly wishes reality to be different from what it actually is. In response to this disappointment with the nature of reality, the suicide turns the "inner" will against his or her own individual body, which is itself merely the "outer" manifestation of that same will, and by doing so the suicide hopes to eradicate the will altogether. This, however, is a vain sort of project. It is, in Schopenhauer's words, "a quite futile and foolish act, for the thing-in-itself remains unaffected by it, just as the rainbow remains unmoved, however rapidly the drops may change which sustain it for the moment."[40] In other words, because everything that exists is a manifestation of the primal will, a person who willfully kills himself or herself is simply continuing the process of willful action that is the source of suffering in the first place! By killing the body, one eliminates an "outer" manifestation of the will while reaffirming ever more strongly the "inner" will. When the body dies the primal will remains, once again to become manifest and to suffer in some other form. When the will turns against its bodily manifestations, it is merely engaging in another project of striving, which is, as we have already seen, the source of suffering itself. The vanity of suicide lies in the fact that in the grand scheme of things, it changes nothing. Just as a rainbow continues to stretch across the sky regardless of the particular drops of water suspended in it, so too does the will continue to pulsate throughout the universe regardless of how many people choose to kill themselves.

All of this might make our existence seem hopeless, awful, and pointless. Even death holds no hope for the cessation of suffering, and if this is so, what are we supposed to do? Should we just continue to grind away and engage in our meaningless and painful projects for all eternity, periodically being recycled by the cosmos to suffer even more? In one sense, according to Schopenhauer, there is nothing else that we can do. As a part of Being itself, we are destined to take part in the eternal cosmic unfolding whether we like it or not. In another sense, however, we do have the option of resigning ourselves to this situation and directing our attention toward understanding the world rather than trying to alter it. While the application of our understanding still constitutes a form of willing, in the course of this particular form of willing we may nevertheless achieve a condition of acquiescence that is the closest thing possible to the denial of willing altogether. It is as if in willing the will to understand the will, the will ceases willing itself to be anything other than will! At the very end of *The World as Will and Representation,* Schopenhauer even seems to suggest that a person who successfully attains this state of comprehension is the closest thing to a holy man that can be imagined. As we increasingly understand our place in the cosmos, we come to a heightened awareness of the interconnectedness of everything that exists. In its interconnectedness, the universe turns out not to be a number of different things but one ever-flowing process of unfolding. The universe is, in this way, no-thing at all. The entirety of particular phenomena that appear to us are best understood as fleeting manifestations of a primal, unitary oneness; a veritable nothing:

> Before us there is certainly left nothing. But that which struggles against
> this flowing away into nothing, namely our nature, is indeed just the
> will-to-live which we ourselves are, just as it is our world. That we
> abhor nothingness so much is simply another way of saying that we will
> life so much, and that we are nothing but this will and know nothing
> but it alone. But we now turn our glance from our own needy and
> perplexed nature to those who have overcome the world, in whom the
> will, having reached complete self-knowledge, has found itself again in
> everything, and then freely denied itself, and who merely wait to see the
> last trace of the will vanish with the body that is animated by that trace.
> Then, instead of the restless pressure and effort; instead of the constant
> transition from desire to apprehension and from joy to sorrow; instead
> of the never satisfied and never-dying hope that constitutes the life-
> dream of the man who wills, we see that peace that is higher than all
> reason, that ocean-like calmness of spirit, that deep tranquility, that
> unshakable confidence and serenity, whose mere reflection in the
> countenance, as depicted by Raphael and Correggio, is a complete and
> certain gospel. Only knowledge remains; the will has vanished.[41]

Schopenhauer's philosophy culminates ironically. In understanding the restless nature of the will, we are counseled to accept its spasmodic eruptions as part of the cosmic order and thus resign ourselves to the nature of Being itself. In so doing, we gain mental distance from the world's tumultuousness at the very same moment that we ourselves participate in that tumult.[42] The end of human suffering comes with the end of the will-to-live, which itself comes when we cease willing the universe to be any different from the way that it is. But the universe is, by Schopenhauer's own account, pure will in the first place and so, in the end, we are left with a strange conclusion that, as has often been noted, may appear self-negating. To find peace is to stop asserting the will, and to stop asserting the will is to accept the universe for what it is. Because the universe is pure will, if we stop asserting the will we must give ourselves over to the will, which by its very nature must assert itself! It seems like a rather hopeless situation.

It is my view, however, that this apparent inconsistency in Schopenhauer's philosophy is not so much an outright contradiction as it is an attempt to express a truth about an inherent incongruity embedded within the core of human life. In life we are constantly pulled back and forth between the desire for peace and the desire for activity. Prolonged peace leads to boredom, and prolonged activity leads to anxiety.

In either case, suffering is always with us. What strikes me as particularly interesting about Schopenhauer's take on this situation is his recognition that the very desire to bring about the end of human suffering is itself a symptom of our dissatisfaction with the world as it is and is thus just another example of the eternal human drama of suffering. As long as we hope, dream, and wish for things to be different than they are in the present, we will be unsatisfied with our world as it is in the here-and-now. This was an insight that Schopenhauer shared with Feuerbach and Stirner. Unlike them, however, Schopenhauer recognizes that as long as we live, there is no way for us to do away with the dynamic and unsettled desires of the will. The best that we can do is to make peace with our own unquiet depths and accept the fact that we are the sorts of creatures who are perpetually driven to be dissatisfied.

Regardless, dissatisfaction with the present state of things is the price we pay for ongoing aspiration and creativity. It is, in fact, the price we pay for being human. Pure bliss would entail the cessation of all striving. To be completely happy would announce the end of progress and change. What would we do if the world was perfect in the way that utopian philosophers claim is possible? According to Schopenhauer's account, we would become endlessly bored, and so a perfect world, ironically, would not be perfect at all.[43] If this is so, then perhaps reconciling ourselves to distressing incompleteness is the real key to salvation. Perhaps we can be happy in our unhappiness precisely because it is unhappiness that spurs us on to do great things, and in doing great things we create testaments to the type of creature that we are. To move forward and to will ourselves to constantly do something new; this may be the most that we can hope for. Is this pessimism? It might be, but it is also the idea that motivated someone like Schopenhauer to set about writing one of the most stunning philosophical masterpieces in the history of the West. Perhaps, then, there is something to be said for pessimism!

Schopenhauer was an important influence on many of the philosophers, artists, and writers who came after him, even though today he seems to be largely ignored by mainstream academics. His philosophy strikes many as too gloomy, too inconsistent, and too "nineteenth century" to warrant serious attention. This is a shame, because what we find in Schopenhauer is a passionate, powerful, and eloquent articulation of a point that is central to all true philosophical thinking. With Schopenhauer, the ongoing and endless nature of human striving is given voice, and it is given a voice that does justice both to the pain and the joy that is involved in philosophical thinking. A philosophical life is not one that is purely happy or purely tortured but rather one that is constantly open to the forward movement of thought regardless of the pains and pleasures that accompany such activity. The criticism that Schopenhauer is too gloomy is probably a result of his reemphasis on the inevitability of mental suffering, and the fact that many people would like to glibly dismiss suffering as unnecessary to life. As Bertrand Russell points out, in this way Schopenhauer's pessimism acts as an "antidote" to shallow optimism and is therefore very "useful."[44] In any case, the charge that Schopenhauer is too negative is not really so much a serious or deep criticism of his philosophical insights as it is an aesthetic reaction against the mood that is conveyed through his writing. This mood of melancholy, sadness, and despair was one that even some of those who embraced Schopenhauer's worldview would seek to overcome and replace with a more "positive" outlook.

© Juneko J. Robinson

FRIEDRICH NIETZSCHE AND POSITIVE NIHILISM

In the philosophy of Friedrich Nietzsche (1844–1900) we find a brilliant attempt to imbue Schopenhauer's work with an infusion of optimism and thus to provide an "antidote" to Schopenhauer himself. In what remains of this chapter, I will briefly trace out the main points of Nietzsche's brand of positive nihilism and contrast his ideas with those of John Stuart Mill, a Utilitarian philosopher whose thoughts provide a stark counterpoint to those of Nietzsche and the other nihilists we have encountered in this chapter. In so doing we will highlight a key point of disagreement that, still today, divides people on the issue of life's meaning: is it more important to be happy or to do great things?

The legacy of Friedrich Nietzsche is one that is shrouded in much controversy and misunderstanding. Today there are still those who mistakenly associate his thinking with the atrocities of the Nazis, although Nietzsche would assuredly have been horrified by those developments.[45] As Walter Kaufmann points out, much of the blame for the misunderstanding of Nietzsche's philosophy can be laid at the feet of his sister, Elizabeth, who took control of her brother's literary estate upon his collapse into mental illness.[46] Elizabeth was married to an anti-Semite by the name of Bernhard Förster, and she was involved with him in establishing an Aryan commune in Paraguay. After her husband's death, and the consequent revolt of the Paraguayan settlers, Elizabeth returned to Germany and embarked on a mission to mold her now ailing and insane brother into the image of a proto-Nazi philosopher-saint. She gained legal control of his writings and set about editing his papers, withholding those writings that expressed ideas conflicting with her own political ambitions. Among the results of her efforts was the founding of the Nietzsche Archives, which became a center of pro-Nazi intellectual activity, as well as the publication of a collection of Nietzsche's notes under the title *The Will to Power*, which presented a harsh and misleading image of Nietzsche's ideas.

Nietzsche's true philosophy has since been reconstructed as his original writings have become available in their intended forms. What one finds upon surveying the broad scope of his books and papers is the articulation of a worldview that places the individual at the center of importance in the world and that admonishes us all to enthusiastically take charge of our lives. For Nietzsche, the uncertainty, the suffering, and the struggle that we encounter in life is no occasion for despair or resignation but rather for heroic self-assertion and adventure. Unlike many of the Left Hegelian thinkers, Nietzsche shuns the notion of making life easier and more comfortable. On the contrary, he teaches us that it is through suffering and struggle that we come to truly understand our potential. As he famously wrote in *Twilight of the Idols*, "What does not destroy me, makes me stronger."[47] Like his mentor Schopenhauer, Nietzsche believes that life inevitably involves suffering. However, unlike Schopenhauer, Nietzsche embraces the hardships of life instead of shrinking away from them. Whereas the feeling one comes away with from Schopenhauer's books is one of melancholy and sadness, Nietzsche's writings leave us feeling exuberant and powerful.

Nietzsche was very influenced by Schopenhauer's philosophy, but he was also troubled by what he considered to be its extreme negativity. In *Beyond Good and Evil* he writes:

> Whoever has endeavored with some enigmatic longing, as I have, to think pessimism through to its depths and to liberate it from the half-Christian, half-German narrowness and simplicity in which it has finally presented itself to our century, namely, in the form of Schopenhauer's philosophy; whoever has really, with an Asiatic and supra-Asiatic eye, looked into, down into the most world-denying of all possible ways of thinking—beyond good and evil and no longer, like the Buddha and Schopenhauer, under the spell and delusion of morality—may just thereby, without really meaning to do so, have opened his eyes to the opposite ideal: the ideal of the most high-spirited, alive, and world-affirming human being....[48]

Nietzsche tells us that he has thought through Schopenhauer's ideas, come to terms with his teacher's vision of the universe, and yet has drawn a conclusion that is opposite to the one drawn by Schopenhauer himself. Although the world lacks final purpose and meaning, although we are destined to struggle and to strive eternally, Nietzsche wants us to affirm this process and not recoil from it in the way that Schopenhauer counseled. Instead, Nietzsche wants us to affirm, rather than deny, the will-to-live, and to throw ourselves into living and experiencing life to its fullest.

The Will to Power

According to Nietzsche, the human organism is a receptacle for the "will to power." This will to power is nearly equivalent to what Schopenhauer called simply the "will." It is a force that energizes humans and gives them the motivation to pursue worldly tasks. The will to power is an impulse toward self-overcoming. It constantly attempts to outdo itself, go further, and expand outward, never resting satisfied and always striving for release. In calling this primal force "will to power," Nietzsche is emphasizing that aspect of the will that is involved in the surmounting of obstacles and the expansion into previously unconquered territories. According to Nietzsche, the will is best characterized as a powerful impulse that is known by the effects it produces in the world. We never see the will, but we see what the will is capable of producing, just as we never see electricity but only its effects. We can thus infer that those individuals who consistently demonstrate the ability to overcome obstacles, conquer hardship, and continue to pursue their goals in the face of resistance are individuals driven by an especially strong and powerful will. On the other hand, those people who lack motivation, who shun challenges and are unable to endure hardship, demonstrate through their actions that they have very weak wills. Both the strong and the weak are driven by the will to power, according to Nietzsche, but the strong have a more vital and dynamic store of this primal force. Schopenhauer's influence on Nietzsche is clearly apparent here, as it was Schopenhauer who initially collapsed the distinction between willing and movement, claiming that the two were equivalent. In this same regard, Nietzsche often claims that there is no such thing as latent potential in human beings, only real actions. A person who claims that he or she has an unexpressed potential for greatness is simply offering evidence for the relative weakness of his or her will. Strong-willed human beings always produce powerful effects in the world because worldly effects are the immediate and tangible product of the overflowing power of the will itself. Thus, the will is something we know immediately by the types of consequences it yields. The will is just the power to produce effects. For this reason, Heidegger tells us, "... will is intrinsically power. And power is willing that is constant in itself. Will is power; power is will.... The expression 'to power' therefore never means some sort of appendage to will. Rather it comprises an elucidation of the essence of will itself."[49]

As human beings navigate within the world, they express their will to power, and this is done both physically and intellectually. "The total character of the world ... is in all eternity chaos,"[50] Nietzsche writes, and so humans must exert their will to power to refashion reality and create order out of chaos. The world as it is "in-itself," independent of the human mind, is without pattern or structure, and only by bending the world to suit our will may we find a purpose and meaning in life. Some people carry out this task by using brute force to alter the environment. Military leaders, for instance, physically conquer territories and force others into submission. Empires have been created and maintained in this way. But there is another more subtle and long-lasting way that the will to power may be expressed, and this is through the production of worldviews and artworks that capture the imaginations of people. According to Nietzsche, the very act of creative interpretation is, in fact, an act of conquering reality, but it is a way of conquering the chaos of the world that is the highest testament to the powerful capacities of the human organism. Unlike physical force, systems of thought and artistry demonstrate their power by changing the way people think. Physical force requires constant application from the outside if it is to remain effective. For this reason, its effects are not as long-lasting and comprehensive as are the effects of ideas. Ideas, as expressed through philosophies, religions, and artworks, have the power to change people from the inside, making them see the world differently by changing their inner perspective on reality. The warrior who subjugates a population with physical force may establish a great kingdom in the short run, but a person who changes the way that people think transfigures the world in a much grander and long-lasting fashion in the long run.

Contrary to Schopenhauer, Nietzsche admonishes us to become ever more insistent in our efforts toward aggressively and forcefully asserting the will to conquer the world around us. While Schopenhauer did have a great deal of respect for the process of artistic creation, it is Nietzsche who insists that the meaning of life is truly expressed in the activities of the artist. Kant laid the foundation for this way of thinking by suggesting that our minds are always filtering and interpreting reality from a subjective perspective, and that for this reason the world as we understand it is a creation produced out of our own process of understanding. Nietzsche takes this viewpoint to the extreme, emphasizing the manifold ways in which human beings can imagine and create new and previously unthought of interpretations of reality. All interpretation, according to Nietzsche, is a kind of artistic process. Without this process, we would be overwhelmed by the chaos and power of the universe. Like artists, we all must take the raw materials of the world and selectively filter through them, organizing and fashioning them into a coherent unity. Just as an artist utilizes paints and canvas to create a picture, so must all human beings utilize their interpretive faculties to put their perceptions of the universe into some sort of unique, comprehensible, and creative order. The most powerful and noble individuals, claims Nietzsche, are those able to enthusiastically affirm their vision of reality and embrace it the way that an artist embraces his or her own artwork.

The Superman and the Death of God

Whereas Schopenhauer thought that life was predominantly miserable, Nietzsche sought a way to affirm and cherish the world of struggle. If one could love one's fate, claims Nietzsche, then we might not only endure life but in fact express joy concerning our never-ending struggles. We might, in fact, actively wish for these struggles to recur eternally and to never end. This would be the ultimate sign of strength, thought Nietzsche. A person capable of living in the world in this manner would be a "superman" (in German *Übermensch*), not in the sense of possessing supernatural powers but in the sense of being capable of facing reality with superhuman resolve and strength. The superman would be the ultimate artist of life, always willing to take responsibility for his or her own role in rendering a new and unique vision of the world.

With the *Übermensch*, Nietzsche established a model of the type of human being who could face the coming of an age in which the comfortable illusions of religion were beginning to fall away. Nietzsche made the observation that although people in modern times still talk about God and Heaven, their words, in fact, sound empty and insincere. It is more out of habit than true belief that most people use the words "God" and "Heaven" these days, he claimed. We mouth the words but then go on to live our lives in a manner at odds with the real meaning of those words. The insights of science and philosophy in the Modern era have ushered in a new way of thinking about reality that is slowly but surely overturning our faith in such absolutes. As we progress farther along the path of modernity, Nietzsche claimed that we move farther down the road of nihilism and the realization that "God is dead."[51] When Nietzsche wrote that God is dead, he of course didn't mean that a being called "God" had ever really existed and had literally died. What he seems to mean, rather, is that Western culture has lost its faith in the otherworldly. The general trend of Western thought since the end of the Medieval era and the beginning of Modern times has been to focus more and more attention on the sort of knowledge and control that we can have over this world and to become less interested in otherworldly truths. In a sense, the transition from Medieval to Modern times might be seen as a repetition of the transition between the times of the Mythopoets and the Presocratics. Both transitions are characterized by a declining interest in the supernatural and a development of interest in naturalistic explanations. Human power, rather than the power of God, becomes the main area of concern. In the Modern world, we are specifically being pulled away from the old beliefs of the Judeo-Christian tradition and toward the newly emerging beliefs of the empirical sciences. Transitions like this are usually painful insofar as they involve the undermining of old beliefs and the reevaluation of our most deeply held values.

But the new sciences, claims Nietzsche, are actually no more "true" than the religion that they are currently overturning. All systems of human thought, he claimed, are human creations. They are attempts by the human mind to impose structure and order on the chaos that is reality. Ultimately, there is no real Truth that exists in the world apart from us. There are only ongoing attempts to make sense of ourselves and our place in the universe. "We cannot look around our own corner.... Rather has the world become 'infinite' for us all over again, inasmuch as we cannot reject the possibility that *it may include infinite interpretations*."[52] The scientific quest for final answers about the genuine constitution of reality

---

B o x 11.1 Nietzsche's Relationship to Darwinism and Freudianism

Even though many of Nietzsche's ideas on human life sound similar to the views promulgated by Darwin's theory of evolution, Nietzsche himself rejected Darwinism.

Darwin is well known for his claim that the engine driving the evolution of the species is "natural selection" and the "survival of the fittest." In this view, the present state of human organisms can be explained by the usefulness of various biological traits. Nietzsche rejects this, stating in a section of *The Will to Power* titled "Against Darwinism" that "The utility of an organ does not explain its origin; on the contrary! For most of the time during which a property is forming it does not preserve the individual and is of no use to him, least of all in the struggle with external circumstances and enemies" (aphorism 647). Nietzsche's point here is that human beings possess and retain many traits that are actually detrimental to their personal survival. For instance, humans smoke, eat unhealthy food, and have curiosity that leads them to risk their own lives climbing mountains, racing cars, and fighting wars!

Sigmund Freud, on the other hand, writes in his *Autobiographical Study* that the findings of psychoanalysis correspond significantly with the philosophies of both Schopenhauer and Nietzsche. Of Nietzsche, Freud writes that his "guesses and intuitions often agree in the most astonishing ways with the laborious findings of psychoanalysis" (p. 67). In particular, Freud was astounded at Nietzsche's awareness of the existence of the human unconscious and of the role played by primal urges and drives in human behavior, particularly sex.

The psychoanalyst Irvin Yalom has written two novels that draw strong connections between the ideas of Freud, Schopenhauer, and Nietzsche: *The Schopenhauer Cure* (2006) and *When Nietzsche Wept* (1993). *When Nietzsche Wept* was made into a movie starring Armand Assante in 2007.

and the beginning of the universe is really just a remnant of the old religious way of thinking that has become a habit for modern human beings. Modern scientists may not realize it, but according to Nietzsche their search for absolute and final answers about true reality is motivated by the same desire that motivated the theologians of the Medieval times. They want to know the first cause, the prime mover, and the first principle of the universe. Their quest, consequently, is no less illusory than the religious quest.

If modern scientists are correct, then there will be a point at which all of the world's mysteries will become unlocked and there will be nothing more to learn. However, this is just a pipe dream and an illusion, like the Judeo-Christian notion of Heaven, according to Nietzsche. The struggle for absolute wisdom will never end, and at some point, claims Nietzsche, we must collectively come to this realization. When we do, we will understand that human life and history have no objective point or purpose toward which they are moving. Everything we do is just the expression of the will to power in differing manifestations. Human beings are simply creatures who, as they navigate through their lives, try to understand and interpret the world around them. Over time, different interpretations emerge, and at various points in time some of these interpretations become more influential and popular than others. But ultimately, no interpretation has final authority as the ultimate and supreme Truth about reality. Will humans ever be able to face this insight? Only by becoming supermen, thought Nietzsche. "Behold, I teach you the [super]man. The [super]man is the meaning of the earth! I beseech you, my brothers, *remain faithful to the earth*, and do not believe those who speak to you of otherworldly hopes!"[53] It is only when we become comfortable with the thought that there is no final resting place in our intellectual struggles, and that there is no world other than the one we create for ourselves, that we will be able to love the earth for what it is. There is no end to our philosophical battles. Instead we can only continue to face the chaos of the universe, try to make sense of it, and produce original and new interpretations of reality endlessly. Supermen would have the strength to endure and take joy in this sort of never-ending struggle.

Nietzsche's philosophy proclaims the virtue of individual strength in this respect. The most noble and virtuous individuals are those who find within themselves the energy and the stamina to face the potentially exhausting task of unending creative interpretation. Nietzsche's writing contains many disdainful attacks against those, like Christians and utopians, who claim to have "discovered" the absolute Truth of the universe. Such individuals, he believes, are weak insofar as they are unable to entertain new ways of thinking or to endure the ceaseless struggle of ongoing interpretation. Because they are constitutionally weak, they desire the peace and comfort that come from having faith in the end of history (like Hegel) or the last judgment. Those who are strong, on the other hand, are those who can withstand the discomfort and the uncertainty of a world devoid of such absolute truths. A superman can laugh and be joyful in the face of the world's chaos. Life, for such an individual, is not a matter of pursuing some sort of final goal but of enjoying the process of living. It is a matter of rejoicing in one's strength, facing the pains and struggles of this world, and affirming the things in this earthly realm as good.

Nietzsche tells us that there are very few people who are strong enough to face the world as supermen. Those who are able to do so often go against the popular beliefs of their time and encounter persecution as a result. These individuals face the wrath of the masses who don't want their faith in conventional forms of belief shaken. Despite his many criticisms concerning the followers of Socrates, Jesus, and the Buddha, Nietzsche seems to have a deep sense of admiration for these individuals themselves. Obviously he doesn't consider the content of their teachings to be truthful, but he recognizes the power and strength of their original interpretations of the world. In this regard, these individuals embody a way of life that Nietzsche seems to believe is quite noble. They forsake a comfortable life among the "herd" of human beings in favor of a dangerous and difficult life of adventure and individual creation. They turn their backs on the pleasures and comfort offered by conventional life and strike out on their own in search of some new way of thinking about the world.

Followers are not the same as the leaders who they follow. Followers create nothing. They simply fall into line with a ready-made way of thinking and find comfort and pleasure in their conformity. Nietzsche claims this to be a sign of weakness. Thus, the followers of Socrates, Jesus, and the Buddha are weak and decadent, he claims. Instead of simply mimicking the beliefs of these great men, one should aspire to be as strong as they were. What this entails is confronting reality with courage and creativity. People should "live dangerously," striking out on their own paths of intellectual adventure regardless of the discomfort and pain that this may entail. It is more important to be strong and creative than it is to be comfortable and safe, claims Nietzsche, and he thus admonishes us to act "… not from love of man but because every great danger challenges our curiosity about the degree of our strength and our courage."[54]

In his advocacy of such a life, Nietzsche's philosophy comes into direct conflict with those popular moral systems that identify happiness as life's highest goal. Hume had claimed that empirical observation proves with a high degree of probability that all cultures hold collective happiness to be the guiding principle of morality. Morals, Hume declares, are just rules that grease the wheels of social interaction. They secure a foundation for the smooth functioning of society and make it possible for large groups of individuals to get along with one another, thus promoting the general welfare and happiness of the collective. Morality is in fact guided by the principle of utility according to Hume, meaning that the standards of right and wrong really, in the final analysis, boil down to those types of guidelines that are useful to society as a whole. Ethics and morality do not derive from God's decrees, but rather are human creations that serve a very down-to-earth purpose. Nietzsche would completely agree with this last point. According to Nietzsche, morality as it is commonly practiced is just a system by which the collective herd of human beings regulates behavior to protect itself from the dangerous nonconformism of the few strong supermen. However, whereas Hume applauds this function of morality, Nietzsche abhors it and sees it as a force of oppression. In his books, most of Nietzsche's venom is directed not toward Hume in this regard but rather toward the British thinker John Stuart Mill (1806–1873) and his followers, whose system of moral philosophy has, during the Modern era, become one of the most influential in all of the Western world. In the remainder of this chapter, I will bring the ideas of Mill and Nietzsche into conversation with one another, first to sharply highlight Nietzsche's own views on morality more vividly, and second to prepare the way for a discussion concerning the undesirable consequences that may result when a culture overemphasizes collective utility and contentment at the expense of individual freedom of thought and action. Philosophy can thrive only when the human mind is free to follow ideas wherever they may lead, and any culture that stifles this impulse strangles philosophy itself. During the development of the twentieth century, a whole variety of political systems emerged that were premised on the idea that the collective is more important than the individual, and as we will see, all of these systems resulted in a great deal of barbarity committed in the name of collective happiness.

BEYOND GOOD AND EVIL: NIETZSCHE CONTRA UTILITARIANISM

The Greatest Happiness Principle

Nietzsche called John Stuart Mill and his followers "boring."[55] He considered them to be weak and pathetic individuals who advocated a decadent and unexciting way of life. This is because Mill's philosophy, known as "Utilitarianism," held that the highest good for human beings was the pursuit of pleasure and happiness. Contrary to what Nietzsche claimed, Mill thought that human beings should try to maximize the amount of comfort and pleasure that they get in this life rather than engaging in dangerous activities that could have potentially painful results. Utilitarianism finds its inspiration in the ancient Hellenistic philosophy of Epicurus. Recall that according to Epicurus, happiness in life is to be found in the pursuit of pleasure and in the minimization of pain. Mill accepts this ancient insight and, like Hume, claims that it underlies all systems of morality and ethics. He claims that if you look for the ultimate principle that underlies all moral discussion, you will find it in what he calls "The Greatest Happiness Principle," otherwise known as "The Principle of

© Juneko J. Robinson

Utility." This principle states: "actions are right in proportion as they tend to promote happiness; wrong as they tend to produce the reverse of happiness. By happiness is intended pleasure and the absence of pain; by unhappiness, pain and the privation of pleasure."[56] Mill believes, then, that the greatest good for humankind is pleasure, which he defines as the absence of pain. This follows, he thinks, because it is only pleasure and the absence of pain that people pursue as ends in themselves. For instance, you don't go to school because it is difficult, frustrating, and challenging but because you believe that the experience will contribute to your ability to make more money, understand the world, or otherwise bring pleasure into your life. According to Mill, the only reason why it is ever right to subject yourself or others to a painful situation is if, in the end, that pain will lead to greater pleasure for a greater number of people.

Nietzsche's complaint against the Utilitarians is that the pursuit of pleasure is really a very undignified goal for life. "You want, if possible ... to abolish suffering. And we? It really seems that we would rather have it higher and worse than ever."[57] Animals pursue pleasure, but humans are capable of so much more. The best examples of humanity are those who forsake personal pleasure and instead endure suffering in the pursuit of creativity and greatness. What if someone like Jesus pursued pleasure instead of sacrificing himself for humankind? Would we think him so noble if he was concerned only with pleasure? Mill's answer to this complaint is, first of all, that the pleasure he is talking about is not necessarily personal pleasure, but pleasure for the greatest number of people. Even Jesus pursued this goal, according to Mill, because he died for the sins of humankind. His suffering was intended to promote the happiness of the entire human race, and so even Jesus was guided by the Greatest Happiness Principle. The people who we consider to be the greatest examples of humanity, in fact, are those who have been guided by the desire for the maximization of happiness, and so the pursuit of pleasure is not antithetical to human greatness.

Furthermore, claims Mill, the sorts of pleasures that he is concerned with are not simply bodily pleasures. The "pleasures of the intellect" are just as important, and are in fact more important, than the pleasures of the body: "... there is no known Epicurean theory of life which does not assign to the pleasures of the intellect, of the feelings and imagination, and of the moral sentiments a much higher value as pleasures than to those of mere sensation."[58] In other words, when calculating the greatest happiness, one must assign greater weight to those pleasures that originate from the "higher" source of intellectual endeavor than to those pleasures that originate from mere bodily sensations. If given the choice between some physical pleasure, like drinking beer, and the intellectual pleasure of reading Nietzsche, Mill would claim that we should always choose the "higher" intellectual pleasure. Many people with "weak" characters do indeed become addicted to the "lower" pleasures, claims Mill, but that is because they are unacquainted with the "higher" pleasures. If they just opened themselves up to the joys of the intellect, they would quickly discover that a greater quality of pleasure is obtained through intellectual pursuits. The special nobility of humans is thus not at all endangered when guided by the pursuit of pleasure. In fact, Utilitarianism, in advocating the pursuit of higher over lower pleasures, is committed to the "general cultivation of nobleness of character."[59]

In this last respect, Mill departs from his teacher, Jeremy Bentham (1748–1832), who held that there is really no difference at all between the various forms of pleasure. According to Bentham, all pleasures are alike. There is no difference between intellectual and bodily pleasures, and the only basis for choosing one pleasure over another rests upon seven criteria: (1) How intense is the pleasure?; (2) How long does the pleasure last?; (3) How certain is the pleasure to occur?; (4) How soon will it occur?; (5) How many other pleasures will it lead to?; (6) How little pain accompanies the pleasure?; and (7) How many other people will benefit from the pleasure? The best course of action, claims Bentham, is the one that takes all of these factors into account and pursues that avenue leading to the maximum amount of pleasure regardless of whether it is intellectual or bodily.

Perhaps Bentham's version of Utilitarianism is less elitist than Mill's. Regardless, what Mill was trying to avoid when he assigned a higher value to the intellectual pleasures was a situation in which he would be advocating the hedonistic pursuit of bodily pleasures at all cost to human dignity. In this sense, Mill was aware of the very point with which Nietzsche was concerned. Imagine a world in which right and wrong is gauged simply by the amount of bodily pleasure produced for the population. This would be a world better suited to a pig than a human being, and as Mill writes, "It is better to be a human being dissatisfied than a pig satisfied: better to be Socrates dissatisfied than a fool satisfied."[60] This, one of the most well-known quotes from Mill's writing, highlights the fact that he was, indeed, quite concerned with the philosophical vitality of humankind. It is the sort of assertion that we would expect to come from the pen of someone like Nietzsche rather than a Utilitarian thinker concerned with the elimination of human pain and suffering. Nonetheless, when Mill wrote these words, he no doubt wanted to remind us that dissatisfaction is not something to be fled from at all costs. Pleasure and collective happiness are desirable, Mill emphasizes, but they are not necessarily the most important things in all the world if they lead us to live lives devoid of continued striving and aspiration.

In the final evaluation, Mill believed that the moral binding force of the Greatest Happiness Principle has its roots in our natural, social feelings for one another. We tend to have sympathy for those we live with, and so we experience a sense of duty toward them. We have a desire to experience unity with our fellow human beings, and this requires that we give equal consideration to their feelings and interests. By working with others, rather than against them, we promote the general happiness and in turn promote our own happiness within society. Nietzsche denied that the most noble human beings were herd animals, but Mill disagreed and claimed that there is nothing nobler than being a cooperative part of the group.

In the United States, our laws and customs are more influenced by Mill than they are by Nietzsche. The whole idea of a democracy, with its emphasis on the equality of individuals and the importance of their prosperity and pleasure, is based on something like the Greatest Happiness Principle. The government is supposed to be responsive to the wants and desires of the people, and in voting, citizens voice their concerns and interests. Such a system has its advantages, but we should recognize that it also has its disadvantages. A Nietzschean critique of democracy would point out some of the same weaknesses that Socrates pointed out in the Athenian democracy thousands of years ago. Sometimes the masses don't know what is best, and sometimes by voting in favor of their own interests they promote mediocrity and small-mindedness rather than face the challenges that are necessary to make themselves great. Usually the herd prefers to remain safe and comfortable, but in doing so it runs the risk of becoming stagnant and lazy, and in the process, of persecuting individuals and minority groups who are the subjects of popular prejudice, fear, and hatred.

For Utilitarians, no less than Left Hegelian utopians, happiness is the purpose of life, and whatever system of organization promotes the overall elimination of suffering is thought by them to be the best form of government. This assertion, however, rests on an assumption about the role that individual human beings play within the collective that Nietzsche would vehemently disagree with. In the utilitarian/utopian way of thinking, individual human beings are regarded as instruments for the furtherance of the "greater good" or the "general welfare." While this may seem a reasonable and positive stance to take toward collective living, it also has the effect of casting individuals as "cogs" within the "machine" of society. When a cog ceases to perform its duty, it is replaced with one that works properly so that the machine may go on functioning smoothly. If this metaphor is applied too directly to social living, the implications become quite frightening, as the history of the twentieth century demonstrates and as we will see in the chapters that follow.

WONDER AND DISTRESS IN KIERKEGAARD, SCHOPENHAUER, NIETZSCHE, AND MILL

As already intimated at the beginning of this chapter, I believe that in the nihilistic doctrines of Kierkegaard, Schopenhauer, and Nietzsche we find the authentic spirit of philosophy powerfully expressed. Such a claim may be open to debate, but it is grounded in the ideas and themes that are taken as foundational in this book. Philosophy, it will be recalled, is a kind of "wondrous distress," which is rooted in an incongruity between the human desire for Truth and the distressing realization of our separation from Truth. Over the course of human thinking, various individuals have sought to resolve this incongruity, usually by appealing to the presumptions of science, religion, or "common sense." During the post-Kantian era, we find a number of thinkers engaging in just this sort of endeavor, moving away from philosophical questioning and openness and instead offering final, dogmatic solutions that purport to diagnose and fix the problems of the world once and for all. By purportedly laying bare the world's deepest truths, many post-Kantians believe themselves to have pierced the "in-itself" that Kant had claimed was beyond our comprehension, and in doing so these thinkers tell us that we may finally overcome the human despair and unhappiness that find their source in our alienation from true reality. The refreshing element that we find in Kierkegaard, Schopenhauer, and Nietzsche is a tendency—more prominent in Nietzsche than in Kierkegaard and Schopenhauer—to steer clear of final, unequivocal answers to the issue of human forlornness and instead to admonish all people to exert their own creative, philosophical powers freely, without restraint and without end.

Kierkegaard and Schopenhauer are less enthusiastic about the open-ended nature of the quest for Truth than is Nietzsche. In the writings of Kierkegaard and Schopenhauer there is a distinctively religious longing for finality. Kierkegaard draws explicitly on Christian faith to retain his hope that beyond this world of pain, struggle, and despair there lies a realm of heavenly bliss. Schopenhauer, on the other hand, draws on Hinduism and characterizes human life as an endless vacillation between boredom and anxiety. This vacillation is not, according to him, something positive, although it is something that we must recognize and learn to acknowledge. Schopenhauer claims that we may be able to aspire toward a quasi-mystical state in which the will-to-live is extinguished in us and thus fall back into something like a Stoic condition of apathy; but it is unclear, taking his system as a whole, how this could ever truly be possible. Given that the entire world is an expression of will, and given that the will is a substance that must strive to express itself, it seems that humans must forever be doomed to endless struggle and trial as long as they continue to exist. Schopenhauer nonetheless finds it difficult to accept this as inevitable and so he flees from this distressing situation, formulating his own unconvincing "solution" to the problem of human suffering. Insofar as Schopenhauer advocates this solution, he seems to move away from philosophical thought and into the realm of mysticism and religion.

On the whole, however, Schopenhauer's system is eminently philosophical in the sense of emphasizing the ongoing and open nature of human thought as motivated by both wonder and distress. According to Schopenhauer, stasis in thought brings discomfort and distress in the form of boredom, and so we must move forward and struggle for something "more" to alleviate this feeling. But in the human realm the will cannot tolerate just any sort of forward movement. In humans the will manifests itself in its "highest grade," rationally, and as such demands Truth itself. This wondrous desire for Truth drives us onward, but, ironically, it also produces the distressing sense of incompleteness and anxiety that is part of any journey that has not yet come to completion. If we emphasize these aspects of Schopenhauer's thought instead of his occasional forays into mysticism, we find the true spirit of philosophy expressed.

Wonder and distress are key themes accentuated throughout the writings of Nietzsche even more aggressively than they are in the work of Schopenhauer. In fact, part of Nietzsche's criticism of Schopenhauer consists precisely in the claim that Schopenhauer did not fully embrace the implications of his own underlying teachings. The flight away from struggle and suffering and into apathetic mysticism was a movement within Schopenhauer's philosophy that Nietzsche sought to reverse. Schopenhauer's inability to face the endlessness of life's struggles was, according to Nietzsche, a symptom of weakness; a sort of remnant of Hegelian utopianism. If the world truly is a place characterized by suffering, struggle, and ongoing activity, then it behooves us to understand this truth, embrace it, and participate fully in it. To adopt a pessimistic attitude toward what really is the case is, in a way, to reject Truth. Nietzsche counsels us instead to remain real philosophers in our wondrous embrace of Truth by throwing ourselves optimistically into the tumultuous and never-ending cycles of aspiration and failure, happiness and despair, struggle and defeat, which are the only stable features of our world. If we aspire to be "supermen," then we may face the world with authentic philosophical heroism, nurturing both wonder and distress in ourselves as we actively continue to exert our own creative powers.

Reading Nietzsche's books, one is overtaken by the energy, the excitement, and the vitality of his philosophical enthusiasm. While the writing of many other philosophers comes across as dry, academic, and hairsplitting, with Nietzsche we encounter a thinker who seems to sincerely take absolute joy in his philosophical adventures, even if at times this joy borders on the precipice of recklessness. It is no wonder that so many people claim that it is Nietzsche who first drew them into the study of philosophy. His passion is contagious and continues to infect people in present times. Nonetheless, there are those who are also repulsed by these same elements in his writings, seeing in them the mania of a madman who is driven more by emotion and sickness than he is by reason and a respect for Truth. It is certainly the case that for the last ten years of his life Nietzsche was insane, and that the works he wrote shortly before falling ill may have been affected by his encroaching mental illness. However, Nietzsche left behind a vast body of writing that predates his break with sanity by many years, and in this work we still find the same passion, drive, and enthusiasm for creative thinking that characterizes his later writings. Whether insane or not, Nietzsche was a genuine philosopher in the sense of loving wisdom and also of recognizing his own separation from Truth itself. Who knows: a bit of insanity may even be a *prerequisite* for engaging in philosophy!

This still does not excuse what many people consider to be an irresponsible and callous streak in Nietzsche's works. The flip side of his advocacy of individual toughness and endless creativity is a tendency toward the merciless dismissal of the felt pain of the weak. Nietzsche is so eager to encourage strength in us all that he sometimes sounds mean-spirited and heartless when it comes to those, like Schopenhauer, who have grown tired of the endless struggle involved in the quest for intellectual integrity. Human happiness seems to mean nothing to Nietzsche. As we saw in his dispute with the Utilitarians, in fact, Nietzsche even unapologetically advocates the perpetuation of human suffering against the propagation of pleasure. It is in these sorts of comments that the Nazis were to find inspiration, but no doubt Nietzsche himself was being hyperbolic when he wrote down many of these thoughts. The main idea that he really seems to have wanted to communicate, and the major theme that we should take away when reading his works as a whole, is that human beings must guard against intellectual and moral laziness if they are to fully actualize their potential as philosophical creatures. We must learn to take joy in the struggle toward knowledge and avoid the complacency that sets in when we think we possess the answers. This is a message with which even the Utilitarian philosopher John Stuart Mill agreed when he wrote that it is better to be Socrates unsatisfied than a pig satisfied. For a human, it is better to remain active intellectually than it is to slide into a state of passive satisfaction. All philosophy demands this.

QUESTIONS FOR DISCUSSION

1. In what ways did Kierkegaard, Schopenhauer, and Nietzsche reject Hegelian philosophy? Are there any aspects of Hegel's thought that you can see reflected in the ideas of Kierkegaard, Schopenhauer, and Nietzsche?

2. What are the differences between optimism and pessimism? In what ways are Kierkegaard, Schopenhauer, and Nietzsche optimistic thinkers? In what ways are they pessimistic thinkers?

3. Are you more of an optimist or a pessimist? Discuss your views on this subject and explore the reasons why you lean toward one or the other of these perspectives.

4. Kierkegaard was a Christian, but he was also extremely critical of Christians. What was it about mainstream Christians that Kierkegaard detested? What are your own thoughts on this topic? Do you think that Kierkegaard was overly critical or do you think he had a good point?

5. Schopenhauer is sometimes labeled an atheist. Do you think this a correct characterization? Why or why not?

6. Nietzsche is equally critical of religion and science. Why is this? Do you agree or disagree with his views on this topic?

7. Would you rather be a happy person or a person who accomplishes great things? Discuss and explore the relationship between happiness, distress, and great accomplishment in life. Are suffering and distress really necessary to be a creative person? If so, are they worth it?

NOTES

1. W. L. Reese, *Dictionary of Philosophy and Religion* (Atlantic Highlands, NJ: Humanities Press, 1980), p. 282.

2. Melville Chaning-Pearce, *Søren Kierkegaard: A Study* (London: James Clarke & Co., Ltd., 1945), p. 41.

3. Søren Kierkegaard, *The Sickness Unto Death: A Christian Psychological Exposition for Upbuilding and Awakening.* Howard V. Hong and Edna H. Hong (eds. and trans.) (Princeton, NJ: Princeton University Press, 1980).

4. Ibid., p. 13.

5. Søren Kierkegaard, *The Concept of Anxiety*, Reidar Thomte (ed. and trans.) (Princeton, NJ: Princeton University Press, 1980), p. 81.

6. Kierkegaard, *The Sickness Unto Death*, p. 14.

7. Ibid., p. 15.

8. Ibid., p. 26.

9. Søren Kierkegaard, *Fear and Trembling*, Alstair Hannay (trans.) (New York: Penguin Books, 1985), p. 49.

10. Kierkegaard's antiestablishment attitudes toward "Christendom" were given vent in a newspaper he published called *The Instant*. In this publication, Kierkegaard

contended that "the Church had become an essentially secular institution, hand in glove with the State and ruled by a bureaucracy whose prime concern was to further the material interests of its members." Patrick Gardiner, *Kierkegaard: A Very Short Introduction* (Oxford: Oxford University Press, 1988), p. 16.

11. Kierkegaard, *Fear and Trembling*, p. 59.

12. The movie *Frailty* plays on this Kierkegaardian insight. In this film, a father of two sons claims to be called by God to kill "demons" that populate the world. Throughout the movie, the audience is led to believe that the father is an insane serial killer. Toward the end of the film, however, it is suggested that, like Abraham, perhaps this man has been called by God.

13. Kierkegaard, *Fear and Trembling*, p. 60.

14. Ibid., p. 65.

15. Ibid., p. 70.

16. Ibid., p. 83.

17. Ibid., p. 109.

18. Kierkegaard, *The Sickness Unto Death*, p. 83.

19. Walter Kaufmann, ed. *Existentialism: From Dostoevsky to Sartre* (New York: Meridian Books, 1975), p. 17.

20. Arthur Schopenhauer, *The World as Will and Representation*, Vol. 1, E. F. Payne (trans.) (New York: Dover, 1958), p. 416.

21. Ibid., pp. 417–418.

22. *The Upanishads*, Eknath Easwaran (ed. and trans.) (Tomales, CA: Nilgiri Press, 2000), pp. 217-218.

23. Bertrand Russell, *A History of Western Philosophy* (New York: Simon and Schuster, 1972), p. 754. The relationships between Buddhism and Hinduism are intricate and complicated. The Buddha grew up within Hindu culture, rebelling against it with his own religion/philosophy. Despite his rebellion, Buddhism draws heavily on the Hindu cosmology and terminology. The most radical departures of Buddhism from Hinduism appear to be within the realm of politics and ethics, and in fact many Hindus regard these departures as legitimate reforms rather than as a rejection of Hindu dharma. Consequently, many Hindus think of Buddhism as a form of Hinduism rather than as a distinct religion.

24. Schopenhauer, *World as Will*, Vol. 1, p. 311. This assertion is, of course, also the first of the Buddha's Four Noble Truths.

25. Ibid., p. 18.

26. Arthur Schopenhauer, *The World as Will and Representation*, Vol. 2, E. F. Payne (trans.) (New York: Dover, 1958), p. 195.

27. Christopher Janaway points out the ambiguity of Schopenhauer's position on this subject. See Christopher Janaway, *Schopenhauer* (Oxford: Oxford University Press, 1994), p. 33.

28. Schopenhauer, *World as Will*, Vol. 2, pp. 197-198.

29. There is much here that reminds one of Descartes.

30. Schopenhauer, *World as Will*, Vol. 2, p. 153.

31. Schopenhauer, *World as Will*, Vol. 2, p. 202.

32. There remains something arbitrary here in Schopenhauer's insistence on the primacy of the will. I think he himself senses this and so tells us that, in the end, "it can

never be demonstrated, that is deduced as indirect knowledge from some other more direct knowledge, for the very reason that it is itself the most direct knowledge" (Schopenhauer, *World as Will*, Vol. 2, p. 102). In other words, the primacy of the will is supposed to be taken as an intuitively obvious truth.

33. Ibid., p. 100.

34. Ibid., p. 149.

35. This recalls Aristotle's discussion of the divisions of the soul. See Chapter 4.

36. Schopenhauer, *World as Will*, Vol. 2, p. 153.

37. Ibid., p. 299.

38. Ibid., p. 309.

39. Ibid., p. 398.

40. Ibid., p. 399.

41. Ibid., p. 411.

42. This all sounds very much like the Stoic doctrine of *apathia* as discussed in Chapter 5. Bertrand Russell for this reason writes, "His outlook has a certain temperamental affinity with that of the Hellenistic age" (*A History of Western Philosophy*, p. 753).

43. This is a point made by Agent Smith in the film *The Matrix*. As he is torturing the character Morpheus, Smith becomes uncharacteristically agitated as he recounts the failure of the first attempt by the machines to produce an illusory dream-world with which to placate their human slaves. It failed, he tells Morpheus, because the dream-world produced by the machines was perfect, containing no pain and suffering. As a consequence, humans "rejected the program" and "whole crops were lost." It was then that the machines realized that they had to program imperfection into their computer-generated reality if they wanted humans to accept it as real.

44. Russell, *A History of Western Philosophy*, p. 759.

45. Bertrand Russell's account of Nietzsche is a perfect example of this sort of distortion and misunderstanding. One gets the sense that Russell has not even read, or at least has not thought very deeply about, Nietzsche's books.

46. Walter Kaufmann, *Nietzsche: Philosopher, Psychologist, Antichrist*, 4th ed. (Princeton, NJ: Princeton University Press, 1974), Prologue, pp. 3-18.

47. Friedrich Nietzsche, *Twilight of the Idols*, in *The Portable Nietzsche* (New York: Penguin Books, 1984), p. 467.

48. Friedrich Nietzsche, *Beyond Good and Evil*, in *Basic Writings of Nietzsche* (New York: The Modern Library, 1968), p. 258.

49. Martin Heidegger, *Nietzsche*, Vol. 1. David Farrell Krell (trans.) (San Francisco: Harper San Francisco, 1991), pp. 41-42.

50. Friedrich Nietzsche, *The Gay Science* (New York: Vintage Books, 1974), p. 168.

51. Friedrich Nietzsche, *Thus Spoke Zarathustra*, in *The Portable Nietzsche* (New York: Penguin Books, 1984), p. 124.

52. Nietzsche, *The Gay Science*, p. 336.

53. Nietzsche, *Thus Spoke Zarathustra*, p. 125. Kaufmann translates *Übermensch* as "overman" rather than as "superman."

54. Friedrich Nietzsche, *The Will to Power*, Walter Kaufmann and R. J. Hollingdale (trans.), Walter Kaufmann (ed.) (New York: Vintage Books, 1968), p. 499.

55. Nietzsche, *Beyond Good and Evil*, p. 346.

56. John Stuart Mill, *Utilitarianism*, in *Ten Great Works of Philosophy*, Robert Paul Wolff (ed.) (New York: Mentor Books, 1969), p. 408.

57. Nietzsche, *Beyond Good and Evil*, p. 343.

58. Mill, *Utilitarianism*, p. 409.

59. Ibid., p. 412.

60. Ibid., p. 410.

Chapter 12

Common Sense and Anglo-American Philosophy

© Juneko J. Robinson

What is the difference between the tender- and the tough-minded?
What is the pragmatic method? What is the pragmatic theory
of truth? How is Russell's logic different from that of Aristotle
and Hegel? What is the difference between knowledge by
acquaintance and knowledge by description? How did Wittgenstein
think he had solved all philosophical problems in his book
Tractatus Logico-Philosophicus? In what ways did Wittgenstein
change his views in his book *Philosophical Investigations*?

THE REACTION AGAINST HEGEL

Reaction against Hegelian philosophy continued to develop throughout the nineteenth and twentieth centuries, not only in the German-speaking world but also in places like the British Isles and the United States. In the previous chapter we encountered a few of the most important thinkers who led the charge against Hegelianism in continental Europe. In this chapter we will examine another group of thinkers, largely from English-speaking parts of the globe, who were likewise concerned with the rejection of Hegel. Though both groups of philosophers shared a distaste for Hegelianism, the directions in which they drove their thinking were, in some important ways, quite divergent. The first group, those originating from continental Europe, came to typify a style of philosophizing that we today call "continental"; the second group, those originating largely from the British Isles and the United States, came to typify a style of philosophizing that today is called "Anglo-American." This chapter will focus on the development of Anglo-American philosophy, its attempt to renew our confidence in common sense, and its uneasy relationship with both science and religion.

In the opening pages of this book I discussed and outlined some of the main controversies that presently exist between the continental and the analytic approaches to philosophizing. Continental philosophy, we saw, tends toward ongoing meditation and contemplation of grand philosophical issues. There is a propensity among continental thinkers to enthusiastically engage in metaphysical speculation concerning issues such as the existence God, the fundamental nature of reality, and the meaning of human life. Thinkers such as Hegel, Kierkegaard, Schopenhauer, and Nietzsche characteristically come to mind in this regard, not only because of the subject matter that concerned them but also due to their manner of writing. They approached their subjects in a literary fashion, writing in a style that was sometimes more poetic than it was strictly logical. This approach to philosophy, in which grand issues are dealt with in a literary and quasi-poetic style, leaves some with a profound feeling of awe and wonder in the face of the enigmas of existence. But just as often it has left readers with the sense that a variety of important issues have been covered over and made to sound more obscure and mysterious than they need to be. In the case of Hegel, this tendency went to an extreme, and much of the reaction against him in the English-speaking world has had to do with trying to correct what is perceived as his undisciplined and obscurantist use of language.

Anglo-American thought, of which pragmatism and analytic philosophy are subcategories, tends to be characterized by the disciplined application of logical analysis to problems that may potentially be solved, and so there is a tendency for thinkers in this tradition to steer clear of grand metaphysical speculation. These philosophers tend to use language in a less literary and poetic manner, and more often they write in a terse, logical, and systematic style. Their concern is not usually with open-ended and ongoing meditation, speculation, and contemplation of grand issues but rather with the clarification and analysis of more down-to-earth problems, usually with an eye toward the resolution of those prob-lems. Whereas the continental tradition of philosophy finds affinity with the humanities, the Anglo-American tradition of philosophy finds affinities with the sciences. In fact, in colleges and universities today you can tell a lot about how particular philosophy departments conceive of their missions by identifying the divisions that house them. In some colleges and universities, philosophy is housed within the school of arts and humanities, or even within the school of English and communications. In others, philosophy is housed in the schools of science or social science. In the former case, it is a good bet that the philosophy department conceives of itself as continental in orientation. In the latter case, it is a good bet that it conceives of itself as Anglo-American or analytic in orienta-tion. It is important to note, of course, that what we see here is a matter of emphasis. All philosophers, whether continental or Anglo-American, strive to-ward Truth and are ultimately willing to defer final answers to the questions that they raise. The difference between continental and Anglo-American philo-sophers lies in the way they carry out their inquiries and in the sorts of questions that they find of primary interest.

I believe that in the friction between the continental and Anglo-American traditions we can detect the manifestation of a tension that always has existed in the heart of philosophical thinking. As a form of wondrous distress, philosophy is forever pulled between two opposing poles. On the one hand, philosophers de-sire Truth. On the other, they recognize how far away from Truth they always are. This friction between the desire for final answers and the recognition of our ignorance drives philosophy forward, but it has also recently split the field into warring factions. Continental thinkers seem to be more concerned with trying to linger with, and meditate on, the mysterious and unknown. Anglo-American philosophers seem to be more concerned with resolving what can be known. In any case, if drawn too vigorously toward either extreme, these thinkers run the risk of ceasing to be philosophers altogether. At its most extreme, continental thought starts to sound much like religion, while Anglo-American thought at its most extreme starts to sound like science.

In the present chapter we will encounter a few of the most influential mod-ern Anglo-American philosophers and scrutinize their efforts to move philosophy in the direction of science. It should be noted, however, that all of the indivi-duals that we will examine—William James, Bertrand Russell, and Ludwig Wittgenstein—recognized at one level or another that philosophy and science are two related, yet separate, disciplines. In the end, as important philosophical figures, the thinkers we now turn to ultimately defended the integrity of philos-ophy as a uniquely important way of thinking.

WILLIAM JAMES

In Chapter 11 we encountered the utilitarian philosophy of the British thinker John Stuart Mill. Mill's philosophy is one of the early influences on the

© Juneko J. Robinson

Anglo-American movement, as is the even earlier thought of David Hume, the Scottish philosopher who was dealt with at length in Chapter 8. What both of these men share in common, and what was inspirational in their thinking to later Anglo-American philosophers, is the down-to-earth, common-sense, and systematic approach that they pursue as they raise questions about reality. Both Mill and Hume start from an empirical standpoint, suggesting that if we just look at the world and observe it, there are certain facts that our common sense will allow us to apprehend. This is a departure from the rationalist approach to philosophy that was popular with Hegel and his followers, and it is an approach that dovetails very smoothly with the advice of the modern empirical sciences. If you want to know what is true and real, they counsel, you need to look at the world carefully, making observations that will ground and substantiate your philosophical claims. Systems of philosophy that stray too far from empirically grounded ideas run the risk of becoming unanchored, overly abstract fantasies. Creativity is all fine and good, but in the realm of philosophy the point is not simply to think new things, after all. Rather, it is to move closer to what is actually true. The problem with ideas that are not anchored in observation, both Mill and Hume contend, is that such ideas have no grounding in the real world of objective experience.

This empiricist orientation toward thinking was a great influence on William James (1842–1910), one of the most important philosophers to emerge out of the United States in the nineteenth century. William James was the brother of Henry James, the well-known author of works such as *The Turn of the Screw* and *The Portrait of a Lady*. William, however, seems to have been more interested in science than in fiction, and so instead of following in the footsteps of his brother, he decided to study chemistry, anatomy, and medicine at Harvard University. He also, at this time, became interested in psychology, a field that was just beginning to become established as a science. His first major publication was a two-volume work titled *The Principles of Psychology*, which is still today considered an important text in the field.

James's interest in science, however, was always tempered by another interest; namely, his interest in religion. The trajectory of James's writing career can be interpreted as an ongoing attempt to reconcile the apparent conflict between these two areas of concern. On the one hand, James advocated "radical empiricism," which is his belief that to know anything, we must make observations and gather data from the world around us. On the other hand, he also held a conviction that religious faith, which is an inner feeling of the individual mind, reveals some sort of truth. Is there any way of establishing empirically and scientifically that claims based on inner, subjective religious feelings have a legitimate claim to veracity? This issue was very personal to James. He was a deeply troubled man who suffered from bouts of depression, and a good portion of his despair was rooted in his concern that scientific materialism undermined the existence of human free will and spirituality. If science is correct, then human beings are nothing more than clever animals, powered by chemical reactions and shaped by natural selection. If this is all we are, what meaning or purpose can life possibly have? Is the point of human life simply to be born, to exist, and to die? Is there nothing more beyond that? Does being a scientist automatically commit one to such a bleak and meaningless view of the world?

Pragmatism

In his attempt to circumvent the determinism that results from a crass materialist description of the world, and to rescue the notion of human free will, James developed a philosophy called "Pragmatism." The term "pragmatism" had previously been coined by Charles Sanders Peirce (1839–1914), a friend of James. When James's version of Pragmatism became very popular, however, Peirce was so appalled by its content that he changed the name of his own philosophy to "Pragmaticism," a name, he wrote, that was so ugly no one would be tempted to kidnap it! It is interesting to note that when William James wrote his book titled *Pragmatism,* he dedicated it not to Peirce but to John Stuart Mill. The dedication reads:

> To the memory of John Stuart Mill, from whom I first learned the pragmatic openness of mind and whom my fancy likes to picture as our leader were he alive today.[1]

Pragmatism is a masterpiece of clear and disciplined writing. Originally delivered as a series of lectures at Columbia University between 1906 and 1907, this book systematically articulates the basis of James's pragmatic philosophy and then applies its insights to an analysis and resolution of a number of traditional philosophical problems. It concludes by addressing the issue of religious belief. In its approach, purpose, and execution, *Pragmatism* is a perfect illustration of the Anglo-American style of philosophizing. It demonstrates a keen sense of logic and the ability to draw clear and consistent distinctions and definitions. It goes on to demonstrate how the careful application of these distinctions and definitions is enough to resolve issues that had previously seemed mystifying. As we will see later, this is also, perhaps, one of its weaknesses. At times, James may exhibit an overeagerness to draw unequivocal conclusions at the cost of authentic philosophical openness.

The Tender- and the Tough-Minded

In his book *Pragmatism*, James tells us that "The history of philosophy is to a great extent that of a certain clash of human temperaments."[2] Starting with this psychological observation, James proceeds to group philosophers into two great, opposing camps. On the one hand there are those who are "tender-minded" and on the other there are those who are "tough-minded."[3] Tender-minded philosophers are characterized by James as "rationalistic, intellectualistic, idealistic, optimistic, religious, free-willist, monistic, and dogmatical."[4] They are, generally speaking, similar in nature to what I have been speaking of as continental thinkers, although James specifically had in mind his Hegelian colleagues (in particular, people like Josiah Royce [1855–1916]) when he compiled this list. On the other hand, tough-minded philosophers are "empiricist, sensationalistic, materialistic, pessimistic, irreligious, fatalistic, pluralistic, and sceptical."[5] They are, in large part, similar to what I have been speaking of as analytic thinkers. This distinction between the "tender-minded" and the "tough-minded," James contends, is indicative of a certain "mental make-up" that has colored and influenced the development of philosophy and that has fractured the field into two warring camps.

The tender-minded philosophers are drawn toward abstraction, romanticism, and monism. They tend to think of the world in terms of abstract principles and to interpret the universe by applying these principles to find a unity behind the plurality of appearances. Think of Kant, Hegel, and Schopenhauer in this regard. All of these thinkers created philosophies that endeavored to penetrate the veil of outward appearances to understand the unity lying behind that veil. There is among these sorts of thinkers a desire to understand the world as it is "in-itself" and to reverence the fundamental unity of all things with an almost religious sense of awe, wonder, and mystery. The tough-minded philosophers, in contrast, are drawn toward concrete facts, observation, and pluralism. They tend to give more authority to ideas that can be verified through sensory experience and thus they are skeptical of the sorts of abstract claims made by tender-minded philosophers. Think of Hume and Mill in this regard. Such tough-minded philosophers understand the world not in terms of mysterious and unseen unities but rather in terms of the obvious and observable pluralities that are apparent to our senses. Therefore, they tend to ally themselves with the empirical sciences rather than with religious teachings that encourage faith in an unseen realm.[6]

The tender- and the tough-minded are psychological types, James tells us, and these psychological types have influenced the development of philosophy in the West. People create philosophies that work to buttress their own perspectives, and both the tender- and the tough-minded have instinctively gravitated toward the sorts of philosophies that reflect their own preconceived notions of what the world is like. Each sort of thinker wants a universe that suits his or her own temperament and consequently "he believes in any representation of the universe that does suit it."[7] Philosophy, then, appears not so much as an objective and independent exercise in the search for Truth but rather as an attempt by the human mind to subjectively create comforting and agreeable worldviews with which it may content itself. People are mentally biased in different ways.

Some find comfort in unity, while some find comfort in plurality. The type of philosophy in which one chooses to believe, James tells us, reflects one's psychological predisposition. To philosophers, this may be a bit of a troubling assertion because it makes philosophy itself a subset of psychology. It calls to mind Plato's complaint that most people only see what it is that they want to see and that most people prefer psychological contentment to real Truth; they prefer life in a cave to life in the real world. Nonetheless, James tells us that in large part this is precisely what the history of philosophy details: the history of clashing human temperaments.

James himself expresses a certain amount of discontent with this situation. He suggests that the division between tender- and tough-minded philosophies in reality is overly simplistic and so does not adequately reflect the real-life needs and desires of an ever-growing number of human beings. Whereas the tender-minded philosophies are not sensitive enough to science, the tough-minded philosophies are not sensitive enough to religion. Because in contemporary times there are many people who find themselves attracted toward both religion and science, he wonders whether there is a philosophical position that might satisfy both of these apparently conflicting desires equally. "You want a system that will combine both things, the scientific loyalty to facts and willingness to take account of them, the spirit of adaptation and accommodation, in short, but also the old confidence in human values and the resultant spontaneity, whether of the religious or romantic type."[8] Can the desire for scientific rigor be combined with the desire for religious meaningfulness in one single philosophical position? James tells us that with his philosophy of Pragmatism he offers a system that does indeed satisfy both of these demands.

James's Pragmatism is both a method of philosophizing and a theory of truth. As a *method of philosophizing*, it offers a technique with which to approach questions, not simply to consider or meditate on them but also to formulate positive answers to the issues posed. In this way, Pragmatism lays out an objective procedure by which we may rigorously investigate the world and resolve philosophical disputes. As a *theory of truth*, Pragmatism offers a definition of what we are after as we engage in this process of philosophizing. We need to know what we are looking for as we search for answers so that we recognize the correct answer when it appears, and the pragmatic theory of truth gives us a criterion by which we may judge true answers and distinguish them from the false ones. In what follows I will outline first the pragmatic method and second the pragmatic theory of truth. Once we have explored and understood these aspects of Pragmatism, we may then see how James applies his insights to the analysis of particular issues, especially issues of a religious nature.

The Pragmatic Method

As a method, Pragmatism operates from a simple and straightforward principle: if the dispute between two or more competing philosophical doctrines is authentic, then we will be able to show that there is a practical difference that follows from one side being correct and the other side being wrong.[9] Suppose, for instance, that Thales and Heraclitus were arguing about the one basic underlying element that makes up the universe. You will recall that Thales claimed this element to be water, while Heraclitus claimed it to be fire.[10] The Pragmatic method instructs us to look for any differences between the practical outcomes predicted by each of these theories. When we do so in this case, it might appear that there are no practical differences. Thales claims that all of the world's tangible and observable qualities result from water. Heraclitus claims that all of those same tangible and observable qualities are the result of fire. Whether water or fire, then, the consequence is the same: the world of tangible and observable experience. Anything that Thales can explain in terms of water, Heraclitus can offer a competing explanation in terms of fire. Consequently, according to the Pragmatic method of James, there may appear to be no serious dispute here. What difference does it make whether the world is made of water or fire? None at all, and so we need not concern ourselves with this issue.

However, suppose that we develop a means of experimentation by which we are able to distill the basic element of the universe and test for it in some way; perhaps by observing the effect it has on a piece of paper. If we are able to do this, then it would appear that there is some sort of practical difference in the consequences that would follow from these competing theories. If Thales is correct, the piece of paper will be become damp. If Heraclitus is correct, the piece of paper will ignite. Once we carry out the experiment and discover which outcome actually occurs, we may then resolve the dispute and pronounce one or the other of these theories the correct one. But this is only possible once we have shown that there are differences in the actual, practical consequences that result from competing theories. If there were no differences in the observable consequences anticipated by the theories, there is no way to adjudicate the correctness or incorrectness of those theories. According to the Pragmatic method, they would amount to the same thing: idle speculation.

As illustrated in this example, James' method is closely allied with an empiricist perspective. Pragmatism demands that we be able to observe and test for concrete results. As James writes,

> A pragmatist turns his back resolutely and once for all upon a lot of inveterate habits dear to professional philosophers. He turns away from abstraction and insufficiency, from verbal solutions, from bad *a priori* reasons, from fixed principles, closed systems, and pretended absolutes and origins. He turns towards concreteness and adequacy, towards facts, towards action and power. That means the empiricist temper regnant and the rationalist temper sincerely given up.[11]

Pragmatism demands that we be able to experience and discern the consequences that follow from competing speculations about the nature of the world. When examining and thinking about various theoretical constructs, we should be concerned with, as James puts it, their "cash-value." This phrase, "cash-value," appears again and again in James's writing, and it is intended to emphasize the importance of observable outcomes in philosophy. Too often, James complains, philosophers have constructed systems that have no conceivable *practical* consequences for how we live life. Theories are not adornments or decorations that we should believe in simply because they are internally coherent and logical. Theories should have some sort of use. They are "instruments" that serve to help us uncover and discover things about the world in which we live. Theoretical instruments prove themselves useful or not useful to the degree that they produce cash-value in the form of empirically testable results. Those philosophies that produce the most cash-value are the most useful and thus by pragmatic standards the most correct.

It is important to point out, however, that as a method, Pragmatism does not commit itself to any particular kinds of results. The Pragmatist, in other words, is not necessarily a materialist or an idealist, a theist or an atheist. All that is required by this method is that we remain open to the observation, investigation, and the substantiation of practical consequences as they follow from philosophical speculations. As we sort through the data of experience, we come to construct a richer and richer picture of the world and our place in it, but we must never become dogmatic or fixed in our opinions. Pragmatically speaking, we should always be open to considering the cash-value of any theory, position, or idea that presents itself to us. We must never dismiss an idea out of hand but always endeavor to consider its practical consequences and uses in the real world of human life. In the debate between materialists and idealists, James himself comes to the conclusion that no practical difference is made if you accept one or the other position. Both positions claim that the world we live in, the world that we observe and interact with, really exists. The only difference between the positions is that one side, the materialists, claim that this world is "run by" matter, while the other side, the idealists (or "spiritualists"), claim that this world is "run by" spirit. Yet the world, whether run by matter or spirit, is already given to us as it is. It has already been created, either by an act of God or by "blind physical forces."[12] Whatever we speculate as the cause of the universe, the universe is nevertheless here, formed as it is and operating as it does. Whether you be a materialist or an idealist, the cash-value is the same: namely, the universe we live in. There is no practical difference in what follows from these theories. "The pragmatist must consequently say that the two theories, in spite of their different sounding names, mean exactly the same thing, and that the dispute is purely verbal."[13] Thus we see that for James and his pragmatic method, there is no need to commit oneself to a single, dogmatic, or final position concerning the nature of the universe. The pragmatic method presupposes no particular stance on materialism, idealism, or any of the other "-isms" we have encountered throughout this book. Instead, it attempts to leave the opportunity open for all beliefs to prove themselves with hard and concrete evidence.

James uses the wonderful metaphor of a grease spot to characterize the manner in which we build up our understanding of the world pragmatically. We have various "spots" of knowledge that spread and grow as we investigate our world. Sometimes these spots merge into one another and thus connections are made between the spots, unifying and enlarging our understanding of reality. As old knowledge merges with new discoveries, there is a gradual and positive evolution that occurs and our learning grows into the future, never necessarily reaching the margins of reality, but nonetheless expanding and progressing to become more and more far-reaching. The sum total of these grease spots, collected together over the course of human history, is what we refer to as "common sense." Common sense is composed of the tried and true store of learning that has endured with us over the course of human evolution. Its contents are those bits of information that we have found to be useful and which articulate with other bits of information in our belief systems. Over time, those ideas that serve no use to us are abandoned and eliminated, leaving our commonsense beliefs in place. This process is ongoing, and so what is part of common sense today may fail to be so in the future. However, the longer and more often that we find our beliefs and ideas surviving and serving us well in our lives, the more confident we become that, in one way or another, they point in the direction of something that is stable and true. Common sense represents a consolidation of past beliefs that the ongoing investigations of science and philosophy serve to challenge, to overthrow, or to fortify. James tells us that never do we know once and for all what is absolutely true, but as we challenge our common sense with philosophy and science, and as we reach out to investigate the world more and more, we tend to build stronger and more useful hypotheses about reality. The pragmatic method both describes this process and recommends it as the most sensible means for coming to understand our world.

The Pragmatic Theory of Truth

"The only literally true thing is *reality*; and the only reality we know is ... sensible reality, the flux of our sensations and emotions as they pass."[14] With this statement, James begins to develop a rather novel, and indeed controversial, definition of Truth. Since the beginning of Greek philosophy, Truth has been understood in terms of correspondence between the mind and the world that the mind comprehends. In this view, the mind acts as a mirror that reflects reality; the more clearly polished the mind is, the better it reflects that which it seeks to picture. Traditionally, philosophers have presumed that we can best "polish" the mirror of the mind through the use of logic and reason, and thus the more rational we become, the better able we are to see the world truly.[15] Truth, in this way of thinking, consists of using reason to understand reality and then to hold a representation of that reality in the mind, the way that an image is reflected and held on the surface of a mirror.

James partly agrees with this traditional conception of truth, and he partly modifies it. James does assert that reality is the "only literally true thing." In other words, the world as it is in-itself, objective reality, is considered by James to be the only "real" truth. This should remind us of Kant and his insistence on the objective existence of the thing-in-itself.[16] However, James goes on to assert that the "only reality we know is ... sensible reality." It follows that the only literally true thing that we can know, according to James, is sensible reality. We are never able to transcend our senses to experience the world as it is independent of our sensory experience. Because we cannot get at the literal truth of objective reality, the next best thing is for us to occupy ourselves with the knowable truths of our subjective empirically derived reality. This idea—that the universe of empirically derived sensation is the only world we are able truly to know—lays the groundwork for what James calls the pragmatic theory of truth. In the pragmatic theory of truth, we never have direct access to the world as it is in-itself. As Kant had already argued, our understanding of the world is never unmediated or direct. Our minds always intervene to actively organize and, perhaps, to distort our perceptions of reality. Yet, James tells us, our sensory experience is the best, and in fact the only, tool that we have to help us comprehend what is really "out there" in the world itself. Thus, his theory begins to shift emphasis away from the unknowable world that exists beyond our sensory experience back toward the world as it reveals itself to our senses. In the course of this reemphasis, James redefines truth as a process that unfolds, rather than as a static thing that is to be discovered once and for all. When the pragmatist speaks of truth, he or she is not concerned with some sort of atemporal property that exists independent of human understanding. On the contrary; truth in the pragmatic sense is just the ongoing process by which the human mind assimilates and incorporates ideas into its commonsense understanding. The truth is an event that happens. As James writes, "The truth of an idea is not a stagnant property inherent in it. Truth *happens* to an idea. It *becomes* true, is *made* true by events. Its verity *is* in fact an event, a process: the process namely of its verifying itself, its veri-*fication*. Its validity is the process of its valid-*ation*."[17]

The pragmatic method is the means by which we investigate our world, observing phenomena and taking note of the consequences that follow from those phenomena. The understanding that we develop in the course of this ongoing process is what we consider the truth. The truth unfolds as we investigate reality. We use new ideas and discoveries as "go-betweens" and "smoother-overs"[18] to aid us in the development and growth of our understanding. Truths are those ideas that we find useful for linking and connecting together otherwise disconnected bits and pieces of our knowledge. Truths are bridges that act as instruments allowing us to pass from one experience to another smoothly. Recalling the metaphor of the grease spot, a truth, in the pragmatic sense, grows as it saturates our minds, creeping outward and assimilating more and more territory. Just as small isolated spots of grease become incorporated by the encroachment of a larger grease spot, so do the isolated and disconnected ideas in our minds become interconnected and joined by those larger, all-encompassing ideas that we call "true." The pragmatic theory of truth tells us that what is true are ideas that we find useful in helping us to unify and make sense of the world we have built up in our minds out of empirically derived sensory experience. This is the cash-value of truth: how well does it work in helping us to comprehend and sort through our conceptions of the world?

Suppose you are building a desk using a store-bought kit. The kit contains a number of different wooden parts and bits of hardware with which to connect the parts. There is also an instruction manual that gives step-by-step instructions on how to assemble the kit. As you get ready to attach the legs to the table top, you read in the instructions that you should use a Phillips head screwdriver to drive the screws. Is this statement true? You look at the shape of the screw heads designed to affix the legs to the table. They have little "x" depressions cut out in them. From all appearances, it certainly looks as if the Phillips head screwdriver is the appropriate tool to use. The Phillips head screwdriver in your toolbox appears shaped to fit the depressions in the screws. However, it is only once you commence with the assembly that you will actually be able to verify that this is the case. Suppose, as you put the table together, you do find that your screwdriver works very well to complete the task. You might, consequently, be inclined to say that it is indeed true that a Phillips head screwdriver is the proper tool for driving these screws. It works to complete the job. This is not to say that there are not other tools that might also work to drive in the screws. A flat head screwdriver might work also, or perhaps even the edge of a knife. You might even be able to use your fingernail! However, the Phillips head screwdriver probably works most efficiently for this purpose, and so from a pragmatic standpoint we would say that it is truly the best choice for the job. In the future there might be some other tool developed that is even more efficient for this purpose, and if this does occur, we would then be justified in saying that it is no longer true that a Phillips head screwdriver is the best tool for the job. The truth of the matter may change in this fashion as we respond to new discoveries and as we adjust our understanding to these new discoveries.

Hegel had written about an absolute Truth of the universe that could potentially be comprehended in a final act of pure knowing. James is quite skeptical of this idealistic aspiration. He doesn't necessarily discount it altogether, but he does seem to think of absolute Truth as an abstraction, as something that cannot be made present and "real" in the here-and-now world. Absolute Truth for James is like a "vanishing-point towards which we imagine that all of our temporary truths will some day converge."[19] What we have in the meantime are just collections of provisional "truths" that are more or less useful as we try to make our way through the world as we know it. James underlines this point by drawing our attention to the fact that many things that were once considered absolutely true—like Ptolemaic astronomy, Euclidean space, Aristotelian logic, and scholastic metaphysics—no longer hold that status in our minds. At best they are "relatively true," which is to say that in an absolute sense they are really false.

The pragmatic theory of truth is verificationist in orientation. Things considered to be true are intimately connected with the means by which we come to verify that they are true. Pragmatically speaking, the truth involves the effects and results that are coaxed out of the world during the course of probing and testing reality. All we have to work with as we navigate through the world are our experiences. We are never able to step outside of our minds to commune and meld with reality as it exists independent of our experience. For this reason, we cannot comprehend the world all at once and as a whole. The best that we can do is to probe and test reality using a pragmatic, scientific method of investigation. As we do so, we look for the consequences and the results of our probing, forming ideas about what we can consistently expect from the world. We then string these expectations together into a vast web of connections that constitutes our commonsense understanding. Common sense is the truth for us, but it is a changeable truth that might be altered and subverted the more observations we put in place and the more experiences we collect. As we weave together a body of knowledge, we strive to create a pattern that hangs together and makes sense, but that pattern is always in danger of disruption so that what was true to us at one point in history might have to be reconceived as false at another point in history. Pragmatically, what is true is what works for us now, but there is no guarantee that what works now will work forever. We certainly may hope that the ongoing process of pragmatic investigation will bring us closer and closer to some sort of ultimate reality, but even if it did end up doing so, we would never know when we had arrived. We would still need to test and probe that reality, taking account of our results forever into the future to try and verify that our subjective understanding lines up with something beyond that understanding. We take things as true as long as nothing challenges those beliefs, but the future, as Hume emphasized, is an open book. We never know what sorts of challenges lie ahead.

Religion

James concludes that the truth is a developing process which involves, first, ongoing investigation of the world; second, the integration of new discoveries into interconnected and useful frameworks of knowledge; and third, the attempt to relate new systems to older forms of understanding. We weave the truth together from bits and pieces of information that we accumulate over time, trying to fit things together and to reconcile the old with the new. Many times we find that the old must give way to the new, and when this happens, the content of what we consider to be common sense changes. In the transition from the geocentric to the heliocentric view of the universe, for example, new discoveries in math and astronomy led to the overthrow of old commonsense truths and to the establishment of new commonsense truths. This happens in countless, though perhaps less dramatic, ways every day. Pragmatically speaking, the truth is never static but rather is always evolving in response to how the world appears to us and according to what sort of use to which we can put our knowledge. The pragmatic theory of truth thus leaves open the door to the potential discovery of an ever-expanding and ever-changing body of truths. It insists that we cannot know everything at once, and so it also recognizes that there are all sorts of things going on "out there" beyond our observational perspective that we cannot fully grasp. "We cannot therefore methodically join the tough minds in their rejection of the whole notion of a world beyond our finite experience."[20] If the existence of a realm beyond finite experience cannot categorically be ruled out, then this leaves open the possibility that the claims of religious thinkers, who espouse belief in God and the afterlife, may actually be correct.

In the final pages of *Pragmatism*, James asserts, "On pragmatic principles we can not reject any hypothesis if consequences useful to life flow from it."[21] Are there any "consequences useful to life" that flow from religious beliefs? Indeed, James tells us that there are. Let us consider the religious notion of a creator God who offers the possibility for the world's salvation. James suggests that many rational human beings find this thought comforting and useful because it offers a practical reason to continue to struggle and strive to live a good life. The life of finite existence can be exhausting, and many people throughout history have found that the only sort of belief that motivates them to continue forward is the promise of a final state of "peace and rest."[22] Throughout history this has worked for many people, and it continues to work for many people today. Pragmatically speaking, then, such a belief must be considered "true." "On pragmatic principles, if the hypothesis of God works satisfactorily in the widest sense of the word, it is true. Now, whatever its residual difficulties may be, experience shows that it certainly does work, and that the problem is to build it out and determine it so that it will combine satisfactorily with all the other working truths."[23] It is important to notice that James uses the term "hypothesis" to characterize the religious belief in God here. He is not saying that by pragmatic methods he has established the existence of a particular form of God with certainty in some realm independent of human experience. Rather, he is pointing out that there is a *possibility* that God exists, and belief in this possibility has proven to be useful to billions of people during the "whole course of men's religious history."[24] Because pragmatic theory holds that truth is a process by which beliefs are built up and survive according to how well they become part of our overall system of "common sense," and because religious beliefs have always been among the most dearly held, comforting, and well-incorporated beliefs in cultures worldwide, those beliefs are, in this sense, "true." We have, in short, a right to believe in the possibility of God and of salvation.

In an essay titled "The Will to Believe," James famously argued for the position that "we have a right to adopt a believing attitude in religious matters, in spite of the fact that our merely logical intellect may not have been coerced."[25] Treated carefully, religious belief is a hypothesis. As stated above, it expresses the *possibility* that God exists. This possibility cannot be refuted by the sorts of facts we gather empirically nor, on the other hand, can God's objective existence, on these grounds, be established with absolute certainty. The existence of God must always remain an open question from the purely scientific perspective. This means that, for the individual, belief or nonbelief in God ultimately hinges on a personal, willful choice. We may choose to believe, we may choose not to believe, or we may choose to remain uncommitted. These are the options between theism, atheism, and agnosticism. Whether or not you believe in God, you have willingly made a choice to adopt a certain stance on the issue, and this choice is based not on absolute proof but on an inner feeling and a personal desire to hold a position. The atheist and the agnostic are not necessarily any less passionate in their choices than is the theist, James tells us. All have decided on the issue in one way or another; the atheist has decided against God, the theist has decided for God, and the agnostic has decided "to leave the question open."[26] But each of their beliefs is based on subjective opinion rather than on objective, positive evidence. For this reason alone, the theist has as much right to believe in God as the atheist has the right to deny the existence of God or the agnostic has the right to profess uncertainty. In the end, because there is no *objective* proof for or against the existence of God, the choice to adopt any opinion on the topic whatsoever must be based on *subjective* feeling alone.

There are, however, purely practical reasons why it makes sense to accept the reality of God as a fact, James argues. An empirical survey of the history of belief in God, as expressed through a wide variety of world religions, verifies that the God hypothesis is, in fact, very useful and productive of good effects for human life. Believing in God helps many people feel integrated within the universe, and it endows them with a sense of meaning and purpose in life. Believers derive motivation and enthusiasm from their religious commitment. These sorts of effects are a direct result of a belief in God's existence, and for this reason, as

James writes in his book *The Varieties of Religious Experience*, the pragmatic conclusion must follow: "God is real because he produces real effects."[27] The effects that James refers to here are not the physical, cosmic effects touted by St. Thomas Aquinas, but the personal, practical effects that follow for those who have chosen to place faith in a beneficent power that is greater than themselves. The proof is in the pudding, James seems to be telling us. Those who choose to believe in God experience positive and useful consequences, and this serves to show, pragmatically, that religious faith works. It has cash-value for human life. As we have seen previously, the pragmatic method tells us that those beliefs that result in the most cash-value are the most correct, and so James concludes that religious faith is true in this pragmatic way of thinking.

The "truth" of religious belief is further attested to by the fact that it has always existed, has always proved its usefulness, and has always found a way to articulate cogently with other beliefs that human beings hold to be true. The ancient Greeks had religious belief, the Medievals had religious belief, and even in Modern times religion has found ways to accommodate itself to the scientific worldview. Faith in God has thus proven itself to be "true" by way of its survival into contemporary times. This Darwinian line of argumentation suggests that religious ideas remain with us due to their survival value. Just as the theory of natural selection tells us that organisms must either adapt or die, so it is with the beliefs we hold to be true. Those beliefs that aid us in our struggle to survive stay with us, and those that impede us in this struggle whither away. Throughout the history of humankind, religious beliefs have never withered away, and this is the truth of religion. It appears always to serve a function for humans. From the pragmatic perspective, those ideas that serve a function and that can consistently be made to dovetail with the other beliefs in our systems of common sense are true for us. Therefore, when we empirically survey the persistence of religious beliefs in all cultures throughout all periods of history, we must come to the pragmatic conclusion that these beliefs are, in a practical sense, true.

Wallace Matson refers to Pragmatism as the "first distinctively American philosophical movement to achieve international recognition."[28] In the philosophy of William James we can certainly detect something of the commonsense, down-to-earth, and practical attitude that Americans have a reputation for promoting. The pragmatist, like a frontier cowboy, doesn't hold much truck with sheer speculation and endless pontification on matters of a purely academic nature. Like a cowboy, the pragmatist wants to get the job done. He wants to get his hands dirty and dive right into the task before him, figuring out what sort of difference he can make in the world. If beliefs make no difference whatsoever, then they are of no real concern to the pragmatic thinker. There is something quite attractive to many people about this manner of thinking. As a reaction against the obscurity of Hegelian thinking, it may serve the purpose of bringing philosophy out of the clouds and of cutting through a lot of useless nonsense that makes no difference to how we live our lives in the world. In this way, Pragmatism may be quite refreshing. It reintroduces us to common sense and encourages us to consider the real-world practical consequences of our beliefs. It is modest in its admission that human knowledge is always incomplete, and thus it keeps us open to the new discoveries and possibilities that the universe has in store for us.

It eschews dogmatism and is friendly toward innovation and change. Like a cowboy riding the range, the pragmatist is prepared to adapt to circumstances, deal with situations as they develop, and utilize the resources that are available to make his or her way through an environment that never completely reveals all of its secrets.

Of course, it is this very same cowboy attitude that might also cause some people to take pause. Like a Wild West outlaw, James might be seen by some as recklessly rebellious. He rejects important traditions and conventions only to replace them with doctrines that have a strange and counterintuitive appearance. In particular, he redefines "truth" to be something that many of us may think is not really "true" at all. In philosophy, Truth has traditionally been conceived as something objective, stable, and independent of the human mind. James, with his pragmatic theory, considers the truth to be none of these things. In his hands, it is transformed into an ever-changing, ever-evolving system of ideas that more or less coheres over time. Things "become" true or "become" false depending on their place within our current commonsense understanding of the world. This of course flies in the face of everything that Socrates or Plato had to say on the issue. If the truth is thought of as anything that "works" for us, then it would appear that everything is, at one time or another, true, and conversely, everything is, at one time or another, also false. But doesn't this just wreak havoc with the notion of Truth? Is James even talking about the same thing as other philosophers who are concerned with the idea of Truth?

For instance, when James tells us that it is true that God exists, what he is really telling us is that for a large number of people, the *belief* in God produces useful effects. But this is probably not what most theists mean when they say "God exists." What they really mean is that there is an entity, God, that abides *independent* of their minds. For James, however, saying that God exists means only that God is a useful idea *within* the human mind. Most philosophers, nonetheless, want to know if the idea of God in the human mind corresponds to a real being that exists outside and independent of the human mind. But James never addresses this sort of question. Perhaps his focus on human mental states is a consequence of his training in psychology. While James does certainly have useful contributions to make in this regard, it may also be the case that his philosophical commitment to "real" Truth is compromised by this focus. As Bertrand Russell complains, "James is interested in religion as a human phenomenon, but shows little interest in the objects which religion contemplates. He wants people to be happy, and if belief in God makes them happy let them believe in Him."[29] But is what makes people happy always true? As Plato held, isn't it the case that contentment and satisfaction with our beliefs often results in ignorance of the real truth? Is the pragmatist, perhaps, like one of the prisoners in Plato's cave?

Pragmatism influenced a whole generation of Anglo-American thinkers, and it remains an enormously influential philosophy today. Its down-to-earth and practical approach to philosophy appeals to many people who see in it an alternative to the abstract, and often baffling, perspectives of Hegelianism and other schools of continental thinking.[30] However, as noted, one of the prices paid by Pragmatism for its clarity and "common sense" is a strange sleight of hand in regard to the truth. The truth, in Pragmatism, starts to take on a distinctively subjectivist appearance and thus departs from the traditional conception of Truth as an objective phenomenon that exists independent of human belief. What is the truth according to Jamesean Pragmatism? Just those beliefs that work for us and that help us to get along in the world. Furthermore, what is true changes over time according to our needs and the state of our learning. This sort of viewpoint is bound to rub many philosophers the wrong way, and among those who did object to James's viewpoint on the truth was the influential analytic thinker Bertrand Russell.

BERTRAND RUSSELL

© Juneko J. Robinson

Bertrand Russell (1872–1970), is arguably the most important of all British analytic philosophers. Nicholas Griffin writes, "Analytic philosophy itself owes its existence more to Russell than to any other philosopher."[31] Such a tribute might seem hyperbolic, but in many ways it is justified. Russell is not only responsible for some of the most significant and innovative developments in modern, formal logic, he also worked tirelessly to popularize an approach to philosophy that showcased the application of these logical methods to traditional philosophical problems and issues. His clear, straightforward, and down-to-earth writing exhibits an analytical style that many admire and that has made his ideas accessible to a wide audience of readers outside of academia. For all of these reasons, along with his activist political spirit, Russell was awarded the Nobel Prize in Literature in 1950. Highlighting the distinctively analytic perspective that Russell brought to philosophy, Anders Österling, in his presentation speech to the Nobel Prize committee, said of Russell:

> His whole life's work is a stimulating defense of the reality of common sense. As a philosopher he pursues the line from the classical English empiricism, from Locke and Hume. His attitude toward the idealistic dogmas is a most independent one and quite frequently one of opposition. The great philosophical systems evolved on the Continent he regards, so to speak, from the chilly, windswept, and distinctive perspective of the English Channel.[32]

In these remarks a sharp contrast is drawn between the "chilly, windswept" English perspective of analytic philosophy and the "idealistic dogmas" of the continental systems of philosophy. This comparison calls attention to the fact that, unlike thinkers such as Kant and Hegel, Russell never once and for all settled on a complete and final system of his own. Rather, he seems to have been concerned mainly with the ongoing and open-ended pursuit of logical inquiry and analysis. His exploration of philosophical topics led him, at various points in his career, to hold and then discard a wide variety of positions. Therefore, what appears to be distinctive about Russell as a philosopher is not so much the content of his writing but rather the style and method of procedure that he developed during the course of his thinking. This style includes an adherence to the principles of logic, a respect for the insights and discoveries of science, and a drive for linguistic clarity and concision. In tribute to these characteristics, Russell has been hailed by many as a champion of level-headed "common sense." On the other hand, some thinkers have criticized Russell's analytic approach for being overly glib and even shallow in how it treats certain traditional philosophical issues. In any case, whether one loves or hates him, it is impossible to deny that Russell is among the most influential philosophers of the twentieth century.

In what follows I shall emphasize the development of Russell's analytic approach to philosophy as a reaction against the dominant Hegelian perspective of his time. After we examine Russell's criticisms of Hegelianism, we may then explore a few of the themes that have held a place of prominence in his own writing. Specifically, we will look at Russell's logic, his theory of descriptions, and his thoughts on the nature and purpose of philosophy. These topics will also provide us with a bridge by which we may then later cross over to discuss the ideas of Russell's most well-known student, Ludwig Wittgenstein.

Russell's Rejection of Hegel

Russell did not start out his life as what we would now call an analytic thinker. Initially, as a student at Cambridge he was, like many others, attracted to Hegelian philosophy. Russell writes in his autobiography that it was under the influence of John McTaggart (1866–1925) that he, for two or three years, cultivated this perspective. Russell even claims that he recalls the precise moment, walking along Trinity Lane, when he first became a Hegelian:

> I had gone to buy a tin of tobacco, and was going back with it along
> Trinity Lane, when suddenly I threw it up in the air and exclaimed:
> "Great God in boots!—the ontological argument is sound!"[33]

Russell's Hegelianism did not last long. His driving passion had always been mathematics and logic, and it seems that Russell ultimately came to find Hegel's own system of logic to be unsatisfactory. You will recall, from the discussion in Chapter 10, that Hegel had claimed "The Truth is the whole." What this suggests, Russell tells us, is that no true statement can be made of anything but the whole. When we talk about particular things within the realm of Being, this means that there is nothing absolutely true that can be said about individuals apart from their connections to all other things that exist. Because, according to Hegel, the truth of all things depends on their dialectical relationship to all other things in the universe, there is "only one true statement,"[34] and this is the statement that encapsulates everything: the Absolute. All other statements can only be fragmentary articulations of partial truths. So, if Hegel is correct, it seems to follow that I cannot say anything that is really true about this particular computer, or this particular table, or this particular pencil. But, Russell insists, that is absurd. We assuredly do utter true statements about particular things all of the time. Hegel's claim that the only real knowledge is knowledge of the whole is ridiculous because if it were correct "there would be no knowledge," and, Russell tells us, "this is enough to make us suspect a mistake somewhere."[35] The mistake, according to Russell, lies in the metaphysical "holism" of Hegelianism.

Hegel had presumed that the universe is something like an interrelated system of properties that both give rise to and reside within an underlying substance. This substance, *Geist*, consists of and contains all other things as aspects of its own Being. To understand the whole, you must understand all of the ways in which particular phenomena are related to one another, and this requires that the mind decipher the underlying logic governing the universe and its unfolding. From the perspective of the finite mind, such a task must commence by abstracting from particular things toward an understanding of how their particularity reflects something of the infinite. According to Hegelianism, to grasp the truth you must think your way from the particular toward the absolute. The logic implied here is a logic of synthesis. Because the Truth is the whole, and because all things are interconnected, we must work to synthesize an understanding of how all things interrelate. The universe, according to this view, cannot truly be understood by analyzing it into its parts. The universe is always more than its parts. It is a "gestalt" that consists of the dynamic relationships generated by way of interaction between those parts. Only after we understand the overarching, dialectical logic of this gestalt will all of the pieces within it make sense. We can't know the truth of the parts until we comprehend the Truth of the whole.

Russell suggests that this Hegelian worldview is a mistake. If it were correct, we could not know anything until we knew everything, and this is just contrary to our common sense, Russell contends. It is clearly the case that we do know many particular and individual things even though we cannot comprehend the universe as a whole. Therefore, there is a fallacy involved in the Hegelian "holistic" view of reality. Instead, Russell tells us, the universe is better conceived of as a collection of interrelated, yet distinct, things which we can know independent of one another. This is what science presumes. Though scientists can never know all things, they can come to know some things through the "piecemeal investigation of the world."[36] This belief, that we can gain real knowledge by examining the bits and pieces of reality, is the basis of Russell's analytic approach to philosophy.

Logical Atomism

It has already been stated that Russell's approach to philosophy is heavily influenced by his views on logic; however, it needs to be emphasized that the logic of Russell is a very special form that differs from the logic adhered to by Aristotle and Hegel. You will recall that in Aristotle's logic, statements are interpreted in terms of a subject/predicate construction, and the structure of these statements is held to mirror the actual structure of the world. Additionally, Hegel's logic is a dialectical form of thinking that interprets the world as an ongoing synthesis of contradictory elements. Generally speaking, in the logical systems of both of these thinkers, the universe is imagined as a fundamental substance that supports and sustains a variety of dependent properties. These properties are thought to be *internally* related to one another insofar as they all share preestablished connections within Being itself. All things exist inside of Being, so to speak, and so only by understanding the relationships that hold between particular things within the "bubble" of Being can we determine the nature of anything at all. The logical systems of both Aristotle and Hegel share the presupposition that all individual things, in their very nature, share an underlying and substantial likeness with all other things by virtue of the fact that all existent things participate in a common substrate that grounds the universe. Individual entities are like flowers that all draw from the same soil for nourishment, and thus any logical system that claims to describe this world must recognize the interconnectedness that binds all things together. All things, in this way of thinking, are fundamentally one.

Russell rejects this traditional way of thinking and instead develops a logical system based on his view that the world actually consists of particular things that are linked to one another only by external relationships. Russell does not presuppose the existence of preestablished connections within Being as a whole precisely because he does not suppose that there is necessarily some sort of underlying unity to all things that exist. Beginning from the way the world appears to our sensory observations, Russell claims that objects in the world are only externally related to one another like free-floating atoms that come into contact and go out of contact with one another. The Russellian world, unlike the Aristotelian or the Hegelian world, is one in which particular things have no necessary, preestablished interconnections. The world is made up of many things that are, in large part, disconnected and which share no underlying, hidden unity. Whereas for Hegel the appearance of disconnectedness is an illusion, for Russell it is the most obvious and commonsensical of all realities. There is no preestablished harmony that governs existence. Rather, as he writes in *Introduction to Mathematical Philosophy*, "... the existence of the world is an accident—i.e., it is not logically necessary."[37] Thus, according to Russell, a new system of logic that resonates with this reality needs to be developed. "Logical atomism" is the name that Russell, at least sometimes, gave to his new approach to logic.

As its name suggests, logical atomism is a system that conceives of logical relationships between statements as akin to the relationships that hold between discontinuous atomic bits of matter. Just as atomists, like Democritus, hold that all things can be explained in terms of the collision of simple and indivisible bits of material substance, the logical atomist claims that all logical relationships can be understood in terms of the connections between indivisible atomic facts. These atomic facts are real states of affairs in the world, and each fact corresponds to a statement (or proposition) that can be expressed in language. The structure of language, and thus of the world, can be understood by understanding the ways in which discrete atomic facts combine with one another in an orderly fashion. Unlike Aristotelian or Hegelian logic, logical atomism does not restrict itself to representing statements in terms of a subject/predicate form. Instead, there are a multitude of differing connections that may hold between the factual atoms of the world and the statements in our language.

In Aristotle's logic, there are only four types of statements:

Universal Affirmative = All S is P
Universal Negative = No S is P
Particular Affirmative = Some S is P
Particular Negative = Some S is not P

Every one of these statements represents the intersection of a subject (S) and a predicate (P). Any translation from natural language into the formal language of Aristotelian logic must endeavor to fit statements into one of these four forms. For instance, the statement "Mary is Joe's wife" would be understood as a Universal Affirmative statement, having the standard form "All Mary is the wife of Joe," or more simply as "All M is J." Here, "Mary" (M) is the subject and "wife of Joe" (J) is the predicate. In Russell's logic this same statement would, instead, be interpreted as representing a relationship between the atomic constituents "Mary" and "Joe." Mary and Joe could be represented symbolically with single letters; say, "m" for "Mary," and "j" for "Joe." These atomic particulars share a relationship with one another; namely, the relationship "being the wife of." We could symbolize this relationship with the capital letter "R." The entire complex statement, "Mary is Joe's wife" could then be symbolized as "mRj." Each element of the statement is thus represented in terms of a discrete atomic particle. You may wonder why this is any improvement over the traditional logic of Aristotle. What difference does it make whether you symbolize a statement in one of these ways or the other?

Russell believes that the improvement his method of notation makes over the older Aristotelian form of logic has, at least partly, to do with its ability to accurately and precisely represent the different sorts of relationships that hold between concrete individuals like Mary and Joe. In the example given above, for instance, the relationship between Mary and Joe is one that is "asymmetrical." To say that Mary is Joe's wife is to say that Mary has a very particular type of relationship to Joe that Joe does not have to Mary. If it is true that Mary is Joe's wife, it is not also true that Joe is Mary's wife. Rather, Joe must be Mary's *husband*.[38] The relationship "being a wife" is, thus, asymmetrical. Using Aristotelian notation above, we represented the statement "Mary is Joe's wife" by writing "All M is J." However, this way of symbolizing the statement gives us no way to make a distinction between this sort of asymmetrical relationship and other sorts of "symmetrical" relationships. This is because "is," which always appears in Aristotelian notation, is ambiguous. It represents a wide variety of relationships without making clear distinctions between them. For instance, suppose we wanted to represent the statement "Mary is married to Joe," again using "M" to represent "Mary," and "J" to represent "married to Joe." We would again have a statement in the Universal Affirmative form that reads "All M is J." The form of this statement appears superficially to be the same as the form of "All Mary is Joe's wife," and yet we know that the real relationship being expressed is fundamentally different. In this latter case, the relationship "being married to" is symmetrical in nature because if Mary is married to Joe it must also be the case that Joe is married to Mary.

We can use another example to further illustrate the point:

"New York is bigger than San Francisco." = "All N is S." (Universal Affirmative)

The relationship "being bigger than" is an asymmetrical relationship. If New York is bigger than San Francisco, then it is not also the case that San Francisco is bigger than New York. Yet this relationship, as represented in Aristotelian notation, looks just the same as the following symmetrical relationship:

"New York is 3,000 miles away from San Francisco." = "All N is S." (Universal Affirmative)

The relationship "being 3,000 miles away" is symmetrical. If New York is 3,000 miles away from San Francisco, then it is also the case that San Francisco is 3,000 miles away from New York.

Thus, at least one problem with Aristotelian logic is that it is not flexible enough to accurately bring out the unique and diverse forms of relationships that really do exist in the world in which we live. Russell's system of notation is better able to depict these sorts of details. For instance, let's take the statement "Mary is Joe's Wife." Above we symbolized this relationship as "mRj," which means "M has a relationship with J." Suppose however, we wanted to show that this relationship (namely, of being a wife) is asymmetrical. We could write the following:

$$(mRj) + \sim(jRm)$$

Here, we have used the symbol "+" to represent the natural language word "and." We've also used the symbol "∼" to represent the natural language word "not." The letter "R" is used here to represent a type of relationship between Mary and Joe. Reading from the left to the right, we can thus see, using this means of notation, that Mary has a certain relationship to Joe, and it is not the case that Joe has this same relationship to Mary. This brings out a sort of detail that cannot be represented in more traditional forms of logic.

Let's also look at how the examples concerning the different kinds of relationships between New York and San Francisco are given more clarity with the sort of notation that Russell suggests:

"New York is bigger than San Francisco." = "(nRs) + ∼(sRn)" (asymmetrical)
"New York is 3,000 miles away from San Francisco." = "(nRs) + (sRn)" (symmetrical)

Here we can tell at a glance that the relationship in the first case is intended to be asymmetrical whereas in the second case the relationship is intended to be symmetrical. This is an improvement in precision and clarity over the older subject/predicate means of interpretation, but it also calls into question an underlying metaphysical assumption that both Aristotle and Hegel had taken for granted. If it is clearer and more accurate to represent the relations that occur in our language in terms of externally connected atomic bits, and if the structure of language mirrors the structure of reality, then it would follow that reality has a structure that is quite different from that suggested by both Aristotle and Hegel. The universe, as described by logical atomism, is not one continuous thing. It is, rather, composed of discrete bits that may or may not become connected with one another in a wide variety of relationships.

Russell developed his system of logic to a very high degree of sophistication in collaboration with other pioneers in the field, including Gottlob Frege (1848–1925), Giuseppe Peano (1858–1932), and Alfred North Whitehead (1861–1947). The aspiration of all these thinkers was the same: the creation of a completely formal language that would not depend on any particular content. A logical system is supposed to be completely *syntactical*, which means that it is a system that expresses universally binding structural relationships having nothing to do with subject matter. A pure logical system should be applicable to any subject. It would delineate the proper order by which we think about anything. As Russell states, "It is one of the marks of a proposition of logic that, given a suitable language, such a proposition can be asserted in such a language by a person who knows the syntax without knowing a single word of the vocabulary."[39] A purely logical language, in other words, is a language based solely on the rules governing relationships between variables. You do not need to know the content or the meaning of the variables themselves to understand the formal relationships between the variables. For instance, in

---

B o x 12.1 Modern Logical Notation

Bertrand Russell was key in the development of modern symbolic logic. At the foundation of this system is the idea that all complex statements are built out of simple, atomic statements that have been connected to one another according to a set of consistent relations.

A number of formal symbols have been introduced by modern logicians to represent the recurrent relationships that hold between atomic statements in our language. Like most things in philosophy, there is little uniform agreement concerning which of these symbols is best to use at all times. However, there is widespread agreement that the relationships represented by these symbols are a real part of our language. Some of the common symbols used today are as follows:

Negation: Usually represented using "–" or "~." Suppose that "A" represents the atomic statement "Alice is nice." The negation of this statement, which would be "It is not the case that Alice is nice," is represented as "~A."

Conjunction: Usually represented using "+" or "&." Suppose that "A" is the atomic statement "Alice is nice," and "B" is the atomic statement "Barry is mean." The conjunction of these two statements yields the complex statement "Alice is nice and Barry is mean." This would be represented as "A+B."

Disjunction: Usually represented using "v," which is taken from the Latin word "vel" meaning "or." Suppose either Alice is nice or Barry is mean. This would be represented as "AvB."

Conditional: Usually represented using "⊃" or "→." The conditional is normally stated in an "if, then" form in natural language. Suppose you wanted to say "If Alice is nice, then Barry is mean." This would be represented as "A⊃B."

the example given above, if you understand the syntactic rules of formation, a glance tells you that "(sRn) + ~(nRs)" represents an asymmetrical relationship, and this can be understood even though no particular type of asymmetrical relationship is referred to. This formula applies to "being the wife of," "being older than," "being larger than," etc. All of these particular kinds of relationships share the underlying formal structure of being asymmetrical. A pure logic should give us the tools to talk about such fundamental structures without reference to content. In this sense, logic is the study of syntax and not of content.

The problem with how we normally speak, according to Russell, is that our natural language is filled with ambiguity. For this reason alone, it is impossible to fully develop a system of pure logic without the creation of an artificial language that is free of ambiguity. "Because language is misleading, as well as because it is diffuse and inexact when applied to logic (for which it was never intended), logical symbolism is absolutely necessary to any exact or thorough treatment of our subject."[40] Russell believed that underneath all systems of thought, including mathematics, there lay a fundamental and uniform logical order. The most major contribution of Russell to the history of philosophy has turned out to be his work on a modern form of logic that seems to get close to this fundamental order. His contributions have since developed into a system of staggering sophistication and usefulness. In addition to becoming a field of philosophical study in its own right, modern symbolic logic has supplied the technical basis for the production of computer programs that keep us occupied, entertained, and connected in a buzz of high-tech activity unimaginable before the twentieth century. We have Russell partly to thank (or curse) for this.

Epistemology

As already noted, Russell is an advocate of a piecemeal scientific method, which characterizes the quest for knowledge as an ongoing and fragmentary endeavor. Human beings never know everything once and for all. Rather, we develop greater and greater degrees of understanding by taking in bits and pieces of information through the scientific investigation of various regions of the universe. Like James, Russell suggests that we should look at the world if we want to learn something about it. Yet unlike James, Russell is not a "radical empiricist." While a good portion of our understanding of reality comes from observation, Russell tells us that empirical observation of the external world is not the sole source of our knowledge. The principles of logic, for instance, are not things that we can see, taste, touch, hear, or feel. Rather, they are principles that are directly knowable by means of mental intuition. Our knowledge of Being is built up, bit by bit, from the apprehension of both empirical and intuitive insights, which like the variables in a logical equation comprise discrete atomic bits of information. We come to truly understand reality when we are able to clearly analyze our thoughts and observations into the basic atomic structures out of which they are constructed and to understand the connections between those structures.

According to Russell, our understanding of the world seems to start "somewhere in the middle."[41] What he means by this is that our normal, everyday, commonsense way of thinking is, on the one hand, built on certain basic but unexamined foundations, while on the other hand it points beyond itself toward a variety of very complicated but unanticipated consequences. When we think and reason, we normally start with a middle level of complexity, taking for granted many fundamentals and not foreseeing all of the possible conclusions that are entailed by our thought processes. In mathematics, for instance, most people are not aware of the fundamental definitions on which numbers and basic arithmetical operations are based, and they obviously are not capable of anticipating all of the possible outcomes that will result from carrying out complex mathematical calculations. Yet this does not prevent people from doing math. The average person takes for granted an awful lot when engaging in the practical, down-to-earth job of adding, multiplying, or dividing numbers. Likewise in our understanding of the general nature of reality, our common sense takes for granted many things and does not anticipate all that follows from the assumptions under which we operate. The purpose of philosophy, Russell believes, lies in its drive to, first of all, analyze our thinking so as to reveal and make explicit its fundamental assumptions, and second, to follow and explicate the chains of reasoning that lead from basic principles toward more and more complicated conclusions. The aspiration toward clarity is a major aspect of what philosophy is all about, claims Russell, and clarity is achieved by analyzing our assumptions and systematically demonstrating what is implied by those assumptions, step by step. In this manner, the philosopher strives to understand, and eliminate, "all the vagueness and confusion that underlie our ordinary ideas."[42]

In his book *The Problems of Philosophy*, Russell undertakes a step-by-step excavation of human thinking, in many ways similar to the project carried out by Descartes in *Meditations on First Philosophy*, and attempts to demonstrate the fundamental constituents from which our knowledge of reality is formulated. Although some of the details that Russell lays out in this book would be altered or even abandoned by him later on, the overall scheme traced out in *The Problems of Philosophy* gives us a good sense of how it is that Russell applies his logical method to the analysis and interpretation of traditional philosophical problems. In what follows we will specifically take a look at the line of reasoning that led Russell to his well-known ideas concerning knowledge by acquaintance and knowledge by description.

Like Descartes, Russell notes that our senses do not necessarily give us direct access to the real nature of the world as it exists in-itself. As an example, he draws our attention to how a table appears to us. The color, texture, and shape of a table may, at first glance, seem to correspond with objective qualities that exist in the object itself, but an instant of reflection shows us that this is not the case. Take the color of the table, for example. When you survey any table carefully, you will notice that it does not have only one, uniform color. Viewed from various perspectives under various light conditions, the table appears to change hue. Under very bright conditions, the table may appear to the eye to be a light brown in color. Under dimmer light conditions, the same table appears black. Change the color of the light and the table appears also to change color. It may even, under certain circumstances, appear to have different colored spots that dance and move across its surface. The changing conditions under which we view the table encourage us to see it as possessing a whole variety of different shades. Thus, writes Russell, "to avoid favouritism, we are compelled to deny that, in itself, the table has any one particular color."[43] The same goes for the texture and the shape of the table. Depending on the perspective we take, the table will appear to have a variety of differing textures and shapes. If I run my hand over the surface of the table, it may feel smooth. But if I look at the surface of the table with a microscope, the texture appears rough. If I look at the table from above, it appears rectangular. But if I look at it from a sitting position, it appears to be unevenly shaped. If there is a real table "out there," it seems, then, we cannot know it simply by appealing to these sorts of *immediate*, commonsense observations. At best, we *infer* the existence of some sort of stable entity that we call the table from the collection of our various observations. The table is never experienced once and for all as it exists in-itself. Rather, we infer the existence of something we call a table only from changing and momentary ideas of colors, shapes, textures, and other sorts of sense impressions. What this demonstrates, Russell suggests, is that our sensory observations do not give us immediate and infallible access to the true nature of the world around us. There is some connection that holds between the world and our observations, but it is not the simple and direct connection that common sense would lead us to believe. The world around us is not exactly the same as the sense impressions that we experience.

To clarify the way in which we infer the existence of an objective world from the experiences we collect by means of observation, Russell draws a distinction between "sense data," on the one hand, and "sensation," on the other. Sense data are the immediate objects of our experience. They are the subjective mind-dependent data that appear directly to our minds and that cannot be doubted away. I may be able to doubt that there is a brown table "out there," but when I think I see the color brown, it is immediately and indubitably apparent that I am experiencing the sense data of brownness. This brownness may not correspond with anything outside of my awareness, but regardless of that fact I cannot deny that I am having the experience nonetheless. Such sense data are bits of information that are known to me directly and immediately by means of "sensation." Sensation is just my awareness of sense data. If the sense data comprise the color brown, then the sensation is the awareness of brown. The reason Russell wants to make this distinction is to differentiate between the thing that is experienced and the formal experience of the thing. Even if the thing that is experienced has no objective existence beyond the mind, we can still clearly mark a division between awareness as such and the object of awareness. To put it simply, the sense data is the thing of which we are immediately aware, and the sensation is the awareness itself.

Having made clear the difference between sense data and sensation, Russell wonders what the relationship is that exists between sense data and the objective world. Granting that it is directly and intuitively certain that I experience brownness, what relationship does this experience of brownness have with a possible world outside of my mind? As Descartes before him observed, Russell admits that there is no absolutely certain way to assure ourselves that sense data correspond to anything outside of the mind. "There is no logical impossibility in the supposition that the whole of life is a dream, in which we ourselves create all the objects that come before us."[44] The sense data that appear to us may, in fact, simply be ideas that are floating around in our minds. They might just be part of our imaginations, conjured up for no particular reason whatsoever. We might be living in a dream world of illusions that has no connection to a world of objective reality outside of that dream world. There is no evidence that can completely eliminate this thought as a possibility. However, Russell tells us, even though this is the case, we must keep in mind that such a speculation is merely one hypothesis among others. Yes, all of the sense data that appear to us may originate from our own minds. On the other hand, it is also possible that the sense data we experience may originate from outside of our minds in the realm of real physical objects. Given that we have these two competing hypotheses, we must ask ourselves which is the most probable.

The "natural view" suggests to us that the sense data appearing to us are the result of an independently existing reality. When I have the sensation of a brown table, my instincts encourage me to believe that this sensation is the result of a stimulus originating from an objective and independent reality outside of my mind. Russell admits that this does not guarantee that my instincts are correct, but it does suggest itself as the simplest, most straightforward, and therefore the most probable means of explaining the appearance of the table. If the sensation of the brown table was merely mind-dependent, then we would expect the table to lack the sort of consistency in appearance that it does, in fact, seem to have. I can reinvestigate the table again and again, gathering more observations over a long period of time. I can leave the room in which the table exists and come back later on to find the table in the same place. Certainly, I may be in the grip of an especially consistent hallucination or of a vivid dream; however, it is much simpler and more straightforward to presume, under the circumstances, that there really is a table "out there" that is the cause of my table-sensations. In addition, Russell tells us, the more often that we find our observations harmonizing with the other observations that make up our world, the more confident we become that these observations are informative of a world independent of our own minds. For instance, the brown table I observe appears to my eyes to have a smooth surface. This visual observation is confirmed when I lay a piece of paper on the table and find that I can write easily on its surface. These two sensations, one visual and the other tactile, seem to harmonize and confirm one another, leading us to believe that there really is some sort of object "out there" that has something like a smooth surface. The more of these sorts of observations that we collect, the more likely it seems to us that the sense data we perceive are not simply random ideas conjured up by our own minds. The more consistent and harmonious our observations, the more likely it seems that they represent, in some manner, a reality independent of our thoughts. We must always remember, of course, that this guarantees nothing. Like Hume before him, Russell encourages us to remain open to ongoing future observations that might undermine our hypotheses about reality. If I suddenly observed the brown table collapsing into a pile of chocolate pudding, I would be justified in wondering whether I was dreaming. Until something unexpected like that happens however, the simplest, and therefore the best, hypothesis is that there is a real object before me that has something like the qualities I recognize as a table.

The sensations we experience do not perfectly mirror the world around us, but they do seem to give us an indication of what the world is like. How is this possible? How do we build up a description of the world out of our sensations of things like brownness, smoothness, shape, etc.? How is it possible that the sense data appearing in the human mind are able to describe the world outside of the human mind?

Knowledge by Acquaintance and Knowledge by Description

Our knowledge of the things making up the world comes to us, according to Russell, in two different ways: by acquaintance and by description. Knowledge by acquaintance consists of those things of which we are directly and immediately aware. Sense data, for instance, are known by acquaintance. When I have the experience of "brownness," I am acquainted with the color brown. The experience is one which requires no further reasoning or analysis. It is basic, atomic, and incapable of being broken down any further. When I look at a brown table, I can always analyze my experience of the table into its component sense data, each of which I know by acquaintance. The brownness, the smoothness, and the shape of the table are all experienced by me immediately through my various senses, and thus I know them by acquaintance. The table itself, however, is never known directly and intuitively. It is an entity that I construct out of the sense data with which I am acquainted. The table is a brown, smooth, and rectangular thing. Each of these atomic sense data contribute to my knowledge of the table, but only by way of a process of mental construction. The entity that I call "the table" is thus built up out of atomic bits of information I have collected together, and with which I am acquainted, to yield a complex description. Knowledge by description is that form of knowledge that results from the process of bringing together bits of information with which we are acquainted.

"All our knowledge, both knowledge of things and knowledge of truths, rests upon acquaintance as its foundation."[45] When we claim to know something, we should be able to analyze that knowledge into its constituent components, and each of those components should be something with which we are directly acquainted. This claim, that all real knowledge is reducible to ideas with which we have direct experience, recalls Hume's empiricism and his belief that all true knowledge is rooted in sense impressions. However, according to Russell, it is not correct to claim that the only things with which we are acquainted are sensory impressions. If this was the sole source of our acquaintanceship, he claims, then we could only know about what happens in the here and now. We would have no way of talking about things past. A world comprising only sense data would be a world in which we simply experienced things like "brownness," "hardness," "smoothness," etc. in an ever-present "now." Of course, this is not the sort of world in which we do live. We experience our world as having a past, and so, Russell tells us, it is clear that, in addition to sense data, we also have acquaintance with things in our memory. When we remember something, we recall things that are not currently present to the senses and thus we are able to reconstruct a past.

There are other things as well with which we are immediately acquainted according to Russell. For instance, we all have immediate and intuitive acquaintance with ourselves. We are self-conscious creatures who can introspect and reflect on our experiences. We find ourselves being aware of being aware of our experiences, and this is something that Russell seems to think sets us apart from other animals. When we gaze at a sunset, we are aware that we are gazing at a sunset, whereas a dog simply sees an orb of light descending in the sky. When we wander through the woods, we are aware of and savor the experience of nature, whereas a deer simply scampers through the trees. This sort of introspection is an expression of an inner form of uniquely human life with which we are all acquainted. Whether or not this means, additionally, that there exists an "I," a unique "me" with which I am also acquainted, Russell is less certain. He suggests that there are reasons to suspect that we are all acquainted with such an entity. For instance, when I speak of particular sense data, like brownness, its seems as if there must be some "I" that exists to be acquainted with that sense data. However, it is difficult to pin down exactly what this "I" is, other than to say it is some subject that must be there to have an experience of other things. Consequently, Russell is content to conclude that the question of the existence of an "I" is a difficult one, and thus he leaves it open as to whether or not we are really acquainted with such an entity.

Sense data, memory, and ourselves are all particular things with which we are acquainted. In addition to these, we are also acquainted with what Russell calls "universals." Universals are general principles, or concepts, without which it would be impossible for us to formulate complete sentences that express truths. Among the sorts of universals with which we are acquainted are abstract concepts such as "whiteness, diversity, brotherhood, and so on."[46] Some universals, like "whiteness," we become acquainted with by means of abstracting from instances of particular sense data. I may observe, for instance, a variety of white things and then generalize from those particulars to an understanding of the quality "whiteness." Once I am thus acquainted with this quality, I may then form sentences concerning white things in general. "These sense data are white" expresses a truth that can be asserted about, say, the visual sensation of snow once I have developed an acquaintanceship with the general concept of whiteness. There are, of course, a whole host of other universals with which we must become acquainted if we are to engage in meaningful discourse. Among them are relations of space and time, resemblance, and various logical relationships. Russell goes into some detail discussing and elaborating on these various sorts of universals, but the upshot of his discussion is to point out that the truths we express in language are possible as a result of our acquaintance with particular sense data in combination with our acquaintance with general principles. When we combine, in sentences, references to particular things and their relationships to general principles, we produce complex assertions that are capable of expressing truths about the world.

By formulating our thoughts about the world in sentences, we are capable of expressing ideas that reflect the order of reality either truly or falsely. All knowledge is based on acquaintance with things like sense data, memory, ourselves, and universal concepts, and these atomic constituents with which we are acquainted are organized by us into complex descriptions of the world. When the formal organization of these descriptions corresponds to the order of things as they actually exist in the world, then we say that the sentence containing the descriptions is true. If they fail to correspond with a state of affairs in the world, then we say that the sentence is false. "Thus a belief is *true* when it corresponds to a certain associated complex, and *false* when it does not."[47] For instance, take the assertion "Desdemona loves Cassio." Here "Desdemona" is a description of an entity (black hair, female, etc.) with which one could potentially be acquainted, as is "Cassio." The idea of "love" is a universal concept that expresses a certain type of relationship with which we may also be acquainted. The full sentence "Desdemona loves Cassio" will be true if there is a state of affairs in the world such that there is an entity corresponding to the description of Desdemona who is having a love relationship with an entity that corresponds to the description of Cassio. If we were to represent "Desdemona" with the letter "d," "Cassio" with the letter "c," and the relationship "Love" with the letter "L," we could symbolize the complex relationship being asserted in this sentence as: dLc. The assertion "dLc" is true if, in fact, there is a d that shares relationship L with c.

The Role of Philosophy

Through the analysis of our linguistic assertions about the world, Russell believes that we can become clear about the structure of reality and our place within it. Even if philosophy does not offer us final and definitive answers to all of our questions, it does help us to organize and make sense of our experiences. Russell's manner of approaching philosophy emphasizes analysis and the reduction of complex forms of knowledge into simple, discrete, and manageable bits of information. If we can understand the atomic particles out of which our knowledge is built, and if we can understand the relationships between those particles, then, Russell contends, we can say that we truly grasp what we are talking about. There is much here that reminds us of Descartes and of Hume. From Descartes, Russell has borrowed the method of analysis and synthesis found in the Cartesian Method. From Hume, Russell has learned to conceive of knowledge as comprising atomic bits of data. The major and original contribution that Russell himself has bequeathed to philosophy is his own formalization of these ideas into a new system of logic, which is useful for clarifying and analyzing our assertions about the world. It is in this way that his writings have since inspired the analytic style of philosophizing, which has come to dominate in the English-speaking world today. Following Russell, analytic philosophers tend to view philosophy as intimately allied with the natural sciences. Whereas science investigates the content of the world, according to the analytic tradition the correct role of philosophy is to investigate the logical form of the world. As Russell writes, the role of philosophy is to "examine critically the principles employed in science and in daily life; it searches out any inconsistencies there may be in these principles, and it only accepts them when, as a result of a critical inquiry, no reason for rejecting them has appeared."[48] In this light, the rightful place of philosophy is a critical one. It must concern itself only with issues that can be addressed by means of logic, analysis, and scientific scrutiny.

In reading Russell's works, one comes away with the sense that philosophy must, while allying itself with science, distance itself from religion and mysticism. In a number of papers, including such works as "Why I Am Not a Christian" and "Mysticism and Logic," Russell expresses the view that when our thinking starts to stray into mysticism, we also stray away from the proper realm of philosophy. "Mysticism is, in essence, little more than a certain intensity and depth of feeling with regard to what is believed about the universe."[49] While mysticism does, Russell admits, inspire thinkers with a great deal of passion and motivation, it also tends to encourage a worldview that must ultimately be rejected by true philosophers and scientists alike. For one, mystics downplay analytic understanding and instead emphasize the role of insight and revelation. Second, mystics tend to view the world as a unity rather than as a plurality. Third, they deny the reality of time, and finally, they deny the existence of evil. All of these characteristics, Russell contends, are in direct opposition to philosophy as conceived along the analytic model. Philosophy must instead remain committed to logical analysis and the piecemeal investigation of the *natural* world.

LUDWIG WITTGENSTEIN

During his lifetime, Russell was a troublemaker. He was jailed for antiwar activities, fired from academic positions due to his supposedly "immoral" stance on premarital sex, and he was quite outspoken in his criticisms of world political leaders. To some, there is an element of incongruity in the photos of this well-bred, well-dressed, pipe-smoking English gentleman sitting among students on city sidewalks as he takes part in political protests. His conservative appearance may seem to stand in contrast to his sometimes radical views on the world, but in reality there is nothing too

© Juneko J. Robinson

strange in this. Russell was committed to the position that logic and reason were important guides in how we should live our lives, and his ideas about morality, politics, and culture were always informed by solid arguments and well-thought-out lines of reasoning. Though his cultural, political, and moral writings have not had the same lasting impact as his writings on logic, they are a testament, nonetheless, to his commitment to philosophy as a way of life, and not simply as an academic discipline. Russell's career would, no doubt, have been much easier and much more placid had he not ventured into the tumultuous and troubling realm of current events and politics. However, it would also have been less interesting and less authentic.

Among the colorful figures with whom Russell was to become intimately associated during his unconventional life was the troubled yet brilliant student Ludwig Wittgenstein (1889–1951). Wittgenstein would, under the tutelage of Russell, make his own important and lasting contributions to analytic philosophy, but he would also go on to rebel against these contributions in ways of which Russell did not approve. In the section that follows, we will take a look at the two major works produced by Wittgenstein, examine the ways in which they resonate and conflict with one another, and briefly examine the influence that Wittgenstein has had on the world of both analytic and continental thought.

Few philosophers have had motion pictures made about them, but Wittgenstein is one of those who has.[50] Born into a wealthy and well-connected Viennese family, Wittgenstein's life was filled with drama, turmoil, and adventure as well as with intellectual accomplishment. It seems that part of the reason for Wittgenstein's emotional travails had to do with the fact that he was a homosexual during a time when this was neither understood nor tolerated. He began his education pursuing aeronautical engineering at Manchester University but soon became more interested in the mathematical side of things and so transferred to Cambridge University to study with Bertrand Russell. He remained at Cambridge for a couple of years before dropping out and retreating into seclusion in Norway. When World War I broke out, Wittgenstein enlisted in the Austrian Army and served with an artillery regiment on both the Eastern and the Southern Fronts. He was captured by the Italians in 1918 and remained a prisoner of war until 1919. It was while a prisoner that he finished the manuscript for the only book he would publish during his lifetime, *Tractatus Logico-Philosophicus*. With the help of Russell, Wittgenstein was able to publish this work and eventually to have it accepted as a doctoral dissertation at Cambridge University, thus fulfilling one of the requirements for the completion of his Ph.D. in philosophy. Because he believed that with the *Tractatus* he had solved all of the major problems of philosophy, Wittgenstein decided to give up philosophy and to become a primary school teacher. Apparently he was not very good at this, and so in 1926 he moved to Vienna and became a gardener instead.

While in Vienna, Wittgenstein supervised the design of a house for his sister, and he also had his interest in philosophy renewed when he became acquainted with members of the Vienna Circle, a group of philosophers who had been inspired by the *Tractatus*. Wittgenstein entered into regular conversations with this group and began to suspect that there were problems with the views he had formulated in his only book. Soon he secured a teaching job at Cambridge and began to work on the ideas that would ultimately become the substance of his second, posthumously published book, *Philosophical Investigations*. Wittgenstein's time at Cambridge was not happy, however, as he was not sociable and had a hard time getting along with others. So in 1947 he resigned his position. Shortly thereafter he was diagnosed with prostate cancer, a disease from which he died in 1951.

Tractatus Logico-Philosophicus

The only book that Wittgenstein published during his lifetime is a short, strange, and yet hugely influential work titled *Tractatus Logico-Philosophicus*. With this book, Wittgenstein initially believed that he had solved all of philosophy's major problems. In the preface, he writes that the main issue upon which such problems hinge is "the misunderstanding of the logic of our language."[51] If we just speak, write, and think clearly, logically, and precisely, our language, it turns out, is a completely adequate tool for fully understanding the world of which we are a part. Philosophical puzzles and conundrums are simply dissolved away when we correctly understand the logical rules which govern the way we speak, write, and think. This is because language maps directly onto reality, revealing the world's true form and thus, Wittgenstein argues, nothing is hidden. If we scrutinize the logical structure of language, we will also come to understand the logical structure of our reality. Consequently, the main purpose of the *Tractatus* is to show that language has a logical structure and to describe how it is that this logical structure maps onto the world itself.

The form of the *Tractatus* is unusual. It is organized around seven main statements. In addition to these seven statements, there are a number of subsidiary statements that elaborate and comment on the main assertions. The secondary elaborations are numbered with decimal points, so, for instance, comments on statement number 1 are listed as follows: 1.1, 1.11, 1.12, 1.13, 1.2, 1.21. The entire book is thus structured as a list of interlocking assertions. This barebones, stripped-down form of writing is intended to promote clarity and precision, although whether or not it really achieves this goal is questionable. In any case, we can get an overall understanding of Wittgenstein's intended argument by, first of all, looking at the seven major assertions that act as the anchor points of the work:

1. The world is everything that is the case.
2. What is the case, the fact, is the existence of atomic facts.
3. The logical picture of the facts is the thought.
4. The thought is the significant proposition.
5. Propositions are truth-functions of elementary propositions.
6. The general form of truth-function is: $[\bar{p}, \bar{\xi}, N(\bar{\xi})]$ [Every proposition is the result of successive applications of negation to elementary propositions.]
7. Whereof one cannot speak, thereof one must remain silent.

Taken together and in summary, these seven statements suggest that our world is wholly composed of the totality of facts that can be expressed through the propositions in our language. Furthermore, following Russell's philosophy of logical atomism, Wittgenstein conceives of the complex propositions in our language as composed of more elementary propositions. These elementary propositions, in addition to representing, or "picturing," the atomic facts that exist in the world, are governed by a formal set of rules. Anything that does not fall within the purview of this rule-based system of language falls outside of the realm of our world and thus we cannot speak of it. These are the main ideas conveyed in the *Tractatus*.

The theory put forward here is usually referred to as a "picture theory of meaning." The world, according to Wittgenstein, is made up of simple atomic objects. These simple atomic objects combine with one another, and these combinations constitute what Wittgenstein refers to as "facts." "In the atomic fact, objects hang one in another, like the members of a chain."[52] A fact, then, is a state of affairs that comes to be out of the interlocking structure of objects. The propositions in our language "reach out" to these facts and "picture" them by reflecting something of their "logical form." "What every picture, of whatever form, must have in common with reality to be able to represent it at all—rightly or falsely—is the logical form of reality."[53] Thus, to say that language "pictures" reality is not to say that it mirrors every single detail in a visual sense. Rather, there is something about the logical structure of language that parallels the logical structure of reality, and it is in this sense that language "pictures" the world. The sort of idea that Wittgenstein seems to have in mind, which was already anticipated by Russell, is the metaphor of a map.[54] When you look at a map of some terrain, what is significant is not necessarily the particular color or shape of the icons on the map, but the formal relationships between those icons. A road that is pictured on a map looks nothing like a road in the real world, but its orientation to other marks on the map shares a similar orientation to the actual road's relationship to things in the real world. You are able to navigate the real world according to the marks on a map because the formal organization of the map is something like the formal organization of things in the world. Likewise, according to Wittgenstein, the formal structure of our language allows us to understand the world because world and language share a common organizational structure. Language is a picture of reality in the way that a map is a picture of physical terrain. True statements are those that map onto reality correctly, and false statements are those that do not map onto reality correctly. The purpose of philosophy, then, is to clarify and analyze our language so that it produces a good map of reality.

Ordinary language obscures logical structure, and it is because of this that philosophy must work to move beyond natural language and create a purely formal system that reveals logical structure clearly. "Most questions and propositions of the philosophers result from the fact that we do not understand the logic of our language.... And so it is not to be wondered at that the deepest problems are really no problems."[55] Once the logical form of propositions is clearly understood and revealed, the truth of a situation becomes self-evident and nothing more is to be said. When we encounter traditional philosophical problems, Wittgenstein is suggesting, this is already a sign that something has gone wrong. When we use language properly, the world "shows" itself. Because language "reaches out" and touches the world as it really is, the careful use of language allows reality to "exhibit" itself. Wittgenstein does not give us any examples to illustrate his point, but if we recall Russell's discussion, from above, concerning symmetrical and asymmetrical relations, we can get a better understanding of what Wittgenstein is probably trying to articulate. Remember that Russell showed how the Aristotelian method of logical notation was not precise enough to clearly exhibit the formal difference between statements like "Mary is Joe's wife" and "Mary is married to Joe." Aristotelian logic, we might say, is akin to the careless use of ordinary language. It contains ambiguities (specifically in its use of the term "is"), which Russell's logic does away with. Russell's notation allows

---

B o x 12.2 Wittgenstein and Popular Culture

Wittgenstein is a thinker who has had a widespread effect on popular culture. He has inspired not only logicians and philosophers, but also filmmakers, comic artists, and novelists.

In 2000, *Time* magazine included Wittgenstein, along with Einstein, Freud, and Martin Luther King, Jr., in its list of the most influential people of the past 100 years (http://205.188.238.181/time/time100/scientist/profile/wittgenstein.html).

The book *Wittgenstein's Poker*, by David Edmonds and John Eidinow, tells the true story of an encounter between Wittgenstein and the philosopher Sir Karl Popper, which ended when Wittgenstein nearly assaulted Popper with a fireplace poker. It was only the intervention of Bertrand Russell that prevented an actual assault.

Two graphic novels, *Logicomix*, by Apostolos Doxiadis and Christos Papadimi-triou, and *Action Philosophers*, by Fred Van Lente and Ryan Dunlavey, contain sections that depict the life and accomplishments of Wittgenstein in comic book form.

The film *Wittgenstein* (1993), directed by Derek Jarman, is an art film that chronicles the philosopher's life and struggles.

Novelists seem to be especially fascinated with Wittgenstein. Among the novels in which he, his name, or his relatives play a part are: *The World as I Found It* by Bruce Duffy, *Wittgenstein's Mistress* by David Markson, and *Wittgenstein's Nephew* by Thomas Bernhard.

---

the real differences between symmetrical and asymmetrical relationships to "show" themselves, and once this is done there is nothing more to be said. The reality of the situation actually becomes manifest through the symbolism; this is what Wittgenstein seems to mean when he writes, "What *can* be shown *cannot* be said."[56] To use an analogous example, suppose you meet a man who has never seen the color red. The only way that you could make him understand what the color red is would be to point at an example of the color. You must make him see the same thing that you are thinking about. By pointing to the color, the color becomes manifest to his consciousness. Now the term "red" maps directly on to this reality, and no more needs to be said about the matter. Likewise, Wittgenstein believes that language, carefully used, points out the structure of the world like a finger pointing to a patch of color.

"Logic is not a theory, but a reflection of the world."[57] Logic mirrors reality, revealing the way things really are within the universe that we inhabit. It does not, however, tell us anything about what exists outside of the universe. Logic only reveals the inner connections that govern the natural world. For this reason, the study of logic cannot help us to step outside of the world and to speak of it as a whole. To do so would be to move beyond the bounds of what is sayable, and we would be reduced to nonsensical babbling. The inexpressible does exist, Wittgenstein tells us, but it is always inexpressible. It is "mystical," meaning that it is beyond language and logic precisely because it is beyond the natural world. For that reason, we must remain silent about it. "Whereof one cannot speak, thereof one must remain silent."[58] Thus, toward the end of the *Tractatus*, Wittgenstein offers his advice to philosophers:

The right method of philosophy would be this. To say nothing except what can be said, i.e., the propositions of natural science, i.e., something that has nothing to do with philosophy: and then when someone else wished to say something metaphysical, to demonstrate to him that he had given no meaning to certain signs in his propositions. This method would be unsatisfying to the other—he would not have the feeling that we were teaching him philosophy—but it would be the only strictly correct method.[59]

The *Tractatus* is both clever and aggravating. Its cleverness lies primarily in the way that it concisely and systematically presents a self-contained theory of language by building upon a series of foundational (though questionable) assertions. It was the ingenuity of this work, in fact, which was to inspire a whole movement in analytic philosophy known as Logical Positivism. Logical Positivists were dedicated to eliminating talk of metaphysics and purifying philosophy in accordance with Wittgenstein's logical suggestions. Regardless of this influence, in many ways the *Tractatus* is even more aggravating than it is clever. It contains very few arguments, but consists mostly of bald-faced assertions and the use of metaphors to make its points. For this reason, its insistence on the model of logic that it promotes feels arbitrary and, as A. C. Grayling complains, it also "oversimplifies and distorts language"[60] by ignoring the many and varied ways that language really does operate in everyday usage. Interestingly enough, this last point did not escape Wittgenstein's own attention. In the years after publishing the *Tractatus*, he would come to question, and even reject, much of what he wrote in this work. His second, posthumously published book, *Philosophical Investigations*, would present a completely different theory of language and its connection to the world.

Philosophical Investigations

Whereas the *Tractatus* presents a "picture theory of meaning," *Philosophical Investigations* presents what could be called a "language game theory of meaning." The early writings of Wittgenstein held that when we use language correctly, the structure of our sentences somehow mirrors the very structure of the world, picturing it to our minds and making everything absolutely clear and unambiguous. The world shows itself through language the way that a physical terrain shows itself in a map. The later writings of Wittgenstein, however, begin to move away from this view. Picturing the world, he now claims, is only one of the functions that language serves for us. There are, in fact, many functions that language serves in addition to picturing reality, such as:

- Giving orders and obeying them
- Describing the appearance of an object, or giving its measurements
- Constructing an object from a description ([making] a drawing)
- Reporting an event
- Speculating about an event
- Forming and testing a hypothesis
- Presenting the results of an experiment in tables and diagrams

- Making up a story; and reading it
- Play-acting
- Singing catches
- Guessing riddles
- Making a joke; telling it
- Solving a problem in arithmetic
- Translating from one language into another
- Requesting, thanking, cursing, greeting, praying.[61]

There is something a bit humorous about Wittgenstein's presentation of this list. It is almost as if he suddenly finds himself in awe concerning the number of varied and different things that we can do with language in addition to picturing reality. "Isn't it amazing," you can almost hear him exclaiming, "that we can make up stories, play-act, sing, etc. using language? How did this escape my attention before?!" Language is, in fact, much more varied and rich in its uses than his previous logical perspective would lead us to believe. The mistake of that perspective, Wittgenstein now recognizes, is not that it is wrong but that it is simplistic. In addition to logical discourse, people use language to express feelings, to give orders, to exclaim, and to joke. A theory that does not recognize that language does more than assert facts, it turns out, is not a very good theory at all.

So if the function of language cannot be explained in terms of a single underlying form of logic, then how do we understand its workings? Wittgenstein proposes that we look at all of the ways that words are actually used and then try, inductively, to come to some sort of conclusion about the overall pattern that is exhibited. Considering the vast multiplicity of uses, as noted above, it is impossible, he decides, to pin down only one legitimate way that language functions. Rather, the parts of speech seem to be like the tools in a toolbox; they are used at different times for different purposes according to different needs. "Think of the tools in a toolbox: there is a hammer, pliers, a saw, a screwdriver, a rule, a glue-pot, glue, nails, and screws.—The functions of words are as diverse as the functions of these objects."[62] So, we use words to undertake and complete different sorts of tasks, just as we take up tools to undertake different sorts of building projects. Just as there are a whole variety of projects that we may use our tools to complete, so are there a whole variety of uses to which we may put our words. There is no one right or wrong way to use language. It all depends on what you intend to do.

Wittgenstein suggests that we conceive language use along the lines of a game. When you play a game, you enter into a way of acting that is governed by the expectations and the norms of those with whom you are playing. You don't necessarily need to know all of the rules of a game at the outset to take part, and in fact the rules of a game can change as you engage in it. What is really involved in playing a game is that you enter into a "life-form,"[63] which means that you take part in a series of activities along with others. It is in the actual playing of the game that the meaning and pattern of play emerge. Likewise, when using language, we seem (as Russell had suggested) to jump right into the middle of things along with others and engage in "language games."[64] We don't, before the fact, learn all of the rules of grammar, the meanings of words, or the logic of language before we use it. These sorts of things come after the fact, posterior to our actual engagement in the activity of thinking, speaking, and writing. We learn by doing, and in doing we make up the rules as we go along.

Logical analysis, then, is an after-the-fact reflection on the things that we have already done with language. To claim, as Wittgenstein did in the *Tractatus*, that there is only one proper way to analyze statements is, consequently, fallacious. Instead, he now claims, there are an infinite number of ways to think about the analysis of statements depending upon the sort of game you wish to play and the context in which it is being played. There is no "single ideal of exactness."[65] For example, is it clearer to speak of a "broom" or of the "broomstick and the brush"?[66] If you are asking someone to hand you the entire broom, it seems much clearer, more straightforward and understandable simply to ask for the broom. If, under these circumstances, you were to ask for the broomstick and the brush, you would probably get some strange looks! Or, even more dramatically, suppose you were to refer to the broom by asking for all of the particular parts that make up the broomstick and the brush themselves. "Please hand me the wood that has been turned on a lathe to form a stick 3 feet long, as well as the straw that has been sewn together with red cotton thread and then affixed with glue to the top of the previously mentioned wooden stick." As Wittgenstein writes, the person you made this request to would no doubt respond, "Do you want the broom? Why do you put it so oddly?"[67] There is no improvement in clarity achieved by analyzing the broom into its component parts. Rather, using the term "broom" is sufficient to make yourself understood. That is how the game of asking for a broom is played. On the other hand, if you worked in a broom museum and were given the task of explaining the construction of brooms to visitors, it might very well be appropriate to discuss all of the various parts of the broom. But then you are playing a different game with different expectations.

The problem with the view of language presented in the *Tractatus* was that "a picture held us captive."[68] Now, in *Philosophical Investigations*, Wittgenstein sees that there is no such thing as an ideal language. There are merely differing forms of life and differing games that people play with their words. We are introduced to these games during the course of interacting with others, and thus language is an inherently social activity. Because participation in any particular language game presupposes that a player has already been initiated into a way of life, all language, in addition to being social, is also a public sort of thing. "We are trained"[69] how to use language, and without such training language acquisition is not possible. Thus, it makes no sense to speak of a "private language." A language must always be shared. There must always be common normative expectations and conventional criteria that govern the particular game that is being played at any given time. A "language" that is not shared with others is really no language at all because a person attempting to use such a system would participate in no negotiation or interplay with others and thus would simply be engaged in a free-for-all instead of an orderly and structured game. Language use, we must remember, is an *activity*; it is not some sort of academic, isolated, and self-contained thing. You must practice the activity to be a part of the game, and doing so is to be subject to the expectations, the reactions, and the corrections of others. If you were not subject to these sort of social constraints, you might *think* you were playing the game. However, *thinking* you are

COMMON SENSE AND ANGLO-AMERICAN PHILOSOPHY

playing a game and *actually* playing the game are two different things.[70] To actually play a game you must participate with others in some sort of orderly undertaking. Without others, you are not subject to systematic correction. You can do whatever you want. And that is not how any game, let alone a language game, works.

Philosophical Investigations represents both a development of some of the ideas that first appeared in the *Tractatus*, as well as a rejection of some of those ideas. Wittgenstein came to see that his original views on the logical structure of language, while not necessarily wrong, were in any case overly narrow. The theory of logical atomism that he initially took for granted is only one among many systems that govern language use. The words, sentences, and statements that we speak and write, Wittgenstein finally concluded, are capable of being applied to an infinite variety of purposes, all of which are legitimate in their own ways. It is ironic that this philosopher who was initially an advocate of a purely analytic approach to philosophy should, in the end, also produce a work that had great impact on the continental tradition as well. With his last book, Wittgenstein turned against the view that the proper role of philosophy consists only in the analysis and logical understanding of language. Ultimately, he seems to have concluded that philosophy consists in the exploration and description of various forms of life. The philosopher raises questions because he does not quite understand the rules of the game. "A philosophical problem has the form: 'I don't know my way about.'"[71] Once the way has been found, once the "fly has been shown the way out of the bottle,"[72] philosophy comes to an end.

WONDROUS DISTRESS IN ANGLO-AMERICAN PHILOSOPHY

The Anglo-American tradition in philosophy embodies characteristics that always have, and always will, be present in philosophical thinking. In the aspiration toward clarity, concision, and logical order, both pragmatists and analytic philosophers demonstrate a serious concern with understanding and elucidating a variety of difficult conundrums and puzzles that lie at the center of traditional philosophical discourse. An emphasis on science and logic have been an integral part of philosophy at least since the Presocratic thinkers began to ask questions and to probe the nature of the universe around 600 B.C., and in the modern Anglo-American tradition we see this plan being applied with renewed vigor and enthusiasm. These philosophers insist that it is not enough to simply contemplate and meditate on the world. To aspire toward real understanding, we must also apply the powers of logic and analysis to our intellectual efforts, breaking the world into manageable bits and pieces so that we can make sense of things in accordance with our finite and limited intellects. All of the philosophers we have surveyed in this chapter recognize that the human mind is not unlimited in its capacities. Our understanding will never grasp everything all at once and as a whole. For this reason, we must approach our exploration of reality bit by bit, reconstructing the connections between things in a stepwise and deliberate manner. This approach has much in common with the systematic procedures of science, and it is therefore not surprising that we should find the Anglo-American movement in philosophy allying itself with the discoveries, methods, and worldviews of the most contemporary, empirically driven developments in fields such as psychology, sociology, biology, and physics. Like the most careful empirical scientists, pragmatic and analytic philosophers recognize that the future is an open book, and until we actually read the words in that book we cannot know what it has to say.

Insistence on the open-ended nature of human learning and discovery gives Anglo-American philosophy a distinct sense of both wonder and distress. In wonder, thinkers from this tradition pursue the unknown, striving to understand reality by breaking it down into pieces, hoping that this will allow them to formulate sensible answers to the complex questions that have confounded past thinkers. There is a distinct sense of optimism here, expressed in the belief that a method, systematically applied, will open up and reveal the hidden mysteries of the world. According to this view, clear thinking and observation are the only necessities to move human knowledge forward in its comprehension and understanding of Being. As we build our understanding of reality from the ground up, bit by bit, we move closer and closer toward the goal of wisdom. Because they are in wonder about what is unknown, these philosophers are also distressed by that which they can't comprehend. Confidence in a method, and optimism about the potential for this method to lead in the direction of greater understanding undergirds all of the efforts by the Anglo-American philosophers to transform their distressing uncertainty into wondrous appreciation. The direction that logical analysis and empirical investigation leads, they assure us, is always toward better and better comprehension of the structure and order of our world.

But this confidence in the methods of analysis and of logic also tends, in some ways, to close down the thinking of Anglo-American philosophers and to encourage them, at times, to become quite unphilosophical in their approach toward learning. One of the aggravating and unbecoming tendencies that we see again and again cropping up in the writing of thinkers like James, Russell, and Wittgenstein is an eagerness to dismiss issues, ideas, and questions that are not resolved neatly and unequivocally according to their own particular modes of investigation. Such irresolvable issues are often labeled as "nonsense" or as "confusions" and thus relegated to the trash heap of things to be ignored. Related to this tendency, we often find these thinkers redefining issues in ways that many of us find questionable. They then offer answers to old questions in terms of their new definitions and seem to expect everyone to be satisfied with the result. James does this with his pragmatic answers to the nature of truth and of God's existence; Russell does this when he argues against the existence of God; and Wittgenstein does this with his logical "solution" to all philosophical problems in the *Tractatus*. Partly because of their commitment to analysis and logic, partly because of their commitment to science, and partly because of their eagerness for answers, again and again we find these thinkers insisting upon unequivocal and final resolutions to issues that many of us do not think have been clearly and finally resolved at all. In the process, there is sometimes present an overly glib and off-putting attitude, a self-satisfied cleverness, that often serves to direct attention away from deeper, enduring, and truly philosophical issues toward the ingenuity and shrewdness of the writers themselves. Wondrous distress gets lost as the personality of a "genius" takes center stage.

This last criticism does not apply to all Anglo-American philosophy, but it is an observation illustrating the potential threat to philosophical openness that looms when a desire for answers and conclusions trumps our willingness to engage in the contemplation of issues from a variety of perspectives. Dogmatism and the rejection of alternate possibilities is always a danger when a thinker, once and for all, settles on a single method by which to approach and resolve issues. With pragmatists and analytic philosophers, we must certainly admire the serious commitment that we find in their aspiration toward answers. However, as philosophers we must also question whether any one method of approach is adequate to solving the issues that have always caused wonder and distress in thoughtful people.

QUESTIONS FOR DISCUSSION

1. The Anglo-American tradition includes both the pragmatic and the analytic schools of philosophy. While they share much in common with one another, these two schools also diverge in many ways. Discuss the points at which pragmatism and analytic philosophy overlap and the points at which they diverge.

2. What is the pragmatic theory of truth? What are the problems with this theory? What are its strengths? Do you agree or disagree with this way of thinking about the truth? Why or why not?

3. Are you more of a "tough-minded" individual, or are you more of a "tender-minded" individual? Discuss and explain. How would you use these terms to classify the various philosophers discussed in previous chapters?

4. Russell's Logical Atomism conceives of language, and the world that language maps, as composed of disconnected particles that are not grounded in any underlying foundation. Do you think this is the correct way to think of language and the world? Compare and contrast the logics of Aristotle and Hegel to Russell's version of logic. Assess their strengths and weaknesses.

5. Do you agree with Russell and the early Wittgenstein that the job of philosophy is primarily to analyze and clarify our language? If so, what implications does this have for Socrates, Plato, the Hellenistic thinkers, and the Medieval thinkers?

6. What did Wittgenstein mean when he wrote "Whereof one cannot speak, thereof one must be silent"? Do you agree with him? How does this viewpoint relate to Russell's claim that mysticism is something that lies outside of the realm of philosophy?

7. Wittgenstein is unusual in being the author of two very different philosophical perspectives. One of these perspectives was articulated in his book *Tractatus Logico-Philosophicus* and the other was articulated in his book *Philosophical Investigations*. Do you think these two perspectives are incompatible with one another? Why or why not? Which of these perspectives do you agree with more?

NOTES

1. William James, *Pragmatism* (Indianapolis, IN: Hackett Publishing Company, [1907] 1981), Dedication.

2. Ibid., p. 8.

3. Ibid., p. 10.

4. Ibid.

5. Ibid.

6. In many ways, this is all a reiteration of the philosophical battle that took place between Plato and Aristotle thousands of years beforehand. Plato falls neatly into the "tender-minded" category, and Aristotle falls neatly into the "tough-minded" category. See Chapters 3 and 4.

7. James, *Pragmatism*, p. 8.

8. Ibid., p. 13.

9. This is a paraphrase of James's point on page 26 of *Pragmatism*.

10. See Chapter 1.

11. James, *Pragmatism*, p. 28.

12. Ibid., p. 47.

13. Ibid.

14. Ibid., p. 86.

15. Richard Rorty offers a criticism of this view in his book *Philosophy and the Mirror of Nature* (Princeton, NJ: Princeton University Press, 1981).

16. Bruce Kuklick argues that the Kantian aspects of James's philosophy are absolutely crucial. When melded with Darwinism, he claims that James's thought exhibits a sort of "evolutionary Kantianism." See Bruce Kuklick, *The Rise of American Philosophy: Cambridge, Massachusetts, 1860–1930* (New Haven, CT: Yale University Press, 1977), pp. 272–273.

17. James, *Pragmatism*, p. 92.

18. Ibid., p. 31.

19. Ibid., p. 100.

20. Ibid., p. 119.

21. Ibid., p. 123.

22. Ibid., p. 130.

23. Ibid., p. 133.

24. Ibid., p. 123.

25. William James, "The Will to Believe," in *Ten Great Works of Philosophy*, Robert Paul Wolff (ed.) (New York: Penguin, 2002), p. 462.

26. Ibid., p. 463.

27. William James, *The Varieties of Religious Experience* (New York: Penguin Books, 1985), p. 517.

28. Wallace Matson, *A New History of Philosophy*, Vol. 1 (New York: Harcourt Brace Jovanovich, Publishers, 1987), p. 448.

29. Bertrand Russell, *A History of Western Philosophy* (New York: Simon and Schuster, 1972), p. 818.

30. I'll always remember the comments of one of my own Pragmatist professors. He was fond of telling students in our seminars that the great thing about American Pragmatism is that it allows you to get things done. "You can't build a toaster with continental philosophy," I recall him complaining; or words to that effect.

31. Nicholas Griffin, "Introduction," in *The Cambridge Companion to Bertrand Russell* (Cambridge: Cambridge University Press, 2003), p. 1.

32. Anders Österling, "Award Ceremony Speech, the Nobel Prize in Literature 1950." http://nobelprize.org/nobel_prizes/literature/laureates/1950/press.html.

33. Bertrand Russell, *Autobiography* (London: Routledge, 1998), p. 60.

34. Russell, *History of Western Philosophy*, p. 743.

35. Ibid., p. 745.

36. Bertrand Russell, *The Problems of Philosophy* (New York: Barnes and Noble, 2004), p. 102.

37. Bertrand Russell, *Introduction to Mathematical Philosophy* (New York: Dover Publications, 1993), p. 204.

38. This example is used by Russell on pp. 42–44 of *Introduction to Mathematical Philosophy*. Today it may not be as intuitively obvious as it was to Russell that the relationship of husband to wife is asymmetrical because same-sex marriage is now such a debated issue.

39. Ibid., p. 201.

40. Ibid., p. 205.

41. Ibid., p. 2.

42. Russell, *The Problems of Philosophy*, p. 1.

43. Ibid., p. 3.

44. Ibid., p. 13.

45. Ibid., p. 31.

46. Ibid., p. 34.

47. Ibid., p. 89.

48. Ibid., p. 105.

49. Russell, "Mysticism and Logic," in *Selected Papers of Bertrand Russell* (New York: Modern Library, 1927), p. 18.

50. Derek Jarman (director), *Wittgenstein*. 1993.

51. Ludwig Wittgenstein, *Tractatus Logico-Philosophicus* (New York: Barnes and Noble, 2003), p. 3.

52. Ibid., 2.03.

53. Ibid., 2.18.

54. See Russell, *Introduction to Mathematical Philosophy*, p. 52.

55. Wittgenstein, *Tractatus*, 4.003.

56. Ibid., 4.1212.

57. Ibid., 6.13.

58. Ibid., 7.

59. Ibid., 6.53.

60. A. C. Grayling, *Wittgenstein: A Very Short Introduction* (Oxford: Oxford University Press, 2001), p. 61.

61. Ludwig Wittgenstein, *Philosophical Investigations* (Oxford: Blackwell Publishing, 2001), 23.
62. Ibid., 11.
63. Ibid., 19.
64. Ibid., 7.
65. Ibid., 88.
66. Ibid., 60.
67. Ibid.
68. Ibid., 115.
69. Ibid., 206.
70. Ibid., 202.
71. Ibid., 123.
72. Ibid., 309.

Chapter 13

Existentialism and the Return to Being

How did the horrors of World War I and World War II inspire existentialist insights? Why was Heidegger so concerned with the question of Being? What is *Dasein*? What does it mean to be inauthentic? What is the difference between Being-in-itself and Being-for-itself? What is bad faith? Why does Beauvoir call women the "second sex"? Why does Beauvoir claim that many women are in bad faith?

NATIONALISM, IMPERIALISM, TECHNOLOGY, AND WAR

As the twentieth century dawned, the stage was being set for two great wars that would soon engulf the globe. Nationalism and imperialism were on the rise in Europe, and this trend contributed to the growth of tension between neighboring states, tension that would ultimately explode into open hostility, drawing all of the major powers into years of violence and atrocity. The rise of industry in the nineteenth century, and the more general triumph of science during the Modern era, led to new discoveries and advances in technology that, while contributing to an increase in the standard of living for many people in the Western world, at the same time also contributed to the oppression and degradation of the poor and of non-Western people residing in territories subject to imperialistic exploitation. As industry required more and more resources, nations patriotically proclaimed their right to procure these resources from other less powerful territories, all in the name of progress and civilization. The great European powers acquired and exploited large amounts of territory in Africa and Asia, turning the people and their lands into fuel for an increasingly rapid program of nationalistic and industrial expansion.

The partnership of nationalism and imperialism with the growth of technology turned out to be a cruel and terrifying combination that ultimately doubled back to threaten Western civilization's own stability. Although armed conflict was never totally absent from the world scene, the scope and scale of twentieth-century warfare were unprecedented and cataclysmic. With the outbreak of World Wars I and II, the nations of the West turned against each other, and the inherent horrors of armed conflict were transformed into something even more terrible by a cold and calculating rationality, which enabled human beings to engineer an increasing number of ways to kill an increasing number of people in an increasingly efficient manner. Over the course of the two world wars, the West would see the introduction of mechanized and chemical warfare, death camps, and nuclear weaponry. Human beings served as fodder for destructive technology; they were transformed into mere *things* that fueled the war machine and that had worth only as instruments for national projects of conflict and domination. This seemed a far cry from the promise of the Enlightenment when human learning was supposed to lead the way toward a bright, peaceful, and hopeful future. For many, on the contrary, it appeared not that human culture was progressing but rather that it was in a state of decline and decay. Human power, cleverness, and ingenuity had a dark side that was becoming increasingly apparent. The world was beginning to look like a very gloomy and absurd place.

In the present chapter, we shall explore existentialism, a philosophy that emerged out of this bleak and distressing period of time. Existentialism is a difficult philosophy to characterize. Many of the key figures in its development reject being called existentialists, and even those who do accept the label exhibit a wide and conflicting array of beliefs. There are existentialists who are atheists and those who are theists. Some existentialists are pacifists and others advocate violence. Some existentialists are on the right politically and some are on the left. What sort of philosophy is it that could accommodate these seemingly contradictory viewpoints? In the discussion that follows we shall navigate the terrain of existentialism by emphasizing one predominant theme that seems to be a recurring preoccupation of all existentialists, regardless of their other disagreements. Reacting against the widespread debasement of human life under the domination of the nation-state, existentialism promotes the idea that human beings are not merely material "things" to be manipulated and controlled like other objects in the world. Unlike rocks or pieces of wood, human beings have the capacity to formulate and act upon their own hopes, dreams, and fears. In so doing, they can anticipate the future and so carve out a path that shapes the very world of which they are a part. Existentialist philosophers claim that human beings, to a greater or lesser extent, may, in this way, freely choose the course and the direction of their life's development. Our personal histories are governed by an ongoing stream of choices rather than by the ironclad laws of physics. Existentialism is thus a philosophy that attempts to remind us of the power we possess to constantly refashion the world and ourselves. Bred in times of war and social decline, the existentialists sought to revive a sense of human dignity, demanding that we all shoulder responsibility for a world that seemed to be spinning out of control.

Before addressing the ideas of Martin Heidegger, Jean-Paul Sartre, and Simone de Beauvoir, three of history's most important existentialist philosophers, I shall first sketch a picture of some of the ideas and events that helped to shape their perspectives. As you may already suspect, there is a gloominess and a mournfulness that haunts existential philosophy. This melancholy mood may be attributed to an intellectual and a cultural atmosphere that ruminated on, and anticipated, the impending decline of Western civilization. While darkness and a preoccupation with death characterize much existential literature, we should be clear that existentialism is ultimately not simply a philosophy of despair but rather one of hope. Like all true philosophers, these thinkers are both troubled by the world but also open to future possibilities for transformation. Both distress and wonder remain prominent features in their thinking.

NIHILISM AND THE DECLINE OF CIVILIZATION

Friedrich Nietzsche

Nietzsche had foretold that the Modern age would be a time of nihilism when Western human beings would be forced to reevaluate their highest values. All that humans had believed in would crumble into nothing, he claimed, and as a result we would have to rethink who we are and what our place is in this world. Nietzsche believed that a major element in the nihilistic decline of Western

civilization stemmed from "contemporary natural science" whose "pursuit eventually leads to self-disintegration, opposition."[1] The problem with science, according to Nietzsche, stems from its presumption of "causalism [and] mechanism"[2] as the governing principles of the world. When applied to the nonhuman realm of inanimate objects, this may have legitimacy. However, when applied to the human world, scientific analysis reduces us to mere bodies whose motions are determined by the laws of cause and effect. While this is certainly an aspect of our physiology, it is not what makes human beings great or noble. The source of human greatness and nobility lies, rather, in the creative spirit, the "Dionysian" impulse, or what Nietzsche most (in)famously called "the will to power." In Nietzsche's time, this creative force was increasingly being subsumed to the constraining power of the national state and mass movements, which attempt to "scientifically" manage human beings in accordance with grand schemes and collective purposes. The result was that a vital and healthy human culture, which is dependent upon the creative freedom of individuals, had ceased to grow and was in the process of becoming stifled and ossified. "Culture and state—one should not deceive oneself about this—are antagonists."[3] When "the herd" takes control, thought Nietzsche, no good can come of things; and this is exactly what seemed to be happening in Europe. Western culture had reached its apex, and now, under the artificially constraining structures of the nation-state, it was in the process of disintegrating into a vicious form of barbarism. Human creativity, which should properly be an end in itself, was now simply a tool of the nation, and human beings were thought to have value only insofar as they served some social/utilitarian purpose. This Nietzschean picture of a world in decay was very influential during the start of the twentieth century, helping to both articulate a common sentiment as well as to shape an emerging worldview that sees science and technology as factors not in the redemption of human life but in its decline and destruction.

Oswald Spengler

Perhaps one of the most popular and widely read "theorists of decline" during this period was Oswald Spengler (1880–1936), whose monumental work *The Decline of the West* was a bestseller in Europe at the end of World War I. In this work, Spengler proposed the idea that history does not unfold along a single linear axis but rather it is characterized by the rise and fall of a variety of distinctive cultures. Every culture, he claimed, is a self-contained entity, which is born, matures, and dies, just like an organism. The problem with the traditional approach to historical research, according to Spengler, is that it tries to impose an artificial uniformity on the totality of the world, leading to a mistaken picture of endless and cumulative human cultural progress. Instead, Spengler tells us:

> I see, in place of that empty figment of one linear history which can only be kept up by shutting one's eyes to the overwhelming multitude of facts, the drama of a number of mighty Cultures, each springing with primitive strength from the soil of a mother-region to which it remains firmly bound throughout its whole life-cycle.... Each Culture has its own new possibilities of self-expression which arise, decay, and never return.... These cultures, sublimated life-essences, grow with the same superb aimlessness as the flowers of the field. They belong, like the plants and animals, to the living Nature of Goethe, and not the dead Nature of Newton.[4]

Culture, then, is like a living, breathing organism that unfolds and grows according to an inner life force. For this reason, its particular manifestations and processes cannot be calculated or manipulated according to the "scientific" laws of cause and effect. Like an organism, a culture grows toward its highest potentiality and then becomes mature. This state of maturity is what Spengler calls "Civilization." Once a culture has reached this highest point of development, it then faces the inevitable decline and decay that all organisms face in their twilight years. During this time of decline, the routinization, rationalization, and formalization of life is a common symptom as the culture attempts to conserve itself against a loss of its vital and creative forces. The concrete manifestations witnessed during this stage of civilization in the West are the development of urban centers, the preoccupation with money, machines, and imperialist expansion. In these we see the energy of humans directed outward instead of inward: toward the manipulation of the outer world instead of toward the inner development of the soul. When a people reach this point in their collective life-history, there is no more to do except fatalistically accept that all of the greatest cultural accomplishments now lie in the past, and that the future holds only exhaustion of the spirit. The destiny of all civilizations, according to this view, is decline and finally extinction (see Figure 13.1).

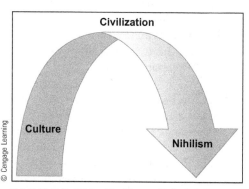

F I G U R E 13.1   The Rise and Fall of Civilizations

H. Stuart Hughes writes, "*The Decline of the West* offers the nearest thing we have to a key to our times. It formulates more comprehensively than any other single book the modern *malaise* that so many feel and so few can express. It has become the classic summary of the now familiar pessimism of the twentieth-century West with regard to its own historical future."[5] It is in Spengler's book that we find a powerful expression of a feeling common to those living through the dawn of the twentieth century.[6] Optimism in human progress and faith in the emancipatory powers of science and technology were on the wane. In their place we find a sense that human culture is an impermanent "blip" on the screen of Being itself. Humans, if not completely insignificant, have at least overestimated their importance, and there is a tragic sense that they have contributed more pain and destruction to the world than beauty and goodness. One also gets a sense that the individual feels constrained, lonely, and isolated in the midst of grand political, social, and natural forces that sweep uncontrolled and unrestrained across the universe. Truly, the atmosphere is one of nihilism, loneliness, and personal impotence.

Totalitarianism

Feelings like isolation, loneliness, uprootedness, and superfluousness are pointed to by the philosopher Hannah Arendt (1906–1975) as factors that contributed to the emergence of totalitarian governments after the end of World War I. Totalitarian movements, like those espoused by the Nazis and the Bolsheviks, exploited these feelings, organizing a despairing mass of people into a forceful mob, giving them a direction, a purpose, and an ideology that helped to alleviate their sense of isolation and impotence. As part of a movement, the masses felt "bound together" and thus "disappeared into One Man of gigantic dimensions."[7] Germany and Russia, in particular, are countries where Arendt claims widespread loneliness took hold of the population during the beginning of the twentieth century, and thus these populations were especially vulnerable to exploitation by dictators such as Hitler and Stalin for political purposes. These leaders were so successful because they were able to conjure up visions of an ideal world and to promise the realization of that ideal world to those who were willing to sacrifice their own freedom and autonomy in the battle for its fulfillment. The irony, according to Arendt, is that the despair that was exploited by Hitler and Stalin was only intensified in the course of their dictatorships. The logic of totalitarianism is such that in "destroying all space between men and pressing men together,"[8] even the inner life of the mind is obliterated, and so the individual necessarily becomes self-alienated, as he or she is transformed into a cog, a gear, or a piece of the collective machine. Under totalitarian rule, a person may find the alleviation of loneliness, but it is at the cost of having any inner life whatsoever. When there is no space left for free thought, when the only thinking that is allowed is that which follows the ideology of the "movement," the individual disappears altogether, and so the totalitarian "cure" for social "atomization" and nihilism actually amounts to killing the patient.[9]

The Nazis and the Bolsheviks carried out the logic of their movements with unflinching commitment. Hitler's concentration camps and Stalin's gulags represent the ultimate outcome of treating human beings as "things" that have only instrumental value for the pursuit of ideal goals. In these camps, human beings were reduced to objects that were to be used for labor, or when they outlived their usefulness, to be disposed of like garbage. When the parts of a machine stop working, one gets rid of them and replaces them with others. The totalitarian way of thinking has no qualms about this and sees any sort of sentimental reflection on the inherent worth of the human individual as "unscientific" insofar as it does not grasp the importance of the fulfillment of some sort of historical destiny. In the concentration camps we see "the insane mass manufacture of corpses," but as Arendt points out, "this is preceded by the historically and politically intelligible preparation of living corpses."[10] The Holocaust and the horrors of the gulags, in other words, would not have been possible unless human beings had first been reduced to something less than human, something that one could justify tossing aside like any other inanimate "thing" without an inner life of its own.

The Muselmann

Perhaps the most shocking and distressing product of the Nazi concentration camps was the "Muselmann." "Muselmann" is another word for "Muslim," but in this context it has nothing to do with adherence to the Islamic faith. Rather, the Muselmann is a type of individual often found in the concentration camps who, just as a Muslim completely submits to Allah, completely submitted to the Nazi expectations for camp inmates. These individuals are described by other inmates as "shell-men," "the living dead," "mummy-men," or "non-men." They had been completely broken by their experience in the camps and had lost all sense of their own dignity, self-worth, or uniqueness. The process of total institutionalization had stripped them of the last remnants of humanness, and so they shambled around carrying out only the most basic, instinctual functions associated with eating, defecating, and sleeping, if they did those things at all. Muselmänner lost the drive to even defend themselves when beaten, or to read letters received from loved ones. Their interior life had been completely extinguished so that they existed as nothing more than flesh, bone, and blood. They were no longer human:

> I personally was a Muselmann for a short while. I remember that after the move to the barrack, I completely collapsed as far as my psychological life was concerned. The collapse took the following form: I was overcome by a general apathy; nothing interested me; I no longer reacted to either external or internal stimuli; I stopped washing, even when there was water; I no longer even felt hungry.[11]

Individuals in this state were "unbearable to human eyes,"[12] as they represented the complete and utter degradation of a human being into a thing, an object, a worthless heap of shambling flesh. The Muselmänner did not retain a sense of who they had been in the past, nor did they harbor any hopes or fears of the future. Rather, they existed in a perpetual "now," which was itself void of any concerns or feelings. Like a rock, or a piece of wood, the Muselmann was simply "there." To endure the

© Juneko J. Robinson

sight of this "thing" one was also forced to become less than human and thus to be degraded as well. The Muselmann was a reminder to others in the camps of what they all might become, and so developing a sense of callousness to this creature was a necessary part of a prisoner's own psychological survival. If personal hope was to be salvaged, then the Muselmann must not be given thoughtful consideration. Yet in doing this, the camp inmate engaged in the same sort of thinking that the committed Nazi engaged in and thus became inhuman as well. As Primo Levi writes, "This is why the experience of someone who has lived for days during which a man is merely a thing in the eyes of man is nonhuman."[13]

The Muselmann represents the culminating triumph of Nazism, or of any other "scientific" system that views human beings as mere objects to be manipulated by external forces for worldly ends. The preeminent danger of the twentieth century was that everyone would be transformed into Muselmänner in one way or another. Nationalism, imperialism, militarism, industrialism; all of these forces were in the process of conspiring to overwhelm human freedom and to sweep us all along like corks on an enormous ocean wave. Human beings, more than ever, needed to engage in an exercise of recollection if this situation was to be reversed. Against the large, impersonal, exterior forces that were threatening to overwhelm us, modern people needed to rescue the fundamental, interior thinking domain that stands as the uniquely human foundation of our existence. Only by understanding who we truly are would we be able to resist becoming something that we were never supposed to be. It was the task of existential philosophy to remind us of this fundamental truth.

MARTIN HEIDEGGER

The Question of Being

Among the first, and most influential, of the twentieth-century existentialist thinkers was the controversial German philosopher Martin Heidegger (1889–1976). Heidegger's overwhelming concern throughout his career was with the "question of Being," and all of his writings are informed by the desire to understand the ultimate "ground," or "Being," out of which humans emerge and build their lives. "Being" is existence itself, in its essence, apart from all accidental qualities, and so if we could understand its true nature we would understand the primal root of all things. In undertaking this task, Heidegger constructed a new way of thinking that was intended to subvert traditional philosophy and to take us back to the "primordial" foundation in which all particular "beings-in-the-world" are rooted. Heidegger thought that if we could be successful in thinking our way back to this ground, not only would we come to understand our own true nature but we would also come to understand the relationship of that nature to everything else that exists. The ultimate goal of Heidegger's manner of thinking, then, was to reestablish the integration of human existence into Being itself. With this, he hoped to resuscitate an "authentic"

© Juneko J. Robinson

awareness of what we are as human beings, what our true potentialities consist of, and to infuse our lived existence with a sense of profundity, awe, and respect. This almost religious aspiration would offer an important corrective to the modern tendency toward viewing human beings through the lens of science and thus of mistaking them for "things" no different from all other things in the world. According to Heidegger, this modern viewpoint is a mistake, and in fact humans are not "things" at all but rather beings that are much more dynamic and full of potential than any other sorts of beings-in-the-world.

When did the mistaken view of humans as "things" first take hold of our thinking? According to Heidegger, to understand this we must look back thousands of years toward the very beginnings of Western philosophy, and in particular to Plato who, as discussed in Chapter 3, directed our attention away from the empirical world (which he thought was a world of illusion) toward the world of eternal, perfect, and absolute Forms. In so doing, Plato succeeded in splitting reality into two realms: one realm which he claimed was more real, and one which he claimed was less real. The highest reality, the realm of the Forms, is what constitutes true Being, according to Plato, and the highest Form, the Good itself, is, furthermore, the most real, most substantial, and most fundamental expression of Being itself. Thus, according to Platonic thinking, even the Forms of Truth, Beauty, and Justice are not as real as is the Form of the Good. Being, then, is most properly equated with one particular "thing," namely, the Good itself, which stands above and beyond every other "thing" below it on the scale of the divided line of existence.[14]

But in this, Heidegger tells us, Plato has falsified and shattered the unity of Being. In his most famous book, titled *Being and Time*, Heidegger insists, "The [B]eing of beings 'is' itself not a being. The first philosophical step in understanding the problem of [B]eing consists in ... not determining beings as beings by tracing them back in their origins to another being—as if [B]eing had the character of a possible being."[15] Here you get the flavor not only of Heidegger's difficult writing style but also of the fundamental problem that he has with the Western philosophical treatment of Being. "Being" (with a capital "B") is not a thing among other things, according to Heidegger, but rather the ground that allows for particular things, or "beings" (with a lowercase "b"), to make their appearance. Tables, chairs, trees, and humans are all "beings." But what is it that makes it possible for these beings to exist? What is it that constitutes "Being" itself, apart from the qualities of individual beings? The question of Being, thus, is a question that is addressed toward the Being of beings, or in other words, it is a question that asks us to consider what it is that first makes possible the existence of all the particular things that do in fact exist in the world. It was a question first raised by the Presocratic philosophers but which needs to be reconsidered in light of our contemporary situation. "Why are there beings at all instead of nothing?"[16] Heidegger asks, and in doing so he calls to our attention an issue that is prior to, deeper, broader, and more universal than any particular, existent "thing." He asks us, in sum, to consider the conditions that are required for the existence of any-thing. In order to successfully do this, however, Heidegger tells us that we must rethink the concept of Being anew and break free from the distorting influence of the Platonic tradition.

According to Heidegger, the influence of Plato's way of thinking is evident in all major Western philosophical figures; from Aristotle, who developed the science of logic and used it to break Being up into little bits and pieces; to Descartes, who, with his dualism of mind and body, split the thinking subject off from the world; to Nietzsche, who completely rejected the notion of Being in favor of constant flux, change, and becoming. The common element in the history of Western metaphysics, Heidegger tells us, is the tendency to assume that human thinking is separate and distinct from Being and that we can understand Being only by focusing our attention on the fragments of existence, looking at them from afar like an astronomer looks at the stars through a telescope. As long as we continue to make this assumption and focus our attention on particular beings instead of Being itself, we will remain alienated, isolated, and atomized. The resuscitation of Western civilization depends on our willingness to develop an understanding of Being that goes to its foundations and that sees human life as rooted in the whole. You will notice here that in his concern with the whole, Heidegger rejects the contention of the analytic philosophers surveyed in the previous chapter. Instead of trying to understand Being by analyzing it into bits and pieces, Heidegger instead wants to encourage us to synthesize our understanding of the world and in this manner aspire toward Truth. In this regard his project is similar to the project pursued by Hegel, and like Hegel, Heidegger continues to be held in very low regard by most analytic philosophers.

Dasein

So how are we to correct our failure of vision? How are we to look past particular things in the world to understand the underlying unity that ties together all that exists? In *Being and Time*, Heidegger suggests a starting point. Heidegger observes that human beings are by their very nature "thrown" into the drama of existence. Before anything else, we exist, and our existence is not separate from Being but is embedded right in the middle of it from the moment we are born. If it was otherwise, we wouldn't be here in the first place. Our own being is a unique manifestation of Being itself, and so the special characteristics of our own human experience of existence should be capable of giving us access to the mysteries of Being, the way that a bridge provides passage to either side of a river. Heidegger uses the word *Dasein* to refer to the uniquely human sort of existence. The word "Dasein" is made up of two German words: *Da* means "there," but it also carries a temporal component, suggesting something like "there-then" or "there-now." *Sein* means "to be." "Being-there" is a common way that this term is translated into English, but perhaps "being-there-now" would be a better translation. What Heidegger's use of the term Dasein high-lights, in any case, is the point that human beings exist in a particular place at a particular time and in a particular way, and that we experience everything in our world from this fundamental starting point; including Being itself. As he writes at the very opening of *Being and Time*, "The essence of Da-sein lies in its existence."[17]

Because we are rooted in Being from the moment we come to be, by ex-amining the essential characteristics that constitute who we are, Heidegger hopes that we will be able to trace our way back to the deepest depths of all existence and consequently relieve our underlying alienation. Remember, Heidegger is not primarily concerned here with our physical mode of existence but rather with the way that we *consciously* experience the world. His starting point is a description of those mental states that are characteristic of the human mode of being. In this regard, one of the fundamental traits that we can discern in Dasein, claims Heidegger, is the fact that it is the only form of being that "in its being ... is concerned about its very [B]eing."[18] This is something that makes us different from all other beings-in-the-world. Part of our essence is the basic fact that we "care" about who we are and what we will become. Unlike other creatures that have no sense of self, we desire to understand ourselves and to fulfill our poten-tial. For this reason, we are always reflecting on the past and planning for the future. Dasein, then, as it cares about its existence, also always steps outside of the bounds of the present and "projects" into other times and places. It conjures up new goals, projects, and objectives, and then pursues them, evolving and changing over the course of its life. In so doing, Dasein reveals itself as "pure possibility" because as humans we are always capable of making choices that are unanticipated and novel. In existing, we constantly run ahead of who we are at any given moment, making decisions to undertake the sorts of projects that fill our lives with meaningful activity.

In sum, Dasein, or human being, is thrown into the world as a being that cares about its existence, and thus it is constantly projecting outside of itself in anticipation of the future and in recollection of the past (see Figure 13.2). In this way, Dasein is inherently temporal. Even though it experiences life from the perspective of the here and now, it nevertheless mentally flees into both the past and the future on a constant basis. It is precisely this "fleeing" that allows Dasein to begin the task of gathering a world around itself. If humans never mentally stepped outside of their own here and now awareness, they would never have an opportunity to create and retain the webs of interconnections that are experi-enced as our lived universe. Without the element of time, we could not string events together into some sort of lasting sequence, and without that, there would be nothing like the everyday world that we experience ourselves inhabiting. What time does for us is to create a sort of "clearing" in the fabric of existence, and thus to make room for the presence of a domain that we can then call our own environment. Just as the building of a house requires that we clear out a space on the ground for the foundation, so the gathering together of a world requires that we clear out a space in Being itself. Time is the tool with

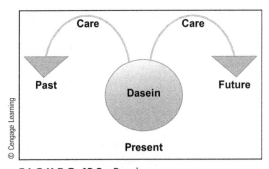

FIGURE 13.2 Dasein

which we are able to do this. As Heidegger writes, "Only in terms of the rootedness of Dasein in temporality, do we gain insight into the existential possibility of the phenomenon that we characterized at the beginning of our analytic as the fundamental constitution of being-in-the-world." In other words, it is time that makes it possible for us to create a world to be-in. It allows us to think outside of the immediate moment, to retain memories and make them "present" to our consciousness, and thus to build a world of relationships around us.

Being-toward-Death

But time is a force that also makes us mindful that there is a point when we will no longer "be-there" and when we will die. Thus, in addition to care and time, conscious human life is constituted by an awareness of death. We are "beings-toward-death." No other creatures, according to Heidegger, have this unique quality as a part of their existence. Certainly, other sorts of organisms in the world "expire," but none of them "dies" in the sense of anticipating and feeling anxious about their own impending mortality.[19] In this, we discover the initially disturbing fact that there will be a time when we will cease to exist. Thus, ironically, part of what makes Dasein unique is its awareness of its potential to no longer be-there. Coming to grips with this fact is difficult for many people, and so they suppress their thoughts about this inevitability and try to forget about death. Yet to suppress this awareness is a mistake that leads down the path of an inauthentic and alienated existence, according to Heidegger. First of all, because "being-toward-death" is an essential part of our very essence, ignoring death is to ignore part of who we are. To suppress an awareness of death is to try to become like a nonhuman "thing," an object that will never die.

Furthermore, to ignore the inevitability of death is to deny the very quality that holds the potential to give our lives an "end" and thus a "totality."[20] What Heidegger seems to mean here is that without the finality of death, particular human lives would never be capable of being "summed up" and given shape or meaning. Imagine a movie that went on forever, without a final, concluding scene. What would be the point? How would we ever be able to say what the movie was about? Without an end, the movie would just be one scene after another, and there would be no culmination that would give us the satisfaction of understanding how all of the scenes were meant to fit together and how they shed light on each other. Likewise, our human lives take on meaning and significance by virtue of our awareness that the actions and activities that we take part in during the course of living will contribute to an overall project that others, after we die, will look back on and appreciate as a whole. "A constant unfinished quality thus lies in the essence and constitution of Dasein.... As long as Dasein is a being, it has never attained its 'wholeness.' But if it does, this gain becomes the absolute loss of being-in-the-world."[21] To die is to no longer be-in-the-world, but it is also to reach a point of completion, albeit a point of completion that can never actually be experienced by the dead person himself or herself. Nevertheless, the ability to die bestows upon us a unique and rather precious potentiality; the potential to leave behind a time-bound memory that others may cherish as a totality in-itself. As Heidegger writes,

> The "deceased," as distinct from the dead body, has been torn away from "those remaining behind," and that is so because he is "still more" in his kind of being than an inner worldly thing at hand to be taken care of. In lingering together with him in mourning and commemorating, those remaining behind are with him, in a mode of concern which honors him.[22]

When we mourn, we don't mourn the body that is left behind but rather the whole person we cared about; the entire life project that we can now see, in retrospect, constituted our loved one. When Heidegger writes about human beings as Dasein, this is what he is ultimately suggesting. We are not just bodily "things" that exist in the same mode as rocks and chairs. To be human is to care about others and the world, to pursue life projects, and to die. All of these are activities and events, not objectively present entities and "things," and as such they are made possible only by our ability to exist in time. As Heidegger concludes, "Dasein is grounded in temporality."[23]

Being is revealed to humans by way of time, and thus the two are very intimately connected to one another for us. Without time, we would not "be" who we are. It is time that gives us the capacity to hope, plan, remember, fear, and mourn, and it is Being that gives us our essence and "nature." Being and time together allow us to gather facts and ideas and to arrange them into a world of our own. But notice, neither Being nor time is a "thing." They are not objects inside of the world. They are the very conditions that allow the world to unfold and to be what it is for us. Being, however, also seems to stand above time, because it is the more comprehensive concept. It is the actual essence of "unfolding" that gives substance and a ground to the passage of time. Time emerges from the human desire to know the essence of Being itself, and so it would not come to be unless Being was there to be cared for in the first place.

Inauthenticity and Technological Thinking

All of this contributes to Heidegger's diagnosis of the disease of his time; the disease that has led to the advent of Nazism, Bolshevism, "Americanism," death camps, and the technological manipulation of people. The root of this disease is our alienation from Being. The problem with modern human beings, according to Heidegger, is that they have allowed themselves to be pulled away from an authentic understanding of themselves as time-bound, unfolding projects, and have instead come to view themselves as "objects" or "animals" alongside all of the other "things" that exist in the world. Certainly, along with objects and animals, we share a relationship to Being. However, our relationship to Being is a different one from that of objects and animals. Human-being, Dasein, is unique in its care for Being, as has already been discussed. But beyond this, because we care about Being and desire to understand it, human beings have the special responsibility to act as the "shepherds of Being."[24] We must shoulder an enormous burden to "guard the Truth of Being."[25] This means that we must be careful to keep the question of Being at the forefront of our thinking and not allow ourselves the temptation of "falling away" from a concern for this issue. In the modern age, this is precisely what has happened. The experiences of isolation, loneliness, uprootedness, and superfluousness described by Heidegger's student Hannah Arendt are symptoms of this much deeper experience of the "forgetfulness of Being" that has resulted in "the homelessness of contemporary man from the essence of Being's history."[26] This "homelessness" about which Heidegger writes is the circumstance of those for whom Being has become a forgotten issue. When a human being no longer cares about the question of Being, that person has become alienated from the very quality that made him or her a human being in the first place. This is the epitome of self-loss and nihilism, and it is the also the height of "inauthentic" existence.

Inauthenticity is clearly operant in the tendency toward what Heidegger calls "technological thinking." Modern cultures, whether they be the fascist culture of Germany, the communist culture of the Soviet Union, or the consumer culture of the United States, were, during Heidegger's time, all focused toward viewing human beings, and in fact the whole of nature itself, as instruments to be utilized for the exercise of human power and greed. At the start of this chapter, I pointed to the Muselmann as a profoundly disturbing example of what happens when human beings are treated as "things" rather than as ends-in-themselves. But this same process is at work everywhere, according to Heidegger, and not just in the death camps of the Nazis. During World War II, the Americans dropped atomic bombs on Hiroshima and Nagasaki, justifying the deaths of hundreds of thousands of innocent civilians by claiming that these people were instrumental in ending the war sooner than it would otherwise have ended. Stalin, the leader of the Soviet Union, destroyed millions of his own countrymen to promote his own agenda and hold on to power during and after World War II. In less dramatic but perhaps no less destructive form, we see technological thinking at work today when advertisers and social engineers use the latest state-of-the-art techniques to manipulate public opinion for the purposes of making money or of winning votes. When humans are treated as objects that are merely "useful" or "unuseful" for particular purposes, we know that technological thinking is operational and that an estrangement from the true nature of human essence, and thus of Being itself, has occurred. This is bad enough in itself, according to Heidegger, but as Arendt reminds us, it may also, further-more, be the prelude to future atrocities.

Being reveals itself in many ways, but the fundamental problem with technological thinking is that it forces Being to reveal itself in an artificial, limited, and restricted fashion that is subject to human power and its whims. Take, for instance, the manner in which the science of behavioral psychology has attempted to "reveal" the nature of the human mind. Psychologists, such as B. F. Skinner, claimed that human beings are "blank slates" whose behavior can be controlled and programmed through the careful and systematic introduction of various positive and negative stimuli. If you want a person to desire something, get that person to associate that thing with a reward. If you want a person to dislike something, get that person to associate that thing with a punishment. By exposing a person to such rewards and punishments, you can, in this way of thinking, shape the human mind to be anything you want it to be. This is all that the human "mind" is, according to behaviorism: a pattern of stimulus and response. But does this account really tell us the true nature and potential of the human mind? Or does this sort of procedure only tell us some of the ways that a human mind reacts under a tightly controlled environment? According to Heidegger, technological thinking is the result of a "will to mastery,"[27] and, in a manner of speaking, it sees what it wants to see, rather than allowing the nature, or Being, of things to reveal themselves according to their own manner of "unfolding." This is the real danger, of course. Technology does reveal a kind of "truth," yet at the same time that it does so it also conceals the fact that the "truth" it reveals is a limited, partial, and fragmented sort of truth. Furthermore, it also perpetuates the lie that human power is capable of controlling, interrogating, and provoking Being into showing itself in its totality as something that is "useful" to human devices.

Authenticity

So what is the alternative? The latter part of Heidegger's writing career was devoted to exploring the manner in which Dasein could execute its duty as the shepherd of Being and thus act as a conduit through which Being might gain its authentic voice. The manner in which this could be accomplished, Heidegger tells us, is through a "turning" away from the rational, logic-based, and technological tradition of Western philosophy toward a new way of pure thinking that refuses to be bound by the rules, laws, prejudices, or goals of past thinking. "Especially we moderns can learn only if we always unlearn at the same time. Applied to the matter before us: we can learn thinking only if we radically unlearn what thinking has been traditionally. To do that, we must at the same time come to know it."[28] So, we must learn about our tradition, not simply to mimic the thinkers of the past but to unlearn their mistakes and to strike out on our own new and original paths. In the process of engaging in thinking for its own sake, and not for some other instrumental purpose, we will find our way back to Being as long as we remain "open" to the call of Being as it makes itself heard in the very language that we use to do our thinking. It is in language itself, Heidegger ultimately concludes, that we will rediscover the wonder of Being itself. "Language is the house of Being."[29] What he means by this is that it is in language that we think, and it is through thinking that we come to understand our relationship to Being. Language creates the conceptual "walls" between which the existence of Being can make its appearance. Just as the walls of a house create the space that allows for the existence of a "living room" or a "bedroom," so language creates a "space" that allows for the advent of Being. In thinking freely and allowing language to take us where it will, we trace out the complicated and unanticipated contours that give shape and unity to Being. Being thus gains a voice through human language, but at the same time Being shapes what is said in human language. Like a wanderer walking along a wooded path, the authentic thinker is one who is enraptured by the journey, unconcerned where this journey will lead, and not at all disappointed if it winds up at a dead end. Like a walk in the woods, the only goal of pure thinking is the unfolding process itself, which, like the unfolding of time, attunes us to the ever-evolving character of Being.

In a number of his later writings, Heidegger increasingly stresses the interrelatedness and interdependency of Being with human existence. It is a mistake, he suggests, to think of Being as something separate from, or "above," Dasein. Rather, Being itself could not exist without humans. As he said in a televised interview with Richard Wisser, "And the fundamental thought of my thinking is precisely that Being, or the manifestation of Being, *needs* human beings and that, vice-versa, human beings are only human beings if they are standing in the manifestation of Being."[30] This reinforces Heidegger's long-standing point that Being is not a "thing" among other things but that it is instead an emergent "unfolding" that comes to be through the language of humans. Without humans, Being would have no voice, and this is why the question of Being is such an important issue for humans to take seriously. As the "shepherds of Being," we have a responsibility to take care of Being and to articulate its mysteries. If we fail to do this, Being remains concealed and humans remain alienated and homeless with no real, deep roots in the world. This is precisely the plight of modern humans, claims Heidegger. In their concern with "things" and with "beings," contemporary humans have neglected their more profound duty to Being. They race around, busily chasing money, possessions, fame, and power. What is true and what is false no longer concern many people. Instead, they pursue whatever sorts of things will bring them the most material rewards in the quickest period of time. In the end, I believe Heidegger's most important message is to call us back from the superficiality of this modern way of life to a more respectful and profound appreciation for Truth itself. He is challenging us to take our words and our beliefs seriously, and to see them in the light of some project that is bigger and more lasting than our own individual lives. What we write and say in language builds the world around us, and we need to take care with the sort of world that we are in the process of building lest we discover that it is not a world in which we want to dwell.

Heidegger and Nazism

It is one of the tragic ironies of history that Heidegger, who was so convinced of the world-building potential of language, should have become involved with one of the most malignant, world-destroying political movements ever to sweep across the face of Europe. In May 1933, Heidegger joined the Nazi Party, and he

---

B o x 13.1   Heidegger's Influence

Heidegger's thinking and writing led to the growth and development of existentialist philosophy, but he has also exerted influence on an incredible number of other fields, including psychology, theology, art, literary criticism, political science, hermeneutics, and environmentalism.

In psychology, figures such as Jacques Lacan, Abraham Maslow, Rollo May, Viktor Frankl, and Irvin Yalom have built upon Heideggerian ideas about the nature of human Being and authenticity, developing unique and groundbreaking therapies and theories of human behavior.

In theology, figures such as Paul Tillich, Emmanuel Levinas, Martin Buber, and D. T. Suzuki have engaged with Heidegger's discussion of Being, relating it to reflections on God and the holy.

In art, Heidegger's writings, especially his piece "The Origin of the Work of Art," have been incredibly influential on artists, writers, and filmmakers such as Terrence Malick, Milan Kundera, Anselm Kiefer, and Philip K. Dick.

In political science, figures such as Leo Strauss, Hannah Arendt, Herbert Marcuse, and Jürgen Habermas have commented on and developed Heidegger's ideas concerning the relationship between the concrete individual and the collective.

Heidegger's critique of technology has been important to the development of the deep ecology movement. His essay "The Question Concerning Technology" is especially influential in this regard.

---

remained a member until the end of World War II. The significance of this episode in Heidegger's career remains a point of incredible controversy, leading many, on the one hand, to discount his philosophy as one that is tainted by totalitarian sentiments, or on the other, leading many to discount the man himself as a poor "shepherd of Being." There is, I think, a bit of truth and a bit of falsehood in both sides of this opposition, and I think we are well advised not to be too quick in coming to unequivocal or overly simplistic conclusions concerning Heidegger's character or his philosophy based solely on the nature of his political involvements. The real issues are very complicated, and we will only have room to touch on a few of the most prominent ones in what follows. Nonetheless, I believe it is of absolute importance to keep in mind that the content of a philosophy is largely independent of the character of the individual who authored that philosophy. Let us not forget that in the United States, the Declaration of Independence, which declares that "all men are created equal," was authored by Thomas Jefferson, who owned slaves. Does this mean that the sentiments expressed in the Declaration are therefore unsound? Most of us would probably not want to make that claim, but would rather recognize that the man, Jefferson, was fallible, imperfect, and subject to the prejudices and temptations of his time. This does not excuse his actions, but neither does it undermine his greatest ideas. The same, I think, might be claimed about Heidegger.

As discussed at the beginning of this chapter, Heidegger was living in a time of discontent. This is the first point that should be considered when trying to make sense of his attraction to National Socialism. It was because of this widespread discontent in Germany that the Nazis were able to ascend to power in the first place, and though their power grab took place rather quickly, it didn't happen overnight. Hitler and his officers promised much, and their movement rose to prominence by exploiting the feelings, the hopes, and the fears of the German people. It was not by peddling atrocity, murder, and mayhem that Hitler was able to gain support for his movement. On the contrary, he promised revolution against the old, decaying order of things, the reintegration of all Germans into one people, and the promise of a rejuvenated national spirit that offered pride and hope for the population. While all of these promises turned out to be lies,[31] the rhetoric of the Nazis promoted a vision of change that was very attractive to a people caught in a time of loneliness, despair, and social atomization. The Germans, collectively, wanted a change, and the Nazis held out the possibility for a radical cultural and political revolution.[32]

Heidegger was attracted to National Socialism, in part, for some of the same reasons as many other Germans. He seems to have thought that there was great promise in this movement, and his involvement with the Nazis seems to have been partly motivated by his hope that a revolutionary change would bring life and vitality back to Germany. As Heidegger writes, "At the time, I saw in the movement that had come to power the possibility of an inner self-collection and of a renewal of the people, and a path toward the discovery of its historical-Western purpose."[33] This is not an outrageous expectation, though it might be naïve. Like many people today in the United States who advocate "getting involved" with the government to change the things that you don't like, Heidegger seems to have wanted to "get involved" in the political life of his country and to help direct what he saw as a promising "movement" toward its positive potential. Again, Heidegger's own words are helpful here:

> What would have happened and what would have been prevented if, around 1933, all capable forces had set out, in secret cohesion, to slowly purify and moderate the "movement" that had come to power? ...
> Those who were so prophetically gifted then that they foresaw what was to come (I was not so wise), why did they wait almost ten years to oppose the threatening disaster? Why did not those who thought they knew it, why did precisely they not set out to direct everything, starting from the foundations, toward the good in 1933?[34]

It therefore seems that one of the reasons that Heidegger became involved with the Nazis stemmed from his belief that by getting involved with them, he could help mold and shape the movement into something positive and beneficial for the German nation as a whole.

Heidegger's actual involvement with National Socialism was restricted to his acceptance of the position of the rectorate at the University of Freiburg, a position that he retained for about a year. It was after delivering a controversial speech titled "The Self-Assertion of the German University" that Heidegger came to be considered unreliable and overly independent. His speech was, thereafter, forbidden to be sold, and Heidegger resigned his position as rector. Top Nazis began to condemn and denounce Heidegger, but he nonetheless remained a party member until the end of the war. Why all of this controversy? The main issues seem to have revolved around the abstract nature of Heidegger's philosophy, his rejection of the racism of Nazi biological theories, and his desire to designate himself and the University as the spiritual center of the Nazi movement. Heidegger's "Nazism" was thus labeled by one of the party leaders as "a kind of 'private National Socialism,' which circumvented the perspectives of the Party program."[35] In sum, Heidegger was a threat to the real program of the Nazis, and his active involvement with the movement ended as this became apparent to those in power and as it became apparent to Heidegger that his involvement would be ineffective at producing any real, positive effects. The Nazis, of course, continued to use Heidegger's name, which was associated worldwide with deep and important thinking, as a part of their propaganda attesting to the cultural supremacy of German culture.

But despite all of this, it has been claimed by some people that there are indeed aspects of Heidegger's philosophy that are compatible with Nazi doctrines and with totalitarianism in general. For instance, Heidegger's call for a spiritual renewal of the people by way of reaffirming their "rootedness" in Being sounds very similar to the Nazi emphasis on "blood and soil." Heidegger's characterization of Dasein as "pure possibility" has resonance with the Nazi principle that "everything is possible."[36] Heidegger's "irrationalism," as evidenced in his criticisms of logic and technology, sounds not unlike the Nazi focus on the importance of "instinct" and "will" over reason. We could multiply these similarities, but all in all they remain interesting parallels and not out-and-out correspondences. In fact, the dissimilarities between Heideggerian philosophy and Nazism are far more profound. Heidegger's criticism of technological thinking is a direct attack on the sort of mechanized destructiveness at which the Nazis excelled. Heidegger's rejection of the reduction of human beings to biological entities is in undeniable contradiction to Nazi race policies. His criticism of the destructive influences of mass movements on the interior life of the individual sits none too well with the mob character of National Socialism.

Certainly, we could continue to search for commonalities and differences between Heidegger's philosophy and Nazi philosophy, but I don't think this will result in much illumination. Perhaps the most important issue here is that Heidegger lived in the same culture that gave birth to National Socialism. This was a culture that was in crisis, that was critical of the state of things, and that was ripe for change. Such periods of time are filled with opportunity as well as with danger. On the one hand, there is the opportunity for new things to be done and old problems to be resolved. On the other hand, there is the danger of merely perpetuating the old problems through impatience and over-hastiness. The sad fact is that when given the chance, the masses often jump at quick fixes rather than summoning up the resolve to confront deep issues over the long run. The consequences of cultural crisis are, as a result, often disappointing and sometimes destructive. Both Heidegger and the Nazis offered paths toward change, but whereas the Nazi program of revolution was political, violent, and coercive, Heidegger's path was philosophical in nature. He sought the spiritual rejuvenation of humanity not through brute force but through deep thinking, and let's face it, this is not something that appeals to most people.

Heidegger's career as a philosopher was forever stained by his involvement with Nazism, yet his ideas were powerful enough to survive this episode and to attract the interest of a diverse group of philosophers, writers, and artists, many of them, ironically, from Jewish backgrounds. Although he sometimes dismissed the notion, Heidegger had himself become the instigator of a new "movement" in thought that became known as "existentialism." It was in France that existential philosophy took hold first and most firmly, and during the post–World War II years it became just as much a fashion and countercultural lifestyle as it was a philosophical perspective. "In the United States existentialism was described as the esoteric creed of Parisian bohemians, and became associated with jazz, cafe singers, and pony tails."[37] The popular image of the existential philosopher was that of a black-clad, cigarette-smoking intellectual who spent the day sitting in a cafe while philosophizing, drinking coffee, and all the while rejecting the boring values of mainstream, polite society. While this image prejudiced some people against existentialism, it also led to a great deal of real-world excitement about this philosophy and the questions that it raises for us.

JEAN-PAUL SARTRE

© Juneko J. Robinson

On the forefront of this new movement in philosophy was the very influential figure of Jean-Paul Sartre (1905–1980). Sartre was undeniably fascinated and influenced by Heidegger's ideas, but he had an uneasy relationship with Heidegger as a man and as a political figure. While Heidegger was a member of the Nazi Party, Sartre fought against the Nazis as a member of the French army and the French resistance. Nevertheless, when he was captured and detained as a prisoner of war under the Germans for nine months, Sartre is reported to have taught his fellow POWs about Heideggerian thinking. After the war, Sartre became a committed communist, and he proceeded to develop his own brand of existential philosophy in directions that would lead to much further friction between himself and his philosophical mentor. Heidegger, in fact, claimed that Sartre's philosophy ultimately bore no resemblance to his own, and that what Sartre described as "existentialism" simply was a reiteration of many of the mistakes initiated by Plato thousands of years ago.

Being-in-Itself and Being-for-Itself

Sartre agreed with Heidegger that addressing the "question of Being" is of primary importance to us. But whereas Heidegger's discussion of Dasein characterizes human beings as immersed in and interconnected with Being itself, Sartre's characterization of the human connection to the world makes a clear distinction between two separate, and incompatible, forms of Being that are forever in conflict with and opposition to one another. Being is not one and whole, it seems, but rather is divided between "two absolutely separated regions."[38] On the one hand, there is "being-in-itself." Being-in-itself is nonconscious material "stuff," like the stuff that makes up rocks and chairs. It doesn't think or make choices because it is wholly self-contained and complete "in-itself." It "is what it is"[39] and nothing more. A rock, for instance, has no capability to choose to be anything but a rock. It is a "thing" with no mind, no freedom, and thus no responsibility for what it is. On the other hand, there is "being-for-itself."[40] A being-for-itself corresponds to what Heidegger discussed as Dasein. It is a conscious, thinking, human being. Being-for-itself "is defined ... as being what it is not and not being what it is."[41] In other words, it is always capable of being something other than it is at any given instance and of electing to pursue new and unanticipated paths and objectives as it projects into the future. What distinguishes being-for-itself essentially from being-in-itself is the fact that being-for-itself can make free choices and thus has responsibility for what sort of life it lives, while being-in-itself has no freedom of choice and so has no responsibility for the course of its own existence. A rock is not responsible for choosing its life project, because it is a being-in-itself. A human, on the other hand, is responsible for the course of his or her life because a human is a being-for-itself and thus has the freedom to make choices. This is a basic, foundational, ontological distinction for Sartre: Being is divided between the in-itself and the for-itself.

TABLE 13.1   Being-in-Itself versus Being-for-Itself

Being-in-Itself	Being-for-Itself
1. Essence precedes existence	1. Existence precedes essence
2. Not free	2. Free
3. Cannot make choices	3. Always makes choices
4. No moral responsibility	4. Possesses responsibility
5. Not conscious	5. Conscious
6. Nonhuman	6. Human

In insisting on this distinction, Sartre picks up on a theme explored by Heidegger. However, whereas Heidegger refused to equate Dasein with a form of consciousness that is separate and apart from the rest of the world, Sartre establishes the experience of being human precisely on this ground. According to Sartre, the human mind exists as an entity, a thinking "thing," which is in eternal conflict with the rest of unthinking, inert reality. Echoing Descartes, Sartre claims that we come to understand our own unique form of existence most clearly when we recognize the power and structure of our minds and that there is one absolutely certain truth upon which all else rests: "I think, therefore I am." As he writes in *Being and Nothingness*, "the *cogito* must be our point of departure."[42] But, according to Heidegger, choosing this as a starting point dooms Sartre's philosophical project from the very beginning. It assumes that human thinking is alienated from its world rather than embedded within it, and this was an assumption that Heidegger had tried to avoid all along.

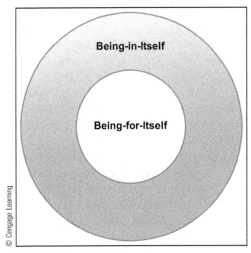

Sartre anticipates these sorts of criticisms and attempts to show that the apparent dualism between being-in-itself and being-for-itself is really only a dualism when considered from the perspective of abstraction. In actuality, he tells us, both of these kinds of Being form a synthesis, such that one depends upon the other for its existence. Human consciousness is contained within Being as a whole; however, it is not continuous with nonthinking existence. It represents a disruption of being-in-itself. It is "like a hole in being at the heart of Being,"[43] as shown in Figure 13.3.

FIGURE 13.3 Being

The for-itself is, in fact, a sort of "nihilation" or "nothing" that clears out a space in the in-itself. This is what creates room for human freedom of thought and rescues human existence from the determinism of the material world. Yet, as a nihilation or hole in Being, the for-itself (human consciousness) depends upon the in-itself. A "hole" by definition represents a vacancy or opening in something. A hole simply can't exist without being taken out of some substance, and so human existence is really part and parcel of a larger "whole," namely, Being in its totality. This recalls Hegel's dialectic of Being, and in fact much of Sartre's terminology, including the in-itself and the for-itself distinction, was first coined by Hegel.[44]

Freedom and Bad Faith

In his famous essay titled *Existentialism Is a Humanism*, Sartre provides us with the most concise and clear formulation of the philosophy of existentialism ever articulated. Existentialism, he writes, is the view that, for humans, "Existence precedes essence."[45] Human beings first exist, and then they live their lives; further, it is through the manner of choosing and living one's life that one constructs an identity, an essence, for oneself. We are, as Heidegger claimed, "thrown" into Being, and from that point on we struggle to make something of ourselves. This view is quite different from the religious view, which claims that God first conceptualizes a notion of human essence and then creates humans according to that image. Sartre's existentialism rejects this and instead posits the idea that human beings have no pregiven essence or soul. Before pursuing life projects, we are nothing. It is only over the course of living our lives, as we struggle and strive, that we pull together a world that gives shape, purpose, and meaning to who we are. As one acts in the world, one becomes a person who is simply the sum total of all the things in which one has engaged oneself. Recall the treatment by Schopenhauer and Nietzsche (in Chapter 11) of this same issue, and it becomes clear the influence they had on the development of existentialist thought.

According to Sartre, it is important to embrace the freedom that we have as beings-for-ourselves and to accept the full weight of responsibility that this status bestows upon us. We only have one life to live, so we had better do all that we can to make sure that it is the sort of life of which we are proud.

Many people, of course, find the responsibility of this freedom too crushing, and so they lapse into what Sartre calls "bad faith."[46] To be in bad faith is to shirk your responsibility as a free creature and attempt to become like those beings in the world that are "in-themselves." Thinking of oneself as a being-in-itself is a great comfort to many people, because it entails never having to take responsibility for your own actions in the world. Think of all the people you know who prefer to see themselves as victims of circumstance rather than as individuals who have made poor decisions in life. To be a "thing" that is pushed this way and that by the contingencies of the world is to free oneself from accepting responsibility for anything. While this is, on the one hand, dehumanizing, it is also, on the other hand, reassuring because it allows one to avoid feelings of guilt, responsibility, and the ownership of poor choices. However, according to Sartre, human beings, whether they like it or not, are not things. A human being is an ongoing process that is constantly open to new possibilities in the future. Human beings live in the present moment at which the future is decided. If they think otherwise they are fooling themselves and being purposefully blind to their own nature. Even if one chooses not to make choices in life, Sartre tells us that refraining from choosing is still a choice. There is no way out of this dilemma. Humans are doomed to make choices, are in fact "condemned" to their freedom, and are thus always responsible for the details of their lives.

Sartre's philosophy places a heavy emphasis on the importance of personal responsibility and freedom in human life, yet it also places an equal amount of emphasis on the unending struggle and difficulty involved in the quest to avoid falling into bad faith. As articulated by Sartre, existentialism is not an easy philosophy to live by, yet it is one that was taken very seriously by him and his life partner Simone de Beauvoir (1908–1986), who was another important existentialist philosopher in her own right. Throughout their lives together, both Sartre and Beauvoir fought against the constraining forces of mainstream society, living in their own freely chosen and very controversial manner. These two individuals, though deeply committed to one another until Sartre's death in 1980, never married, opting rather to carry on their relationship outside of the formal traditions of wedlock. This gesture was probably calculated, like many others in their lives, to help them break free of the suffocating and objectifying gaze of the public, which often tries to neatly pigeonhole people and to look at them as "things" that are there to be ogled for the purposes of mere entertainment. To take on the role of a celebrity is, in a sense, to prostitute oneself and to sacrifice freedom and authenticity for fame and fortune. This is a sacrifice that neither Sartre nor Beauvoir were willing to make. As proof of this, in 1964, Sartre refused to accept the Nobel Prize in literature for his autobiographical book *The Words*. Sartre explained his rejection of this award to Beauvoir in the following way:

> I am entirely against the Nobel prize because it amounts to classifying writers.... What does this prize correspond to? What does it mean, saying that a writer had it in 1974, what does it mean in relation to the

men who had it earlier or to those who have not had it but who also write and who are perhaps better? What does the prize mean? Can it really be said that the year they gave it to me I was superior to my colleagues, the other writers, and that the year after it was someone else who was superior? Does one really have to look at literature like that? ... It's an absurd notion. The whole idea of arranging literature in a hierarchical order is one that is completely contrary to the literary idea. On the other hand it is perfectly suitable for a bourgeois society that wants to make everything an integral part of the system.[47]

All of the fame, fortune, and prestige in the world are not worth the risk of giving up one's dignity and freedom as an individual, according to Sartre and Beauvoir. Conventional "honors" like the Nobel Prize are among the means used by "the system" to buy off and placate free and creative humans, thus bringing them into the fold of the mainstream. It is easier and safer to accept the accolades and rewards of the system than it is to fight against the conventional ways of doing things and to change the very institutions that constitute society. Perhaps one of the important messages that existentialist philosophy has to communicate to us is that "selling out" is never a good option. We must guard against becoming cogs in the social machine to retain our individual dignity so that we may take charge of our lives resolutely and responsibly. Heidegger learned this fact the hard way, and his students, Sartre and Beauvoir included, were committed to making sure that the rest of us never forgot this lesson.

SIMONE DE BEAUVOIR

The Second Sex

Simone de Beauvoir tells us that the lesson against selling out is especially important for modern women to understand and take to heart. In her book *The Second Sex*, Beauvoir applies an existential analysis to the lives of women to show how they have been objectified, and have *allowed* themselves to be objectified, over

the course of history. Women, like all humans, are beings-for-themselves who are, nevertheless, always tempted to give up their freedom and fall into bad faith. The temptation for women to give in to this urge is, perhaps, even greater than it is for men, because women can garner tremendous social, economic, and cultural rewards by conforming to mainstream images of beauty and sexual desirability. Actresses, models, pop singers, and even nonpublic figures like businesswomen, cashiers, and housewives are prone to falling for the lie that their real worth is found in how closely they conform to a standardized image of femininity. This view, that there is some sort of "essence" that defines a woman as a "real woman," is called by Beauvoir the "myth of the eternal feminine."[48] This dangerous myth perpetuates the false idea that there is some sort of timeless notion of femininity against which all women, in all places, should be judged. In our own culture, we see this myth manifested in the idea that a true "lady" is thin, well-groomed, demure, and submissive toward men. Any woman who does not exhibit these characteristics is often denigrated, devalued, and regarded as defective. She is called a "cow" if she is not thin enough, or a "bitch" if she is not submissive to men. These sorts of derogatory terms are symptomatic of the fact that when anyone, and especially women, step outside of the lines of a set of predetermined stereotypes, there are punishments to be faced. Mainstream society expects people to conform, to act like "things-in-themselves" by following the dictates not of their own, individual, free will but of common, impersonal, social rules. Beauvoir eloquently articulates for us the dangers of this sort of bad faith and argues that women must take responsibility for their own lives, refusing to be tempted and seduced, or intimidated and frightened, by those forces that threaten to pull them into inauthentic, shallow, and debased ways of life.

Nonetheless, according to Beauvoir, it is a mistake to hold only women accountable for their submission to the sexist attitudes of society. To do so would amount to blaming the victim. Obviously, men also share responsibility for the way things are, and in *The Second Sex* Beauvoir outlines the existential dynamics that have led to the contemporary condition of inequality between the sexes, highlighting both the domineering male contributions and the passive female contributions that together have helped to establish our stereotypes about the nature of masculinity and femininity. The ultimate point that Beauvoir wants to make is that although the world we live in has been directed along a certain path up to this point in history, it is concrete, living human beings, real-life men and women, who have chosen to follow this path, and we are, likewise, free to choose a different path as we move into the future. The sexism of today may become a thing of the past if we so choose, but this will require a great deal of commitment, effort, and honesty on the part of both men and women. If we are successful, however, the payoff for all human beings, both male and female, will be the realization of authentic "fraternity" and "liberty,"[49] and nothing is more worthwhile, according to Beauvoir.

Beauvoir begins her existential analysis of women by asking a simple, yet far from simplistic, question: "What is a woman?"[50] In the past, it has been held that a woman is "a womb,"[51] but as Beauvoir immediately points out, this is nowhere near an adequate definition. To say that a woman is "a womb" is to claim that it is biology that determines a woman's essence and that anyone born with the appropriate physiology is automatically a woman. Yet it is clear that in the human world, some females are considered more "womanly" than others: "...we are exhorted to be women, remain women, become women. It would appear, then, that every female human being is not necessarily a woman; to be so considered she must share in that mysterious and threatened reality known as femininity."[52] Beauvoir's point is clear. Some females are applauded and rewarded for their "womanly" qualities while those who are not "womanly" are punished and insulted. To be a "real" woman is to be feminine, and there are many biological females who are considered "unfeminine" and so not "real" women. But this still doesn't tell us much because it is not at all clear what it means to be "feminine." Is femininity some sort of natural, inborn essence? Is there an eternal and unchanging quality, something like a Platonic Form, that constitutes femininity as such? Is there, as Beauvoir calls it, an "eternal feminine" that some females are born with? Or is femininity, on the other hand, an artificial construction of culture that has been conjured into existence by human invention?

As an existentialist, Beauvoir's response to these questions is predictable. At the start of Book II of *The Second Sex*, she famously writes, "One is not born, but rather becomes, a woman."[53] The quality of womanhood, of femininity, is something that females are socialized into, and it is this process of socialization that has promoted their oppression across the span of history. The notion of the eternal feminine is thus a myth, a lie, and a fabrication. Like all human beings, women are born free, they are beings-for-themselves, endowed with the capacity to choose and to make of themselves whatever it is that they wish. It is only over the course of living their lives within the confines of mainstream society that women have become imprisoned by the sexist expectations and the social norms that civilization has established over the course of its development. Consistently throughout human history we have seen women subjected to the oppression of men, but it is a mistake to take this as evidence of some sort of natural, necessary state of affairs, claims Beauvoir. Just as we have come to view racial prejudice as something to be rejected and overcome, so must we come to view sexual prejudice as an abomination against all humankind. Just because it has always been so does not mean that it must always be so.

Yet Beauvoir is insistent and unequivocal in stating that we cannot expect widespread social changes to take hold simply by asserting the artificial nature of femininity and then directing individual women to make their own choices about how to live their lives. On this point Beauvoir departs from the radical views of Sartre and returns to the views of Heidegger by highlighting the fact that women, like all human beings, are "thrown" into a world that is not of their own making. We do not choose the world into which we are born, and in being born into a world we are inevitably affected and conditioned by its very character. This is why so many women have for so long accepted and submitted to their subservient position in society. Being born into a sexist environment has conditioned and socialized them into thinking of themselves as submissive. They have come to see themselves as weak and subordinate precisely because the world treats them that way. Therefore, to change women's situation will require more than simply a resolute decision on the part of individual women to act as they please; it will also require that society itself undergo a transformation so that future generations are born into a world in which women are viewed as equal to men.

Otherness

The truth is that women and men *are* equal in their Being, claims Beauvoir, because both sexes are human. They are beings-for-themselves. So what is it that has led to the social inequalities that we see in the world? Why is it that women have traditionally been subjected to the domination of men? The diagnosis offered by Beauvoir focuses on two things. First, there is the fundamental tendency of every consciousness to separate and define itself in terms of "otherness." "Otherness is a fundamental category of human thought."[54] What Beauvoir means by this is that as we make our way through the world, we define ourselves primarily by separating ourselves from those things that are outside and around us. We become aware of ourselves as individuals by drawing a line between our own minds and the other nonconscious and conscious beings in our environment. We develop a sense of ourselves as unique by coming into opposition with those things that are not us, thereby establishing the boundaries of our own identities. This recalls Hegel's discussion of lordship and bondage. How do I know who I am? According to Beauvoir (and Hegel), I know who I am primarily by recognizing the things that I am not, by recognizing those things that are different from me, and in the human community it has always been apparent that there is a basic biological difference that acts as a primary point of separation between men and women. Even though both men and women share a common essence as thinking beings, physically they have different sorts of bodies. It is this visible physical difference, as well as the procreative functions that are attached to these differences, that have been utilized by both men and women as a means of separating and defining themselves as different from one another. Women have wombs and bear children. Men do not. This biological disparity in the human species has traditionally been latched onto as a convenient and obvious way of establishing the social division between men and women. Keep in mind, of course, that these differences are really, according to Beauvoir, largely superficial. In the jargon of existentialism, such biological distinctions are matters of "facticity." They are facts of the world that we are free to interpret as we choose. Just as there is nothing inherent in the color of a person's skin that destines him to be a slave, so there is nothing inherent in a woman's sex that destines her to be submissive. Yet both skin color and sex are biological particularities that have traditionally been exploited as a means of dividing human beings into groups based on "otherness."

Beauvoir points out that in nature, the sexes complement one another, both being necessary to the propagation of the species. This would suggest that it is natural for men and women to be equal partners in life and that instead of opposition and hostility, we would expect their relationship to be characterized by *Mitsein*, or "fellowship based on solidarity and friendliness."[55] However, there have been a series of decisions made over the course of human history that have led us to think of women as "the weaker sex" in relation to men. In addition to the establishment of our identity against that of the "other," Beauvoir tells us that this series of decisions is the second factor that explains women's contemporary situation in the world.

Women and Biology

Women bear children and men do not. From this brute fact of biology there develops a way of life that, beginning in nomadic times, has developed into modern day sexism, not by necessity but by the force of human choice. According to Beauvoir, childbirth (before the advent of contraception) was initially experienced by women as something that happened to them, not something that they consciously controlled: "... she felt herself the plaything of obscure forces, and the painful ordeal of childbirth seemed a useless or even troublesome accident."[56] This feeling continued, so Beauvoir claims, as women went on to raise their offspring, and it was reinforced by the experience of menstruation. Nature governed a good portion of women's lives in an especially visible and dramatic fashion, and thus they felt themselves to be subject to mysterious forces that could not be planned for or understood. As a result, woman developed the habit of submitting to the world as it is. She became comfortable with the repetition of household tasks and did not strive to acquire the skills involved in planning for the future or to exert the willpower required to alter the course of events as they unfolded around her. Woman felt herself to be governed by the whims of an uncanny natural world that claimed her, rather than her mastering it. "In woman are incarnated the disturbing mysteries of nature," Beauvoir tells us, "and man escapes her hold when he frees himself from nature."[57]

Compared to women, men feel themselves to be relatively free from the contingencies of the cosmos. Men don't get pregnant or experience menstruation, and so they are not reminded, as women are on an ongoing basis, of how closely their bodies are related to the natural world. As a result, it is easier for men to develop a sense of their own autonomy and willpower. Beauvoir claims that it is in warrior culture that we see the key point of development in the male psychology as it is transformed into something that is for-itself rather than in-itself:

> The warrior put his life in jeopardy to elevate the prestige of the horde, the clan to which he belonged. And in this he proved dramatically that life is not the supreme value for man, but on the contrary that it should be made to serve ends more important than itself. The worst curse that was laid upon woman was that she should be excluded from these warlike forays. For it is not in giving life but in risking life that man is raised above the animal; that is why superiority has been accorded in humanity not to the sex that brings forth but to that which kills.[58]

Here we see Beauvoir, again, drawing on a distinctively Heideggerian theme. What truly allows men to transcend the in-itself of animal nature and come fully into their own as beings-for-themselves is the willingness to face death and to value some goal or ideal over that of the mere repetition of life as it is. In conceptualizing projects to be undertaken, man finds himself able to think beyond the moment and into the future, thus becoming a conscious, timely being. The warrior is the first step in this direction, claims Beauvoir, because it is the warrior who first starts to think abstractly about the honor of the tribe rather than of his own personal safety. In becoming able to think of something more important than life itself, the warrior demonstrates his own overcoming of the laws of nature and thus he transcends the world of brute material forces. Women, in becoming tied to the domestic realm, where the maintenance of the household, the care of children, and the repetition of daily chores is the routine, take the first step toward a way of life that ultimately will exclude them from the world of public decision-making, public management, and public power. Men have developed into the "superior sex" because of their ability to think into the future and their willingness to manipulate and control the world according to their own plans and projects. Women, on the other hand, have developed into the "second sex" because of their bodily connection to the cycles of nature and their propensity to submit to those cycles. "Here we have the key to the whole mystery,"[59] Beauvoir tells us.

In the course of discussing the relationship between men and women, Beauvoir inevitably draws attention to their physical differences, and some critics have claimed that by doing so she inadvertently lends credence to the notion that there is something "natural" about the social dominance of men over women after all. If it is true that woman has traditionally occupied a passive, submissive position in society because she "remained closely bound to her body, like an animal,"[60] doesn't this offer an account that legitimates the subjugation of women? If it is the very structure of the female body that holds her back from engaging in the sort of transcendence in which men engage, then aren't women destined by their biology to remain submissive? While it is true that Beauvoir believes that the female body, and specifically its child-birthing capacity, is an impediment to freedom, it is not, we must remember, an unbreachable impediment. Men must also overcome the constraints of their physicality to realize their potential as beings-for-themselves. Beauvoir's point is that the history of male domination over women is a history of choices made. For both men and women, the key to transcendence of the physical is a matter of how they choose to *interpret* the body. It certainly is a fact of nature that women have wombs and men lack them. However, it is not a fact of nature that the possession of a womb requires women to be subservient to men. Both men and women have *chosen* to interpret their bodies and their relationship to nature in particular ways, and this in turn has contributed to the way we see the world today. Although our ancestors could have chosen to interpret things differently,[61] today we live with the legacy of the actual decisions that have been made in the past. Do we want to continue in the same direction? Do we want to continue to interpret the possession of a womb as a sufficient condition for the subjugation of half of the human race? Beauvoir's own bold response to these questions is no! Both men and women should now stand resolute and change the course of gender relations by insisting on equality between the sexes.

Another criticism faced by Beauvoir has come from both feminists and anti-feminists who claim that she is hostile to the female body and thus has constructed a philosophy in which women are encouraged to be too much like men.[62] With regard to the first part of this criticism, Beauvoir's supposed hostility to the body is, of course, rooted in her more general existentialist perspective. The body is material substance; it is a being-in-itself governed by the impersonal laws of necessity, and as such it inhibits and resists the exercise of free will, which is the domain of human consciousness and the source of our dignity as beings-for-ourselves. While it may be true that Beauvoir's perspective takes a dim view of the body, it does so to reassert the distinctively existentialist claim that as human beings, we are always more than *simply* our bodies. Humans, women included, are not "things" to be objectified and manipulated. They are freely choosing individuals responsible for their actions. By insisting on this, Beauvoir's philosophical investigation into the nature of womanhood reasserts the full humanity of women and demands that they be treated equally to men and not simply as baby-making machines. She is not so much seeking to denigrate the female body in relation to the male body as she is suggesting that differences in bodily composition and structure are philosophically superficial. What is really important are the thoughts we think and the ideas upon which we act. This is what makes us truly human, and it is a point worth being emphasized again and again lest we forget what happened in the Nazi death camps when humans really were regarded merely as bodily things.

This brings us to a final issue. Did Beauvoir want women to abandon their femininity and to adopt the qualities of men? In the conclusion to *The Second Sex* she writes that the modern woman "accepts masculine values: she prides herself on thinking, taking action, working, creating, on the same terms as men."[63] Was this a call, as many feminists as well as antifeminists have worried, for women to become too much like men? I don't think so. We have to remember that Beauvoir is first and foremost an existentialist philosopher, and as such she is primarily concerned with the issue of Being. The designations "male" and "female" are

---

B o x 13.2 Existentialism in Film

Existentialist philosophy has had an incredibly influential effect on popular culture, and we continue to see this effect in today's media. In particular, a number of successful films deal explicitly with existential themes and issues.

Being There (Hal Ashby, 1979). This film is an adaptation of the Jerzy Kosinski novel of the same name. The title of both the film and the book is a literal translation of Heidegger's term "Dasein." In this film, Chance Gardener, a simple and uneducated groundskeeper, is cast out of his employer's house when the employer dies. Upon being thrown into the outside world, Chance's simple statements about gardening are interpreted by others as profound political pronouncements. He is consequently catapulted to a position of political power.

Fight Club (David Fincher, 1999). Adapted from the book by Chuck Palahniuk, this film chronicles the struggle for authenticity by the main character, who remains without a name throughout the film. It is only after turning his back on the distracting influences of mainstream society that the main character is able to discover who he really is.

I Heart Huckabees (David O. Russell, 2004). The main character in this film is an environmental activist who is in the midst of an existential crisis. He hires a pair of "existential detectives" who endeavor to investigate the details of his life and thus get to the root of his despair. What is especially interesting in this film is the contrast that is drawn between two differing approaches to existentialist philosophy. On the one hand, some characters, in Heideggerian fashion, characterize existentialism as a philosophy that stresses the interconnectedness of all things. On the other hand, some characters, in Sartrean fashion, characterize existentialism as a philosophy that stresses the disconnectedness between humans and the rest of the universe.

certainly expressions of Being, but they are not fundamental and timeless descriptions of the world itself. For Beauvoir, the fundamental struggle that characterizes our world is that between immanence and transcendence, or in other words, the struggle between being-in-itself and being-for-itself. The battle between the sexes is merely one of the many ways that this more fundamental struggle becomes apparent. Men have traditionally emphasized their drive toward transcendence, while women have traditionally emphasized their submission to immanence. Men have chosen to define themselves in terms of the for-itself, while women have chosen to define themselves in terms of the in-itself. This is what has led to the generation of the stereotype that men are naturally active and women are naturally passive. Thus, when Beauvoir calls for women to "accept masculine values," I don't think she is demanding that they take on all of the particular social and psychological characteristics of men but rather that they reassert their own drive toward transcendence, thereby becoming more balanced, more fully human, and more authentically integrated with Being itself. As she herself writes, "no physiological destiny imposes an eternal hostility upon male and female as such."[64] Rather, "male" and "female" characteristics complement and enrich one another, and the world itself is "androgynous."[65] So the point seems not to be that women should become men but instead that both women and men should become fully human in the sense of integrating the full ambiguity of Being into their lives. Only then will "we abolish the slavery of half of humanity, together with the whole system of hypocrisy that it implies ... and the human couple will find its true form."[66]

Despite the various attacks that Beauvoir has sustained from critics across the political spectrum, her philosophy has served to lay a groundwork for the modern women's movement by offering a serious and sustained account of the historical roots of sexual oppression and by offering a strategy for the overcoming of that oppression. Beauvoir accomplishes her task by drawing on the perspective of existentialism, a philosophy that encourages us to reflect deeply on Being itself and to consider how it is that we are related to Being. In raising the question "What is a woman?" Beauvoir asks us to consider the essence of womanhood, and by so doing to move beyond the superficial differences that characterize physical bodies. Beauvoir, like Heidegger, asks us to linger in the presence of the only being that in its Being cares about Being. What we find in the course of this reflection is that to be a woman is to be human, and thus to be equal to men. With her book *The Second Sex*, Beauvoir has made it impossible to ever again presume the inherent inferiority of half of the human race.

WONDROUS DISTRESS IN EXISTENTIALISM

There are many more important figures in existentialist philosophy than have been discussed in this chapter, although Heidegger, Sartre, and Beauvoir are, perhaps, among the most influential of those emerging in the postwar era. These thinkers offer a new vision for what philosophy should be and what its role in human life is. Instead of the coldly rational methods of thinkers like Plato,

Aristotle, Descartes, Hume, Kant, and Hegel, the existentialists emphasize the importance of feelings, emotions, and authentic, lived commitment to ourselves and the world we inhabit. Our natural fears and anxieties concerning human freedom and death are seen by them as means toward a renewed love of the universe itself. By looking at our fears and our worries, they teach us that we can discover not only something about who we are as humans but also something about our place within Being.

Even though the existentialists do offer a unique and novel approach to philosophy, they also, in a sense, bring philosophy back to its essential core. With these thinkers we are reminded of a message delivered thousands of years ago by an Athenian nonconformist by the name of Socrates, who tried to remind his fellow citizens that self-examination and the struggle to understand Truth are more important than anything else we can pursue in the course of our lives. We still consider Socrates to be the father of philosophy, and in the existentialists we can certainly see the family resemblance. For this reason, there are even some contemporary commentators who seek to trace the roots of existentialism all the way back to Socrates, claiming that in his thinking we find the first expression of existentialist sentiment. There is a grain of truth in this contention, I think, not because Socrates founded existentialism but rather because in both Socrates and the existentialists we find something approaching a nearly pure manifestation of the spirit of philosophy as wondrous distress.

The ideas of both Socrates and the existentialists were formulated during periods of war, hardship, and social decline. The Peloponnesian War dealt a death blow to Athenian supremacy over the Greek the world, and likewise the two world wars served to destabilize traditional power hierarchies in Europe. During such periods of tumult and transition, new ways of thinking tend to emerge as people seek to reorient and reconceptualize their place within the world. When routines are running smoothly there is less motivation to question the order of things, or to speculate about possible alternatives to the status quo, than there is when order breaks down. Therefore, the distressing situations encountered during war and cultural transition are likely to also be opportunities for the creative and vital spirit of philosophical thinking to blossom forth.

In the case of existentialism, World Wars I and II provided dramatic and horrifying examples that there was something wrong in the world. Within this context, Heidegger formulated his insight that the distressing feeling of angst is a mode of attunement that focuses our attention, motivates our thinking, and thus serves as a necessary component in our philosophical well-being. Without distress, we would not seek Truth, he tells us. While many people take this as a sign of existentialism's promotion of pessimism and despair, I believe that it is actually a misinterpretation to characterize things this way. As with Schopenhauer, what we find in the existentialist perspective is a corrective to the overly cheery and reassuring view that depicts philosophy merely as a support for the comforting doctrines of commonsense. Instead, philosophy comes into its own only when our commonsense view of the world becomes upset and our minds are opened to consider new questions and to wonder about things unknown. While this process certainly involves the distressing realization of our ignorance, it also requires that the creative spirit of wonder remain active in our thinking. In existentialism, we find both distress and wonder promoted, but never mere despair.

The never-ending pursuit of Being is a key feature of existentialist thinking, and in this we find a further element that is friendly to authentic philosophizing. The emphasis that existentialists place on the contemplation of death, suffering, anxiety, and forlornness are not ends in themselves but are intended as modes of access to something larger than ourselves. These feelings alert us to our alienation from the totality of Being, and in the recognition of this alienation we are inspired to try to mend the rift. The irony is that as beings ourselves, we are already a part of Being, and so we already are, in a way, connected to what it is from which we feel alienated. Paradoxically, as we try to grasp this situation, we always find ourselves falling away from full comprehension because Being is not a thing but an ongoing and open process that projects and expands ever forward into the future. To grasp Being as a totality, it turns out, is not possible, although we are able to get a sense of its abyssal depths and in so doing develop a feeling of respect for its profundity. Like Socrates, the existentialist philosophers counsel us to wondrously aspire toward Being yet also to modestly admit our own ignorance of many of its mysteries. There is always more to learn, to explore, and to question.

Like Socrates, the existentialists are predominantly concerned with understanding the unique and special characteristics of human existence as a prelude to understanding the universe. Although we are a part of Being, and in this way similar to all other beings-in-the-world, we also have our own special mode of existence. It is from this perspective that we must initiate our philosophical quest, and thus all understanding begins from the foundation of self-understanding. As we reflect on our own lives, we gain greater and greater wisdom concerning who we are and what our place is in the world; developing, growing, and becoming more mature along the way. This process of self-expansion, however, must always end with death, and so there is an inevitably tragic element to the search for wisdom. It must always be cut short and remain incomplete.

Existentialism thus emphasizes at least three elements that bring it close to a pure manifestation of philosophical thinking as wondrous distress. First, it counsels us to aspire toward and wonder about the mysteries of Being. Second, it demands that we pay heed to the distress involved in our alienation from Being. Third, it represents our distressing separation from Being as an opportunity for the unending and continued quest for wisdom.

I will add one other important point. Existentialism does not confuse philosophy with religion or with science but rather sees the philosophical impulse as something distinct from any particular methodology or body of doctrines. Science and religion are part of our world, the existentialists tell us, but neither of them exhausts the Truth of that world. Authentic philosophy should always recognize this and be willing to continue questioning the taken-for-granted beliefs that any culture accepts as resolved and certain. In its critical stance toward both science and religion, existentialism carries on one of the most controversial and yet important tasks that philosophy has always played in human history: it unsettles and upsets the accepted beliefs of the day.

QUESTIONS FOR DISCUSSION

1. What influences from earlier philosophers do you detect in existentialist thinking? In particular, discuss the possible influences of Socrates, Plato, Descartes, Hegel, Kierkegaard, Schopenhauer, and Nietzsche. In what ways does existential philosophy overlap with the insights of these thinkers? In what ways does it conflict?

2. In what ways does the existentialist approach to philosophy differ from the approach of the Anglo–American philosophers? Discuss their differences in method and in their metaphysical assumptions about the structure of the universe.

3. Why do you think that existentialism is still considered by many people to be a philosophy of despair and depression? Do you think this view is legitimate?

4. The insights of Heidegger, Sartre, and Beauvoir have been absorbed into psychology and have led to the growth of a branch of therapy known as "existential psychoanalysis." In what ways do you think the existential insights into "authenticity" and "bad faith" may have useful application to psychological therapy?

5. Why do you think that Heidegger became involved with the Nazi movement? In what ways do you think that Heideggerian philosophy is consistent with Nazi ideas? In what ways do you think his philosophy is inconsistent with Nazi ideas? Do you think that Heidegger's involvement with the Nazis discredits his thinking? Why do you think he never apologized for his involvement with the Nazis?

6. Sartre and Beauvoir were criticized for their involvement with the communist movement after the end of World War II. Many people have pointed out the irony of this involvement. In what ways do you think existentialism is inconsistent with the presumptions of communism? What are some reasons why Sartre and Beauvoir might have been attracted to communism?

7. In what ways do you think that Sartre's existentialism differs from the existentialism of both Heidegger and Beauvoir?

8. Beauvoir is one of the philosophical founders of modern feminism, and yet many feminists are very critical of her thinking. What aspects of Beauvoir's existentialism do you think some feminists might find troubling? Why do you think some feminists criticize Beauvoir's form of feminism as too philosophical?

NOTES

1. Friedrich Nietzsche, *The Will to Power*, Walter Kaufman and R. J. Hollingdale (trans.) (New York: Vintage Books, 1968), p. 8.

2. Ibid., p. 44.

3. Friedrich Nietzsche, *Twilight of the Idols* in *The Portable Nietzsche* (New York: Penguin Books, 1984), p. 509.

4. Oswald Spengler, *The Decline of the West* (New York: Alfred A. Knopf, 1937), p. 21.

5. H. Stuart Hughes, *Oswald Spengler: A Critical Estimate* (New York: Charles Scribner's Sons, 1952), p. 165.

6. Hans-Georg Gadamer, in writing about the major intellectual influences on the spirit of early twentieth-century philosophy remarks, "One thinks of the virtually revolutionary effect that Oswald Spengler's *The Decline of the West* had on everyone's souls." Hans-Georg Gadamer, *Heidegger's Ways*, John Stanley (trans.) (Albany: State University of New York Press, 1994), p. 8.

7. Hannah Arendt, *The Origins of Totalitarianism* (New York: Harcourt Inc., 1976), p. 466.

8. Ibid., p. 478.

9. An interesting author from this same time period, Ernst Jünger (1895–1998), counsels us to embrace our role as instruments of the state. In his masterpiece, *Storm of Steel*, he revels in the loss of self that he himself experienced as a German soldier in the trenches during World War I. Ernst Jünger, *Storm of Steel*, Michael Hofmann (trans.) (New York: Penguin Books, 2004).

10. Arendt, *Origins*, p. 447.

11. Feliksa Piekarska, quoted in Giorgio Agamben, *Remnants of Auschwitz: The Witness and the Archive* (New York: Zone Books, 2002), p. 166.

12. Ibid., p. 51.

13. Primo Levi, *Survival in Auschwitz* (New York: Collier Books, 1961), p. 156.

14. Martin Heidegger, *Nietzsche, Volume Four: Nihilism*, David Farrell Krell (trans.) (San Francisco: HarperCollins, 1982), pp. 167–177.

15. Martin Heidegger, *Being and Time*, Joan Stambaugh (trans.) (Albany: State University of New York Press, 1996), p. 5. I have added a capital "B" to those uses of the word "Being" in this quotation that refer to Being-itself as distinguished from particular beings.

16. Martin Heidegger, *An Introduction to Metaphysics*, Gregory Fried and Richard Polt (trans.) (New Haven, CT: Yale University Press, 2000), p. 1.

17. Heidegger, *Being and Time*, p. 40.

18. Ibid., p. 10.

19. Heidegger might be wrong about this. It does appear that elephants mourn their dead, as do whales, higher apes, and dolphins. This does not undermine Heidegger's main point, however; rather, it may simply suggest that these animals may be more human than Heidegger gave them credit for.

20. Heidegger, *Being and Time*, p. 241.

21. Ibid., pp. 219–220.

22. Ibid., p. 222.

23. Ibid., p. 398.

24. Heidegger, "Letter on Humanism," in *Basic Writings* (San Francisco: HarperCollins, 1993), p. 234.

25. Ibid.

26. Ibid., p. 241.

27. Heidegger, "The Question Concerning Technology," in *Basic Writings*, p. 313.

28. Heidegger, "What Calls For Thinking?," in *Basic Writings*, p. 374.

29. Heidegger, "Letter on Humanism," p. 217.

30. Martin Heidegger interviewed by Richard Wisser, transcribed as, "The Television Interview," in *Martin Heidegger and National Socialism* (New York: Paragon House, 1990), p. 82.

31. To verify that Hitler was simply a cynical manipulator of the masses, one need only consult his own book, *Mein Kampf* (My Struggle). In particular, the section titled "Philosophy and Party" outlines Hitler's intended use of philosophy, force, and religion to motivate the masses to revolution. Adolf Hitler, *Mein Kampf*, Ralph Manheim (trans.) (Boston: Houghton Mifflin, 1971), pp. 373–385.

32. For an interesting account of the philosophical basis of Nazism and of its appeal to the German people, see *Nietzsche and the Nazis: A Personal View by Stephen Hicks, PhD* (DVD, Ockham's Razor Publishing, 2006). While I disagree with Dr. Hicks's interpretation of Nietzsche's philosophy, I very much appreciate his comments on the importance of taking seriously the philosophical ideas upon which Nazism is premised.

33. Heidegger, "The Rectorate 1933/34: Facts and Thoughts," in *Martin Heidegger and National Socialism*, p. 17.

34. Ibid., p. 19.

35. Ibid., p. 23.

36. Arendt, *Origins*, p. 441.

37. Norman N. Greene, *Jean-Paul Sartre: The Existentialist Ethic* (Ann Arbor: University of Michigan Press, 1963), p. 3.

38. Jean-Paul Sartre, *Being and Nothingness* (New York: Washington Square Press, 1966), p. 26.

39. Ibid., p. 29.

40. Ibid. See Part II.

41. Ibid., p. 28.

42. Ibid., p. 120.

43. Ibid., p. 786.

44. See Chapter 10.

45. Jean-Paul Sartre, "Existentialism Is a Humanism" in *Existentialism: From Dostoevsky to Sartre*, Walter Kaufmann (ed. and trans.) (New York: Meridian, 1975), p. 348.

46. Sartre, *Being and Nothingness*, Part I, Chapter Two.

47. Simone de Beauvoir, *Adieux: A Farewell to Sartre* (New York: Pantheon Books, 1984), p. 253.

48. Simone de Beauvoir, *The Second Sex*. H. M. Parshley (trans.) (New York: Vintage Books, 1974), pp. xvi.

49. Ibid., p. 810.

50. Ibid., p. xv.

51. Ibid.

52. Ibid., p. xvi.

53. Ibid., p. 301.

54. Ibid., p. xix.

55. Ibid., p. xx.

56. Ibid., p. 71.

57. Ibid., p. 84.

58. Ibid., p. 72.

59. Ibid.

60. Ibid., p. 73.

61. Beauvoir points out that there are, and have always been, women warriors. This suggests that there is nothing that necessarily ties women to the domestic sphere. See *The Second Sex,* p. 70.

62. For an overview of the various criticisms of Beauvoir's account of womanhood see Jo-Ann Pilardi, "The Changing Critical Fortunes of the Second Sex," *History and Theory* 32, no. 1 (February 1993): pp. 51–74.

63. Beauvoir, *The Second Sex,* p. 798.

64. Ibid., p. 796.

65. Ibid., p. 807.

66. Ibid., p. 814.

Conclusion: Philosophy and Wondrous Distress

© Juneko J. Robinson

There are many important and influential figures in the history of philosophy whom we have not had the opportunity to examine here, but simply enumerating the doctrines and ideas of more and more thinkers will not necessarily bring us any closer to a true understanding of the essence of philosophy. In fact, there may even be a threshold at which too much detail threatens to obscure the pattern that, over the course of this book, has struggled to emerge. How close we have come to this threshold, I will leave for the reader to decide. Suffice it to say that as a work of philosophy itself, this book is not intended to be the final word about the figures, movements, and ideas that are presented within its pages. Rather, it is intended to characterize, and indeed to exercise, what I believe to be the underlying spirit of philosophy and to show how this spirit is related to, yet distinct from, other modes of human thinking. In the process of pursuing this goal, it has been necessary to go into some detail concerning names, technical terms, and facts about history. However, it would be a mistake to conclude that the study of these details is itself the study of philosophy. On the contrary, these details merely allow for the expression of an impulse that is the real core of philosophical contemplation itself. One of the main purposes of this book has been to emphasize the point that philosophy is not primarily a collection of facts, ideas, or methods but is, rather, a particular manner of thinking that makes indispensable contributions to the progress and development of human culture.

Philosophy is a mode of thinking that is unique among other modes of human thought. In all of those individuals whom we call philosophers, at least a couple of characteristics remain consistent. First of all, philosophers are concerned with understanding the real Truth about particular things, events, and phenomena in the world. A philosopher wants to know the way things really are, not just the way things appear, and this desire for Truth is, perhaps, the most powerful motive behind the pursuit of philosophy. In contrast, there are many people who simply content themselves with points of view and opinions that make them feel happy. "Why believe in something that makes you miserable?" we sometimes hear people ask. Such individuals are not thinking philosophically. The philosopher is someone who desires the Truth above all else, even if it results in distress, unhappiness, and sadness. It should be emphasized that as a mode of contemplation, we probably all slip into and out of philosophical thinking on a regular basis. Even a professional philosopher can be unphilosophical at times. However, when actually in a philosophical frame of mind, an individual thinks in such a manner that he or she desires to know something, regardless of the consequences that may follow from that knowledge. In this sense, philosophical thinking is insensitive to anything but the Truth, which is its guiding ideal. To come to an understanding of the way that things really are is the primary longing involved in this mode of thought, and for the duration or to the degree that one diverges from this longing, one also diverges from the most fundamental aspect of philosophical thinking.

Although the love of Truth is fundamental to philosophy, it alone is not enough to distinguish philosophy from other areas of study. Both scientists and religious thinkers also aspire toward the truth, and though their thoughts may sometimes converge with a philosophical mindset, it is also clear that they may just as often come into conflict with it. This is because both science and religion share a common element that, from time to time, creates friction with the radical openness of philosophical thinking. In the case of religion, for instance, there is the dogmatic assertion of the existence of a supernatural realm that provides believers with an intuitive and indubitable apprehension of the Truth. So it is that religious thinkers can often be heard to dismiss the skeptical doubts of both philosophers and scientists alike as indicative of minds that are unwilling to recognize supernatural forms of evidence that could settle nagging questions. Understanding reality is, according to the religious thinker, a matter of opening up one's heart and allowing the spirit of God (or the gods) to touch you. Scientists, on the other hand, dogmatically reject the legitimacy of any sort of evidence that is claimed to be of supernatural origin and instead demand that all evidence in support of the truth comes from a source within the natural world. Science has thus developed methods of experimentation and hypothesis-testing that are designed to verify whether there is any tangible, this-worldly evidence to support the veracity of theories and beliefs. If you want to know the truth, according to a scientific way of thinking, you are best advised to open your eyes to the natural world and see for yourself what is there to be discovered.

Both religion and science are therefore premised on the dogmatic assertion that an understanding of the truth must ultimately be derived from an understanding of evidence that originates from a particular realm of the universe. The religious thinker appeals to the authority of the supernatural realm, while the scientific thinker appeals to the authority of the natural realm. In both cases, it is the dogmatism of these appeals that chafes against the philosophical way of thinking. Philosophy, as philosophy, takes no dogmatic stand on the existence or the nonexistence of the supernatural. Rather, philosophy is open to evidence that comes from anywhere, and the philosopher is willing to entertain any sort of argument, no matter what its origin. Thus, the second essential characteristic of philosophical thinking is its openness. It attempts to take nothing for granted and to be open to all sorts of ideas, speculations, and theories that may fly in the face of "common sense." For the philosopher, common sense is something of an impediment, because it limits and imprisons our minds, placing boundaries on the sorts of thoughts that we allow ourselves to take seriously. But how can we really know whether common sense is correct unless we allow our minds the leisure to wander beyond its purview and to question its assumptions? This is one of the things that philosophy is especially good at, and it is precisely what causes it to so often come into conflict with the conventions of science and religion, as well as all other areas of study that are premised on the assumption that the underlying nature of reality has been established categorically once and for all.

Philosophy can thus be thought of as a way of thinking that not only desires to know the Truth but that is willing, in its desire, to constantly question the conclusions that it reaches in the course of its investigations. There is no rest in philosophical thought. At each step, the philosopher attempts to move closer to the Truth, all the while remaining open to the possibility that each step may be a misstep. Final conclusions to issues must always be viewed with suspicion, and the philosopher must always be willing to reexamine ideas or doctrines that appeared at first to be built on certainty. In this incessant drive toward absolute Truth there is also a constant falling away from certainty, and the philosopher must be willing to defer final answers or else falter and become less philosophical than the title "philosopher" demands. It was Aristotle who claimed that philosophy begins in wonder, but now we can see that this is only part of the story. Certainly, to pursue philosophical thinking one must be curious about the nature of Being itself, having a sense of wonder about that which is unknown. However, a philosopher must also possess intellectual modesty, and be aware at all times of the degree to which the search for Truth falls short of its goal. To be in wonder about the unknown presupposes an awareness that something remains obscure to our comprehension. When this awareness evaporates, so too does philosophical thinking. It is then that complacency replaces the anxious drive to know and apprehend more. Because philosophical thinking rests on this drive, in addition to wonder it requires a sort of distressing feeling that something in our understanding remains unsettled. Philosophy begins in wondrous distress.

In this book, we have followed the development of some of the threads of Western philosophy from what are conventionally thought to be its beginnings in ancient Greece. The Presocratics are, in this regard, sometimes pointed to as the very first human beings to engage in a new kind of thinking because of their emphasis on providing nonsupernatural explanations of the world's phenomena. Previous to them, mythic thinking offered explanations in terms of the actions of gods and goddesses, demons, spirits, and other supernatural entities. One of the novelties of Presocratic thought was that it attempted to comprehend the universe naturalistically. By appealing to one or more natural forces, thinkers such as Thales, Anaximander, Heraclitus, Parmenides, and Democritus produced relatively systematic explanations for why the world is the way that it is.

But scientific thinking is also engaged in the search for naturalistic explanations of the world, and so this alone is not enough to help us understand what is uniquely philosophical about the efforts of the Presocratics. Many contemporary scholars fail to notice this fact, and so they make no clear distinction between the philosophical and the scientific contributions of the Presocratics. Philosophy, they claim, is really just the first halting step toward science. As such, it is a movement in the right direction toward the modern, advanced way of thinking, yet it is also in itself underdeveloped and somewhat archaic. This, I think, is mistaken. If it was correct, then science would be the most advanced replacement for philosophy. Philosophic thinking would merely be transitional between the "infancy" of mythic thinking and the "adulthood" of modern scientific thought. It would be legitimate, if this was the case, to gauge intellectual progress and development by how fully an individual or a culture has accepted science, on the one hand, and left philosophy and religion behind, on the other. The best, most advanced state of being would be one in which all questions were answered and all mysteries were solved by an appeal to the forces of nature. Admittedly, there are people who hold this view of civilization, yet theirs is a rather superficial take on what constitutes the progress of human culture. In fact, the sophistication of both individuals and cultures is not simply a matter of their scientific development but also depends on the complexity and depth of their religious, artistic, and philosophical insights. A whole genre of dystopian literature, including classic novels like *1984*, *Brave New World*, and *Limbo*, have pointed out the sort of shallowness and inhumanity that may result from an overemphasis on scientific thinking in our society. To truly benefit humankind, scientific thinking must be accompanied by the kinds of religious and philosophical insights that cannot ever be discovered through experimentation, hypothesis-testing, or observation. Issues concerning morality, ethics, beauty, meaning, and spiritual significance have never been dealt with adequately from a purely scientific perspective, yet these issues are among the most important that we face. Responsible scientific progress depends for its very existence on the guiding values, concerns, and doubts introduced by both religion and philosophy.

Philosophy will not disappear as science advances; nor, incidentally will religion. All of these ways of thinking—religious, philosophical, and scientific—are differing yet related modes by which human beings try to comprehend a universe that resists being summed up and understood in any final and comprehensive manner. Accordingly, the Presocratics were indeed philosophical thinkers. But what made them such was not the attempt to provide naturalistic answers to the mysteries of existence. Rather, as Nietzsche has written, that is what made them scientists. What made the Presocratics philosophers were not the answers they gave but rather the questions that they entertained. It is the propensity to think in terms of questions rather than answers that also makes the Presocratics, and all philosophers, distinct from religious thinkers. Religious thought seeks to offer final answers to the mysteries of Being no less than does scientific thought. The major distinction between the two lies in the character of the answers that they give. For the scientist, answers are framed in naturalistic terms. For the religious thinker, they are framed in supernatural terms. For the philosopher, however, none of these answers is as important, or as interesting, as the questions that have gone unanswered and the issues that remain unexplored.

The concern with asking, rather than answering, questions comes to extreme expression with Socrates. As we have seen, Socrates was predominantly concerned with posing questions, and the answers to those questions were not of primary interest to him. In this sense, it is perhaps with him that philosophy really comes into its own and radically distinguishes itself from other forms of thought. This is why for many thinkers today Socrates is still considered to be the true father of philosophy. With him, the worlds of physical and supernatural existence cease to be of major concern. Instead, it is the world of the mind that becomes his major focus. While reacting against the scientific and religious dogmas of his time, Socrates developed and elaborated a technique that allowed him to engage in an unceasing exploration of thinking itself. Through self-examination, and the examination of others, Socrates revealed that the domain of absolute certainty is very small, perhaps even nonexistent. If prodded sufficiently, the human mind is always capable of asking more questions, and though the desire for absolute Truth may be the very thing that motivates us to formulate speculations, theories, and answers to the mysteries of life, it is this same drive that in turn motivates us to question our intellectual constructs.

Socrates was executed because of the unsettling effects that his philosophy had on the Athenian authorities. It is a rare mind that is able to endure the endless task of facing questions with no final answers. Consequently, the need served by religious and scientific thinking may be a need that most people have at one time or another. We want to rest mentally and feel comfortable and secure in our knowledge of the world. We want to reach a point at which we can stop worrying about things and feel satisfied that we know at least a few facts with certainty. Philosophers like Socrates challenge such complacency and point out that there is very little, if anything at all, that cannot be questioned. Socrates seemed to take delight in bringing this to our attention. Others, however, simply felt threatened by this revelation.

The Presocratics questioned the assumptions of mythic thinking and went on to pose further questions of reality itself. In this they were philosophers. Yet insofar as they offered final answers to their own questions, they exhibited the character of scientists and religious thinkers. Socrates, on the other hand, very rarely offered any final answers to the questions he asked, and when he did, he too departed from truly philosophical thinking. Yet generally Socrates pushed philosophy to its purest extreme. With him, we find a way of thinking that is not reliant upon any particular content but rather upon curiosity, care, and a kind of distress and dissatisfaction with the present state of things.

Some may think it odd to claim that philosophy is motivated in part by distress and dissatisfaction. Philosophers, after all, are often depicted as calm, rational, and serene contemplators of reality. With wisdom doesn't philosophy bring tranquility? We should not forget, however, that philosophy is not the same as wisdom itself. It is, rather, the "love of wisdom." Philosophers are beings right in the middle of a process of aspiration. They are striving toward understanding and wisdom. But when one strives there is a recognition that one is not at the end. There is still distance between the philosopher and wisdom, and that is why such an individual is able to continue in the loving pursuit of understanding. There is a desire to move closer to the ultimate, yet at the same time the presence of this desire reveals the fact that this goal has not been reached. Desire is partially frustrated in the philosopher. Questions remain. If it was possible for an individual to perfectly understand reality, that individual would no longer be a philosopher. That person would be either a superscientist or a god, and as Plato wrote, "None of the gods philosophizes." They have no need to, because there are no questions that remain unanswered for gods.

Few of Socrates' students practiced philosophy with the same purity that Socrates himself did. Many, like Plato and Aristotle, used their teacher's insights as stepping stones to develop religious and scientific doctrines that purported to offer solutions to the world's mysteries. According to Plato, dialectical reasoning and the study of science were tools that would lead to religious enlightenment. The Truth itself would come like a flash, filling our souls, once we had become prepared for its advent. Aristotle, while rejecting some of Plato's more religious proclamations, nevertheless embraced the optimistic hope that through dialectic and science the first principles of the universe could be grasped by the human mind. For both of these thinkers, reality is an open book, and its meaning and message are clearly spelled out for those who know how to read it properly. As for those who cannot, they will, as Plato wrote, remain living in a cave of illusion until forced into the sunlight of objective Truth by those who are truly wise.

Although the Hellenistic philosophers are often considered to be "decadent" insofar as their ideas and doctrines exhibit a pessimistic attitude toward the acquisition of final truths, many of them nonetheless can also be interpreted as reinvigorating the sort of intellectual modesty that Socrates introduced with his thinking. The Cynics and Skeptics in particular were ruthless in their recognition of the limits of understanding. Yet even the Epicureans and Stoics drew on the insights of Socrates, making their greatest contributions to philosophy by turning their attention inward and showing us how the power of the mind can be used to reveal and explore its own inner workings. Whereas Socrates never offered any positive advice beyond imploring us to continue "examining our lives," the Hellenistic philosophers were full of solutions that would alleviate the pain and suffering of living in a world that offered no final rest for our unsettled minds. Drawing on a combination of religious and scientific doctrines, these thinkers ultimately held out the hope for a final point at which all uncertainties, worries, and anxieties would be alleviated. In *ataraxia*, the mind would finally come to peace and rest satisfied with what it had accomplished. At that point, the need for philosophy would evaporate, and unlike Socrates, who hoped to continue philosophizing even in heaven, the Hellenistic thinkers hoped only for eternal rest and freedom from distress and ignorance.

We see the influence of Platonic, Aristotelian, and Hellenistic thinking on the Medieval theologians who proposed final answers to questions about the beginning of the universe, the nature of the soul, and the existence of God. In tackling these issues, thinkers like St. Augustine, St. Anselm, and St. Thomas Aquinas asked many questions, but very rarely were these questions fully open or purely philosophical. Instead, the Medieval theologians already knew the answers they wanted, and so philosophy was for them never an end in itself. It was, rather, a way of thinking intended as an inspiration to push their religious thoughts and beliefs as far as they would go. Philosophy encouraged these men to explore the boundaries of their faith, in the process discovering both the strengths and weaknesses involved in religious thought.

It is interesting to see how philosophical thinking lends itself to the strengthening and exploration of religious belief. We tend to think of faith as something that goes unquestioned. It provides solace in a world where all other things are uncertain. However, despite this feature, unquestioned religious belief also has the weakness of being unjustified. "Having faith" means not having any rational reason to believe, and this is a cause for concern to the human mind. We become distressed when we realize that we have no answer as to "why" we believe in God, the soul, or an afterlife. It's just not good enough to simply believe and leave it at that. The philosophical tendency to question such beliefs, destabilizing though it may be, also has the potential to help us understand the nature of religious thinking and the need that it fulfills. By asking philosophical questions about their faith, the Medieval philosophers enriched and fortified their religious ideas in turn.

Religion and science came into conflict during the Modern Era, and philosophy prospered as a result. Because philosophical thinking is not committed to any particular body of knowledge or set of facts, it may flourish at those times in history when the most is up for grabs. In the Modern milieu, Descartes, Hume, and Kant all recognized and highlighted the importance of key philosophical questions. How do we know what we claim to know? Are there any ways by which we can verify that which we believe to be true? What is ultimately real? These sorts of questions troubled the seventeenth- and eighteenth-century philosophers largely because at that time the institutions of science and religion were locked in a battle over who had the true answers to the mysteries of the universe. In this book we have encountered thinkers on either side of this issue who advocated one set of answers over another, but as I have been stressing, it is not their answers that made them philosophers. It was, rather, the fact that something was in question and that they were engaged in an aspiration toward Truth that made them philosophers. In fact, most of the answers they formulated are of note only insofar as they led to further questions and further philosophical exploration.

This is very clear in the case of Kant. His answer to Hume's skepticism about our capacity to obtain certain knowledge about the world led to the famous distinction between the phenomenal and noumenal worlds. Yet this answer to Humean skepticism only led philosophers in the following centuries to ask more and more questions. The nineteenth-century philosophers, many of them taking Kant as their starting point, proceeded to ask whether there was any possible path toward resolving the apparent disconnect between our subjective comprehension of the world and the Truth of objective reality. Some, like Hegel and his followers, claimed that through logic and mental discipline we could achieve a state of perfect knowledge. Others, like Schopenhauer and Nietzsche, who I have called "nihilistic thinkers," suggested that never-ending aspiration and the desire for more are part of the human spirit, and though the world denies us what we want we are not so constituted that we can just give up on our desires.

In the nihilistic philosophers of the nineteenth century I believe we see the reemergence of the spirit of Socrates. Thinkers such as Schopenhauer and Nietzsche represent a return to the sort of never-ending activity and inquiry engaged in by the father of philosophy. In the case of Schopenhauer, this activity is tinged with pessimism, whereas with Nietzsche it is tinged with optimism. In either case, however, thinking is represented as a process that is undertaken not for the results it will yield but simply for the sake of probing further and further into the nature of Being itself. There is no ultimate conclusion to our struggles. There are no final answers to our inquiries. Time and thinking continue to move on in a never-ending cycle of question and answer. Each question leads to a series of answers, which then lead to new questions. As Schopenhauer claimed, we vacillate forever between feeling anxious for solutions and feeling bored with those solutions. The philosophical mind never rests, though the religious and scientific aspects of that very same mind wish it would.

With Heidegger and the Existentialists we encounter an even more recent expression of this philosophical impulse. In these philosophers, thinking gains full status as an end in itself. Never mind that it may oftentimes cause us pain and anguish; the point of life is not, as the Epicurean and Utilitarian philosophers claim, to be happy. It is, rather, to think freely and to follow our reflections wherever they may take us, regardless of the consequences. This is, after all, what Socrates did. He died, not for the content of his thinking, but simply for thinking itself. Philosophy, though often distracted and influenced by other sorts of concerns, nevertheless still aspires toward an apprehension of Truth that is forever beyond our full grasp.

There is much talk these days that we have started the transition out of the Modern era into something of a "Postmodern" era. Just as the Modern era was characterized by a general movement away from religious faith toward a faith in science, so the Postmodern era, it is claimed by writers such as Jean-François Lyotard, is characterized by a loss of faith in all totalizing views of reality, including scientific ones. The final Truth is seen, in the Postmodern way of thinking, to be something of a pipe dream. It is an abstraction, elusive and unattainable precisely because it is a construction of the human mind. Religion and science are viewed merely as human systems of thinking, not mirrors of reality, and so it is suggested that we content ourselves with endless playfulness in our thinking rather than aspiring toward some sort of absolute comprehension of objective reality. If it is true that our culture has emerged into a Postmodern era, then not only must traditional forms of religion and science come to an end, but so too must traditional philosophy. Without the desire for Truth, philosophy cannot prosper. It will be up to historians to determine whether the accounts of Postmodernists are correct. In the meantime, while the rest of us still wonder and worry about the point and purpose of human existence, philosophical thinking will continue to make its contributions to our culture.

Glossary

© Juneko J. Robinson

A posteriori: Latin term meaning "after experience."

A priori: Latin term meaning "before experience."

Abraham: Patriarch of the three great monotheistic traditions of Judaism, Christianity, and Islam. Abraham is considered by followers of these faiths to be the first monotheist. His story appears in the Torah, the Bible, and the Koran.

Absolute Idea: In Hegel's philosophy, the point at which all conflicts are resolved in a final synthesis. The absolute Idea summarizes the ultimate Truth of *Geist*, or Being itself.

Abstractions: Objects like numbers, geometrical figures, and statements, which do not exist as concrete, physical entities.

Academy: The first formal school of Greek philosophy, founded by Plato ca. 385 B.C.

Adventitious ideas: According to Descartes, those ideas whose source is a stimulus originating from outside of the mind.

Aesthetics: The field of philosophy that focuses on the study of art.

Agnosticism: The middle position between atheism and theism. An agnostic does not claim to know whether God exists or not.

Alexander the Great: King of Macedon (356–323 B.C.). Alexander was the son of Philip of Macedon and was tutored by Aristotle. He is remembered as one of the most successful military leaders of all time. He is credited with spreading Greek culture into the East and initiating the Hellenistic period of history.

Al-Farabi: Islamic philosopher (ca. A.D. 870–950).

Al-Kindi: Islamic philosopher (ca. A.D. 800–873).

Ambiguity: A lack of clarity. A statement is ambiguous if it has more than one possible meaning. For instance, the statement "My car is hot" is ambiguous because it might mean any of the following: "My car is really nice," "My car is high in temperature," or "My car is stolen."

Ambiguous description: According to Bertrand Russell, a description that applies to more than one particular individual. An ambiguous description is usually preceded by "a." For example, "a table," "a dog," or "a motorcycle."

Analysis: The act of breaking something down into its simplest parts to understand it.

Analytic philosophy: A style of philosophy that emphasizes analysis and clarity in argumentation. Analytic philosophers tend to think of philosophy as closely allied with science and the scientific method.

Anarchy: A philosophical position holding that government should be eliminated or that all forms of authority should be distrusted.

Anaximander: Presocratic Greek philosopher of the Milesian School who lived ca. 547 B.C. Anaximander claimed that all things emerge out of a singular substance he called "aperion" or the "infinite."

Anaximenes of Miletus: Presocratic Greek philosopher of the Milesian School who lived sometime during the sixth century B.C. Anaximenes claimed that everything is made of air.

Angst: German word meaning "anxiety" or "fear." In existentialism, angst is a feeling that attunes us to the nature of reality.

Anselm of Canterbury, St.: Benedictine monk (1033–1109). Anselm is the author of the Ontological Argument for God's existence.

Antinomies: According to Kant, antinomies are equally valid arguments that conflict with one another. Because such arguments are logically valid, the only way to resolve such conflicts is to make observations to demonstrate which argument most closely reflects the nature of reality. Because there are some observations that can never be made, there are some antinomies that must forever go unresolved according to Kant.

Antisthenes: Founder of Cynicism (ca. 444–366 B.C.).

Antithesis: In Hegel's philosophy, the entity that opposes a thesis. The thesis and antithesis are resolved, or sublated, in a synthesis.

Apathia: Greek word meaning "apathy," describing the state of mind advocated by Stoic philosophers. In this state, all emotions, or at least all negative emotions, are overcome.

Aquinas, St. Thomas: Dominican monk (1225–1274) who is the author of five *a posteriori* arguments for God's existence.

Arendt, Hannah: German-born philosopher (1906–1975). Arendt was a student of Martin Heidegger.

Argument: A series of statements, some of which constitute the premises and one of which constitutes the conclusion. In an argument, the premises are intended to offer reasons for why the conclusion is true.

Aristocracy: From a Greek term meaning "rule by the best." A form of government in which those who are most qualified to rule are in charge of society.

Aristophanes: Ancient Greek comic playwright (ca. 446–386 B.C.). Author of *The Clouds*, a play that satirizes Socrates.

Aristotle: Greek philosopher (384–322 B.C.). Student of Plato and founder of a school called the Lyceum.

Ataraxia: Greek word meaning "lacking anxiety." Ataraxia is a mental state of bliss that was sought by Epicureans and Skeptics.

Atheism: The belief that God does not exist.

Athens: Greek city-state that was home to many important philosophers.

Atomism: The philosophical belief that all things are composed of indivisible bits of material substance.

Augustine, St.: The Bishop of Hippo (354–430). Augustine is an important figure in the transition from Ancient to Medieval philosophy.

Aurelius, Marcus: Emperor of Rome A.D. 121–180. Aurelius was a major Stoic philosopher.

Authenticity: The state of being what you really are. Authenticity is in contrast to inauthenticity, which is a state of self-alienation. In existentialism, authenticity is praised as the goal of philosophy.

Averroes: Islamic philosopher (1126–1198).

Avicenna: Islamic philosopher (980–1037).

Bad faith: The philosopher Jean-Paul Sartre used this term to refer to the psychological state of a person who denies his or her existential freedom. Bad faith is similar to inauthenticity, except that whereas inauthenticity is an ontological condition, bad faith is a psychological condition.

Beauty: An aesthetic property that produces a particular form of pleasure in an observer. According to Kant, the beautiful is experienced when a human mind resonates with a form in nature.

Becoming: A state of coming to be. In the Hegelian Dialectic, becoming is the synthesis of being and nothingness.

Behaviorism: A perspective claiming that the purpose of psychology is to explain and predict behavior rather than to understand inner mental states.

Being: What is; reality itself; that which underlies all change. The study of Being is called "ontology."

Being-for-itself: According to Sartre, being-for-itself is a designation for human being. A being-for-itself is conscious, freely choosing, and thus responsible for its actions.

Being-in-itself: According to Sartre, being-in-itself is a designation for the kinds of beings that are nonhuman, nonconscious, and incapable of free choice. A rock, for instance, may not choose to be anything. It just is what it is in-itself.

Being-toward-death: In existentialism, an integral aspect of human existence. Once born, humans move inevitably toward death, thus all humans are beings-toward-death. Understanding this is a necessary part of being authentic.

Bentham, Jeremy: English philosopher (1748–1832). Bentham is the founder of utilitarianism.

Berkeley, George: Irish idealist philosopher (1685–1753).

Brahman: The Hindu term for God or Being itself. According to Hindus, all things are part of Brahman.

Bruno, Giordano: Dominican monk (1548–1600). Bruno was burned at the stake for heresy.

Buber, Martin: Jewish philosopher (1878–1965).

Buddha: Founder of the religion of Buddhism (560–477 B.C.). The Buddha was originally a prince by the name of Siddhartha Gautama.

Buddhism: A religion originating during the sixth century B.C. in India. Buddhism shares many beliefs with Hinduism but rejects the caste system and the authority of the Vedas.

Care: English translation of the German term *sorge*. Care is considered by Heidegger to be one of the existential characteristics of human beings.

Cartesian: The term "Cartesian" is used to refer to things that were created or inspired by René Descartes such as the Cartesian Method, Cartesian Doubt, the Cartesian Coordinate System, or Cartesian Dualism.

Cartesian Doubt: A form of skepticism that is used by Descartes as a tool to eliminate beliefs that are not absolutely certain. If an idea can be doubted, then it is not accepted as a foundation for other beliefs.

Cartesian Dualism: The claim by Descartes that the world is made up of two fundamental substances: mind and matter.

Cartesian Method: A four-step method used by Descartes to systematically investigate and understand reality. The steps in the Cartesian Method can be summarized as follows: (1) Doubt, (2) Analyze, (3) Synthesize, and (4) Repeat.

Cartesian skepticism: See Cartesian Doubt.

Categorical imperative: According to Kant, the only sort of imperative that is truly moral in nature. A categorical imperative is a command that holds at all times and under all circumstances. It is in contrast to a hypothetical imperative, which is a nonmoral command holding only under certain circumstances.

Categories of the understanding: According to Kant, there are twelve categories of the understanding that are part of the human mind and which the mind uses to organize ideas to produce the phenomenal world. These categories are unity, plurality, totality, reality, negation, limitation, substance, causality, community, possibility, existence, and necessity.

Catharsis: According to Aristotle, the purging of emotion through laughter or crying. The purpose of comic and tragic plays is to generate emotions in an audience so that these emotions can then safely be released. This sort of catharsis leaves an audience with a relaxed feeling that is psychologically beneficial according to Aristotle.

Causation: The relation of cause to effect. According to Hume, causation is a necessary connection between events.

Chuang Tzu: Chinese Taoist who lived during the fourth century B.C.

Circular reasoning: A fallacious form of reasoning in which the conclusion of an argument already appears, more or less explicitly, among the premises of the argument.

Cogito ergo sum: Latin phrase meaning "I think, therefore I am." Often referred to simply as the Cogito, it was formulated by René Descartes.

Cognition: The mental processes involved in becoming conscious of, or of knowing, something. The act of cognition includes things like perception, thinking, feeling, and reasoning.

Coherence theory of truth: A theory holding that truth is constituted by how well our beliefs cohere, or consistently hang together, with one another. This theory is often contrasted with the correspondence theory of truth.

Communism: A form of social organization in which the means of production are collectively owned.

Complex idea: An idea that is made up of simple ideas. For instance, the idea of an apple is a complex idea made up of the simple ideas of red, crisp, sweet, juicy, etc.

Conditional: In formal logic, the conditional is a connective that combines simple statements into complex statements. A conditional is usually represented by an arrow or by a horseshoe; for instance A→B, or A⊃B. This is read as "If A, then B." A, the antecedent, is a sufficient condition for B, and B, the consequent, is a necessary condition for A.

Conjunction: In formal logic, the conjunction is a connective that combines simple statements into complex statements. A conjunction is often represented by a plus sign or an ampersand; for instance, A+B, or A&B. This is read as "A and B." A conjunctive statement is true when all of its components are true.

Consequentialism: In moral philosophy, the view that the rightness or wrongness of an action is fully dependent upon the consequences that are brought about by that action.

Continental philosophy: A style of philosophy originating with thinkers from continental Europe. Continental thinkers tend to ally themselves with the humanities, whereas analytic thinkers tend to ally themselves with the sciences. Continental philosophers are less concerned with logic and argumentation than are analytic philosophers, and they are more apt to emphasize the ongoing, and sometimes mysterious, nature of philosophical questioning.

Contradiction: A logical relationship holding between two or more statements. If two statements contradict one another, then if one of the statements is true the other must be false and vice versa. For instance, consider the following two statements: The light is on. The light is off. Both of these statements cannot be true at the same time, and they cannot be false at the same time. Thus, they contradict one another.

Copula: In Aristotle's logic, the copula is a version of the verb "to be" that acts to connect the subject and the predicate of a statement. For instance, in the statement "All philosophers are brilliant," the word "are" acts as the copula, connecting the subject "philosophers" with the predicate "brilliant."

Correspondence theory of truth: A theory holding that truth is constituted by how well our beliefs, ideas, or statements correspond with or mirror the objective world. This theory is often contrasted with the coherence theory of truth.

Cosmology: The study of the structure and origins of the universe. The term "cosmology" comes from the Greek words *cosmos* meaning "world," and *logos* meaning "logic" or "reason."

Creationism: The belief that the universe was created by God.

Cynicism: From the Greek word *cynikos*, which means "dog-like." An ancient Greek school of philosophy, founded by Antisthenes, that advocated the rejection of convention and a return to nature. Diogenes of Sinope is perhaps the most well known and infamous of the Cynics.

Darwin, Charles: English naturalist (1809–1882). Darwin is the author of the modern theory of evolution.

Dasein: German word meaning "existence." In Heidegger's philosophy, Dasein refers specifically to human existence.

de Beauvoir, Simone: French existentialist and feminist (1908–1986).

Deduction: A form of argumentation in which a conclusion is shown to follow from a set of premises by necessity.

Definite description: According to Bertrand Russell, a description that refers to a particular individual. A definite description is usually preceded by the word "the." For example, "the table," "the house," or "the haggis."

Democritus: Presocratic philosopher (ca. 400 B.C.). Democritus is credited with being one of the first proponents of atomism, the

view that everything in the world is made of tiny, indivisible particles of matter.

Descartes, René: French philosopher (1596–1650). Descartes is considered by many to be the first Modern philosopher. He is perhaps most well known as the author of the Cogito: "I think, therefore I am."

Despair: The psychological feeling that one's desires cannot be fulfilled. According to Kierkegaard, despair is also an ontological condition that describes the state of all living human beings who exist as separate from God.

Determinism: The belief that all events in the world have been caused by the events and states of affairs that preceded them. Determinism is usually thought to be incompatible with the existence of free will.

Dialectic: A process in which two (or more) individuals engage in an exchange of ideas. Ideally, both sides are transformed by the exchange. According to Socrates, a dialectic exchange ultimately leads to Truth. According to Hegel, it leads to the synthesis of oppositions.

Diogenes of Sinope: Ancient Greek Cynic (ca. 413–327 B.C.). Diogenes rejected convention and taught that virtue is found in the return to nature.

Disjunction: In formal logic, the disjunction is a connective that combines simple statements into complex statements. A disjunction is often represented by a small "v," which comes from the Latin term *vel*, meaning "or." For instance "A v B" would be read as "A or B." A disjunctive statement is true when at least one of its components is true.

Divided line: An analogy used by Plato in Book VI of *The Republic* to illustrate the structure of reality. According to this analogy, the world is like a line divided into lower and higher realms. The lower realm is the realm of visible objects, whereas the higher realm is the realm of ideas and concepts. The point of education, according to Plato, is to direct the mind toward the higher realm of ideas.

Dogmatism: From a Greek term meaning "opinion." Today the term is used to characterize a position that is treated as authoritative and established without further argumentation.

Dualism: The view that reality is made up of two fundamental components, such as mind and matter, noumena and phenomena, atoms and void, the sacred and the profane, etc.

Dynamism: The belief that all things in nature are a manifestation of energy or force.

Efficient cause: In the philosophy of Aristotle, the efficient cause is one among four causes in nature. The efficient cause is the moving cause that imparts form to matter.

Egoism: The belief that all actions are, or should be, motivated by self-interest.

Eleatic School: A school of philosophy comprised of two fifth-century B.C. Presocratic philosophers Parmenides and Zeno, who lived in the Greek colony of Elea. They claimed that all change and movement are illusions.

Empiricism: A perspective holding that all knowledge originates in sense experience.

Engels, Friedrich: German thinker (1820–1895). Engels collaborated with Karl Marx and is considered the cofounder of Marxism.

Enlightenment: 1. A state of spiritual awakening. 2. An eighteenth-century European movement that encouraged empiricism, skepticism, reason, and science.

Epicurus: Hellenistic philosopher (341–270 B.C.). Epicurus was the founder of Epicureanism, a philosophy that advocates pleasure-seeking as the highest good.

Epistemology: The study of knowledge.

Essentialism: A belief that things in the world have essences that can be distinguished from merely accidental, or nonessential, properties.

Eternal feminine: According to de Beauvoir, the eternal feminine is the myth that there exists some sort of stable and unchangeable essence that makes a woman a real woman.

Eternal return: A metaphysical theory claiming that everything that has ever happened or that will happen is part of a never-ending cycle of repetition. This belief was argued for by the Stoic philosophers in ancient times and by Friedrich Nietzsche in modern times.

Ethics: The branch of philosophy that studies the nature of good and evil, right and wrong.

Eudoxus of Cnidus: Greek philosopher (408–355 B.C.). Formulated the idea that the universe consisted of a series of nested spheres.

Euthanasia: Greek term meaning "happy death." Euthanasia consists of either actively intervening to end a sick person's life or allowing a person to die out of mercy.

Evil: The opposite of Good. Evil is sometimes conceived as a lack of Goodness, as is the case with St. Augustine, or as a positive force that actively opposes Goodness, as in the case of Manicheanism.

Evolution: The belief that the present state of things can be traced back to, and is continuous with, the unfolding of the past states of things.

Existentialism: A philosophical movement that emphasizes the question of Being, human existence, and the reality of freedom of choice.

Extrinsic value: Something possesses extrinsic value if it is valuable not in itself but for what it has the power to bring about. Extrinsic value is synonymous with instrumental value.

Facticity: In existentialism, the facts about the world that we cannot change.

Faith: Belief without evidence.

Fallacy: A mistake in reasoning. Fallacies can be either formal or informal in nature. A formal fallacy is a mistake in the formal structure of reasoning. An informal fallacy is a mistake in the content of reasoning.

Fallenness: In existentialism, the human experience of alienation from Being. We are all "fallen" insofar as we experience ourselves as separate and alienated from the totality of Being.

Fascism: A political and religious philosophy originating in Europe in the early twentieth century. Fascism was given its name by the Italian dictator Benito Mussolini, and it held that people should be bound together as a nation under the leadership and guidance of a supreme leader.

Feminism: A philosophical perspective that emphasizes the female point of view. Although feminist beliefs are very diverse and sometimes conflict, generally feminists hold that the female point of view has traditionally been ignored, subjugated, or silenced in popular discourse.

Feuerbach, Ludwig: German philosopher (1804–1872).

Fichte, Johann Gottlieb: German philosopher (1762–1814).

Finite: The opposite of infinite. A thing is finite if it has boundaries or limits. According to many philosophers and religious thinkers, the only thing that is not finite is God.

First philosophy: According to Aristotle, the study of Being. First philosophy can be thought of as the study of those conditions that are necessary for all other things to be. It is first not necessarily in the temporal but in the ontological sense.

Formal cause: In the philosophy of Aristotle, the formal cause is one among four causes in nature. The formal cause is the form, structure, or essence of a thing.

Formal logic: The study of correct and incorrect forms of reasoning.

Foundationalism: The belief that there is a final foundation upon which all knowledge rests and from which all knowledge can be derived.

Four causes: According to Aristotle, a full explanation of anything must appeal to four causes: the material cause, the formal cause, the efficient cause, and the final cause. The material cause is the matter out of which a thing is made. The formal cause is the shape, form, or essence of a thing. The efficient cause is the force that imparts form to matter. The final cause is the purpose or goal of a thing. For instance, the material cause of a knife is the metal out of which it is made. Its formal cause is the sharpness and flatness of the knife. The efficient cause is the cutler. The final cause is cutting.

Free will: If humans are truly free to choose between various courses of action in life, then they are claimed to have free will. Those who believe that humans do possess free will are opposed by determinists who claim that human choices are not free but are instead determined by factors such as social conditioning, character, biology, God, etc.

Frege, Gottlob: German logician (1848–1925).

Freud, Sigmund: Austrian psychologist (1856–1940) who was the founder of psychoanalysis.

Galileo Galilei: Italian astronomer (1564–1642). Spent the last eight years of his life under house arrest by the Catholic Church, which had charged him with heresy for advocating a heliocentric model of the universe. The Church pardoned Galileo in 1992.

Geist: German word meaning "spirit" or "mind." Geist is the term used by Hegel to refer to the universe or Being itself.

Gestalt: The view that understanding does not come from analysis and separation but from examining the form of totalities. The whole is more than the sum of the parts.

God: With a capital "G," a term that refers to the single and supreme creator of the universe. With a lowercase "g," the term refers to any number of supernatural entities that rule over various aspects of nature and/or human culture.

Golden Mean: In Aristotle's philosophy, a middle point between extreme forms of behavior. The Golden Mean is held by Aristotle to be a measure of virtue. For instance, to feel too much fear is to be a coward; to feel too little is to be a fool. Feeling just the right amount of fear is a sign of courage.

Gospels: The books of the Christian New Testament that tell the story of Jesus. There are four Gospels: Matthew, Mark, Luke, and John. The first three are referred to collectively as the Synoptic Gospels because they are very similar to one another.

Greatest happiness principle: In utilitarianism, the principle that what is good is whatever brings the maximum amount of happiness to the maximum number of people while also limiting pain to a minimum.

Heaven: A state or place of spiritual perfection and peace. In the Abrahamic religions, Heaven is a place where the soul resides once the body dies, provided one has lived a virtuous life. In Eastern religions, Heaven is a blissful and serene state of mind achieved by living virtuously.

Hedonism: A philosophical perspective holding that pleasure is the greatest good.

Hegel, Georg Wilhelm Friedrich: German philosopher (1770–1831).

Hegesias: Greek philosopher who lived during the third century B.C. Also known as the "Death Persuader" because of his teaching that in life there is more pain than pleasure on balance, and thus it is best to commit suicide.

Heidegger, Martin: German philosopher (1889–1976). Although Heidegger distanced himself from the movement, he is considered to be the first of the modern existentialist philosophers.

Hell: A state or place of spiritual suffering. In the Abrahamic religions, Hell is a place where the soul is condemned to damnation once the body dies if one has not lived a virtuous life. In Eastern religions, Hell is a tortured state of mind.

Hellenistic philosophy: Those schools of philosophy that flourished after the death of Aristotle until the rise of Christianity under the Roman Empire. Stoicism, Epicureanism, and Skepticism are normally classified as Hellenistic philosophies. Cynicism is also sometimes included in this classification, although many of the Cynics lived at the same time as Aristotle.

Heraclitus: Presocratic philosopher (ca. 500 B.C.) who claimed that all is fire.

Hierarchy: The ordering of people or things according to a scale of higher and lower or better and worse.

Hinduism: An ancient religious and philosophical system originating in India. The Hindus claim that all things in the universe are manifestations of one underlying substance called Brahman.

Hobbes, Thomas: English philosopher (1588–1679).

Holism: The view that the parts of any system need to be understood in relation to the system as a whole.

Humanism: The perspective that human beings are the primary source of value in the world and that all things should be judged in relation to human life.

Hume, David: Scottish philosopher (1711–1776).

Husserl, Edmund: German philosopher (1859–1938). The founder of the philosophical movement called phenomenology.

Hypothetical imperative: According to Kant, a hypothetical imperative is a nonmoral action-directing statement. It tells us what to do under particular circumstances.

Idealism: The belief that the world is fundamentally made up of ideas rather than of some other substance, such as matter.

Ideas: Those entities that are present to the mind when one is thinking.

Immanence: The view that God, the Holy, or the Divine is in the world rather than outside of it.

Immortal: Nonmortal; not capable of dying.

Imperative: An action-directing statement. An imperative commands us to do something. For example: "Love your neighbor." "If you want an ice cream, then clean up your room."

Implication: A relationship between statements in which the truth of one statement guarantees the truth of another. It is said in such cases that the first statement implies the other. For example: "This figure is a square" implies the statement "This figure has four sides."

Impression: An immediate sensory experience. According to Hume, every sensory impression is followed by the creation of an idea, which is stored in the memory.

Inauthenticity: A state of self-alienation. In existentialism, authenticity is praised as the goal of philosophy while inauthenticity is seen as something to be overcome.

Individualism: The view that particular individual human beings have a value that is higher and more important than the value of the collective.

Indubitable: Absolutely certain.

Induction: A form of reasoning in which a conclusion follows from a set of premises with varying degrees of probability. This is different from deduction in which a conclusion follows from the premises by necessity.

Inference: In an argument, the movement from the premises to the conclusion. Inferences may be deductive in nature, in which case the conclusion follows from the premises by necessity, or inductive in nature, in which case the conclusion follows from the premises with a degree of probability. Some philosophers also claim that some inferences may be abductive in nature, in which case the conclusion follows from the premises with a degree of plausibility.

Infinite: The opposite of finite. A thing is infinite if it has no boundaries or limits. God, numbers, and the universe are things that have been claimed at various times to be infinite.

Informal fallacy: A mistake in reasoning that is based on the content of the argument.

Inherent value: The value possessed by something by virtue of what it is rather than by virtue of what it brings about or results in.

Innate: Inborn; not derived from outside influences or experiences. An innate idea, for instance, is an idea that a person is born with.

Instrumental: Useful for some purpose. A fork is instrumental for eating, for example.

Intuition: A type of knowledge that is not derived from argument or implication. An intuition is immediate and involves no inferences. I have an intuitive understanding of the color red. It comes not through argument, but through direct experience.

Irrational: Not rational. Irrationality involves, in one way or another, the failure to "make sense."

Islamic philosophy: The movement in philosophical thinking that is based on the beliefs of Islam. Islamic philosophers claim that the Koran is the word of God as revealed through the prophet Muhammad. Interpreting and understanding the Koran is necessary for understanding any other Truth according to Islamic philosophers.

Jacobi, Friedrich Heinrich: German philosopher (1743–1819). Author of the famous "Letter to Fichte," in which he charged Kantian philosophy with being a form of nihilism.

James, William: American philosopher (1842–1910). Considered to be one of the founders of the Pragmatic movement in philosophy.

Jaspers, Karl: German existentialist philosopher (1883–1969).

Jesus of Nazareth: The central figure in Christian faith. Jesus himself was a Jew, but followers of his teachings eventually broke with traditional Judaism, claiming that Jesus was God incarnate.

Judaism: The earliest of the three Abrahamic religious traditions. The holiest text of Judaism is the Torah, also known as the Book of Moses, which became the first five books of the Christian Old Testament.

Justice: The state in which all things are given their due. Justice is most often thought of as a fair balance between the competing needs and desires of people or between the competing forces of the universe.

Kant, Immanuel: German philosopher (1724–1804). Author of *The Critique of Pure Reason, The Critique of Practical Reason,* and *The Critique of Judgment.*

Kepler, Johannes: German astronomer (1571–1630). Kepler is the architect of the modern model of the universe in which the planets, including Earth, rotate around the sun in elliptically shaped orbits.

Kierkegaard, Søren: Danish philosopher (1813–1855). Considered by some to be the first existentialist.

Knowledge: Understanding or being aware of something. How it is that we obtain such understanding or awareness is studied by philosophers working in the field of epistemology.

Knowledge by acquaintance: According to Bertrand Russell, the kind of knowledge we obtain when we actually experience something. Knowledge by acquaintance is immediate and intuitive. For instance, when we see the color red, we are acquainted with the color red.

Knowledge by description: According to Bertrand Russell, the kind of knowledge we obtain when we build up descriptions of the world from our experiences. For instance, a table is known by description. We build up a description of a table from our experiences of flatness, hardness, brownness, and other qualities with which we are acquainted.

Koran: The holy book of Islam. Sometimes also spelled Qur'an.

La Mettrie, Julien Offroy de: French philosopher (1709–1751). A Cartesian materialist and atheist.

Language game theory of meaning: According to Wittgenstein's later work, language is structured like a game and meaning emerges from playing this game with others.

Lao Tzu: Sixth-century B.C. Chinese philosopher. Author of the *Tao Te Ching,* which is one of the major Taoist religious texts.

Leap of faith: Kierkegaard's name for the act of moving past reason and freely making a choice to believe and to act in the world.

Left-Hegelians: Those followers of Hegel who rejected his conservatism in religion and politics. The Left-Hegelians were atheists such as Max Stirner and Karl Marx, who were more concerned with the concrete issues of individual freedom and prosperity than with abstract ideas about the unfolding of absolute spirit.

Leibniz, Gottfried Wilhelm: German philosopher (1646–1716). Claimed that the world is made of monads.

Leucippus: Greek Presocratic philosopher (ca. 440 B.C.). The teacher of Democritus. Advocate of atomism.

Linguistics: The study of language, including its structure and uses.

Locke, John: English empiricist philosopher (1632–1704). Well known for his claim that the mind is like a "blank slate" until it is written upon by experience.

Logic: The branch of philosophy that studies arguments and that establishes the criteria for correct and incorrect forms of reasoning.

Logical atomism: A perspective on logic, held by Bertrand Russell, claiming that the best and most accurate logical notation is built up out of atomic statements that are connected together into complex statements by way of logical connectives.

Lordship/bondsman relationship: See Master/slave dialectic.

Luther, Martin: German religious reformer (1483–1546). Leader of the Protestant Reformation.

Lyceum: The school established by Aristotle near Athens around 399 B.C.

Lyotard, Jean-François: French post-modernist philosopher (1924–1998).

Malebranche, Nicolas: French Cartesian philosopher (1638–1715). Proponent of occasionalism, the view that mind and body do not directly interact with one another but that God is the only causal agent.

Manichaeanism: A religious belief system established by Mani (216–277). According to Manichaeanism, the world is divided between light and dark forces that are in conflict and struggle with one another.

Marx, Karl: German philosopher (1818–1883). Founder of Marxism and author, with Friedrich Engels, of the *Communist Manifesto*.

Master morality: According to Nietzsche, the form of morality adhered to by the strong. Strictly speaking, a master morality is more like an expression of personal preference than it is an ethical system.

Master/slave dialectic: Also called the lordship/bondsman relationship. In Hegel's book *The Phenomenology of Spirit*, this relationship is depicted as the initiating point of self-consciousness. The master, or the lord, comes into a relationship with the slave, or the bondsman. As they struggle with one another, a synthesis occurs that produces the worker, who contains elements of both master and slave.

Materialism: The view that the world is fundamentally composed of matter rather than of some other substance, like ideas.

Matters of fact: According to Hume, systems of knowledge that are informative but uncertain because they depend on empirical observation. For instance, the sciences of biology, astronomy, and sociology deal in matters of fact. When a sociologist claims that crime is correlated with poverty, this is an assertion that may or may not be true according to what the case

is in the observable world. This is unlike the assertions of math and logic, which express unchangeable truths regardless of what happens in the observable world.

Maya: In Hinduism, the veil that separates our perceptions from the truth of reality.

Metaphor: A nonliteral use of words or phrases. A metaphor is a kind of analogy that attempts to explain or evoke a truth. For example, Plato's Cave Myth is a metaphor in which he likens prisoners trapped in a cave to the human situation.

Metaphysics: The study of the structure of reality. Literally "beyond physics," metaphysics is the study of that which does not change, whereas physics is the study of the motion of matter.

Milesians: The Presocratic philosophers who came from the town of Miletus on the coast of Asia Minor sometime beginning in the sixth century B.C. The Milesians Thales, Anaximander, and Anaximenes are generally considered to be the first philosophers and scientists in the Western world.

Mill, John Stuart: British utilitarian philosopher (1806–1873).

Mimesis: Greek term meaning "mimicry" or "imitation." Both Plato and Aristotle held that all art was a form of mimesis.

Mitsein: German word meaning "being-with." According to existentialists, humans are *mitsein* because they are social beings.

Monad: According to Leibniz, the fundamental unit making up all things in the world. The monad has position in space but is nonmaterial. It is something like a point of force.

Monism: The view that the world is fundamentally made of only one substance.

Morality: A synonym for "ethics." The study of the Good and of right and wrong.

Moses: Key figure in Judaism who freed his people from slavery under the Egyptians.

Moses delivered the Ten Commandments to the Jews and led them to the Promised Land.

Muhammad: Founder of the religion of Islam (ca. 571–632).

Muslim: A follower of the religion of Islam.

Mysticism: A way of knowing ultimate reality that is not based in logic or conceptual thinking. Mystics claim to have a particular kind of "mystical experience" that is self-validating and which reveals the nature of things to them all at once, immediately and intuitively.

Myth: A meaningful story or narrative that purports to deliver some sort of important moral message or metaphysical truth. Most religions use myths to convey their teachings, and some philosophers (like Plato) use them as well. Science rejects mythmaking, although it is claimed by some that science tells its own set of mythic stories.

Myth of the Cave: A story that appears in Book VII of Plato's *The Republic*. The Myth of the Cave likens the lives of humans to the lives of prisoners in a cave. The path out of the cave is a metaphor for education and eventual enlightenment.

National Socialism: A form of German fascism that existed between 1933 and 1945. Known as the Nazis and led by Adolf Hitler, the National Socialists advocated totalitarian control of society, the expansion of the German state, and the destruction of "non-Aryan" people like Jews and Slavs.

Naturalism: The view that the world is made only of natural entities. Naturalism is opposed to supernaturalism.

Natural language: A naturally occurring language, used and spoken by people to express themselves and to communicate in everyday life. Languages like English, French, Japanese, German, etc. are natural languages. Formal languages, like math and formal logic, are nonnatural languages.

Natural law: The law of nature governing both the physical and the moral universes.

Nazi: See National Socialism.

Necessity: The property of being undeniable. If a statement is necessary (such as $Av\sim A$), it is impossible to deny that it is true. If a state of affairs is necessary, it is impossible for it to be otherwise. If a connection between two events is necessary, it is impossible for one event to occur without the other.

Negation: In logic, the denial of a statement. When a statement is true, its negation is false, and when the negation is true, the statement it negates is false. In formal logic, negation is usually symbolized with $\sim$ or $-$. So, for instance, the negation of the statement "A" is "$\sim$A."

Neoplatonism: The philosophical movement started by Plotinus (A.D. 204 to 270). Neoplatonism is a mystical form of Platonic philosophy that claims all things are emanations from "the One."

New Academy: The term used to refer to Plato's Academy when it came under the control of the Skeptic philosophers.

Newton, Sir Isaac: English physicist (1642–1727). Author of the Newtonian laws of motion and the Newtonian theory of gravitation.

Nietzsche, Friedrich Wilhelm: German philosopher (1844–1900) who held that all things in the universe are expressions of the Will to Power.

Nihilism: A philosophical position based on the following three assumptions: (1) The highest ideals are beyond human grasp, (2) This situation is other than it ought to be, and (3) There is nothing we can do about this situation. Nihilists claim that humans are forever alienated from absolute Truth, Being, and Goodness and that life is a constant and vain struggle against a meaningless universe. The term is also used to describe historical periods during which whole cultures fall away from their highest values. The term is commonly used in a very loose and imprecise sense to refer to people and philosophies that are destructive and overly negative.

Normative: The prescription of standards against which something, like one's behavior, may be judged as good or bad.

Noumenal world: According to Kant, the world as it exists apart from human experience. The noumenal world is the "thing-in-itself." We know that it exists, but because it is separate from human interpretation, we cannot say anything about it other than that it exists.

Nous: Greek word meaning "mind." Anaxagoras, Socrates' teacher, claimed that the universe was given form and order by the cosmic force of nous.

Objectivity: A perspective that views things the way they really are. A perspective free from bias.

Occasionalism: The philosophical perspective of Malebranche holding that there is no cause and effect relationship between mind and matter. All causation is attributable only to God. The term "occasionalism" comes from the idea that what seem like mental or physical causes and effects are actually only "occasions" for other events, not actual causes.

Ockham, William: English philosopher (1285–1347). The term "Ockham's Razor" comes from his assertion that a simpler explanation is better than an unnecessarily complex one.

Oligarchy: A form of political organization in which a small group of people govern society.

Omnibenevolence: All good; one of the qualities of the Abrahamic God.

Omnipotence: All powerful; one of the qualities of the Abrahamic God.

Omniscience: All knowing; one of the qualities of the Abrahamic God.

Ontological argument: The name given by Kant to an argument authored by St. Anselm that purports to prove the existence of God. This argument is *a priori* in nature, starting from a definition of God as "that than which nothing greater can be conceived." Because we can always conceive of something greater than the subjective idea of God as it exists in our minds, it follows that God is not just a subjective idea. Because the objective existence of God is greater than the merely subjective idea of God, God must exist objectively.

Ontology: From the Greek words *ontos,* meaning "being," and *logos,* meaning "logic" or "reason." The study of Being.

Optimism: The view that the world can potentially be made better or that it is already good. Optimists believe that human aspirations can be fulfilled.

Ordinary language philosophy: A movement in philosophy inspired by Wittgenstein's posthumously published second book, *The Philosophical Investigations.* Ordinary language philosophers claim that we should focus attention on the way that words are used in ordinary language when we philosophize rather than being led astray by unusual and overly technical uses of words.

Organic: Being organized and structured like a living organism rather than like a machine or a mechanism. Organic structures are integrated so that they contribute to the overall functioning and health of the whole.

Otherness: The quality possessed by something that is not me. According to existentialists, human beings experience the world around them as something other than themselves and then develop their own identity by contrast.

Overman: See *Übermensch.*

Panentheism: The view that the material universe is part, but only a part, of the divine or of God.

Pantheism: The view that the universe as a whole is divine or God. Pantheism is different from panentheism insofar as for the pantheist the universe is identical with God, whereas for the panentheist the universe is only a part of God.

Paradox: A line of reasoning that seems correct in all of its steps but that leads to a contradiction. For instance, if I utter the statement, "What I am saying is false," this leads to a paradox. If it is true that what I am saying is false, then what I am saying is false, and if it is false that what I am saying is false, then what I am saying is true!

Parmenides: Presocratic philosopher (515–450 B.C.). Part of the Eleatic School, Parmenides claimed that all movement and change are logical impossibilities.

Peirce, Charles Sanders: American pragmatist philosopher (1839–1914).

Peripatetic School: Aristotle's Lyceum was referred to by this label because Aristotle taught while walking with students. The term "peripatetic" is a Greek term that means "walkway."

Perspectivism: The claim that the way the world appears is tied to the perspective of the observer. Nietzsche's philosophy is sometimes referred to by this label.

Pessimism: The view that the world is not good and cannot be made better, or that all human aspirations are doomed to failure.

Phenomenal world: In Kantian philosophy, the world as it appears to us. The phenomenal world is distinguished from the noumenal world, which is the world as it exists independent of our perceptions.

Phenomenology: The study of phenomena. Phenomenology does not purport to study things-in-themselves but only things as they appear to us.

Philosopher kings: According to Plato, a just and well-ordered society should be run by those who are the wisest. He claims that either kings must study philosophy or philosophers must become kings.

Philosophy: From the Greek words *philos*, meaning "love of," and *sophia*, meaning "wisdom." Philosophy is a way of thinking that emphasizes raising new questions and undermining old assumptions and that exhibits the willingness to defer final answers all in the aspiration toward greater understanding of ourselves and the world.

Picture theory of meaning: A view advocated by Ludwig Wittgenstein in his book *Tractatus Logico Philosophicus*. According to this view, the purpose of language is to logically map out relationships that exist in the world. In this way it offers a kind of "picture" of reality.

Plato: Ancient Greek philosopher (427–347 B.C.). A follower of Socrates and the founder of the first university, called the Academy. Plato taught that the world of ideas is more real than the world of material existence and that the most real idea is the Good.

Platonic idealism: The Platonic doctrine holding that the most real entities that exist are pure ideas, or forms.

Plotinus: Neoplatonist (A.D. 204 to 270).

Pluralism: A viewpoint that emphasizes diversity and difference rather than similarities and unity.

Popper, Karl: British philosopher (1902–1994); did not get along well with Wittgenstein.

Positivism: A view that science and its methods should be used to reform things as diverse as philosophy, politics, language, law, and society itself.

Postmodern: A movement claiming that the Modern age is coming to an end and that a new cultural age is emerging. Because we are in the middle of this emergence, all we know is that it comes after Modernism; hence the term "Postmodern." Postmodernists reject what they see as the vain search for absolutes by Modernist philosophers and thinkers. They tend to emphasize diversity, difference, and subjectivity and to deemphasize what they see as the tendency toward the construction of "metanarratives" that purport to tell objective stories about the unfolding of objective reality.

Practical reason: In Kantian philosophy, practical reason is the faculty of reason that is concerned with deducing moral imperatives.

Pragmatism: A movement in philosophy that puts a great deal of emphasis on assessing the meaning and truth of ideas based upon their uses and consequences.

Predicate: In Aristotle's logic the predicate is the part of a statement that is joined to the subject by a copula. For instance, in the statement "Socrates is ugly," the predicate is "ugly." It is joined to the subject, "Socrates," by the copula "is."

Presocratics: Those Greek thinkers, starting with Thales of Miletus around 600 B.C., who downplayed myth and developed ways of thinking that are today considered the first steps toward science and philosophy.

Prime matter: In the philosophy of Aristotle, prime matter is matter without form. Aristotle insisted that such a thing does not really exist except as a mental abstraction.

Prime mover: In the philosophy of Aristotle, the Prime Mover is the source of all movement in the universe. In later Medieval thought, the Prime Mover became equated with God.

Problem of induction: The problem of how we can reliably draw true conclusions from our observations of past events. David Hume was the first philosopher to clearly emphasize this problem. He demonstrated that our confidence in such inductive inferences is based on the unstated assumption that the future will be consistent with the past.

Proposition: In logic, a proposition is the meaning or the content of a statement, which is capable of being true or false.

Protestantism: A variety of Christianity that "protests" against the authority and hierarchy of the Catholic Church. Protestants vary in their specific beliefs, but generally speaking they emphasize the importance of reading the Bible rather than adhering to the authority of the Pope.

Psychoanalysis: A branch of psychology pioneered by Sigmund Freud in the late nineteenth and early twentieth centuries. Psychoanalysis claims that the human mind is divided into conscious and unconscious regions, with the unconscious mind being very important in explanations of various forms of human psychological development and disorder. In contemporary times, psychoanalysis has had a great deal of influence outside the field of psychology, finding applications in philosophy, literary analysis, film criticism, and aesthetics.

Pyrrho of Elis: Greek philosopher (ca. 360–270 B.C.). The founder of Skepticism.

Pythagoras: Presocratic philosopher who lived during the fifth century B.C. Pythagoras claimed that the universe has an underlying mathematical structure.

Quantum mechanics: A scientific system developed in the early twentieth century based on the idea that all things can be divided into finite packets, or "quanta," of energy.

Rationalism: A philosophical orientation claiming that Truth is found by reflecting inward on the operations of the mind rather than by relying on observations of the "outer" world.

Realism: The claim that a real world exists independent of our perceptions. Realism is sometimes put into contrast with Idealism, which claims that the world has no real existence independent of our ideas.

Reductionism: The procedure involved in reducing complex features of reality to simpler structures. Reductionists believe that in so doing, we gain a better understanding of reality.

Relations of ideas: According to Hume, systems of knowledge that are internally consistent but which do not relate directly to the outside world. Relations of ideas are certain but noninformative. For instance, math and logic are systems that designate necessary truths; however, those truths are empty insofar as they do not tell us anything new about the world.

Relativism: The view that there are no absolutes and that things such as truth, beauty, and ethics are relative to time, place, culture, and perspective.

Religion: A way of thinking that affirms the existence of a supernatural aspect of reality and that emphasizes the importance of experiencing a reconnection with the supernatural.

Revelation: To have something revealed; usually a valuable truth. Revelations may occur in many ways, both rational and mystical.

Right-Hegelians: Those followers of Hegel who accepted his conservatism in religion and politics.

Russell, Bertrand: English philosopher (1872–1970). A key figure in the development of modern symbolic logic.

Samsara: In Hinduism, the repeating cycle of reincarnation.

Sartre, Jean-Paul: French existentialist philosopher (1905–1980).

Scholasticism: The movement in Medieval philosophy centered in major universities and which focused on systematizing philosophy and theology.

Schopenhauer, Arthur: German philosopher (1788–1860).

Science: A way of thinking based on the assumption that all things in the natural world can best be explained by reference to natural causes.

Semantics: A branch of linguists focusing on the meaning or the content of language.

Sensation: The subjective experience produced when the sense organs are stimulated by input from the external world. Sensation is the awareness of sense data.

Sense data: The immediate objects of inner, subjective awareness. For instance, when I have the sensation of sharp pain, sharp pain is the sense datum.

Simple idea: An idea that cannot be broken down into any smaller components; for instance, the idea of red or the idea of sweetness. According to David Hume, all knowledge is built up out of simple ideas.

Skepticism: 1. The school of philosophy founded by the ancient Greek philosopher Pyrrho of Elis; 2. The view that nothing can be known with certainty, or that nothing can be known at all.

Slave morality: According to the philosopher Friedrich Nietzsche, a form of morality that is adhered to by the weak. Because they do not possess the strength to live as creative individuals, these weaklings band together and produce a code of conduct that protects them and those like them against the strong.

Socialism: A political and economic philosophy that advocates group control of property, resources, and wealth.

Socrates: Greek philosopher (469–399 B.C.) considered by many to be the true father of philosophy.

Socratic Method: A dialectical method of debate practiced by Socrates in ancient Greece and still used today by teachers, lawyers, and philosophers. The Socratic Method is a process of question and answer that is guided by a concern for Truth. Also called "dialectic."

Solipsism: The claim that an objective world independent of human thought does not really exist. Solipsists believe that what appears as an external world is really just a projection of the human mind.

Sophism: A movement in ancient Greece centering on the mastery of logic, rhetoric, and argument. The Sophists were not concerned with discovery of Truth but rather with winning arguments, the manipulation of public opinion, and making money.

Soundness: The quality possessed by a perfect argument. An argument is sound if it has a valid, formal structure and all of the statements it contains are true.

Spengler, Oswald: German philosopher and historian (1880–1936). His book *The Decline of the West*, which describes the rise and fall of world civilizations, continues to have an enormous influence on thinkers around the world.

Spinoza, Baruch: Jewish philosopher (1632–1677).

Stirner, Max: German philosopher (1806–1856). Max Stirner is a pseudonym. His birth name was Johann Kaspar Schmidt.

Stoicism: A school of philosophy founded by Zeno of Citium around 108 B.C. Stoicism advocates the elimination of emotion and submission to fate.

Subjectivism: The view that we cannot understand reality apart from our subjective perspective or interpretation. Subjectivism is in contrast to Objectivism.

Sublation: In Hegel's philosophy, the process by which a synthesis occurs. In this process, apparent oppositions are resolved.

Sublime: A designation for those things that overwhelm the human capacity for perception or conception, but which still bring a sense of aesthetic pleasure. Sublime objects are associated with overwhelming power or number and are in contrast to objects of beauty.

Substance: That which undergoes change but does not itself change. For instance, my mind is a mental substance that has an ever-changing cascade of ideas, thoughts, feelings, etc. My body is a physical substance that undergoes injury, aging, etc.

Superman: See *Übermensch.*

Syllogism: A deductive argument with exactly two premises and one conclusion.

Syntax: A branch of linguists focusing on the form or structure of language.

Synthesis: The point in the Hegelian dialectic at which a thesis combines with an antithesis. For instance, if black is a thesis and white is an antithesis, then gray might be the synthesis of the two.

Tabula rasa: Latin phrase meaning "blank slate." It refers to the claim that the mind contains no innate ideas at birth but becomes filled with ideas through experience. The phrase is usually associated with John Locke.

Technological thinking: According to Heidegger, a form of thinking that views the world as something to be used to serve human purposes. Heidegger claims that

this form of thinking tends to cover over the Truth of Being.

Technology: Any structured system or instrument that offers a consistent means by which to achieve a consistent end.

Teleology: From the Greek words *telos,* meaning "goal," and *logos,* meaning "logic" or "reason." The viewpoint that all things are goal-directed or end-seeking.

Temporal: Having to do with time.

Thales of Miletus: Presocratic Greek philosopher (ca. 600 B.C.). Considered by many to be the first scientist and philosopher. Claimed that all things are made of water.

Theology: From the Greek words *theos,* meaning "God," and *logos,* meaning "logic" or "reason." The study of God.

Thesis: The initial starting point of the Hegelian dialectic. The thesis comes into a relationship with its antithesis, which then produces a synthesis.

Thing-in-itself: From the German *ding an sich.* According to Kant, the thing-in-itself is objective reality as it exists independent of human perception. It is also called "noumenal reality."

Thomism: The philosophical system of St. Thomas Aquinas.

Thrownness: In existentialism, part of human experience is to find oneself existing in a world. We do not experience where we came from, but find ourselves "there" in the world. In this sense, we are "thrown" into that world.

Time: The occurrence of past, present, and future. Some philosophers believe that time is an objective phenomenon, whereas others believe it is only a subjective phenomenon. Some philosophers believe that time is linear, and some believe that time is cyclical.

Timon of Philius: Greek skeptical philosopher (320–230 B.C.).

Torah: The holiest of Jewish texts. Sometimes also referred to as the Book of

Moses, the Torah became the first five books of the Christian Old Testament.

Totalitarianism: Any form of government that attempts to exert total control over all aspects of society, including individual life, economics, art, business, and religion. The most infamous totalitarian governments were the Nazis and the Soviet Communists.

Transcendent: Going beyond the boundaries of time and space. For instance, in the Abrahamic religions, God is thought to be transcendent because He exists outside of the boundaries of the universe.

Transcendental: Providing a ground for something else that is a fundamental element of reality. For instance, Kant provided transcendental arguments that he claims demonstrate the necessity of certain *a priori* intuitions and categories of the understanding, which are themselves fundamental to the human mind.

Transcendental Idealism: The name Kant gave to his philosophy. Transcendental Idealism holds that our reality is the product of sensory input from the objective world, which is organized and synthesized by the mind according to a set of *a priori* intuitions and categories of understanding.

Truth: The quality of actually being the case. Philosophers desire the truth, but they often disagree about what the truth actually is. Some claim that the truth is an objective thing, whereas some claim that it is a subjective thing. Some claim that truth exists in language only, while others claim that truth is a quality of the world to which language refers. Some claim that there are many "truths," whereas some claim that there is only one overarching "Truth."

Truth table: In logic, a table that systematically lists all possible combinations of truth values for logical operators and/or statements in an argument.

Übermensch: According to Nietzsche, an *Übermensch* is a higher human being—creative, courageous, and independent in the face of the death of God. The term has been translated into English as both Superman and Overman.

Upanishads: Ancient Hindu philosophical texts that suggest all reality is an emanation from one underlying substance called Brahman.

Utilitarianism: An ethical theory that advocates the principle of utility as a guiding feature. According to this principle, an action is good if it produces more pleasure than pain overall.

Vagueness: Lack of clarity. A statement is vague if what it means is not clear.

Validity: The quality possessed by a deductive argument if its conclusion follows from its premises. If the conclusion does not follow, the argument is called "invalid."

Venn diagram: Diagrams developed by John Venn to visually illustrate the relationships between classes. Venn diagrams consist of overlapping circles. They are useful in showing validity and invalidity when applied to the logic of Aristotle.

Vienna Circle: A group of philosophers who met in Vienna from 1922 to 1938. They were influenced by Ludwig Wittgenstein's early philosophy and desired to make philosophy more scientific.

Virtue: An excellence. The opposite of a virtue is a vice.

Whitehead, Alfred North: British philosopher (1861–1947). Teacher of Bertrand Russell and coauthor with Russell of *Principia Mathematica*.

Will: The faculty, energy, or substance that provokes action and that makes it possible for us to make decisions.

Will to power: According to Nietzsche, the fundamental constituent of the world. The will to power is a force of tension, struggle, and overcoming manifest in all relationships between living and nonliving things.

Wisdom: Understanding of the whole, or understanding of the most important and highest principles of reality.

Wittgenstein, Ludwig: Austrian/British philosopher (1889–1951).

Xenophon: Greek military man (ca. 430–354 B.C.). Author of some Socratic dialogues.

Zarathustra: The founder of Zoroastrianism, the religion of ancient Iran. Nietzsche uses Zarathustra as the name for the main character in his book *Thus Spoke Zarathustra*.

Zeno of Citium: Greek philosopher (335–264 B.C.). Founder of Stoicism.

Zeno of Elea: Greek philosopher (490–430 B.C.). A member of the Eleatic School and a follower of Parmenides.

Bibliography

© Juneko J. Robinson

Aczel, Amir D. *Descartes' Secret Notebook.* New York: Broadway Books, 2005.

Agamben, Giorgio. *Remnants of Auschwitz: The Witness and the Archive.* New York: Zone Books, 2002.

Altizer, Thomas J. J. *Godhead and the Nothing.* Albany: State University of New York Press, 2003.

St. Anselm. *Proslogion with A Reply on Behalf of the Fool by Gaunilo and The Author's Reply to Gaunilo.* Translated by M. J. Charlesworth. Notre Dame, IN: University of Notre Dame Press, 1979.

Aquinas, St. Thomas. *Summa Theologica.* Translated by the Fathers of the English Dominican Province. Westminster, MD: Christian Classics, 1981.

Arendt, Hannah. *The Origins of Totalitarianism.* New York: Harcourt, 1976.

Ariew, Roger and Eric Watkins, eds. *Modern Philosophy: An Anthology of Primary Sources.* Indianapolis, IN: Hackett Publishing Company, 1998.

Aristophanes. *The Clouds.* Translated by William Arrowsmith. New York: Mentor Books, 1962.

Aristotle. *The Basic Works of Aristotle.* Translated by Richard McKeon. New York: Random House, 1941.

Armstrong, Karen. *Muhammad: A Biography of the Prophet.* San Francisco: HarperCollins, 1993.

———. *A Short History of Myth.* Edinburgh: Cannongate, 2005.

St. Augustine. *The Confessions of St. Augustine.* New York: Mentor Books, 1963.

Aurelius, Marcus. *Meditations,* in *Marcus Aurelius and His Times: The Transition from Paganism to Christianity.* Roslyn, NY: Walter J. Black, 1945.

Bales, Eugene. *A Ready Reference to Philosophy East and West.* Lanham, MD: University Press of America, 1987.

Banham, Gary and Charlie Blake, eds. *Evil Spirits: Nihilism and the Fate of Modernity.* Manchester: Manchester University Press, 2000.

Barnes, Jonathan, trans. and ed. *Early Greek Philosophy*. London: Penguin Books, 1987.

Beauvoir, Simone de. *Adeiu: A Farewell to Sartre*. Translated by Patrick O'Brian. New York: Pantheon Books, 1984.

———. *The Second Sex*. Translated and edited by H. M. Parshley. New York: Vintage Books, 1974.

Beiser, Frederick C., ed. *The Cambridge Companion to Hegel*. Cambridge: Cambridge University Press, 2006.

Buber, Martin. *I and Thou*. Translated by Walter Kaufman. New York: Book-of-the-Month Club, 1999.

Campbell, Joseph. *The Hero with a Thousand Faces*. Princeton, NJ: Princeton University Press, 1973.

Chaning-Pearce, Melville. *Soren Kierkegaard: A Study*. London: James Clark & Co., 1945.

Clark, John P. *Max Stirner's Egoism*. London: Freedom Press, 1976.

Cohen, I. Bernard. *The Birth of a New Physics*. New York: W. W. Norton & Company, 1985.

Cornford, F. M. *Before and After Socrates*. Cambridge: Cambridge University Press, 1986.

Cottingham, John, ed. *Descartes*. New York: Oxford University Press, 1998.

Critchley, Simon. *Very Little ... Almost Nothing: Death, Philosophy, Literature*. New York: Routledge, 1997.

Dahlstrom, Daniel O. *Heidegger's Concept of Truth*. Cambridge: Cambridge University Press, 2001.

Davies, Paul. *The Cosmic Blueprint*. New York: Simon and Schuster, 1989.

Descartes, René. *Discourse on Method*. Translated by Laurence J. Lafleur. Indianapolis, IN: Bobbs-Merrill Educational Publishing, 1983.

———. *Meditations on First Philosophy*. Translated by Donald A. Cress. Indianapolis, IN: Hackett Publishing Company, 1993.

———. *Treatise of Man*. Translated by Thomas Steele Hall. Amherst, NY: Prometheus Books, 2003.

Dorward, Alan. *Bertrand Russell: A Short Guide to His Philosophy*. Elmsford, NY: The British Book Centre, 1973.

Edmonds, David and John Eidinow. *Wittgenstein's Poker: The Story of a Ten-Minute Argument between Two Great Philosophers*. New York: CCC, 2001.

Eldridge, Richard. *Leading a Human Life: Wittgenstein, Intentionality, and Romanticism*. Chicago: University of Chicago Press, 1997.

Epictetus. *A Manual For Living*. Translated by Sharon Lebell. San Francisco: HarperCollins, 1994.

Epicurus. *Letters and Sayings of Epicurus*. Translated by Odysseus Makridis. New York: Barnes and Noble Books, 2005.

Fakhry, Majid. *A History of Islamic Philosophy*. New York: Columbia University Press, 1970.

Feuerbach, Ludwig. *The Essence of Christianity*. Translated by George Eliot. New York: Barnes and Noble Books, 2004.

Gaarder, Jostein. *Sophie's World: A Novel About the History of Philosophy*. New York: Berkley Books, 1996.

Gardiner, Patrick. *Kierkegaard: A Very Short Introduction*. Oxford: Oxford University Press, 2002.

Gilder, Joshua and Anne-Lee Gilder. *Heavenly Intrigue: Johannes Kepler, Tycho Brahe, and the Murder Behind One of History's Greatest Scientific Discoveries*. New York: Anchor Books, 2005.

Goebbels, Joseph. *Michael: A Novel*. Translated by Joachim Neugroschel. New York: Amok Press, 1987.

Grayling, A. C. *Wittgenstein: A Very Short Introduction*. Oxford: Oxford University Press, 2001.

Greene, Norman N. *Jean-Paul Sartre: The Existentialist Ethic*. Ann Arbor: University of Michigan Press, 1963.

Griffin, Nicholas, ed. *The Cambridge Companion to Bertrand Russell*. Cambridge: Cambridge University Press, 2003.

Guignon, Charles. *On Being Authentic*. London: Routledge, 2004.

Hamilton, Edith. *Mythology*. New York: New American Library, 1942.

Havard, C. W. H., ed. *Black's Medical Dictionary*. Totowa, NJ: Barnes and Noble Books, 1987.

Hawking, Stephen. *A Brief History of Time: From the Big Bang to Black Holes*. New York: Bantam Books, 1990.

Hegel, Georg Wilhelm Friedrich. *Hegel: The Essential Writings*. Edited by Frederick G. Weiss. New York: Harper Torchbooks, 1974.

———. *Phenomenology of Spirit*. Translated by A. V. Miller. Oxford: Oxford University Press, 1977.

———. *Reason in History: A General Introduction to the Philosophy of History*. Translated by Robert S. Hartman. New York: Liberal Arts Press, 1954.

———. *Texts and Commentary*. Translated and edited by Walter Kaufmann. Notre Dame, IN: University of Notre Dame Press, 1977.

Heidegger, Martin. *Basic Writings*. Edited by David Farrell Krell. San Francisco: HarperCollins, 1993.

———. *Being and Time*. Translated by Joan Stambaugh. Albany: State University of New York Press, 1996.

———. *An Introduction to Metaphysics*. Translated by Gregory Fried and Richard Polt. New Haven, CT: Yale University Press, 2000.

———. *Nietzsche* (Four Volumes). Translated and edited by David Farrell Krell. San Francisco: HarperCollins, 1979–1987.

———. *Philosophical and Political Writings*. Edited by Manfred Stassen. New York: Continuum, 2003.

Hick, John and Arthur C. McGill, eds. *The Many-Faced Argument: Recent Studies on the Ontological Argument for the Existence of God*. New York: Macmillan, 1967.

Höffe, Otfried. *Immanuel Kant*. Translated by Marshall Farrier. Albany: SUNY Press, 1994.

Holbrook, David. *Education, Nihilism, and Survival*. New Brunswick, NJ: Transaction Publishers, 2002.

The Holy Qur'an: English Translation of the Meanings of the Qur'an with Notes. Translated by Abdullah Yusuf Ali. Indianapolis, IN: H&C International, 1992.

Hourani, George, ed. *Essays on Islamic Philosophy and Science*. Albany: State University of New York Press, 1975.

Howells, Christina, ed. *The Cambridge Companion to Sartre*. Cambridge: Cambridge University Press, 1992.

Hughes, H. Stuart. *Oswald Spengler: A Critical Estimate*. New York: Charles Scribner's Sons, 1952.

Hume, David. *An Inquiry concerning Human Understanding*. Chicago: Open Court Publishing Co., 1927.

———. *An Inquiry concerning the Principles of Morals*. New York: Library of Liberal Arts, 1957.

———. *Of the Standard of Taste and Other Essays*. New York: Library of Liberal Arts, 1965.

———. *The Philosophy of David Hume*. Edited by V. C. Chappell. New York: Random House, 1963.

Janaway, Christopher. *Schopenhauer*. Oxford: Oxford University Press, 1996.

Jaspers, Karl. *The Great Philosophers*. Edited by Hannah Arendt and translated by Ralph Manheim. New York: Harcourt, Brace & World, 1962.

Kant, Immanuel. *Critique of Judgment*. Translated by Werner S. Pluhar. Indianapolis, IN: Hackett Publishing, 1987.

———. *Critique of Practical Reason*. Translated by Lewis White Beck. New York: Library of Liberal Arts, 1993.

———. *Critique of Pure Reason*. Translated by Norman Kemp Smith. New York: St. Martin's Press, 1929.

———. *Grounding for the Metaphysics of Morals*. Translated by James Ellington. Indianapolis, IN: Hackett Publishing, 1981.

———. *Observations on the Feeling of the Beautiful and Sublime*. Translated by John T. Goldthwait. Berkeley: University of California Press, 1960.

———. *Religion within the Boundaries of Mere Reason and Other Writings*. Translated and edited by Allen Wood. Cambridge: Cambridge University Press, 1998.

Kaufmann, Walter. *Existentialism: From Dostoevsky to Sartre*. New York: Meridian, 1975.

———. *Nietzsche: Philosopher, Psychologist, Antichrist*. Fourth Edition. Princeton, NJ: Princeton University Press, 1974.

———. *Philosophical Classics, Volume V: Twentieth Century Philosophy*. Second Edition. Upper Saddle River, NJ: Prentice Hall, 2000.

Kojeve, Alexandre. *Introduction to the Reading of Hegel*. Translated by James H. Nichols Jr. Ithaca, NY: Cornell University Press, 1980.

Kolb, David. *The Critique of Pure Modernity: Hegel, Heidegger, and After*. Chicago: University of Chicago Press, 1986.

Kuhn, Thomas. *The Structure of Scientific Revolutions*. Third Edition. Chicago: University of Chicago Press, 1970.

LaCapra, Dominick. *Writing History, Writing Trauma*. Baltimore, MD: Johns Hopkins University Press, 2001.

Lavine, T. Z. *From Socrates to Sartre: The Philosophic Quest*. New York: Bantam Books, 1989.

Leeming, David Adams. *The World of Myth: An Anthology*. Oxford: Oxford University Press, 1990.

Levi, Primo. *Survival in Auschwitz*. New York: Macmillan, 1961.

Livingston, Donald W., and James T. King. *Hume: A Re-evaluation*. New York: Fordham University Press, 1976.

Marmysz, John. *Laughing at Nothing: Humor as a Response to Nihilism*. Albany: State University of New York Press, 2003.

Martin, Glen T. *From Nietzsche to Wittgenstein: The Problem of Truth and Nihilism in the Modern World*. New York: Peter Lang Publishing, 1989.

Marx, Karl. *Selected Writings*. Edited by David Mclellan. Oxford: Oxford University Press, 1977.

Matson, Wallace I. *A New History of Philosophy: Volumes I and II*. New York: Harcourt Brace Jovanovich, 1987.

Metzger, Bruce M. and Michael D. Coogan. *The Oxford Companion to the Bible*. Oxford: Oxford University Press, 1993.

Miles, Jack. *God: A Biography*. New York: Random House, 1995.

Nehamas, Alexander. *Virtues of Authenticity: Essays on Plato and Socrates*. Princeton, NJ: Princeton University Press, 1999.

Neske, Günther and Emil Kettering, eds. *Martin Heidegger and National Socialism*. New York: Paragon House, 1990.

Nietzsche, Friedrich. *Basic Writings of Nietzsche*. Translated and edited by Walter Kaufmann. New York: The Modern Library, 1968.

———. *The Gay Science*. Translated by Walter Kaufmann. New York: Vintage Books, 1974.

———. *Philosophy in the Tragic Age of the Greeks*. Washington, DC: Gateway Editions, 1994.

————. *The Portable Nietzsche*. Translated and edited by Walter Kaufmann. New York: Penguin Books, 1984.

————. *The Will to Power*. Translated by Walter Kaufmann and R. J. Hollingdale. New York: Vintage Books, 1968.

Ogletree, Thomas W. *The Death of God Controversy*. Nashville, NY: Abingdon Press, 1966.

Palmer, Donald. *Looking at Philosophy: The Unbearable Heaviness of Philosophy Made Lighter*, Third Edition. Mountain View, CA: Mayfield Publishing Company, 2001.

Pearson, Keith Ansell and Diane Morgan, eds. *Nihilism Now! Monsters of Energy*. New York: St. Martin's Press, 2000.

Plato. *The Collected Dialogues of Plato, Including the Letters*. Edited by Edith Hamilton and Huntington Cairns. Princeton, NJ: Princeton University Press, 1989.

————. *The Symposium*. Translated by Benjamin Jowett. Mineola, NY: Dover Publications, 1993.

————. *The Works of Plato*. Edited by Irwin Edman. New York: Modern Library, 1956.

Popper, Karl. *The Open Society and Its Enemies*. London: Routledge & Keegan Paul, 1945.

Reese, W. L. *Dictionary of Philosophy and Religion: Eastern and Western Thought*. Totawa, NJ: Humanities Press, 1980.

Reich, Wilhelm. *Listen, Little Man!* New York: Noonday Press, 1970.

Russell, Bertrand. *Autobiography*. London: Routledge, 1998.

————. *Has Man a Future?* New York: Simon and Schuster, 1961.

————. *A History of Western Philosophy*. New York: Simon and Schuster, 1945.

————. *Introduction to Mathematical Philosophy*. New York: Dover, 1993.

————. *The Problems of Philosophy*. New York: Barnes and Noble, [1912] 2004.

————. *Selected Papers of Bertrand Russell*. New York: The Modern Library, 1927.

————. *Why I Am Not a Christian and Other Essays on Religion and Related Subjects*. Edited by Paul Edwards. New York: Simon and Schuster, 1957.

Sartre, Jean-Paul. *Being and Nothingness*. Translated by Hazel E. Barnes. New York: Washington Square Press, 1956.

————. *Search for a Method*. Translated by Hazel E. Barnes. New York: Vintage Books, 1968.

————. *The Words*. Translated by Bernard Frechtman. New York: Vintage Books, 1981.

Scholz, Sally J. *On de Beauvoir*. Belmont, CA: Wadsworth, 2000.

Schopenhauer, Arthur. *The World as Will and Representation*. Translated by E. F. J. Payne. New York: Dover, 1958.

Silverman, Hugh J. and Frederick A. Elliston, eds. *Jean-Paul Sartre: Contemporary Approaches to His Philosophy*. Pittsburgh, PA: Duquesne University Press, 1980.

Singer, Peter. *Hegel: A Very Short Introduction*. Oxford: Oxford University Press, 2001.

Smith, Huston. *Why Religion Matters*. San Francisco: HarperCollins, 2001.

————. *The World's Religions*. San Francisco: HarperCollins, 1991.

Solomon, Robert C. *In the Spirit of Hegel*. New York: Oxford University Press, 1985.

Spengler, Oswald. *The Decline of the West*. New York: Alfred A. Knopf, 1928.

————. *Letters of Oswald Spengler: 1913–1936*. Translated by Arthur Helps. New York: Alfred A. Knopf, 1966.

Sprintzen, David A. and Adrian van den Hoven, ed. and trans. *Sartre and Camus: A Historic Confrontation*. Amherst, NY: Humanity Books, 2004.

Spyridakis, Stylianos V. and Bradley P. Nystrom, trans. and ed. *Ancient Greece: Documentary Perspectives*. Dubuque, Iowa: Kendall/Hunt Publishing Company, 1985.

Steinkraus, Warren E., ed. *New Studies in Hegel's Philosophy*. New York: Holt, Rinehart, and Winston, 1971.

Stirner, Max. *The Ego and Its Own*. Translated by Steven Byington. London: Rebel Press, 1993.

———. *The False Principle of Our Education*. Translated by Robert H. Beebe and edited by James J. Martin. Colorado Springs, CO: Ralph Myles Publisher, 1967.

Strathern, Paul. *Thomas Aquinas in 90 Minutes*. Chicago: Ivan R. Dee, 1998.

Stump, Eleonore and Norman Kretzmann, eds. *The Cambridge Companion to Augustine*. Cambridge: Cambridge University Press, 2001.

Taylor, A. E. *Aristotle*. New York: Dover Publications, 1955.

The Upanishads. Translated and edited by Eknath Easwaran. Tomales, CA: Nilgiri Press, 1987.

Wilshire, Bruce. *Fashionable Nihilism: A Critique of Analytic Philosophy*. Albany: State University of New York Press, 2002.

Wittgenstein, Ludwig. *Philosophical Investigations*. Translated by G. E. M. Anscombe. Malden, MA: Blackwell Publishing, [1953] 2001.

———. *Tractatus Logico-Philosophicus*. Translated by C. K. Ogden. New York: Barnes and Noble, [1922] 2003.

Wolff, Robert Paul, ed. *Ten Great Works of Philosophy*. New York: Mentor Books, 1969.

Xenophon. *Conversations of Socrates*. Translated by Hugh Tredennick and Robin Waterfield. London: Penguin Books, 1990.

Young, Julian. *Heidegger's Philosophy of Art*. Cambridge: Cambridge University Press, 2001.

Zimmerman, Michael E. *Heidegger's Confrontation with Modernity*. Bloomington, IN: Indiana University Press, 1990.

Zupancic, Alenka. *The Shortest Shadow: Nietzsche's Philosophy of the Two*. Cambridge, MA: MIT Press, 2003.

Index

© Juneko J. Robinson

Abraham, 111, 112–113, 114, 116, 117, 119, 122, 129, 139, 140, 141n2, 260

Abstractions, xvi, 67, 95–96, 146, 170, 189, 190, 191, 197, 201, 206, 220, 242, 244, 252, 254–256, 258, 262–265, 274, 276–277, 289–290, 314, 316, 317, 322, 326, 329, 339, 372, 376, 382, 400

Academy (Plato's), 44, 47, 65–66, 91, 95–96, 105, 108

Aesthetics, 49, 80–84, 214, 215, 232–235, 281–282, 293

Agnosticism, 324

Alexander the Great, 66, 91, 94, 95

Al-Farabi, 125–127, 129

Al-Kindi, 118, 124–126, 129, 140, 142n27

Ambiguity, 19, 308n27, 334

Anabasis, 33

Analysis, xx–xxi, 27, 81, 82, 84, 127, 129, 168, 199, 202, 219, 221, 222, 245, 249, 312, 315, 317, 328, 335, 338, 340, 341, 348, 349–351, 358, 378, 379

Anarchy, 93, 266, 269n6

Anaximander, 6–9, 12, 13, 18, 25, 45, 90, 142n44, 185, 207, 395

Anaximenes of Miletus, 8, 18

Angst, 386

Anselm of Canterbury, 116, 120, 127, 18–133, 135, 140, 142n32, 144, 166, 212, 398

Antisthenes, 93, 96, 97, 100

Apathia, 89, 99, 101–102, 104, 106, 108, 109, 305, 309n42

Apology, 29–30, 33, 43

A posteriori, 111, 128, 135, 220

A priori, 111, 128, 131, 135, 164, 166, 189, 201, 211, 218–220, 223, 224, 227, 232, 234, 236, 237, 238n17, 273, 285, 286, 288, 318

Aquinas, St. Thomas, 111, 116, 125, 128, 132–138, 139, 140, 142n50, 144, 147, 166, 176n4, 188, 212, 226, 325, 398

Arendt, Hannah, 360–361, 368, 371

Argument, 6, 7, 8, 14, 28, 37, 38, 86, 113, 116, 118, 119, 125, 128, 139, 140, 204, 341, 343, 346, 394

to an absurd conclusion, 30

Anselm's Ontological, 129–132, 140, 166, 328

Aquinas's Five, 134–138, 140, 226

Aristotelian syllogistic, 74–76

Descartes' for God's existence, 164–168, 174

Kant on metaphysical, 225–226
Timon's, 104–105
Aristarchus of Samos, 148, 151, 157
Aristocracy, 55
Aristotle, 6, 16, 59, 64–88, 90, 91, 93, 97,
103, 108, 125, 126, 127, 134, 138,
144, 176n4, 176n6, 188, 196, 212,
221, 242, 244, 258, 309n35, 311,
352n6, 364, 387, 395, 397
on art, 80–84
on astronomy, 147–151, 153, 156
on ethics, 78–80
on the four causes, 70–74
on logic, 74–76, 244, 329–333, 351
on the First Mover, 76–78
Aristophanes, 22, 23, 35–38, 39, 59, 60
Ataraxia, 89, 101–103, 104, 106, 108, 109,
114, 398
Atheism, 30, 130, 136, 204, 206, 260, 307,
319, 324, 356
Athens, 20, 22, 23, 24, 29, 32, 33, 35, 37,
38, 44, 62, 66, 91, 93–95, 97
Atomism, 15–18, 24, 25, 71, 102
logical, 329–334, 338–339, 340,
343–344, 349, 351
Augustine, St., 116, 118–124, 126, 129,
133, 140, 144, 178n39, 212, 398
Aurelius, Marcus, 99
Authenticity, 42, 231–232, 362, 368,
369–370, 371, 379, 384, 385, 386,
387, 388
Autobiographical Study, 298
Averroes, 118, 127, 140
Avicenna, 118, 126–127, 129, 140

Bad faith, 355, 376–377, 378–379, 388
Beauty, 48–51, 55, 56, 65, 83, 98, 155,
211, 215, 232, 233–234, 235, 237,
360, 363, 378, 396
Beauvoir, Simone de, 355, 357, 377,
378–385, 388, 391n61, 391n62
Becoming, 46–47, 50, 245, 258–259, 267,
364
Behaviorism, 369
Being, 14–15, 69, 73–74, 123–124,
129–132, 257–260, 284, 287,
291–292, 330, 355–388
being-there. *See* Dasein
being-toward-death, 366–367
forgetfulness of, 368

for-itself, 355, 374–376, 378, 380, 381,
382, 383, 385
in-itself, 225, 240, 248, 276, 355,
374–376, 383, 385
in-the-world, 362, 363, 365, 366, 367,
387
shepherds of, 368, 369, 371
Being and Nothingness, 375
Being and Time, 363, 364, 365
Being There, 384
Bentham, Jeremy, 302–303
Berkeley, George, 183–184
Beyond Good and Evil, 295
Bible, 4–5, 112–116, 121, 124, 125, 129,
141, 151, 153, 156
Brahe, Tycho, 155, 177n11, 177n12
Brahman, 284–285, 287, 288
Brave New World, 396
Bruno, Giordano, 157, 177n13
Buber, Martin, 249, 141n5
Buddha, 281, 285, 295, 300, 308n23

Care, xxiii, 365–367, 368, 370,
385, 397
Cartesian
Doubt, 159, 163, 164, 167, 175
dualism, 172–173
Method, 158–159, 175
Categorical imperative, 211, 228–232
Categories of the understanding, 211,
220–224, 225, 237, 246
Catharsis, 64, 82–84
Causation, 26, 52–53, 98–99, 125, 126,
128, 134–138, 165–167, 175, 183,
184–185, 284, 286, 288, 319, 337,
358, 359
Four causes. *See* Aristotle
Hume's critique of, 194–203, 208
Kant's defense of, 213, 214–216,
220–226
Chaning-Pearce, Melville, 277
Chuang Tzu, 161
Circular reasoning, 132
The Clouds, 36, 37, 38, 59
Cogito ergo sum, 143, 163–164, 166, 375
Collins, Francis S., 136
Communism, 265–266, 269, 368, 374,
388
Conditional, 333
Confessions, 120

Conjunction, 333
Contradiction, 255
Copernicus, Nicoli, 151–155
Cornford, F. M., 5
Correspondence theory of truth, 320
Cosmology, 147, 151, 308n23
The Critique of Judgment, 215, 232–235
The Critique of Practical Reason, 214,
    227–232, 232
The Critique of Pure Reason, 214, 216–227,
    232, 238n6, 238n17
Crito, 33
Cynicism, 38, 89, 92, 93–96, 109

Darwin, Charles, 137, 298, 325,
    352n16
Dasein, 355, 364–367, 368, 369, 370, 373,
    374, 375
The Decline of the West, 358, 359
Democritus, 2, 15–18, 24, 25, 44, 48, 67,
    71, 102, 144, 330, 395
Descartes, René, 45, 143–178, 180–182,
    183, 186, 189, 191, 193, 199–200,
    201, 206, 212, 222, 224, 257, 288,
    308n29, 335, 336, 340, 375, 386,
    388, 399
Description, 311, 315, 328, 335, 338–340,
    346, 349
Despair, 60, 95, 106, 113, 231, 236, 240,
    241, 255, 264, 272, 273, 274,
    277–282, 285, 293, 294, 304, 305,
    306, 315, 357, 360, 372, 384, 386, 387,
    388
Destruction of the Destruction, 127
The Destruction of the Philosophers, 127
Determinism, 315, 376
*Diagnostic and Statistical Manual of Mental
    Disorders*, 162
Dialectic, 154, 208n3, 278, 397
    Hegelian, 242, 247, 249, 250, 252–257,
        259, 265, 266, 267, 269, 273,
        328–329, 376
    Socratic, 27–30, 34, 36, 38
Dick, Philip K., 371
Diogenes Laertius, 12, 65, 110n8
Diogenes of Sinope, 88, 93–96, 97, 100,
    109, 110n8, 144, 212
Discourse on Method, 158, 163
Disjunction, 333
Divided line, 42, 46–51, 67, 125, 363

Dogmatism, xxv, xxvi, xxvii, 20, 44, 86,
    115, 146, 147, 150, 154, 175, 206,
    214, 216, 304, 316, 319, 326, 327,
    351, 394, 396
Dualism, 172, 364, 376
Du Bois, W. E. B., 249
Dynamism, 287, 291

Eco, Umberto, 81
Efficient cause. *See* Aristotle
Ego and It's Own, 264, 271n46
Egoism, 248
Eleatic School, 12–15
Empiricism, 64, 70, 74, 85, 189–191,
    197, 200, 202, 207, 208, 216, 224,
    237, 314, 315, 316, 318, 327, 334,
    338
Encyclopedia of the Philosophical Sciences, 247
Engels, Friedrich, 264
Enlightenment
    historical period, 243–244, 245, 356
    spiritual, 53, 101, 102, 397
The Enneads, 125
Epicurus, 17, 101–103, 105, 106, 144,
    182, 301
Epistemology, 334
The Essence of Christianity, 263
Eternal feminine, 379–380
Eternal return, 98–99, 297
Ethics, 78–80, 100, 183, 202–206, 208,
    214, 227–232, 237, 281–282, 300,
    301–304, 396
Eudoxus, 148–149
Euthanasia, 106–107
Euthyphro, 43
Evil, 40, 56, 90, 120, 121–124, 126–127,
    140, 162, 167, 174, 228, 279–280,
    281, 295, 341
Evolution, 136, 137, 261, 298, 320,
    352n16
Existentialism, 277, 355–391
Existentialism Is a Humanism, 376

Facticity, 381
Faith, xxiv, xxv, 113–141, 157–158, 236,
    262, 272, 274, 277, 279–282, 285,
    297, 298, 299–300, 305, 315, 316,
    325. *See also* Bad faith
Fascism, 368
Feminism, 383–384, 388

Feuerbach, Ludwig, 262–263, 264, 268, 269

Fight Club, 384

Formal cause. *See* Aristotle

Formal logic, 329–334, 342–346

Förster, Bernhard, 294

Four causes. *See* Aristotle

Frankl, Viktor, 371

Frege, Gottlob, 333

Freud, Sigmund, 298, 345

Fukuyama, Francis, 249

Galileo Galilei, 153–155, 157, 176, 201

Geist, 239, 245–247, 254, 256, 257, 261–262, 273, 276, 329

Geulincx, Arnold, 184

God, 2–6, 17, 30, 33, 37, 76–78, 80, 81, 97, 98, 102, 111–141, 151, 153, 155–157, 158, 159, 160, 174, 181, 184–188, 199–200, 251, 259–260, 261, 273, 275, 277–282, 394, 395, 398

arguments for existence of, 127–128, 129–132, 134–138, 165–168, 225–226

death of, 297–301

as a delusion, 262–265

as evil genius, 162

as guarantor of knowledge, 168–172

pragmatic argument for, 323–327

See also Aristotle; Atheism; Geist; Religion

Golden mean, 78–80. *See also* Aristotle

Gospels, 114–115

Grandin, Temple, 223

Greatest Happiness Principle, 301–304

Griffin, Nicholas, 327

Grounding for the Metaphysics of Morals, 228, 230

Habermas, Jürgen, 371

Hawking, Stephen, 137

Heaven, 102, 106, 108, 115, 151, 156, 262, 265, 282, 297, 299, 305, 398

Hedonism, 120, 303. *See also* Greatest Happiness Principle; Pleasure

Hedwig and the Angry Inch, 36

Hegel, Georg Wilhelm Friedrich, 239–271, 273–277, 278, 279, 282, 285, 290, 294, 299, 304, 305, 307, 311, 312, 314, 316, 322, 325, 326, 327, 328–330, 332, 333, 351, 364, 376, 381, 387, 388, 399. *See also* Dialectic; Geist

Hegesias, 106

Heidegger, Martin, 66, 296, 355, 357, 362–374, 375, 376, 380, 382, 384, 385, 386, 388, 389n19, 399

Hell, 151, 156, 157

Hellenistic philosophy, 17, 27, 89–110, 250, 251, 291, 301, 309n42, 351, 398

Heraclitus, 9, 10–12, 14, 15, 18, 19, 88n6, 317–318, 395

Hinduism, 92, 109, 181, 282–289, 305, 308n23

Hobbes, Thomas, 182–183, 208n3

Holism, 329

Humanism, 244

Hume, David, 179–210, 211, 212, 213, 214, 216, 219–220, 222–223, 224, 225, 229, 240, 300–301, 314, 316, 323, 327, 337, 338, 340, 386. *See also* Causation

Husserl, Edmund, 163, 164, 208n4, 238n17

Hypothetical imperative, 211, 228–232. *See also* Ethics; Kant

I Heart Huckabees, 384

Ideas, 14, 34, 182, 242, 243, 276, 314, 321–326, 336–339

absolute, 256–260, 273, 274, 296

adventitious, 165

of cause and effect. *See* Causation

clear and distinct, 159, 168, 169, 170, 171, 172, 189

complex, 179, 194–196

dialectical relationship between, 247–256

of God and self, 199–200, 251

innate, 164–168

John Locke and the origins of, 189–191

Platonic, 44–51, 63n19

relations of, 196–199, 220

simple, 179, 194–196, 202

transcendental, 226–227

Idealism, 32, 183–184, 185, 319

dialectical, 239–260, 265

Platonic, 42–63

transcendental, 211–238

Impressions, 167, 170, 184, 194–207, 216–220, 222, 336, 338

Inauthenticity, 367–369

Individualism, 38, 275
Induction, 203
Infinite, 8–10, 18, 25, 26, 77, 98, 122–123,
    125, 126, 133, 138, 140, 156–157,
    166–168, 169, 175, 186, 188, 199,
    235, 247, 256, 277–282, 298, 329, 334
An Inquiry concerning Human Understanding,
    192, 193, 201, 202, 209n14, 209n27
An Inquiry concerning the Principles of Morals,
    192, 202, 205
Introduction to Mathematical Philosophy, 330
Intuition, 36, 139, 174, 211, 218–224, 227,
    237, 246, 273, 285–286, 288, 298
Islamic philosophy, 116–118, 124–127.
    See also Al-Farabi; Al-Kindi; Aver-
    roes; Avicenna

James, William, 313–327, 334, 350,
    352n16
Jesus of Nazareth, 32, 39, 109, 111,
    113–116, 117–118, 119, 122, 129,
    141n10, 204, 265, 279, 300, 302
Judaism, 92, 111–118, 121, 139, 140,
    141n5, 141n12, 249, 279, 373
Justice, 69, 183, 240
    Platonic form of, 49, 50, 51, 55, 56, 58,
    363

Kant, Immanuel, xxi, 123, 129, 132,
    211–238, 239, 240–241, 242, 243,
    245–246, 247, 257, 258, 267, 268,
    273–274, 277, 281, 283–288, 290,
    287, 304, 316, 320–321, 327,
    353n16, 386, 399
Kepler, Johannes, 155–157, 176, 177n12
Kiefer, Anselm, 371
Kierkegaard, Søren, 272, 274–282, 285,
    304–305, 307, 307–308n10, 308n12,
    312, 388
Kleist, Heinrich von, 240
Knowledge, 50, 70, 104–105, 128–129,
    159–160, 163–164, 168–170,
    189–191, 194–202, 212–227,
    232, 233, 329. *See also A posteriori;
    A priori*
    by acquaintance, 311, 338–340
    by description, 311, 338–340
    pragmatic theory of, 319–325
    Russell's theory of, 334–338.
Koran, 117–118, 125–127, 141n13

Kuhn, Thomas S., xxv
Kundera, Milan, 371

Lacan, Jacques, 371
Language game theory of meaning,
    346–249
Leap of faith, 274, 277, 280
Left-Hegelians, 261–267, 294, 304
Leibniz, Gottfried Willhelm, 185–188
Leiter, Brian, xx
Leucippus, 15–16
Levinas, Emmanuel, 371
Limbo, 396
Lives of Eminent Philosophers, 65
Locke, John, 189–191, 209n6, 327
Logic, xx–xxii, xxv, 6–8, 13–15, 29–31,
    39, 69, 70, 116, 118, 119, 121, 122,
    125, 127, 129–132, 135, 197, 203,
    320, 324. *See also* Argument
    Aristotelian, 74–76, 85, 86, 221,
    244–245, 322
    Hegelian, 239, 241, 242, 244, 245, 247,
    248, 252–259, 266, 269, 273–274,
    280, 330–332, 360, 364, 369, 373,
    399
    Modern, 311, 312, 315, 327–334, 336,
    339, 340–341, 342–346, 347, 348,
    349, 350, 351
    Stoic, 100
    and trickery, 36–38
Logical atomism, 329–334
Logicomix, 345
Lordship and bondage, 248–250
Luther, Martin, 153
Lyceum, 66, 95
Lyotard, Jean-Francois, 400
Lysis, 43

Malebranche, Nicolas, 184–185
Malick, Terrence, 371
Manichaeanism, 120
Marcuse, Herbert, 371
Marx, Karl, 249, 265–266, 268, 269,
    271n46
Maslow, Abraham, 371
Master/slave dialectic. *See* Lordship and
    bondage
Materialism, 2, 18, 25, 44, 182–183, 185,
    208n3, 260, 315, 319
The Matrix, 54, 162

Matters of fact, 196–199, 200
May, Rollo, 371
Maya, 47, 284–286, 288
McTaggart, John, 328
Meditations (Descartes)
  I, 160–163
  II, 163–164
  III, 164–168
  IV, 168–170
  V, 170–172
  VI, 172–173
Meditations on First Philosophy, 146, 159–173, 174, 189, 335
Memento, 84
Metaphysics, 125, 179, 180, 185, 201, 224–226, 238n6, 322, 346, 364
Metaphysics, 68, 93, 126
Milesians, 6–10
Mill, John Stuart, 272, 275, 294, 300–304, 306
Mitsein, 381
Monad, 186–188
Monism, 10, 185–189, 207, 316
Muhammad, 116–118
Muslim, 117–118, 124, 126, 127, 141n13, 361
"My Own Life," 191
Mysticism, 15, 285, 305, 341, 351
"Mysticism and Logic," 341
Myth, 1–6, 7, 8, 15, 17, 18–20, 36, 298, 395, 397
  of the cave, 42, 51–55, 62, 63, 154, 283
  of the eternal feminine, 379–380

The Name of the Rose, 81
National socialism, 294, 306, 360–362, 367, 368, 370–374, 384, 388, 390n32
Naturalism, 18, 37
Nazi. *See* National socialism
Negation, 221, 224, 250, 251, 255, 333, 343
Neoplatonism, 124–126
New Academy, 105, 108
Nietzsche, Elizabeth Förster-, 294
Nietzsche, Friedrich Wilhelm, xxi, 7, 35, 110n15, 141, 230, 238n27, 260, 272, 274–275, 282, 294–306, 307, 309n45, 312, 357–358, 364, 376, 388, 390n32, 396, 399

Nihilism, 212, 240, 245, 274–275, 282, 294, 297, 357–360, 368, 399
1984, 396
Noumenal world, 211, 217–218, 219, 221, 223, 224, 225, 236, 242, 245, 246, 267, 399
Nous, 24–25, 65, 78, 97, 180, 244

Obereit, Jacob Hermann, 240
Observations on the Feeling of the Beautiful and Sublime, 215
Occasionalism, 184–185, 186
"On the Origin of the Work of Art," 371
On the Revolutions of the Heavenly Orbs, 153
Ontological argument. *See* Argument
Ontology, 129
Optimism, 48, 74, 273, 274, 293, 294, 307, 350, 360, 399
Österling, Anders, 327
Otherness, 381
Overman, 309n53. *See also* Übermensch

Panentheism, 260
Pantheism, 260
Paradox, 121, 191, 280, 387
Parmenides, 9, 10, 12–15, 69–70, 71, 395
Peano, Giuseppe, 333
Peirce, Charles Sanders, 315
Pessimism, 92, 107, 109, 212, 272, 273, 284, 285, 293, 295, 307, 359, 386, 399
Phaedo, 24, 26, 31
Phenomenal world, 87n6, 211, 217–218, 219, 223–224, 228, 233, 235, 263, 237, 240, 242, 245, 246, 247, 267, 285, 399
Phenomenology, 208n4, 238n17, 247, 248, 250
Phenomenology of Spirit, 247–252, 257, 260, 267
Philip of Macedon, 66, 91
Philosopher kings, 42, 55–58, 63n19
Philosophical Investigations, 311, 342, 346, 348, 349, 351
Philosophy
  analytic, xix, xx–xxii, xxiv, 146, 241, 312–313, 316, 327–329, 340–342, 346, 349, 350, 351, 364

continental, xix, xx–xxii, xxiv, 146, 312–313, 316, 326, 327, 342, 349, 353n30

and religion, xix, xx, xxiii, xxiv–xxv, xxvi, 2, 15, 19, 61, 101, 102, 108, 109, 111, 116, 119, 127, 128, 138, 139–140, 143–146, 153, 158, 173, 193, 200, 206, 213, 261, 262–265, 282–285, 297, 298, 305, 307, 312, 313, 315, 317, 323–327, 340–341, 387, 394–396, 399–400

and science, xv, xix, xx, xxi, xxii, xxiii, xxiv–xxvi, 1–3, 6, 15, 17–20, 25, 27, 46, 48–50, 60, 61, 62, 67, 73–74, 78, 84, 85, 86, 87, 125, 136–138, 139, 143–175, 176n1, 189, 193, 200, 206, 207, 208, 213, 214–215, 219–227, 234, 236, 237, 238n6, 238n17, 246, 257, 297–298, 304, 307, 311–315, 316–317, 320, 328, 329, 340–341, 346, 349–350, 356–360, 364, 357–369, 387, 393–400

as wondrous distress, xv, xvi, xvii, xix, xxvii–xxviii, 18–20, 38–40, 61–62, 84–86, 107–109, 139–140, 173–175, 206–207, 236, 267–268, 304–306, 349–351, 385–387, 392–400

Philosophy of Right, 243

Physics, 67

Picture theory of meaning, 342–346, 348

Plato, xxiv, 6, 13, 22, 23, 24, 26, 29, 31, 32, 33, 34, 36, 37, 38, 39, 42–63, 64, 65–67, 69, 70, 71, 72, 73, 74, 78, 80, 81, 84, 85, 86, 87, 88n21, 90, 91, 93, 95, 97, 105, 108, 109, 123, 125, 126, 127, 139, 144, 154, 161, 188, 189, 190, 208, 212, 227, 283–284, 285, 288, 289, 317, 326, 351, 352n6, 363–364, 374, 380, 385, 388, 397–398

Platonic idealism. See Idealism

Plotinus, 125

Pluralism, 316

Poetics, 81, 82, 84

Pope Urban VIII, 154

Popper, Karl, 345

Portrait of a Lady, 314

Positivism, 346

Postmodern era, 400

Practical reason, 227–232

Pragmatism, 312, 315–327

Pragmatism, 315, 316, 323

Predicate, 74–76, 88n12, 244–245, 258, 329–332

Presocratics, 1–2, 6–21, 22, 24, 27, 44, 46, 67, 68–69, 86, 87, 90, 92, 102, 145, 155, 185, 212, 298, 349, 364, 395, 396, 397

Prime matter, 68, 70

Principles of Psychology, 314

Problems of Philosophy, 335–340

The Program, 60

Proposition, 330, 333, 343, 344, 346

Protestantism, 153

Ptolemy, 149, 154

Pulp Fiction, 84

Pyrrho of Elis, 103–104

Pythagoras, xxiii, 9, 13, 46, 155

Quantum physics, xxv

Rationalism, 13, 64, 67, 85, 208, 224

Reason in History, 243

Reign: The Conqueror, 94

Relations of ideas, 189, 196–199

Religion. See Philosophy and religion

Republic, 43, 46, 51

Right-Hegelians, 261–262

Russell, Bertrand, 15, 23, 87, 88n12, 88n15, 99, 110n21, 137–138, 175, 178n35, 185, 209n13, 237n3, 241, 285, 293, 309n42, 309n45, 311, 313, 326, 327–341, 342, 343, 344, 345, 347, 350, 351, 353n38

Sartre, Jean-Paul, 163, 249, 357, 374–378, 380, 384, 385, 388

Schelling, Friedrich Wilhelm, 276

Scholasticism, 128

Schopenhauer, Arthur, 272, 274–275, 282–293, 294–295, 296, 297, 298, 304–306, 307, 308n32, 312, 316, 376, 386, 388, 399

The Schopenhauer Cure, 298

Science. See Philosophy and science

The Science of Logic, 247

The Second Sex, 378, 379, 380, 384, 385, 391n61

Sensation, 17, 102, 107, 217, 218, 219, 220–221, 225, 236, 281, 302, 320, 336–338, 339

Sense data, 336–340
Shvetashvatara Upanishad, 284
Simple idea. *See* Ideas
Skepticism, 17, 38, 45, 58, 74, 132, 159,
    174, 212, 213, 220, 225, 228, 316, 394
  ancient Greek, xxiii, 89, 91, 92, 103–
    106, 108, 109, 250–252, 255, 398
  Cartesian. *See* Cartesian Doubt
  of Hume, 191, 199, 200–203, 206, 240,
    399
  Socrates, xxiii, 1–2, 20, 22–41, 42–44, 45,
    47, 55, 58, 59–60, 62, 66, 67, 78, 83,
    86, 87, 90, 91, 92, 93, 95, 96, 97,
    101, 104, 106, 108, 109, 116, 144,
    154, 174, 176, 181, 192, 201, 212,
    213, 227, 240, 242, 244, 248, 250,
    252, 255, 268, 279, 300, 303, 326,
    351, 386, 387, 388, 396–400
Socratic Method, 27–29
Solipsism, 164, 167
Sophism, 29
Spengler, Oswald, 358–360, 389n6
Spinoza, Baruch, 185, 187–188
Stirner, Max, 263–265, 268, 269, 271n46
Stoicism, 89, 92, 96–101, 104, 106, 108,
    109, 110n11, 110n21, 116, 140,
    178n39, 212, 250–252, 305, 309n42,
    398
Strauss, David Friedrich, 261
Strauss, Leo, 371
Subjectivism, 257
Sublation, 255–256
Sublime, 215, 235, 236, 237, 237n3
Substance, 14–15, 74–78, 122, 157, 167,
    172–173, 180–188, 190–191, 221–
    224, 244, 259, 285, 287–288, 305,
    329–330, 367, 376
  composite, 70–72, 73
  material, 3, 8, 16, 24–25, 26, 44, 67,
    68–69, 71, 97–98, 125, 172–173,
    180–188, 330, 383
  non-material, 45, 46, 48, 125, 172–173,
    244, 245
  primary, 75–76, 190
  secondary, 75–76
  thinking, 78, 80, 164, 172–173,
    180–188, 199–200, 222, 245
Suzuki, D. T., 371
Syllogism, 64, 76, 87, 88n15
Symposium, 36, 90

Syntax, 333–334
Synthesis, 242, 245, 246, 248, 251, 252,
    253, 255, 256, 259, 266

Tabula rasa, 189
Technological thinking, 367–369. *See also*
    Philosophy and science
Thales of Miletus, 6–10, 12, 15, 18, 44, 67,
    90, 144, 207, 317–318, 395
Theatetus, 43, 45
Theology, 260, 271
Thing-in-itself, 217, 245–246, 283,
    285–288, 291, 320. *See also*
    Noumenal world
Thrownness, 364–365, 376, 380
Tillich, Paul, 371
Timaeus, 43, 63n8
Time, 122–123, 191, 195, 198, 218–220,
    224, 273, 276, 286–287, 288, 339,
    341, 364–367, 368, 370, 379, 382,
    385
Timon of Philius, 104–105
Torah, 112
Totalitarianism, 62, 360–361, 371, 373
Tractatus Logico-Philosophicus, 311, 342,
    343, 345, 346, 348, 349, 350, 351
Transcendent, 44, 78, 133, 262
Transcendental idealism. *See* Idealism
A Treatise of Human Nature, 192, 193,
    209n14
Truth, 13–15, 157–159, 244–246, 252,
    257–260, 261, 277, 279, 282, 285,
    316, 328–329, 339, 344, 368, 370
  as the goal of philosophizing, xv–xvii,
    xxii, xxiii–xxviii, 19–20, 23, 27–31,
    34, 36, 38–40, 45–46, 48–51, 61–62,
    74, 84, 86, 90, 94, 101, 119–120,
    124, 131, 139–140, 174–175, 201,
    206, 212, 236, 240, 241, 252, 256,
    257, 267–268, 304–306, 313,
    386–387, 393–400
  Platonic form of, 47–51, 55, 56, 60,
    61–62
  pragmatic theory of, 317, 320–323, 324,
    326, 327, 350
  rejection of, 53–55, 103–106, 108, 206,
    212, 213, 240, 298, 299
  as a vanishing point, 43, 226, 322
Turn of the Screw, 314
Twilight of the Idols, 295

Übermensch, 272, 297–301
Upanishads, 284–285
Utilitarianism, 301–304, 313

Vagueness, xxii, 28, 335
Validity, 7, 18, 76, 138, 191, 225, 233, 234, 252, 273, 321
Varieties of Religious Experience, 325
Venn diagram, 75–76
Vienna Circle, 342
Virtue, xxvii, 92, 203, 205, 299
  as a golden mean, 78–80

The Warriors, 33
The Way of Opinion, 13
The Way of Truth, 13–14
When Nietzsche Wept, 298
Whitehead, Alfred North, 333
"Why I Am Not a Christian," 137, 341
Will, 169, 272, 284, 287–293, 308n32, 373, 379, 382, 383
  good, 228
  to live, 291–292, 295
  to power, 295–297, 298, 299, 305, 358, 369
Williams, Donna, 223
The Will to Power, 294

Wisdom, xxiii–xxiv, xxv, xxvi, 12, 29, 34, 37, 38–40, 47, 48, 51, 54, 55, 61–62, 65, 67, 73, 85, 90, 92, 93, 101, 102, 104, 105, 113, 115, 118–120, 124, 126, 168, 169, 175, 181, 199, 207, 213, 240, 246, 256, 259, 267, 268, 273, 274, 299, 306, 350, 387, 397.
  See also Philosophy
The Words, 377
The World as Will and Representation, 283, 291–292
Wilshire, Bruce, xxi
Wittgenstein, Ludwig, 311, 313, 328, 341–349, 350, 351
Wittgenstein, 345
Wittgenstein's Mistress, 345
Wittgenstein's Nephew, 345
Wittgenstein's Poker, 345

Xenophon, 23, 31–35, 37, 39

Yalom, Irvin, 298
Yoga, 285
Yurick, Sol, 33

Zeno, 97

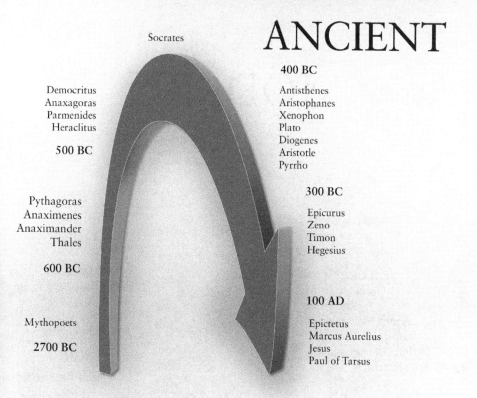

ANCIENT

Socrates

400 BC

Democritus
Anaxagoras
Parmenides
Heraclitus

500 BC

Antisthenes
Aristophanes
Xenophon
Plato
Diogenes
Aristotle
Pyrrho

300 BC

Pythagoras
Anaximenes
Anaximander
Thales

600 BC

Epicurus
Zeno
Timon
Hegesius

100 AD

Mythopoets

2700 BC

Epictetus
Marcus Aurelius
Jesus
Paul of Tarsus

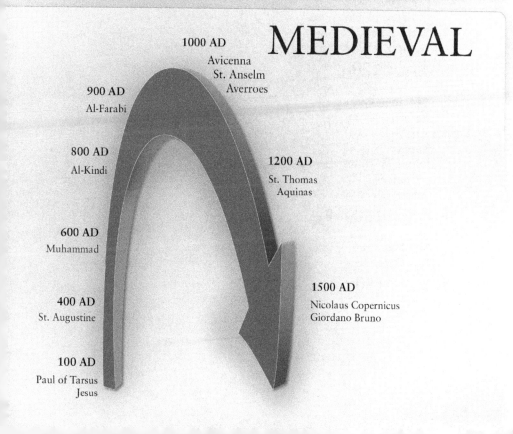

MEDIEVAL

1000 AD
Avicenna
St. Anselm
Averroes

900 AD
Al-Farabi

800 AD
Al-Kindi

1200 AD

St. Thomas
Aquinas

600 AD
Muhammad

400 AD
St. Augustine

1500 AD

Nicolaus Copernicus
Giordano Bruno

100 AD

Paul of Tarsus
Jesus

MODERN

Friedrich Nietzsche
John Stuart Mill
Karl Marx
Søren Kierkegaard
Ludwig Feuerbach
Arthur Schopenhauer
Georg Wilhelm Friedrich Hegel

1800

Jeremy Bentham
Immanuel Kant
David Hume
George Berkeley
Gottfried Liebniz

1700

John Locke
Baruch Spinoza
Nicholas Malbranche
Thomas Hobbes
René Descartes
Galileo Galilei
Johannes Kepler

1600

Giordano Bruno
Nicolaus Copernicus

1500

William James
Bertrand Russell
Oswald Spengler
Ludwig Wittgenstein
Martin Heidegger

1900

Jean-Paul Sartre
Hannah Arendt
Simone de Beauvo

2000
POSTMODERNISM

CPSIA information can be obtained
at www.ICGtesting.com
Printed in the USA
BVHW041734090720
583300BV00010B/14

9 780495 509325